Jean Gerson and the Last Medieval Reformation

Jean Gerson and the Last Medieval Reformation

Brian Patrick McGuire

The Pennsylvania State University Press · University Park

Publication of this book was made possible through the kind support of the Danish Research Council for the Humanities (Statens Humanistiske Forskningsråd)

LIBRARY OF CONGRESS CATALOGING-IN-PUBLICATION DATA

McGuire, Brian Patrick.
Jean Gerson and the last Medieval Reformation / Brian Patrick McGuire.
p. cm.
Includes bibliographical references and index.
ISBN 0-271-02707-3 (cloth : alk. paper)
ISBN 0-271-02706-1 (pbk. : alk. paper)
1. Gerson, Jean, 1363–1429.
2. Theologians—France—Biography
I. Title.

BX4705 .G45M34 2005
282.092—dc22
[B]
2005020446

Printed in the United States of America
Published by The Pennsylvania State University Press,
University Park, PA 16802-1003

The Pennsylvania State University Press
is a member of the
Association of American University Presses.

It is the policy of The Pennsylvania State University Press to use acid-free paper. Publications on uncoated stock satisfy the minimum requirements of American National Standard for Information Sciences—Permanence of Paper for Printed Library Materials, ANSI Z39.48–1992.

Frontispiece: 1502 engraving of Jean Gerson, attributed to Albrecht Dürer. Courtesy of Antoni Kosinski, Princeton University.

To Ann, eternal spring

Contents

List of Illustrations

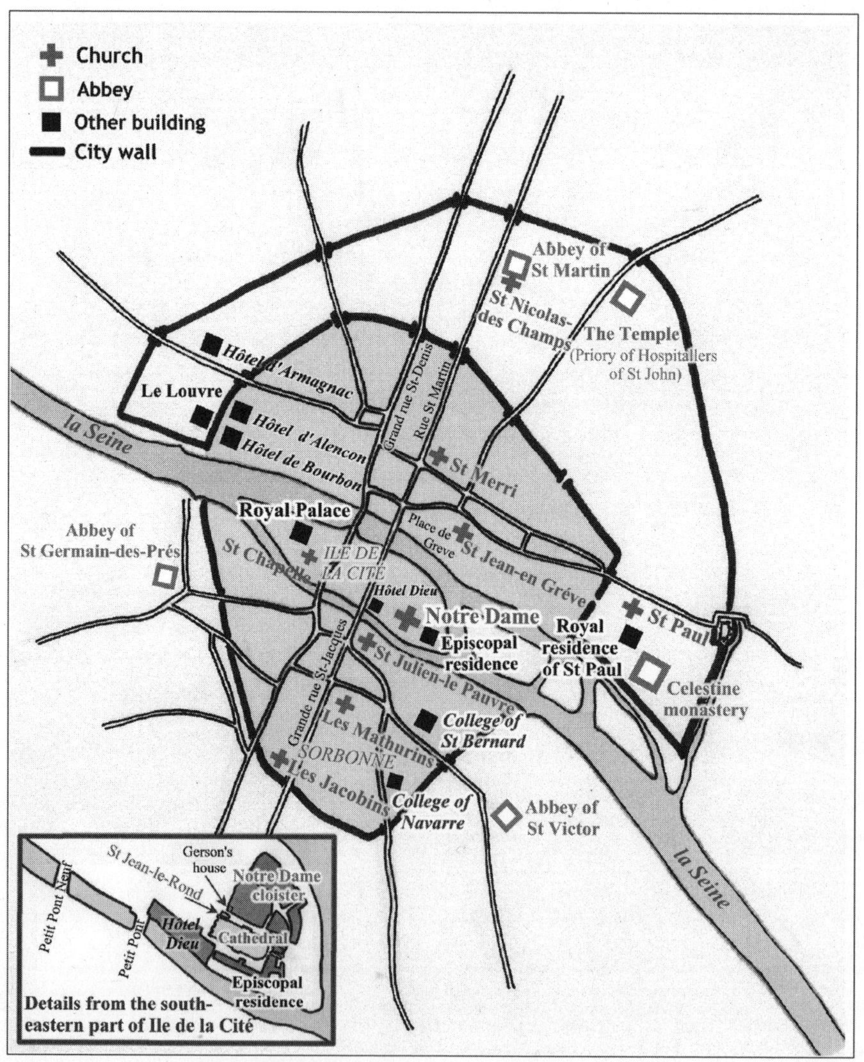
Church
Abbey
Other building
City wall
Abbey of St Martin
St Nicolas-des Champs
The Temple
(Priory of Hospitallers of St John)
Hôtel d'Armagnac
Le Louvre
Hôtel d'Alencon
Hôtel de Bourbon
la Seine
Grand rue St-Denis
Rue St Martin
St Merri
Royal Palace
Place de Greve
St Jean-en Gréve
Abbey of St Germain-des-Prés
St Chapelle
ILE DE LA CITÉ
Hôtel Dieu
Notre Dame
Episcopal residence
Royal residence of St Paul
St Paul
Celestine monastery
Grande rue St-Jacques
St Julien-le Pauvre
College of St Bernard
Les Mathurins
SORBONNE
Les Jacobins
College of Navarre
Abbey of St Victor
la Seine
Gerson's house
St Jean-le-Rond
Notre Dame cloister
Petit Pont Neuf
Hôtel Dieu
Cathedral
Petit Pont
Episcopal residence
Details from the south-eastern part of Ile de la Cité

Map 1 Gerson's Paris. By Johnny Gøgsig Jakobsen, Holbæk

Preface

This biography was written at the end of the twentieth century and in the first years of the twenty-first. It is based on a careful reading of the Latin and French writings of Jean Gerson (1363–1429). Using the life-and-times formula and avoiding any fashionable theoretical approach, I have sought to place Gerson within the context of his age. This age, at the cusp of the medieval and the modern world, I believe has great importance for us today, for in it I find a world that might have been, had the reform program of men like Gerson been given the chance it deserved.

History is made up of stories about people and the societies in which they lived in the past. Gerson's story is part of a larger tale of families and universities, faculties of theology, conciliar reforms, monastic renewals, court intrigue, savage internecine battles, and death by plague. I have tried to bring some of these narratives to life for the reader without dwelling excessively on the brutality of the age, and without waxing nostalgic about its dreams and ideals.

All along I have been aware of the difficulty of conveying Gerson's thought and experience without a tiresome recounting of the contents of his writings. But since many of Gerson's works have been my main source, a summary of them was frequently necessary. It is in these works that I discover him as person, priest, teacher, theologian, and perhaps also mystic. Time and again I return to these sources in order to understand the meaning of his life. Only in the final chapter do I begin to ask how these writings were received by the wider world.

Limitations of space have forced me to forego a broad comparison of Gerson's thinking with that of his contemporaries. Another way to Gerson I did not pursue is a thematic consideration of his writings, in terms of family bonds, ecclesiology, pastoral thinking, and mystical theology. Instead I have followed Gerson chronologically through the course of his life in its various stages. In tracing the development of his thinking, I have sought to determine how the changes in his personal life and in the world around him are reflected in his writings.

Subsequent to taking office as chancellor of the University of Paris in 1395, Gerson, as I came to realize in my earliest work on him, experienced an overwhelming crisis of faith. A second period of turmoil began in April 1413 when he was driven out of his lodgings in the precinct of Notre Dame cathedral. He had to take refuge in the "high vaults" of the church where he reconsidered his earlier attempt to reconcile rival factions in the royal family.

In this period Gerson found in Saint Joseph a person to love and venerate. It was only in the last stage of my research that I began to understand why he expended so much of his time and effort during the years 1413 to 1417 attacking the defense of tyrannicide made by one of his colleagues at the faculty of theology. Until then, Gerson's stance had been a mystery to me, for it seemed to preclude his full involvement in the reform of the Church at the Council of Constance. But as I came to understand Gerson's second great crisis of conscience, I began to appreciate him in the roles in which he saw himself as outsider, pilgrim, and foreigner.

I have come to perceive these crises in Gerson's emotional and intellectual life as fruitful for his self-understanding and for his writings. It was through Gerson that the affective theology of the eleventh and twelfth century, as it developed among monastic writers such as Anselm of Canterbury and Richard of Saint Victor, returned to Paris and provided a new context for scholastic theology. The vehicle of this new theology for Gerson became the brief treatise, partially replacing the accepted scholastic form of questions and answers with a host of authorities. In the midst of the pressures of his work and in response to a church and a society in disarray, Gerson broke the scholastic mold and returned to an older monastic one, more personal and individual.

His writings reveal a rich spiritual and emotional life which, in previous centuries, did not gain the attention or study it deserves. At present, however, I sense among both European and North American medievalists an opening to Gerson as a key medieval thinker and spiritual writer.

I have been encouraged in my work on Gerson by the biographical approach to Anselm of Canterbury used in the 1960s by my Oxford teacher R. W. Southern. His formula, as he once described it to me, was to make no distinction between history and biography, for "history is everything." Initially he used all the available sources on Anselm and his period with which to create a complete portrait of the man. Later, in the 1990s, Southern rewrote this biography and made it much narrower, a meditation on the meaning of Anselm's life and thought. Here the monastic context and Anselm's biographer Eadmer almost disappear. The result is a different kind of biography, one in which Southern spoke directly with Anselm about his writings in terms of his search for God.

Southern's first approach of total biography and his later contemplative meeting with his subject have both inspired me. I make no claim to knowing the landscape of late medieval France as Southern knew Anglo-Norman England; nor am I able to reach the depths of theological understanding at which Southern arrived in his later work. Gerson has no contemporary biographer, as Anselm had his monk Eadmer, to tell me about my subject's everyday life, conversation, and encounters.

Not only because of more limited insight, but also because of more limited sources, I cannot portray sides of Gerson that Southern perceived in his Anselm. In remembering Southern, who died in 2001, I celebrate a mentor and a friend who became a spiritual father.

Another source of inspiration for my biography has been the work of Peter Brown of Princeton. In the last two decades he has been a perennial guide and friend. His biography of Augustine from 1967 has been a model for my writing in the genre. He made the man come alive in the context of his friends and interests. Yet here again, Peter Brown has sources about his Augustine that do not exist for Gerson. Augustine can be seen at the center of a circle of friends, while Gerson's friendships are almost hidden from view. I have done my best to make use of the few instances where a friend (or an enemy) wrote about Gerson, but most of the time I describe the world through Gerson's eyes alone.

A third colleague and friend whose words have given me faith in doing history and biography has been my first teacher of medieval history, Robert Brentano of the University of California at Berkeley. I first heard him speak about Anselm and Bernard of Clairvaux when I was a freshman in the autumn of 1964. Here was a voice that conveyed the excitement and importance of studying medieval history. Through Brentano's open-ended and indefinable approach to the past, I came to believe in the worth of writing history that deals with human feeling as well as with thought. In Brentano's work, as in Southern's and Brown's, I found a spirituality where, at its best, thought and feeling become one.

As with my other models, I cannot reproduce Robert Brentano's insights. But I look to him as a brilliant source of inspiration not only for myself but also for generations of medievalists who first encountered him as undergraduates or graduates at Berkeley. With his death in November 2002, we have lost one of the great teachers of medieval history of the second half of the twentieth century. His fifty years at Berkeley, from 1952 to 2002, were truly a time of flowering for medieval studies, and I want to remember him especially for his course on medieval biography taught in the chaotic spring of 1968.

A fourth person to whom I am indebted and without whose support and guidance this biography could never have appeared is Gilbert Ouy, the gersonian expert sans pareil. Ever since I first contacted him in the early 1990s, Gilbert Ouy has been generous in sending me his articles, criticizing my writings, and providing answers to my queries. In several encounters at his study at Choisy-le-Roi outside of Paris, we have discussed passionately what can and cannot be said about Gerson. Ouy has been the center of a reevaluation of Gerson in terms of the coming of humanism from Italy to Northern Europe. I believe Gilbert Ouy could have written a much better biography of Gerson than I am able to offer, but since he has chosen not to do so, let the inevitable fool step in where a scholarly angel has decided not to tread.

I was privileged in 2001 to be given time to research and write two of the central chapters of this biography, covering the years immediately before and during the Council of Constance (1415–1418). At the Danish Institute for Advanced Study in the Humanities in Copenhagen, I was freed from all teaching duties. I am grateful to the director of the institute, the historian and biographer Birgitte Possing, for memorable conversations and seminars on our common passion.

I also want to thank the fellows and personnel of the institute and especially my colleagues there, anthropologist Christian Kordt Højbjerg and historian Kurt Villads Jensen, for patient reading of my chapter drafts and helpful criticism.*

Others to whom I am grateful are Anthony Perron of Loyola Marymount University in Los Angeles; Russell Friedman of the Thomas Institute in Cologne; James France, Cistercian scholar in Blewbury, Oxfordshire; Pauline Matarasso, translator and biographer, of Oxford; the late Norman F. Cantor, emeritus professor of history at New York University; Bernard McGinn, emeritus professor of the Divinity School at the University of Chicago; Jacques Berlioz, *directeur de recherches* at the Centre National de Recherches Scientifiques, and Hervé Chopin, archaeologist of Lyon, France. In meetings, phone calls, emails and face-to-face conversations, these friends and colleagues have given me the encouragement and guidance I needed. My friend since childhood, Michael West Oborne, has kindly taken me to the sites of Gerson's early life and has, since the 1970s, shared my interest in medieval life and history. I am also grateful to my former student Johnny Gøgsig Jakobsen of Holbæk for drawing the maps according to my specifications. My editor at the Pennsylvania State University Press, Peter Potter, has been a model of dependability and efficiency, a beacon of light in academic publishing.**

I finally want to thank my friend, companion, and wife, Ann Kirstin Pedersen. My everyday life with her, our son Christian Sung Dan, and our collection of once homeless cats in the Danish countryside has been a point of departure for everything else in my existence. The love we have shared since 1967 is the basis of my understanding of the loves Jean Gerson sought in his own life. It is to Ann that I dedicate this book.

Svallerup, Kalundborg, Denmark
The anniversary of Gerson's death
12 July 2005

* Thanks to shortsighted politicians and university administrators, however, the institute's existence will not be extended beyond this year.

** The Press's copyeditor, Brigitte M. Goldstein, has skillfully weeded out many of my "Dinglish" (Danish-English) phrases.

Guide to Readers

In writing a book in a time when standards and practices are constantly changing, I have had to make some decisions that may irritate some readers. I have chosen, for example, to keep Gerson's French name, *Jean,* and also to call his brothers, who had the same forename, *Jean the Celestine* and *Jean the Benedictine,* in order to distinguish them from their eldest brother. Otherwise I have for the most part translated French names into English.

A second problem has been capitalization. There is a tendency nowadays to "downsize" what used to be proper nouns, and I have followed it for the most part. In writing of the medieval Christian Church, I have capitalized the term. When I use "the Church," I mean the international institution as a whole, while "church" refers to local churches. In chapter 11, dealing with the national churches of the fifteenth century, I have also capitalized terms like the Gallican Church, for example. In speaking of the Great Schism (1378–1417), with two or three popes at the same time, I also capitalize the term.

In making endnotes, it is always a question how much information to provide. I have restricted myself to brief references to author and title, and I leave the full information to the bibliography. I have also tried to keep scholarly polemics to a minimum, preferring to concentrate on the narrative of Gerson's life rather than on disagreements among the experts. This practice has been necessary in order to limit the size of this book, which easily could have been twice as long.

In citing from Gerson, I also had to restrain myself. In many instances, I have provided only a reference to the volume of the Glorieux edition and the page number and have included this notation in the text itself, in order to limit the number of notes and to spare the reader from looking elsewhere for a reference.

In some places I have cited a few words or even a whole sentence in the original Latin or French in my text to give the reader a better sense of Gerson's use of language. Here I follow Glorieux's spelling. In most cases, however, rather than intimidating the reader who is not an expert in medieval Latin or French, I have paraphrased the quotations or tried to make their meaning immediately clear.

Biblical references are taken from the Latin Vulgate, the version Gerson used. Here Psalm 9 includes what later was broken up into two psalms, with the result that Vulgate numbering is equal to modern practice minus one.

Frequently Used Abbreviations

Alberigo = *Conciliorum Oecumenicorum Decreta,* ed. Centro di Documentazione, Istituto per le Scienze Religiose, Bologna, curantibus Josepho Alberigo, Perikle-P. Joannou, Claudio Leonardi, Paulo Prodi. Basel: Herder, 1962.

Crowder = *Unity, Heresy and Reform 1378–1460: The Conciliar Response to the Great Schism.* London: Edward Arnold, 1977.

CRSD = *Chronique du Religieux de Saint-Denys,* ed. M.L. Bellaguet, originally 1842; reprinted 1994. Reference according to livre and chapter, with original tome number and reprint volume number.

CUP = *Chartularium Universitatis Parisiensis,* ed. Heinrich Denifle, with volume and number. Vol. 3: Paris, Delalain (1894); vol. 4 (1897).

Du Pin (with volume and page or column) = *Johannes Gerson. Opera Omnia,* vols. 1–5, ed. Louis Ellies Du Pin. Hildesheim: Georg Olms Verlag, 1987. Reprint of the Antwerp edition of 1706.

EW = *Jean Gerson. Early Works,* trans. and intro. Brian Patrick McGuire. New York: Paulist Press, 1998.

Finke = *Acta Concilii Constanciensis,* vols. 1–4, ed. Heinrich Finke. Münster in Westfalen: Regensbergsche Buchhandlung, 1896–1928.

Gl (with volume and page number) = *Jean Gerson. Oeuvres complètes,* vols. 1–10, ed. Palemon Glorieux. Desclée & Cie: Paris, 1960–73. Volume 7 is in two tomes, referred to as 7.1 and 7.2

Hardt = *Rerum Concilii Oecumenici Constantiensis,* vols. 1–4, ed. Hermann von der Hardt. Frankfurt and Leipzig: Christian Genschius, 1697–1700.

Hefele-Leclercq = *Histoire des conciles,* Charles-Joseph Hefele and Henri Leclercq. Paris: Letouzey et Ané. Tome 6.2 (1915) covers 1311–1409. Tome 7.1 (1916) 1409–1430, including Pisa and Constance. Tome 7.2 (1916) 1431–64, including Basel.

Jadart = *Jean de Gerson. Recherches sur son origine, son village natal et sa famille,* Henri Jadart. Reims: Deligne et Renart, 1881.

Morrall = *Gerson and the Great Schism,* John B. Morrall. Manchester, U.K.: Manchester University Press, 1960.

PL = *Patrologiae latinae cursus completus,* ed. Jean Paul Migne, 221 volumes plus supplements. Paris, 1844–1871.

Posthumus Meyjes = *Jean Gerson. Apostle of Unity. His Church Politics and Ecclesiology,* G.H.M. Posthumus Meyjes, trans. J. C. Grayson. Leiden: Brill, 1999.

Rashdall = *The Universities of Europe in the Middle Ages,* Hastings Rashdall 1895, revised by F. M. Powicke and A. B. Emden, vols. 1–3. Oxford, U.K.: Oxford University Press 1936.

Valois = *La France et le grand schisme d'Occident,* Noël Valois. Paris: Alphonse Picard. Vols. 1–2 (1896) for 1378–1394; vol. 3 (1901) for 1394–1407; vol. 4 (1902) 1408–1417, and beyond.

Jean Gerson and the Last Medieval Reformation

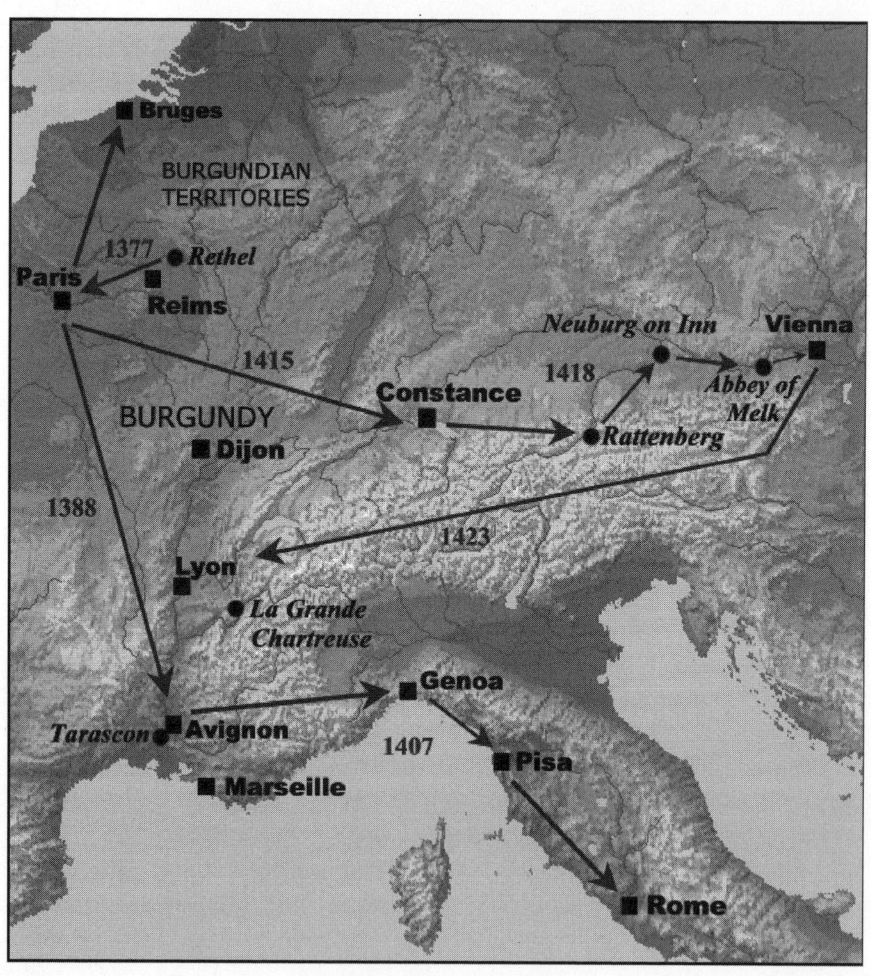

Map 2 Gerson's Europe. By Johnny Døgsig Jakobsen, Holbæk

One Life in the Shadow of Death

To the northeast of Paris lies the county of Champagne, renowned for unforgettable sparkling wines and the great cathedral at Reims. Occupying a prominent place next to the main door of this soaring gothic structure, the statue of a smiling angel survives centuries of unrest, religious war, and revolution since the Middle Ages.

In the early 1370s a schoolboy named Jean may have noticed the smiling angel. The youth, who came from the neighboring county of Rethel, may have gone to school at the great abbey of Saint Rémi at Reims.

Jean was born in 1363 in the hamlet of Gerson, a place that has now disappeared from the map of France. He was probably christened in the parish church at nearby Barby, the first-born of twelve children to a peasant father and mother. Later, at the University of Paris, Jean took his surname from this hamlet and became Jean Gerson, *Maistre Iean Iarson.* Future generations would come to know him as Jean Le Charlier Gerson. Jean, the peasant son, became a theologian and church reformer. Jean, the local boy, became a central figure in an international effort to save and renew the unity of medieval life and culture within the Christian world.[1]

Gerson reached the top of the social ladder at a very early age with unequalled alacrity. In 1395, at the age of thirty-two, he became chancellor of the University of Paris, a title he kept until his death in 1429. One factor that may have contributed to such early success was demographic, the lack of competition in a world where new generations had been decimated, not only in the 1340s but also in the 1360s, when repeated plague epidemics swept through Western Europe. The decreased population left room for growth and change at the University of Paris as well as in towns and villages all over Europe.

Gerson himself may not have been aware that the decline in the population had made it possible for peasants to demand higher wages on the land and aspire for their sons to reach top positions in the church hierarchy. In objective terms, however, Gerson belonged to a generation that was under less economic and social pressure than its predecessors.

After its initial appearance in 1348–1351, the plague returned repeatedly, ravaging town and countryside. But the peoples of Europe also came to build up antibodies against the scourge, decreasing the likelihood of an imminent end of the world through this disease. In the prospect of continuity and renewal of life, the young Gerson could trust in the promise of what we call European civilization and what he characterized as *christianitas,* the spiritual realm of Christendom. Here individual commitment to social goals and religious ideals had a chance to flourish. One person could make a difference by bringing others to salvation and thus assuring his own.

Jean was a gifted child who probably from his early years was considered for service in the Church, the one path a peasant boy could climb in seeking social advancement. Both the hope of worldly success and the pull of religious devotion motivated Jean and his parents. One of Gerson's few memories of his father that he later put down in writing was how Arnaut le Charlier explained Christ's love by stretching out his arms in imitation of Jesus on the cross.[2] Like so many boys who joined the clergy or became monks, Jean Gerson seems to have been especially attached to his mother. Elisabeth la Chardenière came from a leading family in the district and may not have considered herself to be a peasant at all. She was devoted to her children, as she indicates in a letter to Jean's younger brothers when they were living with him in Paris:

> I, being your mother, call upon you now as my two dear children. Since I cannot do so in speech, I address you in this letter. I ask you to listen to me. Do not close your ears to the words of the one who often patiently listened to the crying and wailing of your infancy. Listen then, listen and follow the first instruction of your mother as she gives it.
>
> This is that you fear and love God with all your heart and all your mind, so much so that you for nothing would consent to sin. [. . .]
>
> You would be most unnatural children, may God not allow that, if you forgot me, who has remembered and thought of you, and who will continue to do so as long as it pleases God. Think of my old age and of the great and terrible need that I now have and will have at the last moment of death. Think of the terror and fear I have that my repentance will not be sufficient for my trespasses. . . .

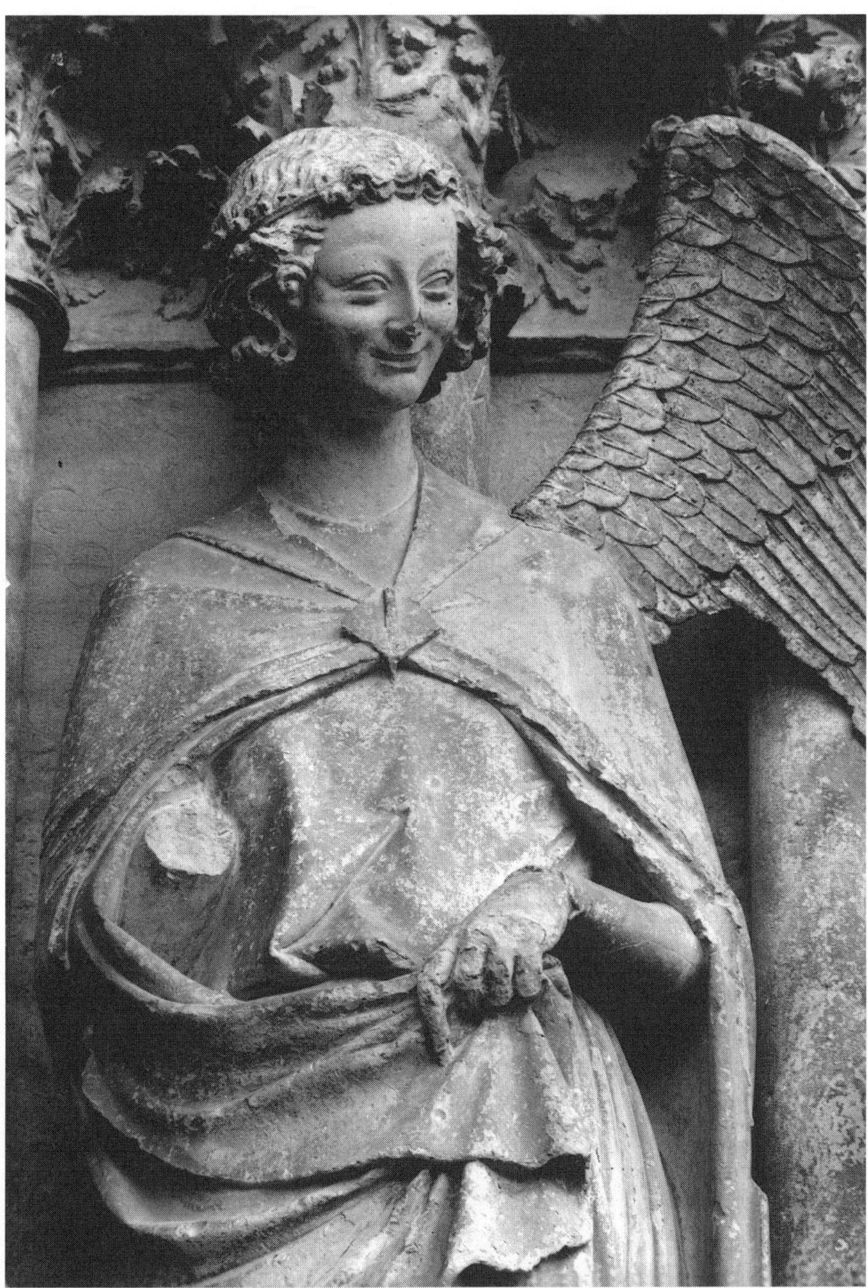

FIG. 1 Smiling angel at the Annunciation. West façade of the cathedral of Reims, thirteenth century. Gerson in his youth may have seen the angel. He certainly passed the cathedral several times when he was at Reims in 1408 for a synod. (Photo by author)

FIG. 2 Cathedral of Reims, site of royal anointing since Merovingian times. (Photo by author)

> Dear children, remember also your good father with whom alone I have lived for such a long time and in harmony in God's service. Take as an example your good sisters and pray devoutly for them, for they do not forget you . . . and make sure that the brother with whom you are living is always pleased with you, as he now is. This makes me so happy that I cannot tell you. In the opposite case I would feel so much pain that it would almost kill me.[3]

This is the one source we have directly from Gerson's mother. It can be interpreted in a variety of ways. Recent scholarship has hinted that the letter may be Gerson's own creation, and not, as it claims to be, Elisabeth's words as taken down *par la main de poncete vostre seur,* Poncete, who was probably Gerson's youngest sister.[4] To my mind, the letter did originate from Elisabeth, even if Gerson edited it later. It is unusual, if not unique, to have the letter of a country woman to her university sons in the late fourteenth century. But the content is not really surprising. Elisabeth may very well have been devoted to her children in the way most mothers (and fathers) usually are, wanting them to be happy and to have success, in becoming good human beings, but worrying daily about them.

Gerson felt a close bond to his parents. He had every reason to consider them to be good Christians who gave him a belief in himself and his possibilities. Arnaut le Charlier and Elisabeth, having brought Jean into a world close to the soil, made sure that he would not have to cultivate it. Perhaps with the help of the parish priest at the nearby village, the young Gerson learned the rudiments of Latin and may have been sent on to the abbey of Saint Rémi. Here he would have been welcome to stay on and become a monk, as one of his younger brothers later did. Instead he either chose or was convinced to try a university education. This meant going to Paris and studying at the faculty of arts.

In 1377, at the age of fourteen, Jean set out for the most populous and important city in Northern Europe. His thoughts and feelings at this juncture in his life remain inaccessible to us. Later, however, in a memorable letter, he indirectly criticized his parents and family for pushing him into a university career and barring him from a more contemplative life. He was writing to one of his brothers who had left him behind at Paris in order to become a monk: "God showed great mercy to you, since you had no relatives or friends who wanted you to become something great in the world and so would have been opposed to your intention. It is, and always has been, quite different for me, as well as for countless other people who read in the book of experience that one's enemies are the members of one's own household. In order that we can take care of their children, they want us never to be children."[5] Here Gerson refers to a passage from the Gospel of Saint Matthew (10:36): our enemies can be the very members of our own family. His next sentence indicates regret that he was deprived of his childhood, for he had to look out for his siblings. He did so by pursuing a career that would bring him position and wealth that he could share with his family. Through a university education Gerson had a chance to gain preferment in the Church. He would have an income that might help him look after his old parents and place his brothers and sisters in religious institutions.

Gerson never forgot his humble social origins or his struggle to reach higher. He felt responsible for providing for his brothers and sisters. The price he paid was a sense of lost opportunities in discovering his own needs. Nevertheless, Gerson attained precisely what he sought. He became a distinguished doctor of theology and chancellor of the university.

Fourteenth-century Europe was perhaps more repressive and less tolerant toward new forms of thought than the medieval world of the previous century had been. But capable young men could still attend university at Paris or Oxford, make a career in the Church, and engage in the intellectual, social, and political disputes of their time. The very word that characterizes the work of the schools, *disputatio,* emphasizes that truth, rather than being something given, was attainable through structured yet free discussion of what previous masters had said or written. The result was often a solution to a problem that earlier generations had not imagined.

The attitude behind this quest for knowledge and understanding was summarized by the eleventh-century teacher Bernard of Chartres: "We are but dwarfs sitting on the shoulders of giants." Thanks to the giants of the past, new dwarfs could attain a high level of knowledge and thereby come to see further than their predecessors.

As a university master, Gerson revealed in his sermons that he had not forgotten the rural world that had formed him. Peasants made up the overwhelming bulk of the population and continued to do so after the Black Death. They had benefited from a relatively warm and dry period in Western Europe, starting in the eleventh century and lasting to the end of the thirteenth. Now the climate was turning cooler and wetter, making the growing season shorter and life more precarious than ever.

Since the eleventh century, the population of Europe had been growing steadily. In many regions, such as the south of England, Flanders and Brabant (today Belgium), as well as the area around Paris, all available arable land was under the plow. Centuries of draining marshes and building water mills and windmills had brought increased productivity, but now the land could barely support the population living on it. Already in the years 1315 to 1317 crops failed, and many areas in Western Europe experienced severe famines.[6]

Some historians have postulated that the rural population that experienced the plague after 1348 had already been weakened by years of crop failures and subsequent malnourishment. Such a direct link ignores the fact that the greatest mortality took place in the towns, where there were both well-fed and underfed people. The plague flea did not distinguish between rich and poor, but the brown rat and its deadly parasite tended to thrive where many people lived in close quarters. Some areas almost totally escaped the plague, while the wealthy often tried to escape to the countryside.[7]

The peasants had always known the dangers of crop failure and disease. For centuries the Church had been reaching out for the rural population. Priests saw to it that the walls of village churches were filled with the story of salvation. In much of Europe, most traces of these wall paintings are gone, but in the small kingdom of Denmark a wealth of such murals survives.

In one illustration from the fourteenth century, peasants could look up at three young and handsome kings on horseback, all dressed up in finery. The kings meet three skeletal figures, with worms emerging from their viscera. The Latin text hardly needed translation into the vernacular, for the pictures speak for themselves: "What you are, we were; what we are, you will be."[8]

Such a reminder of death, *memento mori,* had been a stock theme of Christian art since Late Antiquity. But in the mid-fourteenth century the message had a more immediate application than ever before. Fresh young knights were being cut down by the sword on the battlefield and by disease in their sleeping chambers. High birth, even kingship, was no guarantee of longevity. Almost the opposite was the case. Sons of kings often did not live to inherit their kingdoms. The brave knight and victor at the fateful battle of Crécy, the Black Prince (d. 1376), did not outlive his father, England's Edward III (1327–1377).

The French monarchy, the most powerful and prestigious in medieval Europe, had been rocked by the 1346 English military victory at Crécy. Even though the French greatly outnumbered the English, they were slaughtered because of poor military strategy. The flower of French chivalry had sought to display individual acts of bravery and had attacked the English before the signal to advance was given. The French ended up paying dearly for a classic failure of military coordination. A dynastic conflict with England that stretched back to the thirteenth century now continued in the form of a war whose intermittent recurrences before, during, and after Gerson's lifetime have been summarized as the Hundred Years War (1336–1453).[9]

During this period, France was ruled by a man who obeyed all the rules of knightly behavior and so ended up as a voluntary prisoner in England. John the Good (1350–1364) was not able to organize French material and military resources. His successor Charles V, known as "the Wise" (1364–1380) had much greater success and was well on his way to restoring French hegemony when he was overtaken by an early death.

Besides the monarchy, another great French but also universal institution, the University of Paris, was in crisis. Since the early thirteenth century, the university had been the darling of popes, bishops, and kings and called itself the king's daughter, *la fille du roi.* But the Black Death in mid-century also left its mark here. The Faculty of Medicine tried to counter the disease by circulating a popular pamphlet of good advice.[10] Survivors accused the good doctors of incompetence and even witchcraft, for the pamphlets rarely helped and the doctors' knowledge seemed to come from dark places.

At the more prestigious Faculty of Theology, professors had offered prayers, but their knowledge and disputations may have seemed irrelevant in the midst of continuing catastrophe. The university was being challenged by questions that exceeded the power of academic discourse. At the same time the usefulness of the university to medieval church and society was being questioned.

For more than a century, the masters of the University of Paris had been able to set their own agenda in terms of teaching and research. They had made their corporation into the intellectual center of the Western world. Boldly they had received, interpreted, and partly christianized the writings of Aristotle. In combining "the philosopher" with Christian revelation, the masters tried to understand the world by tackling the contradiction between Aristotle's assertion of an eternal world and the creation account in the Book of Genesis.

In the mid-thirteenth century some masters in the arts faculty (what we would call the humanities) had concluded that philosophy and theology give different answers. Theology had to be respected as a higher science, but philosophy, they insisted, has its own truths. The dispute between the two branches of knowledge ended in a draw.[11] A brilliant master named William of Ockham participated in this discussion. A probable victim of the first outbreak of the plague, he died not as a teacher in Paris but as an exile in Munich. Ockham's philosophical thinking had upset many of his Paris colleagues. He refused to let them multiply mental concepts in trying to explain the ideas we harbor in our minds. Ockham came to be excoriated as a nominalist, one who believes that ideas exist only in the mind as an aggregate of information from the senses. Words and concepts do not necessarily reflect anything that exists outside the mind.[12]

Traditional theologians objected to Ockham's sparse world in which things exist only in themselves and do not necessarily reflect a higher divine world of ideas. For Ockham our ideas do not logically point to a creator. Theology is the result of God's revelation. There is no such thing as a natural theology building on a meeting between human minds and God's creation.

Ockham undermined the idealistic basis of theology, but it was his political thought that made it impossible for him to continue teaching at the University of Paris.[13] A member of the Franciscan Order, Ockham refused to ignore its original ideal of poverty and demanded that the Church as a whole give up its acquisitive ways. He criticized the papacy and insisted, with some of his fellow Franciscans, that Christ and the apostles had lived in a state of poverty their successors in the

Church had abandoned. Ockham had to leave Paris and seek political asylum at the court of the German king.

Another critic of the Church was the Italian humanist Petrarch (1304–1374). After first-hand experience of the papal court at Avignon, he excoriated churchmen not only for a lax way of life but also for the Latin they used. Petrarch demanded a return to the pristine language of Cicero and Vergil, instead of the "barbaric" Latin that had become the shorthand of intellectual discourse in Europe.

Petrarch's successors in Italy believed that the heartland of medieval culture, Northern France, the Rhineland, and the Low Countries, with their gothic art and architecture, had mistreated Rome's heritage. No art or creativity was possible outside of Italy, they cried: *Oratores et poete extra Italian non querantur.*[14] Only they, the new humanists, could recover a lost classical heritage. Petrarch addressed letters to Cicero and wept over the ruins of Rome.[15]

However much Petrarch and his contemporaries tried to distance themselves from the medieval world, they remained very much a part of it. Behind their proud assertions of classical learning, they were devout Christians dedicated to church reform and fascinated by monastic ideals. Petrarch's brother was a Carthusian monk with whom he shared a love for the writings of the fourth-century African bishop, Augustine of Hippo (354–430).[16]

Petrarch called for an end to the residence of the papacy at Avignon, which he called "that western Babylon, worst of cities, very like to hell."[17] At the same time, he enjoyed the patronage of Avignon popes. In prayer and service he remained as much a medieval person as he was the proto-modern figure into which modern scholarship has converted him. In Petrarch's and Gerson's age, a single fervent "Hail Mary" could save a soul destined for hell and thus cheat the devil of his prize.

For sixteenth-century reformers this belief in action or words as meritorious in themselves was a misunderstanding. From Martin Luther on, what mattered was an overwhelming act of faith in one's own salvation. Luther shoved aside the idea of a spiritual treasury of the Church on which all could draw and declared it to be of no value. The new Catholics who emerged from the Council of Trent tried to cut back on indulgences and superstitious practices. For Luther's successor Calvin, we are locked into the fate of our predestination.

The modern world has been built on the assumption that the individual in one way or other is determined, or predetermined, by either inner or outer forces. Not so the world of Gerson. He saw the development of his life as his own decision. Salvation or damnation for him resulted not from a single act of faith or a divine decree, but from choices the individual makes. In spite of their culture's material limitations, medieval people insisted on their freedom as individuals to create heaven or hell for themselves in this life and the next. Theologians had long been teaching that what matters in human life is not so much outward performance as inward intention.[18] An act is not bad or good in itself. It is the intention behind it that decides moral value.

When people in the Middle Ages made choices, they usually did so by thinking of their families. In his Paris years, Gerson never forgot his sisters and wrote to them about what he thought was best for them. Gerson's advice, as we shall see, was that they remain together on the family homestead and not marry.

Medieval society, even more than its modern successors, can be seen in terms of family passions. The knights who fought the battles of the Hundred Year's War acted according to what they thought were family interests. They dreamed of conquest and plunder that they could bring back home. Best of all, they hoped to take captive some high aristocratic figure and demand a ransom from his family. The chroniclers of these wars took such practices for granted and concentrated on bold moments of military prowess instead of on war's grime and chaos.[19] Every knight hoped to come home a richer man than he had left, but many never came home at all.

The family was so important that one priest (admittedly a heretic) went so far as to say that it would be better if members of his family could marry each other in order to keep the family property from being divided. For this man, the prohibition against incest was a real shame, for it meant that families had to ally themselves with each other. If sister and brother could marry, then family lands would be kept intact.[20]

The medieval Christian Church believed in the integrity of the family but not of its lands or material interests. The salvation of the individual was more important than the concerns of the family. God's law forbade incest, and family bonds ultimately had to give way to the love of God for his own sake.

Was it possible to love God and also love individual human beings? How could the two great commandments be reconciled? For many aristocratic and merchant families striving for position and wealth, the family was god. A family fortune could vanish in a moment on the battlefield, or in the premature death of the wife who was meant to bear offspring. Life was nasty, short, and brutish, but behind the secular values of getting and of giving away wealth was the Church's warning that everything passes away except the word of the Lord.

For Petrarch's brother as for many other young men in the fourteenth century, the best response to the fragility of life and the requirement of loving God was to enter a monastic order. Not a traditional aristocratic house with huge possessions and many social privileges, but a Carthusian house, where the members of the community saw each other only in church and chapter house and otherwise lived as hermits. In their isolated quarters such monks could look out on tiny gardens and receive their meals through small openings that did not allow even a glimpse of the brother outside.

The Carthusians had lived since the twelfth century in the countryside, but now they began to move their charterhouses into cities like Cologne and Paris. Here the brothers continued to live in isolation but impressed their surroundings with their hermitages on the fringes of urban bustle.[21]

Austerity and asceticism had long attracted medieval Christians, but the new or reformed orders of the fourteenth century, especially the Celestines and the Carthusians, exercised a special fascination. The Carthusians could boast that they never had to be reformed, for they had never been "deformed." The Celestines could point to their founder, the hermit Peter Morrone, who was elected pope in 1294 and took the name Celestine. Five months later, he resigned, the only pope with the wisdom to give up the keys of Saint Peter. Peter's *gran rifiuto* (great refusal) caught the imagination of Dante, who put him in hell for his lack of courage. But Celestine was relegated only to its vestibule.[22] Dante reserved the lower regions and his full condemnation for popes who, hailing from greedy Italian families, used the office to grab as much loot as possible.

Amid such villainy, the fourteenth century also produced saints.[23] Regardless of Dante's criticism, there were many devoted to the figure of Celestine V. But no later pope ever chose to canonize this remarkable predecessor. Celestine monks, however, remembered their founder by spreading foundations in his name all over France and neighboring areas. The Carthusians enjoyed even greater success. No plague, epidemic, or war could stop the two orders, not until the French Revolution snuffed out the Celestines, while the Carthusians persist to our time. Despite the doubts and hesitations of Jean Gerson, two of his younger brothers ended up as Celestine monks and perhaps attained the contemplative peace for which Jean himself yearned.

One of the most remarkable figures of the contemplative movement of the period is John Ruusbroec (1293–1381), who contributed to a group of Flemish mystics seeking to worship God through the direct experience of divine power.[24] Ruusbroec wrote in his *Spiritual Espousals* of a storm in which two spirits battle each other. These are God's spirit and ours. The struggle is one of love, in which we are wounded by the love of God.[25] Ruusbroec takes the familiar terminology of courtly love and turns it into a language of mystical religion. The individual forgets his or her own existence and becomes united with his or her beloved, God himself.

Theologians like Jean Gerson felt a strong attraction for such an affective union, but they were also afraid of how it might be understood. Gerson reviewed some of Ruusbroec's terms and warned that he was perilously close to pantheism, which dissolves the boundaries between God's being and our own and makes us part of God.[26] Ruusbroec, however, was never officially condemned for any of his writings or teachings. His bold language, referring to the mystic's consuming and devouring God, was generally looked upon as a metaphorical challenge, not a theological assertion.

Ruusbroec's followers attached themselves to a new form of religious devotion, the *Devotio Moderna*.[27] They refused to organize themselves in a clearly defined religious order and remained mostly part of the laity instead of seeking monastic life or priestly ordination. As in earlier centuries, medieval Christianity renewed the language of religious life and experience as it reformulated the meaning of the Gospels.

Franciscan friars were especially willing to encourage devout women to express the content of their mystical experiences. One of these women, Angela of Foligno (ca. 1248–1309), warned that the bonds of friendship in the sharing of such language could be dangerous: "Unless it is regulated by the proper weapons, true love of neighbor, that of devout men and women, either becomes carnal or gets lost in wasted conversations. For hearts bound to one another in this type of imperfect love are extremely indiscreet. This is why for fear of wrongful love, I am willing to suspect the love that is good."[28] Angela exercised great fascination on members of the opposite sex. She believed in sharing spiritual love with them but was wary that this attachment could turn into something physical.

So was Jean Gerson. He read Angela and quoted from her.[29] The fourteenth century was neither obsessed with sex nor oblivious to it. The priests and visionaries of the time did not need a Freud to tell them that sexual desire lies at the basis of much human activity and many a dream and fantasy. The hope of the medieval world, however, was that desire for love could be transformed and spiritualized. The knight would impress his lady not by seducing her but by doing valiant deeds in her honor. The priest would do service to the nun in whom he confided by making her revelations known to a skeptical world. The monk coped with the temptations of the flesh by turning to Mary's help and remembering her Son's sufferings.

The very act of reaching for the love of God was significant. Long before Johan Huizinga's brilliant *Waning of the Middle Ages* appeared in Dutch in 1919 and in English in 1924, historians had pointed to the failure of medieval civilization to live up to its own ideals.[30] Another approach is possible, without romanticizing the content and meaning of medieval life. In considering what emerged from the human wreckage and loss of the Black Death and in concentrating on the life of one person, the historian can see how a wounded medieval world got back into contact with the sources of its own strength and largely healed itself. Theologians like Gerson reinvigorated the belief in the unity of Christendom by pouring their lifeblood into both academic discourse and popular preaching.

It may be easy to see the Black Death as a great turning point of Western history, the end of the Middle Ages and the opening of the Modern Age. This Modern European World, which was based on a belief in technological progress and social improvement, began to unravel after the cataclysm of the First World War.[31] It is too easy, however, to make the Black Death the medieval pendant to the First

World War. However much I admire historians, such as Barbara Tuchman, for using the catastrophes of the fourteenth century to comment on the dilemmas of our own time, medieval culture was able to survive these terrible years and to renew itself.[32]

If the world stank of corpses in 1350, and again in 1363, the year Gerson was born, it was also full of light. John Ruusbroec, who survived the plague, rejoiced in what this light can do: "God bestows his light, and through that light a person responds with a free and perfect conversion; from these there arises a perfect love towards God, and from this love there issues a perfect sorrow for sin and a purification of one's conscience."[33] Beyond the light, the person would find a kind of nothingness, a state that could not be explained in words. As another spiritual writer put it, we here come into "a cloud of unknowing."[34]

The men and women who picked up their lives and began afresh after 1350 could have remained traumatized by what they had experienced. They could have spent the rest of their lives dwelling on the evil they had witnessed. Few seem to have done so. They accepted that they had come to live in a new world. Here war still raged. Plagues broke out again. But there were also prayer and song and even dance. Not only the dance of death, *danse macabre,* so well recorded in the art of the age, but dances celebrating joy in life, as we can see in the wall paintings of a Danish village church.[35]

Jews who survived persecution by Christians attempting to find scapegoats for the plague must have shaken their heads in sadness and called upon God's help. They had no reason to be optimistic about the future. But there was no holocaust in the fourteenth century. That was the doing of the twentieth. Christians might blame the "perfidious Jews," but they were allowed to maintain a necessary place in medieval society as merchants and moneylenders.[36]

Medieval life is full of contradictions. For every assertion about its content or meaning, the historian can make a counterstatement. In the mid-fourteenth century, however, practically everyone believed in God's goodness and mercy. This belief perhaps made it easier to assert that life makes sense. In the aftermath of death, there would be life. The stench of rotting corpses would not remain forever. Spring would return; flowers bloom; the world would be carpeted with green. As the Goliard poets two centuries earlier had sung: "The woods turn green; the bushes sprout leaves; the harsh winter gives way."[37]

After the triumph of death, there was life. In looking at the life of one person who lived between 1363 and 1429, the historian is faced with the challenge of representativity. I allow a dead white male to speak on behalf of an entire culture. But this voice can reveal more than the personal trials and hopes of Jean Gerson.

Always in contact with his social origins, he looked to the countryside as a point of departure for everything in his life. At the same time, Gerson took advantage of the possibilities a great medieval city offered. Its university milieu never constricted Gerson. From his mid-twenties, he was invited to preach at the royal court, sometimes in the king's presence. Eventually Gerson began to speak and write for a European audience on the topic of finding solutions to the papal Schism and reestablishing the unity of the Church. He became, in the phrase of a recent insightful evaluation of his persona, a public intellectual.[38]

Was Gerson a "self-fashioning" individual who made his way up the academic ladder without regard for others and kept aware of the next step he would take in order to profile himself? After an initial review of his childhood and youth, I will seek to locate the man within university and court through his own words. I will look at Gerson's dilemmas of faith and trust in other people in terms of nightmares that have grown large in European civilization and its North American version: the search for community when communities break down; the desire for love when human bonds do not last; the limitations of intellectual analysis when the emotions are left behind.

Jean Gerson was a medieval person who offered hope for renewal and reformation of the Christian Church. But Gerson's reform program was never carried out in full. His life experience as university teacher and church reformer points to the vulnerability of medieval solutions and their later collapse in the bitter reformations of the sixteenth century and beyond. But in terms of contemporary concerns about the breakdown of communities and what might be called the narcissism of culture, Gerson's world is still relevant. From the perspective of the twenty-first century, Gerson and the last medieval reformation of the Christian Church merit renewed attention.

Entering a Troubled World

The Lay of the Land

Rethel, Reims, Paris—the cities the young Gerson came to know still exist today, but now they are choked with traffic and fumes, the blessings of our modern age. In the fourteenth century these places were filled with human and animal noises and smells. Rethel lies about thirty-five kilometers northeast of Reims, on the border between the old province of Champagne and the Ardennes region. It borders the River Aisne which, like so many northern French rivers, makes its lazy way to a distant sea.

A few kilometers west of Rethel, on the way to the ancient Roman settlement of Château-Porcien, the village of Barby is still on the map. Here the church dates from 1880 and is closed most of the time. Across the road, a thoroughfare for speeding automobiles, is the modest Place Gerson. Inside the church, which a kind and ancient lady opens for the visitor, is a nineteenth-century monument to Gerson. The interior, on a November day a freezing waste of discarded spirituality, recalls a warmer, richer time. The church's medieval predecessor was in another part of the village, closer to the river. On this site the local cemetery still provides a place of peace and meditation, but the oldest graves go back only to the end of the nineteenth century.

As for Gerson, the hamlet next to Barby, where Jean, the first born of Arnaut le Charlier and Elisabeth la Chardenière, came into the world on 14 December 1363, no visible trace remains except for a wayside crucifix. According to the nineteenth-century local historian Henri Jadart, the cross marks the spot where a chapel dedicated to Saint Martin once provided a religious center for the village of Gerson. The settlement existed before Carolingian times, as indicated in the *Polyptych of Irmion,* a record of land holdings compiled by a great ninth-century abbot of the monastery of Saint Rémi at Reims.[1]

Until the dawn of the French Revolution, a century after the village itself disappeared, the hamlet of Gerson belonged to this abbey and thus linked the family of Arnaut to the world of the Church. The village of Barby on the west side of Gerson was owned by another monastery, but its parish church of Saint John the Baptist at Barby served both villages. Jean, who indicated in a later poem that he was baptized on the same day he was born, may have been taken to Barby and given his name from the church where he was christened.[2] Or the priest may have come to the chapel of Saint Martin in order to admit the son of Arnaut and Elisabeth into the Christian community.

The hamlet of Gerson once stood where Departmental Road 926 now cuts a swath from Rethel through Barby and crosses the stream called Bourgeron. Here peasants and skilled laborers knew how to make a living from the land. The inhabitants of the late fourteenth century and their monastic owners could draw on centuries of customs and a way of life that combined patience with skill.[3] By the nineteenth century, few remnants of the medieval village remained. Local names

Fig. 3 Sign from Place de Jean Gerson, across from the nineteenth-century church in the village of Rethel. (Photo by author)

and traditions, however, made it possible for the local historian Jadart in 1881 to map out the area.

Such a tiny place may seem an unlikely birthplace of a person who was to become the voice for reformation of the Christian Church that might have guaranteed the unity of Western Christendom. The humblest village, however, could and did in this period provide both political saints like Joan of Arc and theological stars like Jean Gerson.[4]

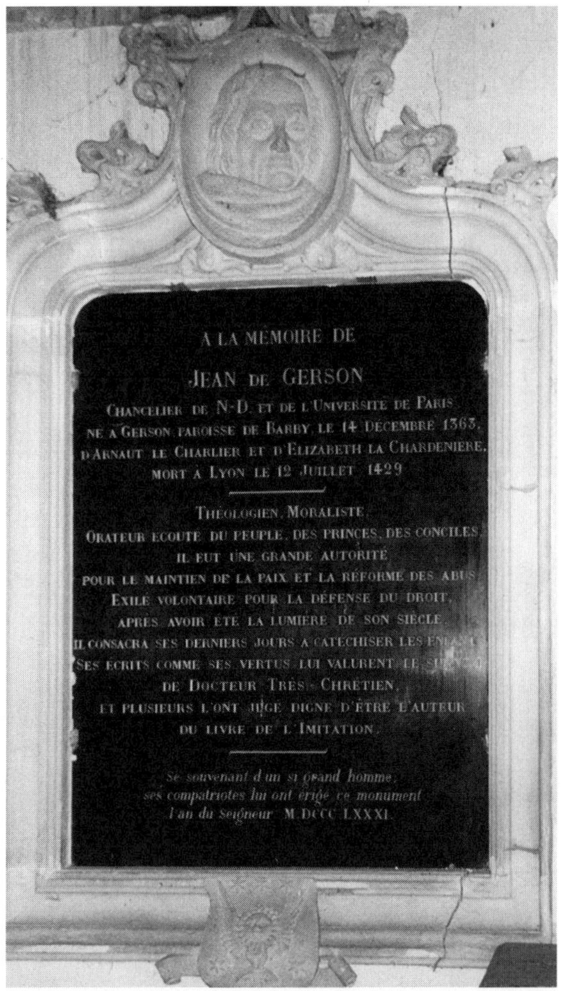

Fig. 4 1881 monument to Gerson in the parish church at Barby. Notice the assertion that he spent his last days teaching catechism to children. The text is more cautious, however, in attributing to him the authorship of *The Imitation of Christ*. (Photo by author)

Medieval Europe was a rural society from where some families sent their sons to the great university at Paris. Jean belonged to such a family, with parents who appreciated their child's intelligence and religious imagination. Arnaut may have been in minor orders, as many men were in this part of the world, a result of the ownership of the land by a monastic institution.[5] The influence of the Church created respect for learning and love of religion. To prove the power of prayer, Arnaut and Elisabeth once suggested to Jean that he pray for apples or nuts and then secretly cast such delicacies down on him from a high place.[6] They understood the literalness of a child's mind and wanted their son to believe that his prayers would be answered.

Years later, Gerson addressed prayers to various saints, prayers that continued and deepened the high medieval tradition of affective appeals to living human beings. Like an earlier theologian, Anselm of Canterbury, Jean Gerson addressed Saint John the Baptist, the patron of the church of Barby. Jean reminded his namesake of all that the saint could do for a wayward, suffering human being. He knew he was not worthy of the saint's help, "But then, alas, who would be worthy of

Fig. 5 Nineteenth-century cross marking the site of the hamlet of Gerson. (Photo by author)

it if grace did not come? I ask for and need this grace, o blessed Saint John, in remembering your name which is full of grace, the name that I carry, even though I do not deserve it."[7]

The Prospect of Life

For anyone born at the end of the year 1363, it was a good idea to reach out for any help a patron saint might provide. Life was not promising and prayer was perhaps the only way to influence an uncertain future. In 1361–62 a new wave of the plague had swept across Europe and had wiped out a good part of the new generation that had grown up after the first and worst years of sickness and death in mid-century.[8]

In spite of war, plague, and economic uncertainty, Jean Gerson came to live to a relatively old age by medieval standards. When he died on 12 July 1429, he was only a few years from his seventieth birthday. Despite repeated outbreaks of the plague in 1375 and later, Gerson seems not to have lived in the shadow of death. Few episodes of illness affected his ability to write theological treatises in Latin and devotional tracts in French. The list of his works is well above five hundred, and new writings from his hand, such as the prayer to John the Baptist quoted in part above, are still being discovered.[9]

The child's father was a village artisan. *Charlier,* meaning wheelwright, indicates that either Arnaut, or one of his ancestors, was given a last name for the profession of making and repairing wagons.[10] In his great poem *Josephina,* written at the Council of Constance after 1415, Gerson describes how Joseph taught his son Jesus the fashioning of objects from wood. The language reveals the author's knowledge of processes only a carpenter or his apprentice could know.[11] It is likely that young Jean was familiar with his father's work and may even have had some training in it.

In later life Gerson remained loyal to his parents and his siblings. He felt that he had to return to his sisters and brothers what his parents had sacrificed for him. "In all truth . . . our good parents, father and mother, once invested their goods and common inheritance for me, your oldest brother, so that I could learn the Holy Scriptures, and so it is reasonable that you can participate and profit from this [knowledge]" (Gl 7.1.158). Thus Jean Gerson explains to his sisters in 1407 why he was writing his *Spiritual Dialogue.* They deserved to be initiated into the insights theological training had brought their oldest brother.

By 1404 both parents had died, while Gerson continued to reflect on what they had given him. His words in the above passage about "biens et heritages communs" indicate that Arnaut and Elisabeth probably owned more than they could have earned from his profession or from working the land they were probably renting from the abbey of Saint Rémi. Elisabeth may well have brought some kind of dowry into the marriage, or the family may have been blessed with an inheritance at a later point.[12]

It is hard to place the family in a world with countless, subtle gradations according to background, education, and family. There is no doubt, however, that its place was modest. It soon became apparent that the oldest boy would enter the service of the Church. Young Jean may have been noticed by the priest of Barby or by a monk from the abbey of Saint Rémi or its priory at Rethel. He would have been taught to read Latin at an early age, paving his way for entry into a clerical world that rewarded intellectual proficiency and did not always discriminate on the basis of social background.[13]

Later in life Jean hinted that if he had been able to follow the path he really wanted, he would have chosen a monastic vocation without the demands of university life.[14] But his family apparently needed Jean to use the university as a social ladder that would perhaps open up career possibilities for his siblings. There could be no chance for Jean, as later was the case for his younger brothers, to withdraw from the world to a monastery. It remains one of the mysteries of Gerson's life, how the boy had been persuaded to set out for Paris. Even though an old Roman road took the straight and narrow route directly to this ancient city, the state of the countryside and the reputation of Paris hardly invited anyone to travel there.

Years of Hope: 1364–1377

Jean grew up in the shadow of what we call the Hundred Years War, a convenient but misleading term for an on-again, off-again armed conflict between France and England. For several years, spanning Gerson's childhood and youth, there was hope for an end to the hostilities and restoration of a strong monarchy in France. From 1364, when Charles V assumed the throne, until 1392, when his son Charles VI first succumbed to mental illness, the country functioned as a political unit able to cope with the English threat.[15]

Through much of the 1370s the English suffered one military defeat after another. There was nothing as memorable as Crécy in 1346 or Poitiers in 1356, and so the period is hardly mentioned in standard history books. But France was led from 1364 until his all too early death in 1380 by a king who slowly rebuilt the monarchy and reestablished its prestige. Unlike his knightly father, John the Good, Charles V did his best to avoid the battlefield and the possibility of capture. He was a brilliant military strategist who realized the importance of preserving an army from the chivalrous deeds of individual knights.

In 1377, the year Jean Gerson left home for Paris, King Edward III of England died. The new king, Richard II, Edward's grandson, was a ten-year-old child leaving England without a "natural leader."[16] King Charles took advantage of the situation and confiscated the duchy of Brittany in 1378. The same year saw an uprising of the Ciompi or day laborers in Florence. So began a series of popular revolts which in 1379 shook Flanders and in 1381 England.[17]

What was it like to grow up in a world where everything in social terms was so stable and yet so fragile? So far as the truths of Christendom and the structure of society were concerned, young Jean had no doubt in his mind. He was a member of God's people on its way to salvation, a pilgrim, a word and concept that came to mean a great deal to him, as he showed with the surname he took from his village. Gerson, he would point out, in Hebrew means "wanderer" or "pilgrim."[18]

Jean Gerson belonged to a society that defined itself through a vision that went back centuries, all the way to Carolingian theological writers. They described the necessary presence of *oratores,* those who pray; *bellatores,* those who fight; *laboratores,* those who work.[19] In his childhood, Gerson would have looked upon his family as workers who made it possible for the monks of Saint Rémi to pray. Such workers may themselves have prayed that their king and his nobles would fight valiantly to restore the integrity of the territory under the rule of the king of France, whose dynasty supposedly went back to King Clovis who, in 496, had been baptized by Saint Rémi, the first archbishop of Reims, and who lay buried in its great abbey church.[20] Every new king of France came to Reims and its great gothic cathedral to be anointed and crowned by the archbishop.

In 1364, and again in 1380, Reims was the scene of this anointing ceremony that guaranteed the continuity of the French monarchy. In later life Gerson visited this city, as in 1408, to attend a diocesan synod and to preach about reforming the Church.[21] But he may have already gotten to know Reims in the 1370s, before he left for Paris. The fact that the second eldest boy in the family, who was also called Jean, became a Benedictine monk (and so was called Jean the Benedictine), indicates a family bond at the abbey. Jean Gerson may have lived at Saint Rémi in order to get a rudimentary education in the Latin necessary for learning the grammar that formed the first part of the arts course at Paris.[22] Or he may have started out as a day student at the Benedictine priory at Rethel and then later have gone to Reims for better teachers.

The history of Reims in the later Middle Ages has been carefully researched. We know a great deal about its bourgeoisie and clergy, living in symbiosis and rivalry.[23] Even today the city is dominated by its two great churches, the cathedral and the abbey. Most tourists make do with the cathedral, restored after the damage of the First World War, an immense cavern of light and darkness inside and amazing statues outside, showing the baptism of Clovis, the resurrection of the dead and the Last Judgment in vivid images of bishops and other lords being pulled by devils into the mouth of hell.

At the other end of the city, in a district it once owned, is the church of Saint Rémi. Of the great medieval abbey only the chapter room is left. The remainder was redone in baroque style and reflects the continuing prosperity of the institution until the French Revolution. Now a municipal museum, the abbey buildings seem worlds away from the neighboring church, also a victim of the First World War but rebuilt with arches and vaults that capture the spirit of mature romanesque architecture on its way to gothic heights. Two towers flank the facade, but most striking are the two lower levels of the west front, the first with five great openings for doors and windows, the second level with five windows that are harbingers of the gothic fascination with great expanses of glass. Above the central window are two more levels, with a portico arcade and a great rose window placed in the center.

The learned Pierre de Celle, as abbot from 1162–1181, began the renovation and expansion of the church. He was influenced by Abbot Suger of Saint Denis outside Paris. Suger, the creator of the first gothic church, dreamed of space and light in a way romanesque architecture could not provide.[24] Pierre and his successor Simon (1182–1198) did their best to add gothic features to the solid romanesque building. Simon raised the walls of the nave and transepts of the church with pointed arches, and today the nave remains a miracle of romanesque sturdiness in the lower level and gothic lightness above.

Did Gerson appreciate what former abbots of Saint Rémi had done for the church of the abbey which owned his village? In all his writings, I find no reflections on church architecture. Gerson reveals little or nothing about his everyday life and the objects that filled it. But his works show us a love of language that perhaps began already in his earliest schooling. His poetry, hardly known even by those who study his theology, is better than its reputation and reached its zenith in his great *Josephina,* on the life of Jesus as experienced by Mary and especially by Joseph.[25] "The bilingual Gerson" made sure some of his central writings appeared both in French and Latin. The first language made them available for *les gens simples,* ordinary people; the second provided contact and dialogue with learned men all over Europe.[26]

The Gerson who wrote in both languages loved to quote from popular sayings, either in the vernacular French or in his Latin translation. He had an ear for what people said and how they described human foibles, and Gerson's works await a researcher to gather together this treasury of folk wisdom. At the same time he added sayings and stories he himself had heard or read in the *Lives of the Fathers* (*Vitae patrum*), a Latin version of Greek sayings going back to Late Antiquity. Another favorite source was apparently Jacques of Voragine's *Golden Legend* (*Legenda aurea*), a collection of saints' lives from the end of the thirteenth century. Here Gerson could find spiritual heroes and villains and moralize about their lives.[27]

Fig. 6 Abbey church of Saint Rémi, Reims, where Gerson's brother, Jean the Benedictine, was a monk. (Photo by author)

At the same time as he read such works of popular medieval Latin literature, the young Jean would also have begun digging into the Latin classics. Like so many schoolboys of his day, he was probably made to memorize the sayings of Cato, *Disticha Catonis,* with their generous serving of Stoic philosophy now seen in Christian terms. In a polemical letter from 1402, in which he attacked the *Romance of the Rose,* Gerson characterized it in terms that came from Cato: "This work could be described in the phrase that schoolboys recite: He is in agreement with no one when he is in disagreement with himself."[28]

Gerson's later writings show his familiarity with Latin poets and prose writers, among them Vergil, Seneca, Cicero, Horace.[29] Gerson seems to have had a phenomenal memory, for he stored away in his mind everything he read and later drew on it with ease for examples or sayings from both classical and biblical sources.

One of Gerson's literary devices later in life was to combine in the same sentence or paragraph quotations both from classical authors and from the Bible.[30] In this way he demonstrated the continuity of truth from the Greeks and Romans to their Christian inheritors. But the Bible remained the main staple of Gerson's intellectual diet. He wove into his writings the words of Scripture, whether Psalms, Gospel narratives, or Epistles, as he had them from the Latin Vulgate. He absorbed so completely the language of the Bible that it at times is hard to distinguish between his own expositions and the biblical language that provides their basis. Here he resembled Bernard of Clairvaux (1090–1153), who was one of his central inspirations and sources.[31]

What distinguishes Gerson from his contemporaries is his desire as a university scholar to make his Latin learning available in French, to women and those without Latin: *je veuil escripre en francois plus qu'en latin, et plus aux femmes que aux hommes* (I want to write in French rather than in Latin, and more for women than for men; Gl 7.1.16). But first he had to store up the necessary knowledge and arrange it in his own mind.

Gerson never seems to have forgotten his childhood learning, for he was one of the first university scholars who took seriously the task of teaching children. Probably soon after 1400, he wrote his *On Bringing Children to Christ.*[32] His great concern was that teachers might drive children away from the faith because of the corrupt lives they reveal to them. "Many parents and masters show either no or little concern for the habits of children or for protecting them by discipline" (Gl 9.673). "Children are daily being incited by the worst kind of talk to do evil, and no one freely stands in the way and urges the part of virtue by inciting them to the good" (675). Gerson was seldom concrete about what such evil involved, but he was especially concerned about the sixth commandment.

In a sermon on the virtues of Saint Bernard, he hinted that university teachers sometimes initiate their pupils into sexual acts: "Such people in the basest manner ruin those whom they ought to have saved and instructed."[33] In writing about children, he recalled his own youth: "Whoever . . . remembers the crimes of his youth and those of so many others, as I am aware for myself" (677).

Gerson's most specific provisions for the education and care of children are found in a collection of rules "for the boys of the church of Paris." Here in 1411 he provided a code for the choir boys of Notre Dame cathedral, warning against anyone "being admitted to spending time with the boys or being with them on the outside . . . so that our youths not be drawn into bad habits because of the evil of others . . . especially when someone can be led to perversion and brought to the most enormous of sins which are not to be named" (688–89).

The masters to whom the boys were entrusted had to be models of Christian life: "The master of grammar, who for the instruction of the youths is to be educated in grammar and logic, should live the kind of life that is appropriate for such a master. It should be arranged that both in the daytime and at night there always be a master with the boys, both in the school and wherever outside the boys may happen to be" (687). Supervision could, of course, hinder initiation into sexuality. Gerson's educational project based everything on sticking to a fixed rule, so that the boys at any given hour would have lessons in chant or song; at another hour, Latin grammar. Each boy was to keep watch over the others and was expected to report on others "if he has heard someone speaking French or swearing; if he has lied; if he has lied about another or slandered him; if he has struck him" (688). If a boy used bad or impure language or touched another boy in an unchaste manner, he was to be reported. Also of concern were boys who got up late or missed lessons, or those who talked in church.

Was Gerson trying to reproduce his own childhood educational world, or was he trying to avoid it? I think he was enshrining standards which he had sought in his youth but which he feared were not followed in the world he knew as an adult. He complained that academic colleagues criticized him for bothering with such trifles as primary education: *allegant officii dignitatem occupandam ad majora* (they assert that the dignity of my office should be concerned with more important matters; 679).

Gerson looked upon the world as a place full of danger and evil. Therefore children could not be left to themselves but required constant supervision: "We will not allow for any reason that boys go anywhere outside the school and church for singing, except with the special permission of their superiors. And then let a master be present, who will see that neither in eating nor in any other way they act improperly or immorally" (*excessive . . . aut inhoneste;* 688).

Perhaps this concern for care and guidance reflects the situation of Gerson after he left the family home and headed for Paris. At home he would never have been alone and would have been entrusted with looking out for his many brothers and sisters. We do not know the birth dates of most of his siblings, but the family grew in the later 1360s and 70s. Gerson's eldest sister was called Marion, the only one who later married.[34] Then came the second Jean, the later Benedictine at Saint Rémi, followed by Jabina and Raulina. Agnes and Pierre died as infants (Gl 2.226). There are two more sisters whose names Gerson does not give, perhaps because they were born after he left for Paris in 1377 and died in youth, thus never playing a significant role in his life.

In the 1380s two more brothers were born, Nicolas in 1382 and a third Jean, in 1384. They both came to study in Paris and lived for periods with their older brother and later became monks. These we call Jean the Benedictine and Jean the Celestine. Finally there was a sister named Poncete, whom we know from the extraordinary letter dictated by Elisabeth and written in the hand of Poncete to her brothers in Paris.[35]

The bonds of family were important to Jean Gerson, and he maintained contact with his sisters after the death of their mother in 1401 and their father in 1404. But already at the age of fourteen, Jean left his biological family to enter into the family of the Church. Probably around the time he set out for Paris in 1377, Gerson received the "crown" or tonsure that made him a cleric and thus set him off from the lay population. This bald spot on his skull would be with him for the rest of his life. It would be some years before he was ordained a priest, an event that Gerson never mentions amid the scattered references he provides in his writings about the events of his life.

But he did commemorate his tonsure. As he told King Charles VI in a sermon in 1405, it was the archbishop of Reims "who gave me my crown" (*qui me donna couronne* Gl 7.2.1166). This would have been Richard Picque (1375–1389), who also came to crown Charles king of France in 1380. In the 1405 sermon Gerson praised Richard Picque for having said to a noble "the lords of France are not such tyrants that they would martyr people for telling the truth." In other words it was possible in France to address a noble, or even the king, and tell him truthfully about the state of the kingdom without fearing for one's life. As we shall see, Gerson also insisted on speaking out and avoiding the court practice of flattery.

From the embrace of his family and its religious observances, the teenager Jean Gerson set out to face a foreign yet receptive world which, by the end of the 1380s, would open to him the royal court itself. But he never forgot his family and its expectations of him.

Entering the World: 1377–1381

A few kilometers northeast of Barby and the now vanished hamlet of Gerson lies another place that had fostered a distinguished university figure: the village of Sorbon. As far as I have been able to determine, no memorial exists there to the Robert whose birthplace gave its name to the college he founded in 1257 even though the Sorbonne took on such importance that it eventually became synonymous with the University of Paris. Robert of Sorbon started out as canon of Cambrai and later became canon of Notre Dame of Paris.[36] His foundation for sixteen theology students, who were divided equally among the four nations of the University of Paris (French, Norman, Picard, and German), had an international outlook in contrast to previous colleges that had been founded with local or regional interests in mind.

Robert, in the thirteenth century, took the name of his village with him to Paris as did Jean in the fourteenth century. In 1387 we find the name *Johanni de Gersonio* as master in arts and student of theology.[37] The young Jean was made welcome at the College of Navarre, founded by Joan, the queen of Philip the Fair, in 1304.[38] A much more ambitious project than the original Sorbonne, the College of Navarre was located on the left bank of the Seine, at the end of the Rue Sainte Geneviève and not far from the abbey of the same name, where Peter Abelard had come to teach in the early twelfth century.

The University of Paris had grown out of the schools whose teachers set up shop on the Ile de la Cité and the Petit Pont that linked the island with the left bank of the Seine. In order to teach, it was necessary to obtain a license from the chancellor of the cathedral of Notre Dame. But the abbot of Sainte Geneviève also had the right to grant licenses, at least to masters of arts. By the beginning of the thirteenth century, the masters had organized themselves into a guild, in Latin called *universitas*. Leaving behind the Ile de la Cité, they preferred the relative independence of the Mont Sainte Geneviève on the Left Bank, stretching up to the abbey. Dante mentions in his *Divine Comedy* a master of arts, Siger of Brabant, teaching in "the Street of Straw" (Rue de Fouarre), one of the few medieval street names still extant in Paris today.[39] Here the masters rented rooms and spread straw on the floor on which their pupils sat and took notes, until the time came when a cleanup was inevitable and the filthy straw was swept away and a new portion added.

The young Gerson would have attended lessons here, but he probably also got some tuition at his own college. He had to pay the masters of arts, whose salary still consisted of the fees they could get from their students, just as in the days of Abelard. But the new college system guaranteed a university place regardless of the student's economic situation.

Gerson was fortunate that he was a *champenois*. Even though his village was geographically located in the county of Rethel and even though it was taken over by the duke of Burgundy in 1364, it was still considered part of Champagne. Its capital Reims exercised an immediate influence on Gerson's village, thanks to the abbey of Saint Rémi's ownership of the land. With this attachment to the county of Champagne, the young Gerson could benefit from the endowment of the dead queen.

As a scholarship student, Gerson may have felt a social distance to the more privileged sons of rich bourgeois and even nobles at the College of Navarre. But his attachment also introduced him to students who, like Gerson, were interested in both classical and theological learning. He met young men whose humanist orientation would place him in the forefront of a new interest in the tradition already embraced by Petrarch. This dedication to the classics and attention to poetic form used to be thought of as an exclusively Italian concern. Recent research, however, emphasizes the existence of a strong current of French humanism cultivated at Navarre by Gerson's generation.[40]

Young Jean worked hard and made a solid impression on his contemporaries. But he also paid a high price, for this country boy seems to have isolated himself in his studies and to have made it clear to others that he was not looking for close friendships. This rejection of human bonds by a scholar who was in contact with the long classical and medieval tradition of spiritual friendship is remarkable in Gerson.[41] He knew the language of friendship and could use it on occasion but in general distanced himself from the practice of friendship and from the investment of time and talk that friendship requires. As he wrote in 1400 to some of the very colleagues at the College of Navarre with whom he had grown up:

> On the basis of experience I would add that nothing is more harmful to mental peace and contemplation, nothing more wasteful of that most precious thing, time, and nothing more of a hindrance to the perfection of those who study, as conversations. I mean not only the base ones, which wholly corrupt good habits, but also those that are extended at length and to no purpose and which fly on the wings of common rumors, or deal with childish jokes and clumsy tales or people's conflicts in opposing each other and similar matters. Here, from morning until night, the day is slowly eaten up and even much of the deepest night.[42]

Jean Gerson was in a hurry and had no time for "shooting the breeze" with his friends. His concern contradicts what often is asserted about our relaxed medieval ancestors, who are supposed to have had little concept of time as something precious and carefully measured out.[43] Gerson apparently had a schedule to meet and books and lecture notes to read and even memorize. He did not want to throw away his time with speculations about other people and what they were doing.

In the traditional English term, Gerson was a "swot," who came from a humble background and was aware of his parents' ambitions and sacrifices. In order to live up to their expectations, and his own, he withdrew into the recesses of his own mind and sought to master the authors required for the arts degree. Toward the end of his life, in 1423, he spoke of the grammatical works of Donatus and the logical ones of Peter of Spain that "are handed down from the beginning to new disciples so that they will be memorized, even if they do not immediately understand them" (Gl 9.475). Here he may have been remembering his own experience as he sat over these bone-dry treatises trying to make sense of them. He recommended much more warmly the theological writings of Saint Bonaventure, but he never denied the importance of the foundation that first had to be built on grammar and logic.

Gerson may have found it difficult to live in the communal atmosphere of a great college, with no chance to withdraw from his fellows. But he must have had moments alone when he experienced the impulses of his own body and the difficulty of the strict self-control the Church required in its interpretation of the sixth commandment. He hinted about his situation in the earliest letter we have from him, probably from the early 1380s. Here he thanked God that he had "not led a life ensnared in vices, especially not of a public kind." But he added, "I do not deal with hidden ones, of which the conscience is judge and to which God, not men, bears witness."[44] The language is vague and may reflect a literary commonplace, so it would be wrong to push its meaning too far.

For many priests, as we can see from visitation records of the thirteenth century, the requirement of celibacy was more an ideal than a reality.[45] Priests who openly or secretly cohabited with a woman had every reason to show tolerance in judging the sexual acts of which they were told in the confessional. Despite the impression sometimes given in popular studies of the Middle Ages that sexuality was the central concern of a repressed population, medieval people seem not to have been as worried about sexual expression as their postmodern successors at times have been.[46] In a society where violence so easily could get out of control, it was pride and anger more than lust and desire that belonged at the top of any list of sins that disturbed and threatened the fabric of everyday life.[47]

Gerson could not even contemplate such a relaxed attitude. So far as he was concerned, there was no possibility of compromise. The one time in his life he realized he was attracted to a woman, he cut her off and used the incident to warn against believing in the usefulness or desirability of spiritual friendships between the two sexes.[48] As far as he was concerned, all such bonds were a delusion. The devil wants us to believe that we become brothers and sisters in Christ. In reality, however, something else is happening.

Is it fair to use Gerson's later writings on such matters and project them back on his childhood and youth? I think so, but any conclusions on the matter need to be hedged with sense and sensibility. Gerson may have had his problems reconciling himself to the requirement of clerical celibacy, but such difficulties do not necessarily provide a central explanation for the core of his life.

The teenage Gerson had much else to think about, including the concern of generations of university students in the Middle Ages and in our time: financial support. This is the central theme of a letter Gilbert Ouy discovered some years ago and which is our earliest source from Gerson's hand.[49] He was writing to a benefactor, likely to have been Pierre d'Ailly (1350–1420), who from 1381 was one of Gerson's teachers in theology and in 1384 was appointed head of the College of Navarre.[50] Pierre opened many doors for Gerson, and for this reason the young scholar may already at this point have been turning to his master, to whom he gave the title "father by filial adoption." "As often as I have come hurrying through the twisting paths of this vale of misery from boyhood to the boundary of my present age, I have been sustained by your willing support."[51]

Gerson compared himself to a "little ship" that was about to be torn to bits by the storms it faces. He piled image upon image, using copious classical references and only a few Christian ones. It is as if he wanted to impress his patron with the knowledge that he had gained as a student at the arts faculty. The letter speaks of Aeneas, Jason, Ulysses, and other figures of classical mythology, who had set out on perilous voyages. "Come then, may your paternity favor my path and may a loving charity not deny help to one who is in danger of perishing."[52]

Having exhausted the ship image, Gerson turned to biblical descriptions of charity, the crumbs he sought from the master's table: "I do not want to be dressed up in brilliant clothes but only to be covered by some moth-eaten garb." Another theme Gerson used is that of friendship: "If all these considerations do not persuade you, then still the fraternal bond of love and the firm knot of attachment with Nicolas, who I hope dwells in heaven, will convince you."[53] We know nothing about Nicolas, but the context indicates he had been a mutual friend of Pierre d'Ailly and Jean Gerson, perhaps a student at the College of Navarre. The mention of this departed friend allowed Gerson to list some of the most famous friendships of classical Antiquity, as well, of course, that between David and Jonathan in the Bible.

Gerson piled one reason after another in order to get his patron to come to his assistance. He even turned to the situation of his parents, who would be socially humiliated if their son had to return to them:

> They earn a meager existence in heat and sweat through their own manual labor. After God they have all their hope in you. Under the shadow of your wings they give me some basic help and nourishment. However modest it is, it is the greatest of burdens for them with regard to their social position, so that they now bear burdens beyond their abilities. I fear, may God forbid, that they will become a parable for the neighbors, a source of ridicule for strangers, and a ribald refrain for base people. Perhaps the iniquitous will turn their contempt against you in murmuring their ridicule against my parents: "Ha! Look at those whom a shady faith has deceived, an empty confidence has disappointed."[54]

Gerson hints here that if he could not remain in Paris, not only would his parents be ridiculed, but perhaps d'Ailly also. Young Jean may have been exaggerating, but he may have been projecting on his teacher a deep fear that the family could become the laughingstock of the village.

The student Gerson used his biblical and classical learning in order to bring home his own insecurity. He added that if he could concentrate full time on his studies, he would get much better results. For the time being, however, he had to spend time in finding ways to earn money and make ends meet. Until now he had avoided doing work that took him away from his studies. But he did not think he could continue in this way.

Such appeals to parents or benefactors were standard procedure in student letter collections.[55] Gerson's lament on his situation, however, is so detailed and specific that I think he was describing his personal circumstances in Paris in the early 1380s. One element is, nevertheless, almost too fortuitous in terms of his argument based on need: "While I was writing the draft of this letter, an unforeseen situation arose, as if fortune had not been sufficiently harsh on me."[56] Gerson had been informed that he would be denied the income from an unspecified benefice, possibly one connected to the abbey of Saint Rémy. Thus he now appeared to be in even more dire financial straits.

This clinching argument seems to be a literary and rhetorical device. The young scholar was mustering every conceivable reason: the duties of a patron, the vulnerability of the student, the social position of his family, the obligations of mutual friendship, and the most recent events in his attempt to get independent sources of income allowing him to continue his studies.

The young man signed the letter with the name by which we know him, *Jo. de Gers.* He knew that his path from Gerson to Paris was only possible if his patron backed him. Otherwise he would have to return to his village and perhaps become a country priest, to the shame and even disgrace of his parents, who clearly had greater ambitions for their eldest son. Elisabeth and Arnaut, as well as their son, might be reduced to the state described in Psalm 68: "I am the subject of gossip for those who sit in the gate, and the drunkards make songs about me."

Jean Gerson was not alone in needing to find a patron to provide what his family could not give him. In the words of one of the leading medieval historians of the twentieth century, "By far the best resource was a wealthy and well-connected family. Failing this, an able man with only modest wealth and family support could succeed if he had a powerful patron."[57] These lines were written about the situation of an Englishman seeking to attend Paris almost two centuries earlier. But the requirement was the same for a Frenchman in the later fourteenth century. Without a well-connected family, the only hope was a well-connected patron. Here Gerson seems to have been fortunate. Someone, probably Pierre d'Ailly, looked after him.

In 1381 Gerson appeared before the chancellor of the University of Paris or his subchancellor, together with four examiners, and was questioned about the books he had read during his arts course. At the ceremony where the license in arts was given out, Gerson may have been called upon to give a collation, a lecture on one of the texts. Here the chancellor would sometimes take part and respond to the "questions" being discussed.[58]

Theoretically the young candidate could be questioned on any of the books he had read in the course of his four years. We are fortunate to have a description by Pierre d'Ailly himself from 1375 listing requirements for what he called the "school of philosophers" and the "school of mathematicians" (Gl 10.419). The first school covered grammar and logic, rhetoric and poetics. Among the authors central to each subject, respectively, were Priscian, Aristotle, Cicero, and Vergil. But there were many others like Ovid, Horace, Juvenal, Seneca, Terence, Sallust, Livy, Valerius Maximus, and Martial. All these authors, and many more, appear in Gerson's writings, indicating that in the midst of concerns about money, sexuality, and academic advancement, he had sufficient peace of mind to absorb the learning of classical and Christian writers.

One might, of course, ask whether the examination administered by the university's chancellor was all that demanding. In the fourteenth century there was a tendency to simplify procedures. Upon assuming office on 15 July 1381, Chancellor Jean Blanchard gained notoriety for his greater emphasis on money payments than on academic excellence when it came to granting the licentiate.[59]

Jean Gerson was to benefit from a patron like Pierre d'Ailly, who challenged the regime of Jean Blanchard and began a reform of the university. In his early years, Gerson was extraordinarily fortunate. He survived what is known as the revolt of the Maillotins in the Paris spring of 1383 and otherwise avoided the ills of plague, war, political intrigue, and academic corruption. Now on his way in university life, the graduate feared returning to his village in penury. But he managed to remain in Paris and begin his lifelong reform of church and society.

Doing Theology for Everyone

Seeking Theology's Shepherd, 1381–1389

The young licentiate in arts did not actually obtain the degree of master, the *magisterium,* until he had begun teaching his subject and was accepted into the university by his colleagues. Since the twelfth century, the masters of Paris had maintained their independence from the chancellor by making sure their corporation or guild had the right to recognize its own members. This is the origin of the word *universitas,* which originally meant not a university in our sense but a guild.[1]

The new licentiate might have to wait six months until he could get his master's cap in the ceremony of *birettatio,* whose descendant can still be seen at Oxford and Cambridge. First, the candidate had to appear before his nation and receive its permission to seek promotion. Then he had to swear to obey the rector, the faculty, and the nation to which he belonged. The evening before the actual inception ceremony, the candidate took part in a disputation known from the time of day as *vesperiae.* The next morning he could show his worth by engaging in a disputation, after which he would be handed the *biretta* and a book from the master of ceremonies, who would give him a kiss, in a reminder of the university's origins in bonds of collegiality and mutual loyalty. This act signified the candidate's entrance into the intellectual community. Finally he could take his seat among the masters.[2]

These formal ceremonies would end with a banquet, paid for by the new master himself. Gerson's begging letter to Pierre d'Ailly could well have been composed at a time when the young scholar was worried about how he would be able to afford the clothes and entertainment required to become a master of arts. Somehow Gerson did get the support he needed. He completed the arts course and began working on a degree in theology. As a new member of the university corporation, he occupied the ambiguous status of both student and teacher which graduate students today hold in university life.

Not all the arts masters, of course, followed this path to the highest degree the university offered, that of doctor of theology. Many of the masters were content with giving lectures year after year on the texts they had known from their youth. But for an ambitious young man like Gerson, the biretta of master of arts was but the first step in an academic career where he had higher expectations.

At times this life must have been hard, even for someone with Gerson's gifts. According to a faculty reform in 1366, the course of studies towards the doctorate in theology was supposed to last sixteen years.[3] The first six years Gerson would have been an *auditor,* attending lectures in theology, the first four years those on the Bible, and the next two on the great textbook of theological questions from the 1140s, the *Sentences* of Peter Lombard. There are lists of the regent masters in theology from this period, and they of course include Pierre d'Ailly, whose lectures Gerson would have attended (Gl 10.420).

At the end of this period, Gerson would have been twenty-six or twenty-seven, just old enough to be allowed to appear before four doctors who would have examined him and given permission for him to offer his first course in the faculty. At this point he was recognized as a bachelor of theology. With the title of *biblicus ordinarius* or *cursor,* Gerson could now lecture on one of the books of the Bible. The second year he would choose a second book of the Bible, a procedure that underlined the biblical basis of theology, which in Gerson's day was still called *Sacra Scriptura.* All theological discourse depended on the revealed word of God as found in the Bible.

By September of 1389, Gerson would have been admitted as a *sententiarius,* a lecturer in the *Sentences* of Peter Lombard, the twelfth-century compendium that in its time was a revolutionary document, organizing the study of Scripture into the discipline of theology.[4] Finally he would have reached the stage of *baccalarius formatus,* the fully formed bachelor, and would have been expected to be resident in Paris and to have participated in disputations at the faculty of theology.

Gerson was still a few years away from the license in theology, which he gained at the end of 1392. We do not have his lectures providing a commentary on the *Sentences,* dated to 1389–90. Every new theologian had to give such lectures, but their importance as original research was in decline by the end of the fourteenth century, and they were often not considered important enough to be preserved for posterity.[5] We are, however, fortunate to have other writings that reflect Gerson's situation at this time. The *Pastorium Carmen,* dated 1381–83, is an exotic and difficult Latin poem, an eclogue in the tradition of Vergil, set in the countryside, but dealing with the dire situation of the Western Church.[6] Here for the first of many times Gerson tried to deal with the fact that since the age of fifteen, he had experienced one pope in Rome and another at Avignon.[7] Thanks to the *Song of the Shepherds,* we can see how the youthful Gerson dealt with the fact that the Christian Church was in the midst of the division between two popes, what historians later came to call the Great Western Schism.

In 1381, when Gerson was just finishing his arts degree, the university had responded to the situation in recommending that there be held a general council. In May that year Pierre d'Ailly argued for this measure before the brothers of King Charles V. But only a month later, when another theological master was sent before the French court to repeat the university's arguments, he was refused permission to speak. Subsequently he was dragged from his bed and thrown into prison. The masters of the university were made to promise to remain silent about the Schism and especially concerning the calling of a council.[8] For the king and his brothers, the true pope was Clement VII, who resided in Avignon, and there was no room for debate.

What better way for a young man trained in classical poetry and rhetoric to avoid this prohibition than to use some of the language and imagery that filled his mind? Here in a manner that would save him from being considered an upstart or rebel, Gerson could express his concern. The *Pastorium Carmen* is by no means great poetry, and some of its verses are technically flawed.[9] It is even harder to understand than Gerson's letter to his patron. But in the poem the young master of arts showed familiarity with a literary genre long neglected in Europe and only recently revived by Petrarch.

The poem opens with a long lament by Pales, the goddess who protects sheep and cattle, over the fact that a fight had arisen among the shepherds. One part of the flock has been taken to the Tiber (Rome) and the other to the Rhône (Avignon). The status of their shepherds is unclear: "Either they both are thieves, or a thief and a shepherd at night have entered the same sheepfolds" (Gl 10.290). The flock is torn apart and "the time has come when there is no guard" to keep watch.

Pales ends her complaint by asking the god Pan why he is virtually deaf to what is going on. He answers that he does not understand why Pales, so dear to him, is weeping in this manner. Pan is a figure of Christ, while Pales represents the Church. With this symbolism, Gerson, as numerous church writers before him, made use of a description of erotic love to represent the love that exists between the Church and Christ.[10] As Pales says to Pan: "You alone are my rest, Pan, my devotion and love" (*sola quies mea, Pan, meus ardor amorque;* 291). Pan, awakened to Pales's suffering, invites her to lay her head on his breast.

It is no good, Pales complains. Her voice gets caught in her throat and she cannot tell all she sees and suffers. Instead she begins a long description of the history of the Christian Church, from its very beginnings in Christ and the Apostles. The language here is more obscure and difficult to follow than ever, but the conclusion is clear. The gift by the Emperor Constantine in the fourth century of areas in Central Italy to the bishop of Rome, the so-called Donation of Constantine, considered until the mid-fifteenth century as historical fact, is lamented as the Church's undoing: "Alas, sad gift, gift dearly bought" (293).

The problem has been wealth (*copia rerum*); an excess of possessions has been the Church's undoing. In the old days the sheep were well fed and well taken care of. Now they are diseased and their milk is not good. They are sick with a terrible cough, and they fight with each other all the time.

Pan tells his beloved to calm down, "You have experienced worse things" (*et pejora tulisti;* 293). But Pales will not be comforted. She refuses to say any more, for fear that the wind will spread her words; perhaps a hint that Gerson feared his words might reach the wrong ears (294).

Pan realizes how serious the situation has become. The one pastor is incapable of bearing the responsibilities entrusted him. The other is such a bad leader of the sheep that the more stubborn ones actually lead him. The descriptions of the two shepherds are so general here that it is difficult to know which pope was intended. (294). Pan insists he will not allow the division of the flock to continue. He concedes that Pales is right that the situation is crucial and something must be done. Pan promises to bring the Schism to an end and makes a final declaration of his love for Pales.

There are many lines in this poem whose precise meaning is not clear, such as the assertion (line 174) that the *cardo* or thistle plant grows profusely and suffocates the violets and fertile fields. Is this a reference to the fact that Clement VII had created many new cardinals and was thus suffocating the Church? The imagery was probably meant to be ambiguous. Gerson was protecting himself from nobles and courtiers who tried to stop public discussion about the Schism.

The poem was written by someone who had dedicated himself to a university career requiring mastery of an impersonal way of discourse. The new master of arts broke away from this training. Abandoning the scholastic form, he turned to poetry in order to plead for reform of the Church. Already here we find the Jean Gerson who was to involve himself in the great issues of his time. For him there was no difference between theology as learned science and as moral commitment. The young arts master, on fire with his knowledge of classical masters and new Italian poetry, was making his way into a dangerous world. His guarded, veiled Latin gave him some protection. It was, nevertheless, an act of academic and political courage to write in such a way.

Teaching Ordinary People

Gerson's commitment to ending the Schism was part of a larger involvement in church affairs. This concern meant that he had to look outside the university community and learn how to convey his views to a larger audience. Ever the teacher, he revealed time and again in his later writings how important it was for him to make traditional Latin theological learning available to ordinary people. He addressed these *gens simples* in several theological primers he wrote in French.

Already in the 1380s, Jean Gerson apparently made his first attempt at such a description of the truths of the faith. The *Doctrinal aux simples gens* has been dated to 1387, and even though there is no decisive proof that it was composed at that time, Gerson may well have composed this work as a young student of theology.[11]

There is a preface added by the archbishop of Reims, Guy de Roye, possibly in 1403, recommending the tract for lay people and asking that the parish priests of the city and diocese of Reims read aloud "two or three chapters" of the work every Sunday.[12] This introduction must have been added to Gerson's briefer and more modest presentation of his purpose: "What is in this little book, priests are to teach their parishioners. [For the benefit of] uneducated priests who do not have theological training and for ordinary people, it is written in French, with clarity and a great deal of deliberation [*plainement, par grant conseil*]" (Gl 10.296). Here is *in nuce* what during the next decades was to become his program of pastoral instruction, a concern of his which only recently has begun to attract attention.[13]

Gerson summarized in ten lines the doctrines of the Trinity, the Incarnation, the Redemption, the Resurrection, and the Last Judgment: "These articles of faith and all the others, you should firmly believe. And if because of your lack of education (*ta simplesse*), you have believed or believe differently in some other articles, your intention ought always to be to believe and hold as holy Church believes and holds" (296). The first requirement of faith is to love God, in order to find comfort "in every tribulation." Gerson told the story of Job and added a tale that he could have taken from Jacobus de Voragine's *Golden Legend*.[14] Saint Ambrose refused to eat at the house of a rich man who told the bishop of Milan that he had an easy life with no problems or sorrows at all. Ambrose realized that the man therefore could not be God's friend and had to be a creature of the devil and he would have nothing to do with him. Sure enough, as soon as Ambrose got away from the place, a great earthquake came and the house disappeared into an abyss (297).

Happy are they, claimed Gerson, whom God visits with tribulations while they are alive, for this is the way to paradise (cf. Rom 5:3). He reinforced the message of Saint Paul with references to the sufferings of Christ, the Apostles, and the first martyrs. His narrative about Saint Ambrose provides the section on charity with a memorable story of the type that priests used in sermons. As the great authority on Gerson's sermons, Louis Mourin, concluded his chapter on the use of examples and quotations: "One is aware of a man who knows how to teach, who arranges his material, and who truly masters it."[15]

Another instance where Gerson strengthened his argument by using an *exemplum* or brief moralizing story appears in his description of love of one's enemy. A desert father kissed the hands of a thief as he was dying: "These are the hands which will bring me into paradise," he said, "for this man has quite often deprived me and taken away from me my small sustenance." Because the hermit had accepted the sufferings the thief had inflicted on him, he could trust in the hope of salvation. The thief was an instrument of salvation, and so the hermit could love the man (298–99).

This anecdote provides an introduction to a brief review of the spiritual and corporal works of mercy and then a presentation of the commandments. Being a good Christian meant for ordinary people fashioning their everyday lives in accordance with these teachings. The commandment to keep the Sabbath required that in attending to God's works, good people should abandon anything that took them away from God. One dangerous activity was dancing, "if it is not for a good and honest reason" (300). It might lead to a number of sins, one of which is laziness, "for it is wasted time" (*car c'est temps perdu*).

Having completed his review of the commandments, Gerson turned to another traditional list that of the five senses (302). Here he did not dally, in contrast to the aristocratic culture of the day exemplified in the Unicorn tapestries now on display at the Musée de Cluny in Paris. He gave much more space to the next list, the seven deadly sins. Avarice receives a great deal of attention. Gerson was especially concerned with wealthy people who refuse to render to the Church what they owe it in terms of tithes and other payments. He extended his condemnation to "bad lords, judges, lawyers, sergeants, procurators and others" (303) and warned against those who are tardy in paying their workers or try to exploit them in other ways.

With lust or *luxure,* Gerson guarded his language, for he did not want to give ideas to lay people about what they might try. He mentioned masturbation and linked it with another "sin so great that an ordinary priest cannot absolve it." Absolution could only be given by a bishop or the confessor whom he had appointed. Gerson in later treatises dealt at length with such "reserved sins."[16] But here he kept silence: "All the other types are so abominable that they are not to be mentioned" (305).

Having reviewed categories of sin, Gerson considered prayers that lay people could say. He devoted most of his attention to the power of the *Ave Maria,* and indulged himself and his readers, or listeners, with several miracles attributed to the Virgin, a literary genre widespread in Europe since the twelfth century.[17] He told the story of a valet who served a young man for fourteen years, a tale found in the *Golden Legend*'s entry for the Feast of the Annunciation, 25 March.[18] The servant was actually the devil but was unable to capture the soul of the youth because the latter prayed daily to Mary. If he had only once forgotten to say his *Ave,* he would have been taken away to hell by the devil (306).

Gerson did not necessarily have this story from reading the *Golden Legend* itself. He may have heard it at home from his parents or the parish priest. His willingness to use such simple anecdotes is shown in another tale. Encouraging people to remember the Passion of Christ and to make the sign of the cross in asking for God's mercy, Gerson described a man who did so faithfully. When he died, devils wanted to take his soul, but on his forehead and chest, where he had touched himself in making the sign, there were beautiful stars. Therefore the devils could not take hold of him (307).

Turning now to the seven sacraments, he ordered his material in the form of lists, a device Huizinga once found tiring but which was popular because it made the material easier to master.[19] Gerson seems to have had difficulty in deciding whether he was addressing parish priests or their parishioners. Normally he speaks to his listeners in the *tu* form, appropriate for a priest reading out instructions to the people.

Describing the Eucharist, however, Gerson seems to have forgotten this lay audience and concentrated on clerical readers. First he claims that for every worthy mass celebrated, several souls are delivered from purgatory (308). From here he digresses, encouraging priests to live up to their duties. He borrows an episode from the *Life of Saint Andrew,* as contained in the *Golden Legend,* and also makes use of Augustine and Gregory the Great in order to encourage priests to celebrate the mass frequently, preferably daily.[20]

At the end of his treatment of the Eucharist, Gerson recalled the laity and encouraged its members to take communion frequently, even every Sunday, and especially prior to dangerous moments in life, as when a woman is about to give birth or a soldier is on his way to war (310). So much for the common assertion that the medieval Church discouraged the laity from frequent communion.

The split audience of the treatise again becomes apparent when Gerson, after a few words on the anointing of the sick, returns to the behavior of priests. If they do not live in chastity, they will become the laughing stock of the people (311). All clerics are to say the office daily and not drop syllables or words in forgetfulness. Otherwise the devil will pick them up and collect them in his sack, a reference to the devil often called "Tutivillus." This story had been popular since the thirteenth century, but Gerson attributed it to the *Lives of the Desert Fathers.*[21]

There is much good advice here of a practical kind that could be helpful in parish life. A possible argument for the assumption that Gerson composed the work in his youth could be that this confusion of intended audiences points to a writer who had not yet done much pastoral work. The young Gerson was willing and able to lift himself out of Latin theological debates and to address ordinary problems of parish life. But he could not help combining general instruction for lay people with sharp admonitions to badly educated parish priests.

Dealing with the sacrament of marriage and parenthood, Gerson warns that when parents do not take advantage of childhood's receptivity for moral instruction, they become responsible for what happens later. "For as is said in a proverb, what a young horse learns when it is trained, it will keep so long as it lasts. What a child learns in its youth, it will hold on to in old age" (*Qu'aprent enfant en sa jeunesse, il le retient en sa viellesse;* 312).[22]

After digressions on marriage and sexuality, Gerson eventually returns to the subject of the seven sacraments and considered penance. He asks what is necessary for a good confession and for satisfaction for sin, ending with an exhortation to sinners to convert to a better life (319). A rather tame description of the joys of heaven (320) stands in stark contrast to lurid descriptions of the monsters, serpents, and other creatures that contribute to the punishments in hell.[23]

In the section on confession, Gerson takes special care to address potential lay listeners: "Do not keep anything back from the priest, for your confession will then be worthless. And do not make excuses for yourself, as clever people do; and don't make your sin greater than it is, for you will be lying" (315). He was laying the foundation here for his later treatises on confession.[24] This passionate appeal indicates how important it was for him to reach his audience. As earlier, he seems to have considered both lay people and their parish priests as his audience: "If you do not declare all your sins clearly, the priest ought to help you to express them better, and any other sins that he thinks that you may have committed" (315).

Gerson underlined the importance of making a full confession. Once again he made use of an *exemplum* or brief moral story in order to make his point: how a hermit saw a fine woman as having a devil chained to her body. It was revealed to the hermit that the woman had sinned in her youth but had never dared to confess. Now she was damned forever (316).[25]

The *Doctrinal aux simples gens* reveals Gerson as a young master of arts who was also a student of theology, perhaps shortly after his ordination to the priesthood. If the *Doctrinal* is correctly dated to the later 1380s, its content shows that he had already committed himself to combining university theology with pastoral involvement.

Making Serious Satire: 1388–1389

The young Gerson who expressed himself in the vernacular concerning his visions of heaven and hell and used popular sayings for lay people also wrote biting sarcasm in Latin. In the late 1380s Gerson took advantage of a period of relative tranquility at the university in its involvement with the Schism. He turned his attention to the role of the Dominican friars in Paris and their teaching about Mary's sinless conception. To Gerson's mind the Dominican Order, and especially its Paris theologian Juan de Monzon, threatened the orthodoxy of the university.[26]

In May of 1387 Juan de Monzon apparently scandalized the masters of theology when he tried to enter their ranks at Paris with his *resumptio*, the final disputation given before the faculty of theology by a candidate for the degree.[27] Here he followed standard medieval Dominican practice and denied that it was necessary to believe that Mary was conceived without sin.[28] The university censored the friar for some of his theses; the bishop of Paris condemned him; Monzon appealed to Rome, with the backing of the General Chapter of his own Order (Gl 10.3). In July 1388, the university sent a delegation to the Avignon pope, Clement VII. It was led by master in theology and coming chancellor of the university, Pierre d'Ailly. In his company was his pupil Jean Gerson.

Apart from his initial journey to Paris itself, this was the first extended trip Gerson took in his life. His writings reveal almost nothing about what he saw, but the young theology student was given a first-hand look at the Avignon papacy and the chance to observe his master Pierre d'Ailly as a diplomat. In a letter written in 1400, Gerson mentions his stay at Avignon: "I affirm that the condemnation of the errors of the forenamed Juan de Monzon was done according to reason and catholic faith. When he was defended at the papal court, I myself was present, being then a bachelor of theology lecturing on the Bible, together with other excellent and most wise men sent as legates from the university."[29] The result was a partial victory for the secular masters of Paris against the mendicants. Because the Dominican General Chapter backed Juan de Monzon, the brothers had to leave the university. Pierre d'Ailly had made his point, but years later Gerson would lament the effect on the university. The Dominicans had been its best preachers, and their departure meant a decline in standards: "Sermons are lacking at the university, even Sunday sermons to the clergy. This development lately has come about like some monster and is hardly bearable."[30]

In 1388, however, the young master had other matters to think about than the way the Dominicans preached university sermons. When he returned to Paris in September, Gerson began his second course on a book of the Bible. His inaugural collation is lost, but we know its theme, the same as the one he had lectured on the previous autumn at the opening of his first course in theology. Gerson spoke on the basis of the Book of Wisdom (8:2): *Quaesivi sponsam mihi eam assumere* (I sought to take her to me as my bride).[31] In the allegorical manner used for such Old Testament passages, Gerson saw here the marriage of the theologian with wisdom. He was already declaring a lifetime commitment: the pursuit of wisdom as his only spouse.

The following September (1389), Gerson as bachelor in the *Sentences* began his lectures by making another collation based on the same biblical phrase. Probably by the end of the year, he also wrote a brief tract attacking Juan de Monzon and especially his position on Marian doctrine. Like the *Doctrinal*, the *Adversus Joannem de Montesono* provides an opportunity to look into the mind of the young theologian. Gerson was casting about for a satisfying mode of expression and experimented with various approaches.[32]

Adversus starts with praise of France, the *Gallia* that "always has been brilliant with men powerful in war and learned in wisdom" (Gl 10.7). This statement is taken almost verbatim from Jerome,[33] but Gerson added his own lament that his country until now had lacked historians and poets to celebrate the accomplishments of its warriors and philosophers. He was probably reacting to Petrarch's claim about the absence of orators or poets outside of Italy. The young theologian was creating a fresh agenda in Northern European literature by assuming the role of the orator celebrating the accomplishments of his country and especially of his university.[34] He thereby marked the arrival of a humanist mentality in France.

Gerson lamented the fact that until his time there had been no one to sing the praises of his countrymen. This awareness left him with sorrow (*dolor*), not the least because hardly anyone had bothered to celebrate the glory of the University of Paris (8). There was almost no historical record of the achievements of the past, and little desire in the present university to preserve this fragile heritage (*tenuis . . . memoria*). Now he himself considered writing about the question of doctrine (*causam fidei*), a central concern in university history although he did not consider his talents in this area to be greater than anyone else's. But he had been present on crucial occasions when the subject was discussed, so he could describe it not just from hearsay but also as a witness (8). At the same time he wanted to provide an account to show his devotion to the university to which, as he said, "I owe everything I am" (*totum me debeo*).

Gerson provided a detailed exposition in literary form of his own inner debate (9) using the Old Testament image of Rachel and Leah to illustrate the difference between the active and the contemplative lives. His subject was theology, yet his approach is light years from the method of question and answer that he and his colleagues used in his lectures and disputations. Gerson was returning to the more personal and individual approach of twelfth-century teachers, such as John of Salisbury, who also described their experiences of an intellectual milieu.[35]

This twelfth-century humanistic and personal quality is also present in the next assertion, Gerson's version of the *translatio studii* idea once uttered by Chrétien de Troyes, the assertion that the center of studies has moved from one location to another.[36] Different authorities traced the origins of the University of Paris to Rome, Athens, Egypt, the earthly paradise, or even heaven itself. Gerson emphasized the preeminence of Paris "in glory and dignity" (9). Thanks to the university, the profession of the faith was nowhere more pure or complete than in France.

In order to maintain its standards, the university made war on the proud. Here Gerson quotes from Vergil (*Aeneid* 6.854) and soon makes clear what he means: the chancellor of the university had required financial reimbursement from men seeking an academic degree. If they refused to pay out, he denied them the license for teaching. Gerson referred to two treatises by Pierre d'Ailly on the matter (11). D'Ailly had opposed chancellor Jean Blanchard, who had not been the first to receive payment for the license to lecture, but who had increased the amounts required to such a degree that the masters had risen up against him.[37] According to Gerson, Blanchard had appealed to the papal curia in Avignon and also to the Parlement of Paris, which functioned as the royal tribunal (11). In 1386, however, he was removed from office.

Gerson's description of the glories of the University of Paris thus became a chronicle of recent university history. He also mentioned an incident at the funeral procession of King Charles V in 1380 when the provost of Paris, Hugh Aubriot, violated precedence and ignored the rights of the masters of Paris. These refused to take the matter lightly and demanded that Aubriot be punished severely (11–12).

Gerson used this defense of university prerogatives in order to point out that if the doctors of theology could be so caught up by such a slight to their prestige, they were rightly all the more outraged when someone threatened the faith itself. Personal injury is nothing compared to damage to the faith. Thus the masters had once attacked even the pope himself, John XXII (1316–1334), "whose highest dignity and great power did not prevent" the doctors of theology of the university from going after him (12). John had asserted that the souls of the just do not acquire the vision of God until after Judgment Day.[38] In spite of what Gerson saw as a general decline of standards, the university in the person of such masters had remained firm.

Recently the university once again had to assert its right to make war on the proud and to overcome falsehood. In this manner Gerson approached the story of Juan de Monzon, whose Latin name, *de Montesono* had invited "many and facetious interpretations." Claiming to avoid such vulgarity, Gerson nevertheless in several places manipulated the name and emphasized the mountainous size of the apparently overweight Dominican theologian. Monzon's capacious body becomes a representation of his inflated mind: *vir corpulentioris staturae sed animi tumiditate ingentior* (12).

Gerson described in detail Juan de Monzon's *vesperiae* or "vespers," a solemn disputation made the evening of the day before the inception of a new master of theology.[39] Once again using Vergil (*Aeneid* 10.640), Gerson described Monzon as "making noise without meaning." The Dominican expressed his "barbaric teaching" in speech "so confused and empty that you would scarcely believe him to have a human brain" (12).

The harshness of Gerson's tone grows in severity as his description thickens. He points to statements on transubstantiation and Christ's presence in the Eucharist which were either incomprehensible or outright heretical. Nevertheless, "this subtle theologian of ours got what he wanted." By using unclear language, which no one understood, not even himself, "he filled the ears of bystanders and made them admire him" (13). Gerson set no limits on his sarcasm: "Lift up your ears, scholars, to such high and deep doctrine; you have not heard, as I think, such things until now."

Gerson criticized students and masters who wanted to be impressed by complex-sounding arguments that really said nothing at all. He broached a theme to which he would return in later years.[40] Academics were pleased by "whatever is unusual" and they believed that "whatever can be imagined is also probable." For such people, "obscurity is a form of cleverness" (13).

Gerson made no attempt to describe Monzon's disputation in terms of its content. Instead he gave a personal account of the emotional atmosphere on the occasion. A key term is *nugae,* or trifles, that conveys contempt for Monzon's mode of argumentation. Normally some months would pass after a master's "vesper" before the *resumptio,* when the actual inception as master took place. But in Juan de Monzon's case, it was only a matter of days (14). Monzon told his potential listeners not to be late for his inception, for they would receive "a new and pleasing teaching." But for Gerson the occasion merely repeated an old story, which went back to Aesop, but also is found in Horace, about the mountain that gives birth to a mouse.[41]

Gerson set the scene for Monzon's inception, with bells being rung, a large audience gathering, and the new doctor trying to arrive in slow procession, "as much as his burning passion allowed him to enter with gravity" (15). He was so eager to take his place that he lost all dignity. Gerson again used Monzon's physical size to represent his inflated arrogance. The Dominican is supposed to have said, "Since I am a doctor, I am permitted to claim as probable whatever pleases me."

The new doctor was lecturing on necessary being and creation. According to Gerson, Monzon confused the attributes of creator and creature and thereby seemed to be restricting God's activity. In postulating a universe where created beings are necessary, Monzon gave them independent existence (15).

This seemingly dispassionate presentation of Monzon is followed up by a much more vitriolic description of his teaching on Mary: "It was little enough for the foul-mouthed doctor to blaspheme God and to cut off his power. He prepares something more obscene. . . . Taking the filthy faeces of the errors with which he was puffed up, he openly poured them into the clearest and purest fountain of Mary" (16). Gerson admits he hardly could contain his anger with Monzon because of what the Dominican claimed about Mary. Imitating ciceronian rhetorical practice, the young theologian stops in the middle of his description of Monzon's reasoning and allows himself an outburst: "But why do I stop? Why do I delay? Behold a rage seizes me, one which I had not intended. My burning heart cannot suppress its anger" (17).

Because Monzon injured Christ's mother, who also is our mother, we her sons cannot remain passive when our mother is molested. Gerson appeals to "sweet Jesus" to punish the blasphemer and asks why the divine Son had not yet struck down the Dominican with a bolt of lightning! Now it was up to Gerson and other theologians to respond by defending the mother's honor. Mohammed in the Koran acknowledged that sin had not touched Mary, but not Monzon (18). He was a heretic. In ancient Rome, anyone who insulted a goddess such as Diana had to pay with death. But in our century someone who defamed Mary was allowed to live:

> *O saeculum nostrum; o mores; o religio!*
> *Dianae spretor perit, et vivit Mariae infamator!*

The refrain is ciceronian, reminiscent of the Catiline orations. How could anyone with such opinions, Gerson asked, be left in peace? Why is the head that is full of such madness not crushed and why is the brain not yet spread out on the street?

After some of the most rabid language of his career, Gerson stops and accuses himself of allowing his bitterness to go too far. He then addressed Monzon directly, using the "tu" form, and appeals to him: "I ask that you not mix in [Mary] with the common lot of men, for she is above men" (19).

Gerson reflected on the scene of Monzon in his doctoral chair. "There is nothing funny about it," he insisted, while he continued to ridicule his enemy. The man tried to hide behind Saint Thomas Aquinas and meanwhile fabricated a new grammar for theology. Monzon is described as rising to his feet, squeezing himself into the pulpit with his bulky chest and breathing heavily while violently shaking his right hand (20).

Some members of the audience made gestures to show that they did not understand what was being said; others were stunned or whispered to each other. Some listeners thought Monzon had done well and was to be admired. Their reaction encouraged him to puff himself up with even greater vigor and to protrude his stomach while he spoke. "He repeated often what had been badly said, or added some madness. Often his words, jammed as it were into a single phrase, run into each other and make him babble, so that vomiting them forth at one time, his capacious mouth is not sufficient for them" (20). By now, claimed Gerson, the scholars of Paris had had enough: *Evicta tandem vero est scholasticorum patientia.* Monzon was practically driven from his chair and had to descend, breathless and almost hyperventilating. Some of the listeners still praised Monzon, but the number of those accusing him was greater. In leaving the school, people broke off into different parties, according to bonds of friendship, the route they were taking, or their association because of common studies or interests.

A few scholars, however, remained behind. They had their eyes on the ground and tried to remember exactly what had been said. They noted how Monzon's body language revealed his confusion: "His face wrinkled with grimaces, his voice unrestrained, so that the motion of his whole body was disordered" (21). The man had to be either drunk or insane.

Gerson's target was not only Juan de Monzon but also other Dominican theologians at Paris, whom he compared to the Pharisees. Gerson added a popular saying that the Dominicans had handed over their key to a great fool.[42] Once again, but in a different manner than in the *Doctrinal,* Gerson showed both a sense of language and an ability for vivid descriptions and memorable phrases. In the last pages of this remarkable and disturbing work, Gerson described the accusations made against Juan de Monzon at the faculty of theology and his condemnation there. Once again he made fun of Monzon, who is said to have been totally inadequate in his own defense. Six masters of theology were appointed to go through the text of Monzon's inception, and they spent more than two months on the job. In the end Monzon was given three days to retract several of his statements. He had not yet done so: "The Jews still await the Messiah, the Britons Arthur, and we still await the third day" (24).

The opening of this work has been justly celebrated as a fresh statement of a French humanism that rivaled what the Italians offered. Yet, at the same time, Gerson allowed himself an inflammatory rhetoric that made use of crass ridicule and scatological language. He indulged himself in the very crass jokes (*facetias*), which he at first promised not to employ. Also he failed to tell his readers that the Dominicans were not alone in their opposition to Mary's immaculate conception as church doctrine.

Medieval writers and their early modern successors, such as Erasmus, Thomas More, and Martin Luther, were not squeamish. They spared no crudity in attacking their enemies. But why did Gerson choose to lash out so harshly at this time? He was kicking opponents who already were in the dirt. By the time Gerson wrote at the end of 1389, Monzon's inception was two years in the past. The Dominicans had been humiliated and were on their way out of the university.

Earlier scholarship has pointed out that the treatise as we have it is only a *brouillon,* a draft, which was never completed.[43] One can imagine that the new chancellor from October 1389, Pierre d'Ailly, was not interested in dredging up all the bad feeling that had been created by the case of Juan de Monzon. Gerson may have written the treatise in order to please his master, Pierre d'Ailly, but did not complete it because of Pierre's negative reaction.

Gerson did not try, as he had done earlier with his pastoral poem, to obscure his meaning. Driven by passion for theological truth and fear of heresy, the man who after his death would be named "the consoling doctor" showed little self-discipline and much vindictiveness. His grasp of rhetoric enabled him to build up an invective that left no room for sympathy, understanding, or forgiveness.

It is important to include such a treatise in a study of Gerson, for it shows a darker side to him. But one can also read the attack on Juan de Monzon as an exercise in wordplay that enabled Gerson to break away from the usual scholastic form and to display his talents and knowledge of classical language and rhetoric. Gerson probably enjoyed himself immensely as he wrote these lines, which I can imagine he showed off to colleagues at the College of Navarre.

This display of scholastic argument, literary talent, and scholarly violence linked Gerson to a tradition that went back to the early twelfth century and Peter Abelard, who looked upon himself as an intellectual knight.[44] In Abelard's *History of my Calamities*, he did battle with his intellectual opponents. The academic world was then and still is a field of battle. The stakes may not be high, but the competition can be fierce and mean.

One reads Gerson's treatise, which has largely been ignored perhaps because of its difficult Latin, with a sense of perplexed admiration for a man with a new vision of the importance of history and rhetoric. Such a treatise points to a young scholar who had a great deal of self-confidence and assumed that others would appreciate his invective. They may well have done so, even though Pierre d'Ailly apparently had no interest in letting such a work become better known.

Preaching for Court and University: 1389–1391

At around the same time Gerson made his harsh attack on Juan de Monzon, he began to give public sermons. Some of these were delivered in Latin to his students and colleagues, while others were preached at court in French. At times Gerson would have spoken in the presence of the king himself, Charles VI, who had recently taken over power from his uncles and had a brief period of competence until he in 1392 became openly mentally ill.[45]

The earliest of these sermons has been dated to 3 March 1389.[46] In preaching to a lay audience, Gerson was clear, precise, relatively personal in tone, and fairly brief. One can imagine the sermon being given, perhaps in the royal chapel of Saint Paul on the right bank of the Seine and with the king listening.

"Seek the Lord while he can be found; call upon him while he is near," began the young theologian, using the words of Isaiah (55:6). Gerson provided three subjects for consideration: the loss of the love of God; the acquisition of his grace and love; the admonition to seek this love at the right time. We lose the love of God by defying him, through pride, or because of disobedience. Gerson gave several Old Testament examples of proud kings, such as Saul, who lost their kingdoms (Gl 7.2.971). As for disobedience, it includes neglect of God's commands. Gerson used a moralizing story or *exemplum* about how an abbot wept at the sight of a woman who was all dressed up. When asked why he cried over such an attractive woman, the abbot replied that he did so both because the lady was damned and because he himself had not spent as much care in pleasing God as she had done in pleasing young men (971–72).[47]

The second major point of the sermon is the question of how and where to seek God's love. We are to look for him not in palaces but in stables. Here Gerson could have been addressing the youthful king directly: "You will perhaps say to me: 'I am in the full flower of youth, and I still have a long time to live'." The answer is that even if life and death seem to be distant from each other, there is nothing closer.[48] Appropriate quotations are given from Seneca and Apuleius. "If you glorify your beauty, wait a little, and you will not have it any longer" (973). All human accomplishments are illusions. They may be with us for a time but soon are gone, or they were never there in the first place. Those who think they are wise are in fact made foolish (Rom 1:22). Ancestry is also no reason for being proud, for the nobler one's ancestors, the more one is obliged to live up to the challenge of their heritage.

Gerson intended to demonstrate to his royal and aristocratic listeners that the trappings of their lives easily turned into sadness, disappointment, and damnation. All that we take for granted in our lives can be deception, as the belief that one has many friends. These will be proven only in adversity. Gerson added a story told by Cicero in order to emphasize that a prince must always act with circumspection, following reason and discipline, for all eyes are on him: "Thus it is asked where the king is, what he is doing. The king sleeps; the king gets up; the king hears mass; the king dines . . . he does not take a leap at Senlis without its immediately being known at Paris" (974).

Kingship is such a burden that many kings in the past either considered resigning (like Augustus Caesar) or actually did so (like Diocletian). Instead of envying princes for their position, one should pity them and help them as much as is within one's power. God is to be found not in the palace but in the stable, and therefore those who live in palaces are to be on their guard.

A second place to seek God is in the temple or church, where one prays and fasts, as during the Lent that was just beginning. A third place to seek God is at the cross and a fourth is in the tomb where the body of Christ was placed. We Christians are to die and to be buried with him. We are to die to our bodies and the pleasure they offer us. Gerson then turned to the final consideration, concerning when to seek the Lord.

A description of the ages of life shows that a person is to seek God in youth, in the heat of the day when one still has strength (977). In old age, the individual loses good sense, discretion, and stamina. Once again the context suggests that Gerson was addressing a young king, who would have been a little more than twenty at the time. There is no hint of flattery here, and yet at the same time Gerson does not preach hellfire and damnation. The possibility of salvation is held forth in the sermon, whose ending describes the path to heaven and the kingdom of paradise (978).

Medieval sermons have long been looked upon as one of the least interesting places for finding human beings. Recently, however, sermons have been studied as evidence not only of religious thought but also of daily life.[49] Gerson's first sermon, however much he composed it in accord with late medieval requirements for such a genre,[50] is close to a real-life situation: the court in all its finery; the young king, perhaps half distracted by his surroundings; the fledgling theologian, possibly wondering how he had come from his hamlet and modest background to such splendor. On 6 January 1391, Epiphany, he once again preached in the presence of the king. His text was the verse from Psalm 71: "All the kings of the earth will adore him." First comes what is known as the protheme, introducing the subject and addressing a prayer to Mary, and then the body of the sermon, in which Gerson defined three types of kingdoms: personal, temporal, and spiritual. In the first, each person must govern himself; in the second, princes and lords must govern others; in the third, the Church is governed (Gl 7.2.519–21).

Gerson admonished the king to look after all three kingdoms, also the spiritual one, because of his role as an anointed ruler. Referring to the ceremony in which the king was anointed with chrism at Reims, Gerson described him as a priestly figure. In spite of all the reforms of the eleventh century and the papal attempt to abolish such a sacerdotal role for kings, Gerson at the end of the fourteenth century was appealing to an earlier view of royal power as sacerdotal.[51]

Gerson referred to the king's title as *roy tres crestien,* most Christian king (522). Thanks to the king's special role, France had a unique place within the Church. Just as in the polemic against Juan de Monzon, Gerson here repeats Saint Jerome's claim that "only Gaul has lacked monsters."[52] In other words, only France, thanks to its kings, had not allowed heretics to thrive. Continuing with his exposition of the personal kingdom, Gerson turns to Seneca, who said that whoever is able to govern himself has a great kingdom. Alexander the Great, "who had the whole world in his power," could not master himself (524). In his personal realm the king must not provide access for his enemies. First of all, he must guard his ears and not believe all that was said to him. The king had a reputation for being eager to believe his advisors: *Vous avez le renom de croire tres voulentiers conseil* (525). Counselors not motivated by concern for the public weal or compassion for the people could be interested merely in their own advancement and thus be willing to deceive the king.

A second means of access to the king's personal realm was the eyes. The king had to keep them from leading him into foolish love (*folle amour*) and was to remember what happened to Troy because of Helen. Such love killed Samson because of Delilah and made David a murderer for the sake of Bathsheba (526). Among other ways of access is especially the heart, where pride can take power. Pride was for Gerson the cause of the division within the Church: "What is it that now subjects Christianity to a most cruel and damaging schism? It is pride and the desire to dominate" (527). Thus Gerson mentioned a subject that had been banned from public debate since the early 1380s. Passing to the second kingdom, the temporal one, he provides examples of good rule. It is the king's duty to follow Vergil's dictum, which Gerson found in the fifth book of the Aeneid: to spare subjects and make war on the proud.[53] Love and harmony are essential for the government of the kingdom. Here Gerson makes use of a familiar story in Livy about how the parts of the body have to work together, or else the body politic will die.[54]

From here Gerson turned to the king's spiritual rule. If he defends the Church, his kingdom will flourish. He can become aware of its needs by listening to "your very humble and very devout daughter," the University of Paris (530). Gerson praised the king for his patience and attentiveness in this area and mentioned how the king recently held audience from prime until vespers for a thousand persons at the Palace of the Louvre. In so doing, he was following "the example of the glorious kings of France, especially of Saint Charlemagne and Saint Louis" (531).

As the king's "little subject and unworthy cleric," Gerson celebrated the "ardent affection" which his master showed for his "third kingdom," the Church (531–32). He once again returns to the subject of the Schism: "Alas, very sovereign king of Christians, you see with great sorrow" how Christianity for twelve years has been divided. One part considers the other to be schismatic and excommunicated, so that hope of salvation is denied. Terrible evils arise because of the Schism. There are wars; unworthy persons are promoted to church offices; dispensations are misused; Jews and Saracens have reason to rejoice (532).

There must be a way, Gerson insists, that would not prejudice the king or Pope Clement, "who by his graciousness provided me with a benefice,"[55] admitting a personal dependency on the Avignon pope. Whichever pope was legitimate, however, Gerson was convinced that the use of force (*via facti*) was not desirable or defendable. An armed attack would undermine the very mission of the Church: "Because it has been instituted for charity, one ought not to fight against charity."

If the kings of old were alive today, they would rather have died a thousand times than let the Schism persist. If King Charles were to succeed in ending the Schism, it would be better than beating a Saracen army. On the very edge of orthodoxy, Gerson thus claimed that a solution would not only benefit the souls in purgatory but even those in hell (534).

Gerson now turned to the king's uncles, the dukes of Berry and of Burgundy and his brother, Louis of Orleans, here called duke of Touraine. They could do a great service not only to God, the faith, Christianity, and the king, but also to their people. Gerson also addressed the nobility as "noble and valiant knights," who are seeking "true honor." Finally he spoke to the prelates of the kingdom (535).

Returning to the king and citing several parallels from biblical texts, especially Maccabees, Gerson asks him to decree public prayers, fasting, and the holding of processions (536). The prayers of a single person can make a decisive difference, as was demonstrated when Ambrose was chosen bishop of Milan, thanks to the cry of one child.[56]

Gerson closed the sermon by addressing Charles as "son of devout prayer." Pope Urban V (1362–1370) was said to have prayed publicly at the king's birth in 1368. Gerson refers to a "miracle" that had taken place, presumably the survival of the infant against all odds. Therefore King Charles should love the Church as his mother, while he at the same time had been saved as a "son of prayer" so that he could restore the unity of the Church. The sermon ends with what borders on a hymn of praise to the king in anticipating all he would be able to do to end the Schism.

Gerson appealed to the best instincts of Charles in order to make him do something about the situation of the Church. Not by sending an army to Italy, as some in the royal circle wanted, but by galvanizing the entire kingdom in prayer, fasting, and processions. The king would spearhead a religious revival that somehow would break the deadlock.

In giving this sermon, Gerson disregarded the political intrigues already evident at the court of Charles VI. Like other medieval political commentators, Gerson believed that if he could gain the ear of the king and make his case sufficiently well, then he could make a decisive difference.[57] Charles no doubt would have listened sympathetically to Gerson's arguments and may have been touched by the final appeal to him as a son of prayer.

Historians, who generally respect naked power more than prayerful rhetoric, may be smiling at such an appeal to popular devotion as a remedy to the Schism. But Gerson's very political innocence shows him walking into a lion's den of intrigue and emerging unscathed. He believed wholeheartedly in the sacredness of kingship but did not curry favor with the king. With no desire to attach himself to the court, Gerson preferred the university and identified with her in his appeal to the king's best instincts.

There is no private journal to tell us what Gerson thought that evening upon returning to his lodgings. But Gerson's admission about his dependence on Pope Clement at Avignon hints that the young theologian realized that he and his clerical colleagues were part of the problem. Gerson believed in the king as a free agent. As the successor of saints, he could lead France and the rest of Christianity out of its dilemma.

Probably already a few weeks later, Gerson preached in Latin for his university colleagues.[58] Taking his theme from Matthew 20:2, "He sent them into his vineyard," Gerson described the University of Paris as a vineyard stretching its vines "from sea to sea and to the ends of the earth" (Gl 5.362).[59] This sermon was preached as an afternoon collation. The same theme had been touched upon in the morning by Pierre d'Ailly, whom Gerson called "my teacher from boyhood and a doctor whom I will always consider as being of the most revered authority." After d'Ailly's exposition, Gerson claimed to fear there was nothing left to say.

The term *praeceptor meus a puero* indicates Gerson looked upon d'Ailly as his guardian even before d'Ailly became his formal teacher in theology after 1381. Gerson may have used a figure of speech, or d'Ailly may in fact have taught Gerson at the faculty of arts. Whatever the official bond, Gerson suggests that Pierre d'Ailly had looked after him from the time he first arrived in Paris in 1377.

Gerson concentrated on the possibilities and obligations of the students. They had been sent to school at an early age because it is easier then to learn; young people are like wax that can easily be formed (366). This image goes back at least to the eleventh century and Saint Anselm.[60] Therefore, "we must labor and not play nor foolishly waste time, which, as Seneca says, is the most precious of all things" (369).

As so often in Gerson, there is an awareness of the value of time. Here in a university sermon is the same sense of time's preciousness as might have existed in the mind of a Paris merchant.[61] Gerson was thinking in terms of working hard for heaven. His ethos of spiritual production and the virtue of efficiency anticipates a later age.

The object of a scholar's efforts is the wine "that makes God and men rejoice" (372). This is the "spiritual understanding of the Scriptures," which theology provides. Gerson describes his wine in so detailed a manner that he conveys knowledge of wines and their quality. He had not forgotten his background in a region still famous for its grapes.

Gerson's theological wine is meant to nourish the Church and strengthen her members. Because of evil men, however, the name of theology has been besmirched and people laugh at the few who cultivate its vineyard. These people are made the butt of jokes (*et in fabulosum suum vertunt jocum;* 372), a phrase that recalls Gerson's early letter to his patron in which he expressed fear that his parents would become the laughing stock of their village.[62]

Gerson concedes that such attacks on the theologians might be justified. Some men when they drink the wine of theology forget friendship and confraternity. Because of their insatiable avarice, they prefer to make a reputation through verbal displays that are like tournaments. By impressing others, they "waste their time in the hope of the basest compensation." They are out to make as much money as possible (373).

Gerson may be referring here to the recent affair of Jean Blanchard and his avid pursuit of money through academic licensing fees.[63] At the same time he warns against "useless matters" which could distract theologians from their true vocation of considering God's revealed truths (374). Through the discipline of theology it is possible to put on the "wings of contemplation" and to fly through the air, "looking down upon odious lands" and seeking God, "who has his vineyards in the mountains" (374).

Gerson develops his image of the vineyard but also anticipates later descriptions he would provide of contemplation as a mountain. He also touches on a theme to which he returned on many occasions and made his personal motto: "Our way of life is in heaven" (*Nostra conversatio in coelis est;* Phil 3:20).[64] This heavenly way of life is available only for those genuine workers, who toil not for their own sake but for everyone (Gl 5.375). Gerson ends the sermon in referring both to Aristotle's *Rhetoric* and to the First Epistle of Peter (376). Here as elsewhere he delights in combining classical and Christian wisdom in the same sentence.

This impressive sermon develops with great ingenuity the image of the vineyard and its workers in order to describe the task of university teachers, especially those in theology. Gerson could draw on his knowledge of classical authors and combine it with Old Testament images, as well as the Psalms and Paul's Epistles. He was confident that through hard work in the vineyards of the Church and the University of Paris, students and teachers could come to the contemplative life and thus to the threshold of heaven.

Gerson was here more concerned with effort than with reward. He drew on the experience of his own early years in Paris. He believed in the value of making an effort and formulated an attitude toward an intellectual life that left behind the old Roman aristocratic appreciation of *otium* as leisurely intellectual occupation, as well as the monastic *otium spiritale,* in which the mind is open to heavenly things because it has abandoned intellectual and physical activities.[65] He firmly believed that each individual had to put forth an effort to reach the heights of contemplation.

Later in 1391, Gerson may have addressed a university congregation two more times: on the Feast of Saint Louis (25 August) and at Christmas (179; 597). A sermon in French is likely to have been preached on the Feast of All Saints, probably to a princely audience (Gl 7.2.992). The theme is hardly one that would be expected from such a joyful day: "The kingdom of heaven has suffered violence and the violent take it by force" (Mt 11:12). Gerson chose to describe the saints as defending the people of God from tyranny, heresy, and unchaste behavior. It is necessary to go to them in order to ward off the attacks of the world and its obsessions. In dealing with heresy Gerson took up for the first time in his authorship the question of black magic and superstition (Gl 7.2.1001).[66] He also characterized the Schism as a form of heresy but chose "to keep quiet about the horrible and damnable negligence of Christians who allow this division."

The longest section of this sermon concerns chastity. Gerson admits that it is not easy, perhaps hinting at what he himself experienced in his teenage years: "To overcome lustful flesh at all times in one's life is more difficult than to suffer death for a brief time. Those who experience it know it" (*ceulx le scevent qui l'espreuvent;* 1002). He gives advice for avoiding impure actions: keep busy; avoid too much food or wine.

He admits that it may seem almost impossible to overcome sexual temptation: "I know it is much easier to condemn this vice than to get rid of it, but it is nevertheless possible." Otherwise one would be preaching heresy. In any case it is necessary to remember that "the kingdom of Our Lord is acquired through pain and effort" (*par peine et par vigueur*). Once again Gerson comes across as an apostle of hard work in getting to heaven.

The sermon ends with four questions concerning paradise, the knowledge of the saints about who is damned and who is saved, the usefulness of praying to one saint rather than another, and the possibility that saints assume their bodies in order to appear on earth. The treatment is both brief and magisterial, without any scholastic question and answer form. This is a much more conventional sermon than some of the earlier ones, and at the same time it is representative of Gerson's usual procedure, providing a theme based on the feast of the day and a scriptural quotation, referring to his audience without using flattery, and at the end clearing up questions of religious observance or theology.

The Gerson who gave such sermons comes across as a confident, disciplined preacher, dedicated to his cause but hardly a fanatic. Drawing on an immense knowledge of his sources, he always maintained structure and discipline in presentation and avoided becoming abstract or difficult to follow. To a king who was young and perhaps only conventionally religious, Gerson spoke of the fragility and brevity of life. He warned aristocrats living in a hothouse atmosphere of sensual pleasure that they risk infamy in this life and punishment in the next. Indirectly he drew on his self-knowledge, but never hinted at his own humble background nor did he apologize for being the son of an artisan. Believing in the virtue of individual effort, Gerson devoted time and energy to sermons conveying religious conviction and intellectual discipline.

Mastering Theology: 1392–1393

As a bachelor of theology (*baccalaureus formatus*), Gerson was expected from 1390 on to take part in university affairs. The Latin sermons we have from this period are probably only a fragmentary indication of his efforts to use his time well and to influence events. On Wednesday 18 December 1392, he graduated to the licentiate in theology. The proceedings were led by Gerson's teacher and university chancellor since 1389, Pierre d'Ailly.[67] The theme of the discourse for the day after his inception Gerson chose, as earlier in his career, from the Book of Wisdom. "I sought my bride," which he interpreted as a description of how the theologian seeks the bride of wisdom. This text is lost, but we do have the *resumptio* given a few days later and it is clear that Gerson here added his comment to one of the questions that he had previously defended at the *vesperiae* or evening disputation (Gl 3.ix).

This work, *On Spiritual Jurisdiction,* deals with the Schism (Gl 3.1). Gerson asks whether it is ever possible to disregard the claims of a spiritual authority. He answers not in terms of canon law but on the basis of practical, almost political, needs. Since the two popes made unity of faith impossible, at least one of them had to give way. This surrender of power, *via cessionis,* Gerson justifies on the basis of present need and the history of the Church. As pointed out by John B. Morrall, a pioneer in reevaluating Gerson's role in the Schism, Gerson dealt not with doctrine but with custom.[68]

The new master of theology at no point appealed to a general council. Anyone who did not work toward ending the Schism was guilty of prolonging it. No pope could cling to power by claiming his own legitimacy if such insistence resulted in the Schism's indefinite prolongation. Gerson's indifference to the canonical tradition of papal plenitude of power made him a *bête-noire* for later advocates of papal infallibility.[69] As far as he was concerned, Church authorities had to be practical and do whatever was necessary, regardless of the possibility that it might be the true pope who is relinquishing power.[70]

There was no solution, however, if the war between England and France were revived. In March of 1392 the English and French met to negotiate at Reims, but King Charles became ill and withdrew.[71] He was back at Paris by the Feast of the Ascension and on 2 June, at Pentecost, he listened to a sermon given by Gerson: "You will receive the power of the Holy Spirit in you" (Acts 1:6).[72]

Once again Gerson combined a powerful evocation of a biblical text with reference to the contemporary situation. He started with the scene of the apostles after the Ascension of Jesus, as they waited in prayer in their locked room. God gave them the solid faith (*ferme creance*) that they needed, and now the king, like every good Christian, should also receive this gift (Gl 7.2.435). Gerson reminded Charles of the promise given by Saint Rémi or Remigius at the baptism of Clovis: the kingdom would be preserved for as long as the kings protected the faith. In order to guard this heritage, pride and lust are temptations to be avoided: *orgueil* and *folle amour* can destroy the kingdom (436). He asked the king to remember that he was *homme mortel* and as weak as anyone else. He was to think of his subjects as people on their way to salvation "and not a pack of curs" (*chiens mastins;* 437).

Besides firm belief, the king should also receive the sword of true wisdom (*vraye sapience*) from the Holy Spirit, in remembering that the apostles were ordinary people who were not learned: *simple gens sans lettres et sans clergie* (437). The question of wisdom brought Gerson to a treatment of the need to know Scripture in order to govern well. If men followed its teachings, then wars would end. When kings become tyrants and abuse their subjects, they lose their legitimacy. He referred to a claim by Saint Augustine that without justice, kings are nothing but thieves.[73] In this connection Gerson quoted the common proverb: "Petty thieves are hung, not the big ones" (*les petits larrons sont penduez, non pas les grands;* 439).

Such statements point to tolerance for criticism and free expression in late medieval France.[74] Gerson warned against the misuse of public funds and pleaded that soldiers be paid enough so that they will not be tempted to plunder the countryside (440). All public officials were obliged to act according to justice. Otherwise "one cannot describe sufficiently the evils that arise from them." Similarly clerics were not to buy and sell church benefices nor to spend their time in trying to put into high office men so ignorant and undependable that one could hardly entrust an apple to them, not to speak of the thousands of people handed over to their care!

With lively language and striking examples, Gerson went beyond the genre of bland and general recommendations that one might expect from a court preacher. Through the Holy Spirit, he said, the king receives strength to resist God's enemies in a *commune alliance* with the powers of the realm (441). Knights should fight together against the enemies of Christianity, and yet they spend their time in fighting each other. In this way Christians make Saracens rejoice. The protracted war between France and England allowed the continuation of the Schism and the loss of the Eastern Church, with the result that "Christian religion will be desolate and almost lost and dissipated" (443). It was wrong for Christians to fight each other, and it is the special task of the kingdom of France and its king to safeguard Christianity.

Gerson was not done. He went on describing the horrors and uncertainties of war. The outcome of battle is always dubious. More than fifty thousand men, he claims, had recently died in fighting between the towns of Ghent and Bruges.[75] "Consider this carnage, this terror and horror. And what will be the case if the war resumes between two so great kingdoms?" (444)

Gerson condemned the belief (which persisted until the First World War and is held even to this day) that war could be good for a country. When war breaks out, terrible things happen. From the war between England and France came *les grands et inexcogitables meschiefs:* acts of vengeance and the pursuit of profit through pillage (445).

A king has no obligation to regain territories lost in war: "In any case, most excellent prince . . . blessed and glorious is the loss which gains the good of peace." Gerson again drew on his knowledge of popular sayings: "It is a good halfpenny that saves a penny."[76] In other words, it is better to give up land than to sacrifice peace and security (447).

For Gerson the only way to end the Schism was to stop the war between England and France. He asks the pardon of the king, his brother, and his uncles, as well as of others present, for his directness: "For it is not temerity or presumption which makes me speak and exhort you to what you now are to do." Love of peace and union made him be so specific (448–49). Gerson hints that the great lords of France would become criminals if they allowed the war to continue.

How did Gerson manage to dwell on war when his subject was the coming of the Holy Spirit at Pentecost? As in his sermon on the Feast of All Saints, he used the day's pious theme to show its opposite. The antithesis of the wisdom of the Holy Spirit was this mindless, evil war which disrupted society and prolonged the Schism.

The king's first public display of mental illness a few months later, in August of 1392, weakened Gerson's hope that Charles VI was the man to end war and Schism. In a state of delusion, Charles, physically attacked some of his own men.[77] Although he subsequently seemed to recover, he soon had a relapse. Charles had days and even weeks when he was mentally competent, but his vulnerable mental state made him subject to his advisors. His brother, Louis of Orleans, did his best to influence, or manipulate, him, and so did his uncle, Philip, the duke of Burgundy.

The three decades from 1392 and until Charles's death in 1422 witnessed endless rivalries around a disabled king, with dire consequences for the kingdom and the Western Church. For Gerson this situation meant that he could not again turn to a king who was in full control of his life and able to make the consistent decisions necessary to cope with the political and military crisis.[78]

A few weeks before the king's first attack of illness, Gerson, on 29 June 1392, the Feast of Saints Peter and Paul, preached at the royal chapel of Saint Paul. He remembered Paul as the teacher of the same Saint Denis who, legend has it, came to France, where he was martyred (Gl 7.2.729).

Saint Paul, too, had on occasion fled from his persecutors. Like a good knight, he knew how to withdraw from a field of battle to avoid being killed, so that he might fight more effectively on another day (729). As for the objection that Paul indulged in too much self-praise, Gerson answered that he needed to do so in order to spread the Gospel. Paul's description of his own acts and sufferings did not stem from pride (731).

Gerson emphasized Paul's gentle side. "As the nurse sometimes speaks incorrectly . . . in order to descend to the speech of the child, then chews its food, then sits on the ground, then weeps and for a brief time makes herself a child with the child," so too, Paul took on different roles in order to accommodate himself to different types of people (734). In evoking the experience of childhood, Gerson was perhaps remembering how his parents had been with him. His description of Paul as nurse also recalls one of the prayers of Saint Anselm, which Gerson knew.[79]

Gerson began his portrayal of Paul by depicting him as a knight of Christ, but in the last part of the sermon Paul the nurse and mother took over. The Pauline epistles with their rich layers of self-description provided a point of departure for Gerson in visualizing different roles. The words with which Gerson described Paul hinted at his own life as a preacher of the Gospel: "He taught, he prayed without ceasing; he pardoned sin" (736). Gerson also remembered Paul as a hermit, dead to the world, and an ideal for the secular priest who, like Paul, lived in the midst of the world and had to protect himself from its lures (737).

If Saint Paul was the ideal priest for Gerson, Saint Louis was the ideal ruler. On 25 August 1392, soon after the king's first attack, Gerson addressed his colleagues at the College of Navarre in a portrait of Louis based on the categories of the kingdom of the self, of one's neighbor, and of God, a division already used earlier in addressing the king (Gl 5.229). In recalling the deeds of Saint Louis, Gerson hoped that his successor somehow would obtain strength to follow in his ways.

"In the kings of France the cult of God has always been alive and well." Gerson quoted from a letter by Pope Gregory the Great and referred to the baptism of Clovis: "Our Remigius, archbishop of Reims, when he baptized Clovis with chrism sent from heaven, was filled with a prophetic spirit and said that this king of France and all its kings would be glorious and strong so long as they kept to this confession of faith, just as they have remained."[80]

Gerson linked the original Frankish kingdom directly with its French successor beginning with the Capetian kings in the 980s. For us, the Franks belong to another world, but Gerson's proto-nationalism is a harbinger of a new perception of French identity, one that would be heightened a few decades later by the appearance of Joan of Arc.

A month later, on the Feast of Saint Michael Archangel (29 September 1392), Gerson again preached at the royal chapel of Saint Paul (292). His text as we have it is in Latin, but the original sermon would almost certainly have been in French. His purpose was once again to urge the country's spiritual and secular leaders to bring the Schism to an end. Before force was used, arguments were to be tried. Theological wisdom was not to be despised (306). Princes and prelates were obliged to seek agreements. Gerson reviewed the original choice of Urban VI as pope in Rome in 1378, the point of departure for the present Schism and asked whether this election had been valid (307).

In dealing so directly in his sermons with both war and Schism, Gerson was facing the central problems of his land and his age. He believed in the unity of the

Church and of Christian culture. His hope lay in a monarchy that traditionally had been the strongest in Europe and which ideologically had its origins in fifth-century rulers. But in counting so much on these distant descendants, Gerson was engaging in wishful thinking. The monarch was for the time being unable to provide his country with a dependable or rational rule.

In the autumn of 1392, however, it was not yet apparent that Charles VI would never regain full control. On 13 September, the king told a delegate to Richard II in England that he had recovered from his illness.[81] On 6 October, the Feast of Saint Denis, the king on his way to Paris stopped at the basilica of the saint, where so many of his royal ancestors lay buried. It was an important moment to establish the king's "gratefulness that he felt because of his restoration to health," in the diplomatic language of a contemporary chronicle.[82]

In June of 1393, the king had a second attack, lasting this time for almost seven months. Because of the French conception of monarchy, which made no provision for replacing an anointed king, and also because Charles at times actually did function, the question of royal resignation or deposition was not seriously discussed. The fact that the king remained on the throne shows how much more stable the French monarchy was than the English, under which Edward II was removed in 1327, and Richard II in 1399. But the result in France was a court filled with intrigue.

Treatments of this period take sides for or against Philip, the duke of Burgundy, the king's uncle, and Louis of Orleans, the king's younger brother.[83] The history of these years, from 1392 and to 1407, when Philip's son, John the Fearless had Louis murdered in a Paris street, is often told in relation to the rivalry between the two dukes. I find it difficult to judge the characters or motives of Philip and Louis. They were princes who tried to fill the power vacuum left by the king's chronic illness. The instability at the very heart of the French monarchy meant that schemes for ending war and the Schism as proposed by Gerson and others could not be realized in a consistent manner.

On 14 April 1393, Jean Gerson was made *aumonier*, almoner or chaplain, to the duke of Burgundy, Philip the Bold. He was given a yearly pension of 200 *livres*. The duke also provided Gerson with two servants and three horses.[84] Probably in December that same year, Philip the Bold recommended Gerson as his candidate to become dean of the chapter at the collegiate church of Saint Donatian in Bruges.[85]

As an advocate of church reform, Gerson well knew the ignominy attached to collecting funds from a priestly benefice without being resident. And yet the entire university system depended on having teachers who gained their livelihoods not only from students, whose fees were erratic, but also from tithes collected in parishes where someone else was carrying out pastoral duties.[86] The Bruges deanship, together with the income from the duke of Burgundy, apparently did not give Gerson financial independence. Writing from Bruges in 1400, he pointed out how he had been obliged at Paris to take on boarders in order to make ends meet: "I am forced in material life almost to beg and to live in a downtrodden way, for in the midst of bitter poverty it is impossible to live according to the golden mean, in accord with the requirements of one's position. Elsewhere I would be abundantly provided for and be able to maintain a household, but now it is necessary in my straitened circumstances to do without and to live with grammar students and schoolboys."[87]

Gerson must have had expenses in looking after the needs of his family at home, whose investment in his education now was expected to pay off. But in view of the patronage from the duke of Burgundy, Gerson may have been exaggerating his problems at a time when he was depressed about his situation at the university and was thinking of giving up on Paris. His search for a prebend at a local church in Paris became both frustrating and humiliating. As he wrote, "I am now forced to pursue a prebend." *Cogor ad praebendam noviter anhelare.*[88]

During these years Gerson could both be grateful and resentful that his financial status depended so directly on the favor of the duke of Burgundy. However enigmatic the duke may have been as a person, he or his advisors seem to have had a sense of literary and artistic quality. The same man also supported the sculptor Claus Sluter of Haarlem by paying for his magnificent work whose fragment at the former Charterhouse outside of Dijon still provides one of the most powerful indications of a transition from late gothic realism to renaissance art.[89]

What did Gerson think about his relationship with the duke of Burgundy? On this he remained silent, even in his outbursts in 1400 when he questioned almost everything else in his life and career. We do, however, have a sermon that must have been preached in the presence of the duke of Burgundy and is dated to 17 January 1393, the duke's birthday and also the Feast of Saint Anthony (Gl 7.2.561). Gerson here did his very best to describe a saint who could be recognizable for the duke, even though the sermon thereby downplayed Anthony's eremitical side and made him a knight in chivalrous combat with the devil.

Gerson began with the text from Wisdom (10:12): "She [Wisdom] in harsh contest gave him victory." Anthony was "like all other human beings" because he was at birth placed on the "most dangerous field of war in this miserable life" (561). Gerson quoted both Job and Seneca in order to show that "this life is a type of chivalry" (562).

We are engaged in making war on the world, the flesh, and the devil. Therefore there can be no joy in being born, for we enter into a vale of tears. The Church has always celebrated the day of the saints' death rather than of their birth, for it is only at death that one can be certain of heaven.

Here, however, Gerson made a concession to his patron: "I do not mean that a Christian prince cannot have a good intention in remembering the day of his birth and in specially honoring the feast of a saint for that day" (563). This is one of the few times where Gerson tries to soften his message for the sake of an important listener. Gerson knew he was speaking to a man whose life was based on celebrations. He gave his patron the benefit of the doubt and claimed Philip was not remembering his birthday or Saint Anthony's feast day "because of vanity or pride" (*non pas par vanite ou par orgueil*).

Anthony here became a knight of Christ who at baptism was given "the glove of justice, the sword of discretion, the belt of temperance" (563). This "noble champion" faced the devil in a "spiritual battle of vices against virtues." For a moment Gerson considered the Cistercian nuns who may also have been listening to his sermon: "Differently, with greater subtlety . . . one could speak to persons who live the contemplative and solitary life."[90]

Anthony was remembered for having fought off various tyrants, of which the first was the flesh. In his youth he was assaulted night and day by obscene thoughts but managed to repel them. He is supposed to have said to the evil spirits of carnal pleasure, *fy de toy, fy,* a phrase that appears in Gerson's later work on purity. If the devil assaults one with thoughts of the flesh, one should tell him, as it were, to get lost.[91] Young people are to follow Anthony and not make excuses, as they do when they say they cannot resist carnal temptation (564). They think they can live chastely in old age, but many do not get old, or else they are stuck in youthful habits they cannot alter (565).

Gerson named Alexander the Great, Julius Caesar, Anthony, Kings David and Solomon, Samson, "and others without number," who had succumbed to carnal temptation. He made Saint Anthony into a model man who through prayer conquered the spiritual fire of carnality (566).

In the remainder of the sermon Gerson considers two other temptations that characterized Anthony's life: despair, because of all his trials and tribulations, and greed, which came when the devil threw gold coins in his path. Gerson could draw on episodes from the *Life of Anthony,* a central text of monasticism and hagiography. But Gerson saw Anthony more in terms of his fighting devils than his shaping a monastic way of life. Gerson knew his source well, as in taking its story of how Anthony reproached Jesus after the saint had experienced a terrible temptation and asked, "O good Jesus, where were you when these enemies were tormenting me so?" (567). Jesus assured Anthony that he was present: "I expected your patience, your loyalty towards me and your victory over yourself in order to repay you. And since you have shown these things, I will make you known in all the world" (567–68).[92]

Gerson recast Saint Anthony as a spiritual hero who could be an icon for the duke born on this saint's day. Anthony was an example in terms of purity, endurance, and lack of desire for worldly goods. However odd it must have seemed to convert a desert ascetic into a knight of Christ, Gerson made the saint relevant for his aristocratic audience.

Did the duke listen? Did such sermons make any difference in everyday life? The duke's new almoner wanted him to live the life of a Christian knight: chaste, brave, and unselfish. The duke, whatever he thought of this exhortation, was favoring a man born in one of his territories and on his way to the academic summit.

When Jean Gerson reached the age of thirty on 14 December 1393, he could look back on his life as the story of arrival at a rank and place many aspired to but few attained. He could write, teach, and preach about subjects dear to him, and he could try to make his words change people's lives.

There was a streak of arrogance in this young man, as when he displayed his knowledge of classical learning. But there was also a commitment to bringing the Gospel to whomever he met. Jean Gerson was completing his education and getting ready for a lifetime of dedication. It is not by accident that he looked to Saint Anthony. How ever much Gerson may have wanted to make the saint into a knight, the Anthony who emerged from his pen remained a solitary figure amid his tribulations. Much like young Jean himself.

Living a Personal Schism, 1394–1399

Facing the Schism, 1394

From January of 1394 on, the University of Paris reentered the public arena in efforts to end the Schism. A delegation of masters to the king, who had temporarily recovered his health, asked that the ban on public discussion be lifted.[1] The masters, among whom Gerson may well have been, received a surprisingly positive answer from the king's uncle, the formidable duke of Berry, known previously for his resistance to university debate on the matter. According to the *Chronique du Religieux de Saint-Denys,* our best contemporary source for these years in Paris, the duke is supposed to have said to the masters: "The prolonged length of this terrible Schism is a matter of shame for the king and for the royal family of France. All the world has grown weary of it. If you find a remedy to which the royal council can agree, we will work to carry it out."[2]

There is no explanation here for the duke's change of mind, but the university took immediate advantage of the opening. On 25 January it was decided that any member of the university who had advice to give about a solution to the Schism was to write his suggestion down on a piece of paper (*cedula* or *schedula*) and deposit it in a sealed box at the Monastery of Saint Mathurin, located in the Latin Quarter, where the university often met. The result was a kind of referendum. More than ten thousand pieces of paper were received, indicating that some contributors had "voted" more than once. The results were reviewed by the members of a committee from the faculties of theology, law, and arts. They concluded that the university had three central suggestions, which basically all boiled down to recommending the *via cessionis,* the voluntary resignation of both popes.[3]

On 26 February, four hundred masters gathered at the Cistercian College of Saint Bernard, another favored university meeting place because of its size. The assembly approved this recommendation.[4] Gerson's name is not on the list of consenting doctors of theology who are described in a manner reminiscent of the *Rule of Saint Benedict* as making up the *majorem et saniorem partem istius facultatis* (the greater and sounder segment of this faculty). His absence in itself proves nothing but hints that he was keeping a distance from university negotiations on the Schism. On 18 April 1394, Gerson was officially appointed dean of the chapter of Saint Donatian at Bruges.[5] The next day he preached an Easter sermon known as *Pax vobis,* from the words said to the apostles by the risen Christ: "Peace be to you. Do not be afraid" (Luke 24:36). Gerson must have been speaking to the court, but the text does not make clear whether or not the king was present.[6] The sermon is one of his classic statements about the position of the monarchy in the Schism.

Gerson considered the peace that the risen Christ brought: "I exhort the king our lord to peace in his kingdom for the good of the Holy Church and of all Christianity" (Gl 7.2.789). The devil was persecuting the Church and allied himself with tyranny, heresy, and especially with greed, the main cause for its division (790). Jesus showed his wounds to us in order to remind us how much it cost to bring peace. We must also be prepared to suffer in seeking peace. All other schisms and persecutions were ended by the intervention of "brave Christian princes." Now "you, my lords most Christian princes who are present here" must do the same (791). The Schism is said to have lasted sixteen years, thus giving us a date for this sermon.

Gerson closed with the warning that unless his listeners acted to heal the Church and cooperated with the university, they could all end up in eternal damnation. Ignorance was no excuse (792). The lords of France would be held responsible for something that had never before happened in the history of Christianity: "Do not allow it to happen that Holy Church, which was established through the deaths of so many martyrs and by the devotion of such great princes, be lost or destroyed in your time because of favoritism to certain people or through negligence" (793).

Who were the "certain people" (*aucunes personnes particulières*) to whom Gerson was referring? He was careful not to name names, and yet he was going far in warning his audience against failing to take appropriate action. He was telling the princes of the royal family and their retainers that it was their obligation to ensure that both popes accepted the way of cession. Otherwise the princes would neglect their historical responsibility to support and defend the Church and so would be deprived of the peace and salvation that the risen Christ offered them.

Gerson's hope that the court would cooperate with the university is reflected in a long statement composed by his colleague at the College of Navarre, Nicolas de Clamanges. This document, which the Chronicle of Saint Denis (*Chronique du Religieux de Saint-Denys*) found important enough to reproduce in its entirety, takes up almost forty pages in the modern edition of the work.[7] Nicolas began with a biblical reference which Gerson would have applauded: "We have sought peace and we say with the prophet, here is confusion" (Jer 14:19).[8] In rhetorical terms as violent as anything Gerson was capable of in his sermons, Nicolas lamented the state of the Church: *O nova et stupenda ecclesie calamitas!*[9]

The plea was sent to the king but was also summarized in a sermon preached at court by doctor of theology William Barrault.[10] But on 30 June the king rejected the university's proposal out of hand and forbade further public discussion of the matter. Anyone who did so risked the king's wrath.[11]

Six months of open discussion had ended, but the university masters refused to accept the "way of silence," as it might have been called. They threatened to suspend all sermons and lessons. Their recommendations had already been sent to Pope Clement VII at Avignon, who according to rumor was apparently so outraged by them that he died soon thereafter, on 16 September.[12] By 28 September the Avignon cardinals already elected a successor, Pedro de Luna, who became Benedict XIII. As a cardinal he was well known to the University of Paris since he had been involved in its negotiations with Avignon that previous summer. But Benedict, like his predecessor, was to be just as much a disappointment to the university reform party as Clement had been.

The brief papal interregnum gave an opportunity to the university to turn again publicly to the Schism. On 23 September the court gave permission for the university to do so, and the masters promised the king to resume lectures.[13] Gerson's role remains unclear, as none of his writings can be dated with certitude to the summer or autumn of 1394. A sermon for All Saints, *Exsultabunt sancti in gloria*, however, is supposed to have been given that year (Gl 5.265–278).[14] The first part of the sermon was apparently intended primarily for his fellow university masters.[15] Gerson dealt with the society of the saints and used what would become one of his favorite biblical quotations, from Saint Paul to the Hebrews (13:14): "We have here on earth no abiding city or home but seek a future one."

After eighteen theological questions concerning the status of the saints, their joy, bodily organs, and so on, Gerson warned against useless curiosity! There was a time for disputation and a time for instruction: "The first in the school, the other in the sermon" (273). *Studiositas*, over-intellectualization, is a waste of time and a distraction from the inner life of the university scholar who seeks the company of the saints.

In the second part of the sermon, which may have been preached as an afternoon or early evening collation primarily for students, Gerson dealt with purity of life (274). A youth who wanted to remain pure had to make sure he had a chaste and uncorrupted teacher, and not one who was a wolf among sheep. Good company in one's own peer group is also essential. Young people were to beware of base conversations and contact. At the same time they were to flee the devil's company, which is found when people do not work hard and instead seek entertainment or leisure. Biblical writings, Jerome, and Horace were all used to make the point that the devil must never find us unoccupied: "Believe not me but the Wise man: lack of occupation has taught many evils."[16]

It is terrible when a corrupted youth is "the cause of perdition of so many souls from his unclean deed, when he transfers his vice like an evil disease from one to another, and indeed to many others, perhaps ten, twenty, a hundred, a thousand" (276). The prospective of the spread of sin horrified Gerson, who asked how amends can possibly be made or sufficient punishment dealt out to such a person.

Here he added an exemplum or moral story about a son who bit off his father's nose in order to show him that if the father had corrected him in youth, he would not have come to such a bad end.[17] To emphasize the same point, Gerson turned to the section on sin "against nature" in the Dominican Thomas of Cantimpré's *Bonum Universale de Apibus* (The Universal Good of the Bees), a thirteenth-century collection of stories for the use of preachers.[18] This one concerns a youth who was corrupted by his master and cried out to friends who came to visit him: "Woe to him who seduced me. What possible help can I ask for from God? Behold, I see hell opening and the demons ready to grab me" (277). The youth despaired of any forgiveness. Gerson ended his narrative with the remark, "Do you understand this terrible story, boys? Do you not shake all over when you hear it?"

The sermon concludes with an appeal to its youthful listeners not to be embarrassed to confess sexual sins. "You will say: How can I speak of deeds so base, sins so awful, to a living man, to the priest? What will he say and what will he do?" Gerson answers by asking: "If you are so much in fear of the priest, why are you not more afraid of God who knows everything?" For those who wanted to repent but could not stop sinning, there was hope. They had to flee lack of occupation and bad company, then pray to a special saint, especially to Saint Mary, and follow Saint Anthony by crying out to the devil in the midst of temptation: "Get off with you and your temptation, wretched devil" (*phy de te et de tentatione tua, miser diabole*; 278).

Such practical suggestions would also come from Gerson in the early years of the next decade, when he wrote about confession and masturbation.[19] This sermon reflects one of Gerson's perennial concerns. He could not separate reformation of the Church from the reformation of the lives of individual Christians.[20] In childhood and youth, they had to be shaped through adherence to the medieval Church's strictures on sexual morals. Gerson's solution was to fill everyday life with study and other hard work, where there was no time for empty conversations. At the same time priests and teachers were to act as saintly role models.[21]

In seeking peace and unity in the Church, Gerson sought peace and unity within himself and those around him. Although he also praised the contemplative life, Gerson believed in the possibility of action. Now it seemed as if he would have an opportunity to make changes.

Becoming Chancellor, 1395

On 1 February 1395, the chancellor of the university, Pierre d'Ailly, had an audience at the royal residence of Saint Paul. He recommended the way of cession as the best procedure for ending the Schism.[22] The next day an assembly of French clergy (later to be called the First Paris Council) opened and more than two weeks later concluded with recommending double cession of office by the two popes and threatening the subtraction of obedience from the Avignon pope if he did not cooperate.[23] Such a threat seemed necessary in order to force Benedict XIII into active cooperation with the French clergy. But Benedict had chosen a tactic of negotiation, delay, and favoritism. On 2 April, for example, he named Pierre d'Ailly bishop of Puy, probably in order to neutralize the Paris opposition.[24]

Two days later, on Palm Sunday, Gerson may have given a sermon known as *Ecce rex tuus venit tibi mansuetus:* "Behold your gentle king comes to you" (Mt 21:5).[25] One theme is the destruction of Jerusalem, which is said to have come about because of the corruption of its three estates: the clergy or academic class was racked by avarice and envy; the secular lords and chivalry by injustice and tyranny; the common people and bourgeoisie by ingratitude and betrayal of loyalties. Gerson condemned those who buy office and oppress others, but he did not go into detail, remarking that *la matière est trop dangereuse,* "the subject is too dangerous" (Gl 7.2.617). He added, however, that preachers must not restrain themselves out of fear or for the sake of flattery. He would rather die than flatter.

The latter part of the text is less polished and more summary, apparently little more than Gerson's notes. The peace of the Church could come only through the *voye d'humilite,* the way of humility: "It will not come through sedition in civil war or by the corruption of money or by occult deception" (621). Gerson thus named three methods already being used to deal with the Schism: the threat of war between the royal princes; the buying of loyalties; and recourse to magic.

At the conclusion of the sermon Gerson prayed for the various people involved in dealing with the Schism, especially the duke of Berry, a central figure in earlier efforts to silence the university.[26] Now the Schism was once again out in the open, but Gerson's recommendation of a "way of humility" indicates he feared the Council of Paris had gone too far in threatening a subtraction of obedience.

On the Holy Thursday after the Palm Sunday court sermon, Gerson addressed an unnamed monastic or religious community that was connected to the university: *Ante diem autem festum Paschae* (Gl 5.50–64). The many references to the Rule of Saint Benedict indicate that Gerson may have been speaking to the Cistercians at the College of Saint Bernard.[27] He told his audience that he would not give the type of sermon preached "by moderns," but would follow "the fashion of the ancients" and give a homily (51). The Schism, he warned, easily could turn into something permanent, like the division between the Latin and Greek Churches. No one had originally intended questions such as the dating of Easter to separate two churches, but this is what had happened. Since the Greeks had gone their own way, their standard of learning had declined and they had slipped into error.

After a long exposition on the question of calculating the date of Easter and an impressive list of authorities, Gerson eventually turned to the Holy Thursday theme of Christ's offering himself for us. Using part of the central passage on charity in Paul's First Letter to the Corinthians (13:4), Gerson defined Christ's love (61). It is not the same as friendship, which is limited to a small circle of people. According to God's command, we are to love without exception. God is our "supreme chancellor," a title probably much on the mind of a man who was on the verge of being promoted to the chancellorship of the University of Paris.

Gerson adapted his language to his audience. He spoke of how we enter into the "school of Christ," a term that evokes the Rule of Saint Benedict's "school of the service of God."[28] Jesus is here our "abbot and leader" (61). Our obligation is to follow "the rule of love and the way of charity" (*regulam amoris et viam dilectionis*) (62). As in the sermon of a few days earlier, Gerson may have been reacting to his colleagues' threats to follow the *via cessionis.* For Gerson the Schism could be resolved only through charity. The disciple of Christ should be ashamed when he rejects patience and neglects charity and becomes angry.

Compared to Gerson's usual attacks on political, moral and ecclesiastical abuses in other sermons from this period, he was calmer here and more attentive to the theme of Christ's overwhelming love for mankind. There is an element of the contemplative reflection which was to become an ever more explicit dimension in Gerson's thought and life.

A few days later, on Easter Tuesday, 13 April, Pope Benedict XIII at Avignon named "Jean de Gerson, dean of the church of Saint Donatian at Bruges in the diocese of Tournai, master in theology," chancellor of the University of Paris (Gl 2.5–6). The appointment could hardly have come as a surprise to Gerson, who in a later letter to Pierre d'Ailly described his master as the cause of his advancement to this office (Gl 5.63). The papal letter reserved the chancellorship for Gerson because of d'Ailly's appointment as bishop of Puy, and it approved of Gerson's occupying the office of dean of Saint Donatian at Bruges and holding the parish church of Champeaux-en-Brie in the diocese of Paris. The latter may have been given as a benefice to Gerson already in 1388 by the bishop of Paris (Gl 10.421). In a sermon from January 1391, Gerson had indicated that the pope in Avignon had approved of this gift (Gl 7.2.533).

In spite of the decisions of innumerable councils prohibiting a plurality of benefices, the pope granted Gerson the right to hold deanship, chancellorship, and parish benefice at one and the same time, provided that these not be deprived of their rightful incomes and that the care of souls was not neglected.[29] We can assume that Gerson, since the end of the 1380s, had a vicar take his place at Champeaux, just as he would have done from 1394 on at Bruges. The University of Paris could not have functioned without such arrangements. Even a chancellor had to depend on such revenue, especially when limitations were imposed in 1385 on income from examination fees.[30] Gerson was entering an office that was venerable and prestigious but did not have its own independent source of income.[31] He was to spend years trying to establish a financial basis for his university position.

The Avignon pope approved Gerson's threefold status, but there is no indication that the new chancellor felt especially obligated to Benedict XIII. If Gerson was in anyone's shadow, he was beholden to his teacher. Pierre d'Ailly had taken him under his wing from the first years in Paris; as the recipient of Gerson's begging letter, he had probably helped him out with his expenses; he had restrained his pupil from going too far in his attack on Juan de Monzon.

Even before he became chancellor, Gerson had seen himself as a defender of orthodoxy. Now, as chancellor, he would play that role in an official capacity which gave him the right to confer the license to teach on graduates of the university.[32] At the same time, he could distance himself from the intrigues of court. In 1400 Gerson claimed that his sole reason for accepting the chancellorship was to get away from the instability of court life (*curiae fluctibus . . . a quibus ut emigrarem sola hec fuit occasio cancellariam postulandi*; Gl 2.18). As Gilbert Ouy once pointed out, Gerson's selective memory (*étrange et pathétique mémoire*) here failed to account for the vital role of d'Ailly.[33] There is no doubt that Gerson was d'Ailly's protégé, much more so than the pope's. At Paris d'Ailly had identified himself as a leader of the reform party, and as bishop he apparently did not feel bound to defend the interests of the Avignon pope. In the years to come, Jean Gerson and Pierre d'Ailly acted as free agents of their own consciences. They were indebted to the university that had formed them but were not its creatures. They were loyal subjects of the crown but could hardly follow all the machinations of royal power once the king's mental illness became chronic. They were tied to the pope at Avignon but could negotiate with the pope at Rome.

The day after Gerson's official appointment to the chancellorship, a delegation from the University of Paris departed for Avignon. On 21 May another legation came from Paris, this time from the king, including the king's uncles, the dukes of Berry and of Burgundy.[34] The account of the negotiations in the Chronicle of

Saint Denis indicates that the pope had no intention of ceding power. At every point he outmaneuvered those who asked him to resign. By July the university delegation had given up.

In the wake of this deadlock, Gerson wrote a very brief statement: *De substractione schismatis,* also known as *De substractione obedientiae* (Gl 6.22–24). He was, however, much more cautious here than he had been in 1392 in his only previous statement about the Schism.[35] Then he had considered the possibility that the pope might err and could be removed. Now his worry was that any drastic action by the university might worsen the situation and make the Schism permanent: "If the University of Paris decides anything in a matter that is so momentous and difficult and which touches a person of the highest office and his supporters, then it is to be feared that the pope and his men, who also are clerics, will make contrary decisions. In this way the Schism will touch matters concerned with the faith and, as it were, become insoluble" (22).

In the next paragraph, Gerson speculated on the likelihood of this scenario. Other universities were issuing statements about the true faith in disagreement with Paris. No progress could be made unless there was consent on both sides to the way of concession. The effort supported by many Paris masters to declare the Avignon pope a perjurer for breaking a promise to end the Schism were useless. The Roman side was even more uncompromising than the Avignon one, so that there was no point in attacking the Avignon pope. If both present popes were disregarded and a new papal election took place, then there might be three popes instead of two, and the situation would be "much worse than the first one" (*multum pejus priore;* 23). The words are prophetic.

Gerson lamented that the faculty of theology had only one vote in four in deciding policy. Despite the expertise of the theologians, the faculty of medicine had just as much to say. He recalled the previous year's decision to set up a sealed box for depositing statements in writing (*schedulae*) about what to do to end the Schism: "This subject has to be treated not only by scraps of paper but also by means of oral statements and exchange of disputations, whether in secret or in public: in this way the truth is best investigated" (23). Gerson believed in open discussion as the best way to reach the truth. The referendum method, he complained, allowed a single man to write a hundred opinions and thus seem to represent a significant faction simply because of the number of pieces of paper with which one person could stuff the referendum box!

Gerson concluded with what he called his own *schedula,* stating that his goal was not to delay the way of cession and the union of the Church but to assure the unity of the Christian faith, without sacrificing the reputation of the university and especially of its faculty of theology. The way of concession was best but it was useless if the princes and clergy of the Roman obedience would not consent to it (24).

This little treatise, closer in form to a modern newspaper comment than to a traditional scholastic statement, reveals Gerson's state of mind shortly after he became chancellor. He would not support a radical break with Avignon that might isolate the university and perhaps lead to a worsening of the Schism. He wanted to follow the procedure used a few years earlier in the expulsion of the Dominicans: first the theological faculty would treat the matter at hand, in full congregation with all its masters, and then the decision could be approved by the university as a whole.

Gerson looked for precedents and believed in the special position of theology at Paris. He based his life on the value of scholastic debate, as opposed to a pseudo-democratic referendum. Most of all, he would do anything to avoid an escalation of responses on both sides of the Schism. In the coming years, Gerson voiced on several occasions his main fear that the Schism would become permanent. If this were to happen, the University of Paris would become a creature of the Avignon pope, a far cry from its former status as the theological arbiter of the Church.

Gerson's contribution seems to have done little to cool the determination of some Paris masters to force Benedict XIII into giving up power by threatening him with an open break. The university made up a list of nine questions to the pope, which were, more or less, bald statements urging him to cede power. In December 1395 the masters sent letters to the cardinals at Avignon indicating that the pope was bound to adopt the *via cessionis*.[36]

Gerson's response to this move is not known. We next find him on 17 January 1396, the Feast of Saint Anthony, in a rousing sermon, *Poenitemini* (Do penance) in the presence of the duke of Burgundy.[37] In contrast to his sermon of four years earlier, Gerson did not portray Anthony as a knight. This time the theme was penance. Just as Anthony had gone into the desert to do penance, so must the duke in following the saint on whose day he was born.

Anthony's life bore witness to the truth of the Christian religion (Gl 7.2.938–940), but three vices block this faith in many people: curiosity, carnality, and iniquity. Amid such temptations, the duke may want to cry out as Anthony once did, "Good Jesus, where were you?"[38] Gerson again used the *Life of Saint Anthony* by Athanasius, but this time, in contrast with his 1393 sermon, he underlined Anthony's trials and tribulations.

A subtheme of the sermon contains a warning against the use of magic and superstition as temptations of the devil (943). Gerson's concern may be connected to the fact that the king, after a period of improvement, had fallen ill again in December, and the court sought any and every cure.[39] Gerson turned to the example of Philip VI (1328–1350), the first of the Valois line. When offered healing by sorcery, he is supposed to have replied, "I would rather die if it is God's will that I die now, for it is in any case necessary that at some time we die" (944).

Gerson warned that self-love (*amour propre*) was in the process of destroying the community of the realm. It must be replaced by a charity that unites the three estates in peace and union: *l'estat de seigneurie, de clerge et de bourgoisie* (946). Self-love brings with it flattery, adulation, and lies. A person deceives his lord in order to seek his own good. Such venality undermines the lord and endangers the lives of his subjects. Gerson did not challenge the system of rewards and benefices upon which the service of any lord was based: "I do not criticize payment for services rendered, or the generosity of the lords; but in every case it should be done with restraint. Generosity must not justify cruelty" (947).

If love of self is a problem in the lay world, it is even worse in the Church. He saw it as a cause of the Schism for "it does not seek anything except its own glory, social status and profit."

Peace had been relegated to a desert more barren than that in which Anthony lived. A place full of thorns, rocks, and ditches, where charity had been cast out. The one hope was that God will take both popes to paradise "so that they will sing there, 'Glory to God in the highest' and we will have peace!" The preacher's desire, then, was for the quick dispatch of both popes!

This outburst is softened by a final prayer for peace, to which he nevertheless added a warning to Philip the Bold and to all powerful lords: "Alas, what will people say in the future when they read the chronicles of France, if the peace of the holy Church was lost in the time of the lords who are here?" (948) This will indeed be a harsh lesson, a shameful tale: *Ha, sire, ce seroit dure lesson, trop peu honnourable narracion.*

The sermon, which started as a conventional exposition on penance in the life of Saint Anthony, had become more specific: a warning that flattery, self-aggrandizement, and self-love would mean the end of the unity of Christendom. In several places, Gerson hints that the great duke's entourage included people who went too far in trying to please their master. He was no longer trying to please. The Anthony he held up as a model in 1396 was a man who felt abandoned by his good Jesus when confronted by the devil, not the attractive and glorious knight depicted a few years earlier. Gerson apparently said what was on his mind. His position at the university and benefice at Bruges did not prevent him from speaking out.

Making a Distance

By the spring of 1396, it must have been apparent to Gerson that his cautious approach to the way of cession was not making headway. In March the university appealed to the future pope and asserted that on questions of schism or heresy, each pope had his own judge: a living pope had to submit to the council; while a deceased pope was subject to his successor.[40] On 30 May, Benedict XIII contradicted this claim. At this time Gerson gave a sermon in French (28 May), but it says nothing about the Schism.[41]

The occasion was Trinity Sunday, and the title comes from the sign of the cross: *In nomine Patris et Filii et Spiritus Sancti* (671–79). Gerson's errand was to praise the mystery of the Trinity, in pointing out the boundaries to human understanding. Untaught men had exceeded in wisdom *toute humaine clergie,* all academic learning, as in the case of John the Evangelist. When Alan of Lille was supposed to speak on the Trinity, he had to declare his ignorance (674–75). If this was the case for so great a theologian, then how could uneducated people claim to grasp such high matters? Often they cannot comprehend other types of knowledge that are much easier to gain.

Hard work is a value that has to be combined with faith. It is necessary to accept that in order to specialize in a field, such as carpentry or money changing, "time and study are needed." This is even more the case with theology: the long training of its teachers enables them to deal with the most arcane matters (676). Toward the end of the sermon, in speaking of the image of the Trinity in the soul of each person, Gerson allowed himself some topical remarks. He laments the fact that many kings and princes did not imitate the persons of the Trinity in terms of their attributes of power, wisdom, and charity. Such men misuse their power, as when they allow sorcerers to claim they are more powerful than God (678). In abusing wisdom, there are people "who hinder the promotion of wise clerics whose duty it is to defend the faith and perform the divine service and prefer to advance others" (679) This complaint would appear again in Gerson's letter from Bruges in 1400 in which he explained why he intended to resign the chancellorship (Gl 1.18).

Finally, Gerson points to abuse of the goodness that comes from the Holy Spirit: "There are the officials who by exaction and extortion burden poor people." These men are like lions who devour such people and their children with "painful torments and death in anguish, and their lords get the least out of it" (Gl 7.2.679). Even though he kept a low profile on the Schism, he showed deep political and religious commitment.

More direct insight into his inner world is gained from his annotations to a document on the Schism authored by the masters of the University of Oxford. He is likely to have gotten hold of this declaration of loyalty to the Roman pope, composed on 17 March 1395 for King Richard II, in the spring of 1396. Gilbert Ouy has identified Gerson's handwritten annotations on the Oxford text.[42] In March the truce between England and France had been extended for twenty-eight years and King Richard II was engaged to Isabelle, the eldest daughter of King Charles VI.[43] It looked as though the new contacts between French and English might encourage a rapprochement also on the Schism and its solution.[44]

In reality, however, the two universities had little to discuss. The Oxford masters in their declaration rejected any consideration of cession as the best way to end the Schism. In pompous, wordy language, which seems old-fashioned compared to Gerson's more pragmatic style, the masters asserted unswerving loyalty to the Roman pope. They refused to contemplate any other settlement than a general council, unless, of course, the Avignon pope conceded that he was in the wrong and voluntarily gave way to the true pope in Rome.

Gerson's annotations are sometimes neutral headlines that pedagogically divide up the text, sometimes brief remarks that show his contempt for the style or presentation of the Oxford masters. In one place he calls their objections childish and empty (*puerilis et verbalis tantum*; Gl 10.327). On several occasions, he attacks them for going too far in their rhetoric (*verba invectiva et injuriosa*; 331, 337, 339). On many points, he notes for himself why he disagrees with individual statements in the document. When the Oxford masters claim that Pope Urban VI was deprived of the possession of the papacy, Gerson notes: "It ought not to be said 'deprived' because his election was invalid."[45]

The Oxford masters simply did not understand, Gerson claimed, what was involved in the way of cession (326). He added here a long note, about four hundred words, concerning the reasons why it would be unrealistic to call a general council. The fact that at the death of one pope another had been elected in both observances showed him that the longer Christendom waited, the more unlikely it became that either pope would voluntarily give up power. Some agreement had to be made so that both popes would concede power.

One of Gerson's central points was that even a true pope can be removed from office if he blocks the unity of the Church. Here he agreed with his colleagues at the University of Paris that the question of legitimacy was not the central one. Unlike the Oxford masters, he did not care who was the true pope. What mattered at this point was to make sure there was only one pope: "Even the true pope, whoever he might be, and those who obey him ought to be called schismatic if they repudiate suitable solutions offered them" (329).

To the Oxford claim that a council would be more effective, Gerson countered that the way of cession by both popes would spare the Church a painful legal investigation. Any review of past actions would cause scandal. Neither side knew who was in the right, with the result that both sides undermined the unity of the Church (332).

As in his first contribution in 1392, Gerson sought a solution he believed would be practical.[46] The word *utilitas* was central for him. It would be served by the cession of both popes (333). Gerson showed impatience with his colleagues. At one point he claimed to be amazed that "reputable men" could argue in a manner "whose ineffectiveness is obvious" (334).

Few times in medieval history do we have access to a document that apparently was meant only for the eyes of its writer.[47] Gerson had no time for long-winded arguments or the belief that either side in the Schism was totally in the right and monopolized truth. It was essential to leave off considerations of legitimacy and to bring the matter to an end without interminable public debates: "As has been said so often, it is impossible to get to the truth through the way of discussion" (337).

This statement may seem surprising from the pen of a scholar whose public life was based on open debate of intellectual questions. Gerson, however, had had enough. Since the year after his arrival in Paris, he had been hearing about the Schism and witnessing fruitless efforts to end it. In one of his most bitter moments, he challenges his Oxford colleagues: "Why do you spend so much time in grieving over our wretchedness, and yet you have remained silent. . . . Where are your writings on the subject of unity? What about frequent processions with tears? By now it is almost twenty years since this dreadful matter started; while you apparently will do nothing except, as you say, call on the power of the emperor. . . . The matter cannot permit further delay, for it will soon be a lost cause" (340). Despite his impatience Gerson did concede one point to the Oxford masters. The idea of a general council might be a good one, he admitted, once union had been obtained (341). The advantage of such a council would be its possible contribution to "the reformation of the entire situation of the Church" (*pro totius ecclesiae status reformatione*; 341). In the years to come, he would insist that the restoration of the papacy and the reformation of the Church belonged together.

For the time being, however, Gerson considered a conciliar solution to the Schism too great of a risk to take. He did not trust that the presence of the Holy Spirit would guide the decisions of the council fathers. A council trying to determine the legitimate pope might "be deceived and err because of false witnesses" or because of other incorrect information given its members.[48]

The council might end in becoming the instrument of the devil. Gerson distinguished between matters of faith, where a general council would be on strong ground, and matters of fact, where it could be led astray. He doubted if it could ever reach agreement (343). Therefore the way of cession was the only "easy, quick, and good way for ending the Schism." The word *brevis* appears time and again in Gerson's defense of the way of cession.

These presumably private annotations reveal attitudes apparent in Gerson's published writings. He worked fast, sought pragmatic solutions, and disregarded many theoretical questions. He had no time for long discussions about conciliar theory or papal power. He sought a resolution here and now. At this point he had no use for theorizing about the basis of papal and ecclesiastical power.

While reviewing the Oxford arguments and preparing arguments against a general council, Gerson was also coping with the more extreme views of his Paris colleagues. In *De papatu contendentibus,* which has been dated to May or June of 1396, he rebuts in twenty points charges made by the Parisian masters against Benedict XIII.[49] The masters had reproached the Avignon pope for taking an oath before his election that he would voluntarily give up power in order to bring the Schism to an end. Now he was being accused of perjury.

Gerson points out that Benedict's cession of office would be useless unless the Roman pope also promised to resign. Benedict, moreover, could not be accused of perjury if he had promised cession only in principle (Gl 6.24). To force him to do so would contradict the meaning of the term, for it would be violence and not cession (25). In any case, the Avignon pope had not rejected the way of cession: he had condemned the assertion that he could be forced to resign (27).

Although Gerson argued for a flexible response to ending the Schism, he exposed himself to the charge of being the instrument of Benedict XIII by making the Avignon pope's delaying tactic acceptable. One recent interpreter has accused Gerson of abandoning the *via cessionis* and accepting a *via discussionis* by which the two popes would meet and work out a solution. Gerson had made himself a creature of Benedict, whose "sincerity" was "open to doubt."[50]

Gerson was, however, far from being Benedict's patsy. The chancellor made it clear that the Avignon pope had to work sincerely for a cession of power. But the Paris theologian's main concern in the late spring or early summer of 1396 apparently was the radical position taken by his colleagues. He warned them that their withdrawal of obedience from Benedict XIII would not necessarily be helping matters and might in fact end up worsening the Schism.

Gerson's fear is apparent in his twentieth and final point: if one pope, in order to defend his position, were to begin excommunicating those with allegiance to the other pope and take away benefices, this would be the start of a tactical escalation which the other pope would employ as well. The Christian religion as a way to salvation would be in danger, for no one could be sure about his status (28).

This nightmare scenario Gerson would describe two years later in much greater detail.[51] As in his annotations to the Oxford document, the 1396 statement reveals a pragmatic Gerson trying to end the Schism before it turned into mutual excommunications and accusations of heresy. He was the proverbial man in the middle or, in his own biblical language, a voice crying in the wilderness.

The Second Council of Paris was held from 16 August until 14 September 1396 and concluded with the acceptance in principle of a subtraction of obedience from the pope of Avignon.[52] The council did not take the full step of withdrawing obedience, for the duke of Orleans continued to negotiate with Benedict XIII. A substantial faction of the French clergy, however, was ready to abandon further discussion and to break free from the Avignon pope.

In that same summer of 1396, Gerson would have been aware of the fate of a priest who was a kindred spirit: Jean de Varennes, a preacher and reformer whose words had reached into the highest circles of society but who at the same time spoke to ordinary people about the truths of the Christian religion. Varennes had been at Avignon as the chaplain of Clement VII and also had been in contact with King Charles VI and with the university.[53] At one point he had withdrawn to the parish church of Saint Lié outside of Reims. Here he gave thunderous French sermons attacking abuses in the Church and especially in his own archdiocese. Among his loyal following was a girl named Ermine whose visions Gerson was to defend a few years later.[54]

Unlike Gerson, Jean de Varennes named names in his condemnation of conditions in the Church. He spoke openly against the archbishop of Reims, Guy de Roye, who on 30 May 1396 had him imprisoned. Two months later Jean de Varennes wrote his defense, a list of the accusations made against him and his responses. It is not by accident that Gerson's eighteenth-century editor included this document in his materials.[55] There is a direct connection between the evangelical preacher and the university theologian. It is likely that Jean de Varennes sent this defense to Gerson from prison.[56] In many of his own sermons the chancellor had already attacked church and court abuses in favoritism shown the rich and privileged and the exploitation of the poor. Now from Paris Gerson witnessed what happened to a preacher who was seen as encouraging people to cast off royal and ecclesiastical officials.[57]

Jean de Varennes denied the charge of inciting to rebellion against the lords, but he did admit that he had preached "so that they stop devouring the people and then the people would stop rising up in rebellion."[58] He admitted that he was attacking specific persons for their privileges and excesses. Charged with preaching that "all the evils that come about in this world come from men of the Church," he more or less conceded the point: "I do not remember having said so, but if I did, then I was not far from the truth."[59]

Jean de Varennes was a dangerous critic for the clergy of Reims, who claimed he had said that from the start of the Schism, the gates of heaven had been closed to humanity. He countered that he had never asserted or even imagined such a thing: *certe non memoror nec vellem me unquam somniasse.*[60] He had, however, probably expressed a widespread feeling of uncertainty about the true pope and a concurrent fear that the sacramental powers of the Church were in abeyance.[61]

Gerson did not participate in the prosecution of Jean de Varennes; nor did he come to his defense. Later in one of his Paris lectures in late 1401, however, he mentioned his namesake: "We have seen in our time and lately how a certain man because of an almost unbelievable austerity of life gathered together a great crowd for his sermons. If only he had joined knowledge and discretion to his life and zeal, then he would have done a great deal of good. But it is true what Bernard has said: zeal without discretion casts out."[62] Gerson criticized lack of training and absence of self-restraint, yet in the coming years he would himself border on the same lack of discretion. Such language, however, he kept within ecclesiastical or university fora. Jean de Varennes had said in French what Gerson would state only in Latin.

In the crisis of the Schism, Gerson may have felt attracted by such a voice. He yearned to speak to the crowds and show them the path to salvation. There would always be something of a revivalist preacher in Gerson, as can be seen from his *Poenitemini* or penitential sermons given shortly after 1400. But most of the time he held back. Praising discretion, he feared to lose it.

Seeking a Home

In becoming chancellor at the great church of Notre Dame in Paris, Gerson was not given a benefice there or a place of residence. "He would have to wait for eight years before he could enjoy all the rights and privileges" of this position.[63] On 20 October 1395 the chapter did concede Gerson a room, called the *barre du chapitre,* near the well in the cloister yard. Here he could hold meetings and conduct business connected to his office (Gl 10.443). He must have continued living at the College of Navarre, where he had probably been staying since his arrival at Paris almost twenty years earlier. His two youngest brothers, Nicolas and Jean, born in 1382 and 1384, arrived in Paris sometime after 1395, in order to attend the university.[64]

Before her death in 1401 their mother, Elisabeth la Chardenière, wrote to the youths urging them to obey their eldest brother and to do well. The letter, quoted from in chapter 1, is an amazing piece of medieval French prose, an example of lay piety: "My sweet children, think often that you are in my presence, that you see me and hear me speaking. Act also in the presence of God when you are alone, as if you were close to me and as if I were looking at you. But also give me as your mother the same as I give you. Pray for me attentively, devoutly, ardently, I who often weep and sigh to God for you."[65] One thinks of Blanche of Castile speaking to her son Louis, the saint *in spe.* But this is a *femme de campagne,* a woman living in the countryside, not a queen, and yet the attitude is the same: the salvation of the children is the mother's central concern. The family is united in mutual love and prayers.

It has been common to idealize Gerson's family and its bonds.[66] But how did such a strong mother figure influence her sons and daughters? Elisabeth asked that her youngest sons read her letter once a week, a type of regulation that her order-seeking theologian son would have applauded. If they sinned, they would make her unhappy: "So that you may remember me, your old and weak mother, and so that foolish youth does not make you forget God and me and yourselves."[67]

Gerson later provided recommendations for the daily lives of his sisters who had remained with the parents in their hamlet.[68] At least one letter from his father informed him that his sisters had formed a domestic religious community. As Arnaut le Charlier wrote his eldest son: "I do not think they will even consider marrying until and insofar as it will be acceptable for us and you."[69]

No source mentions any visit by Gerson to his family home, but in going to Bruges for the first time in October of 1396, Jean Gerson prepared himself to make another home. On 12 October he assumed the office of dean in person. The next day the chapter wrote to its patron, the duke of Burgundy, in the hope that Gerson would reside there permanently, at the duke's pleasure (Gl 10.432). Gerson's first act of cooperation with the chapter was in the publication on 16 October of a new ordinance regulating its recitation of masses of remembrance (434–35).

At Bruges, Gerson at last had his own house. Or at least the hope of one. The dean's residence was in disrepair, so much so that Bruges citizens are said to have made fun of its state. In a letter to Duke Philip and to his chancellor, the bishop of Arras, the chapter of Saint Donatian described the miserable state of the building and asked for their assistance (430–33). Bruges thus promised something that Paris did not: an office as well as a benefice and a residence.

Fig. 7 Burg Square, Bruges, site of the disappeared collegial church of Saint Donatian, where Gerson was dean of the chapter. The Town Hall in front is from the fourteenth century but was restored in the nineteenth. (Photo by author)

Gerson did not intend, however, to give the canons of Saint Donatian the "continual residence" which they desired. Paris was his home, however much he lacked a place to call his own there, and by early January 1397, he was back. He would have heard news about the terrible defeat of the crusaders' army at the hands of the Turks at Nicopolis on 25 September the previous year. In the words of the Chronicle of Saint Denis: "Everywhere there was general mourning. Anguish lays claim to the hearts of all."[70]

It is likely that Gerson was present on 9 January when solemn services were held in churches all over the kingdom for the repose of the souls of those who had fallen in battle. An empty display of chivalrous spirit under the leadership of the duke of Burgundy's son, the future John the Fearless, had ended in massive slaughter.[71]

The atmosphere of gloom may have been partly alleviated by the birth of a son to King Charles and Queen Isabella on 22 January. At month's end the university asked the king to prevent the Avignon pope from conferring any more benefices. The theologian Jean Cortecuisse made the case that "many evils and problems came from the conferment of church tithes and benefices." This was, he said, the "main root" of the pope's refusal to relinquish his office.[72]

Discussions of the matter went on for several days, concluding that withdrawal of obedience would be reasonable and acceptable. In pursuit of this policy, the king sent Jean Cortecuisse and another professor of theology, Gilles des Champs, as his ambassadors to both popes. Gerson later asserted that he had not participated in these discussions and decisions (Gl 6.35). His activities in Paris at this time can be gleaned only from one single document, *Requête pour les condamnés à mort,* an appeal to the king to allow prisoners convicted of capital offences to confess to a priest instead of being led away to the gallows unconfessed, as had been the practice (Gl 7.1.341–43).

Gerson listed five *verités* or truths, all of which emphasized that every baptized Christian had a right to confession in order to obtain God's forgiveness from sin. "Against this law no man can dispense." He warned that anyone who prevented the confession of another person committed mortal sin, even if he were a prince or a secular judge. Going even further, Gerson added in his fifth *verité* that any law that is contrary to the above truths is unjust and is not to be obeyed.

Gerson was on the verge of recommending civil disobedience. The matter, however, seems to have been resolved with no further difficulty. An ordinance of 2 February 1397 allowed for a final confession for those condemned to death. The decision is mentioned in the Chronicle of Saint Denis, with no reference to Gerson's contribution. According to this source, the change was made thanks to the intervention of a certain magnate named Pierre de Craon, who afterwards set up a wooden cross at the place of execution. Here the condemned could stop and confess their sins to a Franciscan friar whose office the same lord had endowed.[73]

For the royalist monks of Saint Denis Gerson did not exist in their reconstruction of the events of the 1390s.[74] It was only after 1400 that this source referred to him at all, and then only rarely. In 1397 Gerson had apparently not yet made his mark on public events. Once again we are limited to one of Gerson's sermons for a sense of his concerns at that particular time. On 2 February, the Feast of the Purification of Mary, Gerson spoke on the theme from Psalm 47:10 in the Vulgate: *Suscepimus Deus misericordiam tuam in medio templi tui* (We have received, God, your mercy in the midst of your temple).[75]

The king was almost certainly not present. He had another attack of illness, which this time was to last until the second week of July.[76] Gerson avoided any direct statement on the Schism. Instead he spoke in general terms of spiritual hunger for truth. This is one of his most allegorical sermons, obscuring as he does his own views behind qualities such as Justice and Mercy. Among his few topical references are two brief warnings against the use of sorcerers. This practice is a great sin and will bring much infamy on those who are its cause (Gl 7.2.1053, 1055). The sermon ends in a prayer for peace and mercy in the Church; only here is the Schism briefly mentioned (1057).

This sermon is not among Gerson's best. He did not show his usual ability to structure and develop his theme and to move from general theological points to specific moral applications. The fact that it is impossible to detect the precise audience from internal references shows how the preacher distanced himself from his surroundings.

The Chronicle of Saint Denis reveals that magicians or sorcerers did frequent the court. They competed with more orthodox attempts to obtain the king's recovery.[77] Public prayers and religious processions were held all over Paris, until finally the king did seem to improve. In July he was able to go to the cathedral of Notre Dame to hear mass and give thanks, but a few days later he had another relapse. The king even asked for his knife to be taken away and for knives to be removed from everyone at court. He is supposed to have cried out: "For the love of Jesus Christ, if there is anyone who is behind this evil, I pray that they not torture me any longer but quickly make sure that my last day comes."[78]

In such an atmosphere Gerson had to be careful about what he said. On the Feast of the Annunciation, 25 March, he gave what was probably another court sermon, *Ave Maria, gracia plena,* concerning the angelic salutation.[79] This time, however, Gerson was more direct in his description of evil and provides a veritable psychomachia or battle of virtues and vices, where Truth is betrayed by Lying Flattery (544). Gerson referred to Saint Louis's warning to his son to beware of bad men.[80] He added the story of a preacher who was asked by a lord whether he governed well. The lord told how his people had praised him for doing so. The preacher answered that the lord was in fact cursed, "because he or his officers pillaged and ravished everything" (545).

Gerson did not need to make direct comparisons between the moral of his story and the state of the kingdom. His point was clear. His next subject concerned chastity and three means to guard it: we are to flee lack of occupation in imitating Mary who worked and studied; we are to flee strong wines and spicy foods; we are to flee all bad company. "The angel found Mary, as says Saint Bernard, all alone in her room, not speaking to Bertha or to Walter."[81] Other people are at best a distraction, at worst an occasion of sin. Gerson recommended reading, physical labor and isolation from others as the best way toward a chaste life.

Gerson attacked those who devoted themselves to the care and adornment of their bodies, which he saw as merely filthy containers. For those who might answer that he was asking the ladies of the court to dress like *femmes de village* or like beguine religious, he said he was criticizing only excessive pride in dress.[82] The lords of France should instead think about the poverty of their own subjects who "according to nature are brothers and often lords according to the gift of grace" (548). It was a trait of noble and royal *courtoisie* to be generous and compassionate, just as it was the greatest *vilenie* (baseness) to deprive people of what belonged to them.

Gerson used the language and ethics of the courtly world to remind its members of their duties. But he went beyond and underlined the Christian view that we are bound to each other in the Lord. We are united in a "natural love that ought to exist between brothers and sisters of one blood" (549). After his restrained February sermon, Gerson was back in form. Again, he excelled as the court preacher who praised the poverty of Mary and Jesus and warned against the evils that plague a kingdom "when women of status turn to what is wrong" (548). Such women Gerson opposed to the Frankish Queen Clotilde, remembered for bringing the Christian faith to her husband Clovis and thus to France.

In the absence of a strong king, Gerson placed his hope in the queen and other women of court. He had to concede their place in society and even their right to a standard of dress. They were to act like Mary and be busy and purposeful. Through the compassion of women, husbands and sons might be reminded of their duties toward their subjects.

No Abiding Home

On Holy Thursday, 19 April 1397, Gerson spoke in Latin to his university colleagues and took as his theme the betrayal of Jesus by Judas: *Tradidit Jesum Judas* (John 13:2).[83] The sermon is a harsh attack on the evil lives of many of the clergy, who like Judas betray Jesus (Gl 5.547): "Be careful then that you do not make yourself like Judas in your life: By being like him in hardness of heart and unrepentant death you will hand yourself over to the just judgment of God" (549).

A churchman imitates Judas when, out of avarice, he makes his soul into a uninhabitable desert, pathless and parched, an abyss of darkness and misery (549–50). Some members of the clergy have a seemingly limitless capacity for consumption of material goods. Like Alexander the Great, they weep at the thought of not being able to contain even one world inside themselves (551). Gerson added other classical stories, as those of Tantalus and Croesus, known for insatiable desire and greed for possessions. He drew also on one of Aesop's fables, about a dog swimming across a river with a morsel of meat in its mouth. When the animal sees the food's reflection in the water, he drops it and dives deep down to chase this illusion.[84] Similarly the greedy man spurns God and pursues shadows. Human beings are never satisfied with what they have and always seek more.

The clergy betrays Jesus by "pretending from its status and name that it alone owns God in a kind of inheritance. But it has been cast far aside from this inheritance through the vice of cupidity" (552). The churchman imitates Judas when he acts the hypocrite and pretends to show faith and devotion when, in reality, he plunders and despoils his brothers, thus betraying Christ once again.

Gerson linked greed to pride, which he held responsible for the protracted Schism. Peace was possible "not by giving gifts or by threats against the souls of those on the opposite side, but only through the way of generous and kind humility" (555). For Gerson the use of force involved in subtraction of obedience would not lead to any good. The Church needed a settlement based on choice, not on compulsion or bribery.

"Doctor, cure yourself," Gerson continued, one of his favorite passages from Luke (4:23). A moral reformation of the clergy was the only hope. He accused the preachers of his day of not listening to their own voices (556). They were hypocrites who ignored the fact that they were going to die. Even at funerals, men laugh and joke, ignoring the inevitable future to which they could look forward.

Gerson accused churchmen of being servants of the devil: "They hand over the eternal one, sell him, prostitute him, throw filth, tear him apart, crucify him" (557). But here he stopped, claiming it was no use to go on in such a manner. Such name-calling would only harden offenders rather than soften them.

Rather than making personal accusations, as Jean de Varennes had done, Gerson now posed theological questions, including whether schismatic priests can consecrate the Eucharist. Yes, they can, if they have the intention to do so according to the observances of the Church. His concern, as before, was to maintain unity of faith and observance, even if there was disagreement on rightful authority. But this sermon remains the harshest of Gerson's attacks on the lives and habits of the clergy: "In the name of God, religion, faith, and piety, shall I speak or be silent? Now, alas, every spiritual function such as the care of souls, confession and preaching is either given up or indiscriminately handed over to the worst sort of people who are filthy, faithless, unschooled, and unlearned. . . . They are so base that they consider insignificant the loss of souls for whom Christ has died" (561). Such men involve themselves in useless disputes on the poverty of Christ when what matters above all is the love of God.[85]

Judas could have been saved if he had asked for mercy. He had an opportunity especially to turn to Mary. Gerson asked his listeners not to let their hearts be hardened or to despair as Judas had done (562). These last lines of hope do not soften this tirade against the abuses of the clergy. Without challenging the Church's authority, Gerson questioned the seriousness of the commitment among many churchmen to the Gospel. Bernard of Clairvaux—and Martin Luther—could not have better expressed disgust with church prelates for abandoning their ideals and living as courtiers without consciences.

Gerson was committed to reforming the Church through preaching, but he did not believe in forcing the hand of the pope at Avignon. For Gerson the best hope lay in an educated, unselfish, and idealistic clergy and in acts of penance and reconciliation by all quarters of society. However naïve his political point of view may seem, it fits perfectly into the Christian belief that adherence to the Gospel can change hearts and minds. Gerson believed that hard hearts could be softened in a religion of love.

The frail hope Gerson might still have harbored for a quick end to the Schism was undermined in the summer of 1397. A triple embassy of French, English, and Castilian delegates traveled first to Avignon and then to Rome. They made no progress and were completely rebuffed by the Roman pope.[86] In the words of one of the central historians of the Schism: "Boniface IX showed the same antipathy [as Benedict XIII] for the ways of council, compromise, and cession." Boniface is supposed to have vowed: "I will never hand over my rights into the hands of anyone. You can tell this to your king. I would sooner consent to stop eating or drinking and to do nothing pleasing to God. I renounce my part of heaven."[87]

Whether or not Boniface ever said such words, the prelate the ambassadors encountered at Rome refused to make even a gesture of compromise. When the news was brought back to the French court, the king, once again functioning, on 12 September forbade anyone to preach or write against the way of cession.[88] Some weeks later he prohibited chapters of cathedrals and other churches from accepting any candidate nominated for a prebend by the Avignon pope.[89] Royal permission had to be given first.

At some time during this traumatic year, Gerson finally left his rooms in the College of Navarre and rented for life a house that bordered on the garden of the college's master.[90] In doing so he showed that he did not expect, at least for the time being, to be given a prebend with a benefice at Notre Dame cathedral, with a place to reside in its great cloister.

Our single source for Gerson's thinking in the autumn of 1397 is a sermon to the university students and masters on the nineteenth Sunday after Pentecost,

21 October. *Vade in domum tuam* refers to Christ's words to the paralytic he had healed (Arise take your bed and go into your house; Mt 9:6). We have both the morning sermon and the afternoon collation (563–96). His major theme concerned the meanings of the word "home," an appropriate concern for a professor and priest who regularly reminded his audiences that our only true home is in heaven.

Gerson divided his theme according to the traditional fourfold division of Scripture into literal, allegorical, moral, and anagogical meanings. The last two are treated in the collation, the first in the morning sermon. Gerson first reviewed the contents of the text in Matthew and made clear that he was speaking to a learned audience. In dealing with the question of Christ's divinity, he made use of Vergil's *Aeneid,* as well as of Durand of Saint Pourçain, an early fourteenth-century Dominican theologian (565–66).

References to Augustine, Suetonius, Josephus, Valerius Maximus, as well as to the near contemporary theologian Thomas Bradwardine (568) recall the Jean Gerson who in his earliest letter jumped from one erudite citation to another, presumably to impress his patron (Gl 2.1–4). After a chain of biblical citations using the term "house," he moved into the allegorical sense. *Domus* means the Church's house (Gl5.572). The greatest danger to this structure is ignorance.

Gerson worried that "human sciences" were being preferred to theological ones. He also was concerned with the students who were getting theological degrees. They were "restless and untrained boys, totally unsettled in their ways. They claim that they have fine blood lines and that their fathers are the friends of kings and dukes: they blend threats with pleas."[91] It is such undeserving youths who attain "lofty seats in the Church's house" (578). Here is the same criticism Gerson later expressed in explaining why he intended to abandon university life.

This description of how unworthy men advance in the Church opens a long discussion on how prelates play up to lay lords in order to obtain advancement. Such churchmen even go so far as to encourage powerful men to satisfy their lust. "Why do they do so? So that they will become dear to them, be loved and feared. What more? So that they can seek entrance to the best benefices?" (578) Gerson was questioning the system that encouraged ambitious churchmen to connect themselves to powerful lords. In warning that the university must not be "forced to be silent" in the face of such abuses (579), Gerson challenged the very system that had brought him to the deanship of Saint Donatian at Bruges.

For Gerson the house of the Church was being plundered by its leaders, who bought their offices in simony. How could lay princes respect the Church and be generous to it when they thereby enabled its priests to "get drunk, live in luxury and drown most basely in all forms of sensual delight" (580). There was no end to abuses, which daily grew worse: "O this mindlessness. What cruelty! Alas, under what a sad and evil star we were born."

After this ciceronian outburst Gerson turned to the disunity of the Church, which could only be remedied by appeals to God's mercy through public processions and prayers (581). He told his fellow masters that it was their responsibility to end the Schism. If they failed, they had neglected the talent given them in the Gospel story. "There is no excuse": the masters of Paris would be held responsible for members of the Church who ended up in the torments of hell or purgatory. These victims of neglect would cry out in accusation at the masters who in life had ignored them. "Where will you flee when your punishment comes, hapless ones? How will you avoid the terrifying hands of the living God, you most lost of all men?"[92]

Gerson was telling his colleagues that if they failed to give good advice to a confused laity and abandoned such people to eternal punishment, then they too would be brought before a frightful judge. The origins of this view are to be found in the Gospel, in some of Christ's most striking parables about stewardship. Saint Benedict, in his *Rule*, emphasized that the abbot on Judgment Day would be responsible for rendering account for all the monks entrusted to his care. As archbishop of Canterbury at the end of the eleventh century, Saint Anselm brought this view with him from the abbey of Bec and looked upon his pastoral responsibilities in similar terms. He had to answer for every soul in his care, to say nothing of every piece of property and even every pig and sheep.[93]

As a secular cleric responsible for the care of students and laypersons, Gerson followed in this tradition and interpreted it in relation to his university colleagues. They could not shrug their shoulders and ignore the world around them. If they failed to administer the talents given them, they would be called to a terrible reckoning.

Gerson concluded this morning sermon with the assertion that many among the clergy had long ago left the house of the Church for other houses (582). Some had chosen the house of Venus with the desire to try everything there. Others went to houses of strife, greed, or curiosity. The image entailed a long string of classical references, but Gerson stopped himself: "It is not right in the midst of such a huge and terrible conflict of the Church to spend time on fables" (583). Instead he turned to a medley of biblical analogies as in the warning: "Men of the Church should see to it that the house of prayer is not made into a place of business."[94]

He began his afternoon collation with homage to Pierre d'Ailly and his treatise on the soul.[95] The sermon was to consider the moral and anagogical meanings of house or home again through a mixture of classical and Christian references. After these preliminaries, Gerson considered the moral meaning of the Gospel text about the paralytic. We are to be ready to open our door to the Lord, but this means our house must be in order, full of the children who are our virtues (590). In looking at the same idea in terms of the life to come, he turned to his favored saying and addressed humankind as *homo viator*, having no abiding place on earth: *qui peregrinans non habes hic, secundum Apostolum, civitatem vel domum manentem* (591; cf. Heb 13:14). There follows another display of his knowledge of classical and late antique writers, from Vergil to Boethius and Lactantius (592).

Gerson once again voiced his skepticism about church prelates, few of whom would be saved (594). He suggested various questions his audience might pose, a familiar device in his sermons. He asked whether in heaven people would eat and drink. No, he insisted, and what about the ensuing problem with getting rid of human waste (595)? It is better to imagine that we will be like the angels (596). Here will be our home "in the land of the living" (597).

The text we have in Glorieux is almost certainly Gerson's later completion of what at the time may have existed only as notes and scattered references. The full text reveals how Gerson saw himself as a man without a permanent home whose motto was Saint Paul's dictum "Our way of life is in heaven" (*conversatio nostra est in coelis*; Phil 3:20).[96] Gerson nevertheless would continue to seek an earthly home.

Preparing a Fateful Decision

Home looked more and more like Bruges. From at least the end of January until early March 1398, Gerson was there again, negotiating with the municipal authorities concerning the repair and reconstruction of the dean's house. The cost was high because of what one document describes as "the inadequacy, neglect, and carelessness" of its former occupant, whose heirs the chapter made pay at least part of the cost of rebuilding.[97]

Probably at this time Gerson wrote to his classmate from the College of Navarre Nicolas de Clamanges. We do not have a copy of the letter, but we do have Nicolas's answer. Like so many medieval letters, it suggests more than it states. Nicolas opened by saying how surprised he had been by the "unbelievable" news he had gotten from Gerson the day before.[98] Nicolas hinted at some imminent confrontation between good and evil. He may have been speaking of the Schism and the situation of the Church, as indicated by his lament that there was no one to erect a wall around the house of Israel.[99]

Gerson's letter, wrote Nicolas, contained an exhortation to patience, while he in reply recommended "constancy, fortitude, generosity . . . which you know are especially necessary in adversity" (Gl 2.11). Otherwise patience is useless and stupid. It would be terrible if Gerson amid the Church's ruin gave up writing and speaking. Nicolas distinguished between private sorrows and public catastrophes. For God and his Church, there must be resistance, not silence. Otherwise Gerson's patient bearing of ills, Nicolas warned, might be construed to be the result of fear and cowardice rather than strength and faithfulness.

Professors of theology, like Gerson, had to be pillars of strength. If they failed to hold up the structure, the whole building will collapse. If Gerson felt he did not have the strength to continue, then he had to trust in God to provide it. He should think of the example of Christ and the moneychangers (Jn 2:17). Jesus did not put up with them; he turned over their tables and cast them out. The same had to be done now.

Nicolas's letter indicates that Gerson had expressed a desire to keep silent and disengage himself from any involvement in the Schism. To a certain extent Gerson had already done so. The letter may have reached Gerson at Bruges, where for the time being he kept a distance from the strident voices of Paris. Gerson's final contribution to the discussion on the Schism, before a long pause, can be dated to the early months of 1398. The *De modo se habendi tempore schismatis* (the manner of acting in the time of the Schism) may have been intended especially for the people of Flanders and especially around Bruges.[100]

Here Gerson describes the Schism as dangerous to "brotherly love." People stop obeying ecclesiastical superiors and avoid the sacraments. In the face of doubt about legitimate authority, Gerson suggests eight points in order to avoid that one faction drive the other out of the Church: "In the uncertainty of the present schism it is rash, injurious and scandalous to assert that everyone who holds one side or the other or all who remain neutral . . . are universally beyond salvation or excommunicate" (Gl 6.29). It is in fact heretical to claim that the sacraments administered by the priests of one or the other faction have no validity, "with the result that priests are not consecrated, children not baptized, and the sacrament of the altar is not dispensed." It is wrong to forbid people from hearing the mass of one priest or another. It is better to seek the union of the Church through the way of cession or the subtraction of obedience or "any other legitimate type of force" rather than to excommunicate the subjects of one allegiance or "otherwise harass and disturb them" (29).

To Gerson's mind the Schism could not be resolved by manipulating or terrifying the laity; resolution could only come from making the pope change his mind. Until then, the Church must continue to offer the means of salvation to everyone. Gerson now admitted for the first time, however, that a solution might only come from forcing both popes to give way. Yet, his central message was still one of reconciliation. If acts of excommunication are issued on both sides, then "one part of Christianity will be permanently separated from communion with the other" (30).

Never before in any previous schism had there been such good reason for doubt about legitimacy. Gerson points to "the variety of opinions among the most learned and outstanding persons on both sides." People were beginning to doubt if the host on the altar really was properly consecrated. What mattered for Gerson was the good intention of those involved. The sacraments were properly dispensed if priest and laity intended to participate in these functions in the manner instituted by Christ. If both sides showed flexibility and made their allegiance conditional, there was no reason to resort to excommunication. This power was given to churchmen not in order to destroy but to build up: *non . . . ad destructionem sed ad aedificationem* (31).

Above all Gerson sought the unity of the Church. The Schism had separated its members not only from their head but also from each other (32). Everybody's talents had to be employed in a concerted effort toward bringing the Schism to an end: "Each according to his portion is obliged according to the gift given by God to seek what leads to peace, the one by praying, the other by preaching, the third by teaching" (32). Otherwise they broke the rule of brotherly love, the central precept to be followed in the midst of uncertainty.

So long as there was doubt about who was the true pope, people were not obligated to follow the sentences or decrees of either one of the pretenders (33). He modified this advice, however, stating that each side should follow the decrees of its leaders "in holding as a fact that which the one believed to be their superior has done."[101]

This kind of hedging has an almost postmodern quality with its emphasis on the construction of a truth rather than its inherent absoluteness. Gerson was not interested in establishing which side was right but in preserving outer unity. He did not give permission to the priesthood and laity to do whatever they wanted, but he was close to advising people to follow their consciences and not to worry. Under the present circumstances, he insisted, "the same man could adore in one place a host which is shown by a person who acts as a priest, and in another place or before others he will not adore it" (34).

Attachment to one pope or another should not be allowed to undermine faith in the sacrament of the Eucharist. The only guideline in such a matter is *intentio recta,* right intention, which is found together with love of God and fraternal charity. If both priest and people, whichever pope they follow, intend to do what is right and make good use of the sacraments, then the sacraments the priest dispenses are valid. Right intention, explained Gerson, is like a straight line going to the same center. There can be many such lines of good intention. So long as they are directed to the same center, which is love of God and fraternal charity, then the lines do not intersect or block each other out.

Here we are close to Peter Abelard's moral theology.[102] Gerson, however, was not trying to develop a theology of intentionalism. He suggested a practical strategy for coping with everyday life while the Schism lasted. Gerson asked for charity and what we would call tolerance and mutual respect. For Avignon and Rome, such restraint was out of the question. Each pope considered himself to be the sole leader of the true Church. But from the vantage point of Bruges, it was necessary to live and let live, for here different groups in the same town supported different popes.[103] In order to fulfill their Easter duty, people felt obligated to migrate from one town to another, amid threats of excommunication from their own priests.

Gerson wanted to stop this escalation. His goal was to make sure the clergy continued to carry out its basic function of caring for the souls in its charge. As a pragmatist, not a theoretician, he considered pastoral care more important than canon law when it came to counseling and consoling his Bruges parishioners.

Back at Paris, Gerson had no parish connection. On 12 March 1398, he asked the Chapter of Notre Dame for a canonry and its prebend there. His rival was a master Gilles Juvenis. The legal proceedings lasted a year and culminated in Gerson's renunciation of his claims.[104] The records of the chapter reveal that on 15 May Gilles Juvenis, who had the title of papal secretary, was able to produce letters in which Benedict XIII asked that cathedral chapters favor papal secretaries for benefices. Unless the chapter chose to defy the Avignon pope, it was a question of time before it rejected Gerson's bid for a benefice.

Thanks at least to Benedict XIII's formal backing, Gerson had obtained the office of chancellor. But no further support was forthcoming from Avignon. He thus had little to lose in breaking openly with Benedict and supporting a French decision to withdraw obedience from the Avignon pope. But here Gerson was not only a pragmatist; he also kept to a moral stance. His views on the Schism still prevented him from following any radical course.

In late March, Wenceslas, King of the Romans and of Bohemia, met at Reims with Charles VI, who just then enjoyed a brief period of good health.[105] The French monarchy tried to coordinate its papal policy with the Empire, which until now had supported the Roman pope. The Third Council of Paris met between 14 May and 28 July 1398 and declared a formal withdrawal of obedience.[106] As Gerson later indicated, he had nothing to do with these proceedings (Gl 6.36). The Chronicle of Saint Denis reproduces the royal decree, read aloud by the royal chancellor. It refers to *ecclesie gallicane,* the Gallican Church.[107] In this phrase lurks the coming splintering of the Christian Church in the West and the establishment of royal churches in early modern Europe.

Pierre d'Ailly was sent to Avignon one last time, but with little effect. For a time Benedict XIII was kept under siege at his papal palace.[108] As late as 1403 he was restricted in his movements, until French obedience was partially restored. But he still refused to yield; the deadlock continued.

None of Gerson's sermons can be dated to 1398. He may have preached, but it is likely that he kept a low profile and did not share his views on the Schism with others. Because of his refusal to approve the withdrawal of obedience, he had marginalized his position at the university. At the same time he failed to clarify his status at the chapter of Notre Dame. Only in Bruges did Gerson enjoy both a title and its full function, but the records of Saint Donatian here cast light only on legal matters and not on Gerson's pastoral concerns.

In August, Nicolas de Clamanges again wrote to Gerson, this time from Langres in Champagne. He tells his friend that he escaped from the plague that was raging at Avignon (Gl 2.12–14). Nicolas described the Church's situation as grave, but this time he gave no advice. He no longer asked his friend directly to involve himself in the disputes of the day.

The one Parisian source that casts light on Gerson's activities is a copy of a decision made by the faculty of theology censoring twenty-eight propositions describing superstitious practices.[109] We know from Gerson's 1396–97 court sermons that he was concerned about necromancers and magicians. As "chancellor of the church of Paris," he had met with his colleagues in the morning in the church of the monastery of Saint Mathurin.

The language of the declaration is pure Gerson, with rich classical references joined to Old Testament examples in a striking synthesis of the type in which he excelled. There is also a precise reference to a sermon of Saint Augustine condemning superstitious observances. The masters of the theology faculty emphasized that they did not attack legitimate science. Their purpose was to point out the errors that "injure, contaminate, and infect orthodox faith and Christian religion."

It is error to seek the friendship and help of demons (article 1); it is wrong to make pacts with demons (3) and to drive out witchcraft by witchcraft (*maleficia maleficiis repellere*; 6). There is no excuse for such practices even if they are accompanied by devout prayers, fasting, continence, and the celebration of the mass (12). It is error to claim that the prophets had their knowledge through such arts (13); it is wrong to believe that such practices can force the free will of a person (15). Exotic substances such as the skin of a lion have no power to drive out demons (20); images made of lead or other materials that are baptized, exorcised, or consecrated cannot have miraculous powers (21). It is error to claim that there can be good or generous or all-knowing devils (23), or that we can attain to the vision of God or of holy spirits through magic (28).

The catalogue provides a sense of what superstitious ideas and practices may have circulated in late fourteenth-century Paris. For our purpose what is important, however, is the fact that Gerson here remained visible, acting as chancellor and exercising the authority of the theology faculty. As in his dealing with the Schism, his efforts must have seemed vain. So long as the king's bouts of mental illness continued, it was impossible to keep at bay people who based their lives on such beliefs and practices.

Gerson himself may, at this point, have wondered whether diabolical forces were at work in his life. On 29 November the prebend which both he and Gilles Juvenis sought at Notre Dame was handed over by the chapter to a third master.[110] Gerson did not give up his bid until the following March, but already on 4 December he attempted to gain another prebend. This time it was the Parisian church of Saint Merry, one of the "four daughters" under the direct jurisdiction of the chapter of Notre Dame. This church would have been a choice prize and an appropriate benefice for the chancellor, who on 4 December pointed out to the chapter that the pope already had given him permission to combine a parish benefice with his office (Gl 10.445). According to the chapter proceedings, Gerson "requested the lords that they would favor him in his right and in justice."

There are forty-nine mentions of this matter in the Register of the Chapter of Notre Dame cathedral.[111] After 21 March 1399, when Gerson gave up his claim to the prebend that finally was given to Gilles Juvenis , there was all the more reason to maintain his bid for Saint Merry. Gerson's state of mind six days later is suggested by a Holy Thursday sermon, *Si non lavero te,* the fourth time he preached on that occasion (Gl 5.498–511).

Christ had said to the apostles at the Last Supper, "Unless I wash you, you have no share with me" (Jn 13:8). Gerson chose to interpret these words as both threat and teaching: *terreat et erudiat haec formidanda nimis sententia.* We are polluted by pride, envy, anger, and sloth (499). The only way to wash away sin is through the ministry of penance. Penance was no lofty subject, for it belonged to daily life. Unfortunately, he lamented, this theme was out of fashion and considered to be an inappropriate one for a sermon: *apud modernos dissolutum, flaccidum et nauseans contemnitur* (500). Gerson asked his colleagues not to lose patience with him or to ridicule him with "base laughter."

After this apology, he attacked all forms of knowledge that lead to pride. Such learning uses subtleties to impress its listeners and drowns in minute matters. It is always gathering knowledge but never comes to the truth. Gerson caricatured colleagues who "seem in their own eyes to be wise." They drown in trivia and tire themselves out but never do anything except to engage in empty argument and useless pursuits. Such masters ought to realize that there is "nothing more difficult than the art of living well, nothing more subtle, sublime, and divine" (501).

Everything he wanted to say, concedes Gerson, could already be found in books written by theologians. But not everyone has time to read everything. Also the spoken word can have a more lasting effect on people. They remember it better. Sermons on moral matters are a necessary part of university life. Gerson dealt with his material in either a rhetorical or a scholastic manner. The first was better suited for his listeners' emotions or affective lives, the second for their intellects (501).

The sermon expresses Gerson's fatigue with scholastic subtleties and perhaps also with the irrelevance of university discourse to the moral lives of ordinary people. As so often in the course of his life, Gerson was fighting to maintain a balance between the life of the mind and that of the heart.

He never forgot his audience, however, in his careful use of a scholastic form of exposition, with definitions and categories. He spoke of what was required from the waters of contrition: they were to be hot, clean, bitter, and life giving (502–3).

He asked how it was possible to obtain the tears of contrition and pointed to the flagellants and what they did in order to provoke tears.[112] He recommended fasting and prayer to obtain the "grace of tears," but he also alludes to the importance of compassion. He cites Saint Bernard's saying that no heart is so hard that it is not softened when it recalls the Passion of Christ.[113]

When contrition is achieved, the priest gives absolution. In accord with the Fourth Lateran Council, confession takes place at least once a year, even though more frequent confession is preferable. Gerson here developed almost a mini-treatise on the elements of confession, an indication of his pastoral concern that would later lead to *On the Art of Hearing Confessions*.[114]

Gerson objected to the practice of "reserved sins." Absolution was given for some sins only by a bishop or by a special confessor appointed by him (506–7). There was disagreement concerning which sins should be reserved for this confessor.[115] Gerson objected that such a practice caused many tragedies: "If all prelates carefully considered how difficult it is and what a burden it is to tell one's secret sins to someone, then I firmly believe that they would never impose such a heavy burden on the shoulders of their subjects, with the result that countless numbers of them are cast into hell" (507). He asserted that recruitment of a thousand special confessors for reserved sins during Holy Week would not suffice. He claimed to know many people who over a period of two or three years could hardly be convinced to confess their sins: "How then will they tell of such things to a prelate or special confessor, especially in the case of children and women, who are most shy?" Prelates who think they can terrify such people end up sending them in their silence into hell! *Credentes terrere subditos occidunt et demergunt tacentes in infernum* (507).

Men trained in questions of morality and theological matters "scarcely know what to say" to such penitents. In what follows here and in later treatises on confession, Gerson laid out his method for gently convincing people to confess actions that they were deeply embarrassed to name or describe.

His complaint about reserved sins gives way to his usual list of various questions connected with the subject at hand. What should the confessor do if he thinks the penitent is lying about being sorry for sin? He should tell him his absolution is conditional. What about the seal of secrecy for the priest? There are no exceptions. What about exemptions from yearly parish confession? They depend on the consent of the curate. Here we find Gerson in his element, identifying scruples of conscience and dealing with them.

The sermon, which has turned into a small treatise on confession, ends in a section on satisfaction for sin. Gerson gives what was standard late medieval advice for confessors: the penances handed out were not to be too heavy.[116] It is better to give a small penance, which leaves something to be made up in purgatory, than a heavy penance, which is not completed and leaves the frustrated penitent on his way to hell. There are some sins, however, so enormous that hardly any penance is enough, as for people who entice others into sin. He was almost certainly thinking of sexual contacts, as between teachers and pupils, one of his major concerns.[117]

Gerson lashed out against "the arrogance of the human heart which more quickly allows itself and others to be damned rather than to be humbled" (511). If it had not been so, then the terrible and fateful Schism would not have lasted so long: *si non esset, non tantum durasset hoc exsecrandum et exitiabile schisma pestiferum*. This is the only mention of the Schism, and the first time since early 1398 that Gerson broached the subject. Even though the sermon is on a completely different topic, he is unable to contain his disgust with what was happening in the Church. Those responsible for continuing the Schism were among the greatest of sinners, lost in their own pride.

This sermon hints at Gerson's frustration with his role as pastoral guide to individual penitents and their confessors. In his experience, canon law on reserved sins hindered individual Christians from getting absolution. Parish priests and not special confessors must be able to comfort and encourage penitent laypersons, to say the words necessary to bring them to salvation. Church prelates and university masters were insufficiently concerned about such matters. Their goal was to preserve their own privileges and prerogatives.

Gerson came close here to dismissing his own group in Christian society, the educated clergy: "How many of them want to seem wise in their own eyes, how many want to be learned and erudite . . . and so they waste their time, their minds and the energy on superfluous matters. They fail to cultivate the good life which is the best teacher. . . . Discouraged and broken they will never find from all their labor anything except vain argument and useless concerns" (501). Only an academic could describe the life of fellow academics in such a way. Gerson felt ashamed and disgusted with colleagues who looked down on pastoral concerns.

From early June 1399 and until late September 1400, Gerson was back in Bruges as dean of the chapter and did his best to reform its daily life.[118] There was little reason to expect anything more from his life in Paris. In the course of 1399, Charles VI relapsed six times into mental confusion and fear.[119] The news reached France that King Richard II had been taken prisoner by his political enemies, and the Chronicle of Saint Denis lamented that the isle of Albion had nourished such treachery in its breast.[120]

The prospect of an end to warfare between England and France vanished. Richard's queen, the hapless Isabelle, would be ignominiously sent home to Paris and her half-mad father, an insult to him and his line. At the same time the plague, which had almost ended the life of Nicolas de Clamanges at Avignon, arrived in Paris (1399–1400) and wreaked its usual havoc.[121] Gerson's departure for Bruges may have been connected with the outbreak, but the main reason for his decision to leave behind his duties as professor of theology was a loss of faith in the university world. Gerson was asking himself if he could continue to be chancellor and still save his soul (Gl 2.17–18). For the time being he had concluded that the university and its learned professors could not be a home for him. If he wanted to seek wisdom and save the souls of ordinary people, he would have to look for another home.

Making a New Home, 1399–1400

Gerson lived as dean of the chapter at the church of Saint Donatian at Bruges from 9 June 1399 and until 22 September 1400.[1] On this first visit in 1396, as we saw in the last chapter, Gerson apparently had no intention to reside there, in spite of the hope asserted by the canons on 13 October that he would stay (Gl 10.432). A few days later the new dean and his chapter published what would be the first of several reform ordinances. Masses were to be celebrated and the divine office observed properly, "in reforming the failings of persons belonging to this church" (*super reformacione defectuum personarum huius ecclesie*; 434).

The names of many canons reveal their origins in what we would today call Flemish language and culture. But in their trade-oriented town, with its guilds and cloth industry, the canons of Bruges knew how to write good French for their patron the duke of Burgundy.[2] Now they had a dean who took their spiritual functions seriously and despised *negligencia* or slackness.

The reform statute for Saint Donatian reveals in its contents something of Gerson's personality. The final point stipulated that the changes would not be valid unless they were confirmed after a year's time.[3] This clause is followed by a sentence redolent with Gerson's caution and prudence: "In this we counsel each to examine his conscience, since even though we do not desire to add more obligations at the present time, we cannot nevertheless change or adjust rightful duties confirmed by our predecessors" (435). Gerson felt he was bound to the decisions of former deans and chapters and yet he and his fellow canons appealed to conscience. The Paris academic was trying to be reasonable and moderate. He wanted a reform from within, in accord with the canons' desires and convictions.

The sources for Gerson's second visit to Bruges (January 1398) concentrate not on chapter reform but on repairs to the dean's house. He conferred on 2 March with the heirs of his predecessor William Vernachten. In the presence of the bailiff and town official, an agreement was reached. The heirs were to provide a hefty sum "because of the insufficiency, neglect, and lack of care" of William, which had resulted in a need for major repairs (443). Gerson was making sure that he had a home of a type he lacked in his rented Paris lodgings at the College of Navarre.[4]

Reforming One Church

Gerson's next stay in Bruges lasted more than fifteen months. The chapter's records reflect his concerns in terms of his everyday life. In the first part of this period, from June to October of 1399, Gerson supported several measures that would make sure the canons of his chapter carried out their liturgical duties faithfully. His extended residence at Bruges gave him time to reflect on his life at Paris and to involve himself in the religious education of his sisters. The frustrated university teacher and administrator became an effective educator and spiritual writer.

On 9 June 1399 the dean and canons at Saint Donatian agreed that they would be present in the chapter room by the time the bell had ceased ringing and would open their meeting immediately afterwards. Once the chapter candle was lit, anyone arriving later would lose his compensation for that day (*denarios suos capitulares illius diei;* 447). The canons also decided on a question of precedence that had apparently been the root of lively disagreement (*altercaciones et questiones*).

In a religious community, such questions can create much ill will. Centuries earlier, Benedict had dealt with precedence in a monastery in his *Rule* (ch. 63). The canons of Saint Donatian had their own regulations. On this particular decision, the proceedings of the chapter note that four canons disagreed. Even in what might seem to be a trivial matter, strong feelings can emerge when standard procedures are changed or even clarified.

Three weeks later, on 30 June, dean and chapter agreed that no compensation or salary was to be given for celebrating Mass at the high altar of Saint Donatian (Gl 10.448). It was important for Gerson that normal ecclesiastical functions be carried out in his church without any special payment.[5] The canons had their prebends as well as supplementary income from attending chapter and other special functions. Gerson looked at compensation for saying an ordinary mass as simony, a chronic concern in the Western Church since its eleventh-century reformation.[6]

A few days later, on 2 July, the implementation of the new ordinances was postponed for a month "for certain reasons" (*ex certis causis;* 449). The new provisions were to be more carefully considered for a month "but nevertheless not to be withdrawn." The reforming faction of the chapter had come across unexpected opposition. Instead of confronting it head-on, the reformers allowed for a "cooling-off" period, after which they expected the necessary changes would be made.

A further indication of tensions is a regulation of discussions during chapter meetings. In cases submitted to the chapter, each canon would be allowed to speak only when it was his turn. No interruptions would be tolerated, and "if anyone did the contrary, the lord dean or the one who will be presiding in chapter, will give him a warning." If the canon did not keep silence, then "he will be made immediately to leave" (450–51).

A decision made on August 16 perhaps reveals the cause of hefty discussions. The customary "salary" given for celebrating masses was reinstated, in spite of the ordinance of 30 June. The reform faction had to give ground, "after many deliberations and negotiations" (449). These privileged canons wanted to follow their distinguished dean but were even more eager to keep a source of income. The text, "for the sake of brevity," leaves out the arguments presented in chapter. This reversion to customary practice was a defeat for Gerson's reform program.

In other areas, however, Gerson was apparently able to join forces with the canons in order to make changes. There was no opposition in chapter to a proposal on 9 July that canons who wanted to pursue studies elsewhere could during their absence enjoy the fruits of their prebends (450). Later that summer it was decided that canons who had houses belonging to the chapter were to occupy them and not to rent them out to lay persons. Absent canons could rent to other canons for the same amount they themselves would have paid. Their residences were not to be used for economic gain. Gerson, who did not have enough seniority or political weight in Paris to become a canon and thus have a residence in the cathedral cloister, would have been particularly sensitive about such a matter.

As often happens in an institution whose members share common wealth, there were squabbles about who got what. Gerson and a majority of the canons opposed those who wanted to deprive the curate of Saint Donatian of offerings to the church. On 27 August they declared that from time immemorial a third part of the offerings had gone to the curate, a third to the chapter, and a third to the church fabric (451).

The most detailed decision concerned the canons' clothing. On 8 October 1399, the matter was deliberated and decreed for a second time, indicating its importance for the chapter (451–52). Canons, chaplains, and other clerics were to "correct and improve themselves under penalty of receiving no income from the church." No cleric or canon of Saint Donatian was to appear in public in a shirt with a belt unless he also wore a cloak. Canons were not to go about in "ample sleeves with indecent fringes and pointed shoes." They were to wear modest tunics or great coats and were to avoid "small gowns with knots in them in the manner of laymen . . . for all these are not fitting for churchmen" (*Que omnia non decent viros ecclesiasticos*). As Vansteenberghe once pointed out, Bruges was the center of the cloth industry, and its citizens loved to display their finery: "Luxury reigned in the cosmopolitan town, and it was almost inevitable that the fashions of the time exercised a certain attraction on the men of the Church."[7]

A week later the chapter proceedings indicate open opposition to reforms. The canon Siger Heilt was deprived for a month of the right to speak in chapter or to be present there. He was accused of having uttered "some coarse and dishonorable words" in the presence of the entire chapter and directed "against the person of the lord dean" (452). This confrontation may have taken place the previous day, 14 October, the Feast of Saint Donatian, when good food and drink might have relaxed normal restraint.

Years later, in 1408, the canons accused Gerson of failing to provide the banquets which his predecessors had given.[8] Saint Donatian's feast day in 1399 may have been the first such occasion when the dean made it clear that he was not interested in wining and dining his canons. On the same day when Siger Heilt was punished, the chapter decided that the new ordinances about dress would be enforced from the vigil of All Saints, a few weeks away (452). On 5 November, however, Gerson told the canons that they had nothing to fear from him. Because of his earlier absence from the chapter and that of his predecessor William Vernachten, doubts had arisen concerning the dean's duty to say mass in the choir. He promised that in his future functions in the church, he would not add new burdens for himself or his successors. At the same time he would not allow future deans to be relieved of the duties they owed in these matters (452–53).

The text of this decision is convoluted and repetitive. Retreating from his program of reform, Gerson tried to assure everyone involved that he would not make changes and made known at the same time that he would be faithful to the practices observed by his predecessors.

A month later, on 11 December, the chapter backed Gerson in suspending from office and from all church income four priests of Saint Donatian (*clerici installati;* 453) who were accused of neglecting their duties, apparently failing to say mass and keeping other observances connected with their positions. Once again, however, a disciplinary decision was subsequently revoked. Less than a week later, on 16 December, the priests were restored to their former positions!

The dean was running into opposition in his attempts to make members of his church fulfill what he considered to be their obligations. Three weeks later, on 7 January 1400, the chapter gave Gerson permission to be absent "as often and for as long as he wished," without prejudice to his privileges as canon of the church (453). On 21 February, he appointed William de Fossa to act for him on spiritual and temporal matters, together with Nicolas Storkin. The decision is slightly odd, for it empowered Fossa but claims to take away nothing from Storkin, previously named as the dean's substitute (453–54).

Gerson was present at the chapter of 10 March and then left for Paris.[9] Illness, however, forced him to return to Bruges for treatment. Gerson's malady may be connected with an epidemic already mentioned at Bruges the previous July. The canons had then decided that because of the "epidemic, which has now begun to flourish," they could leave the town and reside elsewhere until Christmas (450).

This may have been the same pestilence that in 1399 had raged first at Avignon and then at Paris. The canons called upon their saint for help and organized a public procession, with the casket containing the relics of Saint Donatian being carried across Bruges to the Carthusian church.[10] On 1 April 1400, Gerson wrote to Pierre d'Ailly that although he was ill, he was strong enough not only to compose this message but also to formulate proposals to reform the faculty of theology at Paris. He wrote in his own hand: *propria manu scripsi in lecto adversae valetudinis meae* (Gl 2.26). A few days later, on 5 April, the canons of Saint Donatian met without Gerson, who was again described as being confined "to the bed of illness" (Gl 10.454).

At the same time, however, the chapter went ahead with work on the central tower of their church. Its height was to be increased by at least twenty-five feet, so that its bells could attract the faithful and pilgrims. The unfinished tower had, according to the canons, caused sarcastic comments from townspeople and others (454).

Despite the epidemic that may have been a form of plague, life continued. The previous summer, three canons had given the chapter an account of payments made for the repair of the dean's house. Dean and chapter are said to have been well pleased (*bene contenti*) with the work done (450). In accord with the dean's wishes, a wall between his house and the adjacent one of the chanter was made higher and stronger, "to the height of a man and a little more, because of the evident usefulness of the said houses" (449). The dean was to pay half the cost of the wall, while the church's fabric fund was to pay the other half.

With Saint Donatian showing a finished tower, a renovated dean's house, and even a wall to protect privacy and quiet, Jean Gerson could hope that Bruges would remain his permanent home. When he set out in March of 1400 for Paris, his intention apparently was to resign his chancellorship.[11] According to a statement to the faculty of theology (11 March 1400), Gerson claimed that he "no longer wishes to exercise the office of the chancellorship" (455) and suggested master Dominique Petit as his successor. Gerson claimed that the proposal was dropped because of the intervention of the duke of Burgundy.[12]

On 7 July the canon and stand-in for Gerson, William Fossa, presented himself to the chapter in order to establish the dean's continuing residence. A week later, "because of the pestilence and epidemic which now rages," the chapter allowed its canons to go to "any suitable place and wherever it might please them" (456). They would not be bound by their usual duties to say Mass or perform other liturgical functions.

The rest of July as well as the month of August, chapter records note Gerson's absence from its meetings because of illness. On 23 July he made a testament: "Before the canons of the church and me Baldwin [the notary], before the window in the dormitory," for the construction of the church's tower he left 100 pounds, for the repair of his dean's house 150 pounds in Parisian currency (*centum libras parisis*), and for his burial and for observing anniversaries of his death, 160 pounds (455).[13] These sums were to be taken from the sale of his movable goods at Bruges and the fruits of his prebend for the year after his death. As for his burial place, he left it to his executors, including William of Fossa.

Gerson's testament confirms how important the church and chapter of Saint Donatian had become for him. He wanted to help complete the bell tower, but also to make sure his successor as dean lived in the renovated residence he had planned. The document contains no expression of sentiment, but the legacies speak for themselves. Now at the age of thirty-seven, he awaited death and burial in his adopted church and town.

Gerson's executors never had to carry out his testament. The turning point in his illness must have come in August. For the entire month he was absent from chapter. But on 2 September he was back, attending the installation of a new canon. Four days later the chapter under Gerson decided, presumably because the worst of the epidemic was over, that canons no longer could live outside of Bruges. Any canon who was ill but who wanted to enjoy the income of his office had to remain within the walls and enclosure of the town of Bruges (456).

On 20 September Gerson presided over the installation of a new chanter for Saint Donatian. The position of schoolmaster, vacated by the new chanter, was in turn conferred on William de Fossa, who during Gerson's illness had acted on his behalf (456–57). Having made these arrangements, Gerson missed the chapter on 22 September, probably because he was on his way back to Paris after an absence from that city of more than fifteen months. He would not return to Bruges for almost five years.

The chapter's rich materials shed light on Gerson's development as a reformer. After his arrival in June 1399, he did everything possible to tighten discipline. But he quickly met resistance and had to back away from his original hard line and assure the canons that he had no desire to take away their privileges.

Gerson must have gone to Bruges in the belief that here he could make a difference in reforming one church. A little more than a year later, as he was lying on what looked like his deathbed in the corner of the dormitory, he had accomplished much less than he had set out to do. Practically every one of his reform ordinances had been revoked. In bequeathing so much to the church and chapter, however, he showed his continued belief in his position. He had established the type of home that had been beyond his power or influence to obtain at Paris. At Bruges Gerson was able to live the life of a reformer, which had long been his goal. And yet he returned to Paris.

Rejecting Marriage and Praying a New Language

While at Bruges Gerson also began to come to terms with women. It was imperative for him to be an example to other priests. Such a concern perhaps explains why shortly after his arrival in June of 1399, Gerson and the chapter decided that a female recluse, Margareta de Hulst, had to leave the cell she inhabited under the dormitory (Gl 10.449). Such an arrangement of a woman living as an anchorite on the fringes of a male church community, was probably fairly common in the period, despite the efforts of the eleventh-century clerical reformation.[14] Dean and canons wanted to be above suspicion, and so the woman had to go.

Gerson is sometimes said to have been hostile to women,[15] but the truth of the matter, as with so much in history, is more complex than what meets the eye. He came to recognize that women without theological training could have a deeper spiritual life than many learned churchmen and considered his biological sisters to be representative of such women. By the time he got to Bruges, he had probably completed a remarkable treatise in which he tried to dissuade his sisters from considering marriage. In writing his sisters, he began to dedicate himself to the spiritual direction of women.[16]

Like so much else in Gerson's production, it is impossible to give a precise date for his *Petit traitie enhortant a prendre l'estat de virginite plus que de mariage,* also known as *Discours de l'excellence de la virginité.*[17] It was probably written sometime between 1395 and 1399 and so belongs to the years of Gerson's stays at Bruges where he was likely to have gained an impression of women in a parish milieu. Ever since he had left home for the male university milieu at Paris, women had been at a distance in his life. Now he was seeking them out.

The treatise is one long exhortation not to marry. Gerson describes his observations on women in marriage and outside of it. It is much better for them to remain unmarried virgins and to establish a kind of religious life with each other. Not once did he speak of marriage as a sacrament instituted by Christ. He admitted that it was necessary to produce offspring to "increase Christianity," but he assured his sisters that other women would more than adequately take care of that need.[18]

Yet, paradoxically perhaps, he did not want them to become nuns. Gerson did not give his reasons, but his later criticism of laxity in monastic life for women may explain his position.[19] His reasoning, however, may also have been pragmatic.

The five sisters had only limited economic resources and could not all have entered monastic houses, which normally required some form of dowry.[20] Gerson assured his sisters that he and his brothers, who had all entered the Church, would not make claims on the family inheritance.[21] If the girls continued living together, they could use their inheritance to establish an informal religious community. Although Gerson did not use the word "beguine," which by this time was under a cloud,[22] his proposal seems to have been for something of a "béguinage à la campagne," an informal rural settlement of religious women, as opposed to the urban beguine communities in Flanders and Brabant.

The purpose of Gerson's treatise on virginity was not to regulate in detail his sisters' way of life. Such prescriptions would come later. At this point, he wanted to make sure they did not get married, and so he described what marriage might involve. Instead of drawing on traditional literary models, Gerson asked how women experience marriage and combine being married with being good Christians. The result was a fresh, original, and deeply disturbing perspective on married life. Avoiding the usual clerical clichés about weak women, Gerson took the wives's side as he exposed the pitiful weaknesses of boorish husbands: "Look what can and does happen every day. One husband will be a drunkard, a player of dice, a spendthrift, and for each penny that he and his wife will earn, he will spend for both of them. Another husband will be the exact opposite. He will wish to save everything and make his wife and household live very penuriously and impoverished, even in the midst of sickness and childbirth."[23] Gerson imagined a husband who was a gambler: "He will lose in one hour more than he will earn in ten days or in one year, and all the loss and pain will be piled on the poor woman." Angry at his own embarrassment, the drunken husband takes his losses out on the woman and ridicules or beats her.[24]

Even if he is a good man who takes care of wife and children, the husband can run into difficulties. He can lose his job, or if he is a farmer, he can have a bad year and lose his crops. If he is a merchant, he can lose his merchandise. Or the wife herself can become ill, and he can leave her for other women, in excusing himself because he cannot have *compagnie charnelle* with her.[25]

Gerson conceded a rightful place to sexual pleasure in marriage, but countered that it was hardly worth it, considering all the pain and misery of childbearing and nursing, "especially when the man and woman are poor and they have nothing to support the expenses of marriage without endless labor."[26] It is much easier for a virgin who is not attached to anyone to provide for herself and maintain a modest standard of living.

As for the joy of having children, Gerson also had his reservations. Offspring can turn out to be crippled, sickly, or rebellious. They can grow up to be "spendthrifts" and "brawlers." Poor people, moreover, can do little to help their children get ahead in the world. If a woman becomes a widow, she is even worse off in this area. "Her poor children cry and languish at her side and she can do nothing about it. God, what anguish!" *Dieu, quelle angoisse!*[27] If the widow remarries, the children's stepfather may not care for them.

A mother will, of course, do almost anything for her children, and Gerson tells how mothers even sin in order to help them out.[28] Mothers become obsessed with a desire for possessions and thus succumb to covetousness. Their desires give them no rest "night or day" and threaten the salvation of their souls. "Thus they have hell in this world and in the next one."[29]

It might be objected that Gerson as a priest had little or no experience with such matters. But his precise depictions of the woes of married life indicate women had told him of their misery: "It happens that a wife will displease her husband because her body is poorly made, and he will never love her nor wish to have carnal commerce with her. I imagine that in this case, as often happens, nothing can be more miserable in this world."[30] The fault, however, lies not always with the man. Some wives drink and gossip too much, even though they are encouraged by their husbands to be sociable and entertaining, until the point comes when "the husband may suspect his wife of too familiar laughing, looking, and touching."[31] If the wife is beautiful, the husband becomes jealous; if she is ugly, he might leave her. Whatever the case, she is subjected to the man's whims.

Marriage, as Gerson saw it, was prone to suspicion and disappointment. It is hard enough, he wrote, for two friends or brothers to remain together without clashing.[32] Marriage, a far more demanding state of life, leaves even less room for trust and companionship. Husband and wife cannot fulfill each other's sexual needs or live up to expectations. Women get angry with husbands who do not make it possible for them to dress and live in a way that impresses their surroundings.[33] Husband and wife are constantly in danger of losing each other to illness, infidelity, or death. As parents, they risk creating disobedient and concupiscent little monsters. Yet mothers will always want to protect and care for their children, no matter how ill behaved they might be.

As for Saint Paul's assertion that it is better to marry than to burn with sexual desire (1 Cor 7:9), Gerson disagreed. Without openly contradicting the Apostle, he claimed that a married woman has more temptations than an unmarried one. A person's sexual appetite grows when one has a sex life, while an unmarried girl who remains a virgin can much more easily accept the denial of sex.[34] Gerson's arguments are not based on the old monastic view of women as creatures of lust. His point is that the sexual act in itself does not lead to a lasting state of satisfaction. Without distinguishing between men and women, Gerson asserted that the more sex one has, the more one desires it: "Thus when you think that the fire of carnality has diminished because it has been satisfied, it shortly thereafter becomes more ardent or the same as before."[35]

Sexual desire is like lust for food: the more variation the better. Relations with one man or one woman can make one want to try others: "When a woman has gorged herself with one man, she will be tempted by another, because he is handsomer or stronger or cleverer or simply because he pleases her more, even though he may be ugly or awkward. The same is true for men regarding women."[36] Here as elsewhere in Gerson, what applies to the woman is also the case for the man. His view of human behavior and sexuality has a chilling equality: there is no strong or weak sex. Both men and women are controlled by their appetites, once they let themselves go in the least way.

More pragmatically, the married woman can consort with another man and even have children by him without being discovered, while the virgin has no such opportunity. "A wife, especially if she and her husband are hoteliers, tavern keepers, merchants, or other public traders, goes more lightly into this sin than a maid does, because there the peril is greater."[37]

A married woman may have to live without sex for six months, during a husband's absence, "if she does not want to sin greatly against God and her husband."[38] If such a person, used to having sex, can behave in such a way, is it not all the more natural and easy for the unmarried woman to do so permanently?

Earlier in these considerations, Gerson paused to ask his sisters' forgiveness for dealing with such matters "which you should not or ought not to hear, but truth compels me to do so and the great love that I have for you, so that you accept and make use of good advice."[39] He did not want to violate his sisters' "chaste ears." Also he asked pardon from "good married women, especially my dear and much beloved mother" for speaking in such a harsh way of marriage.

The world of women is divided in this treatise between the good sphere of female family members and women of their kind, and the bad realm of taverners' and merchants' wives and the like, who take advantage of a husband's absence in order to follow their desires. Just as Chaucer could not have presented his portraits of lustful women without his background in London, Gerson seems to have been drawing on knowledge of a secular Paris and Bruges, and all the inns in between where he might have noticed people who did what they pleased.

Gerson did believe in the possibility of marital fidelity; but he trusted spiritual marriage more. As he wrote at the opening of this treatise, he wanted his sisters to marry the richest, handsomest, and most loyal husband of all, Jesus Christ.[40] He was thinking in terms of Saint Paul (1 Cor 7:33), contrasting the wife who must spend her time in pleasing her husband with the unmarried woman who can concentrate on pleasing God. With Jesus as groom, the material demands of everyday life recede. His sisters could live a simple life by pooling their resources, thus gaining time for prayer and contemplation. A wife's time is consumed by activities around the desires or needs of her husband or with the acquisition and display of social prominence. Unmarried women could get along in a more modest way and concentrate on their spiritual lives.

The oldest of Gerson's sisters, Marion, had recently lost her husband. Gerson, after expressing his sympathy, claimed that this death was for her own good. God had taken away a "burden" from Marion and thus enabled her to stay with her other sisters: "I firmly believe that God has sent this misfortune of her husband's death for her great good, even though it is hard for her not to be sad."[41] Marion had married because of someone else's desire (apparently the parents') and because of custom and not because of any special attachment: *plus par voulenté d'autrui et par une maniere de coustume que par affection.* Gerson was sure that Marion had found more "rest and pleasure and a greater joy now than she did before in marriage."[42]

How could Gerson know about Marion's inner life? He claimed knowledge on the basis of a letter he had received from his father, describing the good and exemplary life his sisters now led and assuring him that none would marry without their father's or Gerson's permission.[43] He was also told that his sisters had begun to say their prayers, including the Office of the Blessed Virgin, together. Gerson rejoiced: "Even though my sisters are grown-up and come from the village and the working class (*de village et de labourage*), they have learned their prayers. And especially to be praised is the one who after her marriage has wanted and been able to do so. I believe that when one is married, it takes longer before one is able to learn them [because of lack of time]."[44] Once again Gerson's words derive from Paul (1 Cor 7:33): a woman who must serve a husband does not have time for religious devotions, while a woman who serves Christ can concentrate on prayer and contemplation. On the basis of Paul, Gerson fashioned his description of the commitments and demands of "carnal marriage," acceptable in itself but inferior to spiritual marriage.

Gerson assured his sisters that he was not forbidding them to marry. If one of them wanted to do so, then "in the name of God so be it," but she was not to persuade the others to do the same.[45] The sisters should remain together in the countryside and not go to a city. While the parents were alive, the sisters should stay with them. They could subsist on their own toil and on their inheritance.

In closing, Gerson provided "seven instructions" and promised more later. The sisters should dress modestly. They should continue to say their prayers regularly and attend mass. "The rest of the time you should work hard, not to acquire riches, but to avoid laziness and idleness and the revelry which are the mother and cause of all evils, as we can see in girls who live in cities without working (*sans labourer*)."[46] Gerson could have been thinking about wives and daughters of wealthy merchants in Paris and Bruges, women whose main concern was to dress well and to look good. For him they were idle.

His sisters were also to eat and drink soberly, diluting their wine with water and not eating too much meat or spices "which engender lustful desires."[47] They were to confess once weekly and to receive communion frequently. Living peacefully together, they were to avoid forming cliques. There was no requirement of enclosure, as was the case for most medieval nuns. Gerson's sisters could leave the house, but in public were to avoid contact with male strangers and keep away from dances and "other foolish entertainments where there is more harm than good."[48]

Finally, Gerson encouraged his sisters to learn to read French (*que vous peussiés aprendre à lire roumant*) so that he could send them "books of devotion" and write to them "very often with much great joy and pleasure."[49] There was no reason for them to seek out "the burden" (*la charge*) of marriage and to abandon "the liberty" (*la franchise*) found in the single life. In opposition to the twelfth-century dream of romantic love between male and female in marriage, Gerson insisted that marriage is slavery and the single life bliss. But the individual was not to be alone. Gerson envisioned a spiritual community without any institutional framework. His sisters would be under his own guidance, especially after their father's death.

This treatise does not share the misogynous attitude apparent in some writings of advice to women. Gerson belonged to a newer yet also perennial tradition, which had developed since the twelfth century but actually went back to Late Antiquity.[50] Here churchmen described for women a way of life that would bring them to God. Often such men seemed to be expressing their own worries and concerns rather than those of the women for whom they wrote.[51] Gerson, however, was not necessarily projecting his own concerns. He was in touch with his sisters and knew that some women were unhappy in marriage. He was wary of sexual experience for either men or women. Sexual desire could take a long time to arouse but once kindled could hardly be tamed.[52]

Gerson also opposed marriage because of the needs it creates. For the poor, marriage meant a nightmarish number of screaming children for whom a mother might have to go out and steal. In bourgeois circles, marriage as an institution led to conspicuous consumption and display of wealth. Gerson wanted to simplify life for his sisters and so rejoiced that his eldest sister now was a widow.

In writing to his sisters with such conviction about the joys of spiritual marriage, Jean Gerson was coming to terms with his own inner life. He sought fulfillment, union, and completeness in the love of God and wanted to avoid intimacy with any other person. At times he even doubted whether he should be so involved with his sisters, as he later revealed in his *De parvulis ad Christum trahendis* (On Bringing Youth to Christ, 1406). "Once when I was trying to convince my sisters to live in celibacy for life, I experienced something carnal. Confusion due to common custom sometimes disturbed me and my reasoning. It told me that what I was trying to do was extraordinary. I was in doubt, hesitated, and almost tried to abandon the sanctity of my proposal and to withdraw."[53] Gerson here drew on the Christian tradition of separation from all family bonds, while he also admitted the power of such loves. He concluded that he could allow himself a continuing attachment to his sisters, for he knew what was best for them.

By the late 1390s Gerson had reached a new immediacy in his perception of what mattered in the world. He could not cope with either the Schism or university politics, but he could reach out for his sisters and for the embrace of Christ himself. An indication of this new spiritual life is his *Pitieuse complainte et oraison devote* (Gl 7.1.213–16), which probably is from the end of 1399 or early 1400, when he was considering the meaning of his new life at Bruges.[54] It is a wonderful little prayer, in the tradition of Saint Anselm, calling upon God's grace and expressing a sense of helplessness and defeat but also hope. However, Gerson was writing not in Latin or for monks or powerful women, as Anselm had done. The dean of Saint Donatian was thinking of non-aristocratic women like his sisters whom he sought to convince not to marry or, in his own words, to enter into a spiritual marriage with Jesus. Gerson called Jesus "true spouse of virginity," the loving and ever-faithful husband of his treatise on virginity.

In the tradition of mystical writing represented by Bernard of Clairvaux, Gerson described a soul that once had been united to Jesus in spiritual marriage. It had betrayed its spouse and had been lost, burying itself in the cesspool of worldly affections and making itself "stinking and displeasing to God and all the saints" (214). Such a soul feels horrified by itself and turns to God for protection from torment and death.

Saint Anselm's first and probably earliest meditation similarly dwells on the soul's horror in seeing the depth of its sin.[55] But Gerson more quickly than Anselm introduces the person of a "sweet Jesus" who takes pity on the soul. Gerson switched from the third to the first person singular and plural, making the soul's plight into a direct cry for help: "For this, savior Jesus, our advocate and mediator, our emperor and our brother, who alone knows my misery and my weakness, if it is true what I know and believe of your sweetness, I implore you in your piety and mercy to remove all my iniquity through pure and clear contrition and total penance" (215). Jesus has the power to transform the heart of the sinner. The language of prayer becomes poetry describing Gerson's vision of the beautiful face, the "sweet look" which embraces him with its understanding.

Probably about a year later, Gerson appended this prayer to the conclusion of his treatise *La mendicité spirituelle* (280). There it has remained ever since, lost in the jungle of Gerson's writings and unknown to all but a few experts. But just as eleventh-century spiritual writings began to emerge from obscurity some decades ago, Gerson's prayers are now gaining new attention. Perhaps they have been ignored because they are so transparent, direct, and naive in language. But Gerson wanted his sisters and others to have these simple and unpretentious statements because he found it imperative as a churchman to reach lay people and enrich their inner lives.

Advising for Daily Life

At the end of the treatise on virginity, Gerson promised he would write more about edification and regulation of life. Probably in the winter of 1399–1400, he sent his sisters a letter. He began with the statement that they already had "sufficient letters and books" instructing them on how to serve the Lord (Gl 2.14). Telling them how busy he was, he had "taken the opportunity to stay up this night in order briefly to write you." This time he intended to provide "brief and concise advice about what one is to know in particular about each day and especially concerning the subjects of meditation."[56]

Gerson arranged the days and nights of his sisters in patterns of activity that was by no means original but would fill up their hours and thus hinder the idleness he feared so much in himself and in others.[57] Different days of the week were to be dedicated to God, the angels, the prophets and apostles, the martyrs, confessors, or to the passion of Christ or to Mary and holy virgins. Each day included a request for one of the gifts of the Holy Spirit, from fear of God to knowledge, fortitude, counsel, understanding, and wisdom.

Huizinga once showed contempt for such prescriptions, which he characterized as a kind of *horror vacui,* a fear of emptiness and desire to make use of all available space or time.[58] But Gerson was not recommending mindless busy-work. He was aware, he wrote, that various forms of reading and meditation had a different effect on different people: "For I well know how often that which moves one person to devotion does not so easily affect another. Therefore each of you should do what God will teach her."[59] Gerson's only claim was that his method suited him: his sisters would eventually have to find their own approach.

The letter ends with advice about how to enter into prayer, in remembering one's sins and asking for God's mercy. The great danger for the person who wants to regulate her religious life is pride. Instead of counting on one's own abilities or good works, we must entrust ourselves to God: "Be careful that you remain in this meditation and prayer until you feel that your heart has no confidence whatsoever in itself but only in the mercy of God."[60] At the same time as the individual puts herself in the presence of God, however, she can appeal to the saints, on the basis of their own lives. They can even be "convinced" by means of argument. Prayer, however, is a journey not only to heaven: whoever prays must go all the way into hell "in order to avoid and fear it."[61]

There is nothing revolutionary in this type of language, but by writing in French Gerson made himself useful to people without school training, especially women. He provided an outline for lay spiritual life anticipating by two centuries the recommendations of Saint Francis de Sales.[62]

A further indication of Gerson's continuing concern for his sisters and through them for any layperson is the *Nine Considerations*.[63] This advice can be summarized as a spirituality of everyday life: "Each evening a person ought to withdraw by herself for a little while and think about what she has done that day" (Gl 7.1.1). If temptations of the flesh come, then make the sign of the cross and tell them to go away. If this does not work, then pinch yourself or otherwise cause physical pain in order to "forget the unfaithful will and evil desires."[64]

Each sister should find someone in whom she can confide. Each of them should be careful about how they speak to each other. Daily, whether in the evening or in the morning, they should agree on what work needs to be done. If someone is not needed at work, she can spend her time in prayer or study (2). These recommendations end with brief prayers in Latin. The sisters' religious education thus included learning by heart Latin prayers whose meaning they quickly would come to grasp.

Here Gerson specifically addressed his sisters, but in his *Montaigne de contemplation* he came to see them as representatives of lay Christians who had been long neglected in their daily lives and spiritual aspirations.

Resigning the Chancellorship

Probably early in 1400, Jean Gerson took stock of his life. He had failed in his attempt to reform the chapter at Bruges. He could not remain there indefinitely without resigning the university chancellorship, and now he had to make his decision.

We have a remarkable statement from Gerson's hand in which he considers his position (Gl 2.17–23), and which deserves comparison with the opening chapter of Augustine's *Confessiones* or Abelard's *Historiae calamitatum*. The text has traditionally been called a letter, intended either for his teacher Pierre d'Ailly or for the chapter of Notre Dame at Paris. This central source for Gerson's life is a memorandum in the form of a meditation[65] that reviews his life and examines his conscience. He was apparently not defending his situation to others. His goal was self-understanding.

Sixteen times in the first part of this statement, Gerson uses the passive form of the verb: *cogor* (I am forced). He shows how his present way of life is forcing him to act in a way contrary to Christian ethics. As chancellor he had to "struggle with the most importune and even most oppressive people to the point of sinning."[66] He had to promote unworthy candidates to degrees "because of the consideration of others" and to bow to the demands of "very great lords" whose names he chose not to mention. He had taken the job of chancellor, he says, in order to avoid the intrigues of court life, and now was amid even more intrigue.

Gerson's everyday life at the university had been full of "the rumors that infect the place." Without peace of mind, "spiritual matters quickly are dispersed." He had to write pointless sermons, and had no time to say mass or his prayers. When he did find time, he was so distracted by his thoughts that he could not concentrate. This inner turmoil upset him greatly and gave him a guilty conscience.

Besides sacrificing his spiritual life to the worries of his job, Gerson complains that the material rewards of the chancellorship were limited. Because of its modest income, he had to find ways to make ends meet, for example by taking in student boarders. Forced to hold two offices, he went against the long tradition that forbade churchmen to do so. In becoming dean, he got a necessary income, but thereby failed to be resident at Paris. He thus broke the oath he had taken as chancellor and caused "murmuring and damage."

Gerson had long been looking for a benefice and, after he had renounced one claim, was "forced to pursue a new prebend." This was at the parish church of Saint Merry, as we saw in the last chapter. He thereby risked scandalizing other people, who called him "a two-headed monster." Instead of being an example for others, he was "forced to follow the crowd in doing what I do not want or what is not permitted."

Gerson suffered "from every evil tongue." "These tongues," he adds, "rage against me in an intolerable and irrational way, and they are expert in knowing how to reach their target." He refers to "a certain conspiracy here unnamed," perhaps a court intrigue. Betrayal was everywhere in political life: "The times are full of dangers and everywhere replete with the seeds of sedition."

This list of attacks, criticisms, and slanders that Gerson experienced describes the precarious position of any university administrator or political figure, whether in medieval or modern society. But Gerson did not limit himself to the external onslaught: the situation affected his own self-esteem. "For the time being, no good can be attributed me," he laments. He asks whether he is doing "more harm than good" and worries about "how small is the hope of doing any good." He concludes that he was wasting his time in preaching to Paris academics, "who do not seek their own salvation." It was better to stay away from Paris and concentrate on Bruges: "It should be considered what good can be done at Bruges solely by the example of life, without any words."

Gerson wanted to transform the spiritual lives of people around him. Now he sensed that his project was not working. At least not in Paris. So he had to stick to Bruges, where his example could make a difference and where he thought he could avoid the debates and polemics of which he had grown tired. He searched every corner of his soul, not to defend his record, but to put his mind at rest and end the moral double bookkeeping between Paris and Bruges. Facing his doubts he wanted to order his life.

Gerson characterizes himself without flattery: "It is my nature and custom in terms of action to be wholly inept and inert, full of scruples and fear, most easily upset, so that I continually mull over something more than a thousand times."[67] Here is the hesitant intellectual, knowing all the arguments and not being able to decide on a course of action. This state of mind left Gerson at the mercy of the powerful, and yet he was determined to avoid pleasing them, as he saw other theologians do: "These learned men are willing to dance about, altering and varying their songs, that is their doctrines, according to the whims of such magnates."

Much of what Gerson thus far had done in his life left him with a feeling of inadequacy and guilt. But he could also defend his behavior, as toward the members of his family. He admits that "carnal consideration could in the end overcome me," for his parents could not take care of his brothers and sisters. Gerson was willing to look after their material and spiritual needs, as already indicated in his writings to his sisters. Toward his brothers he did not hide his desire to help them advance, presumably in a university career: "I by no means act without masculine courage nor do I lack concern for the younger ones who would climb to the heights."

Family was important, but not personal advancement at the cost of moral integrity. In Gerson's language, "one must flee a fire without taking one's own possessions, as I violently ripped myself away from what was surely a profitable way of life at court." He had acted not out of fear but from conviction, and thus he might do the same with his academic career. What he needed now was peace of mind: "It should be considered how much love for God there is in the quiet of contemplation." Gerson looks to the example of others who had abandoned burdensome positions. Such were Bishop Gregory of Nazianzus (d. 389) and Pope Celestine V (d. 1296).

The last lines of the memorandum show that Gerson intended to resign the chancellorship: "In the end I think that no one is in doubt that it is permitted in accord with all laws to resign such an office, to hand it over to a superior either to enter a religious order or to live differently, especially for one who has been provided with another benefice." The position at Bruges was sufficient for Gerson's religious and material life: "I am sure, with every certitude, that in such a matter I will find what is necessary and what is best for me." He relies on his own self-knowledge: "I know myself and my own ways." This is not the renaissance individualist immortalized by Jakob Burckhardt but a medieval interiorized person, a successor to Saint Augustine, the bishop, and Saint Anselm, the monk, looking into himself, and there finding God's grace to provide integrity.

Gerson concedes that his decision might provoke criticism: "And so that they do not accuse me of changeableness if now I so passionately flee that which I once so diligently pursued [the chancellorship], let them know that my knowledge has grown with age and experience, and my hopes have been greatly frustrated. One thing, indeed, is certain: the wise man changes his ways with the times."[68]

The dream of youth here gives way to a sense of limitation, an awareness of his own needs as a person, and a program for interior life. In the end the once proud academic puts himself into the hands of God: "I know how little it ought to matter that I be judged by a human court, for he who judges me is the Lord" (1 Cor 4:3–4). Gerson would ignore "popular rumor" and live "in simplicity of conscience."

Sticking to the Pauline mode of self-assertion in Christ, Gerson anticipated the "Here I stand" position of Luther. And yet Gerson, unlike Luther, did not have to abandon his spiritual and intellectual formation. Following his conscience, Gerson trusted that he would find peace within the world that had made him.

This process of self-discovery has been the path of Christians from Paul onwards. Gerson's Damascus was not as dramatic as Paul's, nor did it lead him away from mother Church as Luther's awakening would. The chancellor faced his own scruples and fear. Behind them he discovered that he believed in his life. He could face leaving academia and exposing himself to the charge that he was running away from what he had "once so diligently pursued."

When Gerson realized that he could abandon his earlier life, he was also able to contemplate living it in a new, more complete way. As I pointed out earlier in this chapter, in early March he sent his request for being relieved of the chancellorship to Paris but withdrew it subsequently. Gerson's assertion that his patron the duke of Burgundy was decisive in making him continue as chancellor is probably an exaggeration (Gl 2.29). If he had been truly determined to resign, he would have done so, regardless of the duke. But now that he had worked through his own doubts, he could return not only to his own double life at Paris and Bruges but also to the Schism.

In a letter of 1 April 1400 to his teacher and benefactor Pierre d'Ailly, Gerson dealt for the first time in two years not only with personal concerns but also with the situation of the Church in general. After having withdrawn into himself, he was ready to face the world around him: "Reverend father and special lord, I turn the powers of my mind to our condition and order, if there is any order at all in this our time of tempest. I can consider the general disaster of the Church, which is so much to be pitied because its size and merits have been diminished in a decline of religious feeling."[69] Here is the Latin scholar playing with the idea of *ordo,* but also the moral preacher looking at a church in turmoil. The Schism meant not only an administrative split but also a much more fundamental challenge to religious expression (*pia affectione*).

Pierre d'Ailly's whereabouts during these years after the French withdrawal of obedience to the Avignon pope are hard to determine, but he seems to have remained mostly in his diocese of Cambrai.[70] In the meantime there were more negotiations between the royal court and the Avignon pope, under the leadership of the king's brother.[71] Benedict XIII, a virtual prisoner in his palace, refused to budge. Gerson and d'Ailly kept aloof by resisting pressure from Paris colleagues to force Benedict to resign.

In going to Bruges, Gerson had distanced himself from the Schism. Now he was back in the fray and turned to d'Ailly. Pierre had set Gerson up as chancellor, and their relationship may have become a genuine friendship.[72] Now he would no longer appeal to d'Ailly but consider his friend's situation in dealing with the Schism. "I have already wasted innumerable writings and words [on myself]," claimed Gerson.[73] He knew that his mentor normally showed a "modest and most composed way of being," but d'Ailly had confided that he found his position as bishop difficult. It was to be expected that "the pastoral burden" made his friend "anxious and full of sorrows, and in the end subjects you to dangers of soul and body."

Was Gerson repeating what d'Ailly had told him or was he thinking mainly of himself? Whatever the case, Gerson encouraged d'Ailly to face reality, as he himself had done: "There is no doubt that conditions get daily worse when each person adds something to the heap of iniquity and no one reduces it. If you are in doubt, take a look at the hateful Schism. Here, in the most evident passivity of former pastors, the worst customs have been slowly allowed to take root."[74] Quoting Seneca, Gerson described how practices, which once were considered to be vices, had become habits: "I speak as someone with experience." He used the example of the Feast of Fools, the yearly world-turned-upside-down festivity against which he later wrote a brief treatise.[75] Here the clergy dressed up and mocked itself, a practice Gerson found sacrilegious. Bishops failed to curb such misbehavior. Even worse, they neglected their duty to provide good preachers to reach the people. Instead they concentrated on protecting their own rights and possessions. Dioceses hired the best canon lawyers in this pursuit, while hardly any bishop would dream of employing a theologian to deal with spiritual needs (Gl 2.25). "These affairs are, I am sure, all the more known to you, the more experienced you are in them, and so all the more burdensome, for whoever increases knowledge also increases sorrow" (Eccles 1:18).[76] Gerson was skeptical about the advantage of knowing a great deal, but he was not rejecting the training d'Ailly had given him: "What I have begun, I will in pious boldness complete, for I have great trust in your devotion, since I love you greatly." Gerson assures d'Ailly that he would not resign from the chancellorship. He would not closet himself in his dean's house at Bruges, nor would he continue to ignore the situation of the Church in the Schism.

Gerson was back in the ball game. He concludes with a list of "what seems necessary to be done." Even though bed-ridden, as he himself writes, he made the list in his own handwriting, a blueprint for the reformation of the teaching of theology.

Gerson's main concern here was to replace useless teachings by useful ones. Linguistic and logical niceties, especially about the persons of the Trinity, were a waste of time. There was no use trying to push language beyond its reasonable limits in order to describe the godhead. The faculty of theology instead had to concentrate on moral and ethical questions, to prepare its candidates "for the education of the people and the solution of moral questions in our times."[77] The faculty should draw up a "little treatise . . . on the main points of our religion, and especially on its precepts, for the instruction of uneducated people." This is precisely what he would do in coming years, providing catechisms for the faithful.[78]

Theology had to be a practical subject, concerned with human life as well as with divine nature. Therefore Peter Lombard's *Sentences* once again had to be commented on in all its parts, including its ethical content and not just the teaching on God's existence and nature. "This text is hardly read any longer except for its first book," he complains. Students of theology were to devote themselves to the other books of the Lombard, as well as to the Bible.[79]

It might be necessary for the chancellor to refuse bestowing the licentiate in theology to masters concerned only with speculative matters. But Gerson was aware of the limitations of his own office, and so he concluded, "It would be more wholesome that in such a matter the chancellor proceed in agreement with the faculty." But his agenda was set: a return to the moral theology of early thirteenth-century masters such as William of Auvergne, bishop of Paris (d. 1249).

The letter to Pierre d'Ailly, together with his earlier memorandum, marks a change from frustrated isolation to renewed participation in academic life. Jean Gerson had reached the summit of his profession and then had tried to withdraw from it. Now he again involved himself, returning to Paris in the autumn of 1400 to begin fifteen years of energetic teaching and writing in both practical and speculative theology. The man who said he always was plagued by fears and self-doubt had found a new language for both prayer and argument.

Ascending Contemplation's Mountain

Probably in April and May of 1400, Gerson wrote the first statement of his new theology, the *Montaigne de contemplation* or *Mountain of Contemplation*.[80] He explains that he chose to write in French rather than in Latin, for women rather than men, because of the desire for spiritual instruction he felt in many women, especially his sisters, who could read French but not Latin. They had every right, Gerson insists, to be in contact with the learning of the Church Fathers and later theologians: "Therefore, nothing is more fitting, in writing to my sisters, who by

God's gift set out some time ago to live without marriage, than to teach them how they will please God by always serving him in constantly loving and honoring him. The lack of learning of my sisters cannot keep me from going ahead, for I intend to speak only about what they can fully grasp according to the understanding that I have seen in them" (*Selonc l'entendement que j'ai esprouvé en elles*; Gl 7.1.16).

Gerson was embarking on a new program of education in the spiritual life. Close to the surface of this text is the writer's own experience. Taking his point of departure again from the words of Saint Paul, this time concerning humility (1 Cor 3:18), Gerson laments that pride limits our understanding of God's ways: "The result is that some clerics are hindered in pursuing such a life, for they will not allow themselves to be humbled, nor to hand over their understanding of the mysteries of the incarnation of our Lord and the humility of his actions. . . . That is why many great scholars have wished at times that they had remained in a state of simplicity, like their mothers, without knowing Latin."[81] Gerson may have been thinking of Saint Monica and her son Augustine, but also of himself and his own mother. During his period of doubt and hesitation, he apparently had wished for the seemingly uncomplicated piety of his mother.

But now he had gotten beyond such regrets. He could accept the usefulness of knowledge, "provided one has the grace to use it well and humbly" (Gl 7.1.17). The danger is always arrogance, an attitude latent in Gerson's earlier writing. With this warning he could distinguish between two types of contemplation, one based on knowledge alone, the other coming from affectivity. The second is a higher form, found in the mystical writer Saint Denis, our Pseudo-Dionysius, who Gerson thought was the martyr Saint Denis, the patron saint of France. Gerson believed that "ordinary people" (*les gens simples*) could obtain the wisdom that provided the basis for such experience. Thus he could counter proud colleagues: "Simple Christians who have firm faith in the goodness of God and love him ardently have more true wisdom and a greater claim to being called wise than any scholars who have no love or affection for God and his saints."[82] Basing his argument on William of Auxerre's *Golden Summa* from the early thirteenth century, Gerson asserts that uneducated people can "know God better than any scholar or philosopher will be able to do through reasoning based on God's external actions." He emphasizes individual experience as opposed to school learning. In taking up where spiritual writers of the twelfth century, such as Bernard of Clairvaux, Hugh and Richard of Saint Victor, had left off, Gerson fostered a rebirth of twelfth-century spirituality, inspired by the affective language of the Psalms, where the fear of the Lord is the beginning of wisdom.[83]

Sketching what is necessary to get beyond the world's love and to come to God's, Gerson exhorts his readers, and especially his own sisters, to read or listen to the lives of the saints.[84] They may experience adversity and tribulation, but to reach contemplation, they had to go through the three degrees of humble penitence, a secret place in silence, and strong perseverance.[85]

The remainder of the *Mountain of Contemplation* describes this growth and development in the soul. Humble penance requires hard physical work, as well as fasting and other forms of self-denial (chs. 17 and 18). His sisters did not need to find some isolated spot in order to follow such a regime: "For the way of hermitage or reclusion is found not only in the woods and deserted places, but anywhere that one can pursue it in escaping from the confusion of the world and all its cares and occupations."[86] This sentiment recalls the Carthusians, who at that time had begun founding their houses of reclusion in the midst of cities. It is not surprising that Gerson came to form many intellectual and spiritual bonds with these monks.[87]

A person who chooses humble penance and then proceeds to the second stage might at first receive no spiritual consolation but may enter "a state of listlessness" (*langueur*) in which the desires of the world are gone but have not been replaced by a sense of God: "Then this person will suffer harsh assaults" (Gl 7.1.30). Even when she begins to feel better, she may remain "between two states, neither wholly dead to the world nor wholly alive in God."

In this situation, in apparent silence and solitude, this person can discover she is not alone at all. She has to contend with "a very harmful and damnable companion in the guise of herself, with her fantasies, thoughts, and bouts of melancholy" (32). Gerson recalls Saint Jerome's complaint that desert solitude led him into all kinds of fantastic imaginings, with the women of Rome dancing around him.[88] But the chancellor may also have been describing his own state when he tried to cut himself off from other people: "Such phantasms will make terrific noise and chatter on at length. At one moment they will put one image and then another before a person; now they bring her to the kitchen, now to the market; then they will tell her about filthy carnal pleasures and show her various attractions, songs, and such vanities that draw one to evil and to sin."[89]

Gerson still advises his sisters to seek some secret place. This might be in their own dwelling or elsewhere where they could be alone. Like Virginia Woolf, Gerson believed in the importance of "a room of one's own" (*en sa chambre, s'elle l'a seule*; 33). He recalls one woman who because of illness had to keep for a long time to her room. She told him that she was afraid of losing the solitude that it gave her: "I don't know what I will do when I lose this little room, for there [will be] no place where I can concentrate on my thoughts about God and myself."

Gerson assumed that everyone needs times and places for withdrawal. The twelfth-century contemplative tradition had been a monastic and elite one, conveying itself in Latin and assuming that women belonged to a more practical world. Certainly there were female recluses in that period whose visions and spiritual insights had fascinated churchmen.[90] But such women almost had to trap such men to make them listen. Now Gerson was actively seeking out women to whom to give spiritual advice.

He gives practical pointers on body postures in prayer. Here he drew on the writings of William of Auvergne: "A person should prepare herself in the manner that will serve her best, whether kneeling, standing, sitting, bowing, or leaning up against something, or perhaps lying down. I refer to the situation when a person is alone and can act in such a way without eccentricity, for in church one should follow the others."[91] William also recommended "standing up and bending over on the left arm." Gerson was certain that William himself had tried this position!

In returning to thirteenth-century expositions of the spiritual life, Gerson made a clean break with contemporary scholastic discourse. The works of William of Auxerre and William of Auvergne had been virtually forgotten in an increasingly abstract Paris scholastic theology. Now Gerson found inspiration in an earlier combination of moral theology and practical advice.[92]

Gerson also wanted to keep people from going overboard in the discipline connected with the contemplative life. Excessive asceticism can lead to depression. Some people find out "through experience that it is much better for them to be in company and to do physical work, for then they will not brood" (34).

Above all else, Gerson believed in a sustained effort: "There is nothing that hard work and diligent effort cannot overcome" (*N'est rien que labeur et diligence ne vinquist*). These words are emblematic of his way of life. At the same time, however, Gerson did not claim that what was good for him was appropriate for everyone else. He was aware that some had to pull back from contemplation because of the dangers of depression or other forms of mental imbalance.

In the last part of the treatise, Gerson defends himself against those who consider this way of life to be "deranged and depressed": "Instead of the occupations that worldly persons have on earth, in their narrow and petty concerns, contemplatives concern themselves with something much larger and greater than the whole world, that is, with God. Those who have experience know what I mean."[93] Gerson was describing his own pursuit.

The final stage on the mountain of contemplation is strong perseverance. Here it is not possible to rest. If one does so, one slides back down the mountain (ch. 35). In this section Gerson developed most fully the image of mountain climbing. There are many moments when one is tempted to give up. Some people think they are at the top even though they are far below, while some actually reach contemplation but "they are too quick to rejoice and boast about this achievement." And so they fall from the place they have achieved.

There are several false summits. The only way to keep going is to put one's trust in God's grace "and to proceed according to his movement and his will" (44). There are many hindrances to the final achievement of contemplation, as for those so hungry to hear God's word that they spend too much time in spiritual reading. They rest here and stop advancing (ch. 36). Then there are people who do reach the top and think that this has become "their inheritance." Only in descending do they realize that "the grace of God put them there and held them for as long or as short a time as pleased him" (45).

Gerson reminds his sisters of what he earlier had written them and provides a list for spiritual reading. Richard of Saint Victor was better for educated clerics, while *The Clock of Wisdom,* which deals with the marriage of the soul with divine wisdom, is named as a more recent work than Bernard's *Sermons on the Song of Songs.*[94] The spiritual marriage in the Song might be dangerous, however, for "one easily can slide into thoughts about carnal marriage" (47).

Less problematic is Bernard's recommendation to dwell on the details of Christ's life (ch. 38). Another procedure (ch. 39) would be to go from one saint to another in "spiritual begging" (*mendicité spirituelle*), the title of the much longer treatise that Gerson perhaps wrote later in 1400 (Gl 7.1.220–280). He recommends the prayers of Saint Anselm, of which some were in French (49). He refers to his own prayer to Jesus but warns that "all the writings of the world will never serve so much as strong perseverance with God's grace does . . . for one cannot describe or engender affectivity through writing or talking."[95]

Gerson knew he could not create feelings, but he did try to organize and discipline the emotions. People could become aware of what they were thinking and be helped to channel their feelings in the right direction. In entering this area of religious sentiment, he assumed a task that most of his university colleagues would have considered either beneath their dignity or beyond theology. The religious writer, he saw, might engender expectations and create frustrations. In the end the person seeking contemplation was alone with God's grace.

Gerson anticipated Luther's *sola gratia:* grace alone brings salvation. But the individual could be prepared for the reception of grace. Gerson was poised between the old monastic theology, beautiful in form but elitist in its view of the world, and the new protestant theology, radical and at times rabid in its rejection of human effort.

However much he resigned himself to the grace of God, Gerson was an activist. The insights he conveyed in his writings could make a difference for others. He began with his sisters and from them sought to inspire and encourage every devout man and woman. The way of contemplation involved hard work. The person must "have a great amount of time" and not be caught up in other pursuits, but must stay in one place "regardless of whether devotion may or may not appear." Wait for half an hour, he exhorts, and then for another half hour, even if the effort is exhausting: "Often in the last half hour she will profit more in terms of contemplation than in all the preceding time, and more than someone else will do in ten days or even in a month" (52).

At about the same time as he wrote *The Mountain of Contemplation,* Gerson made further recommendations for the daily lives of his sisters, the *Onze Ordonnances* or *Eleven Rules.*[96] Instead of seeking to imitate a monastic community, they should simply follow "the law of Jesus Christ."

In this voluntary community with no vows, the sisters should confess once a week and receive communion once a month. Anyone who spoke unkindly should ask for forgiveness, or else be excluded from sharing meals with the others, just as in the *Rule of Saint Benedict* (ch. 25). Every day part of a good spiritual book should be read aloud, for the benefit of all. Certain types of communal work also lend themselves to common prayer. At fixed times the sisters should pray together, even at midnight, if possible.

They should dress in simple clothing and not sleep in the nude. Hard work was essential, "not so much in order to gain riches as to rid yourselves of idleness, laziness and indolence, which are the mothers and causes of all evils" (56). Faithful to a tradition going back to the Desert Fathers, Gerson praised the contemplative life but was afraid what might happen if someone had a free minute.

The sisters were to let their supervisor, presumably Gerson or their father, choose one of them "as prioress." Here, more than in the *Nine Considerations,* he laid out a framework for daily life without, however, going into great detail. He asked his sisters to "begin little by little in this way of life." He was confident that the Lord would give the grace of perseverance so that they could reach perfection with "the true spouse of virginity and loyal friend of chastity" (Gl 7.2.57).

These last lines were a repetition of the first lines of *Jhesus, vray espous de virginité, Jhesus de chasteté loyal ami* (Gl 7.1.213), the same prayer that he had appended to *Mendicité spirituelle.* One prayer or treatise for his sisters led to another; one set of rules required further elaboration. Finally in the *Mendicité,* Gerson went beyond addressing his sisters alone and wrote for a general audience, concerning what he called "the secret parliament of the contemplative person to his soul and of the soul to the man" (220).

Preparing University Reform and Writing More Books

In the spring and summer of 1400, while Gerson distilled his spiritual life into advice for his sisters and all good Christians, he also began proposing reforms for the University of Paris. On 27 April, he wrote to his colleagues at the College of Navarre, where he had studied and lived for so many years before leaving for Bruges, about his attempt to resign the chancellorship (Gl 2.29–30).

Two days later Gerson sent a much longer and more detailed letter to the same audience, in which he spoke about his health and detailed his views on the intellectual life (30–35). Quoting Ecclesiastes (12:12), Gerson proclaims, "There is no end to making more books." He laments the fact that "outstanding men of the greatest genius and wisdom" had written much that now was ignored. He is worried that he, like so many others, would fill parchment and the minds of students with empty thoughts.

This was not necessarily pure rhetorical humility. He was uttering the thoughts that had long plagued him: "We do write, but our sentences have no weight, our words, no number or measure. For all that we write is flabby, mean, slack. We do not write what is new. Instead we repeat what is old but treat and transmit it in a new way. . . . How much wiser it would be to make use of what already has been well invented, rather than to invent what is sought for."[97]

Warning against arrogance, one of his favorite themes, Gerson summarizes the goals of university education in three areas. First is the requirement to learn the subject of the schools, conventional theology. But this is not enough. Students must also be introduced to "that which edifies, regulates, and forms the way of life of those who read the subject."[98] Knowledge in itself is useless. As pointed out before, learning had to provide a basis for ethical considerations. But these are insufficient without a third competence: students of theology had to learn not only to live well but also to convey their knowledge and insights to others. They had to become good preachers.

All three elements are combined in a proper university education. One of these alone is not only insufficient but could be downright dangerous: "The first scholastic concern puffs up and disturbs a person when it lacks the second element of edification." The second is also inadequate, while preaching without a basis in the other two "does not so much instruct others as repel and ruin them."

Gerson provides a reading list within each area. For the first he recommends commentaries on the Lombard's *Sentences* by scholastics such as Saint Bonaventure and Thomas Aquinas. He warns against more recent masters who have turned theology into logic. For the ethical category he draws on patristic and monastic literature, including Augustine's *Confessions* and John Cassian's *Collations,* as well as the *Lives of the Desert Fathers,* with their anecdotes of wisdom. But William of Auvergne's *Divine Rhetoric* was also relevant. Then there are the works of pagan classics: "I recommend them and, as it were, as a pilgrim I run through them, both for their abundance of moral statements, for the style and elaboration in the words and for the special expertise of poems and stories, and finally for a certain pleasure in the variety of what one can read."[99]

This approach to university education was syncretic: many areas were useful, and one was not to be favored over another. Much had to be combined in order to create the complete scholar and preacher. Within this discipline, he recommends the practice of disputation, to be carried out in a calm and modest manner, without "stubborn animosity." In the practice of edification, however, it was silence that was necessary. Gerson exhorts his colleagues, just as he did his sisters, to withdraw for some periods from the company of others to obtain spiritual rest and renewal: "It is even necessary at one point to take time off from prior study, since it cannot wholly provide the peace of mind of which we speak" (Gl 2.34–35).

Gerson here states his memorable warning against empty conversations. As a student, so he claims, he never had time to dissipate himself in such a manner.[100] Here is Gerson the man apart, the loner proud of what had made him, but also the country boy with a smoldering anger toward an aristocratic world of which he never could be a part: "So great among us was the difference of background and studies."

Amid such recollections, Gerson almost loses the thread of his exposition. At letter's end he returns to the subject of preaching, the third area necessary for the theologian. He recommends Gregory the Great's *Pastoral Care.* His devotion to good preaching can be seen in another letter from the spring or summer of 1400, again to his colleagues at the College of Navarre (36–42). He laments the fact that the Dominicans, a few years earlier, had been thrown out of the university. Gerson admitted that he was one of those responsible for their removal, after the affair of Juan de Monzon. University sermons were important for warning and reforming arrogant teachers and undisciplined students. Without the Dominicans, this function was being neglected.

As in the previous letter, Gerson states that the university was not living up to its obligation to train good Christian men, who should be both learned and devout. He even was concerned that some teachers corrupted their pupils, as he would describe in more detail in a later sermon.[101] Gerson worried that the state of the university had gotten to a point where it was almost irreparable: "In this my meditation I see these dangers and am confounded by them. I am shaken at the same time by lamentation and weeping. I really can find no sufficient answer to what I should do or how I should take care and by what means I can rightly win people over."[102] He considered writing to individual teachers but found this to be too overwhelming a task. Also there were many he did not know. He could also write a collective letter, but this might be a waste of time, "since many of the teachers either would ridicule the zeal of my humble self and assert their own rights, or they would become enraged, or accuse me of presumption." Here was an old dilemma: the limited power of the chancellor, going back to the twelfth century, when the masters weakened the office.

Gerson's solution was university sermons on the moral and spiritual problems of students and teachers. Consequently, he suggested that everything possible be done to bring back the Dominicans and delineated his own state of mind and actions: "Let each see to it that he repairs this damage with diligence and keenness, insofar as he receives from above the ability or grace to do so. Once all desire for rivalry has been put aside, let him then look for peace and pursue it. This is what I am trying to do now. This is what I on my behalf offer in these writings."[103]

In the first months of 1400, in spite of his failure to reform the chapter at Bruges, Gerson came again to believe in the power of individual action to improve the institution to which he had dedicated his life. Bruges had given him a physical home, but now he was thinking of returning to the university whose members he hardly trusted: "I know the way men behave in public. I know how different they are in their judgments and opinions. I know what implacable and untamed feelings reign in the hearts of some and how much enjoyment in contradicting others flourishes in their unrestrained tongues."[104] He realized that any effort on his part to bring back the Dominicans would make him liable to the charge of being fickle. First he had helped get rid of them. Now he wanted them back. But he was ready to eat his words and take on the hypercriticism of the same academic milieu he had tried to leave behind at Bruges.

In the last letter to his colleagues at Navarre before returning, Gerson repeated a perennial worry. There were too many books in circulation. He regretted that students and even colleagues were eager for his own unfinished works, while they failed to read much better writings, less popular because the students looked at them as old-fashioned: "It delights them to transcribe, the faster the better, or to study more recent compilations rather than old ones. They are like boys who, even though the most unripe fruits are more sour, eat them more avidly than ripe ones, which are healthy for the digestion."[105] Then as now students (and their teachers) followed the latest academic fashion and spoke in whatever language was the latest jargon.

Gerson could have felt flattered that his writings were considered desirable. He claimed that he could not prevent his household from being plundered for his drafts, which he would rather consign to the flames. And yet, at the same time, he hoped that the reading of his incomplete work would create a thirst for the real thing: "Who knows in the end if, once small rivulets have been tasted, students will be drawn by their sweetness to imagine more savory things from their sources" (Gl 2.43).

Gerson was torn in his reaction. A radical part of him wanted to destroy all incomplete writings before they could be illicitly distributed. A reconciliatory side hoped that by some *felix culpa* or happy fault, the reading of his jumbled thoughts would inspire students to go to the Gospels or to patristic or classical literature.

By September Gerson was strong enough in body and mind to return to Paris and resume his life there. A vital indication of his state of mind is provided by the letters to his colleagues. Another hint is provided by a poem, *Against curiosity in writing more books.* Its message is close to that of the letters and so probably belongs to this period:[106]

What will be the end of writing? Alas this anxious care!
Are there not enough works of wisdom already written?
They are wise, I admit, but sometimes they are foolish.
In changing chapters each age has its own taste
And pursues its own study.
When a man is old he does not wish for the same as the boy
Or learned youth does.
Thus the book pleases the child by its newness.
Each person is inordinately satisfied with his own writings.
Just as each beast loves its own offspring
and its own nest is more beautiful for each bird.
As gluttonous time gives way to death, you see the same happening with writings.
Fortune rejoices in change and brings variation.
She gives birth to new ages and renews the world:
Similarly the pen destroys the wax, rubbing it away
and renewing it.
Or music develops in notes and reaches the ears,
now sad, now attractive.
The studious crowd at Paris once dedicated its genius to poetry and to the figures of rhetoric.
Theology was renewing its scholars of olden times,
But fortune, alas, forbids that such men multiply.
There are as many different minds as kinds of language.
Go now and write books that last forever.
The eternal book is one which in pure light
You are to seek to look upon.
Then knowing everything, there will be an end.
And so Solomon says: honor God and keep his commands.
This is what every man must do,
And then books will end.

Gerson returned to Paris in September of 1400 in order to honor God and keep his commandments. He was ready to employ his talents in working ceaselessly as teacher and preacher. He would write more books than ever, many of them brief pamphlets in contributing to current debates, some of them long treatises of learned theology. There would be no end to books in his life. Gerson had reconciled himself to living once again with two central offices, separated by almost three hundred kilometers. The contradictions of a double life at Bruges and Paris would continue.

Returning to the Summit, 1400–1403

When Jean Gerson returned to Paris at the end of September 1400, he probably moved back into the rented house he had left fifteen months earlier.[1] Here, next to the garden of the Grand Master of the College of Navarre, the churchman who had probably enjoyed one of the finest ecclesiastical residences at Bruges contented himself with a more modest way of living.

Gerson spent days and nights writing. From October 1400 until October 1403, when he left for the papal court, he produced sermons and treatises that in bulk match those of his earlier career. He knew what he wanted to do: preach the gospel of repentance and reform church and university. He involved himself again in efforts to end the Schism and joined a university delegation to Benedict XIII.[2] He helped end the withdrawal of obedience which had existed since 1398 in the kingdom of France and elsewhere.[3]

During these years, Gerson also set out to join mystical with scholastic theology, a task not successfully attempted by any respected Paris master since Bonaventure in the mid-thirteenth century.[4] At the same time, he continued his campaign to define boundaries between acceptable and wrongful forms of human contact.

The death of his mother on 8 June 1401 left only faint traces in Gerson's writings,[5] but he continued to give advice to his sisters, who remained on the family homestead. With his brother Nicolas, Gerson revealed himself most clearly as a caring brother trying to exercise control.

Caring for the Self in the Family

A few months after their mother's death, Nicolas joined the Celestine Order, a reformed Benedictine congregation that traced its origin to Peter Morrone, better known as the hermit-pope Celestine V (1294). Three weeks after Nicolas's profession on 11 November 1401 at the Celestine house of Villeneuve-lez-Soissons, Gerson wrote to his brother and described how "the laxness of my mind has shown me how I still am not wholly capable of loving heavenly things." He describes his reaction to his brother's profession as he returned to Paris: "Your absence then seemed to me more of a burden and my fate harsher than usual. I sighed for you as an ox that is separated from its mate. The trauma of separation from you was devouring me. It caused great pain and mangled my soul. Amid my thoughts and my words about you, tears that were not asked for came to my eyes."[6] Such a narrative may have literary models, such as Petrarch's letter to his brother,[7] but Gerson no doubt was telling how it felt to part from Nicolas, after his brother had lived with him in Paris. First he tried to counter the tears by remembering that Nicolas had found happiness in his new way of life. But this thought was quickly overwhelmed by "a great crowd of carnal affections" which confronted Gerson with his brother's "bodily weakness" and "cried out at the unbearable hardships in the austerity" of the Celestines. A voice told him that if Nicolas had remained with him, he could have saved his soul and at the same time given his brother a "necessary and pleasant" company (Gl 2.46).

Doing his best to dismiss the voice as "base sensuality" only concerned with "the comfort of the body," Gerson extricated himself from what he considered to be a temptation: "I was badly shaken by these voices, and I almost came to agree with them. But I struggled as reason illuminated by faith regularly struggles in the good Lord. This sense of reason strongly congratulated you on your status and sighed deeply at mine, nor was it fooled."[8] The ascetic regime of the Celestines was an integral part of their vocation, and Gerson encouraged his brother to follow it and not give up. It was better for Nicolas to deal with such demands than to return to the tempest of the world, "where the worst and most contagious society everywhere pollutes" and where "monstrous crimes are part of everyday life."

Gerson warned Nicolas not to "waste away" in his spirit if he sensed "creeping into your soul that treacherous softness (*mollities*) I now described concerning myself." The word is the same term Gerson used to describe masturbation.[9] Nicolas was to beware of a spiritual self-indulgence, which in Gerson's mind was just as dangerous as physical self-gratification. Instead Nicolas should thank God for the grace given him: "It is he who from your boyhood has shown mercy to you, giving you a good and God-fearing heart compassionate on those in affliction. He has added from above his mercy, to drive you away from the evil world in which you would have been plunged irrevocably, if you had obtained your licentiate or master's degree in arts. Since you were close to this result, accept from others such a conjecture."[10]

Nicolas apparently had almost finished his course of studies at Paris and his elder brother had looked forward to his remaining there. Instead Nicolas withdrew to a religious order whose observances Gerson found excessive, a concern reflected in a later letter to Nicolas, this time about their youngest brother Jean.[11]

Gerson tried to convince himself that Nicolas had made the right decision in fleeing the world. But he could not keep back one last reproach, even as he claimed that Nicolas was more fortunate than he had been. The passage, already quoted early in chapter 1, indicates that even after his return to Paris Gerson questioned his way of life: "God showed great mercy to you, since you had no relatives or friends who wanted you to become something great in the world and so would have been opposed to your intention. It is, and always has been, quite different for me, as well as for countless other people who read in the book of experience that one's enemies are the members of one's own household (Mt 10:36)" (Gl 2.47).

Gerson asserts that he had never been allowed to be a child. His parents had chosen his career so he could look out for family members. His loyalty to family bonds meant a kind of love that in his eyes was less harmful than so many others, but one which meant that he had to ignore his own needs.

The letter ends conventionally with requests for prayers for family, starting with the departed mother, "another mother of Augustine" toward her sons, as she had shown herself in the letter to Nicolas and young Jean. Gerson exhorts Nicolas to read Augustine's *On the Psalms* "in one of the volumes that I know you have with you."

Gerson's doubt about Nicolas is also transparent in a letter written two days later to his superior. He feared that Nicolas would not be able to handle the ascetic regime of a Celestine house because of his *fervorem indiscretum* in a "religious observance that in itself is harsh." He pleads: "Show yourself, I ask, to be attentive to him in such a way that he makes known to you all his needs, even his bodily ones."[12]

Gerson's youngest brother, Jean the Celestine, later became his literary executor and so made sure this letter survived. Why did Jean allow such criticism of his own order to become part of his brother's heritage? Perhaps Gerson had ended up saying "the right thing" about overcoming doubts and dismissing them as "treacherous softness." In Augustine's manner, it was acceptable to admit temptation and lack of belief so the individual may triumph over them. Gerson provided a necessary "happy ending" for his reservations and fear. But I sense that Gerson did not approve of Nicolas's decision, just as the case would be when Jean joined the Celestines.

Gerson needed Nicolas and Jean. He wanted to make decisions for his brothers and his sisters. In reaching out to his siblings for affection, he sought to make himself indispensable to them. With Nicolas, as with young Jean, this regime was only temporary. With his sisters, except for Marion, who apparently remarried, Gerson seems to have exercised control for a longer period.[13] Significantly, he restricted his search for affective attachments to members of his family.

Gerson was dealing with a major dilemma in Christian life: how to replace the bonds of the flesh with those of the spirit? His response was a classic one: to make one's parents or siblings into one's closest friends, for everyone else was a potential temptation. In Gerson there is none of the carefree joy in friends that Augustine expressed. Gone is the optimism of twelfth-century monasticism that a friend is the guardian of the soul and a sure path to heaven.[14] Only family will do. But then family too can be a disappointment. With brothers and sisters now at a physical distance, Gerson turned to writing, teaching, and preaching as his outlets for emotional and spiritual life.

Getting a Prebend at Paris

While seeking inner balance, Gerson continued his quest for a steady income. Since December 1398, he had been trying to get a prebend at the church of Saint Merry, which included a canonry at Notre Dame cathedral.[15] In February 1399, this position was handed over to a master Jean Willequin. After Willequin's death, a canon of Notre Dame, Pierre de Ogero, conferred the prebend on his nephew. In August 1400 Gerson, still at Bruges, applied for the post through his lawyer. Another applicant for the same position, Nicolas Le Sellier, temporarily abandoned his claim when he was promised another prebend.

In September 1400, the chapter's inquiry into the matter continued, and Le Sellier again submitted his application. On 8 April 1401, the chapter handed over the matter to legal experts. The decision issued on 20 May left it up to Pierre de Ogero to confer the prebend and canonry on whomever he chose. Gerson and his rival both appealed to the pope. The outcome of this appeal is uncertain, but on 6 July the nephew of Pierre de Ogero handed over the position to yet another person, Raoul le Gay, in an exchange of prebends with him.

Gerson was clearly not in the good offices of the canons of Notre Dame, for he never came close to getting this prebend. On 15 December 1400, he had been called before the chapter on the business of both the prebend of Saint Merry and the seal of the chapter. Two days later he gave his consent to the decision that the canons "dispose of the seals of the chapter accordingly as it will seem best to them" (Gl 10.459). The wording implies criticism of Gerson for his past behavior, even though as chancellor of Notre Dame he had the right to hold the seal. Whatever his university position and theological reputation, the canons did not trust him!

Nevertheless, Gerson's position with the chapter of Notre Dame would eventually improve. In January 1403, the canons asked him to give one of the sermons at the capitular synod in March (462). Gerson never did so, for the university went on strike and so the traditional sermon was not given. But the invitation shows that Gerson and the chapter had reached an understanding. By the end of 1403, as we shall see (ch. 7), Gerson did finally get a prebend.

An indication of an optimistic and hopeful attitude in Gerson shortly after his return from Bruges is found in a sermon probably given on the Feast of All Saints, 1 November 1400 (Gl 5.604–10), that celebrates the saints' bliss. Here he again used the image of an ascent of a mountain, recalling his vernacular *Mountain of Contemplation*. But in speaking to academic colleagues in Latin, Gerson employed many more biblical and patristic references.

The following March (1401), Gerson gave a Holy Thursday sermon to his colleagues on the text from John 13:3: "The father gave all things into his hands" (405–19). Each Christian as the brother and friend of Christ obtains the government of all things. There is a triple entitlement in filial adoption, triumphant victory, and reciprocal love (407). We can rejoice in sharing in Christ's gift: "Mouth, tongue, mind, senses and strength resound in confession, jubilation, benediction, and praise." The individual can take part in Saint Paul's words, "I can do everything" (Phil 4:13). Recalling the words of Jerome, we can live "as if we had nothing and possess everything."[16]

This sense of power and possession arises because "the just man has total dominion" (413), richer and more perfect when it comes from grace rather than from civil or political justice. Thus lordship as given in the Gospel is free (*gratuitum*; 414). The just man knows that everything belongs to him (*sciens omnia esse sua*; 415). In such evangelical ownership a person burns with meditation's flame and is lit up by divine love. "Those who have experienced it know what we are saying," Gerson added, hinting that he himself had felt this love: *Sciunt experti quod loquimur.*

Did Gerson at this point in his life have a mystical experience?[17] Perhaps not in the sense of any vision, but the man who earlier seemed to have lost faith in his vocation and life was now full of hope. The grace he experienced freed him from the need to possess anything. Having nothing, he had everything, for grace's lordship confounds greed: "All these things are mine, as I do all things towards others" (416).

This is not the Franciscan ideal of poverty as a voluntary way of life. For Gerson it was not necessary to enter a religious order or take vows (417). Poverty lives within the mind that is aware of itself (*in animo sibi bene conscio*). In this new state of grace, we are more complete than ever before. And so we can stop being anxious. The Father will hand over everything into our hands, as he did when Christ asked him to do so on Holy Thursday.

The Gerson who preached to his colleagues with such trust that God would provide was a different person from the one who in 1399 had abandoned Paris to avoid the moral dilemmas of life as a university administrator. In facing himself, Gerson came to terms with his roles as pastor, teacher, and reformer. He could work for his goals in having faith and trusting that all would be well. The Father whom he shared with Christ would hand over everything, and so he was not to wander about in worrying about many things: *Non necesse habet ut evagetur anxius aut turbetur erga plurima* (419).

Teaching a New Generation

Two months later, in a French sermon probably at the church of Saint Jean-en-Grève, Gerson preached how difficult it could be to have faith (29 May 1401). Once he had experienced temptation concerning a matter of belief. It was only when he gave up and humbly accepted his own inadequacy that he felt *une clarté d'entendement,* an illumination of understanding (Gl 7.2.1043): "I know a man who, after being overwhelmed by temptation concerning an article of faith, was suddenly brought into such light of truth and certitude that there remained in him no trace of doubt, and no hesitation. There was only a great calm, instilled in him by the one who commands the waves (cf. 2 Macc 9:8)."[18]

Gerson here as elsewhere uses the example of his own experience to encourage others, recalling twelfth-century spiritual writings. He added this personal, even intimate, dimension, occasionally to his scholastic treatises, as in his lectures on the Gospel according to Mark, probably initiated in the autumn of 1401. He began with the mission of John the Baptist described in its first chapter,[19] mentioning his own life in terms of sharing the desert with the Baptist: "It pleased the fatherly providence [of God] . . . to place me for some time in the desert of tribulation and a certain solitude" (Gl 3.57). Now he could combine his spirituality and theological training in addressing his students in a fresher and more direct manner than that of his own teachers.[20]

In the first lecture, Gerson explained his method as a commentary on the Gospel text for the sake of study and charity (28). Thus it was not necessary to cite multiple authorities, for this practice was often just a kind of showing off (*ostentationem*). In the text from Mark 1:3, we find John as the voice of the Word of God: "The voice of one crying in the desert, 'Prepare the ways of the Lord'." His voice contrasts with those of many in Gerson's time, who fail to cry out, "for they are made into dogs that cannot bark" (31). Gerson may have been thinking of the Dominicans, the *domini canes,* the Lord's hounds, still banished from the university.

There are many pitfalls for those who would teach and preach well. Each path, however good, has its dangers. On the one side is contemplative life, which offers insight but also threatens with *phantasticas illusiones* (33). The active life involves the person and sometimes traps him in the world (34). The only way to combine the two lives is to investigate oneself, as John did before he began to preach (36).

Gerson continued such self-examination in the lesson which later became his treatise *On Distinguishing True from False Revelations.* The original commentary in the schools (Mark 1:4: "John was baptizing in the desert") is dated to the end of 1401. The finished treatise he sent to his brother Nicolas the Celestine in early 1402 (Gl 2.49).

By sending this work to Nicolas, Gerson maintained contact with him. Warning against the devil's wiles, he tried to establish a criterion for separating "angelic revelations" from "demonic illusions." There was every reason to be on guard "in this final hour just before Antichrist comes," for now "the world is like a senile old man, who lets himself indulge in many fantasies and illusions that are like dreams."[21]

It is not always wrong to reveal apparent visions to others, so long as there is an element of "edification or guidance" (Gl 3.41). Gerson, however, was critical of those who wanted "to titillate the prurient ears of bystanders." This is a waste of time. Ever concerned with the right use of time, he resented people who told useless stories. Outward behavior can indicate whether they are worth listening to. Gerson warned against those who fast excessively and "weaken their brains with excessive tears" (43). They are obliged to follow the advice of others, as he himself sought to warn his brother Nicolas against too much asceticism.

Gerson related the story of a woman whom he had recently met at Arras, perhaps on his way from Bruges to Paris. For days at a time, she would not eat and then would stuff herself. She could not explain why she acted as she did, except to say that "she was unworthy to eat food" (44). The woman admitted that she took no advice from her confessor or anyone else. In fact she had not been to confession for more than six months:

> I admit that I was filled with fear and horror. Hiding my true feelings, I nevertheless began to point out that these are the traps of the demon, and that she was dangerously close to insanity. She had a frantic look on her face and her color was like that of someone close to death. [. . .]
>
> I continued in my questioning. If she really felt this way about herself, how could she maintain a form of abstinence without the advice of someone else and do something so unusual and not regulated by others, who were holier and stronger than she was? She began to make up some vague answers, which I cannot remember.[22]

The woman needed advice. Gerson saw her bulimic behavior as a danger sign. He criticized her for what he called "singularity," lack of discretion, and arrogance.

But he also implied that she was mentally ill and needed help, something she refused to admit.

Gerson saw the woman of Arras as symptomatic in an age when people refused to listen to others. He even concluded that "the accumulation of the greatest evils that we now experience and suffer from in the Schism is the result of this disease of indiscretion, by which no one will let anyone else give advice."[23]

The immediate audience of these warnings, besides his students, was Gerson's brother and his fellow Celestines. "Excessive abstinence" was even more dangerous than "drunken overeating" because the former can cause "brain damage and mental disorder" (44). Gerson recalled that Saint Benedict, famed for living in his youth in solitude, warned monks against such a practice (45). Only those who have been tried and tested on the path of asceticism should go to its extremes. Otherwise the results might be disastrous, both physically and spiritually.

Besides discretion, the person who believes to have received a revelation must show charity. Gerson warned against mistaking other forms of love for charity: "It is not safe for holy women to live together and enjoy familiarity with even the most religious of men."[24] He excoriated the Beguines and Beghards for "their excessive love that was disguised as devotion" and referred to a Marie of Valenciennes with her teaching on love. This was probably Marguerite Porete who was burned as a heretic in 1310.[25]

Here Gerson explained how he had confused spiritual with physical love, when he became close to a nun: "Love slowly grew, but not wholly in the Lord, until the man could scarcely be separated from the woman, if she went away, without trying to visit her or thinking constantly about her."[26] When he was apart from the woman for a longer period, he realized what was happening: "Then the man felt for the first time that this love was not pure and completely sincere and chaste. He realized he would have been heading for great evil unless God in his goodness had averted it. All passionate feeling (*omnis . . . vehementia*) is a most dangerous companion for virtue, whether it comes from love, zeal, correction of behavior, or similar matters."[27]

Whether in seeking the love of another person or that of God himself, we have to restrain ourselves. Gerson imagined his listener or reader seeking the vision of God. For every instance when it may come, there are many more manifestations that are false, hypocritical, or tragic, as in the case of mental illness. One has to be critical and yet also believe that God chooses some people to speak with his voice, whether they are educated or not. But in order to avoid misunderstandings and scandal, an educated clergy has to show discernment.

In commenting on Mark 1:5–6, concerning how the crowds came out from Jerusalem to see John, Gerson said he was speaking "outside of the ordinary lessons" and was doing so "not so much in a university lecture as by way of intimate conversation" (*neque tam magistrali locutione quam collocutione familiari*;

Gl 3.57). This he sought through "an everyday manner of talking" (*quotidiano loquendi more*) thus transforming scholastic discourse. Without abandoning the traditional apparatus of authorities and proofs, he insisted on teaching in plain speech and inviting dialogue.

The rhetoric of Gerson's theology was easily understandable. He criticized the dry logical terms he thought had come to France from England: "The theologians of our time are called verbose sophists . . . [who] abandon what is useful and understandable . . . and give themselves over to naked logic or metaphysics or even mathematics" (62). The result was confused and obscure language. Instead of profiting the faith through edification, such terminology made listeners laugh and ridicule its silliness.

Gerson contrasted the theology of his time with John the Baptist's message. He had made himself understandable, without seeking popularity. A preacher such as Jean de Varennes, whom Gerson considered to be a demagogue, was no John the Baptist. If the priest of Reims had combined knowledge with humble discretion, he would have done much good (62).

Gerson's teaching in theology during these extra afternoon lessons was more a form of preaching than traditional exposition and biblical exegesis. From the end of 1401 there were two more commentaries on the first chapter of Mark. One of them concerned what the Baptist ate and was a point of departure for a treatise defending Carthusian monks' refusal to eat meat.[28] The other compared the contemplative and the active life, a favorite theme now expanded with reflections on the Church's situation (63–77).

The solitary or contemplative life is not limited to prayer but can include preaching and ministration of the sacraments (71). The contemplative life is superior to the active one, but within the Church, a mixed life may be necessary. It may even be a sin to fail to help others, and so a person at times has to give up the contemplative life (73).

There follows a discussion on the Church's use of its endowed goods. Here Gerson deals with the so-called Donation of Constantine, the "gift" of Rome and its surroundings to the Holy See by the Emperor Constantine before he moved his capital.[29] In Gerson's day the historical basis for the Donation had not yet been challenged,[30] but he believed it would have been better to have abandoned such a privilege (75). The Church had concentrated too much on increasing its temporal goods and jurisdictions: "No small cause of its destruction (*suae desolationis*), both in spiritual and in temporal matters" (76).

Gerson decried churchmen caught up in feasting and hunting, in promotions of the unworthy, "in seeking high office and benefices," in base forms of pleasure, and much else. Such abuses would end if churchmen lived in "moderate poverty." He contrasted the wealthy prelates of his own day with John in the desert but did not agree with Jean de Varennes that the Church had to be transformed. His *paupertas modesta* recalls the "modest use" (*usus moderatus*) adopted by most Franciscans, allowing for possessions without exorbitant accumulation.[31]

The Church needed a material basis without making wealth the goal of its existence. Having asked his students to be critical of the Church, Gerson turned to the lives and attitudes of the students themselves. In the autumn of 1402 his *Against the Curiosity of Scholars* warned that they were not to waste their time by delving into useless matters.[32] This time the key passage was: *Poenitemini et credite evangelio* (Repent and believe in the Gospel, Mk 1:15).

First he considered the meaning of penance John preached (Gl 3.226–28). He made use of the Fourth Book of Peter Lombard's *Sentences* and thus criticized his colleagues for their almost exclusive concentration on speculations about the nature of the Trinity in the First Book.[33] He looked for a new theology of ethics, where the Lombard could provide inspiration.[34]

More than the *Sentences*, however, Gerson upheld the Bible and especially the New Testament. He thus reminded theologians that their subject still was called *Sacra Scriptura*. From the need for penance, he turned to the danger of curiosity as a manifestation of the pride and self-sufficiency which make penance impossible (229–30). Curiosity went with *singularitas*, the study of exotic and unusual teachings (230). Philosophers had sought to go beyond the limits of natural reasoning. Adapting Anselm's concept of God as the being of which no greater can exist, Gerson said philosophers try to restrict God, subjecting his power to "rules of necessity" (231). Referring to propositions condemned in 1277, he said that the correct answer to the question of the world's eternity is that God follows his own will (232). Philosophers think that they can limit possibilities according to what they find around themselves in the world. But God can do anything, and so the philosopher as well as the theologian should admit his ignorance (233).[35]

Such considerations lead to specific criticisms of the Parisian intellectual milieu as in the rivalry among teachers: "If someone says, for example, of Duns Scotus or John of Ripa or another Franciscan doctor: 'This doctor has less good sense in this or that area,' then there appear, in accord with the variety of religious orders, different allegiances and tastes. Some people get angry and are eager to contradict" (239). Such empty competition leads to singularity and error. In the university milieu, teachers have to learn to avoid such rivalries. At the same time, they are obligated to keep disciplines separate from each other. Theologians have to learn not to be philosophers, and should refrain from adding logic, mathematics, and physics to their study.

Those who spend their time in attacking the teachings of others are subject to empty curiosity. It is better to create peace than strife (241). Yet, Gerson himself attacked the followers of Duns Scotus for their logical distinctions, which they applied even to the divinity. "All matters are not to be referred to logic alone." He could not reconcile the followers of Scotus with the simplicity of God, for they had "a thousand ways of imagining how to cut up, divide, constitute, cut to pieces" their metaphysical forms. This "crowd of terms" (*grandiorem terminorum congeriem*) was made to grow so that it filled a thousand manuscripts. A long life would not be sufficient for reading them all![36]

Gerson had no time for such foolishness. The introduction of new terms, especially by the Scotists and when dealing with the Trinity, had to be limited. "If you add a million terms to explain this secret of faith, you will know nothing more fully . . . than this one truth, which is explained by the fewest number of words" (244). He warned against introducing distinctions based on different essences into the godhead (246). Such a practice repeated Plato's mistake in "abstracting things" (*quidditates*) and making them into real existences outside the soul and God. Gerson's solution was that of Albert the Great and Thomas Aquinas, who spoke of God in terms of analogies that are not real distinctions but descriptions on the basis of comparisons from what we find in the world around us.[37]

Summarizing his case, Gerson warned: "Let any form of subtlety, however nuanced, be left behind." Such verbal entanglement was like a spider web (247). "Let us learn not so much to dispute as to live, remembering our end: *Discamus non tam disputare quam vivere, memores finis nostri.*" There is no greater virtue than clarity, and yet many consider the more difficult the mode of expression to be the more attractive. Such people are guilty of wasting time, instead of using it wisely (248).

Gerson saw here the construction of a new tower of Babel. To avoid this confusion of voices and academic languages, he preferred a single faculty of theology in all of Christendom, or at least in all of France (*tota Gallia*), for here was one pure source, *unicus et praecipuus studii theologiae fons incorruptus.* Its theologians were enjoined to keep discussions to themselves and not engage in them in the presence of members of other faculties (249).

Gerson's criticisms of the Paris milieu, and especially of the Scotists, show impatience with those seeking new ways of interpreting overused passages in Peter Lombard's *Sentences,* "in constructing a multiplication of readings beyond number." These were nothing but "tedious toil" (*taediosi laboris*) that created "more confusion than edification" (249). Instead of such futile scholastic exercises, Gerson asked for a hidden or mystical theology, obtained "more through penance than through human enquiry." He thus announced his next set of lectures.

Gerson was not a pure "nominalist" who followed William of Ockham in limiting abstract ideas to purely mental concepts. In attacking the Scotists, he showed sympathy for Ockham's cleanup of intellectual categories and skepticism concerning their use in dividing up the godhead. But he was also fond of the mild platonic "realism" he found in Saint Bonaventure, whose *Soul's Journey into God* was one of his favorite theological works. Here as in much else, Gerson was an impatient pragmatist, asking that intellectual analysis be made useful to Christian life.

Ultimately, he sought edification, a word that was, though reduced today to its moralizing dimension, understood by him in a wider, less pietistic sense. He did not seek easy solutions, but watched the clock and asked, "What is this leading to?" When the outcome seemed dubious or superfluous, he abandoned word games for the sake of practical results.

In moving into the subject of mystical theology itself, Gerson remained the pragmatist, for he composed both a speculative and a practical treatise. The first was based on lectures given in the autumn of 1402; the second probably came five years later.[38] Both treatments he later revised. At this point, it is sufficient to look briefly at the *Speculative Mystical Theology,* which Gerson introduced in his prologue as the fulfillment of his promise to his students to show "whether it is better to have the knowledge of God through repentant affectivity" (*per poenitentem affectum*) rather than through an investigative intellect (*per intellectum investigantem;* Gl 3.250).

The answer was obvious. Mystical theology was built on the exhortation of John the Baptist to repent and believe in the Gospel. It requires contemplation, which comes at the peak of human mental activity. We start this process in cogitation, which can lead to meditation, but we seldom, if ever, reach contemplation. This requires not only that the mind be cleared of all distractions but also that the grace of God be poured into it.

Gerson had many sources of inspiration for the ascent to contemplation: the language of the Psalms and of the Wisdom literature, Saint Paul, and Pseudo-Dionysius. In all of these writings hidden knowledge of God is based on personal experiences, and their theology is "more perfect and more certain" precisely because what comes from experience is "known with more complete certitude" (253).

In order to attain such necessary experience, we must first believe. Gerson took as his point of departure Anselm of Canterbury's "I believe so that I may understand." He wanted his students to seek the experience of what they already believed on faith and to speak to each other "by learned reasoning" about the contents of their faith.[39] In doing so, they will be more careful in judging uneducated persons who claim similar experience: "Such people are to be admired for their affective lives when there is found nothing contrary either to faith or to good morals" (256).

As in *Against Curiosity,* Gerson shows his impatience with any abstractions that divide God into intellectual categories. "Otherwise the object will be separated from itself in terms of a real distinction" (257). Immediately afterwards, however, he drops the discussion, which he categorizes as "not very useful," something to be dealt with by masters in arts or logicians, not by theologians.[40]

Contemplation is not easy to attain. It is difficult enough to concentrate on one train of thought, as is obvious for "anyone who tries to study" (268). If we succeed, however, cogitation's free flow is replaced by meditation. Far beyond is contemplation, characterized by a state of rest, fulfillment, and stability (288). While meditation moves from one object of concentration to another, contemplation stays fixed on its goal of divine love: "To explain these matters, an endless succession of words could be added, but for those with experience, these few mentions are sufficient. For those who lack experience or are untrained or who put their effort into using human assistance to raise up the mind to a state of loving, no words will ever be enough for them to fully understand this process" (289). By characterizing mystical theology in this way, Gerson accepted its nonverbal content. Whether drawing on written sources or on his own experience in prayer, he found that words failed him.

For the requirements of an examined life, however, Gerson had many words. He used what he thought was Saint Bernard (actually William of Saint Thierry) to point out that speculative theology is incomplete without mystical theology, while the latter can exist without the former. No one can understand the meaning of Paul's words or those of the prophetical literature of the Old Testament, "however much these are bandied about in a superficial way, if he does not take on the affectivity (*affectum*) of their authors."[41] Theology as *Sacra Scriptura* had to be more than pure analysis of words and concepts. Ultimately not only experience was required to understand them. Love had to be present, "for love itself is knowledge" (*amor ipse notitia est*).[42]

Gerson here uses a saying by Gregory the Great, one of the most challenging assertions in all patristic literature. Time and again in his writings, Gerson returned to Gregory and especially his *Forty Gospel Sermons.*[43] In the *Speculative Mystical Theology* he turned to Saint Anthony in the desert and Paul in his epistles. From the first he took a description of prayer.[44] In Paul he found a desire to attain "that which surpasses all understanding" (Gl 3.290–91; cf. Ph 4:7). "The school of prayer" is the way to mystical theology, while "the school of learning" has to take second place: "The school of religion, which seeks affectivity (*pro affectu*), excels the school of erudition, which seeks understanding (*pro intellectu*)" (291).

Turning to Hugh of Saint Victor and William of Auvergne (291), Gerson outlines a development of the mystical tradition from the Old Testament and the Gospels to the affective theology of twelfth- and early thirteenth-century Paris. He does not reject the speculative theology in which he had been nurtured, but argues that the intellectual life "without love or affection . . . is now arid, now restless, curious, ungrateful or puffed up."[45]

Gerson did not consider this process leading to union with God to be easy or common. It is a challenge for everyone, and there are many pitfalls. One is the ambition to merge totally with God, even to annihilate one's own existence. In a letter he also wrote in 1402, Gerson dealt further with this phenomenon.

Addressing a Carthusian brother, he responded to *The Spiritual Espousals* of John Ruusbroec (1293–1381). Although most of this work was acceptable, he did find fault with the third book: "The author imagines . . . that the soul . . . ceases to be in the existence it formerly had in its own genus, and it is converted or transformed and absorbed into the divine being" (Gl 2.57). Gerson warned against imagining any such disintegration of individual human identity.

In both letter and treatise Gerson, on the one hand, encourages everyone to seek affective knowledge of God; yet, on the other, he worries that people might misunderstand what happens to them. He was concerned about those whose "insufficient instruction" made them liable to "fall into the most dangerous errors" (62). Such was his view of Ruusbroec, an interpretation that some scholars today would challenge.[46] Just as much as Gerson seemed to offer the possibility of experiencing divine love, he feared the process.

Gerson was looking for a way to describe how the individual can reach out for God without entering into false pride, ascetic fanaticism, or sentimental affectivity. In April 1402, he wrote to his brother Nicolas and his Celestine superior. The chancellor recommended what he found in one of Bernard of Clairvaux's *Sermons on the Song of Songs:* a description of how a penitent soul moves from contrition to solitude and finally to perseverance.[47] He thanked God that he had seen this development and had outlined it already in his *Mountain of Contemplation,* even though "someone might accuse me of rashness for overstepping my territory in treating this material, which is most profound and hidden" (54).

Probably that same summer, on 20 August, the Feast of Saint Bernard, Gerson spoke to the Cistercians about mystical theology as experienced in the life of their patron.[48] Showing an excellent grasp of the hagiographical sources, Gerson portrayed Bernard in terms of his growth from contrition to solitude and perseverance. What might have been a conventional summary of a saint's life took on topical relevance when Gerson decried the existence of teachers in Paris who, instead of leading their pupils to understanding, tried to have sex with them. His message gained in immediacy as he took on the *persona* of his subject, speaking as if his was Bernard's own voice: "I warn you, good youth, and I repeat the point again and again in warning you: beware of the company of evil youths or of men of ill repute. You know how the worst conversations corrupt good habits, and so all the more do touching and actions. Oh, what habits! What crimes! No, I mean what deaths! Oh, most heinous of crimes, for that association is to be feared in the worst form of contagion."[49]

These words underline the sermon's central message: the inner life of the soul is enriched through separation from other people. Contrition and asceticism are not enough. Distance from others, which he found in Bernard, was essential. He ignored sources indicating the presence of friends and companions in Bernard's life.

The path to mystical experience seemed to exclude closeness to others. And yet, Gerson was seeking out his brother Nicolas by trying to instruct him in the mystical life. Hungry for affective bonds and afraid of them, Gerson turned to Nicolas, to his sisters, and to his students, while keeping, at the same time, a careful distance.

Preaching Repentance

Gerson's role as preacher has been divided into three periods: the court preacher (1389–1397), the popular preacher (1401–1404), and the preacher on grand occasions, *des grandes circonstances* (1404–1413).[50] During this middle period Gerson gave sermons in various Parisian churches and made use of passages on penance from the first chapter of Mark that also inspired his university lectures.

Probably on 25 August 1401, the Feast of Saint Louis, Gerson gave the day's sermon at his own College of Navarre, in honor of the great king and saint whom he regarded as the ideal monarch. The theme was Christ's words: "Consider the lilies of the field, how they grow" (Mt 6:28).[51] Louis is presented as a model for scholars and teachers because with little formal learning he reached the stage of *consideratio,* the ability to weigh and measure spiritual values, to integrate them in his actions, and thus to live by them (Gl 5.152).

The ruler who lives according to this standard "alone considers the condition of the whole republic and alone . . . places before the mind's eye his own self and the care of all that needs to be done" (153). Such rulers are necessary not only in civil society but also in the Church, whose situation Gerson called "our disaster" (*calamitate nostra;* 154). The kingdom of France had been "placed as a garden and field," brilliant in its beauty, fertile with its lilies and inhabitants. The river irrigating this rich garden was the University of Paris, divided into four streams, its faculties. Their waters reached beyond France, for by them "the entire earth is watered."[52]

Continuing with the image of cultivation, Gerson likens the saint-king to a farmer, who had taken good care of his field of France (157–58). Finally he turns directly to his listeners, first the young students (*adolescentes*), by warning them against laziness and sensuality (160). He reminds their teachers of the great responsibility they assumed in caring for their pupils' welfare: "Youths flow now more than ever from the whole kingdom of France to the flower-filled garden of the University of Paris" (161). It was not enough to teach them grammar. Gerson condemns (*O mores, o tempora*) the corruption of the minds and bodies "of certain adolescents": "There lurks among them a terrible contagion, and no one considers it, no one stops it" (*serpunt inter eos nefanda contagione, nemine considerante, nemine prohibente*). This is the same language Gerson used with Cistercian scholars.

The "healing hand" of the confessor was the only way to extricate the evil serpent coiled within the sinful youth. His warning was most likely directed against same-sex relations among students or among students and teachers. He called the latter "not instructors but destroyers" (*non instructores sed destructores*; 162) and reminded his listeners of the mother of Saint Louis, who told her son she would rather he died than commit a mortal sin. Gerson's concern, however, was not limited to what we today call homosexuality. For the first time he alluded to the teaching of the *Romance of the Rose*, against which the following spring he would write an outright attack (163).

Sexual behavior was not his only theme, however. He asked teachers to be kind to their students, to answer their questions, to avoid harshness in correcting them. For Gerson the spoken word (*viva . . . vox*) was the basis for all learning. Close contact between teacher and pupil makes a profound difference: "It can hardly be said how eagerly we imitate those we like" (163). Gerson asks that in both the Rue du Fouarre (Street of Straw), where liberal arts teachers had been lecturing for centuries, and in "houses," presumably the many college residences of the university, "salvific and joyful things" be told "instead of the usual jokes and stories." He praised one master, Renaud Gobart, who "told me that he had never or scarcely ever read . . . a lesson with his disciples without adding a word of salvation."[53]

Turning from adolescent pupils to young masters, Gerson warns against avarice (164–65). Finally, he reminds the mature men that they had reached the height of consideration and should remember that they could attain contemplation, in following Paul's saying: "Our way of life is in heaven" (Phil 3:20), a phrase that was to become Gerson's personal maxim (165).

At the end of the sermon Gerson returns once more to Saint Louis, a man who had reached the height of consideration and contemplation. The text adds, in good academic form, a list of spiritual masters who had written on the subject of consideration: Dionysius, Augustine, Gregory, "and the more recent" Bernard, Hugh and Richard of Saint-Victor, "and after them" Bonaventure (167). From Gerson's vantage point the view back over the centuries is breathtaking. Here, as in his French sermons, Gerson was attentive to the background of his audience. At the College of Navarre he could speak on the basis of a long tradition of teaching and meditation on the Christian faith, while in parish churches he concentrated on the texts of the Gospels themselves to make it possible for his audiences to visualize scenes from Christ's life and dwell on their meaning.

In a series of sermons grouped under the general theme of repentance, *Poenitemini*, preached from Advent of 1402 through Lent of 1403, Gerson set forth detailed recommendations for the daily life of Parisian citizens. All around him he saw the seven capital sins, from gluttony and lust to avarice, sloth, anger, envy, and pride being committed, prompting him to ask for change.[54] Five of the twelve sermons—of which several contain both the morning address and the afternoon collation—concern lust or its opposite, chastity. The first was preached on the Right Bank, at the parish church of Saint-Germain l'Auxerrois on 10 December 1402, the Second Sunday of Advent. The day's gospel reading describes the second coming of Christ (Luke 21:25–33). After translating the Gospel into French—his regular practice in these sermons—Gerson added a brief commentary (*notes literales;* Gl 7.2.813). It is no good, he said, for people to believe that they can follow the impulses of lust in youth and then later amend their ways (816). In a rare description of the terrors of hell, Gerson alluded to what was in store for those who did not repent.

The bulk of this sermon enumerates some of the "daughters of lust." The first is fornication. Here Gerson followed a practice that characterizes his future sermons: he anticipates various questions of a type his listeners might pose. Can someone who lives in concubinage repent without physically removing his companion (*sans bouter hors sa compaignie;* 818)? Yes, this should be done as soon as possible, but on the advice "of his wise priest or confessor." What is worse, to go from one person to another or to stick to one companion in concubinage? "I say that in evil there is nothing good, and according to different cases the one . . . is worse than the other." Should one give absolution or communion at Easter to someone living in this state who refuses to leave it? No, if the case is notorious in the parish; but yes, if the matter is a secret known to the priest alone.

Concerning the second daughter of lust, adultery, Gerson states that in one sense the married man sins more than the married woman, for "he should show more virtue in resisting," while the woman sins more because her behavior endangers the legitimacy of the family line (819). What about having intercourse purely for pleasure? This is not mortal sin if it is not sought outside of marriage. A man is allowed to know his pregnant wife without sin, so long as he does not injure the fetus. Here, however, Gerson avoids going into detail: "I am silent for the present and in public" (819).

The sermon's information concerning marital relations provides insight into sexual practices in Gerson's time, or at least his perception of such behavior.[55] In individual cases, he shows some flexibility. Usually, for example, a priest who has had "carnal company" cannot celebrate mass the next day. But there may be situations when he has to go ahead, as at Easter when his parishioners are obligated to hear mass (820).

Why did Gerson include questions concerning unchaste priests in a sermon for the laity? He may have wanted to show his audience that he required the same standards from the clergy as from others. Gerson's posthumous title of "consoling doctor" seems appropriate in view of the moral advice he gave in such sermons.[56] His third *Poenitemini* sermon, from 17 December 1402, asks whether every carnal thought is a sin. Gerson distinguished between what happens when a thought first comes into the mind and various stages of consent (826–27). What he describes is not new in moral theology, but as with his *Mountain of Contemplation,* he enriched theological discourse by using the vernacular.

With contemplation as with sexual behavior, Gerson addressed good women. Thus a woman who knows her confessor is in love with her does not have to confess her carnal thoughts to him. Instead, she should ask the priest for leave to confess elsewhere. If he refuses, she should nevertheless go to another confessor (828).

Gerson's recommendations sometimes indicate he was describing what he himself had experienced. Thus he cited a long list of what a person can do to avoid succumbing to sexual temptation: he can spit, injure himself, talk to himself, immerse himself in cold water, get quickly out of bed, think of hellfire or temporal fire (829). Gerson transferred into the world of lay Christians some of the counsel that long had circulated in monastic circles, as in the *Vitae patrum,* the Sayings of the Desert Fathers. The same standard applied to everyone. Good advice from monastic sources was welcome for laypersons.[57]

Just as Benedict's *Rule* encourages the monk to look down and not directly into his brother's face, Gerson exhorts his audience to follow the same practice: "I know someone who hundreds of times keeps from looking at others."[58] He may again have been applying the Pauline "I know a man" expression in order to draw on his own experience.

On many moral questions, Gerson did not give clear-cut answers but anticipated what used to be called "situation ethics." Dealing with nakedness, he said it is not necessarily a sin to look at oneself in the nude (829). It depends on one's purpose and intention. The same is the case with viewing nudity or sexual acts in animals, paintings, or elsewhere. As for books that incite to lust, those who have them should be forced by their confessors to burn them or tear them up. Gerson mentions both Ovid and "parts" of the *Romance of the Rose.*

He asked whether one should be naked in the bath with children and discouraged his listeners from doing so when their offspring were more than two years old. "Even though those of four or six years do not think anything bad of it, nevertheless after they come of age, the recollection comes to them and tempts them grievously."[59] Was Gerson recalling his own childhood or something he had heard in confession? There is much here that shows a fear of sexual awakening in adolescence. He recommended that children sleep in separate beds, or at least the custom he knew from Flanders where brothers shared beds with brothers and sisters with sisters (831).

In the next *Poenitemini* sermon, in which he lashed out against the *Romance of the Rose,* Gerson added a section that showed continuing concern with children. One should not kiss or hold, especially in a private place, naked children (838). A child likewise should refuse to be embraced or kissed by an adult. If it happens, then the child should confess the matter. In the previous sermon, Gerson had asked if kisses are always sinful. No, he could imagine some that are "honest," such as the kiss of peace in church or those given "in public and according to custom of the country, and because of friendship or family, without contemplating something evil" (830).

The general principle for Gerson was that each person had to examine his own conscience to determine right or wrong: *Je renvoye chascune personne a sa conscience.* A seemingly innocent kiss can be a person's undoing, as when Dido kissed the son of Aeneas, Ascanius, and thus conceived what Gerson considered to be her wrongful love for Aeneas. "Lust has no faith or loyalty, reason or law." Every form of spiritual love easily turns into a carnal one: *l'amour espirituelle de legier glice en la charnelle* (830).

It would be all too easy to conclude that Gerson was obsessed with sex and control of its expression. As so often, however, there is more than restrictive authority in Gerson. He could show a gentler side, as in a sermon on chastity in marriage, from 7 January 1403 (857–61). He took his point of departure from the day's Gospel, which told how the twelve-year old Jesus disappeared for three days when he went up to Jerusalem with his parents (Luke 2:41–51). After imagining Mary's pain at the prospect of losing her son, Gerson praised her marriage. Here begins a series of questions about marital behavior. Can a woman, without first getting her husband's consent, vow that she will not have intercourse or that she will attend church or be abstinent? She can decide never to ask for intercourse, but she cannot free herself from fulfilling her marital duty when the husband asks for it (861). As for abstinence, a woman is not to fast so much that she makes herself weak and ugly. She can vow to go to mass on Sundays, but on other days her husband can forbid her to do so, because of household needs: *selond la necessite du mesnage.*

As for pilgrimages, a woman is not to go to distant places. If the pilgrimage site is close by, the wife should still beware of the company she keeps on her journey and get her husband's consent. In general the woman has to make sure that her husband has no reason for jealousy. The same also goes for the husband. There is no double standard here.

More such questions followed in the afternoon collation (862–68). If a woman says she does not feel well, should her husband refrain from asking for intercourse (*non demander sa compaignie*; 863)? Yes, if the husband believes his wife is telling the truth. But what if he wants sexual relations and it is a feast day and the woman has received communion that same day? "I say that she is to obey her husband." It would be better, however, if both husband and wife took communion and agreed to abstain from sex that day.

As for the upbringing of children, Gerson recommends gentleness and cites Anselm's teaching: "Note the example of Anselm that one does not benefit children by hitting them too much."[60] Our Lady when she found her lost son spoke gently (*doucement*) to him, and parents should imitate her. Mothers should concern themselves with the welfare of their children and protect them from "bad nurses, drunkards" whose sexual mores are questionable.

Gerson distrusted domestics. Elsewhere he claimed that they were often responsible for giving boys their first experience with the opposite sex.[61] He reminds his listeners of Bernard's mother, remembered in her own time and apparently also in the fifteenth century because she chose to nurse her own child instead of handing him over to someone else.[62]

Gerson used the expression *notez* to refer in a kind of shorthand to known cases or examples. When he wrote, for example, *notez de la mere saint Bernard,* he apparently left a reference for himself without the details. This method must have been a way of making sure that the sermon did not become too long: examples could be added if there was time.

There is an exceptional vernacular sermon whose length and detail provide a good indication of how Gerson preached and even of the impact he is likely to have had on his listeners. This is the *Ad Deum vadit* (To God He Goes) from Good Friday, 13 April 1403. It ends the *Poenitemini* series and, with its collation, fills seventy pages in the Glorieux edition (449–519).

The opening section reveals Gerson's technique in visualizing the feelings and experiences of the participants in the drama of salvation. He imagines Mary's goodbye to her son when he left her to go to Jerusalem and face his accusers: "Adieu, my lovely son, my only joy, my only solace" (*Adieu beau filz . . . ma seule joye, mon seul confort*; 450). These words Mary spoke "perhaps in silence," in the midst of sobs, "because sorrow kept her from speaking" while she held her son: "You embrace him tenderly and put your face on his shoulders or on his chaste countenance."

Gerson's portrayal of Mary, as if he had witnessed the scene, represents a central element in late medieval spirituality. The individual Christian expressed devotion through empathy or even total identification with Jesus and the saints, especially in relating to Christ's Passion.[63] In the latter part of this first long passage of the sermon, Gerson, rather than speaking to Mary, takes on her own voice. She calls on her son and tells him he could escape the death that awaited him. But then she accepts what he is about to do and assures him she will be with him: "I cannot leave you; everywhere you will go I shall be, and to all your dangers I will abandon myself" (450).

Gerson's dramatization goes beyond the biblical text itself. His visualization of the mother's concern for her son does not sentimentalize the events of the Passion. In a stream-of-consciousness approach through which he imagines the feelings of the participants, he concentrates on Mary but also addresses Mary Magdalene, Martha, Judas, and Jesus himself.

Gerson structured the sermon and collation around narratives that combine everything the four gospels say about the Passion of Christ. He divided the narrative into twenty scenes, perhaps inspired by the relatively new practice of following the Stations of the Cross.[64] Gerson asks Mary where she was when her son was in the Garden of Gethsemane. Just as an angel came to comfort Christ, so too, he reasons, an angel must have come to comfort her. The scene ends with a prayer to Jesus as "our final hope and sole comfort" (460).

Later on, Gerson imagines how Mary must have felt to be kept outside while she could hear the sounds of her son being whipped. In a made-up conversation of Mary with John the Apostle and Mary Magdalene (469), he answers, presuming his audience wanted to know where Mary was when Jesus was taken away. Since there is no clear statement in Scripture, he uses *de conjectures* "without any presumptuous statements but in order to move to religious devotion."[65]

No heart is so hard that it cannot be moved by this death, Gerson proclaims (513). One would like to know the reaction of the members of the congregation during this sermon. In a letter dated sometime between 1397 and 1403, the distinguished humanist and secretary at the royal court, Jean de Montreuil, wrote that if Gerson were to give a sermon at Reims on the Passion of Christ, he would hurry there and prefer Gerson to any other preacher. He had a talent "to move his listeners."[66]

Gerson's Good Friday sermon, as well as many of his earlier *Poenitemini* sermons, is a reminder that, ever since the end of the twelfth century, sermons in the vernacular were becoming standard fare, at least in town churches, not only on feast days but also on Sundays. In the thirteenth century, the friars had emerged to preach sermons in opposing heretics. Now Gerson wanted secular clerics trained in theology to give sermons just as grounded in affective theology as the best Franciscan presentations.[67]

Whether sermons—or more modest homilies—were preached in all parish churches is an open question. For Gerson, however, there was no doubt that pastors had a duty to preach.[68] His dedication to affective interpretation of the Gospel text could have inspired not only lay listeners but also many of his students.

Seeking to End the Schism

Jean de Montreuil reappears in a letter from 1400 in which he claimed that the two finest preachers in Paris were Gerson and his colleague at the faculty of theology, Jean Courtecuisse.[69] Two years later, on 15 April 1402, Courtecuisse used his preaching abilities to call for a general council made up of members of the Avignon obedience to judge Pope Benedict XIII on charges of heresy and perjury.[70] Gerson now dropped his longstanding hesitation about involving himself openly in the Schism and began to write down his views on what was to be done.

Already in February of that same year, representatives from the university at Orleans stated at the royal court that they had never consented to the withdrawal of obedience and so asked for its restitution.[71] The king's brother, Louis of Orleans, was doing his best to represent the interests of Pope Benedict at court, in opposition to the duke of Burgundy. Gerson had long been caught in the middle: his chancellorship came from Benedict; his Bruges office from the duke of Burgundy. By now Benedict's sincerity for compromise with his Roman rival seemed minimal.

In the first indication of his direct involvement (April or May 1402), Gerson insisted he was seeking the unity of the Church and would do so "in following the counsel of the king and kingdom [but] according to my ability and my vocation."[72] However, he did not question the withdrawal of obedience. But to those who wanted to declare Benedict a schismatic or heretic, Gerson issued the warning that such a step might have a catastrophic effect: "The present Schism would be worsened beyond repair, like the Schism of the Greeks and Latins, a most cruel and pernicious division would arise in this kingdom" (Gl 6.35).

In reply to those who would accuse the University of Paris of having planned such a course of action against the Avignon pope, Gerson insisted that he had never been present at any university discussions of the matter. During the last year or two (in the period since his return to Paris), said Gerson, he had done his best to avoid discussing the matter (*totum dimittitur indiscussum*).

He did not deny that such deliberations previously had taken place at the university and even at the faculty of theology. But he had kept away from them. In a statement entitled *Replicationes*, he replied to Courtecuisse and his allies concerning what they considered to be Benedict XIII's criminal behavior. The Avignon pope had the right to decide for himself whether he would relinquish the office (39). No pre-election oath bound him, as his opponents claimed. Whatever accusations might be brought against him concerned only his actions once he became pope. Even if his opponents' allegations were true, they were insufficient to convict him of being a schismatic (40–41).

So long as Benedict showed willingness to be corrected, his insistence on remaining in office could not be considered "pertinacious" (*pertinax*), a key word in the debate. Only someone who refused advice and correction could be legally deposed. Gerson saw Benedict as having been led astray by bad advice. He believed some understanding could be reached without Benedict's removal from office by force.

Another tract from this period, *On the Schism*, lays out more arguments for delaying drastic action (42–51). "A legal hearing (*discussio juridica*) has to be held before a competent judge and with the party being heard" (44). The only competent judge of a pope was a general council of the Church, but such a council could not be convoked without papal authority (45). If such a council were called, the

Church would risk even more confusion than was already the case. It was no good saying that God would not permit such a council to err, for this guarantee covered only matters of faith, not of fact (47). Benedict's possibly schismatic status belonged to the latter category.

Gerson also warned that the accusations would not come from one side alone. The pope and his allies would accuse cardinals who had abandoned him of rebellion, and he would be able to declare heretical some of the writings against him. "And perhaps many will be accused of many crimes both in faith and in morals, crimes that ought to be punished by death and where the perpetrators deserve according to laws and decretals to be disinherited for themselves and their descendants. And so it is easy to say that a horrid cleavage would come about" (*horrenda scissura fieret*; 47). In the rest of this work, Gerson presents one potential disaster scenario after another, as in the case that the proposed council might be split. Then the faithful would not feel obligated to follow its decision. It would become a laughing stock, a development that would endanger all future councils. One new schism would lead to another, "and we will be ridiculed and defamed . . . forever, as a tale and a joke" (*in fabulam quoque et derisum*; 49).

Just as the young Gerson had worried that his parents might become the butt of local jokes if their son, because of lack of money, had to return without finishing his degree (ch. 2), he now fretted that the authority of the Church, and especially of its theologians, would be held up to contempt. "And so we expose ourselves to such dangers if we seek a council" (49).

Another scenario in which the Church was divided by a failed attempt to end the Schism involved "civil division" in France. In a prophetic statement anticipating the events of coming centuries, Gerson warned that the princes of the realm would use "the appearance of religion" to attack each other. He feared that such a pretext would be all the more attractive to the many in France who had never themselves consented to withdrawal of obedience. The only solution was that the matter be discussed by the princes of the blood together with "some experts" (*cum quibusdam peritis*), presumably theologians (50).

Through such control, Gerson hoped to avoid any public debate that might lead to anarchy. Otherwise, the entire kingdom would be left as prey to "those who lie in wait" (*insidiatores*) and who are "more than ready to plunder and devastate" (51). Gerson foresaw the possibility of an English invasion.[73]

Another attack on the Courtecuisse approach is Gerson's *On the Council of One Obedience* (51–58). Here he lists six reasons why such a council should not be held. Any open debate about the divisions already present in the Avignon observance would only cause further splits. It would be impossible to decide who had the right to preside at such a council since there was no precedent for making decisions in such a forum (51).

Gerson adds historical reflections that indicate he was beginning to review the basis of papal and ecclesiastical power. In a sketch of the history of the Church's acquisition of temporalities, especially from the time of Constantine, he decries the abuses after the Church was given benefices and began to administer them. Perhaps it would be best, he suggests, to return to the pristine state of poverty, or at least to the intermediate situation, when each prelate had his own jurisdiction. This would mean that the pope would not be able to reserve offices or to levy huge taxes "to sustain the condition of the curia," which, in Gerson's view, had grown out of all proportion.[74]

These developments meant a need for a reformation of the entire Church: *reformationem universalem ecclesiae* (55). Such a change, however, could not take place in a council of only one obedience. The pope should give up any claim to jurisdiction over the temporal affairs of individual dioceses while, at the same time, retaining his universal authority over matters spiritual. The pope's position would only be enhanced if his office were not involved in secular administration: "Was not Christ the most perfect pope; was not similarly Peter?" (55).

Gerson conceded that the office of pope had evolved and that he now was charged with administering all spiritual things. This task, however, had to do with matters of faith and not "with human traditions in ruling the temporalities of the Church" (56).

Amid the uncertainties of the Schism, Gerson was beginning to express ideas that in the coming years would galvanize the reform party and contribute to a conciliar movement whose repercussions are still present in the Roman Catholic Church.[75] For the time being, Gerson's mission was to inveigh against a special council before allegiance to the Avignon pope was restored. He was, however, beginning to think again about possible solutions if a council were held.

If both popes refused to obey such a council, they would be openly schismatic and could be deposed. Afterwards a new election could be held (57). This procedure was to be tried at the Council of Pisa in 1409. Its weakness lay in the possibility that both popes could refuse to follow the council's decision, thus leaving the Church with three popes instead of two.

In seeking to end the Schism, just as with questions of ethics, Gerson was a pragmatist, looking for a middle way between rigorism and indifference. In 1402 his concern was to restore allegiance to Avignon. He told his colleagues to stop discussing how they had gotten into such a mess and who was responsible for it (Gl 5.60). Only a fresh start would enable them to tackle present questions, leaving aside past offenses.

Gerson knew that many of his colleagues did not trust Benedict, who in the past had failed to keep apparent promises. It was necessary to leave options open and give Benedict the benefit of the doubt. To show his own reservations, Gerson recommended only a partial restoration of obedience. The pope was not to punish the cardinals who had abandoned him. The benefices and annates and other incomes the pope had lost during this period were not to be restored to him. The crimes of which the pope had been accused were, for the time being, not to be discussed. Such a reconciliation would provide a more amicable settlement than one that tried to establish who had acted rightly or wrongly (61).

Such steps were in Gerson's mind a prelude to a general council. If the other side refused to compromise and have such a council, then at least those in the Avignon obedience had a clear conscience about the matter: "We have delivered our soul from the Schism" (61).

Gerson expanded several of these points in a work Glorieux entitled *On the Restitution of Obedience* but which may well be part of the former treatise. Even if Benedict did act wrongly, it was essential to put up with him in the interest of the greater good of the Church (63). Gerson wanted to believe in Benedict's good intentions, and would not discuss the past, such as the circumstances under which Benedict was elected pope and any oath he might have taken. Furthermore, the sacraments administered during the withdrawal of obedience were valid. Whoever questioned them had to concede that it was impossible for the time being to know who was in the right (64).

Beyond his pragmatism, Gerson was willing to consider larger issues. Papal office exists not for the exaltation of an individual but for the good of the Church. Therefore the functions of the papacy can be altered according to the Church's needs. The pope's temporal functions could hardly be considered as having been instituted by Christ. Reason demanded that the pope and cardinals had sufficient incomes, but they still had to respect the rights and prerogatives of bishops (64).

Gerson was moving toward an institution where the bishops to a large extent administered their own affairs, while the pope's leadership would be limited to spiritual matters. In this process he recommended discussion as opposed to mutual recriminations and excommunications. In what looks like a memorandum to Pierre d'Ailly, Gerson states that the chancellor and the faculty of theology dealt only with questions of faith. Since allegiance to the pope did not belong to this category, "the chancellor cannot rationally, according to his office, usurp this matter as one to be treated in his faculty."[76] Gerson repeated his earlier statement that the secular power had to be involved in these deliberations, as well as the bishops. It was their task to reach an agreement. The faculty of theology could only give good advice (68–69).

Gerson had some success in convincing his colleagues at the university to follow this middle way. Once again Jean de Montreuil is our informant. Apparently after Jean Courtecuisse's fiery speech on 15 April 1402, Gerson managed by his arguments to dissuade thirty-three of forty-four theological doctors from following Nicolas's attempt to have Benedict declared a heretic and schismatic (Gl 10.472–73). In March 1403, Benedict, probably with the help of the duke of Orleans, escaped from Avignon.[77] A month later his brother Charles VI gave an audience to representatives of the university at Toulouse, who demanded the restoration of obedience to Benedict.

On 28 May 1403, the duke of Orleans assembled the bishops of France at the royal residence of Saint Paul in Paris. According to the *Chronicle of Saint Denis*, Louis won over the king to his arguments and then took the cross from the altar and asked the king to swear the restitution of obedience: "I return fully and entirely under the obedience of the Lord Pope Benedict, and I affirm by the holy cross of Our Lord that so long as I live I will show him an inviolable obedience as the true vicar of Jesus Christ on earth and have him restored to obedience in all the provinces of my kingdom."[78] On 30 May 1403, Pierre d'Ailly preached a solemn sermon at Notre Dame cathedral to mark the occasion. A few days later on 4 June, Gerson contributed to the general rejoicing by giving one of his most optimistic sermons. The theme *Send forth your spirit* (255–65) was taken from the Vulgate Psalm 103:30 (*Emitte spiritum tuum, et creabuntur; et renovabis faciem terrae*) which describes the Holy Spirit's renewal of the earth. Gerson celebrated the restitution of obedience "through which we as it were have been recreated" (256).

Gerson saw the restoration as bringing renewed unity to the "house of France," the new Jerusalem which John the Evangelist saw descending from heaven (261). Now there was hope for reformation of the universal Church, also in France (*pro spe reformationis in ecclesia tam universali quam particulari in Gallia;* 263). In order to make this transformation possible, Gerson once again asked that the bitterness and recriminations of the past be forgotten. "And so let the old give way and all things be new" (264).

Letting bygones be bygones was an attractive formula but not one that would be followed. "The union desired and sought by all," was still years away. But Gerson now had room to maneuver. In the face of the charge that he was Benedict's man, Gerson in 1402 and 1403 distanced himself from Avignon without abandoning Benedict completely.

Warning against Seduction

Gerson's writings during this time, after his return from Bruges, reflect a remarkable variety of concerns. The busiest year seems to have been 1402, when lectures on mystical theology, tracts on the restoration of obedience, and sermons on penance poured forth from his pen. In addition, he began, in May of 1402, a campaign against the *Romance of the Rose*, the French poem with its allegory of sexual conquest that apparently had become the vogue in humanist circles close to the court.[79] Here he was joined by Christine de Pizan, a courageous widow and professional writer.[80] Christine turned to Gerson for support and possibly for guidance. One historian even speaks of "an intellectual friendship" between her and the chancellor.[81]

Christine wrote against the *Romance* in the conviction that its blatant sexual message degraded women. Gerson opposed the poem because he found its content an incitement to sexual acts forbidden by the Church. Although their approaches were quite different, there was ultimately agreement between Christine and the chancellor though, as elsewhere in his life, Gerson kept his distance and did not seek a close friendship with a woman.

Instead of writing a learned treatise in Latin, Gerson composed an allegory in French as a kind of anti-allegory to the *Romance*.[82] He imagined that he awoke to find himself in the "Court of Christianity," where Justice sat on the throne, with Mercy on one side and Truth on the other. Other virtues were also present, and their purpose was to judge the Fool of Love, who had written the work. Chastity herself inveighs against this man's teaching. In eight articles, she summarized the message of the poem, which in her view encouraged sexual activity outside of marriage and ridiculed anyone who wanted to live a celibate life, whether cleric or widow. In the seventh article, for example, Chastity complains that the Fool of Love recommended a form of free love: "He promises paradise, glory, and praise to all the men and women who perform carnal acts even outside of marriage, for he counsels through his own person and his example that they try all types of women without distinction."[83]

It was impossible to prosecute the Fool himself, for he had long since died (Jean de Meung, the author of the bulk of the poem, was looked upon as the poem's Fool). However, several people appear at the allegorical court to defend his teaching. One admits that there was "evil" in the book, but "each should take the good and leave out the evil" (Gl 7.1.304). At this point Theological Eloquence intervenes. She apparently represents Gerson's view. Reviewing the contents of the poem, she shows that it violates Christian ethical standards and could "sow evil teachings in the hearts of people."[84]

Eloquence asserts that the poem conveys questionable matters in an indirect manner, not through the author directly, but via the Fool or through *La veille*, the old woman, who defends sinful behavior. Often it is difficult or impossible to perceive what the author himself means: "What grieves me the most is that everything here incites the flame of lust, even when he appears to be reproving it. Even those who are quite chaste, if they let themselves study, read, or listen to it, will be all the worse for it."[85] Gerson felt compelled to counter this dangerous message on every point, for Jean de Meung was a clever opponent who knew Christian as well as pagan literature on the subject. Thus Theological Eloquence has to correct the use the *Romance of the Rose* made of Alan of Lille's *On the Plaint of Nature*. This celebrated poem from about 1200 laments the popularity of male-male sexual bonds, which were supposed to be so common that the future of the human race was in danger. Thus Alan was construed as having encouraged heterosexual fornication in order to avoid same sex bonds. Eloquence could only reply, "It would be a ridiculous form of surgery to try to heal one wound by another or to extinguish one fire with another."[86]

Theological Eloquence, like Gerson in some of his sermons on penance, demands that the *Romance* be destroyed, as well as everything else with prurient content, whether written or pictorial. Human weakness was already too evident in this area to avoid our becoming "even more on fire and thrown into the depth of vices" (Gl 7.1.315).

At this point, Gerson says he awoke from his dream and found himself in his study. It was the hour of vespers on 18 May 1402, and he began to occupy himself with "less fickle matters" which could "occupy my heart": two sermons, one on the Trinity, another on the Eucharist. As ever, he had many projects and the completion of one meant it was time to turn to the next.

But the matter was not at rest in Gerson's mind. A few months later, probably in October, Gerson wrote to Pierre Col, an important court figure and successful canon at Notre Dame. Col represented the party that favored the *Romance* and saw no conflict between its message and that of acceptable moral behavior. He had written a now lost letter to Gerson, apparently praising him for his learning, but the recipient refused to be flattered.

Most of the response was taken up with a list of the *Romance's* errors, without any attempt to be allegorical or entertaining in form.[87] Gerson accused Pierre Col of sharing the heresy of Pelagius, the belief in the innate goodness of the human person. Besides having supposedly said that a child of two or three is in the state of innocence, Col also had claimed that only the lover can judge what is wrongful in human passion. To which Gerson retorted: "It is as if it is necessary that all who are to judge rightly and without corruption first must be corrupted by the same vices."[88]

One by one, Gerson went through Pierre Col's arguments in favor of Jean de Meung's teaching. Citing biblical practice, Col could claim that it was not problematic for Jean de Meung to write about female genitals. Gerson retorted that his correspondent must have been using a different Bible from his (Gl 2.66). Col had described how even theologians can fall in love (perhaps recalling Peter Abelard) and that such a love might well one day strike Gerson. His response was that "this position seems more intent on slandering theologians than on dealing with the question in a pertinent way."[89]

Here is Gerson's only reference to Christine de Pizan, whom he called "an outstanding woman" (*insigni femina*; 67). Col had tried to use her to argue that deception in love is sometimes necessary even though Christine's position was the exact opposite. Pierre Col had in Gerson's view misrepresented the facts and had tried to escape from them by using the perennial academic ploy of claiming that the text in his source was corrupted.

Gerson decided not to go into further detail because he did not want to make better known "such base and contagious material" (68). He realized that the more he attacked the *Romance,* the more prominent he made the book and the debate about carnal love. Gerson was dealing with Pierre Col's charge in his lost letter "that I wrote what I did so that people, who we know seek what is forbidden, would be provoked by a great flame and encouraged to re-read this poem." If there was any deception, Gerson insisted, it came not from him but from the author of the *Romance:* "For while he condemns carnal love, whose praises he has often sung, does he not desire . . . to make people more easily attracted to it?"[90]

The letter contains a personal element and a polemical tone which show how deeply Gerson involved himself in the debate. He may himself have experienced the attraction of a work both elegant in form and popular in the humanist circles to which he belonged at the College of Navarre. It was tempting to play with Jean de Meung's ideas and regard his suggestions as subtle intellectual entertainment, and thus to avoid looking at the poem in a literal way. Ultimately, however, the poem is about the rape of a woman when the rose is taken by force.

For Gerson such a matter was deadly serious. As he told Pierre Col: "Now it is time to stop joking, good brother, for you are worthy of backing a better cause. You have got to stop this lust either to conquer or to gossip (*vel vincendi vel garriendi*)."[91] He claimed that if he discovered his own brother had composed such a work and had refused to repent, "then I would no more offer prayers in our Lord Jesus Christ for him who had died impenitent than I would pray for someone who was damned" (70).

Gerson's opponents had claimed he had not really understood the poem. Pierre Col had challenged him to reread it so that he could see its true meaning. Gerson countered that Col instead should read the fourth book of Augustine *On Christian Doctrine.* Here, and not in Jean de Meung, Col would find the meaning of rhetoric: "You will perhaps be ashamed for boldly claiming things that you have not fully considered."[92]

Why was Gerson so concerned with this question? He was rejecting the misogyny fashionable in his day among clerics and academics. He was telling other men that they had no right to play about with their sexual fantasies. The unrestricted expression of lust could undermine the very fabric of society. Unlike Christine, his primary purpose was not to defend the dignity of the female sex. But like her he saw that the teaching of the *Romance of the Rose* could not be reconciled with the message of the Gospel.

At about the same time he wrote to Pierre Col, Gerson composed the statement *Against the Corruption of Youth.* In what appears to have been an open letter to church and civil authorities, he complained that young people were being exposed to pornographic images and writings. Often those close to home were responsible for infecting youth, even mothers and nursemaids (Gl 10.28), while fathers just smiled at what was taking place. Obscene songs and gestures were allowed in public, sometimes even in churches on certain days. He alluded especially to the Feast of Fools, against which, the same year, he wrote a polemic, for it turned holy ritual upside down in a carnival atmosphere.[93]

Gerson felt that his advice was being ridiculed and his listeners instead were "turning toward fables."[94] The only way to stop such practices was the threat of punishment by civil authority, the same as happened with theft, arson, the murder of pilgrims, or the counterfeiting of money. Here as with the Schism, Gerson turns to secular power to cope with the issues of the day. He seems unaffected by the debates of the eleventh and twelfth centuries about the separation of secular and religious powers. He was the offspring of a Gallican church that had squarely allied itself with the monarchy, first in the pious image of a thirteenth-century saint king, later in the questionable propaganda of his grandson, Philip IV (1285–1314).

Gerson believed in an alliance between the princes of the realm and the most learned theologians and bishops of France. His faculty of theology was to set a moral agenda for the reform of church and society. It was necessary to convince the secular powers to follow this lead. His problem was not the princes but privileged clerics who liked to dabble in pagan philosophy and were attracted by irony and a taste for sexual freedom.

In our own age of Internet pornography with endless images of all manner of human coupling, it is perhaps hard to imagine how in another culture much less hardcore images could become matters of such concern. Gerson apparently could not get such pictures out of his head. He worried that they were also circulated among those whom he taught. He was afraid that the ironic stance of their superiors would lead students to believe that it was acceptable at least to fantasize about various forms of sexual behavior.

Gerson had hurled himself into a debate where he was bound to look like a sore loser, a sex-obsessed cleric, and an object of ridicule for those who could claim he did not know how to read a text in all its subtle meanings. His opponents, he complained, charged that he too one day would succumb to the "mad love" (*amorem . . . insanum*) he claimed to despise (Gl 2.67).

Setting Limits on Human Power

Gerson exposed his inner life and made it accessible to others. His writings reveal a priest and teacher in the mold of Saint Augustine who too had wrestled with his sexuality and had placed it in a fuller social and human context. For Gerson as well as for Augustine, the Gospel offered many forms of love but, except in marriage, separated these attachments from sexual expression.

Gerson's opposition to the *Romance* stemmed ultimately from his passionate search for the presence of God. His desire was to understand his own yearnings and those of his fellow Christians. The six-part treatise *On the Life of the Soul* says more about Gerson's vision of existence than does his polemic against sexual license. Probably in the first months of 1402, he presented the completed treatise to Pierre d'Ailly. In the Glorieux edition the work fills almost ninety pages (Gl 3.113–202). In a covering letter he told d'Ailly that he had felt flattered when his former teacher appeared at one of his lessons, probably the previous autumn, and afterwards asked Gerson to send its text to him (Gl 2.63).

Gerson obliged d'Ailly not only with the lesson of that day but also with the whole series of lectures. He used the occasion to thank his master: "You also promoted me in the office of chancellor in which I succeeded you, even though I was not of equal merit."

After the usual protestations of humility to be expected in a medieval author, Gerson outlined the work, based on the theme from Acts 17:29: "In him we live and move and have our being" (64). His purpose was to describe the life of grace first for beginners, and then for the more perfect, and finally for the most perfect, where "the life of the soul . . . finds stability and consolation through contemplation."

The *Spiritual Life of the Soul* begins with a consideration of moral acts in the light of divine law and right reason (Gl 3.124). The main subject of much of the treatise is the relationship between divine law and human acts. There is no precise correspondence between God's law and the canons of the Church. These often deal with temporal matters and do not bind the individual Christian under pain of mortal sin (134). Human laws are the result of traditions or authorities and do not obligate the individual in the same way as divine law does (135). Thus canons issued by the pope are to be respected, at least in order to avoid scandal, but it is not always necessary to follow them.

Gerson countered the point of view forwarded by Wycliffe and his supporters at the time that legitimate authority and lordship could only be exercised by those in the state of grace. "The entitlement of charity" was not necessary for the exercise of dominion, yet such power was not an immediate reflection of divine law.[95] Papal power belonged to this category: a pope could be challenged and even deposed (152). Gerson did not specifically refer to the withdrawal of obedience, but such a move clearly belongs under the extreme cases treated here.

A superior authority, even a pope, "can decide nothing that is adverse to the truth of natural and divine law" (152–53). Here Gerson set forth a maxim that would be one of his guiding principles: papal power is given "not to destroy but to build up" (*non in destructionem sed in aedificationem*). He excoriated canon lawyers for "being out of their minds" and "glued to their texts."[96] A pope could be deposed, or at least deprived of obedience, when the Church as a whole judges him to be acting in conflict with divine law (155).

Gerson was dealing here with the same questions as in his brief treatises on the papacy from this period. But now he looked at larger questions of principle and concluded that no human legislator can punish the violation of his laws with the threat of eternal damnation (158). When the pope acts as head of the Church in temporal matters, he cannot claim his decisions are binding under pain of mortal sin.

In this treatise Gerson distanced himself from canonists who for centuries had been erecting an edifice of papal authority in all areas of life. He contrasted their rigorism with the gentle yoke of Christ (*ad leve jugum et suave vocavit*; 161) and made generous use of Bernard of Clairvaux's treatise *On Precept and Dispensation* to show that human rules should not be turned into divine principles. Just as a monk can break the rule of his cloister without necessarily committing mortal sin, so too a member of a Paris college can abrogate the oath he has taken to his institution without going to hell (182).

Rules and regulations, to Gerson's mind, had gotten out of hand with each authority, whether monastic, civil, academic, or papal, claiming sovereignty. Although he respected human decisions and traditions, these were not to be elevated to principles with eternal value (165). Laws must be tailored to individual needs and situations and cannot claim universal validity. Laws claiming "to apply to every age, every people and country" are made by men who "are out of their minds" (168).

Several times in the treatise Gerson compares the prerogatives of authorities in the secular church with those of an abbot: "Prelates of the Church do not have any more power to bind their subjects to something not handed down in the Rule of the Gospel professed by all Christians than do abbots have the right to obligate their monks beyond what is found in the profession of their Rule" (170). It was natural to compare lay and monastic life, for both were ultimately shaped by the principles of the Gospel. Twelfth-century writers such as Bernard, who had concentrated on monastic perfection, thus became an inspiration for Gerson's attempt to define Christian life in general.

The law of charity, the final end of all legislation, restricted the right of ecclesiastical authorities to use excommunication as a vehicle to enforce their decisions. No such sentence was to be given, he insisted, unless an individual was unwilling to listen to the Church (171). Gerson thus seemed opposed to the concept of *ipso facto* excommunication: the idea that an act in itself placed a person outside the Church.

In this connection, Gerson warns that one person can never be certain of another's spiritual state. No member of a parish should avoid his priest because the latter is thought to be guilty of sexual sin. The only justification for withdrawing from a priest's authority is a sentence of excommunication published by the priest's superior. Otherwise the laity is not to draw its own conclusions. After all, Gerson insists, it is easy "to say of parish priests that they are public fornicators if by chance they are seen having conversation or modest contact with women" (172). A woman may have frequent visits from a priest who is trying to change her way of life. Some saints are even known to have consorted with public prostitutes. In general priests "are to be judged not by their subjects but by prelates" (173).

To a certain extent Gerson would tolerate priests who have concubines (176). It would be "far worse" (*longe deterius*), he rationalizes, if the priest approached other women in the parish. Here again is Gerson's attempt at reconciling the requirement of celibacy with the facts of everyday life. Sometimes rules that cannot be maintained have to be changed. Gerson did not suggest abandoning celibacy, but he considered it the result of a conscious choice made by the Western Church and not a requirement found in the Gospel.[97] What mattered most was to maintain parish and sacramental life. If rules regarding behavior were kept strictly, then almost all priests would be unable to perform their functions. Parishioners would come to doubt the efficacy of the sacraments the priests administer (177). In such a situation, the Church would be plagued with teachings such as those already rife among the Wycliffites in England.

Because of his concern for the parish, Gerson tolerated lax priests to some extent. But he showed no tolerance for church authorities that used excommunication to protect their temporal interests (177–78). In pastoral life, as well as in his response to the Schism, Gerson was a pragmatist who wanted to counter strident voices. What mattered most was extending the means of salvation to everyone.

Here he recalls a personal anecdote. He once had been verbally attacked for preaching that sinners are not obligated to confess immediately after sinning but can wait for the times of year set aside for confession. If people were made to think that their confession and repentance had to be immediate, then they might easily despair about doing so. "And so I will wrongly think that I am healing wounds when I am actually making them worse" (195).

Building up, not tearing down. This was Gerson's program, in the midst of a legalistic age where many voices were calling for justice and even revenge on those who did not obey. It was necessary to cut back on all demands. Within university colleges, for example, there were so many oaths to be taken that they had become, like so much else, "a horrid burden" (*o quam horrendum onus*; 196). As in interpreting monastic rules, moderation was necessary. At the end of the treatise, Gerson imitates Petrarch by engaging in a dialogue with a model from the past. The theologian here speaks to Augustine about the requirements of what the medieval Church knew as his Rule for canons: "Now you order, father, that we do not speak in the cloister, that we be composed in the movements of the body and chaste in the impulses of the eyes. Do you wish then that if any of these actions are performed . . . that the person be guilty of a capital crime and do you wish that he be punished by hell's eternal death?" (198). An Augustine who wanted to call men to the gentle yoke of Christ could not possibly be so restrictive.

By using the voice of Augustine, Gerson resorted to the same rhetorical device as in his sermon on the Feast of Saint Bernard, where he virtually became Bernard, or in his great sermon on Good Friday 1403, where he spoke freely with Mary and invented her dialogue with others. Augustine, Bernard, John the Baptist, Mary, and Jesus himself all spoke to him in the drama for the human soul.

Jean Gerson heard many voices during these years, and he was no longer afraid to make his own voice heard. In the autumn of 1403 he joined a delegation of Paris masters who, with the blessing of the princes of the realm, headed south. Gerson was ready to meet the man who had been humiliated, imprisoned, maligned, and challenged. The chancellor depended on Benedict XIII for his own future at Paris but knew he had to keep this same man from deciding the future of the Church.

Gerson conceded that prelates are princes who have authority from God to rule their people through law and institutions, even if these laws are not divine. Human laws are "to be accepted as healthy admonitions and are not lightly to be spurned" (202). The question was if such a principle could fit a pope who until now had refused to compromise and considered his authority to be divinely given.

Would Gerson be able to find reason and compromise in this man? Or would his efforts to influence events lead him to new disillusionment? In considering his response, Gerson found consolation in Saint Jerome's use of a classical tag: "I sang for myself and the Muses, even if no one else would hear."[98] Would anyone listen to Gerson or would his song remain his alone?

Guiding and Controlling, 1403–1408

At some level Gerson must have known that how ever much he cared about himself and others, he had very little control. He has been compared to much more efficient churchmen such as the archbishop Simon of Cramaud.[1] Simon can be seen as the real leader of the Gallican solution to the Schism, for Simon was willing in the 1390s to take the drastic steps of deposing popes that Gerson at the time wanted to avoid. This man took charge of several Paris church councils, while Gerson stayed away or remained silent.

Gerson, in these years, was torn between a yearning for love and fear of its consequences. This search for union and the flight from it are evident not only in Gerson but in medieval Christian culture as a whole. If God is love, then why must individuals who seek God avoid loving each other, if such loves become carnal? If God is friendship, as Aelred of Rievaulx stated in the twelfth century, then why does his friendship exclude all others?[2]

Gerson did not pose such questions because he refused to concede any such dilemma. The love of neighbor had to be a love totally subordinated to the love of God. And yet Gerson did love other people. It hurt him that his brothers Jean and Nicolas did not love him as he needed. He turned to his sisters with good advice and planned their lives. He asserted the unity of experience and, at the same time, was afflicted with thoughts of his own passions. In what follows here, I will consider some aspects of this duality in terms of a desire to guide and control.

Maintaining Standards but Making a Difference

The complexity of Gerson's inner life during these years emerges in two sermons given in the presence of Pope Benedict XIII: the first at Marseilles on 9 November 1403, the second at Tarascon on the Feast of the Circumcision, 1 January 1404. The first sermon has been looked upon as close to flattery, or at least as a eulogy belonging to a genre of "typically rhetorical productions."[3] The second is supposed to show a "sudden and remarkable change of tone," the result of Gerson's realization that Benedict was not sincere about his claim that he was willing to resign the papacy, if necessary, for the good of the Church.[4] If we look at the Marseilles sermon, however, its praise for the pope is only half the story, for a conflicting message is evident.

Gerson began with a line from the Psalms, "Blessed be your inheritance" (Ps 27:9). The word *benedictus* provided the pope's name and suggested the blessings that Benedict could bring to the Church. It was up to him to hinder further calamities to his inheritance, which was the Church (Gl 5.109). So far the tone is positive, almost effusive, but now come Gerson's reservations. The pope cannot perform his functions without the support of "the most outstanding, potent, and Christian kingdom of France" (110). Gerson holds up as a model of peace the concord the university lately had reached with the Dominican Order.[5] He admitted that the pope had himself recently had to live through many "tribulations and sufferings" (112), but since obedience to him had been restored, there was new hope.

Gerson reveals that his intention is by no means flattery. Benedict is a Jonas thrown into the sea from the ship of the Church. The Jonas figure failed to obey God's command and so is punished. In the end he is saved and has to seek reconciliation with God, as Benedict now must do. An unnamed person has come to the papal court and threatened Benedict, but the pope responded by being merciful and listening to the man, instead of having him arrested. Who now would still insist on calling Benedict "stiff, austere, and vindictive" (*te rigidum, te austerum aut irae memorem*; 113)? Gerson thereby cites the very words probably used by Benedict's opponents. As with the comparison to Jonas, the preacher's apparent flattery contained a critical undercurrent.

Gerson's reservations are also apparent in his use of the parable of the servant who did not forgive what was owed him and so was himself not forgiven (115; cf. Mt 18:32). Benedict had to show generosity or no generosity would be shown him. He had a duty to save the sheep entrusted to him and to render account for them on Judgment Day. Using the language of the *Rule of Saint Benedict* (ch. 2) concerning the abbot's obligation toward his monks, Gerson states that the pope had been placed in his office not for the destruction of these sheep but for their strengthening (*agnoscat quoniam positus est non in destructionem sed aedificationem;*

116). Such verbal opposition became a favorite mode of expression in Gerson's writings advocating reform of the Church through a general council.

In the second part of the sermon, in which Gerson presents to Benedict the *rotuli* or lists of university graduates seeking benefices in the Church, his language takes on a milder tone. But these passages are more concerned with the merits and needs of the University of Paris than with praising Benedict. Gerson was certainly thinking of getting jobs for his colleagues, perhaps also his youngest brother Jean, whose name can be found among the masters of arts who had begun theological studies.[6]

The second sermon to Benedict, seven weeks later, begins with the circumcised Christ, in accord with the feast day at hand (68). There follows a discussion about the disagreement that led to the first council in Jerusalem concerning the necessity of circumcision (Acts 15). This case introduces the question of whether a council is superior to the pope (72).

Gerson criticizes those who insist on observing human laws and so spurn the "living law founded in eternal law" (73). The Schism could not be ended by human laws unless the superior divine law was consulted (74). In *Spiritual Life of the Soul* (1402), he had already taught that an appeal to divine law allowed going beyond the usual categories of canon law, in order to find novel solutions for the Church's situation.

Secondly, Gerson emphasizes the greatness of the child Jesus in humiliating himself at the circumcision. This act contrasted with Lucifer's attempt to exalt himself. Gerson warns the pope against following Lucifer's path and thinking that he had been exalted (75). The preacher here hints that Benedict had allowed the flattery of others to exalt him beyond his rightful station.

Gerson's third consideration criticizes prelates who put excessive burdens on their subjects. One instance is the reservation of sins. The number of acts that require a special confessor is so large that many people are kept from making proper confessions. Gerson promises to deal with the question elsewhere.[7] He adds criticism of the papal office stating that it is "monstrous to see the head usurping all the offices of the members" (77). The curia had become like the devil's court.

The fourth consideration constituted Gerson's most direct challenge to Benedict's position. Sometimes a prelate, who is obliged to show humility through preaching and penance, would do best to resign his post (78). He should remember the words of Saint Paul that we cannot justify ourselves (1 Cor 4:4). Many prelates think they act out of magnanimity but live in arrogance and presumption. Their ambition to stay in office can harm the Church.

The language implies that Benedict lacked humility. Gerson was not contradicting his previous sermon, only making more concrete his questioning of the papal position. Pride will only listen "to its own opinions" and cannot be persuaded by the warnings, counsel, or experience of others. "Woe, woe to the church or religion or anyone" subject to such a pestilence! (79)

Gerson warns that unless there was immediate action, the Schism would become so deeply rooted that it would become permanent, like the break between the Greeks and the Latins (84). The only solution is to follow the charity found in divine rather than in human law. Since the Schism was an epidemic without a previous human remedy, new laws had to be instituted for its cure. No solution was to be rejected, even if human laws seem opposed so long as divine law was kept (85). Gerson excoriates those who "stick to naked texts" and ignore equity in the meaning he found in Aristotle.[8]

It was necessary to follow the principles of the Gospel. Gerson could not tolerate people, presumably at Benedict's court, who obstinately defend "human inventions" and forbid any discussion of papal power. They have the audacity to claim, "it is an article of faith that Benedict is pope" and that "the pope in no situation can be called to a council, and that without him there is no salvation" (85). Others claim that the pope cannot sin, or that he is omnipotent, while some insist that all who do not obey him are outside the state of grace.

Gerson was repeating general principles from his *Spiritual Life of the Soul* but was now applying them specifically to the situation of church and papacy. He even suggests the possibility of using force if a pope abuses his power: *vim illatam vi repellere* (86). Here he immediately turns to the pope's well-known assertion that he would accept anything, including martyrdom, in order "to procure the unity of the Church." Gerson could only conclude, "How much the more then [would he accept] the abdication of his own position, for how could he give his life, if he were unwilling to desert his vestments, crown, or miter?" (86).

The shepherd is obliged to give up his flock if this is the only way in which he could save it (88). Everything has to be tried, except that which is sinful. Human justice must give way to divine. As for a general council, Gerson now asserts that such a council would not err: *pium est credere quod in tractatione praesentis materiae non erraret* (89). It would be guided by the Holy Spirit. He dropped his earlier assertion that, since such a meeting would deal with questions of fact rather than of doctrine, its decisions might be in error.[9]

As the Dutch scholar Posthumus Meyjes has written in his superb exposition of the development of Gerson's thought on church reform, the sermon has "hardly a single idea which cannot be found somewhere in his earlier writings."[10] At the same time, however, Posthumus Meyjes saw a "greater integration" of Gerson's ideas in this sermon. This new synthesis enabled him to abandon the gentler solution of the way of cession.

Something must have happened as a result of Gerson's renewed contact with the papal court.[11] Gerson may have realized that he was dealing with a person who refused to distinguish between his own office and the good of the Church. The coming years would confirm that nothing, not even the Council of Constance, could convince Benedict XIII to resign. In the end he would be limited to a tiny area in Spain, but unlike the pope in Rome, he would never resign office.[12]

Gerson and his colleagues were now ready once again to distance themselves from the man to whom they had pledged new obedience. Four days after he delivered the sermon, on 5 January 1404, Gerson wrote to the duke of Orleans, Benedict's firmest ally at the French court, trying to soften the impact of his words. First he made light of himself and compared himself to a puppy that pursued peace "by barking as much as I can."[13]

Gerson's mild opening is followed by a defense of his policies toward Benedict. He points out how he had previously resisted the withdrawal of obedience from the Avignon pope: "But after our Lord Benedict is said to have accepted the way of resignation and other actions asked for as being appropriate for the peace and reformation of the Church, I, in all humility, spoke to the contrary, in the face of no small expression of hatred and amid dangers, [for I said] that Benedict was to be defended as not having irreversibly lost the papacy."[14] Gerson recalls the risk he had taken in believing in Benedict's good faith. He adds that he had been "forced" to go as the university's legate to Benedict and asks the duke to consider the sermon in its relation to the controversy's development.

Gerson's appeal apparently fell on deaf ears. At a later point, perhaps in 1405, he wrote to Pierre d'Ailly and lamented that he had been misunderstood: "Those who are present at a sermon not only distort what has been well said but staunchly assert statements as having been made that in no way have been uttered."[15] He is supposed to have claimed that a dying man can gain the same forgiveness of punishment and guilt from an ordinary priest as from the pope. Gerson insists he had never said such a thing: his assertion was that confession to any priest is sufficient. The pope could give special indulgences for remission of punishment for sin.

Gerson's protestations may seem a little naive in view of what he was facing. In Benedict's presence he had made claims that undermined his right to be pope. Now Gerson protested that his message had been twisted out of shape: "How many things, O good Jesus, have been told to me about the same sermon that I never said or even thought?" (Gl 2.79).

Controlling His Own Life

Six weeks earlier, on 18 November 1403, Pope Benedict XIII had handed over to Jean Gerson the curacy of the Parisian church of Saint Jean-en-Grève, located on the Right Bank of the Seine.[16] The benefice was in future to be incorporated into the chancellor's office. On 24 December of the same year, he was given a canonry and prebend in the chapter of Notre Dame.[17] Gerson was not personally present for this nomination but was represented by a procurator. The first appointment reflects the Avignon papacy's desire in the autumn of 1403 to win over the scholars of the University of Paris. The position at Notre Dame indicates acceptance by the canons that their chancellor was too important to be passed over for a prebend at his church.

Saint Jean-en-Grève was a desirable parish and also one where Gerson was well known for sermons given there. At Avignon he got what the university's delegates considered to be their due. After years during which the university had made no official requests to the pope for benefices for its members, their time had come.

It has been claimed that after being wounded by Gerson's Tarascon sermon, Benedict XIII, in his displeasure, deprived him of his new appointment.[18] This is an oversimplification. As late as a year later, on 15 February 1404, Gerson informed the chapter of Notre Dame that he had received from the pope "the union of the church of Saint Jean-en-Grève with his chancellorship," to be effective after the death of its incumbent (Gl 10.469). Gerson's situation was jeopardized not by the pope at Avignon but by the abbot of Bec, who claimed the right of appointment to this benefice.[19] It was not until 1409, as we shall see in the next chapter, that the question was settled. Gerson was granted the church, but only as a personal gift for his lifetime.

It was common for benefices to be contested in this manner. What is remarkable is that after years of seeking a canonry at Notre Dame and of being outmaneuvered, one of these was placed squarely in his lap, even though he was far away. From 1395 to the end of 1403, Gerson had acted as chancellor of the church of Notre Dame without having a prebend or residence there. On 6 June 1404, however, the new cathedral canon was able to buy an unfurnished house in the cloister of Notre Dame for 80 francs (469–70). Gerson's new home was located to the left of the entrance, near the cloister gate, which led out onto the Rue Saint-Christophe, on the north side of the church and across from the tiny church of Saint Jean-le-Rond on the northwest corner of the cathedral. Gerson's house opened out into the cloister yard with a well and led to the room granted him in 1395 for his official functions.[20]

The chancellor probably lived here for a time with his youngest brother Jean. With the prospect of an income from Saint Jean-en-Grève, Gerson no longer had to take in students as boarders (Gl 2.19). But by becoming a full-fledged member of the chapter, he had to attend morning meetings up to three times a week, participate in the liturgy daily, and accept special commissions from the chapter. Its records show that he was faithful and did not take advantage of the concession that members of the university could be excused from some meetings.[21]

On 25 June 1404, Gerson's name was added to those *provisores* or supervisors who looked after the Hôtel-Dieu, a combined hospital and poorhouse stretching along the banks of the Seine next to the cathedral itself (Gl 10.470). The same day he was also, together with master Jean Rolland, given charge of the choirboys of the cathedral. Finally he and four other canons were asked to collect the statutes of Notre Dame "into one volume."

Thanks to a sermon from 8 October 1406, we can see that Gerson's concern about the Hôtel-Dieu was more than perfunctory. In the king's presence, Gerson explained why the royal family, considered the founders of the institution, was obligated to show continuing support. The king, in Gerson's eyes, was priestly (*sacerdotal ou pontifical*; Gl 7.2.714), for he had been anointed at Reims by the "holy oil, which comes from heaven." In this capacity the royal house of France had shown mercy and provided refuge for all who had come to it in need. Gerson listed those who now required help: poor infant orphans, invalid laborers, honest women who had kept their chastity and worked hard to gain an income. Such people cross the frozen Seine in the midst of winter, in order to make clothing. Their work apparently supported the institution, but there was also a great need for personnel to clothe, feed, and console the many sick residents. It is enough of a task to look after the needs of one sick person, Gerson commented, while here the number seemed endless! No one, he insisted, could know what it was like unless they had tried to help: *nul ne la scet qui ne l'assaye* (715).

"Charity had grown cold" because of the poverty of the people and the imposition of heavy taxes. At the same time, the royal treasury had defaulted on its payments: "The [royal] treasurer and [his] receivers fail to pay that which they owe by just title in alms, in order to satisfy their excessive vanity" (716). If the situation did not improve, the only solution would be to abandon the Hôtel-Dieu and close its gates. Then, as Gerson said to the king, the poor of your kingdom will have no place to go. They will die and even the dead will not be buried.

Gerson was just as harsh on the king as he had been on the pope. But his real target was the royal officials who administered such matters in the name of the king. The sermon indicates that Gerson's supervisory position at the Hôtel-Dieu was more than a title. The huge building has long since disappeared but in the fifteenth century it was a constant reminder to the canons of Notre Dame that their church was more than an institution catering to the glory of monarchy, nobility, and bourgeoisie. They were responsible for the sick, the poor, the maimed, and the insane. These were cared for by a group of sisters and brothers whose community is sometimes mentioned in the chapter statutes.[22] For Gerson the presence of the Hôtel-Dieu was a solid reminder of the charity that was part of the Church's mission.

In the summer of 1405, Gerson had to leave his duties at Paris temporarily and travel to Bruges. After the death of his patron, Philip, Duke of Burgundy, on 27 April 1404, and the accession of Philip's son John, Gerson's position at the chapter of Bruges had become insecure. A cleric who seems to have had Duke John's favor challenged Gerson's office claiming that he was not administering it properly because of his long absences.[23] By now he had not been to Bruges for several years. This time he managed to salvage his position, but the same cleric later would resume his attack.

On 10 September 1408, Gerson asked the chapter of Notre Dame of Paris to accept "that the chancellorship is not a dignity (*dignitas*) but a plain office (*officium simplex*)" (Gl 10.492). The distinction was important. A dignity was an office with a benefice to support it, while an office was simply that: a position that did not in itself provide an income. Since the reforms of Pierre d'Ailly, the chancellor in theory was not allowed to take payment for the examinations that were held under his office.[24]

In April 1405, the Parlement of Paris reversed Gerson's refusal to accept the examination of a certain master Jean La Dorée (473–74). The chancellor had apparently been trying to assert his position in charge of recognizing examination results. But here, as in the question of taking fees, his office was restricted to purely symbolic leadership.

Gerson's attempt to have the chancellorship defined as a simple office indicates a desire to clear himself of the charge that he was holding multiple benefices. He was probably also facing the possibility of losing his position at Bruges and would have to depend on the curacy of Saint-Jean-en-Grève. After the death in 1404 of his patron Philip of Burgundy, Gerson's strategy was to ally himself with his fellow canons at Notre Dame and to show loyalty to their institution.

Besides looking after the Hôtel-Dieu and the choir school, Gerson was also involved in a heresy case. Jean Marmet, chaplain in the church of Saint Benoît, was put into the prison of the bishop of Paris on suspicion of heresy (468–69). After examining the question, Gerson stated that it had nothing to do with matters of faith. Marmet was only guilty of signing a certain statement, apparently one in which a woman handed herself over to the devil. In May he confessed to the canons that he had done so "out of carelessness and negligence" (469). Gerson was reluctant to prosecute a fellow cleric, even though he spoke and wrote against forms of superstition, apparently rife in Paris, especially because of the king's illness and hopes that magic might help him.[25]

As member of the chapter of Notre Dame, Gerson also had to deal with the authenticity of the relics of Saint Denis, the martyr-saint who as patron of France was still thought to be the same as the mystical writer whom we today call Pseudo-Dionysius. The monks of Saint Denis outside Paris claimed that they had in their possession almost the entire body, including the saint's cranium. At the same time the canons of Notre Dame laid claim to a large part of Saint Denis's head in their collection (476–77). Both skulls could not belong to the same person, it was reasoned, and so began a heated dispute.

In November 1406, the bishop of Paris, Pierre d'Orgemont, wrote that Notre

Dame had "a large portion of the head of Saint Denis the martyr." This was considered to be one of its "main relics" and was regularly shown to the people (477). The bishop referred to a sermon on the authenticity of the relic given recently by Gerson on the Feast of Saint Catherine. The sermon is lost, but we do have a letter from Gerson to the Abbot of Saint Denis (8 October 1408) in which the chancellor laments the division between the two churches. He admits that there could be multiple relics of the same saint or of his or her body parts.[26] So long as neither side could be convicted of bad faith or deliberate error, it was better to allow the cult to continue in both places without one side challenging the other.

Gerson's reasoning here parallels his discussion about the veracity of claims to the papacy. What mattered was not who was right in an absolute sense but who had the right intentions. "Error and falsehood in religious matters require the presence of wrongdoing."[27] Canon law and historical arguments were not enough for determining the rightfulness of a pope or the authenticity of a relic. It was also important to avoid scandalizing the faithful or depriving them of the symbols of authority they needed.

It may seem that Gerson was indifferent to the truth. But what he was saying was much more basic: on questions where absolute truth cannot be established, the consequences for those affected should be considered. It was necessary to have relics to place ordinary people in contact with the power of the saints. It was important to gain consensus about who should be pope, without settling the claims of one side or the other.

Gerson had more important matters on his agenda than squabbles about relics. He had to cope with a world where honor seemed to matter more than the Gospel. The bishop of Paris was keen to get the canons' consent to a monument for himself behind the high altar of Notre Dame. The canons asked that the bishop "lower the tomb which he had made in the church, which is too high" (475). A decision on 29 January 1406 led to further negotiations, which dragged on for weeks.

Gerson's response to such concerns was to avoid losing patience and concentrate on his own inner life. In his *Practical Mystical Theology* he described the type of person who promises himself, "You on this day, at that hour, will be free of all occupations; then you will most assuredly be ready for tasting the sweetness of contemplation" (Gl 8.29). Gerson was probably speaking about himself, caught up as he was in so many duties and looking forward to moments of undistracted prayer and a sense of union with God: "But when that day comes, the person will feel a bitter aridity in his soul and a sense of revulsion toward the spirit. He will not only be repelled by prayer and spiritual reading but also will be plagued by darkness and confusion. By contrast, when a person has had no particular expectations, 'it will come freely, though not hoped for at that time.'"[28] Purposeful involvement did not leave him with the peace and sense of fulfillment for which he yearned. Instead his dynamism in facing external challenges could turn into depression. Like the conscientious student who tells himself that once exams are over, he will be free to enjoy life, or the hardworking teacher who looks forward to doing real research during school vacation, Gerson knew that hard-won leisure, rather than leading to intellectual or spiritual fruitfulness, could end in fallowness and even depression.

Gerson's depiction later on in the same treatise of an interior state of being may well be a reflection of his own situation. He speaks of forbidden passions against which one must struggle: "Then our souls that have been purified and sanctified will sometimes have to bear the attacks of blasphemies and the vilest impurities, even in old age and in solitude. These temptations are of a type that is unknown to us so long as we live in the world among the average and more adolescent temptations of the flesh and the world."[29] What does he mean here? The statement may be related to reminders in the *Lives of the Fathers* that one is never too old to encounter temptations of the flesh.[30] But his parallel warning against blasphemy speaks of another temptation: the desire to say obscene words in even the most holy moments, as in the presence of the Eucharist. Gerson during these years had to account for such impulses. In his brief treatise, *Against the Temptations of Blasphemy,* he ascribes such "suggestions" to the devil, whom God allows to get past the outer defenses of the soul. The best way to deal with such temptations is to laugh at them (Gl 7.1.413). As with barking dogs, one should not stop and confront them but continue on one's path.

Gerson was drawing on a monastic tradition that began in the Egyptian desert and reappeared in the twelfth century. Personal experience was a point of departure for giving moral and spiritual advice to others. As we saw in the last chapter, however, Gerson went beyond his predecessors and intended his advice for all Christians, lay and clerical. In providing a list of questions of conscience together with the Celestine Pierre Poquet, Gerson used the same approach. Again the question was how to deal with temptation. One should confront "empty or harmful thoughts" by saying to them: "You come at a bad time. I do not now have time or opportunity to reply to you: Wait for a while until I do." With impure or blasphemous thoughts, however, it is better to spurn them by not answering them or fighting with them: "I know a certain man who when such [thoughts] come usually smiles at them in his mind, as if showing contempt for them."[31]

Such passages indicate that Gerson may have had trouble in controlling his own thoughts. His solution was not heroic struggle but ironic distance. Ever passionate, he tried to cool off, to talk himself out of obsessions, to comfort himself when depression came. Inspired by Petrarch as model,[32] Gerson conveys much more of his immediate self. This may seem surprising for a scholastic theologian, trained for decades in the strictest school of reasoning. After Bruges, however, Gerson had succeeded in synthesizing thought and feeling. Would this union remain an intellectual construct, or would it enable him to influence the lives of others?

Controlling the Lives of Family Members

From 1404 until 1413 Gerson lived comfortably in his cloister residence at Notre Dame. For a time his youngest brother, Jean, was with him, but sometime before 1408 he followed the lead of Nicolas and joined the Celestine Order. Gerson's reaction is indicated in a letter to Nicolas, probably written soon after his return to France from a mission to both popes, a journey that lasted from April 1407 and possibly until May 1408. The letter was probably written after Gerson and d'Ailly, on their way home, had visited Nicolas's monastic house near Avignon.

Already early in the letter, Gerson felt obligated to defend his commitment to young Jean: "The law of love is such that in speech or in writing, friends enjoy visiting each other, instructing each other, and consoling each other."[33] A surprising assertion from a man who elsewhere showed skepticism about the value of friendship! Gerson, however, needed to justify his involvement with Jean. He added that he had a right to influence Jean's life "because of my own experience and because of the learning I have acquired." His knowledge enabled him to detect the danger that can arise for youths who "frequently believe that spiritual illness is great health" (Gl 2.87).

Both his brothers by now had rejected his guidance and chosen lives of which Gerson did not approve: "Understand, brother, what I say. This is my situation, which began long ago and now continues: I am cast aside; I am told what to do. I do not wish to say any more. . . . Do not persist in this manner for your own sake or your own opinion in defending your way of life. If you do so, you will willfully harm the one who loves you in truth" (87). First Nicolas, and now Jean, had left their Paris home and thus distanced themselves from their elder brother. He refused to accept this situation and made a plea to Nicolas for love: "Let us communicate with each other as those who love, if we really do love each other" (*Communicemus ut amantes, si amantes*).

Only now, a third of the way into the letter, did Gerson make clear what the problem was. Nicolas had told him during his visit that his letters to Jean upset the youngest brother: "They deprive him of sleep and give rise to a plague of fantasies in him" (88). We are not told about the contents of these letters, but when Gerson met with Nicolas, the two had apparently disagreed about why their younger brother was having problems. For Nicolas the reason was obvious: "It did not come about, you will say, because of the strictness or condition of his religious life. It was the contents of letters that caused this overstimulation by their sting. Unwillingly he goes over them again and again, nor can any effort remove them from the house of memory. These letters obtrude upon him against his will and attach their beaks to his mind. And so his head gets disturbed. He lacks sleep. His brain twists about in dizziness."[34] Gerson asked how his "two or three letters" (which unfortunately we do not have) could have such a result. It was much more likely that young Jean's state came from "harsh fasting, excessive vigils, a rigorous program of vocal prayer, a strict collection of readings, and similar practices" (88–89). Anyone who had to maintain such a program would be in danger of losing his sanity.

Gerson denied that his advice may have contributed to Jean's state of mind, but he conceded that Jean had asked him to stop writing. Grudgingly he gave his consent: "If nothing hinders his peace and quiet nor will disturb it except my letters, then I freely, or even gladly, will stop them. But in my mind this explanation lacks any probability."[35] Gerson closed the letter by turning to Nicolas and warning him against a "sensual attachment" (*libidinosa . . . affectio*) to Jean, which might keep him from the advice "given by others." If Nicolas was not willing to listen to Gerson, it was because his attachment to young Jean was of the wrong kind.

Was Gerson not resentful that a second brother had left his company in Paris and chosen an ascetic religious life where he would be virtually inaccessible? Years later, after Gerson had left Paris and could not return because of the political situation, he regained contact with his youngest brother. This fascinating letter is available to us apparently because Gerson's literary executor, the same Jean the Celestine, did not see the tensions in it that I find. Jean could have looked upon the letter as an expression of fraternal love. But a close reading reveals Jean's resentment that his eldest brother's attachment meant a form of control that the young Jean refused to allow.

Gerson's sisters, in contrast, appear in the available sources to have accepted his intervention in their lives. The death of their father in 1404 meant that he probably became their spiritual guardian, and except for the eldest, Marion, who remarried, they remained in the family home. The *Spiritual Dialogue* was probably written on Gerson's long journey abroad and is an indication of continuing concern for his sisters. He constructed an imaginary conversation with them in which they asked for his advice:

> Full brother by blood, but more in spirit, we your five sisters, have renounced mortal marriage for this life and the next. We have followed your advice in the grace of God and the holy commands of our good father and mother, who have left this world to a good end in God's mercy. . . .
>
> Several times already you have drawn on your knowledge and study of the Holy Scripture diligently to teach us, in person as well as in letters, treatises, and sermons. But now, as you may notice, it has been a long time since you have visited or instructed us. How often and how zealously we have wished for this, and not without reason.[36]

Gerson acknowledged his debt to his sisters. Just as their parents once had invested their "common good and inheritance" in his education in theology, he wanted to return this offering and give its benefits to his sisters. The dialogue that follows is meant to be structured on four days of discussion but actually stops in the course of the second day. Gerson wanted to make theological discussions on grace and free will understandable for his sisters and thus for anyone who read French and was interested in the spiritual life. He indicates that he was in contact with other women seeking the same kind of guidance, for he mentions a certain Agnes in Auxerre: "This devout woman, who had served God as an irreproachable virgin from her birth until her old age, asked me which verse of the Gospels is the most valuable cure or protection against all temptation. I answered that it was humility, as was revealed to Saint Anthony when he saw that the world was full of traps and sighing cried out to God, 'O Lord, who will escape them?' He was told: 'Humility.'"[37]

Agnes told Gerson that the greatest sign of humility is the sign of the cross. He agreed with her, and his description of their conversation hints that he did not approach the holy woman as a theological master instructing an ignorant female listener. He took it for granted that both participants had something to contribute. At times Gerson structured the dialogue as an argument, as in replying: "My sisters, I understand your objection, which is true of course and not contrary to what is said" (Gl 7.1.178).

Did Gerson really care about his family members, or do such treatises and letters indicate that the brother made use of his family in fictional dialogues and letters in order to assert the superiority of his learning and acumen? One historian has argued that rather than showing genuine brotherly love, Gerson approached his siblings in terms of his position of authority in the Church.[38] Another researcher has taken the opposite view and has criticized me for being too hard on Gerson in his attempts to care for and control women.[39] I would prefer to see Gerson as the brother who wanted to be in charge but also needed to be loved and appreciated. Behind his good advice and theological language, I find jealousy, insecurity, tenderness, desire for intimacy, and a search for lasting bonds.

The historian, looking back over six centuries, should, of course, be careful about any generalization concerning human feelings. But one final clue to Gerson's family bonds may appear in, of all places, a sermon for the Feast of All Souls, given in the Paris church of Saint Severin, probably in 1404.[40] The text is a traditional one, the lines from 2 Maccabees (12:44–45) stating that it is a holy and pious thought to pray for the dead. We who are in this world think about those to whom we are bound by family or other friendship (*en compagnie de lignage et d'autre amictie*; Gl 7.2.1031). Thus family bonds are the prototype of friendship, and Gerson hints he was thinking of his own family. His own father had died only six weeks earlier, on 14 September.

There follows a description of the content and power of prayer. Affectivity can turn completely to God and become pure prayer. At times prayer can lead to contemplation. As in the *Mountain of Contemplation,* Gerson considers here too the possibility that lay people without Latin theological learning could attain mystical insight (1032–33). He also discusses various ways in which prayer can profit the dead. There is a brief passage on the value of indulgences, a subject whose general absence from his writings indicates that it was not yet a central question for theologians. The faithful need not worry if they alone participate in the Mass and other prayers for the dead. In this way they could help their dead loved ones (1037).

Gerson never specifically mentions his father, but his evaluation of prayers for the dead indicates that the sermon was an intellectual response to the loss he felt. His own prayers and those of his friends and family members could make a difference for loved ones. In involving himself with members of his family, Gerson sought balance between caring and controlling the lives of others. He was afraid of letting his emotions take over, but he also refused to reduce his religious belief to purely intellectual categories.

Controlling the Lives of the Young

Concern for the spiritual well being of others also led Gerson, perhaps already in 1406, to provide a Latin guide for confessors, *On the Art of Hearing Confessions.*[41] Such works were common in the later Middle Ages, but Gerson's stands out for its directness in telling the confessor how to make the penitent reveal the precise content of sins.[42] He encourages the confessor to be alert to sexual transgressions: "It is known by experience that those guilty of such matters scarcely ever tell them in confession, unless they are encouraged by the most attentive artfulness, questioned, and finally taken captive in them."[43] In order to give the penitent the necessary confidence to entrust such matters to the confessor, the priest has to be calm and neutral: "Let the confessor above all be careful not to be harsh, melancholic, and rigid from the beginning. If he does so, he will soon close the mouth of the terrified sinner. His speech should at first be affable and if the situation sometimes requires it, he can show a certain familiarity concerning matters that are not sinful."[44]

Only by putting the penitent at ease could the confessor create the right atmosphere. But then come the hard questions: "Were you ever, from the time you reached the age of reason, in the company of servants or friends, and especially in bed? If you were, did you ever hear anything evil said to you, as often happens, about impurity and women? If so, did you speak in a similar way? And did you desire such evils? If so, did you ever want anyone to touch you in an indecent way, or did he you?"[45]

Once these questions have been posed, the priest can conclude whether masturbation had taken place. It can happen without seminal emission: it was a matter not of physical maturity but of consent. Such a passage indicates that Gerson was especially thinking of boys in their early teens, those he would have met in the school at Notre Dame.

Our author was writing within an established tradition, which saw the priest as the soul's doctor.[46] He used this image in making the confessor into a specialist, a surgeon who was to excise the cancer of sin. Gerson made specific what earlier had been implied in manuals for confession. The priest had to uncover every single detail from the penitent: "He is to be asked for how long and how often, and with how many it happened, and at what time of his life, and if some were of his own family. Finally, he is to be asked in what part of his body his lust or that of the other person was fulfilled" (Gl 8.15). When the priest poses such questions, he is to "proceed by being quick and indirect, in saying without changing his facial expression: 'Well then, I see that you did something similar with such and such.'" In this manner the confessor could reach the truth before the penitent realized how serious such actions are.

Gerson believed that boys often were intimate with each other and with male servants. Once they admitted such bonds, they would be more willing to concede contacts with women: "First of all if they at the age of five or six years ever lay in bed with female servants, as is common for boys" (15). Previous manuals for confession had for the most part discouraged priests from going into detail, for fear that suggesting intimate acts might give people ideas.[47] Now Gerson told the priest to find out everything. Whether the confessor liked it or not, he had to go ahead: "Someone might consider that he either does not know enough or does not wish to ask about such matters, because he perhaps is a shy and inexperienced surgeon, turning pale or unable to control himself in the face of such foul and terrible wounds. I will admit that caution is necessary, and one should not descend into these abominations with any sense of ease."[48]

Gerson placed a heavy burden on the confessor, who was obliged to uncover the soul's interior. In an even more specific treatise, probably from this same period, *On the Confession of Masturbation*, Gerson advised priests how they could trap young men and expose them as liars when they tried to deny that they masturbated. After speaking of other subjects, the priest is to maintain a familiar tone and then ask the youth: "'Friend, do you remember that you ever in your boyhood, around the age of ten or twelve years, experienced your rod or shameful member being erect?' If he says no, he is immediately convicted of lying, for he wants to flee and is afraid of being taken, since it is obvious that every boy experiences this in his body, when he has warmed himself in bed or elsewhere. Therefore he is all the more to be urged to tell the truth" (71). Once the youth concedes that he has experienced physical arousal, he is to be asked about his reaction: "What then were you doing so that it not be erect?" And so on and so on. At the beginning of this brief treatise, Gerson excused the "obscenity of the material" and his language "because of the need to teach remedies." Even when the penitent admits to holding and rubbing his penis, the priest was still to ask for more details: "Friend, I believe you, but for how long? For an hour or a half and for so long a time that the rod was not erect any longer?"

In Gerson's mind many adults, both men and women, were "infected by such a vice" but had never confessed it (72). Therefore it was the confessor's duty to use almost every form of cajolery to make the penitent admit that he (or she) indulged in such behavior. In *Art of Hearing Confessions*, Gerson indicated that in principle his advice was to be applied to both sexes: "I think that with women the reverse order is to be followed in making investigations: First, they are to be asked about intimacy with each other; afterwards with men or children. But I do not have complete experience on this matter."[49]

Even if Gerson's writings are examined within a literary and pastoral context, his great interest in the sexual behavior of boys is quite apparent. Before drawing any conclusion, however, it is necessary to consider a third work from this period, *On Bringing Youth to Christ*, probably also written soon after he took charge of the cathedral school. Gerson chose as his theme the stirring words from the Gospel of Matthew (18:6): "Whoever scandalizes one of the least of these little ones, it is better that he have a millstone fastened around his neck and be drowned in the depth of the sea." He interpreted this passage not only allegorically but also literally as a dire warning in the care of the young. Parents and teachers, he fulminates, allow the young to be exposed to "ignominious and salacious pictures and writings" (Gl 9.673–74), a reference to the debate about the *Romance of the Rose*.[50] In order to bring youth back onto the road leading to Christ, several methods must be followed: public preaching, secret admonition, the discipline of teachers, and confession. The last of these is the most effective way.

As in the other treatises, Gerson regrets that it is difficult to get young people to confess sins of a sexual nature. The priest has to deal with the "tyrannical force of modesty, even more so in women," which holds back the truth from the confessor (Gl 9.676). It can be harder to get people to open their mouths in confession than to make the mute speak: "Whoever then remembers the crimes of his youth and many other things, as I am conscious in myself, he should devote himself to this task, which deals with sins and their remission. Let him turn the sinner from the error of his ways and free his soul from death. You especially who teach and direct youths, be faithful in the discipline you maintain for them" (677). Once again Gerson takes himself as point of departure, hinting that as a young man he had experienced difficulty with sexual control. Now in adulthood, and as an ordained priest, he could make use of this knowledge in assuming that young people also needed guidance.

The teacher or confessor was obligated to find out who it was who "infected" the others. Gerson refused to accept the claim of his colleagues that the people who confessed to them "are not that kind": *Tales nulli sunt* (677). "The public correction of one [person] can keep others from freedom of sinning and of sinning in such a way [though] modesty does not allow [the sin] to be named" (678). In other words, if no one owns up to forbidden behavior, potential penitents will have no language in the confessional for describing their actions. So they will say nothing. But if one guilty person admits to the act, then the confessor can encourage others also to confess it.

There is no specific reference to sins of the flesh, but the mention of modesty and the context indicate Gerson's concern. He concedes that his attention to such matters did not receive universal approval. He had been told that theologians, or those entrusted with high office in the Church, should steer clear of the personal direction of souls, especially the young: "In my case this concern has led to tale-telling and the intimation of impropriety, as if there be a stench of something bad here."[51] Gerson had apparently gained a reputation for being too interested in boys.

Four reasons, he said, had been advanced to make him abandon his involvement. There was too large a gap between his way of life and that of the young; he should dedicate himself to "more important matters"; the times and places when and where he heard confessions were suspect; finally others were bound to attack his involvement simply because such a concern was unusual for someone in his position (679).

The responses reveal how Gerson looked upon himself and his commitment to pastoral work. To the first criticism he said that the confessor has to persuade young people he is their friend before they will confide in him. This is the same strategy he recommended in the *Art of Hearing Confessions.* To the obvious example of Christ's closeness to the young, Gerson added that of Socrates, but here he had to qualify his statement: "O if the censorious Catos of our age saw [Socrates], how much they would have laughed and made fun of him, even though we do not allow ourselves license to play with the young so that we seem to practice any abhorrent rashness or impurity in gesture, word or touching" (680–81). Socrates turned out not to have been so good an example, apparently because he was notorious for admitting physical attraction to handsome youths. Gerson had to make it clear that he did not relate to the schoolboys in such a way, but defended establishing psychological intimacy with boys in order to get them to confide in him. Some later admitted that they otherwise would never have confessed their sins, "even if they were in danger of death and on the point of being damned": "Admit then that in this benign condescension there is efficacy. . . . I have known some men who had heard confessions for many years and said they hardly ever or never were able to find someone infected by certain vices who previously had revealed them to anyone. Nor would they have been able to have gotten hold of these penitents unless they had done so with great care and gentleness, and by a certain pious trick" (*pia quadam fraude*; 681). In defense of his practices, and to counter the charge that he was too interested in the sexual behavior of youths, Gerson pointed to the results he had gotten: he got boys to tell him what they never before had admitted and would not tell anyone else!

Gerson answered more briefly the other accusations. There was no activity more important than that of saving souls. He achieved the best results not when he gave public sermons but when he spoke to youths individually. At the same time, he did not neglect the duties of his chancellorship (681–82). As for time and place, his conversations took place in the church itself and in public view. Finally, it made no difference that his predecessors as chancellors had not engaged themselves in this way. He used a maxim from Terence: Each has his own way of being.[52] In this connection he championed what he perceived was a new practice. If someone were forbidden to act in a good way only because it is a novelty, then society would be in trouble.[53] Finally he justified his activity on the basis of permission given him by the bishop of Paris and the consent of the youths' teachers:

> But my friends repeat what has been said: your adversaries, they say, slander this new practice as if it is a result of curiosity, falsehood, uselessness, too much superficiality or something of the kind. These are not new objections for me, my dearest friends. All of them I have myself considered and dealt with in myself (*Omnia dudum praecogitavi, et mecum ipse peregi*). For what human action can ever take place which will be devoid of criticism or negative or fatuous interpretation? (683)

If there was anything impure in his teachings or activities, he would willingly face God's just judgment. Finally, the children themselves bore witness to his innocence, for they came freely to him and he in no way forced them to confess. Time and again he had seen, also with adults, how people came to him in coldness but went away in tears. He had managed to console them. This was also the case with his sisters, where he once had wondered whether it was right for him to be so involved with them:

> Once when I was trying to encourage my sisters to live in a permanent state of celibacy, I experienced something carnal. I was afflicted by thoughts that emphasized vulgar custom, for they told me that what my devotion [to the sisters] sought was unusual. I was hesitating and thrashing about and almost decided to give up the holiness of my intention and to withdraw. But then finally, with God's help, I turned my eyes from the earth into heaven . . . and so I breathed again and felt that I was on solid ground. (684)

The *aliquid carnale* was apparently not sexual involvement, but a concern that he had failed to follow Christ's exhortation to leave behind the members of his biological family in order to join a spiritual one.

A few lines before, Gerson took the Pauline "we know no one according to his humanity" (*secundum carnem,* 2 Cor 5:16) and transformed it into the expression that "no one knows what is in a man except the spirit of the man which is in him" (683). Gerson wanted to separate himself from people and yet gain the most intimate knowledge of them. His description of the suspicions he aroused shows that medieval people did not need Freud to tell them that many human actions are motivated by conscious or unconscious sexual desire. But the chancellor insisted his motives were pure. At the same time, he tried to use his own position to give higher priority to the education of the young.

Did Gerson protest too much? He tried to convince himself and others that he did not abuse the privilege of his role as confessor to pry into sexual behavior. If we are what we talk and write about, then Gerson was a man worried about control over his own sexuality. In allowing himself such freedom in discerning boys' sexuality, he gave this subject an important place in his own life. Gerson leaves behind, in his own word, an odor or stench of what might, with an oxymoron, be called "auditory voyeurism." He had an apparent need to know about others, especially boys and young men. There is no element of naiveté in his prescription of what the confessor should do and what he risks. At one and the same time Gerson needed to control others so that he could control himself.

Guiding Students in Mystical Theology

Probably in the autumn of 1407, before Gerson left for his mission to the papacy, he gave a second set of lectures on mystical theology. While his teaching on the subject a few years earlier concentrated on speculative aspects, Gerson now provided a *Practical Mystical Theology.* He published the two treatises together in March 1408 and returned to them later at Lyon as one of his most important works, summarizing his concerns from the first years of the century.[54]

"Each person should wait for God's call" (Gl 8.19). God's grace is essential, and so human effort is secondary, "although such effort should not be completely neglected" (18). Gerson was no Pelagian, but he did believe in the saving value of hard work. This treatise contains much advice about the effort that the individual Christian could exert in order to come to the knowledge and experience of God. Thus it is worthwhile that we strive to know ourselves and make use of our natural powers and inclinations (21).

One type of person is the "gentle and friendly heart" which naturally seeks love: "Very easily drawn to the tranquility of contemplation, such a soul considers now the passion of the Lord, now the dignity of God and his love for the soul, and now the good and sorrowful lives of male and female saints of the past. . . . The feminine sex is especially endowed in this capacity, and so it is often called pious and devout."[55] Gerson may have been thinking of his sisters and their religious lives. He was speaking to an all-male audience and thus indirectly encouraged its members to be attentive to the women they knew and to respect their interior lives. Gerson advised his students to avoid thinking that mystical theology is found only in "subtle and varied cognition." It also can involve direct experience:

> For often when there is less cognition, there arises more affection. "Love enters when knowledge remains outside." Those who rejoice imitate the sound of the timbrel or harp. They do not know much about the harmony of the song, but they have enough in rejoicing through their exuberant dance. . . .
>
> You similarly, in that which you read, hear, see, speak, or think, convert it immediately into affectivity, as if you breathed it from within, smelled or tasted it.[56]

Gerson was close here to Hugh of Saint Victor and the Victorine emphasis on the affective life.[57] Theological training based on logical investigation of authorities in scholastic discourse was not enough. He asked his students to seek the experience of God.

At the same time, Gerson did not hesitate to combine pagan with Christian wisdom: "In the final analysis, God has given nothing to mortals without our expending great effort, as the poet says."[58] Horace could be used to tell students of theology that they could not sit around and wait for the grace of God to manifest itself in their lives. They had to work hard: "Blow on the fire, give it life, do not give up on reading, meditating, and praying until the spark of devotion, however tenuous, emerges" (31).

Gerson's good advice included the question of a suitable time and place and even bodily positions for prayer and meditation: "One person stands, the other kneels, while a third is prostrate with the whole body. Another stoops forward or lies on his back. . . . Or a person lifts up his eyes, as much as he can; another turns them downward. Yet another marches around here and there; another stops in his tracks; and another person takes a stroll" (35). Each person should do what seems best in order to prepare for the state of contemplation. Some people, "but only a few," could be inspired by physical enjoyment in dancing and music. For these favored persons, "lust has no place and unclean impulses do not take over" (36).

Gerson was optimistic but at the same time pragmatic. He recommended choosing a time when food has been digested (presumably to avoid falling asleep) and no one is in the vicinity to watch or listen to "the heavy groaning, the sighing erupting from deep within the breast, the bitter cries, broken-off complaints, humble prostrations, teary eyes, the face now full of blushing shame, now of chalky pallor" (36). The process of contemplative prayer involved the entire body: it was not the quiet meditative posture favored today in some religious communities.

However, he also warns against pushing the body too far. The person who pursues contemplation "will need more renewal through food and sleep" (38). He thus departed from a long tradition of asceticism going back to the Desert Fathers, for "the body needs to be nourished in order to aid the mind. It should not be destroyed by overeating or self-starvation" (39). Each person should be aware of his own situation, perhaps an allusion to Gerson's Celestine brothers and what he considered to be excessive fasting and other observances.

Much more than restraint in eating, Gerson required silence and solitude so that there be room for prayer. He excoriated his own colleagues: "Why is there, alas, such a paucity of contemplatives, even among learned and religious churchmen, indeed even among theologians, unless because scarcely anyone is able to stand being alone with himself long enough so that he can come to meditate?" (41) This is vintage Gerson, dissatisfied with the gap between what was taught and what was lived. For him a faculty of theology was not just an institution of learning; it should prepare students for a life of prayer.

Mystical theology involves not only affectivity but also understanding. He envisions a world that is returned to God through contemplation. In this process the soul, through love, enters a divine darkness, "where God is known ineffably and extra-mentally" (45). Here Gerson stops short, admitting that he has reverted to the "speculative dimension" of mystical theology (46). He makes one final effort to describe the process in terms of human experience, recalling the distinctions drawn by Bernard of Clairvaux and closing with the language of the Song of Songs.[59] Finally he adds a "list of some teachers who have spoken of contemplation," mixing standard works with more recent ones.[60]

Gerson's earlier *Mountain of Contemplation* anticipated many of the insights and teachings found in his *Practical Mystical Theology.* A reader who expects to find a detailed how-to guide in terms of reaching mystical experience will be disappointed. But Gerson did encourage his audience to seek the contemplative life. He was careful not to reduce the experience to something physical, even though he considered sense impressions and even bodily positions. His recommendations to a large extent leave it up to the individual to find his or her own way.

Gerson was addressing students who would one day direct church and society, but who, at the same time, yearned for a life of contemplation. He was sure that "a spiritual thirst will goad you on" (46). Such a thirst needed to be controlled and directed through human effort linked to divine grace.[61]

Guiding the Laity in Two Languages

From the time Gerson returned to Paris from Bruges in the autumn of 1400, he wrote moral treatises of instruction for the laity and parish priests. The importance of these works is apparent from the number of copies that survive in fifteenth-century manuscripts, especially the so-called *Tripertitum,* consisting of a guide to the commandments, *Le miroir de l'âme* (also called *Le livre des dix commandemens;* Gl 7.1.193–206); one preparing the penitent for confession on the basis of the seven capital sins, *Examen de conscience* (393–400); and thirdly advice on dying, *La science de bien mourir,* also called *La médecine de l'âme* (404–7). Gilbert Ouy has recently shown that all these works were probably written first in Latin and then translated by Gerson himself into French.[62] Trained to express himself in Latin, Gerson used the language of the schools and then turned to the vernacular. Ouy's bilingual edition shows how Gerson wrote in Latin, then translated into French, and finally improved the Latin version.

One Latin passage, which is briefer in French, is found in the exposition of the commandment "Thou shalt not commit adultery." Here the Latin provides more information about the types of sexual sins.[63] In general, however, the French text contains the essence of what is given in Latin.

Gerson sent off this work to a bishop, as we know from the covering letter, which probably can be dated to before March of 1404.[64] It contains the protestations of humility that one would expect in such a dedication, but Gerson apparently thought well enough of the result to encourage the bishop to make use of the work, or any similar one, so that "on each Sunday and feast day the content of divine law will be made known everywhere in your diocese." As in the *Doctrinale* much earlier, Gerson imagined his work being read aloud to the people or at least paraphrased as part of the homily at mass. He was concerned that sermons did not contain enough information about the commandments "either because of . . . ignorance or the neglect of the preachers" (Gl 2.72).

This work, together with the other two in the *Tripertitum,* was addressed to the widest audience. It can be dated to 1404 or the years immediately afterwards.[65] The prologue explains that it was to be used for four types of believers: parish priests; the laity or religious who are unable to attend church to hear sermons dealing with such matters; young people who are to be taught about the essence of the faith; finally those who care for the sick and work in hospitals. Gerson railed against the ignorance of parish priests, one of his stock themes. But he also encouraged parents to make sure that their children's schools had teachers who were well informed. All entrusted with the care of children were to make sure that they were properly taught. Those who had failed in the past could now do penance by making use of Gerson's writings. Such an action would provide satisfaction for sin and be better than a corporal work of mercy! In addition, he asked that the secular power issue a decree in support of the dissemination of these books and that church prelates give indulgences to those who did so.

The three treatises making up the *Tripertitum* contain standard fare. Their very predictability and sobriety probably assured a longstanding success. Gerson was skeptical about the training priests normally received and tried to compensate, thus taking a first step toward a program of education not fully carried out until the Council of Trent a hundred and fifty years later, with its creation of seminaries for educating priests.

Much more detailed and theologically challenging is Gerson's work (perhaps as early as 1400–1401) on how to distinguish between mortal and venial sin (*Le profit de savoir quel est péché mortel et venial;* Gl 7.1.370–89). It may have been originally intended for his sisters, as hinted at the end of his preface.[66] But as elsewhere, he expressed himself in such a general way that his teachings were relevant for everyone.

Gerson warned against women who put others into danger because they like to show off their clothing or beauty or ability to dance (371–73). They should act modestly, but they need not go to the other extreme and practice exaggerated asceticism. It is not necessary for a woman to dress in a sack or make herself look ugly. Gerson provides advice on many topics here. If a person who goes often to confession feels no sense of devotion, then she should do so more rarely. But if she profits from frequent confession, she can confess even daily. The same is the case with frequent communion: daily communion can be good for the soul (383). Gerson's acceptance of this practice is surprising in view of the often assumed reluctance among priests to allow lay people to receive the Eucharist on a daily or even weekly basis.[67]

Ordinary people were to keep humbly to their faith and not be too curious about its substance (385). Priests were not to encourage *simples gens* to "make great investigations about such truths." Gerson, nevertheless, did encourage lay people to be well enough informed so they can judge their own moral behavior. His approach as "consoling doctor" is reflected in many of the brief moral treatises which came from his pen during these years. He warned against scruples (*Contre conscience trop scrupuleuse;* Gl 7.2.140–42). God wants us to serve him only in reasonable ways. We should not go overboard, for as the proverb says, nothing that is too much can be good.[68] Therefore, forget past failures; do not be concerned about incomplete confessions of long ago; do not try to live as a solitary if you have to be in a community; give your love to God without worrying too much about hell; maintain a firm intention not to sin in future, but if you do sin, just ask for God's pardon. If a person is in doubt, make a general confession. When the enemy persists, it sometimes is best just to laugh at the thoughts he sends. There is no sin for as long as complete consent is lacking (142).

Directing Secular Clergy, Monks, and Religious

Such comforting considerations are expanded in *Treatise on different temptations of the enemy.*[69] Here Gerson may have been thinking of people living in religious communities, whether or not they had taken vows. Again he may have been reflecting on the situation of his sisters. He worried that they might go too far in their observances. Sometimes, he wrote, the devil encourages us to exaggerate our fasts or to go on great pilgrimages (Gl 7.1.344). This can be a temptation to pride. Or the devil can trick us, as in making it seem right to get angry in order to correct someone else. The enemy may counsel silence when bad things are said about someone because of our fear of displeasing the slanderer (345). Likewise the devil may tell us to show discretion in fasting and so stop us from fasting altogether.

Gerson was suspicious of anyone who claimed to be in direct contact with God as his "holy and devout friend" (*saincte et bien devote et amie;* 346). The enemy may give us a false security in thinking that we are doing right, or he may upset us by telling us we are at fault. He may paralyze our good intentions and make it impossible to pray (347).

In general the devil likes to make us impatient with what we are, so that we want to be something or someone else. Those who are in the religious life desire marriage, while the married want to escape (348). Members of religious communities imagine how much more good they could do if they lived alone, while solitaries think it would be better for them to live in the world (348–49). The enemy may delay us with pious thoughts when we have duties toward those others with whom we live. This is the temptation of *singularité, qui est très mauvaise* (349).[70]

Gerson's multiple cases show great understanding of human emotions. He says, for example, that we become melancholy when we think another person is speaking or acting in a certain way in order to hurt us. Divisions occur between husband and wife, sister and brother, friends, or people in the religious life: "But the enemy acts sometimes so that the person hides in her heart such resentments that grow all the more and do greater harm because they are kept inside, and the other person is not given a chance to explain herself" (Gl 7.2.350).

Gerson may have been drawing on his knowledge of people from the confessional or could have been thinking of his relationship with his brothers in Paris. He may have referred to his own experience when he described how the devil sends troublesome thoughts especially when we are trying to pray (353). We can worry about sinning, but if we do not consent, then there is no sin.

A further indication of Gerson's directing the spiritual lives of the clergy and religious is a sermon delivered to a synod on 26 February 1404, shortly after his return from his first mission to Benedict XIII. It has been entitled *On the Life of Clerics* but is also known as "Do penance and believe in the Gospel" (Gl 5.447–58; cf. Mark 1:15).

This is one of Gerson's strongest attacks on clerical abuses, and the strength of the language shows that Gerson had the same awareness as would many sixteenth-century reformers about what was wrong within the Church. Gerson saw the clergy abusing its privileges, as when houses of prayer became places of trade and dens of robbers (453). Priests gossiped about secular matters or concentrated on church incomes "which we seek even though they are not owed us." Gerson reminded his listeners of the sacred images found in their churches: "The cross and the crucified, should they not remind us that we are to do penance?" (453). Also saints' images should show us "that we must enter the kingdom of God through many tribulations." Finally, places of burial in the churches remind us of the transience of this life.

In this sermon Gerson completed the theme of penance on which he had begun to preach years earlier. Then he had spoken to lay audiences, but now he was dealing with clerical colleagues, reminding them of their duties. He alludes briefly to the "blasphemy" involved in yearly games or entertainments that take place in churches and which he attacked in greater detail in his little tract on the "Feast of Fools."[71] True penance was more necessary than ever because of the Schism. People had all kinds of doubts about behavior and authorities: "I know that some are worried by scruples and questions about reserved cases and the power of the keys and other dilemmas with which the present schism is filled" (456). What mattered, Gerson insists, is to do penance and to trust in God. He uses one of his favorite *exempla,* concerning how Saint Anthony was saved from the traps of devils not by knowledge but by humility.[72]

In a final list of the eight cries of woe issued by Christ, Gerson accuses some of his colleagues of contributing to these laments because they "despoil widows and the simple"; they promote members of their own family to office; they misuse oaths; they squeeze tithes out of their parishioners but neglect much more important matters; they are fanatical about the cleanliness of the sacred vessels in church but neglect their own uncleanliness. Woe to the hypocrisy of those who pretend through external actions that they are holy but within are full of hypocrisy (458). They are the whitened sepulchers Christ called the Pharisees. Finally, woe to those who pretend to show reverence to the saints and who cultivate their burial places, but do not imitate them. And so "a horrendous conclusion": the clergy left behind the house of the Church almost deserted, as the synagogue had been deserted.

Even though Gerson was not challenging the authority of the church hierarchy and was speaking to clergy and not to peasants, his message was close to that of Jean de Varennes.[73] In April of 1408, after he had returned from his second mission to the two popes, he went almost directly from Paris to a diocesan synod at Reims, where he spoke "On the office of the pastor" (*De officio pastoris;* 123–44). Here he went into even greater detail about what was required from the good shepherd of souls. He laments that many prelates look down on the function of preaching and leave it to impoverished theologians or the mendicants![74] Bishops are more interested in choosing the men who cultivate their fields than those who take care of the spiritual cultivation of the people.

The elevation of the status of preaching and better education of the clergy, however, are not enough. Priests also need experience of the lives of the people who are to be taught (129). Gerson the country boy reminds his clerical audience to consider who it is they are teaching.

Gerson lays out twelve concrete recommendations for what the Church needs to do. There had to be more and better hospitals for the sick, and these should offer care of the souls as well as bodies. Churchmen are not to burden the poor with excessive taxes or "oppressions" (134). Gerson cites Bernard of Clairvaux's *On Consideration* as a warning against plundering of the poor. He is skeptical about making new church foundations when old ones are in need of maintenance and repair (135). Vicars should have enough to live on, and so the holders of benefices should be provided with decent incomes for their stand-ins.

Gerson's moral tone and ironic stance recall twelfth-century treatises on clerical reform, as when he denounces some clerics for being more devoted to their dogs than to the poor in their parishes.[75] He worries that some schools and religious houses had become houses of prostitution, "with no regard for gender, order, status, family, age, bond of holy religion, matrimony, spiritual affinity, or shame for the parts of the body" (139).

A remedy for such practices he found in the sacraments, and the final section of the sermon reviews all seven, in warning against a chronic lack of respect toward them by both people and clergy: the laughing and talking going on in church, the buying and selling, and Gerson's special concern with the Feast of Fools (140). His main point, however, was that the clerical church had to be visible and available to the people. Bishops and other officials should make visitations; otherwise the people see only the mendicants and poor men who preach without authorization (143). Gerson recommends annual provincial synods, of the very type he was attending at Reims. He further asks if the time had not come for a general council of the entire Church.

This sermon is the fullest statement so far of Gerson's program for church reformation.[76] He also wrote to a new bishop a briefer list of needs without as many details (Gl 2.108–16). In both cases, Gerson thought of the Church in terms of the bishops. He is often seen in terms of his contribution to the debate on the status of the papacy, but his ecclesiastical thinking focused on parishes and bishoprics. At Paris and Reims, as well as at Bruges, he involved himself with everyday concerns, even about how to keep dogs from urinating on altar cloths.[77]

The Gerson who worried about neglect in parishes by no means idealized other forms of Christian life. He criticized monastic institutions, especially for women, and had doubts about the advantages of solitude. To a hermit living outside Paris, Gerson wrote a rule and told him that his choice had not shown "sufficient discretion." He had earlier worried about the hermit's wrong attitudes. Now, however, he accepted the life the man had chosen: "Many things are to be tolerated because they have been done, even though they are displeasing."[78]

Gerson preferred the combination of active and contemplative life possible for a parish priest or university theologian. To his sisters he also recommended both physical labor and regular periods of prayer (Gl 7.1.56). In exercising control, Gerson showed both care and concern.

Controlling Aristocratic Violence and Encouraging Good Government

If it was hard to control parish priests, bishops, hermits, and devout women, it was practically impossible to direct lay aristocrats. After the death of Philip, the duke of Burgundy, in 1404, the first sign of unsettled times was a tragicomic incident in the summer of that year during a procession of clerics and scholars from the university to the Parisian church of Saint Catherine. A young retainer of the king's chamberlain, Charles of Savoisy, accidentally or on purpose ran into them. He was pulled off his horse and slapped. Insulted, he returned to his master, who ordered his horsemen to attack the procession.[79] What followed is described in an oration, "Be merciful" (*Estote misericordes*), given a week later by Gerson before the Parlement of Paris (326–40) in which he asked that mercy be shown not in forgiving the guilty party but in requiring justice from it.

Gerson was particularly angry because the aristocrats had beaten up scholars whom he called "my sons the schoolboys" (*mes fils les escoliers*). There had been "terrible noise and cries and clamor" (330). Even the church building had not been safe. Armed men had penetrated into its interior and stopped the mass. Some of the women present tried to hide youths beneath their clothes. When barbarians had plundered Rome, they had spared those in churches, but these new barbarians had not done so.[80]

If such an outrage could take place in the center of France, "near the king's residence, the Parlement and the Chastelet," what then might happen elsewhere in the kingdom? (331) In 1413 Gerson would himself come to experience the rage of the Paris mob. Now in 1404, he was shocked that the capital city could be the scene of such violence. What will the king's subjects say when they realize they are safer in the forest or desert than in a "city that is the most noble and strong and great of all in the kingdom of France"? (332).

The university's reputation, he warned, would suffer from the incident. Parents would hesitate to send their sons to Paris to study, for fear of their safety. Equity required equal treatment of rich and poor (339). If the Parlement did not punish the malefactors, then it could be said that its court instead was punishing the very poor who had been attacked.

The judgment on Charles de Savoisy and his men came a month later. It gave compensation to the university, as described in the *Chronicle of Saint Denis,* our richest source for politics and life in Paris during these years.[81] The author ignored Gerson's speech, perhaps out of dislike for a representative of the church that defied his monastery with the relics of Saint Denis. The first mention of Gerson's existence in this chronicle is in connection with an important sermon from 7 November 1405, *Vive le roy.* The compiler decided not to provide its entire text, but he did summarize its content.[82]

Gerson spoke in the aftermath of an apparent reconciliation between Louis, the duke of Orleans, and the new duke of Burgundy, John the Fearless. In order to understand the sermon's significance, it is necessary briefly to review the political events of the preceding months, as recorded by our Saint Denis monk. The situation at Paris was unstable in the summer of 1405. When the duke of Burgundy arrived in Paris, the queen left the city with the duke of Orleans for Melun. She tried to get the dauphin, the duke of Guyenne, to be brought the next day, but when the duke of Burgundy heard of the attempt on the youth's "indecent" removal, he rode at top speed through Paris and managed to catch up with the group that was taking the dauphin to the queen.[83]

The rest of the summer various negotiations took place about the dauphin, while military forces were being gathered on both sides: "And since between them there seemed to persist an unquenchable hatred, thoughtful men feared that the division of the princes would harm the kingdom and lead to the dangers of war."[84] The citizens of Paris appealed to the old duke of Berry as a go-between, who subsequently ordered the city's gates closed and iron chains made for them.

On 29 August 1405, the clergy of Paris, together with the members of the university, held a solemn procession. When the rector as well as some of the professors approached the queen and the duke of Orleans to enable a settlement, she refused to listen to them and the duke answered them in French and told the delegates to get back to their schools where they belonged: "By returning you will then through your studies rightly fulfill your ministry, for if the university is called the daughter of the king, then it has no business in dealing with the government of the kingdom."[85]

The duke thereby dismissed the view shared by Gerson that the university, as the king's daughter (*fille du roi*), was to give him wise and loyal counsel. The duke of Orleans may have been so harsh because he looked upon the university as an ally of his rival, the duke of Burgundy. But his words were prophetic. The international role of the University of Paris, which reached its height during these years, was coming to an end. The university that had allied itself so closely with the monarchy would either be victimized by a weakened monarchy or monopolized, as later in the fifteenth century by Louis XI.[86]

The troubles continued through September of 1405, and the threat of civil war increased, especially when a troop of men tried to make its way into the duke of Berry's residence. According to the *Chronicle,* many Parisians thought that the duke of Orleans would attempt to remove the king from Paris by force.[87] On 20 September, the duke of Orleans assembled his men on a field outside Melun, while on the same day three thousand Burgundians occupied the village of Argenteuil near Paris and the surrounding countryside. Many nobles and bourgeois in the Ile-de-France took refuge inside the gates of Paris, and peasants fled into fortified towns, abandoning their crops to pillage by the troops.[88]

At this juncture the chaos ended. On 17 October, the queen and the duke of Orleans returned to Paris, and the two dukes gave all the signs of reconciliation required in a society based on rituals: "With peaceful embrace and shaking of hands and giving of oaths, they bound themselves to remain in peace."[89]

In the chapter immediately following, our chronicler mentions Gerson and uses his sermon *Vive le roy* to show the university's desire to support reconciliation. Gerson began with the state of the kingdom as seen by the University of Paris: As the king's daughter she finds disturbances and wrongdoing everywhere: *Elle voit turbacion partout, meschief par tout:*

> She sees in many places harsh oppression of the people: instead of justice violence, instead of mercy rapine, instead of protection destruction, instead of support subversion, instead of pastors pillagers, instead of defenders persecutors. There are violation of virgins, the prostitution of married women, arson in holy places, the profanation of the sacred, the murdering of many; and see what is worse and horrible, that people kill themselves out of anger and despair over obligations that they cannot bear. (Gl 7.2.1138)

This description belongs to Gerson's protheme or introduction. The princes' dissension had divided the kingdom, and the people had paid for the result. He appealed to the good examples of past kings, such as King John the Good (1350–64), who kept his word and "for this reason returned to England" when his ransom was not paid (1143).

Gerson considered the university's role, perhaps in response to the duke of Orleans' order for scholars to keep to their books. The university seeks peace. Its members must react as knights do and defend what is right. "Can the university . . . close its eyes?" It cannot let the kingdom be destroyed and remain silent in the face of evils (1145). It must speak the truth to its father the king and in doing so represent "not only all the kingdom of France, but all the world, since from all places come or can come those eager to acquire learning and wisdom" (1146).

Dealing with the king's first life, his physical one, Gerson called for prudent men of state to surround him. They should not overwhelm the king with work or other pressures, "as one has often seen to his great harm" (*en son grant preiudice*; 1147). He almost blamed the king's illness on his counselors. But instead of dealing at length with the king's health, Gerson moved quickly to the dauphin's situation and emphasized the importance of his education. He was to be well taught, in the tradition of Saint Louis (1148). Gerson's hope, Louis of Guyenne, was eight years old at the time and would die at the age of eighteen.

The king's second life is his political one (1149). Here Gerson mentions the cardinal virtues necessary for good rule. He warns against flatterers, and once again emphasizes the central role of the university in advising the king or his council (1151). It was necessary to speak out openly, no matter what the consequences; dissimulation was no solution (1153).

It is not easy to sum up Gerson's political message in these many pages. The king was not to exceed his rightful power. The tyrant oppresses with foreign troops, exactions. He oppresses places of study and defies all assemblies of the people (1158). Gerson may have been thinking of the duke of Orleans, but he could just as well also have feared the duke of Burgundy.

The tyrant, Gerson warned, cannot long endure; he seldom dies a natural death: "It is right that death . . . comes to those who exercise tyranny. Also nothing that is violent can last" (1159). Gerson paraphrased the biblical warning about living and dying by the sword (Mt 26:52). Such a statement would be qualified much more carefully after the murder of the duke of Orleans in 1407.

A long section warning against flattery (1161–64) leads to a call for an assembly of the whole country, a meeting of "nobles as well as clerics and bourgeois, to deal openly with the deplorable state of their country" (*le miserable estate de leur pays,* 1165). The inhabitants of Paris, "where there are the riches of the kingdom" have no idea about the situation in the countryside. Gerson apologizes for speaking out so boldly, but he was aware of the sufferings of students, who came from all over the country with stories of woe (1165–66).

The nobility needed to be better educated, in order to assure that it ruled the country well. Its children should be brought up by clerics who teach them stories of military valor (1168); nobles should live in frugality not luxury, as the great rulers of old from Caesar Augustus to Charlemagne did (1169); they should pay their soldiers well, for otherwise these will pillage the countryside, as had already happened.

Gerson details the situation for poor people outside Paris. Some of them had to survive on almost nothing. With six small children, "they ask for bread and cry out in the rage of hunger." Soldiers come and plunder the hen or four chickens that the family owns (1170), and then beat up the man and the woman and set fire to their house. When people reach such a point, some of them despair and commit suicide (1171). It is the king's duty to control such violence and to protect the rural population. For the time being, however, loyal subjects are harassed more by the kingdom's own soldiers than by its enemies, presumably the English (1172).

Another source of oppression is greedy officials (1173). Gerson's critique is so graphic that it cannot be dismissed as the usual themes in sermons to princes encouraging them to have loyal advisors. Gerson saw in the growth of a university, such as the one at Orleans, which educated lawyers, a threat to the prospect for justice. "You have certainly heard of the good lady who saw the students at Orleans and asked what they were doing." She was told they were studying to become judges and lawyers. "Alas, she said, there is only one procurator in our region and the peace is thereby almost totally destroyed. What will happen with such a great crowd?" (1174–75)

This sermon is the closest Gerson came to laying out a political sketch of how France should be ruled. He recommends the calling of the Estates General, as a century earlier in the time of King Philip the Fair, and asks for legislation limiting consumption. He compares the simple knight of his day with King John the Good. The knight now has more food, drink, and clothing than the king once had. Greek and Roman princes had once also passed sumptuary laws. At the same time, taxes should be more fairly distributed, rather than overburdening one part of the population (1178–79).

The final section concerns the spiritual life of the king and the kingdom and again emphasizes the role of the university and the advice it gives. If it had existed in the time of Mohammed, then his religion would not have gained so much power (1182–83).

In closing this magisterial exposition, almost fifty pages in the Glorieux edition, Gerson indulged in a type of laudatory rhetoric from which he normally restrained himself. He called on "all good French people who in devotion, joy, and exaltation will make and do make this beautiful cry: *Vivat rex, vivat rex, vivat rex; vive le roy, vive le roy!*" (1185).

Upon reviewing such a sermon, it is difficult to agree with scholars who insist that the beginnings of national feeling belong to a later period.[90] Gerson used the monarchy as a rallying point for all who lived within the kingdom of France. In his summons to moral and political reform, he frequently made use of shared symbols in French history. The king was anointed by God himself through the archbishop of Reims. He had a duty to look after all estates of the realm, especially the weak. Gerson asserted a social contract and warned against its abrogation.

Losing Control over Church and Society

Gerson's grand plan for the reform of the kingdom came to naught, thanks in part to the dukes of Orleans and Burgundy. But the immediate aftermath of his sermon was a rare show of unity against the Avignon pope, Benedict XIII, who had tried to impose a tithe on the Gallican Church to pay for a proposed journey to Italy. Some of the university members would have been affected, but they claimed exemption from such payments. According to the *Chronicle of Saint Denis,* the dukes ordered the papal collectors not to "harass" the university.[91] When Benedict persisted, its members met and decided to suspend all sermons and lessons, a strike that lasted until the end of January 1406.[92] Probably in November 1406, Gerson issued a brief memorandum on how to end the Schism (*Acta de schismate tollendo;* Gl 6.97–98). He saw a danger that it might continue for generations. There was no reason to continue fruitless discussions about the origins of the Schism or the justice of either side. Human laws had failed to resolve the dilemma, and now it was time for divine law, which could disregard the usual canonical procedures. Thus the pope of one obedience might choose to transfer his rights to his rival, like the true mother in the story of Solomon who willingly gave up her child in order to save its life (1 Kings 3).

Each obedience might hold a general council, in which both popes voluntarily gave up power. Another possibility was for the two colleges of cardinals to meet as a single body in order to choose a pope whom all would accept, "either now or at an opportune time and place." This scenario was the one adopted a few years later at the Council of Pisa.

"Men's traditions" had been observed "too literally, if not to say pertinaciously" (98). Union was to be sought "in conformity with divine and evangelical law rather than through the literal-minded assertion of human laws and of one's own side's worldly honor or its victory through a devastating war." Gerson imagined each side was still jockeying for military support so they could force the rival to resign.[93]

In November 1406, news of the death of the Roman pope, Innocent VII, gave a new incentive for ending the Schism. Gerson again took up his pen for another brief catalogue of suggestions and possibilities. If the Roman observance elected a new pope, he warned, the Schism would just continue. The new pope might, of course, willingly offer cession of power, but this was uncertain, as prior experience had made clear! (*Hoc autem quantum sit incertum experientiae priores manifestant;* 99).

Gerson suggested that the cardinals of the Roman observance choose to make Benedict pope, thus ending the Schism. Whatever happened, however, people were not to blame each other for the past; instead it should be possible to seek some kind of "general absolution." Benedict, even if he were the true pope, might be required by the Church as a whole to resign (103). A third possibility was that representatives of the one obedience met with those of the other. They could then proceed to a common election, something greatly to be preferred to any future one-sided action.

In conclusion Gerson recommended that the king send delegates to the Roman cardinals to convince them to delay the election. The French request was to be made in general terms, without committing the cardinals to elect or to exclude Benedict. Gerson was careful not to appear as the enemy of the Avignon pope, but he was not his staunch supporter either. What mattered was a quick solution.

Behind these concise statements, there is a note of impatience, different from the tone of Gerson's earlier sermons on the Schism. He may have been writing for the Fourth Council of Paris, a meeting of the clergy, which opened on 17 November 1406.[94] After the election of Gregory XII as Roman pope on 30 November, there were heated debates about how to proceed. Finally, on 4 January 1407, the council made a partial withdrawal of obedience from the Avignon pope, who no longer was to have any say in ecclesiastical temporalities. The French clergy and the University of Paris would cease asking Avignon to recognize benefices and other ecclesiastical sources of income.

On 26 January 1407, Gerson addressed the council, but his sermon is lost.[95] It was decided to send an embassy in the name of the king and the university, and among the delegates were Gerson and Pierre d'Ailly, as well as the Pierre Cauchon who almost a quarter of a century later would be instrumental in the trial and condemnation of Joan of Arc.[96] Gerson's departing words were preached on 18 March in the cathedral of Notre Dame on the verse, "Go in peace" (Luke 7:50). They expressed optimism that the thirty-year old Schism now was drawing to its close (Gl 7.2.1095). Gerson and his colleagues believed that "the one of Rome," as he called Gregory XII, had accepted the way of cession.

The delegation first went to Benedict XIII. On 17 May Gerson gave a sermon before the cardinals at Avignon. We do not have the text, but the *Chronicle of Saint Denis,* probably thanks to the presence of its abbot in the delegation, provides a summary.[97] Gerson emphasized the centrality of the king's role. He asked the cardinals to go to Benedict and get him to give up the papacy. If he did not do so, the greatest scandal was in store for the Church. Finally, he suggested that both colleges of cardinals meet in order to elect one pope.

The papal response was not encouraging. The next evening Gerson and d'Ailly, together with Philippe de Villette, the abbot of Saint Denis, had a private interview in Marseilles with Benedict to get him to give his formal consent to the way of cession. As he had done on numerous previous occasions, Benedict refused to give more than vague assurances and would put nothing in writing.[98] Gerson, d'Ailly, de Villette and the king's secretary, Jacques de Nouvion, drew up a memorandum, *Reasons for delaying a withdrawal of obedience,* arguing that in spite of their disappointment with Benedict, nothing drastic should be done until their delegation had seen the Roman pope. Afterwards, however, they might have to react *rigidissime,* in the most severe way possible (Gl 6.106).

In this document Benedict is still called pope, while his Roman rival is merely referred to as "him of Rome," thus maintaining the earlier French attachment to Avignon. The delegates argued that if they withdrew obedience from Benedict at this point, they would weaken their bargaining position in Rome.

In Italy the Paris delegation had no more success than at Avignon. The frustration of Gerson and Pierre d'Ailly is reflected in a letter of 15 September 1407, addressed "to the most reverend father and lord, the Lord Angelo, who at Rome has had himself called Gregory XII."[99] They described their disappointment in a man whose name indicated "an angel divinely sent." Angelo was not to be more concerned with power than with charity (Gl 2.85).

Sometime between February and May 1408, Gerson and the other ambassadors returned to France and to a university that already had declared the two popes to be schismatic. Paris was dominated by a sense of foreboding after the murder on 23 November 1407 of the duke of Orleans by the duke of Burgundy's henchmen.[100] After fleeing the city, John the Fearless returned on 28 February, and on 8 March at the royal residence of Saint Paul, the theologian Jean Petit launched a defense of the murder by arguing that it was a justifiable act of tyrannicide. Since the duke of Orleans had tried to rule France as a tyrant, the duke of Burgundy had done the kingdom a necessary service in getting rid of him.

Gerson, whose position long had been tied to the dukes of Burgundy, did not react publicly. He had other immediate concerns: the culmination of the long dispute with the abbot of Bec over the church of Saint Jean-en-Grève. On 19 February 1408, he was granted a personal title to the benefice, but the original papal provision attaching the church to the office of chancellor was quashed.[101] The abbot of Bec protested, and so the matter dragged on.

In terms of the Schism, Gerson tried as ever to cope with a difficult situation by avoiding drastic solutions. Probably in the course of 1408 he wrote another public memorandum, concerning what the bishops should do during the new withdrawal of obedience.[102] This brief work, which has generally been ignored, provides a fascinating picture of a church without a papacy, one in which bishops would cope by being resident in their dioceses. They would keep their officials honest and confer holy orders only on deserving men, thus avoiding men who had concubines or who made money as usurers or merchants (Gl 6.108–9).

Gerson envisions episcopal visitations and suggests that a bishop send a doctor of theology with one or two bachelors [of theology] on his behalf (110). Here as elsewhere Gerson asked for a central role for theologians, not only as teachers but also as reformers. Such visitations would also include a canon lawyer and a notary to write down everything that was to be corrected. Parish priests were to be examined in terms of their condition, diligence, and learning (111). Gerson was certain that many of them were ignorant of the most basic sacramental forms, thus causing danger and scandal. Unless God in his mercy supplied what was missing, such priests would neither be able to baptize nor to absolve from sin (111).

Priests were to inform their visitors about the status of their parishioners: whether any were excommunicate or in temporal need. As for priests who live with concubines, they are not to be subjected to extreme measures. If they feared that if their women were sent away, they might behave even more badly. Gerson repeats here his earlier recommendation that unless a priest guilty of concubinage had been convicted in a church court, and denounced for his crime, he should be allowed to continue with his sacramental functions. "For if he is tolerated by his prelate why should he not be tolerated by his subjects?"[103] Otherwise, Gerson warns, the way is left open to infinite scandals and dangers. The holy men who formerly held the opposite view "did not see how deeply rooted evils are and how impossible it was to maintain the ancient rigor of church discipline" (113).

Gerson was not cynical, but he was skeptical about the possibility of changing priests' behavior. To some extent he was asking that monogamous clerical concubinage be tolerated. It was more important that parish priests were properly educated, used the right sacramental formulae, made church teachings available to parishioners, and were available for confession instead of having to send them to special confessors. Here as elsewhere Gerson recommends scaling down the clerical apparatus for reserved sins.[104]

Gerson pictured a decentralized Church, without reference to papal authority, but with bishops who took seriously their pastoral role and made use of theologians in contact with the people through visitations and sermons. His vision of church reform took into account everyday life in the parishes and the needs of the laity. He did not despair of clerical celibacy, but he certainly reduced expectations. Most of all, he sought to avoid a situation where the laity would come to doubt the efficacy of sacraments administered by priests who live in concubinage.

In the spring of 1408, Gerson had to turn from his moral and pastoral concerns to a much more immediate political question. The provost of Paris, William of Tignonville, had the previous autumn hanged two clerics.[105] For Gerson this action was a threat to the exemption from secular law for churchmen. Before the royal court, he insisted on the importance of punishing a secular official who had ignored the privilege of clergy.

In Gerson's eyes the provost was guilty of murder. Envious ambition had created a division between spiritual and temporal jurisdictions (Gl 7.2.610). Tignonville, in usurping the judgment of spiritual persons, had committed a crime.

The university had stopped lessons and sermons, but the provost had disregarded its protest and attended mass in spite of being excommunicated. Gerson said that he, as chancellor, had to deal with the question of the suspension of teaching, and so he could not ignore its cause (613). If Tignonville were allowed to get away with his crime, then the whole kingdom would be in danger. Gerson used the word *tirannie* (614) and thus invited comparison between the present case and the fact that a few weeks earlier, on 8 March, the theologian Jean Petit had justified the duke of Burgundy's murder of the duke of Orleans on the grounds of tyrannicide.

The sermon walks a tightrope, suspended between one form of killing and another. Gerson asked for punishment for someone who violated the exempt status of clerics and had them killed, while remaining neutral on the question of the killing of the duke of Burgundy.

Making Peace Come

"Let peace come," Gerson exhorted his audience a few months later (*Veniat pax,* 4 November 1408; Gl 7.2.1100–123). He was addressing the dauphin and through him the nobles who wanted the duke of Burgundy to be punished for his crime.[106] This group, later called the Armagnacs, had every reason to be suspicious of Gerson as the duke of Burgundy's man, and the sermon can be looked upon as a courageous act.

We have waited for peace and instead confusion reigns, Gerson began, borrowing a line from Psalm 88. The members of the university had done everything possible to provide peace in the midst of dissension, with public sermons, processions, delegations, and other means (1102). But now peace needed to come to the Church with the Schism's ending, in spite of the fact that "the one of Rome" had backed away from a promise to give up power (1103). As for his opponent, Gerson now publicly denied the Avignon pope's legitimacy. He referred to him in almost insulting language: "As for the one over here, what good can we say of him?" (*Et de celuy de par de ca, que en pourrons nous de bien dire?*; 103).

The solution would have to emerge at a council to be held at Pisa. In the meantime, everyone must pray for peace, which could come only to men of good will. The Schism could end only with God's help, "and as through a miracle." The task was beyond human strength (1104).

Spiritual peace in the Church, however, first required temporal peace in the kingdom of France (1105). Gerson referred to his sermon *Vive le roy* from 1405 and said that since that time he had occupied himself more than ever with this peace. Princes and nobles were not to assert their rights to such an extent that they ended up destroying peace. The university asked them to think in terms not of compensatory justice (*justice afflictive*) but of peace (1109–10). The point here seems to be that those who had been outraged by the murder of the duke of

Orleans had a legitimate grievance. But the need for peace should outweigh any call for justice and retribution.

Once again, as in *Vive le roy,* Gerson described the devastation brought about by war, where innocent children perish (1111). He added a new plea: the desire of the souls in purgatory for peace. When men war against each other, they do not have the time to remember the faithful departed with prayers and masses. The central Christian teaching, moreover, is pardon for offenders. If we do not forgive those who offend us, then we will end up as the faithless servant in the parable to whom Christ said, "I pardoned you, why do you not grant pardon?" (1112; cf. Mt 18:32).

Gerson assured his audience that the souls of King Charles VI, of Duke Philip of Burgundy and of Louis of Orleans were, "if it pleases God," in a state of salvation. All of them there asked for peace. The duke of Orleans when he heard of the conspiracy against him had told a monk, Pierre Bourguignon, "I pardon with a good heart everything, as I obtain pardon from God" (1113).[107]

War brings joy only to pagans, who see the divisions of Christendom. Also the enemies of the kingdom of France rejoice, such as the English, who "very happily would see civil war among us" (1116). Gerson questioned the code of honor behind aristocratic and chivalrous behavior. Jesus had not sought to guard his honor but allowed himself to be killed and did not ask for revenge (1117). Similarly one of King David's advisors encouraged him not to take revenge on his son Absalom (1119; cf. 2 Samuel 14).

Peace among the nobles would lift an intolerable burden from the people (1121). It would benefit all estates, *de segnorie, de chevalerie, de clergie et de bourgoisie* (1122). Gerson appealed to Christian values of forgiveness and reconciliation, which had taken centuries to emerge in the discourse of medieval life. In speaking in such a manner, he contradicted the demand for strict justice, which, a few years earlier, he had called the essence of mercy. Now mercy meant abandoning what justice required. In accord with the teachings of Christ and with the duke of Orleans' own alleged request, he asked for peace.

In 1408 Gerson had to face the possibility that the French monarchy, for him the hope of university, church, and people, would disintegrate. He believed in the power of the monarchy. If the king was disabled, then at least his son could be given the right teachings that would inspire his tutors and protectors.

Probably this same autumn, Gerson wrote to his mentor Pierre d'Ailly a letter that indicates continuing contact and even friendship between the two men. In it he accepts d'Ailly's weariness of the world he saw around him: "Everywhere are emptiness, madness, and falsity" (Gl 2.105). For a time it was necessary to seek solitude and also to look forward to the solitude of heaven, which Gerson surprisingly called "a deserted place." Here the stray sheep could come, while the ninety-nine had been left behind and thus apparently would not be saved! This strange twist to Christ's parable, implying that most people would never get to heaven, indicates a basically pessimistic view of life. Most of those we know in this life will not be with us in the next. Instead we can look forward to relief in heaven's solitude. "We often act like big children in our adversities, so that we wax angry in public affairs. We are indignant with ourselves or our neighbors and do not seek help. Nor do we flee, by looking to him who ought to save us from weakness of spirit and the tempest (Ps 54:9), just as the child who has fallen should seek help not by himself but from the father or mother who looks after him."[108]

This is a letter of spiritual consolation. There seems to be no political motive behind Gerson's words, no attempt to make use of d'Ailly's influence for any specific purpose. The chancellor is diplomatic, claiming that his advice is meant primarily for his own sake: "I am not presuming to teach you, merely attempting to deal with my own folly and goad myself out of my laziness" (106).

Gerson was hardly lazy, and for once, I think, he was using a literary convention, a commonplace of modesty. But this letter is not conventional, no more than his sermon to the princes. In seeking to comfort his teacher as well as in asking for forgiveness instead of revenge, Gerson looked to the sources of spiritual consolation found in the Sermon on the Mount.

Do we here detect a new voice in Gerson? Or is it a question of circumstances that bring out aspects of the religious heritage and theological learning he previously did not need to emphasize? Gerson's inner life remains an enigma, but it is during these years, from 1403 to 1408, that he revealed the struggle within him between affectivity and discipline. Seeking to control himself and those around him, he appealed to a divine law that is far beyond human legislation. Such a law could provide solutions for the Schism of the Church, just as the law of love and forgiveness in the Gospels could correct princes brought up to be arrogant and self-righteous.

As a conscious heir to twelfth-century affectivity, Gerson sought to trace the individual's movement toward God. With his own experience as a point of departure, he could provide advice for his sisters, give warnings to his brothers, and offer his students insights into mystical theology. The more Gerson speaks of love, however, the more vulnerable he becomes, as when he tried to defend his attachment to youths whose care was entrusted to him.

We end in dualism, the care and concern that turn into a need for control. In his certitude and contradictions, Gerson represents a central and misunderstood period in Western history, one that combined high ideals and deep human insights but failed in providing lasting and fruitful communities. For the moment, however, Gerson was about to contribute not to a failure but to a success, the beginning of the end of the Great Western Schism.

Losing Control and Finding a Loving Man, 1409–1415

During these years Jean Gerson remained for the most part in Paris and continued teaching, preaching, and writing. But his life was anything but placid. His scrupulous care for church and society contrasts with a loss of control. He lost his benefice in Bruges and finally gained one in Paris. He was driven from his lodgings and had to take refuge in the vaults of Notre Dame cathedral. He expressed regret for his initial decision not to speak out against the assassination of the duke of Orleans.

Gerson now chose sides and challenged a teaching on tyrannicide that defended the duke of Burgundy and his supporters. This was a decisive move, which threw him into the political cauldron and identified him with the enemies of Burgundy, the Armagnac faction. At the same time, Gerson chose a new spiritual champion. During the darkest days of 1413, when he lost his Paris home, Gerson was convinced that he escaped the mob under the protection of Saint Joseph. He thus became sure that the Church would accord Joseph his rightful place at Mary's side in the celebration of a feast day for their marriage. Gerson was convinced of the need for such a chaste husband and affectionate father. This loving man could give him the spiritual warmth he sought and feared in his own affective life.

Surviving in Everyday Life

On 23 March 1409 when the Council of Pisa opened, Jean Gerson was not present. Various explanations have been given for his absence, including his teaching duties at Paris, but the most likely reason is more mundane.[1] Gerson was in the midst of futile efforts to save his benefice at Bruges, while negotiating at the same time for the Parisian church of Saint-Jean-en-Grève. On 27 March Gerson appeared at the Parlement in order to defend his possession of Saint-Jean (Gl 10.493–98). The abbot of Bec had claimed the right to dispose of the position, and now the two parties reached a settlement according to which the chancellorship would be united with the benefice, but only during Gerson's lifetime.

A few weeks earlier, on 2 March, the cathedral chapter of Notre Dame had decided to wait until its coming chapter general to discuss the matter of a union of this benefice and the chancellorship.[2] In the meantime Gerson had apparently seen that his chances of linking the university office with a church benefice were limited, and so he reached a compromise to satisfy both Bec and the university. After years of trying to establish a better material basis for the chancellorship, he could provide for himself but not for his successors.

As for Bruges, it was a much bigger headache. Already in 1405 Gerson had been challenged in his deanery. In February 1408, trouble arose again and Gerson asked the king, the duke of Burgundy (whose father had been his champion), and the faculty of theology in Paris to get a certain William Bourgois to return the revenues belonging to Gerson as dean, which he had seized.[3] The chapter at Saint Donatian discussed the matter, and in the course of its proceedings of 1 June 1408 several grievances emerged. The two central questions were the cost of repairs to the dean's house and Gerson's failure to hold customary annual banquets for the canons. Gerson's representative, André de Curia, produced the accounts and showed that besides the small amount received from his predecessor, Gerson himself had paid the sum of five hundred Parisian pounds for repairs (501).

The canons decided to continue to allow their dean to receive his office's income, so long as he handed over fifteen pounds for future building work and promised that income from his prebend in future would support costs. As for banquets, the canons announced they would continue to enjoy them, whether or not the dean was present! The expense would be paid directly from the deanery's revenues.

After settling with the abbot of Bec for his Paris benefice, Gerson returned to Bruges at the end of July 1409. On 5 August he spoke before the chapter and said he had spent more on the dean's house than his predecessor had done and would continue to do so. As for the banquets, he would pay if it was his duty, but he refused to burden his office with new expenses. The cost belonged "more to the church than to himself." He was already supporting "great burdens" in repairing the dean's house (501).

In his absence, Gerson would be represented in chapter by the chanter, the schoolmaster, and Nicolas Storkin. Gerson asked each and every canon if he was content with this arrangement. In the protocol they all replied affirmatively, *nullo contradicente.* At this point Gerson could add in triumph that the rumor (*fama*) that everyone wanted to get rid of him was false (502).

All seemed to be well. On 24 July 1410, the newly elected pope, John XXIII, confirmed Gerson in his deanery at Bruges and his benefice at Paris. But on 5 December 1410 and again on 17 March 1411, the canons took possession of all the movable goods in the dean's house in order to pay for their banquets.[4] From 1 November 1410 on, a professor of theology, Amand de Bremmont, challenged Gerson's right to his office. On 30 June 1411, the chapter officially removed Gerson as dean and replaced him with Bremmont (502–4).

These developments could only have taken place with the acceptance of John the Fearless, duke of Burgundy.[5] After the murder of the duke of Orleans on 23 November 1407, Gerson had not shown his patron the support that other theologians did. Just as the duke's father had set Gerson up at Bruges, the son now used his influence to deprive him of the deanship.

Gerson's long absences from Bruges made it difficult to deal with the situation. Every late medieval cleric who lived in one place and drew income from a prebend at another church had to face such conflicts. The university teaching system was based on absentee clerics who collected from a plurality of benefices, and here Gerson and his circle saw both dangers and disadvantages to themselves and to the faithful.[6] Even church reformers needed regular incomes, while the churches from which they received prebends had to be looked after.

The loss of Saint Donatian may, of course, have been almost a relief to Gerson after years of rumors, political dependency, and journeys back and forth to Bruges, especially since at almost the same time he obtained economic security with a benefice at a nearby Parisian church. Here he could earn his keep, as it were, by providing sermons and probably also by administering the sacraments.[7]

The records of the chapter of Notre Dame show Gerson's absence from its meetings from 24 July to 20 August 1409. He was then at Bruges in a final attempt to save his prebend there. Back in Paris in the autumn of 1409, he defended secular masters and parish priests against new privileges the mendicants had been granted by the pope elected at Pisa, Alexander V. In the spring of 1410, Gerson also intervened in a question about the settlement of debts before entrance to a religious order.[8]

On 6 May of that year Alexander V died, and his successor John XXIII was elected on 23 May. In a letter to his brother Nicolas, dated to 1410, Gerson offers some personal reflections on the situation at Paris, where civil discourse had broken down and war was rumored: "In whatever corner of the world, what security or peace is to be hoped for?"[9] Gerson explained that he had decided to remain in place in Paris and to do there what the Lord wanted. Here he would await "a richer prebend in that great church, not in Paris but in paradise, to which we head by different paths" (Gl 2.140). The passage alludes to an understanding reached with Nicolas. After his initial resentment over his two younger brothers' decisions to leave him for the Celestine Order, Gerson had finally come to accept their vocation.

For more than a year he kept to a daily routine of lecturing to the students, responding to queries with brief theological treatises, and presumably also preaching on the Right Bank at Saint-Jean.[10] His schedule was interrupted, however, by a bout of illness which kept him from attending chapter meetings at Notre Dame from 19 September 1410 until 21 March 1411 (Gl 10.499, 509). During this time his friend Nicolas de Clamanges wrote a letter to comfort him, which indicates that Gerson had frequently been ill in the course of his life.[11]

In March of 1411, Charles of Orleans, the son of the murdered duke, wrote to the University of Paris and asked it to condemn Jean Petit's defense of tyrannicide from 1408.[12] Apparently no one did anything in response. The Parisian masters feared the duke of Burgundy and a coming civil war. A meeting of prelates and magnates was held at Easter to discuss affairs of state. It was established that the duke of Orleans and his allies had not obeyed a royal ordinance from the preceding year to put down their arms.[13] After 24 June of that year both dukes were barred from entering Paris. In September 1413, Gerson recalled in a sermon the university's fruitless efforts to make peace between the dukes.[14]

From the end of 1411 open civil war raged until August 1412, when a treaty was agreed upon at Auxerre. It was during this time that Gerson probably issued a warning against tyranny which at least one modern interpreter has misunderstood (Gl 7.1.360–63).[15] Basing his teaching on Aristotle, Gerson showed how the king exists *pour le bien publique,* for the public good, while the tyrant is interested only "in his own profit and will" (361). There was no contradiction between Aristotle and Christian ethics. A lord is obligated to protect and defend his subjects, and so in Seneca's words, "No victim is more pleasing to God than a tyrant" (362). There is no claim here that anyone has the right to kill a tyrant. God will dispose of him through his just judgment (363).

Another brief statement of Gerson's position may also come from this period. Known as *Cedule de la commission,* in reference to a royal commission providing counsel for the king, it asked why the kingdom was embroiled in civil war. There had been abuses not for the last three or four years but for thirty or forty (Gl 10.399). It takes a long time for God to take vengeance, but in the end it comes. The lords of France had abused their powers and reduced their subjects to beasts or serfs (400). They had failed to look after the poor and wretched and had abused the holy office of the Church. They had misused aids and other levies for the defense of the realm and deprived the people of what they needed in order to live: horses, livestock, bread, wine, and anything else that might nourish them (401).

The document records the devastation resulting from civil war, with "the entire kingdom reduced to poverty so that a few people of modest background can be enriched." This kind of abuse was caused by the king's dwindling health and his children, a rare public reference to the king's mental illness. The first Merovingian kings were restored to power because they reformed themselves (403). But nowadays money was wasted on marriages, alliances, and wars, "which have been made in this kingdom for more than thirty years" and from which "little or nothing has come." Gerson also attacked the levying of 30 million gold coins in aid or taxes (404). This statement has been viewed in connection with a passage in the *Chronicle of Saint Denis* about an attempt to raise money.[16] The clergy and members of the university were asked to help finance an expedition against some of the princes who had been disloyal to the king: "The chancellor of Notre Dame of Paris, speaking in the name of the clergy, said that they had nothing to live on except limited incomes and that it was not in their power to make a grant."[17] Any concession to the royal treasury would be a waste of money. Also, anyone who burdened his subjects with unjust collections was unworthy to be king. History showed that princes who act in such a way were rightly deposed.

Gerson was playing with fire. According to the *Chronicle*, some lords claimed that he asserted that the citizens have a right to remove their king. But when doctors of canon law actually considered what Gerson had written, they declared "in the king's presence that he had wished only to refer to examples" taken from history.[18]

There is no doubt, however, that Gerson was questioning the very foundations of civil authority. He was asking whether Augustine was right when he said that when justice is removed, kingdoms are nothing more than bands of robbers.[19] He was skeptical in regard to princes, and yet he kept a distance from the central question: whether it was acceptable for God-fearing citizens to turn against secular power and remove a tyrant.

Later, when the worst seemed to be over, Gerson could look back on these years, 1411 to 1413, and speak of their "violence and . . . threats," as well as corruption in gifts and promises, undermining the state.[20] He came to consider the attempts from 1408 to 1412 to reconcile the dukes as wrong, for they had involved deceit and strong-arm methods. In the fall of 1413 he disowned his earlier efforts to patch up the torn fabric of French society.

Gerson came to choose sides because he himself became a victim. On 27 April 1413, tensions in Paris, which had previously been kept just beneath the surface, exploded, with the revolt of the Cabochiens, a powerful guild of butchers of Paris led by one Simon Caboche.[21] In a later sermon, Gerson described the Cabochiens as low class people who exercised tyranny.[22] If we look at the governing ordinance adopted by the Cabochiens, however, it reveals a faction interested in reforming the processes of government, eliminating corruption, and establishing a new and more enlightened civil service.[23] Unfortunately these proposals had hardly any effect on the course of events.

In the streets of Paris, no one associated with the Armagnac party was safe. The king's cousin, the duke of Bar, was taken prisoner, as well as many others. As Gerson later lamented in a sermon to the king:

> Sire, I can well say as one with experience that in your daughter the university there are hundreds upon hundreds and even more young masters threatened with death and destruction. Not only they themselves but also their fathers and mothers and all their families. And for no reason other than that they had abandoned and shown contempt for everything [else], in order to serve you loyally. . . . They wished to salute you in saying, "May the king live forever" (Daniel 2:4). (Gl 7.2.1010)

In the spring of 1413, it was not clear who was on the king's side, for he was lost to the world. But in early July, Charles VI again emerged from his mental darkness and a new settlement was arranged between the dukes at the Peace of Pontoise (26 July). On 4 August the dauphin, the duke of Guyenne, left his residence at Saint Paul, escorted by the dukes of Berry and Burgundy. The dauphin, presumably on his father's orders, freed several prisoners, including the duke of Bar.[24]

The next day, there was a meeting at the university intended to give thanks for the return of domestic peace. Here Gerson spoke in a sermon lost to us in which he asked the dauphin, the duke of Guyenne, to bring about lasting peace. A few days later Gerson again gave an address, this time in the course of a procession that followed the main south-north road intersecting Paris, to the church and abbey of Saint Martin-des-Champs.[25] He spoke in this lost oration on the Psalm text (4:8), "In peace I shall both lie down and sleep."[26]

Healing the Schism

Before considering the consequences of Gerson's traumas, we must return to the year 1409, prior to the civil disturbances. The chancellor did his best during these years to fulfill his normal duties at the university: he held examinations, gave sermons, attended meetings of his own faculty and of the university as a whole.[27] However, always on his mind, from his vantage point in the corner of the cloister of Notre Dame, was his dream of ending the Schism, which by then had lasted more than thirty years.

He had abandoned the idea of *via cessionis,* according to which one or both popes would voluntarily give up office. Now he saw the way of a council as the only possible solution. The new pope, however, would still govern the Church. Gerson was no revolutionary; he had great respect for the papacy in its long history and had no desire to replace it with the council.[28] But in his *On the Authority of the*

Council (dated between November 1408 and March 1409) he asserts that the Church exists whether the papacy is vacant or not and can function without a pope, for its authority then devolves to the bishops (Gl 6.114–15). Opposing Ockham's teaching that the Church can exist even in a single woman, Gerson pointed to the bishops as a collective guarantee of the Church's continuing existence. Ever a believer in hierarchy, Gerson could not imagine a situation in which episcopal hierarchy disappeared.

A council, he insisted, cannot err, while a pope can, unless he speaks together with the council: *papa potest errare in fide, sed non est possibile papam cum concilio ecclesiae erronee in materia fidei sententiare.* A council can be convened without the summons of the pope, and it can pass judgment on any matter of doubt concerning the spiritual direction of Christians (116). Possible rivals for the papacy have to submit to the decision of the council (117).

Gerson anticipates here the coming council of Pisa: "In that most holy meeting to be held in March, in which the faith and condition of the universal Church is to be discussed, all catholic Christians who wish to be present are to be received" (119). The council was open to all, and it could summon the pope (120). Its decisions were binding on every Christian (121). What was important for such a council was not to discuss law but to reform the Church (121). If a papal contender refused to submit to the council's decisions, he was to be declared heretical and unable to exercise authority over the faithful. The people, nevertheless, had to obey a heretical pope until the council released them from obedience (122–23).

Gerson had great expectations of the Council of Pisa. At the end of January 1409, he addressed the English delegation on its way to Pisa, his *Propositio facta coram Anglicis.* In what is more a sermon than a theological treatise, he saw in the healing of the Church a new expression of the prophet Hosea's vision: "The sons of Judah and those of Israel shall be gathered together" (Hosea 1:11). Rejoicing in his reunion with, among others, the Oxford masters who earlier had been his adversaries, Gerson cited the Psalm verse (132:1) concerning how good and joyful it is when brothers live together in unity (Gl 6.125).

Following his opening remarks, Gerson criticized the view that only the pope can summon a council (129). He referred to the writings of his teacher Pierre d'Ailly and of Henry of Langenstein, both of whom had long before seen the need for a general council (130).[29] Gerson may here have been apologizing indirectly for his own tardiness in coming around to this point of view. It was the Church's prerogative to institute a new way of electing the pope. At the same time, it can depose him. The example of the early Church was essential for Gerson, for the first councils, as mentioned in the Acts of the Apostles, were convoked without papal summons (133). Here too, Gerson followed Pierre d'Ailly, who, in a statement from 1 January, had mentioned the early councils as described in Acts, especially the Council of Jerusalem, and their leadership not by Peter but by James.[30]

Turning from history to political theory, Gerson argued that any free human community has the right to assemble, as attested to by the practices of "confraternities and many other assemblies based on love" (*conventionibus caritativis*). Gerson was no democrat, but he did believe in a basic human right to form associations and to regulate their functions (133–34).

Concluding, he answered the question whether the Schism had been necessary by rejecting the explanation that men have to commit evil in order to make good come about (134). The *Propositio facta coram anglicis* shows Gerson at his rhetorical best, bolstering his arguments with historical background, biblical texts, clear distinctions, and relating developments in the Church to those in society as a whole.

His next effort was a *Tractatus de unitate ecclesiae* (On the Unity of the Church), the fullest expression thus far of his conciliar thinking. Positive law, he began, cannot block the Church's unity. Canons regulating papal authority have to give way to God's law. A community has the right to seek unity by untraditional means or schism will become permanent (136). The Church has no less a right to secure its own unity than any other civil, mystical, or natural body (137). Once again, Gerson is thinking in terms of a fundamental right any human institution enjoys in looking after its own interests.[31]

Gerson's argument here combines a concept of natural law and a utilitarian point of view: any measure necessary to restore the unity and regular functioning of the Church can and should be followed. The pope has a duty to give way for the sake of the Church. Its own positive law must provide the necessary authority for a council to find a "quick and healthy end" in bringing about union (138).

Gerson reveals himself here as an impatient master, looking not only for what would work but also what would work quickly. He took comfort in his favored philosophical principle of *epikie* or right reason, as a basis for turning to the authority of the council.[32] Thus loyalties or friendships have no role to play in dealing with the papal contenders. He turned to a classical example to defend what the king had to do in abandoning his previous ally, the Avignon pope. When Cicero was accused of being unfaithful in his friendship with Caesar, he answered: "I never loved Caesar except insofar as he seemed to love the republic." When Caesar became a tyrant, Cicero abandoned his friendship.[33] Gerson thus indicated that the papal Caesar at Avignon had become a tyrant by refusing to liberate the Church, and so he no longer was owed friendship. Nothing should be allowed to block the reestablishment of unity (139).

How far can a council go in doing so? Gerson considered the use of force against a papal claimant. He could be imprisoned, and if he refuses to give way, he could be accused of schism or heresy. One might even deprive him of office and even of his life (*dejicere ab omni honore et gradu, immo et vita privare*; 140). Despite the possibility of such drastic measures, it was also necessary to show restraint. There is no reason after the Schism's ending to punish one side or another for not being obedient to the true pope. Many can be excused on the basis of their zeal for union. What is necessary is not prosecution but reformation in the Church; otherwise things will revert to their earlier state: *recidivatio prior fiat* (141).

Gerson again turned to the concept of right reason and used a popular saying he could have gotten from Gratian's *Decretum* or Bernard's *Sermon on the Song of Songs* (50:5): "Necessity has no law" (143). He warned against the tyrant who claims to be acting for the sake of the state and says, "I am ready to die." He may have been thinking of Benedict XIII's claim prior to his election (144).

On 26 June 1409, the archbishop of Milan, Peter Philarges, a Cretan by birth and member of Oxford and Paris universities, was elected as Pope Alexander V at Pisa.[34] The Avignon and Roman popes remained in place, but with few followers, for France, England, and a large part of the German-speaking world accepted the Council of Pisa's choice. When the news reached Paris, Gerson wrote a sermon, ostensibly for the Feast of the Ascension, which he clearly hoped would come to Alexander's attention (Gl 1.124).

Satan tries to block the replacement in heaven of the number of fallen angels with human souls, he began, thus lifting the Schism onto a cosmic plane with a theological assertion that had been around for centuries.[35] Now with Christ, the new Lucifer, penitent souls are brought into their paternal home (Gl 5.206).

However, the Church which Christ had founded has become the subject of tears. Wherever we look, there is no peace (208). Eight hundred years ago, Moslems had thrown off the gentle yoke of Christ. The Greeks had separated from the see of Peter, and the Latins were now also torn by Schism (209). In the past the solution had been to hold a council, and here Gerson repeated what he had said to the English delegation: in the early Church it was not necessarily up to the pope to call a council. Nicaea, for example, was summoned by the Emperor Constantine and not by Pope Sylvester.

Gerson warns Alexander against disappointing the hope invested in him. Following the allegorical practice popular in late medieval culture, he has *Ecclesia* or holy Church question the pope, almost accusing him: "You now call yourself servant of my sons; if you are not so, why do you use this name?" (210) He also reminds the new pope of the task ahead. Merchants were now hastening to the Indies. What about missionaries? What about the return of the Greeks? The Church is impatient and wants results now: "Hurry father, hurry, so that the hour does not pass" (210)

Gerson says he has no desire to "teach Minerva," in the classical maxim (211). But this is exactly what he does in providing good advice for the pope. To gain greater authority, he takes on the *persona* of the Church and laments her misery. It had descended into "the calamity of the present times," and life of earth had become like hell, "where there is no order but eternal horror" (212–13; cf. Job 10:22).

Prelates sought to enrich themselves and get new privileges (213). They acquired new lands, houses, and other possessions, while they lusted for the fruits of benefices, held *in absentia*. Prelates bore arms and made war. Gerson repeats some of the criticisms found in his earlier works, but intensifies them by taking on the identity of the Church itself. She laments that her offices are given out based on greed or family bonds rather than qualifications (214). She condemns warriors who are supposed to defend her but end up betraying her. Once the martyrs had protected her from tyrants, as did the Church's learned doctors from heretics. "But now what am I to do when my friends and relations have come and stood against me?" (215; cf Ps 37:12).

No sixteenth-century critic could have said it better (216). It was up to the new pope to restore *pax ipsa christiana*, torn apart by the Schism. The best the pope can do is to follow "the Gregorian example," presumably of Pope Gregory I, and call together as allies in so great a task "the best and most prudent clerics and members of religious orders" (217).

The fullest statement of Gerson's teaching on the governance of the Church is *De auferabilitate sponsi*, concerning the removal of the spouse from its bride, the Church.[36] It takes as a point of departure Mark 2:20: "The day will come when the spouse will be removed from them." It has been dated to between 15 June and 8 July 1409, just prior to the arrival in Paris of the news of Alexander V's election (26 June).

Gerson asserts that it is Christ, not the pope, who is the bridegroom of the Church, and he can never be taken away from his beloved. Thus the pope can be removed, and he can also renounce his post (Gl 3.299). A general council representing the Church can remove the pope, who is only vicar. The pope need not be present at such a council (300). If the pope acts in a tyrannical manner, he can be resisted by force. A law which dissolves unity and is adverse to the public good is not to be followed (301). As so often, Gerson turns to Aristotle's concept of right reason, but he also speaks of necessity's law and cites biblical examples.

Certain statements in this treatise have been used in the past to make Gerson look like an anti-papal revolutionary.[37] His point of departure, however, was a monarchical church with Christ as king. The pope is Christ's vicar, and so Gerson dismissed the assertion, which he tied to Marsilius of Padua, that each bishop is pope in his own diocese (298–99). The pope is not sovereign: when it is a question of custom, he has no right to make canons to be observed uniformly. Such an attempt may have made the Greeks break with the Latins. The demand for conformity "daily provides much ammunition for fighting" and brings to mind the complaint of Christ, "For the sake of your traditions, you have emptied the word of God" (Mt 15:6; Gl 3.299). Gerson does not deny papal plenitude of power but points out that Christ gave the keys of heaven not to one man or office but to the unity of the Church (302). He turns once again to the early councils and how Peter had to explain himself (Acts 10:34).

Withdrawal of obedience from one or both papal contenders had to be done with great caution, so that disobedience would not become a habit (305). Gerson warns against the assertion that it is acceptable for a subject to kill a leader because he is a tyrant "by using fraudulent and treacherous means and without any authority or judicial declaration."[38] For the first, and perhaps only, time before the Cabochien uprising of 1413, he apparently clarified his position on the question of tyrannicide.

Gerson tried to define the precise circumstances in which a pope could be deposed. Only a general council could take such action (307). The pope kept his jurisdiction not because of holiness but because of the Church's acceptance. He rejected the Wycliffite and Hussite concept that any exercise of political power or dominion depends on the state of grace.[39] A council could remove such jurisdiction, but in accepting that the offices and benefices conferred by a pope remain valid until he has been officially deposed. Gerson wanted no debate about the legitimacy of papal appointments or, even worse, about the validity of sacraments conferred by priests anointed by the bishops of one faction or the other. With his usual impatience, Gerson asked for a quick end to the Schism (309).

The pope could be removed not only for heretical or idolatrous acts but also if he were captured by the Saracens and the Church needed a functioning head (311). Then a council could create a new pope. Also, if the Greeks were willing to return to unity on condition the pope was removed, a council could oblige them! Any pope could be deposed if this action was for the greater good of the Church.

The fathers of the Council of Trent and their successors in the Roman Catholic Church, especially from 1870 until the 1960s, would have rejected such proposals. The question of a pope's removal, or even of his voluntary resignation, remains as much a question of debate in the twenty-first century as it was in the fifteenth.

Gerson's radical suggestions for possible future action should not distract from his pragmatic desire to get on with the business of the Church.[40] After the Council of Pisa ended on 7 August, he did not wait for long to see what the new pope would do. In December 1409, Gerson attempted to shape events by addressing king and court with one of the last of his great public sermons, "For peace and union." His goal was to end not only the Western Schism but also the much older break between Greek and Latin Christians.

Gerson took the words of the angels (Luke 2:14) contained in the Christmas gospel reading: "Peace to men of good will." He invented an allegory, with Bad Will opposing Good. The first asked the university why it got itself involved in so much trouble (Gl 7.2.764). How could it even try to reunite the Greeks and

Latins when it could not create accord among Latin Christians, to say nothing of peace between "two little kingdoms" like France and England? (764)

Good Will replied that now was the time for the French Church to pursue unity. The pope was a doctor of theology, a statement made twice in the sermon (766, 773). He was of Greek background and had *grande experience.* Since the members of the university came from all parts of the world, it was their duty to spread the message of peace and union. In this way they would show their love of neighbor and oppose Cain's damnable response: "Am I my brother's keeper?" (767; cf. Gen 4:9) In working for what is good, all men can join together, whether they be Turk, Jew, pagan, or Saracen. Thus there is a common basis for cooperation or at least peace among humankind (768).

From here Gerson, in the person of Good Will, considers the possibility of a future reunion between Greeks and Latins. He asks that the Greeks accept the decisions made by the Roman pope. The Church could not have two leaders, while secular society could have many (769). There could be only one jurisdiction, but outside there was an area of political life which the pope could not touch. Gerson contradicted those who used Boniface VIII's 1302 bull *Unam sanctam* to claim universal jurisdiction for the pope.[41]

Gerson opposed papal universalism by distinguishing between local or regional laws and customs, which could vary, and the principles which should guide the Church as a whole. Thus married priests were possible in the East (771). Also the manner of baptism may vary. Moreover, the requirement of yearly confession and communion of the Fourth Lateran Council of 1215 was the decision of a Western council and so did not necessarily apply to the Eastern Church. The Greeks, he assures his audience, have their own laws and customs that deserve respect. Similarly the *Esglise de France* has its freedoms, "notwithstanding that opposition which some people from the Roman curia might like to provide" to a Gallican reformation.[42]

In celebrating and defending a Gallican church, Gerson quoted what the duke of Lancaster is reported to once have said to the duke of Burgundy: "We have in England clerics who are very clever in their fantasies, but those of Paris have true and secure theology" (772). He apparently looked upon his Oxford colleagues as dreaming masters, while Paris was the seat of orthodoxy. At the same time, support for the university helped avoid tyranny in France: *le royaume de France n'est point gouverné par tirannie quant il aime les estudes* (773).

Gerson sought to convince the princes to take advantage of a new situation. First the court should send legations to those who still supported the other popes: the Spaniards, the Aragonese, the Scots, and the people of Hainault. The union of the Western Church would be furthered by similar efforts for union with the Eastern. Gerson said nothing about Constantinople's perilous situation. But he thought it was time to reassert Christian unity. He invoked the example of Saint

Louis, who twice had risked his life by going "across the sea, against the misbelievers" (776). Gerson did not ask for another crusade: the concept of crusade seems to be absent in his writings. But he did think that the prospective union of the churches might be God's will in preparing the end of the world, one of the rare times Gerson dwelled on this theme.

This remarkably concrete sermon ends not in a grand vision but in a specific request that the king order his council to arrange for letters and embassies to further the agenda of union (777). As so often, Gerson praised the value of hard work and quoted Vergil to the effect that it overcomes all things.[43] He looked forward to a new council where the Greeks might be present. Here the university would play a leading role.

Christmas of 1409 provides a date for the seeming triumph of an alliance between university learning and the French monarchy. For a moment Gerson could be an optimist, even though he knew the court was divided by suspicion and hatred after the murder of the duke of Orleans. He closed with the words of Paul, "I can do all things in him who comforts me, Christ" (Phil 4:13). This quote did homage to the saint honored at the site of the sermon, the royal residence of Saint Paul.

A great distance remained, however, between words and deeds: the schism with the Greeks would continue, and the princes would pursue their own deadly divisions. But in one sense Gerson was right: the Western Schism was almost over. It would be misleading to see Pisa as merely leading to three popes instead of two. Gerson knew that the geographical areas that still maintained allegiance to the popes of Avignon and Rome were unimportant. In investing so much in the decision of the French church to help elect a pope of Greek origin, Gerson believed that the reformation of the Church finally could begin.

Stopping the Mendicants

Those who advocate reformation can easily get sidetracked. From the winter of 1409 until the spring of 1411, Gerson, as chancellor of the university, apparently had other matters to contend with. He concentrated on a Franciscan scholar, Jean Gorrel, who at his licentiate in December of 1408 defended the rights of the mendicants to hear confessions without reference to the position of parish priests.[44] When Gerson got wind of these theological assertions, he did his utmost to stop Gorrel. On 2 January 1409, the faculty of theology met at the College of Navarre and ordered Gorrel to recant.[45]

Disputes between secular priests and mendicants had by now been going on for almost two centuries. In the 1250s the problem had centered on the place of the mendicants in the university corporation.[46] In the 1380s Gerson had accused the Dominicans of opposing church teaching on Mary's immaculate conception.[47] But now a Franciscan was challenging the exclusive right of parish priests "to preach, hear confessions, give the last rites, bury the dead, or receive tithes" (Gl 10.32). These functions were given them not by Christ but by an early pope, Dionysius. Gorrel also asserted that "the friars have competence in a more basic and essential manner than do curates to preach and hear confessions" (33). The power to do so was based on the mendicants' Rule, while parish priests were merely following a pope's instructions.

In January 1409 Gorrel conceded that he had "scandalized" many by making such claims at his *vesperiae* (the evening lecture completing the theological doctorate). He now stated that the right to preach and hear confessions belonged to prelates and parish priests "principally and essentially," while it is given to the mendicants *per accidens* as a privilege. The parish church is the "fitting and ordinary place" for the laity to receive the church's sacraments.

Gorrel claimed that he had not been trying to take away power from curates but had merely been seeking to remedy abuses, as in the payment of tithes (34). He also conceded that a confession could be repeated. Thus a priest could require his parishioner who had confessed to a mendicant to confess again, presumably to fulfill the requirement of the Fourth Lateran Council that all Christians confess once a year in their parish church.

The mendicants were apparently not satisfied with this outcome. In the summer of 1409, they appealed to the new pope, Alexander V, who himself was a Franciscan. In October he issued *Regnans in excelsis,* a bull criticizing those who claim that the mendicant brothers had no fundamental right to preach, hear confessions, or administer the sacraments.[48] He referred to an earlier bull of Boniface VIII giving the friars the right to preach in their churches and in public places except at the hour when church prelates choose to preach. The friars were not to give sermons in parish churches unless they were invited to do so. Also friars could hear the confessions of lay people, *non obstantibus* (not withstanding) the decisions of the Fourth Lateran Council and other papal decisions requiring them to confess once a year to their own parish priest.

For almost two centuries, the Lateran canon had provided the foundation which gave secular priests priority in administering the sacraments. Gerson saw the challenge and the following February, probably in the cathedral, replied to the papal bull with a French sermon entitled *Quomodo stabit regnum eius* (How will his kingdom stand? Luke 11:18).[49] Glorieux has entitled the sermon "Discourse on the act of the mendicants," but it is a much broader statement of Gerson's views on the structure, mission, and prerogatives of the Church whose hierarchy reflects the celestial orders, with its nine choirs of angels (Gl 7.2.980). The earthly hierarchy, however, has been disturbed, because of this bull which the mendicants "extorted" from the pope (982). Its contents could not possibly reflect the pope's views, for he was a "great theologian" and would never have allowed such a statement to be issued. According to university masters, Gerson claims, "everything was done without [the pope's] knowledge, and against his choice, or at least without his advice or deliberation, as happens with busy people," who hand over to others important questions because of the pressure on them.

The pope would surely change his position, as soon as he realized the seriousness of the matter. Instead of attacking Alexander V personally, he chose to follow standard medieval practice of criticizing the advisors of a person in authority. For Gerson, the Fourth Lateran Council's canon allowed no exceptions: only one's own parish priest is to administer the sacraments, at least during Eastertide when confession and communion are obligatory. No substitutes or replacements were possible (985–86).

Parish priests could not be expected to give sophisticated sermons. Their duty is to provide for their parishioners the basic tenets of faith. Nor are they obligated to preach daily, "as is often done at Paris this Lent" (985). From here Gerson turns to earlier papal decrees (986). The mendicants could only preach because of special privileges granted to them. Their work in the Church supplements the sacramental foundation provided by secular priests (989).

Gerson would have known that badly educated parish priests could rarely sound as convincing and attractive in their preaching as the well-trained mendicants. But the laity was to find in the parish its "spiritual father and the gate through which we cross to God" (991). He attacked the mendicant claim to be living in greater perfection because of the poverty vowed by members of their orders. There can be greater perfection in having riches, as from benefices, and using them well than in having nothing and having to beg. Mendicant poverty "can create cares, theft, and deception, and other evils" (992), while a parish priest with a regular income can concentrate on his work. Jesus did not beg. Already in the time of Peter, converts brought their wealth with them into the Church. Ever the son of modest country people, Gerson saw nothing attractive in a life based on poverty.

Gerson sought to demolish, once and for all, what we might call the corporate myth that better priests emerge from religious communities than from parish life. For centuries Christian renewal had been headed first by monks and later by friars.[50] Now Gerson, as secular priest and theologian, wanted his type of churchman to spearhead a new reformation. Since he saw the origins of the priestly order in the Gospel narrative, it was a matter of theological urgency to defend its prerogatives.

Two weeks later, on 5 March 1409, Gerson joined with other masters of theology in a formal protest against Alexander's bull. They saw it as "an instrument of malice and persecutions of prelates, curates and lay persons" and they accused the mendicants of "machinations . . . which attempt to supplant the status first instituted by Christ for prelates and curates."[51] Gerson's personal hand can be seen in the recommendation that "in each parish both in cities as well as outside in villages" there be "small treatises in French, containing in general the content of precepts." The parish priest could either lecture on them or read them aloud in order to teach the unlearned (*simplices*).

The language here is clear and precise. It has the stamp of Jean Gerson. On the same day this declaration was made, several professors of theology launched a more detailed attack on the bull, again because it set aside the Lateran canon requiring yearly confession and communion in one's own parish church (Gl 10.35). The professors asserted that even the pope could not alter the "status of the universal Church" and reminded him that he would have to "render account" (a term they may have taken from the *Rule* of Saint Benedict) for his actions before God.[52] The bull's terminology was called confusing and misleading (37). Dominic and Francis had never made such claims against their lords the bishops (38): "For who can tolerate or admire men who beg for bread from the people and [at the same time] deprive their superiors of their preeminent rights?" The statement concludes with a terrifying vision of a mendicant takeover of the Church which supposedly had happened already in Italy. The mendicants might come to breed a new heretical sect, as indicated in a reference to the Spiritual Franciscans and their use of Joachim of Fiore's teaching on the Eternal Gospel.[53]

The complaint ends with an appeal to the next council. Here the "hierarchical and basic order of the Church, with prelates and parish priests, of which the pope should be defender, not destroyer" will have to be maintained "undisturbed."[54] A comparison between Gerson's February sermon and this statement two weeks later indicates that the chancellor authored this attack on the papal bull. He defended the *ordo . . . essentialis ecclesiae* that priests and bishops belong to an order instituted by Christ, while the mendicants make up a later and secondary institution.

During the next two years, while Paris and the surrounding countryside slipped into civil war, the dispute continued. After the death of Alexander V in May 1410 and the election of John XXIII, the mendicants appealed to the new pope. In June he issued a bull that set aside his predecessor's decision. For the Parisian secular masters, however, this was not enough. In November the university rejected both bulls and the following spring it asked the pope formally to revoke *Regnans in excelsis.*[55]

As mentioned earlier, Gerson was ill from September 1410 until March 1411, so by April he may have been well enough to help formulate this final statement in the dispute. The pope was not only to recall his predecessor's bull. It was to be "destroyed and buried." The masters lectured John XXIII on papal practice: "It is not, most holy father, unaccustomed or unheard that decrees of prior popes are corrected, interpreted or wholly annulled by their successors. In fact it is worthy of great praise and sometimes necessary."[56]

The University of Paris also asked that the next council be held in France, a safer place than dangerous Italy and more convenient than Spain or "places beyond the Alps," presumably the German speaking world. The letter also asked that university men be given the posts they deserve, and that no preference be given to the ignorant or rich. Cooks and bakers were accorded benefices, complained the masters, simply because they were in the service of powerful lords! Finally, the university requested that a local judge should handle disputes over benefices, to avoid spending large sums of money and risking one's life in going to Italy. The university referred to "a very old privilege" prohibiting its masters from being summoned outside the walls of Paris for any legal case.[57]

The masters of the University of Paris considered themselves to be the center of the intellectual world, and Gerson, as one of them, felt entitled to tell the pope what he could and could not do. The pope needed the university, and though we have no record of any immediate response, a year later (April 1413) Gerson, as chancellor, received from John XXIII extensive powers for the coming three years to give absolution for sins otherwise reserved to the papacy, to commute vows, and in general, to act as a spiritual judge for the university's members (Gl 2.153–54).

The university-mendicant controversy, however surrealistic in the midst of greater problems, cannot be dismissed as intellectual dreaming. It expresses a consciousness that the University of Paris and especially its faculty of theology remained at the core of the Church's *magisterium* or teaching authority. The theologians under their chancellor felt qualified to interpret papal decrees and even to ask that the coming council be held in France.

The faculty's letter to the pope takes its point of departure from the central role Paris and its university had long played in the Church. For Gerson it was paramount for the future of Christendom that university theologians continued to make their voices heard on moral and doctrinal questions.

Summarizing Teaching

The Gerson who probably was behind this tough statement to a new pope could also express himself in a much more considered manner. At some time during this period, he provided a summary of his views on the position of various types of prelates or officeholders in the Church, together with parish priests, in contrast with the status of members of religious orders.[58] Episcopal status is not subject to the pure will of the pope, as is the status of the mendicants (Gl 9.29). The bishops are not to be hemmed in by laws and restrictions, as in the reservation of cases to the papacy. Papal monarchy is placed above the bishops, but it was not instituted by Christ, and the government of the Church can change according to different places and times (30). As elsewhere in his writings, Gerson showed a sense for historical development.

As for parish priests, they are obligated to preach God's word according to their limited learning, while prelates can go into greater detail (31). Parish priests have an exclusive right to preach and administer the sacraments in their own churches. They can receive tithes, offerings, and incomes from burials so that they have enough on which to live.

As for the *privilegati,* members of religious orders, Gerson basically repeated what had already been said in the critique of Jean Gorrel's statements. The mendicants may preach in their own churches and in public places. They also may do so with permission in parish churches. But they are not to solicit burials (34). Also in preaching to the laity, they should not expose the clerics' or lords' vices, thus "nourishing rebellion" (34–35). Priests are to hear confessions of women and youths "only in public and open places," a concern that continues in our time.[59]

In summing up his recommendations for both parish priests and religious, Gerson pleaded for less competition, for they, "like crows, hack at each other" and so create bad feelings about churchmen among the laity.[60] Stepping back from polemics, he sought cooperation and less "pharisaical rivalry about the preeminence of one's status."

Another controversy to which Gerson dedicated himself in these years concerned the case of a knight who, in 1402, had entered the Carthusian Order and five years later left his monastery, ostensibly to pay his debts (Gl 10.29–30). In 1409 both the Carthusian Order and the extramural monk appealed to the University of Paris for advice in the matter. In 1410, Gerson contributed a statement on members of monastic or religious orders and individual debts. A person burdened by debt is not to be admitted into religious life unless the order agrees to pay the debt (Gl 3.316). He pointed to the Celestine Order, which he knew well. It did not receive novices until it had established whether or not they had outstanding debts. Someone who considered entering a religious order should first satisfy his creditors, but it was acceptable to replace a vow to give money with a vow to enter a monastery. But a person cannot use entrance into the order as a way of avoiding his obligation (317).

Gerson had the greatest respect for contracts and financial obligations. His university position had brought him into contact with an aristocratic world where contracts were made and broken in relation to considerations of honor and prestige. He had no sympathy for such maneuvering: we must pay our debts, no matter what. The only loophole he provided for the wayward knight-monk was that he might get his creditors to accept prayers "and other works of religion" as alternative payment (319).

In May, after the runaway Carthusian had rejoined his wife, Gerson made a further statement. He denounced the publication of some writings ascribed to his own name, but which had been abbreviated and distorted.[61] He, therefore, now decided to take a specific stand concerning the case at hand. First of all, the knight had not properly ordered his affairs before entering the Carthusians (320). Also the monks had not been sufficiently careful in checking with the man's creditors. Even though the brothers might now expel him for hiding his debts, he was still bound by his vows to abstain from meat and to live in continence (321). Thus he could not legally return to his wife.

A week later, on 28 May 1410, Gerson, as chancellor, and the faculty of theology issued a full statement. The man had been received into the order without proper care (324). But he had made a valid profession and now must return. The statement more or less repeats what Gerson had written previously. What is interesting is the postscript of statements by individual masters of theology, thus adding nuances to the collective conclusion.

Everyone agreed that the debts had to be paid, that the knight should return to the monastery, and that he could not rejoin his wife. But opinions were divided about how to bring about this result. One theologian asserted that the husband and wife could both work off their debts through manual labor in their respective monasteries.

Gerson's function as theological expert for the Carthusians is one he would resume later, especially after the Council of Constance. He had already written a defense of the way the Carthusians abstained from eating meat.[62] In his last years at Lyon, one of his main contacts with the outside world would be with these monks. Suspicious of the mendicants and their desire to run the affairs of the Church, Gerson respected the Carthusians for their contemplative life.

In spite of all his reservations about canonists and their views, Gerson was invited in April of 1410 to address colleagues about to be made doctors of canon law at Paris (Gl 5.218–29). He set theology above canon law, yet both deserve respect. Canon law is necessary for the regulation of temporal affairs, as in questions of church benefices (227). Here arise questions where theologians have no say at all. Sometimes, however, theology and canon law can be combined. Theologians are often unwilling to deal with anything except matters of principle. Some act as if all else was beneath them. At the same time, canonists should remember that they had to deal with more than individual cases and *particularibus conclusionibus*. They were also responsible for asserting general principles.

In the intellectual life of the Church, theology comes first. It provides primary concepts and definitions, which it may share with canon law.[63] The object of theology, the Gospel, remains changeless, while the object of canon law, the decrees of the Church, can be altered. Again Gerson emphasizes the Aristotelian rule of right reason or *epikie* (228). No clear principle exists in canon law or theology on how the temporalities of the Church are to be administered. Good practice lay somewhere in the middle between extreme claims that the Church has nothing or that it owns everything.

In this congenial yet slightly patronizing address, Gerson praises intellectual activity in general: "An intense consideration of possible questions, beginning in childhood or from adolescence, not only teaches but also illumines the intellect, in so far as one gets practice in principles inviting speculation."[64] He speaks about his own passion and asks colleagues outside the faculty of theology to join him.

Other addresses and treatises from the Paris years cannot be dated any more precisely than the years between the return from Bruges until departure for Constance, 1400–1415. Gerson's *On the Passions of the Soul,* however, may have been completed soon after 1408 as a postscript to his works on mystical theology (Gl 9.1–25). He deals here with the spiritual passions which come from God and are directly mediated by him, as in the case of the amorous soul found in the Song of Songs (13). The content betrays Gerson's perennial interest in mystical or ecstatic experience, but he was not ready to provide his own commentary on the *Song of Songs.* He examines the way passionate language influences a person, as in giving a sermon. Enthusiastic preaching was acceptable, "so long as truth and discretion are observed." Ever the teacher, Gerson turns to Augustine for guidelines: *sicut arguit Augustinus Quarto De doctrina christiana* (23).

Here Gerson returns to one of his chronic concerns: teachers' abuse of pupils. We should always be on guard, and it is actually "more tolerable to allow hateful division to arise between some people rather than that they stain themselves with unchaste love" (24). For the sake of good rule, princes may be motivated by passion for fame, and for the sake of learning, youths may compete with each other. Gerson did not like such rivalry, but it kept gifted people busy and was preferable to physical closeness among students or between them and their masters: "Nothing is more sublime, but nothing is more dangerous and more subject to temptation, than to walk on the path of amorous affection."[65] Love is to be feared as the "most violent of the passions."

Making Rules

Gerson may have been thinking especially about the boys at the choir school of Notre Dame cathedral who were in his charge. During these years, and perhaps in April 1411, Gerson drew up rules of regulation for the school.[66] I already presented some of these rules in chapter 2, but here they deserve more detailed treatment. Before all else the school's master was to be *incorruptissimus* (Gl 9.686). He was to treat the boys with respect (*reverentia*), so that there be "no base or obscene word, nor any lustful or dissolute gesture or touch." The master was to avoid excessive closeness with any one pupil, and he was to prevent any demonstrations of close friendship (*familiaritates*) among the boys, either in the house or the street, in choir or the sacristy or at the altar. Any of the boys who did form such bonds were to be beaten. Some (presumably the most difficult) were to be brought before their superiors. Woe to any master who scandalized the boys! To him applied Christ's words that it would be better to be drowned in the depths of the sea with a millstone around his neck (Mt 18:6).

The teacher was frequently to exhort the pupils to love God and seek heaven; he was to remind them of the danger of sin, to tell them that God sees everything and that they have a guardian angel. "Again they are especially to be taught to guard themselves chastely from all impurity, whether it be of the heart through thoughts, of the mouth through speech, or of deed through base touching" (687). In such cases they are in danger of losing not only their chastity but their very souls.

The boys were never to be left alone. A master was always to be present to supervise them, day and night, "in the house as well as outside, wherever the boys happen to go." Their chant master was not to teach them bawdy songs.

Not all the rules, however, concern purity. The hours of instruction were to be in the morning and then from vespers until supper. Like monks, the boys were to take their meals while being read to. They were to get individual tutoring: *coram uno magistrorum veniant separatum* (688). If a boy spoke French, swore, lied, engaged in impure touching, slept over, missed the hours in church or talked there, the others were to report him. Gerson seems to have been thinking in terms of monastic life, where it had long been customary to "proclaim" another brother who broke rules.

Gerson forbade all games that might encourage avarice or impurity. A lamp before the statue of Holy Mary was always to be kept lit in the boys' room, so they perform only acts that do not shun the light.[67] They were not to move from one bed to another. Nor were they to make cliques or associations where a few kept themselves "apart from the others" (688). They were not to have pets.

No outsider was to be given access to the boys without special permission, "especially when such a person may be perversely inclined and prone to the most gigantic sins, which ought not to be named" (688–89). The servants employed by the school were not to show any familiarity with the boys. When they were disobedient, the boys were to be punished with rods, not whips. They were not to eat excessively. They were to have clean clothes. If they got sick, they were to be cared for. The master of the school was to be held responsible twice a year for its accounts.

In choir the boys were to "sit at a distance from each other" and keep silent, especially at mass. Here they were to act "like angels of God, so that anyone who sees them will say that these are truly angelic boys, and the kind that the immaculate Virgin would have in her church, most celebrated in the whole world" (689).

Gerson closed his list of recommendations by expressing pride "in our church" of Notre Dame, with its ancient customs that the boys were to learn for its liturgy. He placed the choirboys in a rich tradition, but his main concern was that these angels should not touch each other or in any way become physically close to their master, to each other, to the servants, or to any outsider.

I have not presented this list in any logical manner but have more or less followed its own order, or lack of it. This review reveals how the sexual concern is a recurrent theme. Gerson seems to have been more worried about boys' physical contact than about the content of the curriculum. The "horrendous sins" to which he referred were of a sexual kind. He felt no need to be subtle or indirect in expressing his worry.[68]

Elsewhere in his pedagogical works, however, Gerson could provide advice without emphasizing sexual matters, especially when he was addressing the youths directly. His *Donatus spiritualis* is a spiritualized grammar, with the parts of speech turning into moral statements (689–700). A participle, for example, is defined as "human cognition according to nature and according to God, so that each man knows what he is or ought to be according to God" (695). Only someone trained in the treatise on grammar by Donatus, as Gerson's pupils would have been, could appreciate the playfulness and liveliness of these pages which for most of us remain difficult to decipher.

A final indication of Gerson's concerns in this period is a syncretic work that has been called *Regulae morales* or *Flores spiritualium moralium* (Gl 9.94–132). Its sections on the sacraments appear to be conventional moral theology, but the descriptions of the capital sins perhaps bring us closer to Gerson's own mind. In this work Gerson, in scholastic fashion, summarized the learning of a lifetime. At the same time, however, he imitated the old monastic florilegia, bringing together knowledge and providing a convenient catalogue.

Each of the 157 points listed in the work summarizes an area of moral theology. A full treatment of Gerson's teaching would have to work through these bald statements, often unsupported by evidence, and try to separate out the common monastic-scholastic inheritance from Gerson's nuances.[69] He saw moral good as depending on the end sought and accepted the complexity involved in judging the morality of actions. "No desire for something forbidden . . . is in and of itself a mortal sin" (101).

To get a sense of Gerson's teachings on the capital sins, we can look at some of his tenets on pride. Hiding one's sins is in itself not hypocritical and can be prudent (103, nr. 32). If someone does what he is capable of, in making good use of the gifts God has bestowed, then God will provide this person with what is necessary for salvation.[70] In the more pragmatic language of a later ethos: God helps those who help themselves. At the same time, however, no one is to look upon a feeling of spiritual consolation as in itself an infallible sign of the presence of charity. Here we can be in danger of a diabolical illusion (106, nr. 46). As so often, Gerson gives with one hand, comforting his reader, and takes with the other, warning him never to let down his guard.

If it were not for their pious intention and desire to act in harmony with the Church's intention, many Christians would be accused of idolatry in adoring images (106, nr. 47). Gerson tried to be fair and reasonable about popular religious practices, and it is during this period that his theological expertise in terms of popular devotion was tested. On 11 March, probably in 1413, Gerson wrote in a hurry (*raptim*) to the Carthusians of Basel, in response to a request from an undisclosed source in the town that he as theologian evaluate a practice that had arisen there of honoring individual saints by using the prayer "Our Father" to praise them.[71]

In his reply, Gerson stated he did not trust the messenger to be able to understand the subtlety of his response.[72] In general he seemed irritated at being pulled away from his other pursuits and required to write an on-the-spot opinion (Gl 2.151). His answer was not to those who had sent the messenger but to the Carthusians. Their office, he wrote, was not to preach, and so they could not have been involved in the dispute and were "beyond all suspicion of hatred, rancor, or jealousy."

The immediate question was whether a brother James of Bingen had gone too far when he had condemned as heretical the practice of addressing saints with the title "Our Father." Gerson was sympathetic to his concern but found the violence of his language and his manner of preaching questionable. He had upset uneducated people and had spoken *nude et crude*, preferring exaggerated statements, "as if he delighted in speaking grandly, glorying in filling untrained ears with new and unusual matters" (151). "I, however, do not judge him," he added, even though he had indeed stamped James of Bingen as a dangerous figure.

Any judicious preacher should address the unlearned congregation "in simplicity and according to its custom." As in the case of Jean de Varennes, Gerson was wary that attacks on the clergy might be misunderstood.[73] The practice of praying to the saints in such a manner was to be tolerated and even excused. It could, in fact, even be "praiseworthy, because of our weakness," for we are blind to what God really is.

The criticism of this letter was directed at the preacher, not the people. Gerson was more concerned with literal-minded critics than with naively devout people. But, as so often, he took back part of what he conceded. He added a cautionary postscript, warning against what he considered to be a common belief that if someone says so many "Our Fathers" or fasts in a certain way or repeats a given prayer, then he will automatically obtain whatever he asks for (152).

The affair was not over. In March of 1413, Pierre d'Ailly, made a cardinal in 1411 by Pope John XXIII, was sent as his legate to Germany. In 1414 he reached the Rhine valley.[74] D'Ailly had the preacher James of Bingen appear before him, and the man expressed willingness to accept judgment on his teaching. James was required in public to recant his former equation of the "Our Father" cult with heresy. The gersonian scholar Vansteenberghe compared the statement prepared for James with the text of Gerson's letter and demonstrated that d'Ailly was using the terms already employed by Gerson about Bingen's preaching.[75]

Assuming that Gerson received and answered the Basel query on 11 March 1413, he had other things on his mind. The Cabochien uprising would come six weeks later and Paris must already have been rife with rumors.[76] When the worst did come, Gerson, like other university professors, was ordered to pay a tax to support the new regime. When he refused, an attempt was made to capture him, but he escaped to "the high vaults" of Notre Dame. In reprisal the mob plundered his residence: *on le voulut prendre; mais il se bouta es hautes voultes de Notre Dame de Paris; et fut son hotel tout pille et robbe.*[77]

Gerson had become a refugee in his own church. He apparently had to abandon most of the books, papers, and memorabilia of a lifetime while spending weeks in the sanctuary of the cathedral.[78] The man who in dealing with the people of Basel had sympathized with *les gens simples* had now become their victim.

Turning to Friends

How much could Gerson now count on his friends? Or did he really have any? One shadowy figure surfaces from the sources. André de Curia was the cleric who acted as Gerson's secretary in providing the accounts of the deanery at Bruges showing that Gerson had paid for repairing the dean's house. Officially he was Gerson's chaplain at the church of Saint Christopher in Bruges.[79] When his master lost his position there, Gerson apparently called him to Paris. On 4 July 1411, the chapter of Notre Dame gave André, "priest chaplain of the lord chancellor," the chaplaincy of Saint Louis in the cathedral (Gl 10.510). On 31 August that same year, however, another person took possession of the chaplaincy, and it was not until 3 February 1412 that André entered into possession of the revenues he theoretically had from the chaplaincy, described as *litigiosa,* prone to litigation.[80]

This is apparently the same André who accompanied his master to the Council of Constance and died while on the road with him afterwards. On 10 August 1418, Gerson wrote to his Celestine brothers Nicolas and Jean that the thought of death was with him, especially since "the holy death of my most beloved and faithful companion André" (Gl 2.217). André may have been Gerson's confessor, but certainly was his assistant at the chapter of Notre Dame. We know nothing of the man's background. Could Gerson first have met him in Bruges? Or did he bring him there from Paris, perhaps an attentive student who came to serve his master for a lifetime?

In Gerson's choice of words to describe his bond with André, *comes* is less familiar than *amicus* would have been. Gerson did not draw on any of the rich expressions of friendship which he knew so well, as seen in his earliest extant letter.[81] But the presence of André indicates that even Gerson, with his reserve about affective relationships, was not always alone and to some degree had another person in his life.

A much more visible personality is Gerson's classmate from the College of Navarre Nicolas de Clamanges, a humanist writer now also gaining recognition as a spiritual figure.[82] Several letters from Nicolas to Gerson survive from this period, but none of them indicates a close friendship. In the first, dated to 1409–10, Nicolas wondered about what looked like the miraculous punishment of a sacrilegious act. We cannot demand miracles from God, but he does sometimes intervene in a miraculous way, as apparently in the case at hand (129–30).

Such a letter could have been written to anyone with a theological background. It is more a demonstration of orthodoxy than an individual message for Gerson. The next letter is even more conventional. War rages, but God has his designs. His ordeals may mean to punish or purify us, and we should make the best of them. Ultimately God will have mercy on us (132).

Perhaps at the beginning of 1411, Nicolas addressed Gerson, who had been complaining of ill health. Clamanges made appropriate noises about the usefulness of suffering and the welcome one should give to infirmity. It is worthwhile to suffer as Christ did. As the soul grows stronger, the body becomes weaker. When you were young, he wrote Gerson, and still had much heat in your body, you had to fight against the savage beast: "You could not fully overcome it since it was often superior and overcame you, dragged you, took you captive even though you were doing your best to resist" (144). Here it looks as though Nicolas was not just describing the trials of youth in general but was recalling what he knew from their student days.

Clamanges compared Gerson's situation to that of Saint Paul, who once called himself an unhappy man and asked who would free him "from the body of this death" (Rom 7:24). Gerson should not be sad and upset but instead rejoice that he had to sustain similar trials.

In the most ambitious letter from this period (146–50), Nicolas shared Gerson's passion for personification and made himself into France, speaking to the princes and describing her distress. They were not to commit such a terrible crime against their mother, a reference to the ongoing civil war that dates the letter between 1410 and 1412. Gerson is again merely the recipient of Nicolas's statement, and nothing indicates a close bond.

Was Nicolas using his contact with Gerson to remind his Parisian colleagues of his existence? Gerson seems to have been Nicolas's excuse for a display of penmanship that combined biblical knowledge with stylistic aptitude. Nicolas clearly wanted to remain in touch with Gerson, but one wonders if this desire was motivated by a need for recognition.

It is, of course, difficult to read letters in terms of human feeling, especially when they are written by intellectuals trained in classical rhetoric, as Gerson and Clamanges were. But what about the bond between Gerson and his former teacher, Pierre d'Ailly? Here we have an important letter, dated to 18 August 1409 or 1413 (125–28). One interpreter has seen the content as Gerson's criticism of d'Ailly for neglecting the spiritual life.[83] I am not so sure. Gerson was continuing the type of advice he had given him earlier (78–80). In both cases d'Ailly seems to have asked Gerson for guidance and even consolation.

The initial section of the letter speaks of the desire of the soul for union with God, quoting from the Psalm verse, "I remembered God and took delight" (Ps 76:3). In order to reach out for this experience, one must be weaned "from temporal delight." Here Gerson could have begun an intimate review of d'Ailly's life. Instead he dedicates most of the letter to a list of relevant literature, like a helpful teacher with a star pupil. If there is criticism of d'Ailly, it is very mild, a hint that he needed peace of mind through the pursuit of the contemplative life. Only by drawing forth the taste of Scriptures and their innermost meaning could he find what he needed (Gl 2.126).

There is, however, a personal note at the end of the letter. Gerson claims to have written to d'Ailly "alone and secretly, so that I will not be accused by everyone of too much speaking as if I would seem to be teaching my master" (128). He never forgot who his teacher was. Even though this statement may be a polite cliché, it shows a continuing bond.

The same might be said in connection with Gerson's brother Nicolas. In a letter to him dated 1410, Gerson initiated a practice that in coming years would become his trademark: instead of issuing personal statements, he concentrated on answering various theological questions posed by his correspondent. Here it was a question of the words used in confession for absolution. Gerson reviewed various formulae but left them mainly to the priest's discretion (137).

The elder brother here wrote about indulgences and for the first time warned against their abuse. In the old days, he said, a plenary indulgence was scarcely given even if one went to the Holy Land. Nowadays indulgences are handed out all too arbitrarily. He also considered a certain Psalm verse, which was supposed to secure salvation. Gerson was skeptical: no supernatural power can be attributed to such practices unless they are based on the Scriptures or other divine revelation (139). As in the Basel case, however, Gerson took into consideration "the unlearned and pious" who trusted in God's power. Such people need instruction through sermons so that they place their hope in God's help and not in such gimmicks. "Nevertheless we must sometimes take into consideration the fragility and weak devotion of men."[84]

The list of answers to Nicolas's queries continued. What happens, for instance, when a priest gives absolution to a sin which he does not have the power to absolve? In saying the office, if one has a devout thought about some other matter, is it better to pursue it or to concentrate on the words of the service? Gerson answered that if such a thought helps lift the person into the realm of contemplation, then it is to be welcomed, but only if it happens in a natural and effortless manner (140).

Appended to the body of the letter were several notes and comments from the recipient. Earlier in this chapter I considered the letter's remarks about Gerson's insecure situation in Paris. He even hinted at his former differences with Nicolas, in asking that "each of us through good works carry out his own vocation" (140). This may be an allusion to Gerson's earlier difficulties in accepting Nicolas's choice of the Celestines or in letting go of their youngest brother Jean.

The letter hints at reconciliation but also suggests resignation. Do not seek peace on the outside, Gerson ended, but daily look within yourself and flee rumors (141). Encouraging Nicolas to read the forty-fifth chapter of Jeremiah, where the Lord says to Baruch, "I am going to break down what I have built," Gerson prophesied that nothing could be done to stop imminent disaster in France. The Lord, however, would protect and preserve those who trusted in him.

Gerson's tone here had become more distant than in his earlier dealings with Nicolas. And yet with Pierre d'Ailly, Nicolas Gerson, and even with Nicolas Clamanges (where only letters to Gerson have been preserved), there remained a desire for contact, information, and good advice. Unlike the gregarious Augustine, Gerson is likely to have spent many hours alone, far from any friends. He had duties to perform, treatises, and sermons to complete, teaching to prepare. The late medieval cleric was much less a social being than his late antique predecessor. But Jean Gerson also needed to communicate his interior life to others. He learned how to express his affectivity indirectly through giving intellectual guidance. He no longer exposed his inner self to his brother Nicolas, but the feelings were by no means dead.

Giving Way to the Body

Gerson's inner life partly disappears from view in these years, as he tries to cope with the outer world and its growing chaos. Two treatises from this period, however, provide an important commentary on his attitude to the body and its functions. The first is called either *On the Dignity of the Celebration of the Mass* or *On Nocturnal Pollution and Preparation for the Mass,* while the second also has a double title, *On Determining Chastity* or *On Daytime Pollution.*[85] Gerson opens the first with what appears to be a very personal remark:

> I have frequently and for a long time been in doubt, especially after I was ordained priest, if someone who was polluted by a nighttime dream should refrain from celebrating the Mass. Similarly I am aware of many [priests], especially members of religious orders and most recently one above all. These have been greatly disturbed by scruples and hesitation on the matter. Their religious devotion encourages them to celebrate the Mass, but fear of committing an offense restrains them. (9.35–36)

As so often in his theological career, Gerson set out to write a relatively brief treatise of good advice for fellow priests and members of religious orders. This time, however, he had to ask for indulgence "if perhaps I have to speak in an impure way" (36) for there was no other way to treat what he here called an illness.

So begin a number of *considerationes* in Gerson's familiar manner, starting out with free will and choice, as well as the individual's worthiness to celebrate the Mass, and ending with detailed instructions on how to cope with bodily functions. As in the treatises on confession and on masturbation, Gerson wrote in Latin with directness and detail he would not have used in French.[86] He asks when it is that a person gives consent (Gl 9.38–39). In other words: when semen flows in sleep, to what extent can the individual be considered responsible?

Gerson was dealing with a subject that had so far mainly been a concern for monks. John Cassian in the fifth century had devoted his attention to the matter.[87] Now the same discipline was required for secular priests as had long been expected from monks.[88] Just as devotion to the life of Christ had moved from the monastery to the city streets of Europe, so too concern with bridling sexuality was no longer limited to the monastery but also involved ordinary parish priests.

Gerson's absorption of a monastic ethos can be seen in his borrowing from a story about Saint Bernard. When a monk was plagued by so many scruples that he did not dare to say mass, Bernard told him, "Go, brother, and celebrate the Mass on the basis of my faith."[89] In the original story, contained in a Cistercian collection from about 1200, the brother felt unworthy, not about saying mass, but about receiving communion.[90] In calling the tale to mind, Gerson changed it and adapted it to his own subject: the sense of inadequacy many priests feel about carrying out the liturgy that brought Christ onto the very altar in front of them.

Gerson admitted that it could be "praiseworthy" to abstain from saying mass because of a feeling of unworthiness. But it could be even more worthwhile to go ahead and celebrate in spite of doubts and scruples and thus benefit oneself and others (Gl 9.40). Here he used a maxim from Ovid: "He who is not present today will be less fit tomorrow."[91] The adage provided a point of departure to address the troubled priest: "You are distracted today, less devout, less recollected, greatly tempted by the world, the flesh or the devil. I certainly believe you. But you should realize that they who persecute you do not sleep. Tomorrow there will be the same enemies opposing you and laying traps for your devotion, in the same way they do today" (40). Gerson combined Ovid and Ecclesiastes (9:10) in urging that whatever one can do, one should do here and now.

Gerson's closeness to what once were monastic concerns is revealed in his use of the literature of the Desert Fathers. He took a story he said came from the *Lives of the Fathers* about Evagrius, who thought he should take communion only once a year. Some of his colleagues stated that if he was worthy only once a year, he thereby admitted he was unworthy. By this logic Evagrius was presumptuous in taking communion at all. Why then should someone else, who also knew he was unworthy, refrain from taking the sacrament several times? So once a year meant virtually any time![92]

Gerson did not have the scruples the young Luther felt. "There were," Gerson pointed out, "some saints who were convinced by reason that they should never say mass." He may have been thinking of Francis of Assisi, who felt unworthy to become a priest. Such people can be admired, but their examples are not necessarily to be followed (40).

Having established the principle that priests are unworthy to say mass and yet must trust in God and go ahead, Gerson from the fifth consideration deals with the specific circumstances of nocturnal pollution: "No form of pollution that is begun and completed in sleep is a mortal sin" (41). If a person in wakefulness has an impure desire for pollution and this takes place after he falls asleep, then he has sinned. But if he wakes up in the morning and is pleased that the pressure has been removed from him, then, according to Thomas Aquinas, nothing untoward has happened. We must not indirectly cause nocturnal emission, but if it happens, there is no reason to regret it.

In the sixth consideration Gerson is even more specific: "I saw (*vidi*) another religious and sober person who for ten years and more was vexed almost daily by this passion" of nocturnal seminal emissions (42). The matter was to be left to medical doctors, although one such doctor had said that all his efforts to stop nocturnal emissions had been unsuccessful. Gerson's advice was to avoid worrying too much. A person can become excessively obsessed with what to eat or how to sleep, to avoid anything that might provoke an emission (43).

Our bodies are not under our immediate control: "No impurity of the body by itself impedes the celebration [of mass], for it is an accidental matter, unless the reason concurs or consent is given in the soul" (43). When a man experiences seminal flow in sleep, however, the next day he can be plagued by the recollection of his dreams. It might be best to skip saying mass (45). But if there is no one else to do so, then one might have to go ahead anyway. What matters most is to examine one's conscience and consider all the circumstances involved. Because the question is so individual, it is impossible to generalize (46).

In his references to hesitation, doubt, and guilt, Gerson may well have been describing his own situation. Here as elsewhere in his writings, he made use of the Paul's expression, "I know a man" (2 Cor 12:2): "I know a man who in truth came to realize that he never could attain a quiet and serene disposition in celebrating mass because he was in doubt about his own efforts and labor, care and preparation, through confession or otherwise. And so he offered on the altar of his heart the oxen of pride and spoke with a contrite and humble heart."[93] The man admitted to himself that he was unable through his own efforts to become worthy to say mass. Gerson at this point described a vision "a certain person" experienced in his sleep. Again, it is likely he was speaking of himself. The man was thrown into a sewer and tried to keep himself from drowning by holding onto a stick covered with excrement. But the stick kept sinking, and at the same time exuded an unbearable stench. The man realized his own hopeless situation, abandoned the stick, and turned with all his heart to God (46).

The stick, explained Gerson, represents our own efforts (*industria*) of trying to keep from drowning. The only thing we can do to save ourselves is to place our trust in God. The more we try on our own, the more we sink into depravity's abyss, where we sense nothing except the foul and horrid stench of our own doings.

Gerson formulated here one of the central moral principles of his teaching: we must make an effort to do what we can (*agat nostra industria quod poterit*; 47), but in the end we can only hand ourselves over to God's mercy. If someone had a thousand years at his disposal, he would still be unable to make himself worthy to celebrate mass. So the person "at first hesitates, trembles, and shakes" but then can speak to God and say that he finds no mortal sin in himself and that the Lord is not only just but also merciful (Ps 129:7): "Woe to me if I am not to be judged with the greatest of mercy! What can I know if my vices lie hidden within me? I deserve to be blinded; I who have been deprived of my spiritual vision and have abused it when I saw the good but spurned its fulfillment. This one thing I know, that with the Lord there are mercy and redemption in abundance" (47). Gerson's advice was to trust in the Lord. He wrote in language that goes back to Anselm of Canterbury concerning the fornicating soul that can turn to God for forgiveness.[94] The passage ends with an address to the soul which comes close to the language of the *Imitation of Christ* and helps explain why French scholars used to consider Gerson the author of this pious and popular tract:

> You are unclean [my soul]. Then go to be cleansed at the font of purity, which cannot be contaminated. You are hungry. Go to be fed with the living and indestructible bread. You are ill. This will be the most effective medicine for your weakness. You experience an emission and cannot be healed by doctors or by your own exercises, then through the fullness of faith, as the woman who had a hemorrhage of blood touched the thread

> of Jesus's garment (Luke 8:43) . . . you touch the holy victim so that you be cleansed. (Gl 9.48)

I cannot imagine a more eloquent summary of late medieval spirituality, with its doubt, pain and simultaneous hope. Looking to a merciful God as incarnated in his Son, the lonely soul "will have Christ as a faithful companion and most generous host" (48).

We do not have to bother ourselves with overscrupulousness about "matters which do not deserve attention, such as bodily impurities" (49). Gerson chose to disregard what happens to the communion host when it enters into the stomach, as if it thereby could be made filthy. The soul can enter into the mountain of contemplation and leave behind the senses which brought it there (50). The hermit pope Celestine V (Peter Morrone) once had a dream in which he was invited with his donkey to enter into the royal hall of heaven. "Here the donkey left behind on the path a tribute of its stomach." Peter was horrified and tried to back away, but he was addressed by a voice from the throne. Such cleansing was natural and necessary, he was told.

The donkey represents our lower nature, which can "rise up and challenge" the soul. We must trust in God to lift us up (50). It is significant that Gerson used this anecdote about Pope Celestine. During these years Gerson's teacher Pierre d'Ailly wrote a new saint's life of the one pope who had voluntarily resigned his office.[95] Peter was a hero because he had given up the papacy, something men like Benedict XIII were unable to make themselves do. He was also praiseworthy because of his ascetic life, which he managed to spread to others by founding the Celestine Order. Despite Gerson's reservations about its extreme asceticism, he saw the Celestine founder as a sensible man.

The second treatise about "pollution" is perhaps even more direct in its sexual language than the first. Here Gerson dealt with emissions from the genitals that take place when we are awake. His language suggests he was aware that both men and women in a state of sexual arousal, voluntary or not, can emit a lubricant here (51). He also considered how sperm can build up and be ejected, even in a wakeful state, without the full consent of the will. A confessor who is obliged to investigate a penitent's sexual sins may become so aroused that he experiences seminal emission without willing it. A priest who has to ride out to visit his parishioners may be so stimulated by being on a horse that he also experiences emission. So long as one does not take "carnal delight," no mortal sin is involved (57). What matters is not flow of semen, but consent to sexual pleasure (58).

As in the previous treatise Gerson advises that the person who feels arousal should do his best to ignore it, instead of fighting it directly (60). He refers to advice given in his "treatise in French on the remedy against temptations of blasphemy."[96] If the temptation becomes very bad, one can cry out, bite the tongue, say, "Go away, away with you, filthy thoughts; go far from here; you have come at a bad time; I have other things to do."[97]

Gerson also warned against close friendships which, even though not wrong in themselves, can create an atmosphere of sensuality that lurks beneath an edifying surface (61). In spite of such suspicion, he also warned those in charge not to overdo their zealousness. It was no use trying to keep young people apart, "forbidding spiritual conversations" or not letting them study together. Earlier in the treatise he complains that parents worried about their daughters kissing men and their sons' involvement with girls. "Why then do they not show equal concern in keeping their children from touching themselves or others in a base manner?" There was much greater danger of sin here, "for such things do not create so much shame" (53).

It may seem almost hypocritical when Gerson writes that we can allow ourselves to be pleased by the act of pollution, "not because of the pleasure but because it brings relief to the body."[98] But he warns especially the young not to "pretend one thing and do something else" (*prætendens unum et agens alterum*; 62). One could end up almost praying for physical release and yet acting as if one did not desire it. For Gerson the best response was to replace the temptation with other thoughts, instead of facing it directly.

It is admittedly difficult for priests in the confessional to have to dwell in detail on sexual matters and not be affected. He advised the confessor to assume a bodily position which "will provide the least stimulation, as when he stands or kneels" (63). His conversation with the penitent should be brief and limited. Sometimes, however, the confessor has to be affable in order to get the penitent to go into detail. If the priest is aroused, he should go on with the confession, even if it leads to involuntary seminal emission.[99]

All this good advice, partly a repetition of what Gerson wrote earlier in his treatises on confession, may seem hard to follow. Instead of judging Gerson on the basis of twenty-first century secular Western values, however, it might be more fruitful to ask what he was trying to achieve. He inveighed against excessive, unnecessary, and unhealthy control of the body, conceding what we might call its biological functioning. At the same time, he excluded any deliberate acts seeking sexual pleasure. A priest should be able to carry out his sacramental functions without becoming overscrupulous.

What Gerson did not consider, except in his phrase about "pretending one thing and doing another," is that it is virtually impossible both to control the body and at the same time to let go. May a priest pray for a wet dream? May a confessor look forward to a penitent known for providing sexual narratives? How could any human being both want and not want sexual release? There was a thin line between hypocrisy and self-awareness.

Gerson dealt frankly with difficult subjects while seeking to provide comfort and hope to his readers. He took an old discussion out of its monastic or eremitical context and applied it to the pastoral and sacramental life of the Church as a whole. He advised others to follow the path he had chosen for himself, casting away the crutch of his own filthy efforts and trusting in a merciful God who would rescue him.

Facing Fear and Tyrannicide

In 1413 Gerson had every reason to flee to a merciful God. The Cabochien rising in late April threatened his life. On 27 June the chapter of Notre Dame gave him permission to continue his residence inside the church "because of the wickedness (*malignitatem*) of the times" (Gl 10.514). He is noted as still being *in ecclesia* in July, August, and early September (513). Already in mid-July, however, the canons of Notre Dame expressed hope for a peace treaty "among the lords of the royal line." At the end of the month, they decided to provide funds for the needs of the city of Paris.

On Friday 1 September, the dukes of Orleans and Bourbon entered Paris. Many of the citizens bore the colors of the day, black and red, with the motto embroidered on their clothes, *le droit chemin* (the right path).[100] The next day the lords of the realm took an oath of peace before the king. Gerson knew that Jean Petit, in his defense of the duke of Burgundy, had preached that an oath that can be replaced by a better form of action loses its validity. This is one of six points Gerson attacked in his sermon before the king of 4 September, *Rex in sempiternum vive* (May the king live forever; Gl 7.2.1005–30).

Glorieux entitled this sermon *Discours au roi contre Jean Petit,* but the duke of Burgundy's theological champion is never named here, and the sermon is much more than an attack on Petit's justification of tyrannicide. Gerson used the occasion to give the Armagnac party, in the words of the sermon expert Louis Mourin, "more than one reproach that they had deserved."[101] Mourin admitted, however, that Gerson had taken his time (four years) before choosing to speak out against tyrannicide.

The sermon dismissed the revolutionaries of the spring as *gens de petit ou nul estat,* people of no account, who were out for their own gain (1007). The France they disturbed had received centuries earlier, at the baptism of Clovis, God's promise that royal lordship would continue so long as faith and justice reigned in the kingdom (1006). Gerson believed in an alliance between monarchy and church, a vision that continued in French Catholic circles right through the nineteenth century.

It was God's miracle that the kingdom had emerged from the chaos of that spring (1008). He lamented what Paris had to experience. Now the people of the city were seeking to follow "the right path" (*le droit chemin*): "This is the royal road which goes neither to the right nor to the left, which is clear and public, without corners . . . frauds and deceptions" (1009). Gerson sought a middle ground between Burgundians and Armagnacs. Support for the monarchy meant refusing to take sides. As in almost all his court sermons, he hardly ever hinted at the fact that the king for much of the time was lost in the fog of his mind. Gerson hoped that the French people would rally behind their monarchy now that they knew "the difference between royal domination and that of some popular elements" (1010).

Gerson asked the king, the queen, and the dauphin to "guard and favor all the good subjects . . . chivalry, clergy, and bourgeoisie, without overwhelming them with intolerable charges and other oppressions, so that with all their hearts they will greet you and say, May the king live forever." He asked the monarchy to make sure "all men of arms be quickly and completely ejected." He mentioned specifically the English, but he was also thinking of the princely factions, for he warned against inciting civil war: *gardez vous de mouvoir guerres civiles* (1011).

This sermon can be seen as a continuation of his *Vive le roy* from 1405, as in its contrast between the king's inner and outer lives. His inner life requires, for example, that the king be given time to be alone with himself to think. The Roman hero Scipio is said to have spent two hours every morning with himself "so that he could better decide what needed to be done" (1012). Historical examples and Old Testament parallels are cited for asserting royal authority. Gerson reminded the king that the university had participated in an attempt two years earlier to make peace in the kingdom (1017). To no effect. Since then, he claimed, "a hundred thousand persons are dead and your kingdom impoverished."

Gerson's proposals here to improve the civil service and provide officials with decent salaries reflect what the Cabochien ordinance, now a dead letter, had tried to gain.[102] If royal officials had sufficient incomes, he argued, they would not plague the poor. Beyond individual reforms, however, he saw a need for strong royal authority as an alternative to ducal factions. His text here is full of references to civil war in late Republican Rome. The only *chemin* forward was the king's, and so if someone asked, "Which side are you on?" the only "good reply" was to be "I am a true Frenchman; I belong to the king and to no one else. This is the royal way, this is *le droit chemin*" (1019).

Here we find national feeling *avant le mot*.[103] Gerson believed in attachment to monarchy as the basis for an identity he traced back to the time of Clovis. A shared belief in community was the only way to avoid more conflict. At this point, after establishing the principles of good government, he turned to the question of tyrannicide. Even the king cannot give leave to kill a man who does not deserve to die. Gerson saw the spread of false teaching on tyrannicide for the last six years as a cause of the disturbances (*turbation*) that had taken place that year. He listed seven assertions connected to this teaching, again without naming Jean Petit (1020–22).

The formulation that one has a right to kill on one's own authority goes beyond what Jean Petit had said in his 1408 sermon.[104] Gerson, however, was not analyzing a sermon. He was combatting an attitude he believed the sermon had fostered: that it was not only legitimate but even praiseworthy to kill a tyrant.

It was Petit's final assertion Gerson found most damaging: "Every time one does something that is better, even though it is what one swore not to do, it is not perjury but contrary to perjury" (1022). In other words, it is acceptable to violate an oath if one's action is morally better than the result of keeping the oath. The duke of Burgundy was thus released from his previous oaths of friendship with the duke of Orleans because it was more beneficial to kill the duke as a tyrant than to maintain the alliance sworn between the dukes.

Gerson reasserted the standard medieval view, most vividly conveyed by Dante when he put traitors in the deepest recesses of *Inferno,* that perjury is even worse than homicide. Perjury cannot be defended even to save a city or a kingdom (1023). Evil things are not to be done in order to bring about good results. In the language of our age: the end does not justify the means. Any defense of perjury undermined the very fabric of human society.

The chancellor and his colleagues were ready to offer their lives in order to protect the truth: "Perhaps someone will kill us for speaking the truth: so what? (*quoy de cela,* 1027). In coming years Gerson would pursue the question of tyrannicide and almost flog it into the ground. In this first public declaration, however, he considered much more broadly how the kingdom had to rid itself of factions and how to provide peace for all. Closing the sermon, he brought in a new theme, not only calling on Mary but also mentioning the "virginal spouse of Our Lady, Saint Joseph the Just, whose marriage signified the most perfect union and conjunction there is, that of God and his Church" (1030). Here he made known a new concern for promoting the cult of Saint Joseph.

Within a few days, in a statement in the name of the university, Gerson joined defense of tyrannicide to a host of heretical views he claimed to find around him.[105] He here warns against "errors which rise up in our times, some orally, some in writing, some in deeds or acts" (Gl 10.175). There follows a list of fifty-five statements. In dealing with the excommunicate, for example, he had heard it said that "these ought not to be allowed confession, even at the moment of death." His conclusion: "This is heretical. They sin mortally who knowingly hinder [the administration of] this sacrament."[106]

On 6 September, Gerson summarized for the university the seven assertions he had already condemned in his sermon before the king. The faculty of theology expressed its full support for his conclusions (174). The possibility that Gerson might be physically attacked or "in some other way be molested" was mentioned. The faculty promised support for its lord chancellor. The statement does not mention the other faculties. Gerson lacked the support of the faculty of canon law and of the Picard nation in the arts faculty, which remained loyal to the duke of Burgundy.[107]

By early October, resistance to Gerson came to the surface. He felt compelled to compose, in French, a "response to criticisms." He opened by repeating a quotation made in his sermon of 4 September from Gregory the Great: "It is more righteous that scandal be permitted to arise than that truth be deserted."[108] He criticized the university, and thus also himself, for not speaking out earlier and claimed that "there would not have come about so many horrible evils in this kingdom if some people had risked death in resisting the errors which have taken root from our evils" (Gl 7.1.217). Gerson made a half-excuse by quoting the common proverb: *vaut mieux tard que jamais* (better late than never). Just as he liked to mix classical and biblical quotations to make the same point, he had a love of the language of everyday life with its common sense and brevity.[109]

Now was the time to regret past behavior: "It is certainly to be believed that many have repented of their delay and procrastination resulting from human or worldly fear in this matter" (217). Gerson was referring to himself as well as to his colleagues. Now they knew better and would have to behave accordingly, showing courage and not giving any clemency to their enemies.

In November a meeting was called by the king and the bishop of Paris for churchmen to discuss the matter of tyrannicide. Summarizing the previous years and looking back with regret, Gerson here explained: "In the teaching of the faith and the spreading of good morals there were not sufficient freedom and opportunity for me and those like me, because of the threats and terrors we experienced, some in secret, some in public."[110] . He added, however, that he had taken no part in the strong-arm methods of these years. It is likely that he had kept silent in order to protect his integrity and avoid being used by others. He had done the same earlier, when he had disagreed with efforts to withdraw obedience from the pope at Avignon.[111] Then as now, however, his unwillingness to speak out made him appear to be an accomplice in what had taken place.

On 1 December 1413, the entire University of Paris, in congregation at the church of Saint Mathurin, deplored the actions of the preceding years but concluded that the king was more to be pitied than accused for approving them.[112] This is a rare indirect reference to the king's illness. The statement describes how some university members had been forced to flee Paris, hide in churches, or keep silence. Gerson may have been one of the authors of this declaration.[113]

The day before, 30 November, Gerson had intervened at a synod or "council of the faith" in Paris and stated that he had no desire to attack Jean Petit personally (Gl 10.180). His one interest was to extirpate error. A careful review of the proceedings of the council shows that Gerson was very much in a minority in his eagerness to condemn the six points taken from the sermon of Jean Petit.[114] On 18 December, Gerson reviewed point by point virtually all earlier writings on the subject, especially some key passages in Thomas Aquinas (181–216).

On 23 February 1414, the council condemned Jean Petit's justification of tyrannicide.[115] But Gerson did not stop here. On 4 December at the royal residence, the Hôtel Saint Paul, in the presence of the king, Gerson gave a sermon "according to instructions given by the university" (*Ecce rex*; Gl 5.243–55). Our text is in Latin, and there is no indication that it is a translation made after Gerson's death of the original French text, as was the case with many of his French works. He must have delivered the sermon in French but later wrote it up in Latin, perhaps to be certain that his message was not misinterpreted.

Gerson began his remarks stating that he had previously sent a work with "twelve considerations" to the duke of Burgundy, but had reduced these now to four. The first is that peace among Christians cannot come about "without truth or against the truth of faith and morals" (244). He referred to the recent sentence of the council against Jean Petit and added his favorite quotation of this period that it is better for scandal to arise than for truth to be deserted.[116] Here he added a statement which went to the very heart of political events. The treaty of Chartres, which had pardoned the duke of Burgundy, was invalid, because "it favors and nourishes heresy in asserting that the death of the duke of Orleans was for the good of king and kingdom."[117]

The sermon's second consideration asserted that there had been no stable peace in the kingdom for seven years because faith and good morals had gone into exile. Louis of Orleans was not subject to the duke of Burgundy, who therefore had no right to seek his death. No prior warning had been given; there was no judicial sentence against Orleans. The two lords had sworn oaths to support each other and had shown signs of friendship in public and private. Worst of all, the duke of Orleans had no suspicion or warning that he would be struck down "like a dog" when he was returning to his own residence from a visit to the queen. The key word here is *viliter,* basely or vilely (246).

Gerson did not deny that the duke of Orleans might be looked upon as a tyrant, but the circumstances of his death did not conform to any of the conditions necessary to justify such an act. For the first time he accused the duke of Burgundy of pertinacity in his crimes and errors, thus indicating that he was in danger of being condemned as a heretic. He had made "the entire kingdom, from the king to the lowest person, act heretically, insofar as he was able, in his actions, as well as his words and writings" (249).

In the third consideration, Gerson claimed that peace was disturbed because mercy, the sister of peace, was either lacking or had been turned into cruelty. We all have a duty of fraternal correction, which sometimes can require harshness.

There is no excuse for delay when truth is required. He referred to a canon of Gratian that "error which is not resisted is approved."[118] Gerson moderated this statement by pointing to the violence of the times and the threat posed to those who might have spoken out against his theses: "This has excused others, even if not from everything, yet from something" (250). As earlier, he was referring to his own silence.

Eager as always to make use of historical precedents, Gerson reminded the king of how the Paris faculty of theology had spoken out a century earlier, in criticizing the teaching of Pope John XXII on the beatific vision. The king had then convoked masters of theology at Vincennes for their finding. Afterwards it was made known that the pope's teaching was wrong.[119] The episode demonstrated that the faculty of theology "does not easily err in matters of faith" (251).

What mattered to Gerson was the faculty's right and duty to speak out on questions of theology, notwithstanding possible retaliation from popes, dukes, or kings. For the sake of truth, the duke of Burgundy must publicly acknowledge his sin and error. Church prelates or doctors of theology who had hesitated in speaking out were now to receive "fraternal correction." If a pope favored Jean Petit's justification, he might even be removed from office (251).

Gerson's fourth consideration was that a stable peace required justice. Two months earlier, on 9 October, the duke of Burgundy had made a declaration on the matter at the church of Cambrai. At first, Gerson claimed, he had "rejoiced," but when he had read the text, he became "sad that it was different from what I believed and instead of purging him made him all the more filth-ridden."[120] Now it was necessary for the duke to publicly revoke this teaching.

For the first time Gerson openly took sides not only in terms of principles but also in relation to persons. He had long distanced himself from the Burgundian camp. His loss of his Bruges prebend shows that already by 1410–11, he was considered to be in opposition to the duke. He had kept silent back then, but now he spoke out against the duke and embraced Louis's son Charles as the new duke of Orleans. Although he claimed to have no desire to harm Burgundy, he forewarned the duke of the possibility of eternal damnation and the disinheritance of his posterity (presumably because of a heresy charge). The chancellor claimed he sought only the duke's "absolution, salvation, and reconciliation." Then the four virtues could meet and embrace: mercy, truth, justice, and peace (cf. Ps 84:11).

So ended the sermon. The chancellor had chosen sides and would have to live with the consequences of his political as well as moral commitment. The council of faith to which Gerson referred repeatedly had not been an official diocesan synod, merely a consultative assembly. And Gerson had not gotten the unanimous support he had sought. As long as the Armagnacs remained in Paris, so could he. But nothing would ever be the same again.

Loving a Father and Husband

When Gerson emerged from his refuge in the cathedral in August 1413, he had not only escaped with his life: he had also gained a new life. His spiritual renewal is apparent not only in his decision to pursue the question of tyrannicide but in his readiness to promulgate the cult of Saint Joseph as a loving man, the tender father of Jesus, and the loyal husband of Mary.

The gersonian scholar Max Lieberman noticed several decades ago that Gerson's writings from this period about Joseph mention miracles for which the saint was responsible.[121] Gerson never stated categorically that he had experienced one of these miracles, but his celebration of Joseph's closeness to those in need hints at this possibility. Gerson's first desire upon resuming his normal life was to publicize a new feast day for the marriage of Joseph and Mary. In a letter of 17 August 1413 that was addressed to "all churches," especially those dedicated to Mary, Gerson called for a day to commemorate their marriage.

Joseph up to this time had no universal cult in Western Europe and was often portrayed in art and in plays as a rather silly old man, tired and peripheral to the

Fig. 8 The conventional view of Joseph as an old man. He makes the birth soup for Mary, before the flight into Egypt. She worships the Christ child as in a vision of Birgitta of Sweden. From Mørkøv Church, Denmark, about 1450. The workshop of the Master of the Ice Fjord. (Photo by author)

great events he witnessed.[122] In his writings from this period Gerson thundered against such a conception, which he found lodged in apocryphal accounts of the infancy of Christ.[123] Instead Joseph should be seen in terms of what is said and implied in the first chapters of the Gospel of Matthew and Luke, where an angel told him about the coming birth of a child, and where he expressed doubt about his own relationship to Mary. For Gerson it was important to mark the fact that Joseph, once enlightened about God's will, went ahead and married Mary. He described their wedding as one full of joy, of the type the Parisian bourgeoisie celebrated in his time.

Gerson mentions composing a liturgy for the feast of the marriage of Joseph and Mary. This source has hardly been noticed, even though Gerson's position in furthering the cult of Joseph has long been apparent. His liturgy reveals particular aspects of Joseph's life he wanted to emphasize. The first reading, for example, is from Matthew 1:24–25. "In that time Joseph arising from sleep did as the angel of the Lord ordered him and received his bride; and he did not come to know her until she had given birth to her first-born son, and called his name Jesus."

In the homily for this reading, Gerson expresses the joy of "every age and state and sex" in this marriage (Gl 8.56). If there is reason to rejoice in matrimony when it takes place among sinners, how much more happiness there should be in a marriage "where virginity had performed nuptials" and where there was no concupiscence. Gerson joined this celebration of a virginal marriage with a verse from Isaiah (62:5) prophesying that a young man would come to dwell with a virgin. The chancellor imagined Joseph as a young man, full of energy and potency, able to take care of his wife and son by hard work, and not the broken-down, tired figure of popular imagination.

The Matthew quotation, however, was problematic, for it seemed to indicate that Mary and Joseph later had physical union and could have conceived other children. In other writings Gerson regularly returned to the polemic between Saint Jerome and Helvidius on the virginity of Mary.[124] In the liturgy for his proposed feast, however, he concentrated on the scene of the wedding as such.

The second reading, for example, describes how a wedding takes place "among almost all peoples" (56). Friends are summoned and come in their finest clothes. There are lavish food, music, and song. Gerson refers to the nuptials of Ahasuerus and Esther (Esther 2:18), that of Tobias the younger and Sarah (Tobit 11:18), as well as others in the Old Testament. There is also a spiritual celebration of a wedding in the *Song of Songs.* And finally we have the Gospel parable condemning the man who entered the wedding feast without proper dress (Mt 22:11).

In the third reading, Gerson surmises that Joseph would have followed the custom of his people and have held a wedding feast. Once he understood how Mary had conceived her child, he called together parents, friends, and relatives. The poverty and asceticism of his holy life did not dampen his celebration (Gl 8.56).

Gerson's method here is common in his spiritual writings: on the basis of what was to be found in a biblical text, he imagines what else might have happened. It was a matter of piety to go behind Scripture and consider what it implied.[125] Acting as a combined cultural historian and fictional dramatist, Gerson considered Joseph's life and choice. Since he was a Jew and was faithful to the social practices of his religion, his wedding to Mary would have taken place according to standard observance.

In the third reading, Gerson asserts that Joseph knew Mary from friendly visits (*ex familiari visitatione*) to her each year in Jerusalem, where she lived in the Temple (58). He was related to Mary by blood because Anne, her mother, after the death of her husband Joachim, had married Joseph's brother, Cleophas. According to Jewish custom of the time, Joseph took Mary to live with him in Nazareth. It is here that the solemn rite of marriage would have taken place.[126]

In describing the marriage as maintaining virginity, Gerson used the story of Cecilia and Valerian, perhaps taken from the *Golden Legend* for 22 November. Mary had told Joseph that she was with child but did not have sexual experience. Joseph was struck by "so great a novelty" (*tantae novitatis*), but subsequently an angel appeared to him and explained how it was God's will.

This third reading provides a point of departure for most of Gerson's later writings on Joseph and Mary. His central message is twofold: their union was a real marriage; it combined marital love with sexual abstinence. As a man whose way of life required chastity and sexual abstinence, Gerson found in Joseph a model, a loving man who embraced a woman, who brought up a child, and who at the same time remained calm, content, and pure.

Gerson admits in his letter to all churches that there was nothing doctrinally necessary in his description of the marriage. Nevertheless, "we affirm that the marriage should be venerated in a solemn office" (64). His liturgy for such a solemnity would be taken not from "apocryphal or doubtful texts" but from Holy Scripture itself. Only the readings reflect his own theological considerations. Everything else is biblical. The feast could be held on the Thursday of Ember week in Advent, since the previous Thursday used the gospel, "The angel Gabriel was sent" (62).

Gerson wanted a man who was virile and chaste, loving and affectionate, happy and fulfilled in his vocation. Joseph, Mary, and Jesus made up the ideal family, with no conflicts or shadows in its existence, except those that came from the outside world. Such themes are expressed in greatest detail in Gerson's *Considerations on Saint Joseph,* written between August and late September 1413. The text takes up more than thirty pages in the Glorieux edition and provides the basis for his later poem, the *Josephina.*

Gerson saw Joseph as the father of Jesus because he was the one who "nourished, guarded, and served" him through his own labor. "He showed all the care a good and loyal and wise father can and should provide for his true son."[127] Fatherhood is thus not biological: it is a function that is assumed when one takes on responsibility for a child. Joseph *became* the father of Jesus by acting as his father; in taking him by the hand, feeding him, comforting him, teaching him, Joseph *was* his father.

Gerson may well have been thinking of his own father, for the chancellor emphasized the bond between Joseph and Jesus in terms of the latter's subjection to a carpenter. The word he uses is *charlier*, the surname used by Gerson's father, while he calls Mary a *texeresse*, a weaver, reminding us of his mother's surname, *la chardinière*, a carder of wool (Gl 7.2.67).

Gerson imagined how Joseph taught Jesus his trade. He also "carried him, fed him, kissed him with his permission and out of paternal friendship" (68). Joseph did not feel any sexual temptation in his relationship with Mary or others (69). This state Gerson contrasted with what others experience: "Whether we desire it or not, our carnal concupiscence rises up all of a sudden when some desirable or pleasant object is offered to it."

Joseph and Mary are presented here not only in terms of their chastity but also as representatives of a royal line. Thus it is the duty of royalty and aristocracy especially to celebrate them (Gl 7.1.70–71). To the argument that this is a novelty in the liturgy, Gerson replied that it was natural that as time went on, new feasts were introduced as truths of the faith were "successively preached." He cited the examples of the Feast of the Nativity of Mary, which was brought in much later than that of the Assumption of Mary, as well as Corpus Christi and the Feast of Saint Anne: "For God wants our devotion to be directed to one thing more than to another, but this should be according to the truth and good intention, for holy novelty can be pleasing, with no reason for criticism" (71).

In suggesting *saincte nouvelleté*, Gerson became an early representative of the view that newness can be good. He was treading warily, however, and belonged to both medieval and modern worlds. In proposing a new Joseph, and thus a revised spirituality of the Incarnation, he was still faithful to medieval Christianity's traditional way of meditating on the Bible. First in monastic cloisters, and later in theological schools and now also in parish churches, old texts took on new meaning. Gerson was bold not because he was innovative but because he made his findings available at the parish level. He thought about Mary and Joseph in French and tried to promote their cult not only among his colleagues and the aristocracy but also the *gens simples*.

In a letter to the old duke of Berry for support,[128] he reviewed many of the themes he had previously suggested in greater detail in his *Considerations*, but he also used more personal arguments. The duke was renowned for his devotion to Mary, Gerson argued, because of gifts of relics and vestments both to Notre Dame of Paris and the church of Bourges. The canons of Notre Dame had rewarded the duke with four solemn masses a year during Ember days. It would therefore be appropriate, suggested Gerson, that on the Thursday of Ember Tide before Christmas, the Gospel "Joseph getting up from sleep" be said (Mt 1:24) and the feast of the virginal marriage of Joseph and Mary be held.

Gerson also called to mind the duke of Berry's friendship with Pope Clement VII, who is supposed to have shown special veneration for Saint Joseph. He added that other prominent churchmen also favored the cult: Gerson's teacher d'Ailly, now cardinal of Cambrai; the Celestine Pierre Bourgignon; and finally Henry Chiquot, a master of theology who at Chartres had bequeathed incomes to the church in his will for a commemoration of Saint Joseph.

Gerson apparently never got an answer, probably because the duke did not want to be identified with a theologian who had chosen sides against the duke of Burgundy, Berry's nephew. But the letter indicates that other centrally placed theologians were also thinking about Joseph. Pierre Bourgignon was Pierre Poquet, the general of the Celestine Order with whom Gerson collaborated in writing on questions of moral theology.[129]

The letter mentions Gerson's view of Joseph as a man who was physically close to Jesus, and who nurtured and cared for him. This theme was greatly expanded in the *Josephina,* which he may have begun to write in 1414 and finished at the Council of Constance. He felt drawn to a quiet love between Joseph and Mary, as when he saw them withdrawing into Joseph's room "to speak perhaps more openly of how to arrange their wedding" and of whom to invite.[130] It was at this point, Gerson imagined, that Mary told Joseph about her miraculous pregnancy.

In loving a man like Joseph, Gerson could reach out for a life where sexuality and affectivity were separate. But what had happened to the reform of the Church? In the midst of his concern with virginity and his condemnation of tyrannicide, the goal of transforming the Church in head and members seems to have receded. Gerson's lack of concentration invites us to ask why the conciliar movement failed. Where were you, Jean Gerson? The answer may well be that he was at his prayers, meditating on a wedding, a marriage, and a family that could give him the peace and harmony he could not find in the conflicts and disagreements around him.

Defending Truth and Failing Reform, 1415–1418

The Jean Gerson who set out for the Council of Constance in the first days of February 1415 was one of the most distinguished leaders of Western Christendom. For more than thirty years he had been teaching and preaching the truths of Christianity, and for at least two decades he had been active in attempts to bring the Schism to an end and reform the Church. At the same time, he had time and again shown an awareness of the problems of everyday life in parishes and bishoprics, as in his contribution in 1408 to a model diocesan synod at Reims (Gl 5.123–44).

In his years at Constance, Gerson did not succeed in getting his reform program approved by the council or by the new pope, Martin V, elected on 11 November 1417. When Gerson left Constance on 17 May 1418, he was aware that the new pope would make it difficult, if not impossible, to carry out the reform plans that in 1415 had seemed a necessary part of the council's three-fold agenda: to elect a new pope, to combat heresy, and to reform the Church "in head and members."[1]

Gerson's failure to adhere to his agenda of reform was connected to his efforts to ensure the condemnation of Jean Petit's defense of tyrannicide.[2] In the baggage he brought to Constance were nine articles that had been condemned in Paris in February 1414.[3] Almost from the first, he did all he could to make the council confirm the Paris result. Gerson soon met with opposition from churchmen allied with the duke of Burgundy and made very little headway. But he refused to give up, even after his appeals to the council had been rejected. For him, as we saw in the last chapter, it was a matter of conscience, his individual responsibility to speak out and compensate for his silence during the years 1408–1413.

At least one recent conciliar historian has remarked that the tyrannicide issue "distracted Gerson from fulfilling his proper influence in the council or in the French nation."[4] But once he had realized his error in keeping silence and trying to patch up the quarrel between Orleans and Burgundy, there was no going back. Gerson's integrity compelled him to act in a way that was politically unwise, for it distracted him from church reforms at Constance. However, as we shall see, Gerson knew what he was doing.

The Way to Constance: January–February 1415

The council formally opened in November 1414 and had its first solemn session on 16 November.[5] Not many churchmen were present then, but the main participant, Pope John XXIII, had accepted the invitation to convoke the meeting, apparently in the belief that it would confirm him in office. By this time, however, there may have been some kind of understanding that John would have to resign so that

Fig. 9 City of Constance, showing locations of council events. From Hermann von der Hardt, *Rerum Concilii Oecumenici Constantiensis*, vol. 4, Frankfurt 1699.

Constance could elect a new pope who would be acceptable to the entire Western Church.[6] In January 1415 Pierre d'Ailly, whom John XXIII had made a cardinal, revealed his intentions in writing to him about "a gentle way" to resign the papacy.[7]

On Christmas Eve 1414, King Sigismund, the emperor-elect, who would be a key player in the proceedings, arrived at the gates of Constance and made an impressive entrance into the city.[8] He and his retainers found a town of moderate size, with perhaps six thousand inhabitants, now beginning to swell with the council participants and their servants. A pictorial map of the town inside a magnificent collection of council documents published in 1699 shows its location on the edge of Lake Constance, the great lake that today provides part of the boundary between Germany and Switzerland.[9] Constance was within the dominions of Sigismund, but was equally accessible from the south and west. The politics of the area were more settled than those of northern Italy, but in having the meeting here, Sigismund countered any possible attempt by the French to hold the council within their kingdom.[10]

At an early point it was decided to vote according to nations, and for most of the council's duration there were four of them. The German nation, including the Bohemians, Poles, and Greeks, met in the chapter house of the Franciscan priory, while the English nation, including all of northern Europe, held its meetings in the Franciscan refectory. The Italian nation gathered in the refectory of the Dominican priory, while the French made use of the Dominican chapterhouse.[11] The Dominicans had built their impressive priory on an island adjacent to the cathedral of Constance. The Spanish nation, once it was recognized later on, met in the Augustinian monastery, while plenary sessions took place in the cathedral itself.

The council met in a place of cultural and ecclesiastical importance, one of the few areas in Western Europe that in the early medieval centuries had been spared invasions from Viking hordes and Moslem pirates. Nearby monasteries, like Reichenau and Saint Gallen, had pristine libraries stacked with manuscripts attractive for Italians and Frenchmen with humanist scholarly interests.[12]

The council, however, also had chosen a site characterized by an unhealthy climate. The medieval town was circumscribed by the waters of Lake Constance (Bodensee) and the Rhine River. In the oppressive summer heat and amid excessive crowding, epidemics broke out, as Gerson himself mentioned in 1417 (Gl 6.280–81). This is the only hint to his own reaction about his more than three-year residence at Constance. Nothing in his writings tells us about where he stayed during the council, what he ate, if he had periods of illness, and whether he had enough funds to meet his expenses.

Earlier in his career, glimpses of Gerson's everyday life appear in the proceedings of the chapters to which he was attached, first at Bruges and later at Paris.

No similar community at Constance was involved in Gerson's practical needs and problems, and the surviving diaries of prominent council members make little mention of him.[13] He was apparently not a leading political figure like Pierre d'Ailly or Sigismund, who appear prominently in all accounts.[14] Gerson at Constance is visible in his own writings and in those of his enemy Martin Porrée, the Dominican bishop of Arras, who represented the duke of Burgundy and attacked Gerson for his campaign against the defense of tyrannicide.

Our story begins with the chancellor still in the Paris he loved. On 5 January 1415, a solemn requiem mass was held at Notre Dame Cathedral for the repose of the soul of the duke of Orleans, with Gerson preaching. This sermon is lost, but a contemporary chronicler, Monstrelet, summarized its message, approving the results of the Council of Faith in Paris the previous Lent, when a copy of Jean Petit's defense of the murder of the duke of Orleans had been burned. Gerson preached that much remained to be done, but he was "prepared to maintain and

Fig. 10 Procession to the cathedral of Notre Dame on 5 January 1415 to hold a requiem mass for the repose of the soul of Duke Louis of Orleans, the brother of King Charles VI. Gerson was present and gave the sermon, now lost, "more desirous of exciting a war against the duke of Burgundy than of appeasing it." Nineteenth-century illustration from *The Chronicles of Enguerrand de Monstrelet.*

defend what he had said against the whole world." Monstrelet was not enthusiastic about the trouble thereby created. He described Gerson as "more desirous of exciting a war against the duke of Burgundy than of appeasing it."[15]

A few days later, before the king and his council at the Hôtel Saint Paul, Gerson, representing the university, recommended quickly sending royal legates to the council. His main concern, however, was to further his campaign to condemn teachings in defense of tyrannicide. He turned to the Italian cardinal present at the meeting and asked for a heresy trial in the Roman curia. If the pope did not take such an initiative, he would be aiding heresy. Gerson repeated Gratian's dictum: error which is not resisted is thereby approved.[16]

Also in January or the first days of February 1415, just before he left for Constance, Gerson spoke at Saint Mathurin, the church where the university met.[17] He stated that whoever cooperated with the duke of Burgundy's attempt to justify the killing of the king's brother, Duke Louis of Orleans, was a mortal enemy of the duke and his salvation. Such a person risked condemnation for promoting heresy and was subject to both spiritual and temporal judgment. Everyone should consider how he had until now concealed (*dissimulaverit*) the truth because of favoritism, fear, or negligence. Such a person, if he persisted, was to be judged as *impeditor pacis.* In Gerson's view the dispute about tyrannicide was responsible for the breakdown of peace in France (Gl 10.208).

We hear nothing about the immediate response to this appeal, but the Burgundian faction had its supporters at the university. In August, with the chancellor far away at Constance, the faculty of law and the Picard nation in the faculty of arts formally disavowed his actions (535–37).

Before leaving Paris, Gerson had questioned what his role at the council should be. On 8 January 1415, he declared that he would not go there as representative of the church province of Sens (in which Paris was located), nor for the university. He nevertheless did not wish "wholly to deny that he would go there" (517). On 4 February, Gerson asked the chapter of Notre Dame's permission to attend the general council. The dean of the chapter then "recommended to the same [Gerson] the business of the church" (*ecclesie negocia*; 517). Before the end of 1415, Gerson wrote from Constance that he represented university, church province, and king all in one.[18] After the council he repeated the claim (Gl 6.299).

By 8 February Gerson had left Paris for Constance. At a meeting of the chapter, the dean showed the seals of the church handed over to him by the chancellor, "and he reported that it was his right to keep them while the chancellor was absent or if he died" (518). As Glorieux wrote so succinctly: *Il n'y devait plus jamais revenir:* he would never again return to Paris (Gl 1.128).

Already on 21 February, Gerson and the university delegation arrived in Constance,[19] and so it is unlikely that the chancellor made a final visit, however brief, to the hamlet from which he had taken his name (129).

Abandoning Reform: March–October 1415

At the second session of the council on 2 March, Gerson could have witnessed Pope John XXIII's solemn oath that he would abdicate to make way for a pope accepted by all of Western Christendom.[20] On 20 March, however, John fled Constance and made his way to nearby Schaffhausen, an area not under Sigismund's control. Thanks to Duke Frederick of Austria, this pope would play for several weeks a game of hide-and-seek with the council until he was captured and imprisoned.

Gerson's response to these events can be seen in what may be his best-known contribution at Constance, a sermon preached on the Saturday before Palm Sunday, 23 March 1415, *Ambulate dum lucem habetis* (Walk while you have light). He urged the council fathers not to give up faith in what they were doing and reasserted his principles about the governance of the Church, which the council itself would formally adopt a few weeks later.[21] Gerson dramatized his own contribution by saying that he had been asked only the previous evening to give this morning sermon "to elucidate the truth concerning the agenda which this sacred council seems required to carry out" (Gl 5.41). The council was God's own instrument of the reformation of the Church and an expression of the mystical body of Christ (42–44). A pope was obliged to obey a general council that was "created by legitimate authority at a given place from every level within the hierarchy of the entire Catholic Church." The council had an obligation to listen to all persons sharing the faith who wished to address it, so that questions of faith and morals were treated in the manner required.[22] The essence of Gerson's definition was incorporated into the conciliar decree of 6 April, *Haec sancta.*

The Church can be gathered in general council without the express consent or order of the pope (Article 9; 45). If such a council makes a decision to be accepted by the pope for ending a schism, he is bound to accept it (Article 10). Furthermore the council can prosecute anyone in the course of removing error and is to show special regard for no individual (*sine personarum acceptione*; article 11)—a phrase of central importance in Gerson's attempt to block the efforts of the duke of Burgundy to use his influence at the council.[23]

Here Gerson's actual sermon ended, but the Glorieux edition adds a parenthetical remark that the "kind reader" should take into consideration that the speaker, the chancellor of Paris, pressed by lack of time, did not add proofs to these considerations. These, however, can be found in the writings he had produced during the Council of Pisa, when he was in Paris, "in a fuller and more solid argumentation" (45).

This insertion indicates that Gerson had intended in this his first address to the council to speak more about extirpating error. He was hindered, however, "partly because of his friends' persuasion, partly by lack of time."[24] These remarks probably were added by Gerson's youngest brother, Jean the Celestine, when he later edited the sermon. His central role in preserving the gersonian legacy is only now beginning to be understood.[25] Jean wanted future readers to distinguish between the sermon his brother actually preached on the council's function and his addition about heresy and tyrannicide. This second section, just as much as the first, indicates Gerson's concerns during the first weeks of his stay at Constance.

For the time being his colleagues had persuaded him to hold back, but the additional text shows that he wanted the record of his sermon to include an attack on the duke of Burgundy. Gerson repeated what he had said before the king on 4 December 1414: a conditional declaration of faith or confession is not sufficient to purge oneself from an accusation of heresy (253). Anyone who has publicized error must purge himself before a legitimate judge (Articles 8 and 9; Gl 5.49). He was thinking about the duke of Burgundy's insistence in October that he, as a good Christian, followed the faith of his fathers. This was not enough!

To the possible charge that by concerning himself with a single case of heresy, Gerson undermined the council's goal of restoring unity in the Church, he answered that it was the council's task both to fight heresy and end the Schism (50). The adoption on 6 April of *Haec sancta* placing the council above the pope was thus for Gerson not the victory it might appear to be.[26] On 11 April he issued a statement listing conclusions necessary for the council to support. It had to accept that the recent council in Paris had acted rightly in condemning Jean Petit's propositions. Those in error were to be compelled to make amends, and anyone who refused to do so was to be condemned for supporting heresy (Gl 10.208).

A memorandum, probably written by Martin Porrée, a champion of the duke of Burgundy, describes Gerson's activities from April to November 1415. On 11 April, in a large room belonging to the cardinal Pierre d'Ailly (*in stupha magna*), in the presence of many prelates, abbots, doctors, especially from the faculty of theology, Gerson "after many harsh words" read aloud a statement "which he first had cast down at the feet of the said lord cardinal, in contempt, because he had not immediately been given an opportunity for reading it out as he wanted." Then he went into a rage (*inde totus furiosus videbatur*; 529). Despite the author's hostility, it would be no surprise if Gerson, immersed in his campaign against tyrannicide, acted in this way.

The memorandum continues that on 7 June after lunch, in the presence of the cardinals of Cambrai and Florence as well as many others, Gerson said there were certain errors in the kingdom of France. Nine of them had been condemned by the bishop of Paris, and the chancellor was willing to defend this decision "until the fire" (530). The next day, Saturday at vespers, in the house of the cardinal Zabarella of Florence, and in the presence of Sigismund, the matter was discussed with the help of Pierre d'Ailly. On Sunday in the great hall of the Augustinians, at three in the afternoon, Gerson reviewed the propositions condemned at Paris.

On Wednesday 12 June in the same place, again with Sigismund present, Gerson returned to the question once more.

And so on. The account is not a mere polemic against Gerson. It tells how the council tried to hand the question of tyrannicide over to commissioners before whom Gerson was allowed to argue his point. Sigismund involved himself and thus must have been convinced the matter was of importance. On 17 June Gerson asked the commissioners to go ahead quickly (*celeriter*) and confirm the Paris condemnation (531). The same term is found in his own deposition from 15 June *Coram vobis* (Before you).

Gerson's fullest statement came on 9 June, *Quoniam desunt* ("Since they lack," also called "Rejection of the nine assertions"; 208–16). A vassal is not a legitimate judge of his lord and has no authority to condemn him to death. The rule of law is to be observed: even a king cannot kill a traitor until he has warned him, summoned him to court, and seen him convicted (211). If a king cannot do so, then all the less can a vassal: "So that no one who has not been warned or defied can be killed."[27]

On 6 July 1415, the same day as it passed sentence against John Hus and anathematized many articles of faith attributed to him, the council firmly condemned the following statement, in future to be known as *Quilibet tyrannus:* "That any tyrant can and should be licitly and meritoriously killed by any vassal or subject of his, even by treachery, blandishment or adulation, notwithstanding an oath previously given, or an alliance made with him, without waiting for the sentence or mandate of any judge."[28] The council fathers summarized in a single sentence the nine propositions ascribed to Jean Petit that had been condemned at Paris. Apparently thanks to the desire of Sigismund to settle the matter, they captured the essence of what Jean Petit was thought to have said in defending the killing of the duke of Orleans.[29]

For Sigismund the matter had been concluded. He set off on 18 July for Nice to meet ambassadors of the recalcitrant Benedict XIII. The council was getting through its agenda. On 28 April, John XXIII had promised to abdicate, and a month later, on 29 May, the council solemnly deposed him.[30]

The Roman pope was not as difficult as John had been or as Benedict XIII continued to be. On 4 July 1415, Gregory XII abdicated, after having his representatives at Constance "convoke" the council, thus insisting on his own claim to legitimacy but making the gesture of voluntary cession. According to later papal accounts, the Roman pope had been the true one all along, and Gregory XII's resignation without the taint of heresy contributes to a conception of Roman Catholicism as an unbroken continuity.[31]

The fact remains, however, that from July of 1415 until October of 1417, there was no generally recognized pope in the Western Church, and the council was *de facto* in charge. For Gerson the council primarily existed in order to legitimize the results of the council of Paris. In August he sent a new memorandum to the commission appointed by the council and asked why it was delaying his demands and petitions. He was not satisfied with *Quilibet tyrannus* and indicated that the person backing the condemned theses was extremely powerful. Some council fathers in his eyes were afraid "the honor of a great prince will be harmed and seditions arise" (219). But much more was at stake, Gerson insisted, the very honor of the council, of the faith, and of God himself.

For the moment, however, he resumed his place as one of the theological leaders of the council. A few days after Sigismund's departure, Gerson gave a sermon entitled *Prosperum iter faciet nobis Deus* (God will give us a fruitful journey, Gl 5.471–80). He borrowed his opening line and theme from Psalm 67:20. Our enemies lay ambushes on the road (Ps 139:6) and so we cry out with Saint Anthony, the desert father, who said we can hardly avoid all the traps set for us (473). The original story in the *Lives of the Fathers* had concerned humility, but for Gerson it was a question of the scandals that undermined the council's work.[32]

The roads to Sion mourn, he lamented; the scandal of heresy is multiplied beyond number.[33] But we can rejoice in the holding of a general council for the threefold goal of ending the Schism, extirpating heresy, and reforming the Church (473). In considering the first goal, Gerson pointed to the decree *Haec sancta* from 6 April as assuring the supremacy of council over pope. As for heresy, the council had shown its authority in judging John XXIII and the Bohemian John Hus "without favor or fear or concern for persons" (475). Both had powerful supporters, but neither went free. Errors are not sufficiently destroyed if those who favor them are allowed to go unpunished. We must speak according to a fixed rule, Gerson insisted, taking his cue from Augustine.[34]

Finally Gerson touched on the reformation of morals and the Church in head and members. Here he limited himself to questions of the relationship between pope and church. Although the council cannot diminish papal plenitude of power, it can see that it is used according to established laws. Once again Gerson used the very recent case of John XXIII to show that in the future popes had to resign on the demand of the council either because of "rightful usefulness or pressing need" (*pia utilitas vel urgens necessitas*; 478). In the past popes had put aside decisions of general councils and granted privileges and exemptions at will without clear reason or utility.

The regular holding of general councils would limit such papal abuses in the future. Here Gerson anticipated the decision made at Constance in October 1417, *Frequens*, calling for such councils to meet every few years. He admitted it was difficult to hold a general council. All matters could not be referred to it, but the danger of abuse of its decision-making powers did not dispense the pope and other prelates from holding councils (478).

Gerson turned to Aristotle's three types of polity and their opposites: monarchy (tyranny), aristocracy (oligarchy), and timocracy (democracy). He praised the combination of monarchy and aristocracy found in France. But the best polity would also include the third element, timocracy (478). In Aristotle this form of government applied to those who owned property. In applying the term to council representation, Gerson probably meant participants who did not come from the Church hierarchy but had some claim to be heard, such as theologians. No Christian could reject such a council "since it proceeds through the common consent or assent of all or, as it were, of all" (479). Gerson was no democrat, but he wanted the council to have a broad basis.

The Church had been weakened by the rarity of such meetings, and now their reestablishment would provide better control of those in authority (480). As for concrete proposals for what could and should be reformed, Gerson said this was neither the time nor the place for such matters. The council should not pass too much legislation, which would be a burden to implement.

Was Gerson indicating that particular reforms should be made primarily at the diocesan level, as at Reims in 1408? Whatever it was he had in mind, he did not elaborate. He instead concentrated on the question of tyrannicide and was not especially concerned with other questions of heresy. In the judgment against John Hus, he apparently played only a very small role.

Before leaving Paris, he had responded to a letter from the archbishop of Prague and had condemned what he believed was Hus's teaching, especially concerning the validity of sacramental actions by priests who lived in sin (Gl 2.162–66). Gerson may well have misunderstood what Hus meant, but any reading of Hus's remarks and self-defense at Constance reveals how difficult it is to know what exactly the man intended to say.[35] For Gerson the decision on John Hus's orthodoxy had been made before he ever came to Constance. He could tell himself that the case of Hus was securely in the hands of others while he concentrated on his own agenda. While Hus prepared his martyrdom, Gerson was simply elsewhere, making amends for the years when he had not spoken out against the defense of tyrannicide.

In his first year at Constance, however, Gerson did involve himself in other matters. On 21 April he gave a sermon, *Obsecro vos,* based on 1 Peter 2:11: "I beseech you as foreigners and pilgrims (*advenas et peregrinos*) that you abstain" (Gl 5.398–405). Gerson saw himself as an alien or outsider (*advena*) whose faith could be enriched by prayer.

Sometime after May 1415, Gerson was placed on a commission to deal with the cases for canonization of three Swedish saints (Gl 10.528). We hear nothing more about his involvement here, but on 3 August 1415, he summarized in *De probatione spirituum* (On the discernment of spirits) his doubts about the veracity of the revelations of Birgitta of Vadstena (Bridget of Sweden), though he did not attack Birgitta directly.[36] The council had already accepted her as a saint, and he had no desire to denounce her revelations. Such an act, he warned, "would pose a threat, perhaps great, of spiritual harm to the Christian religion and the devotion of the faithful."[37] As so often in his career as a theologian, Gerson was looking for a middle way between skepticism and gullibility: *medium aliquod vel expediens inter haec extrema* (Gl 9.179).

No one can test the revelations of others on the basis of knowledge of the Scriptures unless this person has personally sailed on "this mystical sea of various affections." "What does the inexperienced person know of such things?" (*Inexpertus autem talium, quid novit eorum?*; 170) Here Gerson was in contact with the monastic theology of the twelfth century, which takes experience as a point of departure for every kind of spiritual discernment and wisdom.[38] The difference between the theologian and the contemplative is comparable to that between the person who is learned in the art of medicine and the one who has had long practice in the field (180). The two skills, however, can be found in the same person.

In providing criteria for judging the genuineness of a personal revelation, he warned especially against pride and the deception it creates. Here he could turn to one of his preferred sources of Christian wisdom, the Sayings of the Desert Fathers. Occasionally the devil approached these men in the guise of an angel or a Christ-figure. One of the Fathers had answered such an apparition: "I do not wish to see Christ here. It is enough that I see him in glory." Another had told the demon that he was not worthy to see Christ.[39]

Such stories are presumably Gerson's indirect response to Birgitta, who assured her surroundings that it was Christ who spoke directly to her. Gerson asked those responsible for discernment of spirits to be careful. What at first seems good for the edification of others may end up scandalizing many. Gerson mentioned both the preaching of Jean de Varennes and that of John Hus. Also, why should we depend on divine intervention to show us the way when we can learn God's truth through our own efforts (*humanam industriam*; 183)? We have no right to insist that God speak to us so we know what to do. As ever, Gerson believed in doing what one can.

In evaluating apparitions, it is often best to suspend judgment, neither seeking visions nor trying to drive them away. When a woman claims to have visions, it is necessary to consider what kind of person she is, how she lives with her confessors and teachers, if she is constantly telling others about what she sees, and what else she talks about (184). Gerson was skeptical about such women and even accused some of having an insatiable itch (*prurigo*) to talk to and even to touch men. He quoted Vergil's description of Dido, who could not get the image of Aeneas out of her head.[40]

Gerson appears here less receptive to the revelations of women than he had been some years earlier, when he was closer to his sisters and their spiritual lives.[41]

His guide now was Saint Bernard, who asserted that he never knew when the presence of the Holy Spirit would come over him.[42] As Christ had said to Nicodemus, "The wind blows where it will" (John 3:8).

Gerson finishes the treatise with an apology for having written so fast (*cursim*). He is handing the question over to wiser men, who should know, however, that "there lives a man, whose name is in the book of life, to whom several times and in several persons it has been given to experience and practice all that has been said" (185). He may have been referring to himself.

We hear no more about discernment. For the rest of 1415, Gerson's writings at Constance deal solely with the question of tyrannicide. On 22 August he repeated his denunciation of the nine assertions ascribed to Jean Petit (538). Just as he is recorded as saying at Notre Dame in January, he again promised that he would not stop denouncing these teachings so long as he lived: *non intendo desistere quoad vixero.*

In September Gerson took a slightly new path in his *Nova positio* (New position). He attacked the view that the council had no business in condemning philosophical or moral propositions. Since such matters were connected with faith, the council had to deal with them (Gl 6.146). He also opposed the assertion that in order to condemn an error, one has to name the persons associated with it. This is not always possible, for the person in error can be a powerful tyrant or enemy of the republic (147–48). Gerson was thinking of the duke of Burgundy. It is a problem, he added, that a powerful tyrant could pay clever lawyers to make sure he does not have to appear before a church court. In such a case it is better to condemn a teaching in general terms (precisely what the council had done in July).

The third assertion Gerson opposed was that prelates below the pope cannot condemn theological errors. Apparently the duke's supporters claimed that the bishop of Paris's condemnation of the nine propositions went beyond his authority. On the contrary, Gerson insisted, when error arises, bishops and inquisitors can and must use their authority (148–49). Otherwise the Church can hardly function. He complained that the papal court had become the habitat of the mendicants, who had tried to usurp theology for themselves at the expense of the bishops and secular university theologians (150). The bishop of Paris had a much more competent group of experts on which to base his findings: "It is necessary that such judges be theologians who are very learned and incorruptible. And how rare is such a type of person in the Roman curia, as, alas, experience has taught."[43]

Gerson decried the placement of canon lawyers rather than theologians in the heart of the Church's administration, also as judges of the faith. He dismissed such persons as "sycophants and book-men" (*adulatores vel textuales homines*), who had said that the pope was not subject to a general council, that he cannot commit simony in handing over benefices, that no one can say to him, "Why do you act in such a way? (*Cur ita facis?*)"[44]

How did Gerson make sure that his *Nova positio* and similar relatively brief polemical tracts became known among the council fathers? He could not always count on being asked to give sermons to the council fathers through which to convey his point of view. It has recently been shown that Gerson was the first at Constance to use the university technique of *pronunciatio.* He would announce that, on a given date and time, he intended to read aloud a new work, perhaps in a parish church. All those interested were invited to come and write down his statement, word for word, in a *Gruppendiktat*(group dictation) . The result was more than a *reportatio,* lecture notes taken by students. It was expected that each copyist got the text exactly right.[45]

Despite such methods, Gerson's teachings could be manipulated and misunderstood. In October 1415 Martin Porrée set forth twenty-five doubtful propositions, of which twenty-two were ascribed to Gerson, two to his ally the theologian Peter of Versailles, and one to d'Ailly (Gl 10.220–25). Gerson had said, for example, that tyrannicide in some cases can be justified. Porrée tried to turn the tables on Gerson and claimed that the council decision *Quilibet tyrannus* allowed no exception to its prohibition of tyrannicide.

On 30 October Gerson replied in a *Summaria responsio* (226–30). He compared his point of view to what Thomas Aquinas had written in *On the Rule of Princes,* which does not concede a general right to tyrannicide but, at the same time, does not totally exclude it. Porrée had also criticized Gerson for attacking the teaching that the Church could exist in a single woman.[46] According to Porrée this view would deny the pious belief that after the death of Christ and until the resurrection, the whole Church existed in and through Mary. Gerson replied that his purpose had been to attack Hus, who had claimed that the Church is well ruled without the pope (227).

It is almost impossible always to safeguard a written statement from misinterpretation and misunderstanding, especially in the face of an opponent intent on undermining one's credibility. But Gerson, like John Hus, either claimed that he had not been understood properly or that he had not said what was ascribed to him.[47] Gerson was supposed to have said he would prefer to have Jews and pagans as his judges in a matter of faith rather than some of the council fathers (229). His words, he said, had been rendered *nimis crude,* all too crudely. His statements were true "in their proper forms and if one takes into consideration the intention of those who were asserting them and their reason for expressing them" (230). The same cannot be said, Gerson insisted, for the nine assertions of Jean Petit which had created great scandal and in their proper forms were erroneous.

For the first time Gerson had to defend his own orthodoxy. But the Burgundian party apparently got nowhere in its attempt to make him look like a heretic. Instead he remained on the offensive, as in his *De protestatione circa materiam fidei* (On profession with regards to a matter of faith) from 29 October. It is not enough for someone attacked for specific wrong beliefs to make a general profession of faith and to say something like, "The faith of the truth is enough for me; it is enough that I be saved in the faith of my parents" (Gl 6.158). Clearly thinking of the duke of Burgundy's assurances (Gl 5.253), Gerson required a specific profession of the articles of faith. Even then, the person who has erred is not thereby absolved from responsibility for his past. He is still liable to perpetual prison and the loss of his offices. But the Church can show mercy (Gl 6.161).

Church authorities can only judge a person on the basis of what can be seen in external behavior (165). Someone who is under suspicion has to purge himself, but here the Church takes into consideration local and individual customs and habits. In one situation a given behavior causes suspicion. Elsewhere it is perfectly acceptable. In one place people can use vulgar language about God and mean nothing by it, while elsewhere it can indicate lack of belief.

Gerson concluded that he had written "on the run": *velut in transcursu* (165). He was, as ever, in a hurry, and yet his focus on tyrannicide brought his conciliar commitment to a standstill. Another indication of his concern is in *Considerationes duodecimae de pertinacia* (Twelve considerations on pertinacity; 165–67), dated also to 29 October 1415. Pertinacity or obstinacy is present when someone asserts an error and refuses to be corrected. A sign of such pertinacity is that the one teaching the truth becomes the object of hatred and is persecuted. He was apparently thinking of the treatment the duke of Burgundy was inflicting on him.

In October 1415, Gerson did also manage to consider the subject of simony (167–74). In a relatively brief treatise, he commented on the massive conciliar criticism of John XXIII and his practices and asserted that simony is not a heresy (172). Simoniacs, however, can be suspended from office, because they are excommunicated *ipso facto* by the very deed itself. In all cases, however, there was to be "respect for the immensity of God's mercy and the fragility of human beings," so that "the salvation of the community and of the many be taken into consideration" (173).

The relative mildness and humane concern Gerson showed in dealing with simony are not at all evident in a sermon of 21 October, *Oportet haereses esse* (It is necessary that there be heresies; Gl 5.420–35). Once again he went through what he considered to be the heresies of Jean Petit, taking the nine assertions condemned at Paris. The ninth of these, in which perjury could be defended if it brought about some greater good, he considered the most perverse of all. It undermined the very fabric of the state: *in subversionem graviorem totius reipublicae* (427). He reminded the council fathers that there had been more theologians at Paris to condemn the nine assertions than were present at the council (432). The present blatant disagreement among theologians concerning a matter of faith and morals scandalized laypersons. The council had to pull back from the brink of moral anarchy and avoid further delay on the question of tyrannicide.

Gerson warned that no one is to usurp a power that has not been granted to him as a right. No one is to function at one and the same time as judge, witness, and interested party in a case. A century ago the political philosopher J. N. Figgis recognized Gerson and the conciliar movement as the point of departure for modern parliamentarian government.[48] In Gerson's desire to contradict any general defense of tyrannicide, we also can see him as concerned with what we now call human rights.

A few days after Gerson preached this sermon, many of his countrymen died at Agincourt (25 October 1415), a massive defeat for the French army and its cavalry. They had not learned the lessons of Crécy and other battles where the English were faster, better organized, and more flexible in their strategy.[49] Until this point, the French delegation had dominated the council, but now the French were losing their political hegemony. Within a year a Burgundian alliance with the English would be a fact, while Agincourt also encouraged King Sigismund to seek an English alliance.[50] Agincourt turned the tables on the Armagnac faction of the French nation and its representatives at Constance: the supporters of Charles, the son of the murdered Duke Louis of Orleans, under Charles's father-in-law, the count of Armagnac. Gerson's theological position lost ground in the face of a changed political and military reality.

Experiencing Defeat: November 1415–November 1416

For Gerson the question of tyrannicide was independent of politics and had to be settled in relation to divine law. November and December 1415 saw a preliminary climax to earlier discussions. The council handed over the question of the nine assertions to a commission.[51] Pierre d'Ailly made a full statement of his position, to which Gerson referred and which he claimed should have provided sufficient authority for a condemnation.[52] On 13 November Gerson composed a brief reply to Martin Porrée. He said the bishop of Arras was twisting the question by asserting that the Paris condemnation of tyrannicide had dealt with cases of "inevitable necessity" (Gl 10.230–32). In other words, Martin Porrée made it look as though the person who resorted to tyrannicide acted on the spur of the moment, without planning and premeditation, in order to defend his own life or those dear to him. In Gerson's view the bishop of Arras misrepresented the statements ascribed to Jean Petit.

On 4 December 1415, Gerson gave his response to the council's commission. He virtually ordered the council to condemn the nine assertions "for now it has been excessively delayed" (*jam nimis tardatum est*; 232). After a careful review of previous literature on tyrannicide, he went through the nine assertions, comparing the French text of the Paris condemnation with equivalent Latin terms

(234). He also used canon law, quoting from the Council of Lyon in 1245 on homicide in terms of the hiring of assassins, killing without prior warning, and leaving the victim no chance to confess.[53] He again took Martin Porrée to task for presenting another case than the one contained in the original nine assertions (247). The man must be out of his mind (*delirat*), Gerson proclaimed, for he was contradicting himself (250). Finally he repeated what was to become his refrain: the defense of tyrannicide takes away the very foundation of peace within the state (*omnem pacis stabilitatem*; 253). It would make it possible to turn against one's superior without warning and without prior resort to any legal redress.

On 8 January 1416, Gerson asked for a university-style disputation to be held, with two masters of theology representing one side and two the other (254). Two days later, however, the commission closed its enquiry. Depending on how they are counted, fifty-one or sixty-one masters of theology opposed the decisions of the Paris council, while twenty-four supported them.[54] On this basis, the three cardinals, who had been appointed on 15 January by the council to judge the matter, responded to an appeal from the representatives of the duke of Burgundy and revoked the decision of the bishop of Paris concerning Jean Petit's teaching.[55] In the following days the French delegation protested to the council, but to no avail.

The duke of Burgundy had done everything possible to influence this outcome. He made gifts of some of his best wine to the cardinals, and he may in other ways tried to have influence the masters who were voting.[56] While his father was known for his interest in art and literature, Duke John the Fearless is remembered for two violent deaths: his assassination of the duke of Orleans in 1407, and his own murder in 1419 at the hands of the henchmen of Charles VII, then still dauphin. In between these killings, the duke bullied or bought his way out of his problems.

On 2 February 1416, the Feast of the Purification, Gerson preached a sermon that reflects his state of mind: *Suscepimus Deus misericordiam tuam* (We have received, God, your mercy).[57] Going through the biblical text concerned with the presentation of Jesus in the temple, Gerson emphasized the role of Joseph. He asked why there is no feast "among the Latins" for Joseph (Gl 5.542). More than halfway through, however, Gerson made a rhetorical full stop. Dramatizing his situation, he combined a biblical with a classical quote. First Isaiah: truth stumbles in the street. Then Vergil: like Aeneas, he said, "I held back in horror."[58] He was appalled at the sight of truth prostrate and in ruins, for he had come face to face with error. It was being claimed that bishops are not to define the truths of faith and that error could not be denounced unless someone could be named as responsible for it. A third assertion was that judges of the faith were not to be concerned if truth regarding moral behavior is neglected in everyday life, for such questions are not matters of theology.

Gerson's language here indicates how the decision of the masters had shaken him. "What can I say," he asked, "what can I reply, when I have been so struck and shaken in the secret place of my meditation by a sense of pity weeping for the truth, which has been so basely treated?"[59] Could he not be satisfied with the faith that everyone shared and avoid investigating its meaning? No, he had an obligation to do so, because he was a theologian at the University of Paris, "the mother of studies" (545). Quoting from Isaiah, but referring to his own shame, he sighed:

> *Vae mihi quia tacui aut quia non celerius, patentius, crebrius et constantius memet istis erroribus opposui.*
>
> Woe to me because I was silent (Isa 6:5) or because I did not more quickly, more openly, more often and more consistently put myself in opposition to these errors.

Such self-recrimination, Gerson admitted, might offend his audience: "I know that another subject would have been more pleasing for many, but none is perhaps at this time more useful or more urgent. If I sought only to please people and capture popular acclaim, I would now perhaps be walking amid great and wondrous matters and investigating different questions. But one must imitate him who says: I, God, teach you that which is useful (Isa 48:17), not that which is subtle" (545). As with his students, Gerson reprimanded his council audience for preferring abstract theological speculation to moral questions. He refused to try to please. Instead of the *studiosa speculatrix* (intellectual curiosity) in the sermon's opening, he had turned to what was necessary.

It is the fathers' duty to reprove anything that threatened the observance of the Ten Commandments. Bishops can, in their own dioceses, define errors in faith and morals and condemn them as heretical. They can define error even though those in error have not previously been judged. They are obliged in their pastoral duties to accept that the moral precepts of the commandments derive from natural, canon, and civil law. Finally it is up to bishops to defend the truth, even unto death. They must accept Gregory the Great's statement that it is better to allow scandal than to desert truth, one of Gerson's favorite quotations during these years.[60]

The same day Gerson wrote a memorandum on the right of bishops to define questions of faith (Gl 6.174–75). A few weeks later, in an expanded statement on the same subject, he pointed to examples from Paris, Oxford, and Prague, in defending a tradition that local bishops could make use of the expertise of university scholars in their dioceses (177). Gerson concluded that the cardinals' revocation of the sentences of the bishop of Paris tended to support heresy and immoral behavior: homicide or murder, committed through treachery, and the use of perjury. Until now he had been careful to distinguish between his role as theologian and his respect for the consensus of the Church in terms of its *magisterium* or teaching authority. But now the council had entrusted the definition of faith to three cardinals whose motives Gerson suspected. He could not live with their conclusions.

On 19 March 1416, Gerson turned to the council as a whole, on the basis of an appeal that had come "on behalf of the most Christian and illustrious lord Charles, king of the Franks, through his orators, ambassadors, and messengers" (Gl 10.254–55). He was probably referring to a brief issued in Paris on 2 March in the name of King Charles VI. Here the king asked Gerson and other members of his delegation at Constance to act as a wall to protect God's house (cf. Ezekiel 13:5) by resisting a decision in which justice was rejected (Gl 10.540–42).

On 5 May Gerson made mention of this and similar letters in a sermon to the general assembly of the council: *Deus judicium tuum regi da* (God give your judgment to the king, cf. Ps 71:1; Gl 5.190–204). Normally cautious about involving royal power in the affairs of the Church, Gerson now chose to bring the French king into the center of the debate.[61] The king had shown mildness when he did not seek revenge for the injury done to him when his brother was killed (191). But one must distinguish between vengeance for a death and the abrogation of divine law.[62]

Gerson spoke of the vicious reaction to his own role in the tyrannicide affair. It would be wrong, he said, to try to reject all the false things said against him "and to bite back those who bite" (*mordentes remordere;*, 192). Such a quarrel was for dogs, while Gerson wanted to follow Christ's example and that of King David, who when he was cursed by someone, did not attack him (2 Sam 16:11–13). His actions until now had shown only love and a desire to make men mend their ways so they could save their souls (192–93). Happy is the man who imitates Christ, in tolerating injuries done to himself but in attacking without mercy the injuries done to God. He quoted from the office for a martyr, in praising the saint who "fought until death and did not fear the words of the wicked."[63] In such language Gerson saw himself as a potential martyr.

Gerson was incorruptible, unlike many council fathers who wanted to be able to return to places where the duke of Burgundy had influence and where it would be a question of muddling through with the everyday life of the Church in spite of the troubles that plagued France and Burgundy. Forcing his listeners to face the situation, Gerson invoked the words of Cicero: "In the midst of arms, laws are silent. He who hears will understand."[64] The reference to the machinations of the duke of Burgundy is transparent.

How could such an august assembly of "most learned experts in both laws" have spent almost eleven months discussing a teaching that is "so patently heretical, even sacrilegious, as if it were a question of a proposition that was in doubt or possible or perhaps true?" Even uneducated lay people, whether they were Christians or Jews, pagans or barbarians, knew the truth of such matters (197).

The speaker is the same Gerson who threw a fit of anger in the apartment of Pierre d'Ailly the year before. He could be both emotionally direct and politically incorrect.

Gerson rejected the charge that he had involved the king in a matter where he had no desire to be implicated (200). He was not trying to make the king, his council, the universities, prelates or clergy of the kingdom obey him. At the same time, however, he could not prevent them from defending a matter of faith. Gerson described his own involvement as independent of the king's and as fitting for a theologian.[65]

The commissioners appointed by the council had tried to summon him to Dijon, of all places (the capital of Burgundy). It would have been safer for me to go to Babylon, he commented. He did not intend to pursue legal action against any person. If the matter had been treated in purely theological terms, with no personal interest involved, then Gerson claimed he would not have had to appeal to the king's authority. But now the question had gone to lawyers and notaries, and the opposing faction, he hinted, had stooped to bribery and payments.

Here Gerson brought the person of the murdered Louis of Orleans into the debate. His blood cries out to God and to this holy council, he exclaimed (201). His death had been unworthy, infamous, and now the council fathers were to show him the mercy for which he could not ask in his dying moments. As for his heirs, Louis had three fine sons: one was a hostage; the other a captive held in England. They had not betrayed their king and kingdom. If these youths had the opportunity to stand before the council, if they could speak with tears, they would cry out, "Give justice to our father and to us" (*Date patri, date nobis justitiam*).

Normally Gerson did not make use of such pathos. He addressed personally his "reverend father and lord," the bishop of Arras, with whom he said he once lived in a familiar and benevolent way, presumably in Paris. Of the other main council henchman for the duke of Burgundy, Pierre Cauchon, Gerson spoke as "most beloved compatriot, whom I love in truth." If they wanted the duke's temporal and spiritual salvation, why did they not condemn the deed against Louis of Orleans, an act which Duke John's most prudent father, Duke Philip, would never have committed?

Gerson tried to give Martin Porrée and Pierre Cauchon an alibi. They had been in Italy when the murder took place. If they had been nearby, he was sure they would have advised the duke against such a crime. He repeated a story about Duke Philip, who abruptly left the room while he was being addressed. He went to find his doctor and cried out, "Blessed is the man who does not walk in the counsels of the wicked" (Ps 1:1). The father, unlike the son, did not want to follow the advice of evil men. Gerson recalled how Duke John after the killing admitted how horrified he was by the deed. He told the princes of the royal blood that the devil had made him do it, a story also found in another contemporary source.[66]

If the death was unjust, Gerson continued, then its justification was worse, and the defense of the justification worst of all. Therefore it was necessary for the council to condemn Jean Petit's work as heretical and injurious to royal majesty, so that "its memory be eradicated from a Christian people" (Gl 5.203). Such a condemnation, Gerson claimed, was what King Sigismund had asked for before he left Constance on his journey of reconciliation. The king of France was asking for the same result, as did the University of Paris and many others.

Gerson subsequently deposited several documents relative to the case, including *Octo regulae,* summing up what he saw as the role of the theologian, especially at Paris, in asserting truth and condemning error (Gl 10.256–60). He emphasized the central role the University of Paris, and especially its theological faculty, had played in the Church.

In this sermon, *Deus judicium tuum,* Gerson showed that he would not accept the decisions made first by the council's commission, and secondly by the committee of three cardinals. He insisted that the council fathers reconsider the matter, in appointing new commissioners, both theologians and legal experts. Not surprisingly, the cardinals in a letter of 15 May to Sigismund reaffirmed their decision but were willing to have the question submitted to the council.[67]

Gerson risked his reputation by giving a sermon that defied an unspoken consensus: with the condemnation the previous April of the statement *Quilibet tyrannus,* tyrannicide as a moral question had been resolved. The fathers were not willing to go further and investigate in detail the teaching of Jean Petit, while the cardinals were apparently only too happy to undermine the position of the bishop of Paris and his university theologians in defining articles of faith.

On 25 April 1416, King Sigismund, after an unhappy stay in Paris and a falling out with the Armagnacs, went to England.[68] Gerson's potential champion had other business at hand than the judgment of tyrannicide. For the moment Gerson had to accept defeat. At Pentecost (7 June), he gave a rousing sermon on the theme "The Spirit of the Lord has filled the whole earth" (Wisdom 1:7). Apparently Pierre d'Ailly was supposed to preach but was confined to bed with a fever and asked his former student to take his place (Gl 5.524). The sermon says nothing about tyrannicide. It tells of the coming of God's spirit into the life of the individual. Gerson described the first Pentecost, the speaking in tongues and the spread of the Church (529). Then he explained how the spirit of God continues to fill the earth (530). Amid a wealth of quotations from the Church Fathers, he also described how he had read about a woman who had died at Pentecost after she had heard a sermon on the transformation of the self into God through love. She had been sighing so much that the people around her told her to be quiet because she disturbed them and they thought she was a hypocrite. She was so filled with the spirit that she could not contain it and "her blood vessels and nerves were ripped apart and she expired" (532). Gerson chose to believe she was a saint, a martyr to love, and he quoted the Song of Songs (2:5) to imply that the woman had died because of the love she felt.

Encouraging the council fathers to seek the spirit of God, he assured them that they could show their love of God through their actions (534). Saint Paul, after he was taken into the third heaven and heard secrets, said, "Our way of life is in heaven" (*nostra conversatio in coelis est,* Phil 3:20), one of Gerson's favorite quotes. But Paul then returned to this life and faced the confusion around him. Here Gerson's ideal was King David, who ruled his kingdom while living in "intimate compunction" in God's presence, as shown by his Psalms. To David as an Old Testament example, Gerson added King Sigismund as a contemporary model. He had demonstrated "unbelievable hard work in the active life" but also a "spirit of devotion . . . in devout conversations" which led to "compunction with tears: these I saw and experienced with these eyes," Gerson said, perhaps pointing to his own face: *His oculis vidi et sensi* (534).

Gerson was not the type of preacher to flatter, and Sigismund was far away. In recalling the lives of outstanding figures, he sought to combine religious devotion, political integrity, and inner harmony. A harmony he sought in his own life; but he rarely found such peace. On 4 July 1416 in the Franciscan priory, a memorandum asking for further negotiations on the question of tyrannicide was handed over to deputies of the four nations (Gl 10.543). But after 11 July, the commissioners to whom the council had entrusted the matter stated that they could not find "any hope of agreement" and passed its resolution along to the council itself.[69]

On 5 October Gerson, in the king's name, appealed to the council to resume considering the question. It had now been under discussion for fifteen months, "with many irritations, expenses, and burdens" (261). His arguments were the usual ones. He repeated Gratian's assertion that error, which is not resisted, is approved.[70] Also, as the apostle exhorted (James 2:1), we are not to show favoritism in expressing our faith: *Nolite in personarum acceptione habere fidem Domini nostri Jesu Christi.* The teaching on tyrannicide is looked upon by many, Gerson claimed, as more dangerous than the articles of John Hus the council had condemned.

The day of the appeal, the matter was handed over to the cardinals by the ambassadors of the king of France and the University of Paris (544). The next day Gerson issued a memorandum, repeating the council's declaration from 1415 and saying that each prelate and doctor had a duty to stamp out the heresy resulting from the defense of tyrannicide (262–63). Otherwise the council's intention in condemning the statement *Quilibet tyrannus* was frustrated.

Until this time Gerson had been asking the council to confirm the Paris condemnation of nine articles attributed to Jean Petit. Now he was in retreat. His goal was merely for the council to enforce its own decision from the previous year.[71]

He still linked the nine assertions from Paris to the *Quilibet tyrannus,* but his point of departure was the council's own definition and not that of the diocesan synod.

Gerson regretted that some people said the council was weak (*debile*). They argued that "it is not a good idea for it to condemn [the nine articles] even if they are heretical but should delay" the question (269). He knew it was being said that the council was acting out of hatred, not from a desire for truth. In a remarkably frank statement, he conceded that people could say that due to the prosecution of the matter, scandals and conflicts had arisen at the council which were "harmful to the cause of church unity" (269). But there was no looking back now; the council had to stand up for the truth, whatever the cost.

In Paris on 10 August, 12 September, and 22 October 1416, masters and bachelors in theology subscribed to the condemnation of the nine assertions (544–45). On 10 October, the court issued a letter of encouragement to its ambassadors in the name of King Charles. The king praised their efforts to establish the unity of the Church and sent them master Guillem du Boys (546–47). There is nothing specific about tyrannicide, but the letter in itself indicates regular communication between Paris and Constance. On 11 October, a royal safe conduct was issued to Jean Gerson, who is described as having been sent by the king himself to the council "for the reform of the Church and certain other difficult tasks." The letter was said to provide Gerson with a *laissez-passer* for himself and up to thirty persons, with horses, mules, arms, gold, silver, and household items (547–48).

Was Gerson contemplating a return to Paris? There are no other sources to shed light on his intentions, but he may have been preparing himself for the consequences of defeat. On 20 October the commissioners dealing with the question rejected the appeal as frivolous. Their response is one of the few brief documents in this seemingly endless controversy: "They answer that jurisprudence does not deal with baseless appeals."[72] Gerson could now have used his safe-conduct and returned to Paris, but he remained at Constance.

For the moment the council had other matters to deal with, especially the attempt to handle the most recalcitrant of the three men who had styled themselves pope. On 5 November, a commission was appointed to deal with Pedro de Luna (Benedict XIII), who stayed at a safe geographical distance from Constance and refused to recognize the council's authority.[73]

Gerson was at the time caught up in his devotion to Saint Joseph. In a sermon on the Feast of the Nativity of Mary from 8 September 1416 (*Jacob autem genuit;* Gl 5.344–62), he reviewed the same biblical texts as in his *Considerations sur Saint Joseph* from 1413. He dealt not only with what Scripture contained but also "what could have happened and can be believed in pious religious faith."[74] He considered the sterility of Saint Anne and how she came to marry twice after the birth of Mary and the death of Joachim. Each marriage brought forth a Mary:

Mary the mother of Jesus, Mary Cleophas, and Mary Salome.[75] Gerson dwelt at length on the noble lineage of Joseph and Mary and said that it might be challenged because they both devoted themselves to servile tasks. But in this manner an example was set "to all, also nobles, to keep them from passive leisure" (*inerti otio*; 348).

Gerson went on to questions about childbearing, virginity, and lust or its absence in Joseph. He asked why Joseph was normally painted as an old man in religious art and said that this practice was to make his chastity more credible (352–53) and the faithful not to expect anything carnal of Joseph and Mary. As a result, there was no feast day for their marriage, which did not seem to be a real marriage. Gerson chose, however, to view Joseph as a young man and referred to a depiction of him as such in Germany. The journey to Constance had apparently opened Gerson's eyes to an alternative vision of Joseph in art.

Joseph and Mary on their travels would have spoken about the mysteries of the redemption. "Who would not give [a great deal] to have been present at such conversations?" (355) As in so much of the devotional literature of the period, Gerson made biblical stories come alive by expanding them. He imagined Mary and Jesus at Joseph's death and quoted from his incomplete *Josephina.* Mary kisses her husband "with chaste lips." "My husband, she cries out, are you going away/ Do you desert and leave behind a widow to suffer terrible things?"[76]

On the surface the sermon has the form of a stream of consciousness but in reality it is carefully structured, providing listeners or readers with word pictures to intensify their grasp of biblical texts. He who carved out the dawn and made the sun was subject to a carpenter, Gerson reflected. English cannot capture the wordplay of his Latin: *subditus fabro is qui fabricavit auroram et solem* (358). Jesus was subject to Mary and Joseph, even though he ruled the universe. The sermon also describes a spiritual birth of Christ in the devout soul. This is the blessed nativity in which the boy Jesus is held and kissed with the most chaste embraces (360).

Gerson asked the council to institute a feast for Joseph. He denied his request would contribute to a multiplication of feast days that would keep ordinary people from doing their work. He agreed with d'Ailly and others that there was a need for fewer feast days, but outside the laity and among ecclesiastics, the virginal marriage of Joseph with Mary and his happy death could be celebrated.[77] Thus it would be possible to initiate a solemnity to be kept only by the church hierarchy. Joseph's virtue and strength would ensure the strength of a renewed church in its one pope (362).

The day before this sermon was delivered, Gerson wrote to the chanter of the cathedral of Chartres, Dominic Petit, and recalled how his dead colleague, Henry Chiquot, had shown special affection for Joseph, had written about his genuine marriage with Mary, and had sought to sponsor a feast to be held for their nuptials.

He promised to send the sermon he was writing for the next day to the chanter, along with other works on the same subject (Gl 2.167–68). Gerson made proposals for the possible date and content of the liturgy for such a feast day and recalled that such a feast already existed in some places, such as on 19 March among the Augustinians in Milan (169).

Probably sometime after this sermon, Gerson made a brief summary of the truths of the faith required for salvation (Gl 6.181–89). The bishop is responsible for making sure that the precepts of the Ten Commandments or Decalogue are held not only implicitly but also explicitly (188). At the Council of Constance, Gerson commented, there were certain persons who in delaying the condemnations of the nine assertions in the matter of homicide, perjury, and treachery were not to be blamed. They awaited a final judgment on the question, presumably from the council itself. These lines indicate that Gerson had not yet received the response of 20 October dismissing the appeal. His initial reaction after that date remains unknown to us.

A letter dated 28 September to his brother Jean, who at the time was prior of the Celestines at Marcoussis south of Paris, indicates renewed contact with his family.[78] He wrote that one can pray to persons whose holiness of life is known, even though the Church has not canonized them. One can include prayer to innocent children "of our family" who are assured of salvation because they died after being baptized (Gl 2.172). Such prayer also encompasses "our parents and relatives" whom we address in the heavenly glory "that we in piety believe them to have and which does not take away natural and in-born love but increases and perfects it."

During these months in the autumn of 1416, council business apparently did not greatly involve Gerson and left him time to compose his one tract from this period showing a continuing interest in the reform agenda. A brief treatment of simony (*Ad rationabilem contra simoniam et simoniacos reformationem*; Gl 6.179–81) asked that it first be effaced from the hearts of men. Only then could come its removal from the Church in head and members. Gerson worried that any radical extirpation of simony would create greater dangers through excessive restrictions. Churchmen had to receive compensation for carrying out their duties. A cleric was not to buy an office, but having one office, he had a right to an income.

Such a point of view made good sense, but Gerson did not demonstrate his teacher Pierre d'Ailly's awareness that there was a radical need for reformation. In his *De emendatione ecclesiae* (On the repair of the Church), d'Ailly reviewed papal and episcopal administration, the abuse of offices, the state of monasteries, and the needs of the laity.[79] Only with regard to the latter were his criticisms and proposals sketchy. Otherwise the reader gets the sense of a man who knew intimately the institutions he was criticizing and could provide a concise evaluation. D'Ailly warned that unless the reform was carried out *celeriter* (quickly), there would be a disaster. After "such horrendous thunder," d'Ailly foresaw other events even "more horrible."[80] These words, melodramatic as they are from our vantage point, sound like a prediction of the reformations of the sixteenth century. But what is valuable about this treatise is not its apocalyptic opening. It is the specific, measured language in what follows, based on criticisms of practices already prevalent in the twelfth century, as d'Ailly himself shows by aptly referring to Bernard of Clairvaux's advice to a pope, *De consideratione*.[81]

Some of d'Ailly's terminology sounds almost gersonian, as in the assertion toward the end of the treatise that the council has a duty to exhort princes to do what they can (*faciendo quod in se est*). Then they will gain God's forgiveness.[82] While Gerson in this autumn of 1416 seems almost passive, or at least very cautious, d'Ailly's suggestions for reform are full of energy and reflect first-hand experience.[83]

Salvaging a Life and a Church: January–August 1417

On 1 January 1417, Gerson described himself in a letter to his youngest brother Jean the Celestine (Gl 2.199). This is a remarkable statement, almost a spiritual testament, and a point of departure for later illustrations showing Gerson as a pilgrim bearing a coat of arms:

> I have meditated upon many things in my heart. Finally my mind reached up into the heart's *affectum,* so that it placed before itself a heart, fixed and burning with the golden sign of a Tau [the Greek letter "T"], in the midst of a sapphire-like heaven, with the golden color of sun, moon, and stars radiating forth, so that I as a pilgrim and a stranger, for thus Gerson is interpreted, in constant meditation remember the assertion of the heavenly pilgrim Paul: "Our way of life is in heaven" (Phil 3:20).

As ever, Gerson saw himself as a wanderer and foreigner (*peregrinus et advena*), but now he illustrated in detail his contemplative goal. He wished to lift his heart out of the battles of this world and fly up to the heights of heaven. Addressing the Lord himself, he expressed a belief that such a meditation contained no deception: "For you, Lord, have expanded my heart, while in free flight it has been given to it to pass over the wide heavenly fields of Holy Scripture." In the study of theology Gerson had soared with the wings he had earlier described in his *Mystical Theology*. Later artists used this description to represent Gerson in flight with wings attached to the Tau-crossed heart.[84]

Gerson added that his heavenly view of Scripture's fields gave him "vivid and effective speech" to explain their allegorical, moral, and anagogical meanings.

There was no separation of the heart's meditation and the head's analysis of language and meaning in Scripture. All led to Gerson's joining the Church's prayer found in the preface to the canon of the Mass, *Sursum corda* (Lift up your hearts).

Closing the letter, Gerson referred to his brother as "consort of my pilgrimage: to you with me and for me with you there ought to be one heart and one soul" (Acts 4:32). The younger brother would now be able to know, with the cooperation of the one who turns whatever hearts he desires (Prov 21:1), that he had fashioned their hearts with his seal (Ps 32:15).

Gerson's language here is even more replete with biblical allusions than usual. The image of the pilgrim was standard in medieval thought and life, but Gerson made it his special icon. He added that he as a pilgrim carried a shield, whose letter Tau was the Hebrew letter painted on the foreheads of those to be spared from the exterminating angel (Ezek 9:4).[85]

Gerson was moving away from Constance and readying himself for his final journey. He knew where he was going and wanted to show that his life had meaning and integrity. He had absorbed the discipline of theology and felt he could combine its insight with the fire of divine love. Unlike Thomas Aquinas, he was not about to cast his learning away at the end and to declare it to be nothing but straw.[86] Gerson would accept an identity as both theologian and pilgrim/stranger to the world around him, and the Lord would protect him, as he had the Israelites.

Not many days later, on 17 January 1417, Gerson preached a sermon for the Feast of Saint Anthony (*Nuptiae factae sunt*; Gl 5.376–98). This day had also been the birthday of Gerson's patron, Duke Philip of Burgundy. In the first sermon he had preached for the occasion, when Philip was still alive, Gerson had stretched the image of Anthony and tried to make a spiritual knight out of the hermit.[87] Now he was under no such constraints, and he combined a portrait of Anthony, the ascetic, with a description of the wedding feast at Cana, in accord with the Gospel reading. Gerson recalled his former sermons in the presence of Duke Philip and added that he prayed for his salvation and that of his offspring. This gesture of reconciliation to Duke John was made "without a spirit of falseness or adulation" (387).

Anthony had followed Christ's counsel of perfection in selling everything and giving it to the poor. Once he had done so, nothing could stop him from his search for God. Taking a story found in Cassian's *Conferences*,[88] Gerson told how Anthony in the midst of meditating felt the rising sun shine on his face. He addressed it and asked, "Why do you keep my mind from contemplating heavenly things?" (388)

This sermon's Anthony was not only a hermit; he was also a man of conviction who wrote to princes and emperors with total freedom of expression and reminded them that they were responsible to "a terrible lord, terrible among all the kings of the earth" (390; cf. Ps 75:13). With no fear for king or magistrate (cf 3 Esdras 3:21), Anthony acted according to his conscience alone. Gerson seems once again to be skirting the debate on political power and tyrannicide. Anthony was also remembered for his fight against heretics. Old and solitary and still unable to read, he left his hermitage and spoke at an assembly in the city of Alexandria (396). Gerson closed the sermon urging the council to show the same zeal in fighting heresy.

Was Gerson stretching out a hand of reconciliation to the duke of Burgundy? Perhaps he thought he was doing so by mentioning Duke Philip and praying for the entire family. A treatise he wrote soon after he gave this sermon reveals Gerson's inability to keep his perennial cause out of his writing.[89] He dwelt on the allegory already used in his sermon based on the wedding feast at Cana: the spiritual nuptials of Christ and his Church depicted in the Song of Songs (Gl 6.190–210). He quickly turned to excoriating those who ignore the Gospel and concentrate on papal decretals and decrees.

The question of tyrannicide surfaces again, but Gerson waits until the last sections of the sermon to be specific. After a long review of the question of mendicity or begging and the possession of property, he describes two types of people. The first claim faith is sufficient if it concurs with their parents' beliefs, clearly a reference to the duke of Burgundy (206). Secondly, there are those who complain that in seeking peace and union, their efforts lead only to disturbance and division. Would it not be better, they now ask, to dissimulate instead of forcing a solution to the problems at hand?

In Gerson's view, such people were out of their minds. They drink the wine of Scripture but because of corrupt morals are infected by fever and lose their senses. Their tables are full of vomit and filth, the heresies they throw up (206). Gerson said he knew examples of such a curse at the council, for it had only allowed an incomplete investigation of questions related to doctrinal truths. There now had to be a full examination of the nine assertions of Jean Petit. The faithful had a right to know the Church's position (207). Gerson ignored the commission's work and insisted that the council as a whole must deal with the Paris condemnation. Its failure to do so was causing great scandal, for it appeared to be the result of cowardice (*ignaviae;* 208). In the future princes would be able to say that John Hus and his errors were condemned because they attacked prelates and the clergy, while churchmen had dismissed the errors of Jean Petit because they only challenged princes and laymen.

He concluded that many at Constance were heretics or at least associated with heretics, since many on the one hand affirmed that the defense of tyrannicide was erroneous in faith and morals, while others said it was orthodox (208). Still others claimed that this teaching was not to be condemned by a judgment of faith, for its content did not pertain to faith. "It is clear," Gerson concluded, "that such contrary assertions cannot persist in purity of faith and without open scandal in the entire Church" (209).

A question of faith should be treated simply and openly, in a discussion among experts, with no element of personal interest. Gerson argued, as he had done earlier, as if the matter involved only theological truth and not the political position of the house of Burgundy. He hinted, however, that it was because of political fear that the council avoided dealing with the question.

On 27 January 1417, Sigismund was back at Constance.[90] In Gerson's mind, the renewed presence at the council of the man behind *Quilibet tyrannus* made possible a return to the question of tyrannicide. Sigismund, however, was in a new situation. Now allied with the English, he had no reason to support the concerns of the French at the council.

On 25 March a member of the French delegation, Nicolas of Capella, launched a complaint with Sigismund for having been arrested after he left Constance. Captured near Basel, he was imprisoned in the fortress of Riehen (Gl 10.549). Nicolas was apparently on a diplomatic mission for the French nation. He claimed that he and those like him were being persecuted, "even unto death" because of their connection to Gerson: *quia conversatus fui cum domino cancellario Parisiensis doctore meo.* He blamed the duke of Burgundy for what had happened.

Help was not forthcoming, however, for it was apparently Sigismund who was behind the arrest, in order to hinder communication between the Armagnacs at Paris and the French delegation at the council.[91] The matter was discussed at Constance, and the bitterness between the Armagnac and Burgundian factions remained as intense as ever.[92] But now Sigismund was siding with the Burgundians, and Gerson could expect nothing from him.

In spite of such disappointments, the chancellor managed to complete the fullest expression of his teaching on power in the Church: *Tractatus de potestate ecclesiastica* (Gl 6.210–50).[93] For Gerson it was already a fact that future popes would have to obey the decisions of coming councils. He thanked God for having "freed his Church from the pestiferous and pernicious doctrine"—which had nourished the Schism—that the pope was superior to a council and not bound by its decisions (229). He had in mind the April 1415 decree *Haec sancta.* But he admitted the difficulty of carrying out necessary reform, for when he looked around, so much needed to be done. In monastic life, the Carthusians were perhaps the only order where "regular discipline" flourished.

This treatise provides a historical sketch of the development of papal power and mentions the extreme view that the pope cannot possibly commit simony, for he owns all church goods. This interpretation had been prominent before the Council of Constance but now, Gerson claimed, had gone underground where, like a creeping cancer, it spread its poison (238). What was needed was good sense (*moderatrix discretio*) to remedy the ills of the Church.[94] Ecclesiastics can have temporal goods and are not to be despoiled by the secular power unless they have been heretics or rebels. While the pope and his curia preside over church possessions, the head is not to usurp what the members have (239).

Gerson repeated his earlier definition of a general council, including the important point that no member of the faithful who wishes to be heard can be excluded from an audience.[95] Different people in the Church have different functions, some consultative, some executive. Learned lay people, such as philosophers, could give advice, but definitive decisions were up to the bishops and higher prelates. Other church officials who had the care of souls, however, could also have a voice (241–42).

Gerson asked that the Roman curia in future make use of theological experts who were not corrupt in their way of life. As always, he wanted theologians to play as important a role as canon lawyers (248). He saw his own kind of expertise as the basis for any reformation of the Church. But such knowledge had to be wed to virtue.

Gerson had pulled back from the theological brink to which he had come in the autumn of 1416. At that time he seemed willing to distance himself from everything happening at Constance unless it concerned tyrannicide. Now he was returning to the larger question church governance and the exercise of power by churchmen, individually and in the council.

Another sign of Gerson's new commitment is his involvement with the case of Pedro de Luna (Benedict XIII). On 8 March the council had summoned Pedro, and from 22 April a commission of inquiry heard the case against the last papal holdout.[96] A few days later Gerson submitted a collection of statements (*articuli*) demonstrating that Pedro was a heretic and had erred because of his obstinate refusal to accept the authority of the council and thereby the Church (265–77). In the tenth article he emphasized the importance of Christ's words in Matthew 18:15–18 as the rightful basis for the governance of the Church. If another member of the Church sins against you, then you must go and point out his fault when the two of you are alone (267). If he refuses to listen, then you are to take one or two other members of the Church with you, so that every word may be confirmed by the evidence of two or three witnesses. If the person is still recalcitrant, then you are to tell the entire Church what has happened. If the offender still refuses to listen, let such a person be to you "as a gentile and a tax collector." In other words, he no longer belongs to the Church, for "whatever you bind on earth will be bound in heaven and whatever you loose on earth will be loosed in heaven."

Gerson's attention to these lines in Matthew has not previously received much notice.[97] He was considering the question of papal power and Church governance without sole emphasis on Matthew 16's apparent assertion of Peter's position. Christ's recommendation in Matthew 18 looked upon discipline in the Church as first an individual matter but ultimately as a collegial question: the entire Church in the end had to decide whether a dissident member should be excluded.

In such a scheme the pope was a son of the Church and thus the brother of each member. Peter himself showed he accepted this status as brother rather than father, for in the Acts of the Apostles he accepted fraternal correction: "He then perceived the Church as the assembly of the faithful."[98] Thus if the pope sins, he should be corrected as any other brother.

In the second section, Gerson used this ecclesiology to deal specifically with Pedro de Luna. As Benedict XIII he had claimed on several occasions that anyone who appealed from him or withdrew from his obedience was excommunicated (271). This assertion was heretical. In responding to a recent summons, Pedro de Luna showed that he still maintained this position and did not accept the council's authority. Since the pope is the brother of every Christian, the Church has the right to call him before its assembly to be judged (274).

Pedro was supposed to have stated after a synod at Perpignan that if the whole world said to him that he should give up the papacy, the final decision was up to him alone (276). He flirted with heresy in claiming that a general council could not be assembled without a papal summons. Gerson concluded that Pedro was a perjurer and schismatic but not necessarily a heretic *proprie dictus,* properly speaking, unless he could be condemned on the basis of his own writings and sayings.

The Council of Constance went further and in its thirty-fourth session on 5 June 1417 declared Pedro to be heretical, because his pertinacity had prolonged the Schism. On 26 July he was formally deposed.[99] With all three former popes legally out of the way, the council now had to decide whether to go ahead with a papal election or first secure the Church's reform. Another question was how to elect a new pope. The cardinals asked for a traditional vote among their number alone, while the council's nations wished to delegate electors to join the cardinals.[100] Discussions lasted until October, but we have no evidence of Gerson's participation.

In the same month as the council deposed Pedro de Luna, Gerson wrote a letter to the Dominican preacher Vincent Ferrier (Gl 2.200–202). He began with traditional assurances of friendship, together with praise for Vincent's success in convincing the king of Aragon to withdraw obedience from Benedict XIII. Practically everyone, Gerson asserted, was expecting the end of the Schism after almost forty years. He wished Vincent would himself come to Constance, a second Council of Jerusalem, for its participants were the successors of the apostles who had first met there.

After this *captatio benevolentiae* in the classic letter-writing style, Gerson came to his request. He was aware that much was being said about Vincent's sermons "and especially about that sect of the Flagellants." In the past this cult had been condemned by the Church, and Gerson knew that Vincent did not approve of it, but neither did he "effectively reject" the Flagellants.[101] Because of all the rumors about Vincent, it would be best to come to Constance to dispel them: "I know and have experienced a thousand times how often different and false things are said about those who preach, partly because of the ignorance of the listeners, partly because of the arrogant malice, contempt, or envy of some people" (202).

Gerson may have been thinking especially about his Tarascon sermon before Benedict XIII and how it had been misinterpreted (78–80). He considered the present matter important enough to recruit the support of Pierre d'Ailly, who added a postscript, stating that he also had heard of Vincent's sermons. D'Ailly also exhorted Vincent to come to the council.

This cautious letter shows concern that the Flagellants were endangering the Church. A month later Gerson wrote an attack on them (Gl 10.46–51). "The law of Christ is said to be a law of love," he began, and so Christian life should not take on superfluous burdens. Christ's blood is shed once and for all, and no Christian is obligated to maim himself to obtain forgiveness for sins. In the past, flagellation had been used as a penance, but it was done only after the judgment of a superior and without the drawing of blood (Gl 10.47). The practice took place only in approved religious orders and among a few devout persons.

Gerson's central point was that it was sufficient for salvation, especially for laypersons, to observe the precepts of the Decalogue. There was no need to join a sect that was cruel and bloody (Gerson added to his Latin the French term *sanglante*).[102] The Flagellants challenged the Church's authority, for they decreed their own penances and ignored parish priests. Individuals who whipped themselves as a penance were not to be condemned, provided they obeyed wholesome advice (*monitioni salutaryi*; 50). If people wanted to do penance, the best purgation consisted in the work they did each day. It is better to bear God's whips without murmur, rancor, or hatred against one's superiors or persecutors, whether just or not, than to get impatient and angry and to whip oneself to blood.

Gerson was returning to the kind of pastoral theology that had been his major concern. Perhaps also in the summer of 1417, he considered another question of spiritual direction: how to concentrate on prayer and direct the mind and heart. The first treatise, on meditation, starts with Psalm 18:15: "May the meditation of my heart be always in your sight."[103] People who seek contemplation can experience temptation and even illusions of the devil. Fantasies and depressions can lead to insanity (Gl 8.83). He pointed to the stories of Pygmalion and Narcissus, where a woman's stone image or a mere reflection in the water had become objects of infatuation and empty love. When the host is elevated, some people think they see God crucified or believe they hear the voices of Christ or the saints.

Gerson referred to earlier writings on distinguishing true from false revelations: *Scripsi jam pluries talia.*[104] He worried that people let their imaginations run away with them and feared fantasies where, "as is commonly said, there is neither head nor tail."[105] He loved the popular phrase and may have missed the opportunities he had in Paris to write and preach in French instead of Latin.

The next treatment on spiritual life, *De illuminatione cordis* (84–85), is very brief, while a third one, *De simplificatione cordis,* is fuller (85–97). It takes its title from the opening of the Book of Wisdom, "In simplicity of heart seek him."

Gerson covers familiar ground in defining mystical theology. Such passages hint that in the summer of 1417, he was reviewing the language, thoughts, and experiences of a lifetime. Holy doctors had already expressed themselves in learned writings about our return to God, but Gerson, as earlier in letters to his sisters, sought a way to make meditation accessible for those not trained in philosophy or metaphysics. He quotes Hugh of Saint Victor's familiar phrase that when love enters, cognition remains outside.[106] Love itself is a certain kind of cognition or understanding, he added, taking a phrase from Gregory the Great.[107]

The uneducated person who meditates or prays will seek a heavenly father who is benefactor, redeemer, savior, judge, and friend. Gerson adds an anecdote about how his parents, in order to convince him to ask for God's favors, would cast apples or nuts or other goodies to him from a high place, such as the stove, when he was on his knees, with his hands raised. Then they would clap and say, "See, son, how good it is to pray to God who gives such things to those who pray."[108]

Gerson seems to have been taking stock of his own life and defining his identity, as he had started doing with the letter to his youngest brother on 1 January. The anecdote, however, is only one of many in this treatise to show how the individual Christian can simplify his or her life in order to concentrate on what is really necessary. We read in the *Ecclesiastical History*, Gerson continues, of a certain woman, Blandina, "if I have the name right," who was interrogated and tortured but refused to give any answer to her interrogators except, "I am a Christian."[109]

In our search for God, we can begin our meditations with physical things but must rise above them. Gerson tells of a certain youth, still alive, who was so fixated on his love for a certain woman that he swam across a river where he thought he saw her on the other side. There also "lives one who chastely exercised himself in reading the meditations of Anselm, and in drawing himself to affective love" became so upset that the very sight of the manuscript where the meditations were written made him nauseous and dizzy.[110]

Gerson was probably conveying personal experience. He opens these two anecdotes with the phrase *Vivit adhuc* or *Vivit,* just as he did in the story about the child whose parents threw goodies down to him. The very concreteness and sensuality of the language in Anselm's meditations may have overwhelmed Gerson. In seeking the experience of God, he could not cope with the immediacy and power of Anselm's images.[111]

Immediately after the Anselm anecdote, Gerson repeats the saying of Angela of Foligno, already mentioned in his *Distinguishing true from false revelations,* that love is the most violent of all the passions and so must always be kept under control.[112] This warning provided a bridge to another anecdote, concerning a woman who was still alive. She lived chastely with her husband and apparently had no sexual commerce with him (94). She sought out advice from persons known for their sanctity and was drawn to the love of now one, now the other. This practice was more an expression of her *furor* than of *amor.* Not having control of herself, the woman could not moderate the violence of her love. If it had not been for men who were stronger and more virtuous in their love, the woman would have come to a very bad end, not only before God but also in the sight of men.

Gerson was worried about such people, not only because he was skeptical about such women but also because he had spent a lifetime trying to exercise control over himself and his own affective impulses. Our eyes must always be on the Lord, he insisted, so that he will keep our feet from the trap (Ps 24:15). Only by concentrating on the love of God can we be saved from the dangerous embrace of other loves. Gerson added yet another anecdote, a variation on Aesop's fable about a fox and the cat that once talked about how to avoid attacks from dogs. The cat said she had but one way out: climbing a tree, while the fox claimed to know thousands of exits: "I have a bag full of them" (95). When the dogs arrived, the cat scampered up the tree and was safe, while the fox was mauled by the dogs' bites. One leap into the tree would have saved it, but the fox wanted to display its cleverness. A single moral precept is more profitable, if it is exercised through continual use, than many others whose application is neglected.

The little treatise is full of such anecdotes of moral and spiritual wisdom. Gerson seems to have returned frequently to his own experience, as when he remembered a "pious woman" who felt sorrow at losing some of her children. Thinking of the spiritual trials of her soul and of others, she managed to convert "temporal sadness into something spiritual and then into joy" (96). Was Gerson here remembering his own mother's reaction to the deaths of some of his siblings?

A third treatise, *On the Direction of the Heart,* repeated an earlier letter-treatise on the value of prayer and attentiveness in prayer.[113] New sections, however, deal with the cult of the saints and gifts offered them: a rooster for boys, a hen for girls given to Saint Christopher and John the Baptist, while someone prays to Saint Hubert when bitten by a rabid dog. There are "innumerable particular observances" for which Gerson saw no rational basis, but he accepted human weakness (108). He therefore would not forbid the association of material objects with saintly power.

Gerson was also aware that some Christian festivals came from pagan rites. On the Feast of the Purification, commonly called *Candelaria,* burning candles were carried in honor of Saint Mary, in the same way that the Romans had borne candles in honor of the goddess Ceres (109–10). It was not necessary to forbid making offerings on such feast days, whether they were chickens, loaves of bread, wine, horses, or images made of grain, so long as they were meant to honor God and the saints and to sustain his ministers.

It is wrong, however, to try to tempt God through the invocation of his saints, as if such a ritual compelled him miraculously to provide some temporal good. Also requests made out of curiosity are to be avoided, as when someone asks to be shown the Virgin Mary before death. Uneducated people who live in the countryside without preachers or teachers to guide them can, nevertheless, have direct recourse to the supernatural and receive help because of simple faith. Similarly religious and hermits can trust in divine help through their prayers. In praying and living well, they are doing all that is in their power (*faciunt totum quod in se est*).

The group that can be in the greatest doubt about whether they are using their capabilities (*si fecerint vel faciant quod in se est*) is made up of those with positions of leadership, whether they be kings, judges, prelates, or theologians. But everyone should pray and have faith that in doing what he can and using his own abilities, directing his heart to God, he can expect God's help. We can join the Old Testament figure Jehosaphat in saying: "Since we do not know what we must do, complete us; beyond what we have done or could do, we have only this left, that we turn our eyes to you" (cf 2 Chron 20:12).

Is there a link here with Martin Luther? Gerson had by now spent a lifetime worrying about the value of his own efforts and had concluded that ultimately, after doing what he could, he had to trust in God. He was optimistic, not only in evaluating his own possibilities as a learned cleric, but also in responding to the religious practices popular among the uneducated.

Some people believe that if they say an "Our Father" five times before the image of the crucified, they will have a thousand days or twenty thousand years of indulgences. We are to be very careful about such matters, he warns, but he did not condemn belief in indulgences. As in so much else, he sought a middle way (*via media;* Gl 8.112). Piety of faith accepted whatever seemed likely to strengthen religious devotion. A man could make use of a practice that was not necessary for the faith but still useful. Similarly, Gerson said, he could perform "some pious acts" for his father's soul, not because he had to do them but because he had seen his father in a dream. "This is better than if it [the dream] were wholly rejected" (112–13).

Sermons should restrain pious practices instead of giving them room for expansion into superstitions (113). This treatise underlines why editors by the opening years of the sixteenth century came to call Gerson "the consoling doctor."[114] Our age, so sensitive and even allergic to paternal roles, might also call him patronizing. But he showed openness and responsiveness to the religious impulses of ordinary people. Only in a single aside did he mention tyrannicide, bemoaning the fact that the matter had been discussed at the council "by now for almost three years" and still dragged on (107–8).

In August he wrote a brief treatise *De necessaria communione laicorum sub utraque specie* (On the requirement of communion for the laity under both kinds;

Gl 10.55–68). Gerson and his colleagues understood the Bohemians to have claimed that a person does not receive the body and blood of Christ unless both bread and wine are taken.[115] He began his response by providing general guidelines for how Scripture is to be read, not by taking the literal content of individual passages, but looking at them in relation to each other. Although Christ said that we cannot be saved unless we eat his flesh and drink his blood, he also spoke of himself as the bread of life and said nothing of wine (61). It is dangerous for uneducated people to read Scripture on their own. They cannot possibly have the necessary routine and insight to see its content in context. Thus the errors of the Beghards and the Poor of Lyon arose because many lay people had vernacular translations of the Bible (58).

Gerson was adamant about the laity and Scripture, but in reviewing communion practices, he was much more flexible. He admitted that sometimes communion could be given to lay persons under both kinds (60). He encouraged the council in dealing with the question to make use of the great number of theologians gathered there, not only from the University of Paris, but also from other universities (63).[116] Such theologians saw the practice of giving lay people communion only in the form of bread as a result of a great increase in numbers of the faithful during the time of the Church Fathers.

Communion wine was no longer distributed, a procedure that avoided dangers and scandals. Wine could easily be spilled, was difficult to transport, and needed to be kept in clean receptacles untouched by laypersons. Some laymen have long beards, which get in the way when they drink from the chalice. If wine is stored away after consecration, it can go sour and become vinegar; in the summer flies are generated, and no matter how carefully the container is covered, it is horrible to drink from, also because so many people partake of it. And what container, Gerson asks, can be fashioned large enough for the wine that would be necessary at Easter, when ten to twenty thousand persons in a parish might take communion? Also what about places where wine was scarce and very expensive?

Gerson tried to be practical but also took into account differing customs of different churches. It would be wrong, he said, for a Latin Christian in the Greek Church to take communion in the form of unleavened bread, for this was against standard practice there. One should show respect, but this also meant following the customs prevailing in the Latin Church and not requiring communion under both kinds (65).

Back to Tyrannicide and a Papal Election: August–December 1417

The Gerson who in the summer of 1417 wrote about questions of religious practice may have hoped to turn to the reform agenda that would transform the

Church in head and members. But just as he may have been ready to leave the vexing question of tyrannicide behind, a new development forced him to return to it. In February of 1416, the Dominican John of Falkenberg had written what he called a satire against heresies. He claimed that it would be legitimate to kill the Polish king and all the Poles because they were aiding the pagan Lithuanians against the Teutonic knights. A year later Falkenberg was imprisoned for this assertion. The council ordered an investigation of the matter, which lasted all summer.[117]

Meanwhile the Poles appealed to the French nation, and we have its protocol on the matter of 30 April to 9 July 1417.[118] On 15 August Gerson issued his own brief opinion (Gl 10.280–84). He repeated his general principle that any kind of teaching that persuades, orders, or approves the killing of persons under the pretext of tyranny or any other crime, without reference to the order of divine law, is heretical. To praise homicide is in itself evil and is contrary to Scripture.

Gerson's main enemy remained Martin Porrée, who on 4 August made a statement against the council's commission dealing with matters of faith and its condemnation of Falkenberg.[119] The bishop of Arras described a completely different type of killing than the one to which Gerson referred. One person has a right to kill another without legal judgment not only to save life, property, or comrades but also to maintain catholic faith against heretics, infidels, and apostates. Thus Christian princes had a right to kill heretics and infidels.

Falkenberg had other powerful advocates, and the affair dragged on. The Poles did not get the condemnation of his teaching that they had hoped the French nation would secure for them. Once again Gerson was unable to gain acceptance of his agenda: the condemnation of almost any defense of tyrannicide. His brilliance and involvement were insufficient to convince his colleagues at Constance to make a politically inconvenient decision. The Teutonic Knights must have protected Falkenberg, and behind them the duke of Burgundy's men offered a second line of defense.

In the summer of 1417 Gerson was faced with a dilemma concerning priorities for the council. Sometime before 19 August, when Pierre d'Ailly gave a sermon on the coming papal election, Gerson wrote what Glorieux has entitled a *Memorandum for the Election Prior to Reform.*[120] He asked whether it was advisable to delay the papal election until after completion of the reform agenda for which the council was also responsible. Could one say, "this reformation cannot be done well if the pope is presiding [over it]" or did such a statement smack of the heresy of Hus? (Gl 6.279) Could it be claimed that pope and church could not be fully reformed unless they gave up the temporal goods with which they had been "excessively endowed" by secular powers? Gerson also asked whether Sigismund had the right to exercise any jurisdiction over churchmen without the special mandate of the council. Would the assertion of such a right be error, endangering ecclesiastical liberty?

Until this point, Gerson seemed to favor Sigismund's intervention. And while he normally afforded secular rulers a wide role in the Church, he was now apparently having second thoughts. More radically, Gerson considered ideas which in slightly different forms had already been rejected by the council: the Church's liberation from all property and its existence without a papal head.

In his solutions Gerson pulled back from radical conclusions. The Church cannot be left until the end of the world without a single pontiff. Every baptized adult Christian, according to his position within church and society, had to contribute to the speedy election of the pope (279).

This pragmatism in accepting papal election before church reformation contrasts markedly with Gerson's intractability in the tyrannicide debate. There he seems to have withdrawn into his own moral universe and concerned himself primarily with a categorical requirement of conscience. Here, in risking an election that threatened to eclipse the reform program at Constance, he looked beyond his own aspirations and provided a sober evaluation of the political and social status quo.

Gerson worried that after such a long stay in Constance, people were tired out, not only council members but also the city of Constance "with the whole surrounding countryside" (*cum tota patria circumvicina;* 281). Secondly, "according to the learned in astronomy and medicine," there was a danger "of pestilence of the air." There was, in fact, an epidemic at Constance that same summer and early autumn. Among the most distinguished of the victims was Cardinal Zabarella, who died on 26 September.

A third reason for wanting to get on with the election was the "divisions, hatred, and dissension" that had arisen during the council between Sigismund and some of the nations, and also among the ambassadors of various kings and princes. Gerson said such divisions were "notorious." He did not specify, but he may have been thinking especially about the deep hatred between Burgundians and Armagnacs.

A fourth reason for electing a pope as quickly as possible was wars and other conflicts raging throughout Europe in the course of which church goods and monasteries were being attacked. A papal election would provide support to beleaguered clerics.

Fifthly, Gerson pointed out, with striking honesty, that in spite of two years with "peace, love, and concord among the nations" (an optimistic or ironic summary of the council so far), not one single reform article had been passed concerning the power of the pope and the status of the college of cardinals. Anyone who did not work for the election but dedicated himself to reform risked being charged with prolonging the Schism and not caring about the danger inherent in a headless Church (281).

As for the objection that once the pope was elected, reformation would become impossible because he would block it, Gerson answered as if he were in the midst of a scholastic *quaestio:* "I answer: either the said reformation can be canonically made without him and his consent or not" (281). If the answer is yes, then it is absurd to say the pope will block it when he thereby would cause his own deposition. If, however, the reform could not be made without him, then the present situation in the Church could not continue. A pope, in other words, was necessary for the reform. If he later stood in its way, the council could depose him, as it had previous popes.

Many churchmen may do what they could to please a new pope and therefore not exercise the liberty of speech and action they now showed in a popeless Church. Such people, he complained, "are not friends of truth when they would deny it out of favor and fear" (282). Thus, no matter what the circumstances, they were useless for the necessary reformation of the Church! As in the tyrannicide debate, Gerson refused to consider political expediency.

Once there was a pope, everyone would probably want to leave Constance, so no one would be left to carry out reform. Gerson countered that anyone who genuinely desired the reformation of the Church would find such an objection repugnant. Whoever wanted reform would stay at Constance until the task was completed (282). Even if only a few churchmen remained, they could continue the task, for in them would rest the council's authority. Gerson's final reason for going ahead with the papal election was the scandal caused by the "long wait for a future Roman pontiff." As elsewhere, he considered the laity's reaction to unsatisfactory behavior by the clergy.

Gerson chose to be optimistic and to believe that a future pope would carry out the reform agenda that the council had outlined.[121] The council not only had to act in the interests of the Church; it had to be *seen* as acting in such a way and not to be under suspicion of setting itself up as the Church's executive organ. Plenitude of power still resided in the pope for everyday affairs of the Church, and for Gerson it was high time to return to this state of affairs.

The rest is history. After the procedure was agreed upon in October, with thirty representatives from the nations joining the college of cardinals, the electors withdrew on 8 November into conclave in the merchants' meetinghouse on the harbor in Constance, where they would be safe from outside interference. By 11 November, they had their pope, Odo Colonna, a member of an old Roman noble family. A cardinal, he had not distinguished himself in any way at the council but thus probably had the advantage of not appearing to be a strong personality. He took the name Martin V, after the great bishop and thaumaturge of the fifth century whose feast day it was.

Apparently Sigismund found the new pope acceptable precisely because he was not French, while the Italians could rejoice. The papacy could now at last return to Rome, where the Colonnas were part of the very fabric of the city. The long period of French influence over the papacy was coming to an end. In coming decades, the Gallican Church would have to deal with popes who had never seen Avignon or Paris.

For Gerson such political and cultural considerations did not exist. He welcomed a pope acceptable to all except for the few remaining supporters of Pedro de Luna. Now the Western Church was again one. Pope and council could go ahead in reforming Western Christendom and also in reuniting it with the Eastern Church.

As earlier, however, the question of reform for Gerson was eclipsed by other matters. Within a few days of the election, Martin Porrée composed a report, intended for Martin V, on the history of the case of Jean Petit. Porrée claimed that the whole question of the nine assertions had been introduced at the council against the will of the "lord then pope" (presumably John XXIII), the emperor, and also the French king (Gl 10.549–52). The statements condemned at Paris had been made up by Gerson and had nothing to do with what Jean Petit originally had said and written in his justification of tyrannicide. Gerson, so claimed Porrée, had gone against the instructions given him by the French king. After the matter had been disputed by the commission appointed by the council, a period of three months was given to study the matter. When the vote was taken, sixty-two refused to condemn the assertions, while twenty-six voted for the condemnation, including Gerson and twelve or thirteen others of his colleagues who, according to Porrée, had sworn while still in Paris to pursue the matter and to defend the bishop of Paris and his decision. Otherwise, claimed Porrée, they would not have been given any stipend for attending the council. They were chosen, he insisted, solely on the basis of their willingness to oppose Porrée's lord, the duke of Burgundy (550).

Gerson and his followers are said to have tried all kinds of ways to hinder the decision of the council's commission from being made public (550–51). Now they were asking that the new pope convoke his cardinals so that the matter of Jean Petit be taken up again. The sentence of the bishop of Paris had usurped papal jurisdiction.

Whatever the truths or distortions that this statement contains, it shows that the new pope was almost immediately confronted with this dispute. But now with the triumph of the coalition of the English and German kings and the duke of Burgundy, Gerson had no backing. Martin Porrée made it clear in his brief that he expected papal support for his lord the duke of Burgundy.

Apologizing: January–May 1418

Gerson did not let go. In February of 1418, he issued a statement, *Considerent zelatores* (Let those who are zealous consider), on the council's extirpation of heresy and error (Gl 6.301–2). Some of the council fathers, he wrote, had neglected the question of tyrannicide, while others had ignored it. Others had been concerned with the personalities involved and their fear for them (*ad personarum acceptionem et humanum timorem*). Yet other churchmen had openly denied justice in matters of faith and morals; some were driven more by avarice than by desire for church reform. There were persons who denied the authority of bishops in extirpating heresy in their own dioceses. Some churchmen were corrupt and could be bought, while others wanted to undermine the actions taken by the council. Yet others were culpable of negligence in failing to follow the instructions given to the legates of king and university; some wanted to threaten theologians and those preaching the truth, especially when the persons in error were powerful men and princes. Some wanted to nourish or sustain homicide and perjury, or to avoid the correction of heretics, and some even wanted to delay the enforcement of general obedience to the new pope, *quod absit* (Let it not be!).

Gerson added that since the council had failed to deal with these questions, the matter should be brought, "if it so pleased" before the lord pope (Gl 6.302). This statement exists only because it was copied into a *Dialogus apologeticus* written in September of 1418 by Gerson at the abbey of Melk in Austria (296–304). The work is structured as a conversation between master and disciple, *Volucer* and *Monicus,* where the first represents Gerson's point of view, but is not necessarily Gerson himself, while the second seems to stand for Gerson's brother Jean the Celestine. After the citation of the above statement from February, Monicus asks his master if there was a papal response. Volucer answers that nothing happened, and the matter "has continually gotten worse until now." There had been an appeal to a future council on behalf of the Polish lords (302). The outcome was a papal bull forbidding such appeals, and Volucer concluded that this reaction "completely destroys, as those who read it assert, the basic strength not only of the Council of Pisa but also of Constance and of all things . . . which were decided or done at them" (302–3). The bull especially undermined the agreed procedure for future papal elections and the removal of any usurpers. In forbidding appeal from the pope in cases of faith, it was "plainly against God's law and the decrees of the council."

At a distance of several months from the events of the spring of 1418, Gerson summed up papal rejection of the decree *Haec sancta,* which had placed council over pope. He saw that the reestablished papacy was hindering the kind of open debate on questions of faith that had taken place at Constance. Historians traditionally date the end of the conciliar movement to the bull issued by Pius II in 1460, *Execrabilis,* which condemned the "horrible abuse" of appealing from a pope to future councils.[122] But Martin V had anticipated Pius by more than four decades.

At the closing session of the Council of Constance on 22 April 1418, the Poles were still asking for condemnation of Falkenberg. Martin's answer came on 10

May, just a few days before he left Constance for Italy: a prohibition against any such appeals to a future council.[123] In the meantime Martin drew up concordats with the churches of France, England, and Germany respectively. Although it would be premature to speak here of national churches, these agreements anticipated future papal strategy in dealing with kings. In return for recognition of the pope's supreme power in the universal Church, Rome accepted a certain "national" identity for the various churches. Gerson himself regularly spoke of the *ecclesia gallicana,* and Martin V simply recognized the fact that kings in France, England, and elsewhere now dominated church affairs in their countries.

If we compare the results of the concordat in terms of the practice of indulgences, we can see how Martin negotiated different strategies and thus left the matter open for later adjustments.[124] On matters of religious practice, as opposed to those of faith, Martin was willing to compromise, so long as his authority was acknowledged. But when we look at the actual reform decrees made at Constance in Martin's name in March of 1418, they covered only a few of the areas decided upon the previous October.[125]

Shortly after Martin's bull of 10 May 1418, Gerson issued his response in *An liceat in causis fidei a papa appellare* (Whether it is permitted in matters of faith to appeal from the pope; 283–90). He returned to the council's decision *Haec sancta,* that even the pope has to obey the council, and he briefly went through some of the reasons stated in his earlier treatises on papal authority for limiting its exercise. If there is no appeal from the pope, then it should follow that Peter, recognized by all as the first pope, should not (as described in Acts 11) have been liable to criticism for his practice of accepting uncircumcised converts to the new faith (284–85). Peter had said in his own Epistle that we must always be ready to satisfy those who ask from us "an account of the faith and hope in you" (cf. 1 Peter 3:15). This kind of petrine accountability provided for Gerson a model so that every pope had to account for his doings and sayings and be ready to revise his point of view.

If the new pope's decree were carried out, it would be impossible for a future pope to be judged or deposed through a general council, even if he were guilty of criminal acts or had caused scandal to the Church. But such a procedure had just taken place at Pisa; it had also been carried out when kings and princes recently had withdrawn their obedience from those whom they or others judged to be popes (285–86). Martin's very legitimacy as rightful pope would thus be undermined by his own decree: "The former John XXIII would be considered still to be pope, as before; and thus [it would be that] our most holy lord Pope Martin is not legitimately elected nor is pope, because the same lord and his cardinals refused to observe as inviolable the decisions made in the conciliar manner (*conciliariter*) through the sacred Council of Constance. But the same lord of ours many times said the opposite" (287). Gerson was referring to the statement of Martin V at the tumultuous closing of the council that he confirmed all that had been done at Constance *conciliariter.*[126] The pope whose election depended on his acceptance of the council could not thus forbid appeals to future councils.

Gerson claimed that he argued in this manner not in order to criticize Pope Martin. He chose to conclude that Martin's bull could be read as saying it is not allowed to appeal from the pope's judgment in any and all cases (290). As one recent historian has written, it is hard to accept this interpretation, for Martin quite obviously meant nothing of the sort.[127] Gerson was, however, looking for a way to reconcile loyalty to this much-needed pope with the aspirations and decisions of Constance. He even suggested, apparently with no touch of irony, that the question of papal authority could be avoided if the pope gave the Poles what they wanted and condemned the teaching on tyrannicide. In this way he would eliminate "any favoritism of persons" (*procul abjecta quavis acceptione personarum;* 290). The Poles would not need to appeal, and the pope would demonstrate his independence. Gerson implied that Martin would thereby humble the powerful Teutonic Knights, who were protecting Falkenberg.

At about the same time, Gerson considered the same question of papal authority in *De sententia pastoris semper tenenda* (Whether the sentence of the pastor is always to be kept; 291–94). He argued for the rights and prerogatives of the Gallican Church as exercised by the king. Gerson asked for return to its "ancient and legal liberties," both in the collation of benefices by bishops and in ecclesiastical elections. He opposed royal to papal authority and in some matters considered the king as head of the Church in his own realm, as in calling for assemblies to deal with ecclesiastical questions. Gerson was by no means giving *carte blanche* to royal supremacy, but on the basis of historical experience, he proposed an alternative to papal supremacy.

In yet another statement, which can be dated to May of 1418, Gerson dealt with the power of excommunication and once again described the Church in terms of Matthew 18: "If your brother sins against you" (294–96). It was not contempt of ecclesiastical power when someone refused to obey a papal mandate whose result would be the destruction and not the edification of the Church (295). There is a legal and moral right to resist, for a person can demand accountability by questioning even the pope (296).

Gerson's last contributions at Constance have for the most part been ignored. But his conclusions are important for every historian of political thought. Gerson expressed a rudimentary conception of fundamental human rights based on conscience and the right to criticize even the highest authorities.

At the same time, he defended a vision of the Church as made up of ordinary parish priests as well as the religious orders and the hierarchy. When the Dominican Matthew Graben's treatise on the perfection of religious life became known at Constance, Gerson realized that it placed members of religious orders on a higher plane than parish priests. He countered that the word *religio* referred to the Christian religion as such and that it can be practiced without the taking of vows. One can live outside a religious order and do everything to reach perfection in the Christian life (Gl 10.72).

A layperson as well as a religious can live decently and adequately in communities without property and have nothing except the results of manual labor. A layperson or a priest can live in chastity and obedience without taking religious vows. Such statements have been seen as Gerson's defense of the Brothers and Sisters of the Common Life,[128] but his primary goal was to ensure the status of parish priests. Ever since the 1390s, he had opposed the claims of theologians who were members of religious orders, especially the Dominicans, and now he asked the pope, who he pointed out was a secular priest, to extirpate a teaching that placed members of religious orders in a superior category (72).

After he left Constance on 17 May 1418, Gerson headed east, away from the territories controlled by the duke of Burgundy. From Melk in September, as we have seen, he wrote his *Dialogus apologeticus* and tried to explain in the *persona* of Volucer why the Council of Constance had not condemned Jean Petit's teaching on tyrannicide. He did not accuse the council, but he said he could not excuse many who were present there (Gl 6.297).

Gerson pointed out that the king of the Romans (Sigismund), at least in the early stages of the council, had been eager to get tyrannicide condemned. Monicus (representing Jean the Celestine) asked, just as we might, whether it was reasonable to continue with the issue once the council in general terms dealt with tyrannicide in *Quilibet tyrannus.* Furthermore, why was the stranger or foreigner (*advena*), referring to Gerson himself, so caught up in pursuing this matter? (299)

Volucer here answers on behalf of Gerson and says that the chancellor was responsible for matters of faith: "You have known his profession; you experienced what kind of zeal [he showed] with respect to our religion; you know that he is free from all bonds of worldly needs, and how he, once he readied himself in spirit, could fight all the more for the truth" (299). Gerson, explains Volucer, had been sent by the king, the university, and the Gallican Church for the province of Sens. He had clear instructions and letters to pursue matters of faith, the reunification of the Church, and the reformation of morals in head and members.

Volucer defends what happened at the council but concedes that Constance failed to confirm the condemnation of the nine articles ascribed to Jean Petit by the Paris council of faith. But Constance, in not rejecting the Paris condemnation, implicitly approved it! (300) The council wanted it to be understood that its *Quilibet tyrannus* implicitly covered all the nine assertions. This is very much after-the-fact rationalization, for it does not explain why Gerson at the council had not been satisfied with the declaration and kept asking for a specific condemnation of the nine assertions.

Monicus is not content. He insists on a full review of all that had happened at the council. Volucer chooses not to give it, but instead explains how Gerson at this point looked upon his role. The foreigner (*advena*) had spent much time with his teacher, the cardinal of Cambrai, whom everyone knew to be "most wise and prudent." Someone better acquainted with the matter could tell the story better, but Volucer knew for sure that the pilgrim (Gerson) in his zeal for union tolerated many things which otherwise would have been "neither tolerable nor to be tolerated" (*nec tolerabilia nec toleranda*; 303). He had come to accept bringing an end to the Schism as the council's central concern.

The reform of the Church could not be made by the council "without the leadership of a beloved leader, both prudent and dependable." Apparently such a leader never really emerged. Now Volucer claims he looks forward to seeing what the former members of the council will do at home in their own church provinces and kingdoms. They will be involved not in passing superfluous new legislation but in enforcing the canons that already existed in abundance (303–4).

In these lines I find Gerson's explanation for what had happened at Constance: after the first year under King Sigismund, there was no leader. In the face of terrible divisions between the Burgundians and the French, to say nothing of the French and the English, Gerson had to accept the papal election and postpone his reform program. Now the reform would have to continue on the provincial level.

Meanwhile Volucer advises Monicus not to waste his time in applying remedies "by speaking to the deaf: Where there is no one to listen, says the Wise man, you will not pour forth your speech" (Ecclus 32:6). Monicus had to be satisfied with the status quo and should be grateful that God had taken him away "from these cares." Now he could take pity and weep (304).

In this way Gerson, in the spring of 1418, consoled himself. Accept the outcome of the Council of Constance, he told himself. Accept even the pope's attempt to weaken or even destroy conciliar authority. He was turning inward to his own spiritual life. Glorieux in his list of the sermons given at the Council of Constance proudly recorded that Gerson with his nine contributions comes in first place: *Gerson vient en tête* (Gl 10.522). What difference did it make that the chancellor was so popular? He had failed to convince the council to tackle central religious and moral questions. Now he chose to put these matters behind him, taking stock of his own life and accepting that physically and spiritually, he was a pilgrim and a foreigner, with no abiding home. Jean Gerson could now entrust himself to the comforting hands of his beloved maiden, theology.

Wandering as a Refugee and Finding a New Home, 1418–1429

In 1418 Jean Gerson became a political refugee and had to remain outside his country of origin in order to protect his life. Like so many people before and since, Gerson could not return to the place where he had lived and worked, for it was ruled by men who considered him to be an enemy. Because of the network of contacts he already had in Paris and widened in Constance, Gerson could count on the sympathy and hospitality of both secular and church rulers. He was thus spared the degradation and humiliation with which most political refugees have to live, also in our time: the necessity of convincing the authorities of another country that they are genuinely in danger and are deserving of asylum.

Physical protection, however much it guarantees survival, provides only a fraction of what the refugee or exile has lost: a sense of belonging and having an everyday life in which to work and participate in society. The refugee is an outsider, pleading for his cause and his life, but is rarely allowed, or allows himself, to become part of the new world he or she enters.

Gerson had long been mentally and theologically preparing himself for refugee status. As a youth he had been uprooted from his family and thrown into the cauldron of city life. He had experienced the insecure life of the university student, looking for powerful and generous patrons and worrying about returning in shame to the family home. He had dreaded how it would be to have neighbors laughing at the ambitions of his family on his behalf.[1]

Jean the son of a skilled laborer found his identity in the name of his birthplace, the hamlet of Gerson, a word by chance resembling the Hebrew word for pilgrim, foreigner, outsider, wanderer. The wayfarer (*peregrinus*), as he called himself in his *Consolation of Theology*, made his way from Paris to Bruges to make a new home, but his attempt to reform the canons of Saint Donatian made him unwelcome there. Back in Paris, he accepted his position, with its lack of steady income, as chancellor of the university. After many frustrations, he got a prebend at Notre Dame and became a canon.

Jean Gerson acquired a house in the corner of the great cloister, just inside the precinct. Here he could write his lectures and sermons, on Sundays crossing the Seine to preach at the church of Saint Jean-en-Grève. He supervised the affairs of the great hospital next to the cathedral and looked after the teaching and treatment of choir boys.

It was a rich and full life, even if it was lived in the shadow of foreign war, the king's periodic insanity, dissension in the royal family, recurrent outbreaks of plague, and the seemingly endless Schism between rival popes. Gerson dealt directly or indirectly with all these matters, though his position was vulnerable once his patron, Duke Philip of Burgundy, was dead and his unpredictable and brutal son had replaced him. After Duke John took responsibility for killing the king's brother, Gerson worked for reconciliation. But he came to realize that in so doing, he compromised the Decalogue's command: Thou shalt not kill. In remaining silent, he felt he became an accomplice to a cold-blooded political murder.

The Council of Constance became for Gerson a welcome opportunity to answer any equivocation about tyrannicide, especially as expressed by his colleague Jean Petit. While others concentrated on Hussites or church reform, Gerson demanded his colleagues support the Paris condemnation of Petit's warped theology in defense of the duke of Burgundy. Once the influential Sigismund had lost interest in the matter, the council's general condemnation of tyrannicide was no longer a viable issue. Gerson suffered one humiliating defeat after another, but he refused to let the matter rest. He was fighting for his moral life and acting as the conscience of Christendom. But the Western Church had other matters on its agenda.

In his exile after the council, Gerson consoled himself, as we shall see, with a new understanding of theology. It provided comfort on the road that led him to a brief stay in Austria in the wake of Paris massacres in June of 1418. In the autumn of 1419, after the duke of Burgundy himself was assassinated, Gerson was able to return not to Paris but at least to a French-speaking city, Lyon. Here he found a new patron.

In the last decade of his life, Gerson remained dedicated to church reform and to questions of conscience. Although unable to compromise on basic principles, he was not rigid when it came to individual human beings and their moral dilemmas. These last years even reveal a touch of humor or self-irony, just a hint that Gerson could smile at himself and the world. The dour curé of later illustrations to his printed works has little to do with this passionate urban hermit giving advice on almost every subject between heaven and hell.

Any in-depth study of a historical figure is bound to reveal surprising and complex personality aspects. Few human beings fit into any neat categorization. Gerson wrote enough for the attentive reader to catch him in almost every mood and intellectual ambience. At one moment he seems almost to reject the entire inheritance of scholastic learning, while a few pages later he uses logical definitions with solid rigidity. Gerson, the refugee and exile, was mentally ubiquitous during these years.

Seeking and Finding Political Asylum

The first place we find Gerson after he left Constance in mid-May of 1418 is at Rattenberg, a fortress near the border of Tyrol and Bavaria. It is here, on 27 July, that he completed his epic poem, the *Josephina,* in praise of the love and marriage of Joseph and Mary.[2] It is also likely that Gerson at this time composed some of his poetry lamenting the situation in France and especially in Paris.[3] The entrance of the Burgundians into Paris and the expulsion of the Armagnac leaders had led to the June massacres, killing up to fifteen hundred people,among them Gerson's colleagues Jean de Montreuil and Gontier Col.[4]

Gerson's *Deploratio super civitatem* (Lament on the City) presents the most complete expression of his near-despair at the news of the savageness of the French civil war. In highly rhetorical language, he imitated the lament of Jeremiah at the destruction of Jerusalem but also included a humanist evocation of the glory that once was Rome but was ruined in civil conflict: "The city once strong, which all praised, now full of iniquity and blood; the ancient city of the fathers, which for years dominated many, now divided against itself" (Gl 10.407). The scenes of carnage are so graphic, the streets running with rivers of blood and filled with cadavers, that one might imagine Gerson had first-hand knowledge of the events at Paris. But he took his description from well-known sources.

Behind the carnage were betrayals of trust: "A light suspicion is the cause of most heavy death. No place is sacred and immune to harsh and terrifying killing. Nowhere is faith intact" (*Nusquam tuta fides*; 409). Now, as in 1413, *turbacio,* civil disturbance, swept the streets and churches of Paris, with "impious fury, blasphemy, lying calumny." The breakdown of law and order was accompanied by a moral collapse.

During these years Gerson returned time and again in his writings to this scene of betrayal, the ruin of social trust, and the violation of God's laws. For him the crime of tyrannicide and even worse its justification had dissolved human bonds and initiated the evils that followed in France: *quae causa totius pene turbationis inclitum Franciae regnum discerpentis ut aiunt, seminarium fuit* (Gl 9.228).

His *Deploratio studii parisiensis* (Lament for the University of Paris) summarizes in seventy-six verses Gerson's anguish over the fate of his university (Gl 4.4–7). Again Christian and classical symbols are combined: both the angel of peace and Pallas Athene weep at the sight. The temple, fortress, and asylum of learning has collapsed. In the end Gerson calls upon the dauphin to repair the ruins. Already before he had left Constance he had written a long letter on the education of the then-fifteen-year-old dauphin, the future Charles VII (Gl 2.203–15). This teenage boy was seen as the only hope for the future of France, of Paris and its university.

At Rattenberg Gerson managed to get beyond his dark visions by turning to the comfort in theology which Boethius once had sought from philosophy. The *Consolatio Theologiae* was probably not finished before the autumn of 1418.[5] In the meantime Gerson moved north and east, to another fortress town, this time in Bavaria, Neuburg am Inn, just south of Passau, where the Inn meets the Danube.[6] Here on 10 August he wrote a remarkable letter to his two Celestine monastic brothers, Nicolas and Jean, in which he provided a summary of his life. He started with his favorite Pauline quotation: "Our way of life is in heaven" (*nostra conversatio in coelis est,* Phil 3:20), telling his brothers not to worry about his bodily pilgrimage or his physical situation. Think of me, he asked them, "as if I were dead and lost on the earth," (216–17). The brothers were only to ask that their eldest brother gained the peace to be found within the heavenly Jerusalem. He asked them to greet their elder brother (Jean the Benedictine at Reims), as well as their sisters, for he did not have time "at the present to send letters, and so it is enough that they receive and believe in my speaking through you" (217).

He included a four line poem in French about the *Science de bien mourir,* how to die well, and lamented the death of his "beloved and constant companion André," who must be André de Curia, his chaplain since Bruges days and apparently with Gerson at Constance.[7] Now with the loss of André, he thought of what the protomartyr Stephen had said before he died: "Lord Jesus, receive my spirit" (Acts 7:59).

Gerson added some verses from the Psalms on the same theme of handing oneself over to a merciful God. Ever the teacher, he explained why these verses were so important to him. They show how God freely acts in us and provides refuge, opening up the gate on the inevitable day of death "so that our spirit is not confounded while it speaks with its enemies in this gate" (217; cf. Ps 68:13). He depicted himself as solitary and waiting for death, but in the very last line, as a postscript, he added to his brothers that "my companion (*comes*), master Jacques de Cerisy, who is alone with me, greets you." Even Gerson, our lonely wanderer, had his secretary and associate with him. Medieval people, even celibate clerics, usually had each other's company.

Avoiding the Alps, whose physical reality he never described in his writings, Gerson apparently followed the Danube, for we next find him at the great Benedictine abbey of Melk. Here, in September 1418, he probably wrote his *Dialogus apologeticus* (Gl 6.296–304). This exchange, as mentioned in the previous chapter, contains a dialogue between two figures, *Volucer,* representing wisdom and contemplation, and *Monicus,* more youthful affectivity, the image of his brother Jean the Celestine.[8]

From here it was not far to Vienna, where a new university had been founded in the latter part of the previous century, as was happening elsewhere in German-speaking areas. The Hapsburg duke, Frederick of Austria, the rival of Sigismund in Constance, invited Gerson there, but the only manifestation of the distinguished theologian's presence is a poem of thanks he must have written on leaving: *Carmen in laudem ducis Austriae.* Gerson contrasted the miserable state of France, where those who sought freedom had been condemned, with "happy Austria." The one who had been chancellor of Paris University had come as a foreigner (*advena;* Gl 4.170) to "happy, studious Vienna," where the duke had "provided a place with the freedom of his outstanding college." Gerson asked Jesus to reward the duke, but the poem is more about France than Austria. The nightmare vision of massacre would not go away.

The poem has been dated to September 1419, just after Gerson would have heard that the supporters of Duke John of Burgundy on 10 September had killed him at their meeting on the bridge of Montereau (Gl 4.xxv). If Glorieux is right, Gerson deliberately left out all mention of the murder. Nowhere in his writings do I find any gloating over the death of Duke John.[9] Once the duke was gone, however, Gerson could contemplate returning to the French-speaking world.

But not to Paris. The Burgundians were still there, with their English allies, and Gerson remained *persona non grata.* Instead he went to Lyon, which was loyal to the dauphin and out of Burgundian reach. The archbishop, Amédée de Talaru, had probably made Gerson's acquaintance at the Council of Constance. Our wanderer may have arrived at his new home already by November.[10]

Lyon was a great city, not nearly as large as Paris, but with an even more distinguished past as the former capital of Roman Gaul.[11] Even today its Roman ruins, especially the former theater, are impressive, and in Gerson's time they would have been even more prominent. The archbishop had long called himself primate of Gaul, and his cathedral, located near the confluence of the Saône and Rhône close to the oldest part of the city, housed dozens of canons.[12]

Jean Gerson was not the first distinguished theologian and church exile who received the hospitality and protection of an archbishop of Lyon. In 1099 Anselm, archbishop of Canterbury, whose prayers and meditations Gerson knew, had stayed there. His companion and biographer Eadmer described how the two of them arrived after Anselm's falling out with the Anglo-Norman monarch William Rufus: "When the council was over, we obtained permission and left Rome. Our return journey was beset with many dangers but, by God's protection, we escaped them all and came to Lyon without harm. Here we were received with great honour and joy, and invited to stay by the venerable archbishop of the city, Hugh, so we fixed our abode here, having lost all hope of returning to England while King William was alive."[13] Anselm was fortunate to have such an admirer to describe settings that we can only dimly perceive in Gerson's life. Eadmer remarked that Anselm "was treated not like a guest or a foreigner, but like a native and lord of the place" (*non sicut hospes aut peregrinus, sed vere sicut indigena et loci dominus*).[14]

Anselm could feel at home anywhere. He had long been preparing himself for this exile, and he could almost enjoy it in the company of the archbishop, a friend to whom he had already written of his bond back in the early 1080s. Gerson at Lyon would remain, in his own words, not a citizen (*indigena*) but a foreigner (*advena*).

In December 1419, Pierre d'Ailly, who had settled in Avignon, wrote that he would be coming to Lyon for the dauphin's visit. He asked his former pupil, who also was Gerson's fellow canon at Notre Dame, Gérard Machet, similarly in exile, to recommend him to the archbishop of Lyon so that he would find a suitable place to stay (Gl 2.222). In January 1420, when the dauphin came to Lyon, he provided Gerson, as well as Gérard Machet, with a sum both for their longstanding services to the monarchy and "to help them to bear the losses and damages which they suffered recently in the city of Paris by the rebellion that took place there."[15] Gerson received 200 pounds, while Machet was given 100.

We have no evidence that d'Ailly did come to Lyon, but Gerson remained in contact with him and lectured him almost paternally with warnings against excessive interest in the stars. D'Ailly insisted that astronomy and theology could agree with each other, while his former pupil had much greater reservations about the matter (218–19). As for d'Ailly's death on 9 August 1420, no source records Gerson's reaction. He occasionally mentions his former teacher fondly, but no epitaph or poem survives to publicize his feelings.[16]

Ever since the eighteenth century, writers on Gerson have asserted as a fact that he lived at Lyon during these first years with his brother Jean, who was prior of the Celestine house founded here a few years earlier.[17] The careful researcher Max Lieberman pointed out in 1967 that Jean the Celestine remained prior of the house of Marcoussis near Paris until 1421, when he became prior of the Celestines in Lyon.[18]

Gerson lived in the cloister joining the collegial church of Saint Paul to the parish church of Saint Lawrence. The latter church building was torn down during the French Revolution, while Saint Paul has been greatly altered in the course of time.[19] Gerson's colleague Gérard Machet, now canon of Saint Paul, had found refuge in Lyon already in 1418, and so it was appropriate for Gerson to follow his lead.[20] Here we find Gerson in his last years, in a collegial church far from the cloister of Notre Dame of Paris. He never became a canon at Saint Paul, perhaps because he wanted to emphasize that he remained chancellor and canon of Notre Dame.

A myth has grown up about Gerson at Lyon that he went back to teaching schoolboys, as he had done at Paris.[21] In 1858 Gerson's first detailed biography showed there was no evidence for this assertion,[22] but it continues to appear, just as the claim that Gerson found his first lodgings with the Celestines.[23] A sadly neglected statue of Gerson across from the front of the church of Saint Paul shows him as a curé together with a boy who could have been his pupil. This is the later nineteenth century's version of the legend that Gerson during his last years was close to youth.[24]

The only evidence for Gerson's continuing involvement at this time with youth is an expression of concern for the sexual exploitation of schoolboys by their teachers, one of his perennial worries (Gl 9.562). Our best external source for him in these last years is a letter, probably of May 1423, written by his youngest brother, who must have visited him regularly at his new and final home (Gl 10.554–61). It is addressed to a certain Anselm (who may be Oswald) of the Grande Chartreuse, and ends with our earliest list of Gerson's writings (Gl 1.20, 23–26). The Carthusian had apparently asked for this list, an indication of the great interest these monks showed for Gerson's work.[25]

Jean the Celestine described his brother as someone whose writings "delight, enlighten, and complete the mind" (Gl 10.555). He compared Gerson's conclusions with the teachings of the Church Fathers and emphasized his brother's respect for them. Gerson was not happy when people asked him for copies of his own works. He preferred to recommend Augustine, Gregory, Cassian, Bernard, Richard of Saint Victor, Anselm, and so on (556).

Like his brother, Jean the Celestine questioned the proliferation "of useless, curious, and harmful books" (557), but he defended Gerson's production of more books because they were "a decent occupation" (*honesta occupatio*). They drew on Holy Scripture as a "deep well" whose waters never dried up and so provided new insights. Another image for Scripture was that of a table filled with all different kinds of food, appropriate for different types of people (558). Jean explained how his brother had written for various needs, as doctors provide varying treatments to cure the sick.

Only here, after several pages of justification for learning and writing new things, did the Celestine turn to a portrait of his brother. First he described Gerson in Paris as a "solemn ambassador" both of King Charles and the University of Paris. Because he was "a most faithful and watchful dog" who barked for truth, he was deprived "of home, country, city, relatives, friends, offices, and possessions" (559). For this reason he had sought refuge "in this outstanding city of Lyon."

Here Jean Gerson was "leading a most quiet life and one so solitary that you would believe him to be a hermit except that he has not yet sought the depths of the desert but dwells in the midst of his people."[26] Many of them asked, "What is someone so solitary doing here? Why does he not emerge in public?" It was expected that Gerson would contribute to calm "quarrels which rage so bitterly everywhere."[27]

According to his brother, Gerson in receiving visitors to his house, did involve himself. He showed them a "happy and pleasant face," with the "wisdom which he sought from youth to take as his bride: there he rests with her and makes conversation all the day" (559). Gerson's way of life (*conversatio*) showed "no bitterness nor his manner any regret, only happiness and joy." He was not hemmed in by the walls of his narrow cell but extended his concerns "to the ends of the earth and the distant sea" (560). Considering all places with his "eye of reason," he

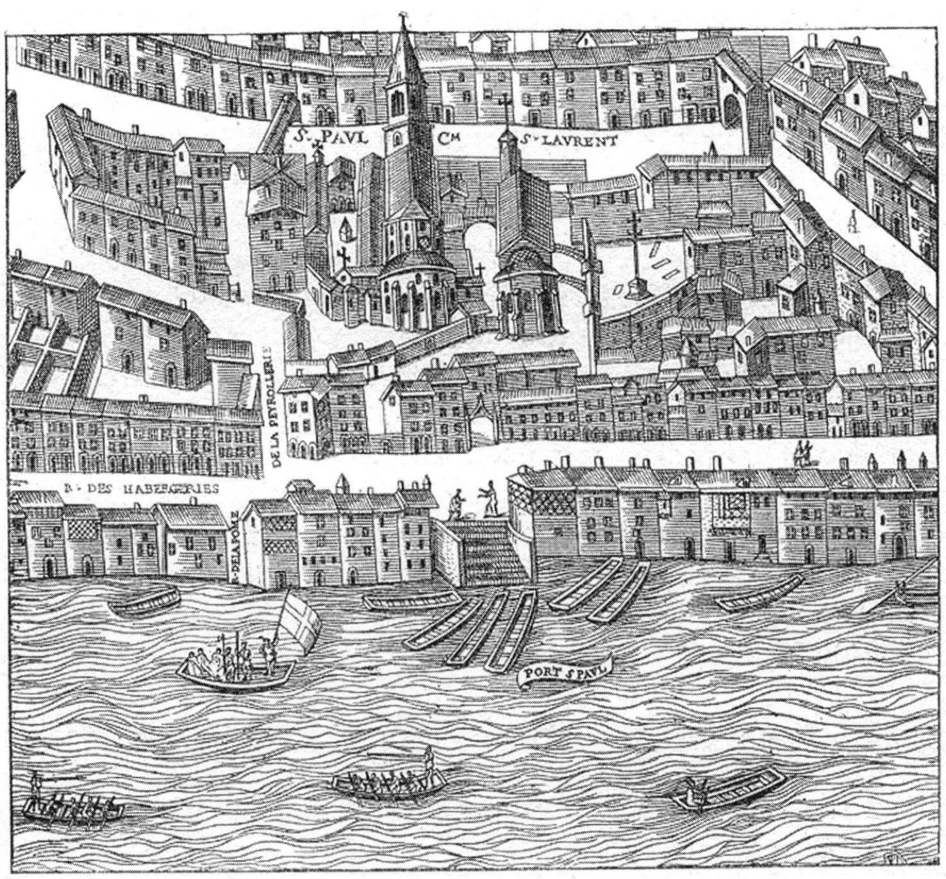

Fig. 11 Port of Saint Paul, Lyon. From a 1550 pictorial map of Lyon, showing the churches of Saint Paul and Saint Lawrence, joined by buildings where Gerson is thought to have lived. Source: A.-L. Masson, *Jean Gerson* (Lyon, 1894).

FIG. 12 Gerson as a curé and teacher of the youth of Lyon. This nineteenth-century statue stands across from the west entrance of the church of Saint Paul. From A.-L. Masson, Jean Gerson

FIG. 13 Nineteenth-century print of the old district of Saint Paul, with church façade and tower. Source: A.-L. Masson, *Jean Gerson* (Lyon, 1894).

looked upon "the various states of men, now prosperous, now adverse." He made himself, in the Pauline mode (1 Cor 9:22), "all things to all people," "now through thanksgiving in applauding them, now in pious prayer in helping them, exhorting them, having pity on them."

Jean the Celestine here summarized perfectly the Carthusian ideal of the hermit in society, at a time when such monks were moving their residences to cities. Remaining apart from the population, these new hermits involved themselves in the world.[28] As a Celestine, caught up in a similar urban monastic asceticism, Jean knew exactly how to describe his brother's way of life. We can see it in the larger context of the *Devotio moderna,* but we do not have to borrow from northern spirituality to understand what was happening in what today is southeastern France.

The brothers found inspiration in the literature of the Desert Fathers. Through prayer and hospitality Jean Gerson remained in the world but could also live as a semi-hermit. What is surprising here is not the ascetic ideal: it is Jean the Celestine's description of how his brother found joy in his new vocation. Jean did not ignore where Gerson was coming from: the description of this serene and happy life is followed by Gerson's tears over the terrible state of France. Here he is "another Jeremiah, seeing the suffering of his people and its burdens." The language is close to Gerson's *Deploratio* on the destruction of Paris (Gl 10.560). The

Fig. 14 Façade of the *manécanterie,* next to the cathedral of Saint Jean, Lyon. Originally a refectory for the canons, but from the fourteenth century onwards a school of chant. (Photo by author)

Celestine depicted Gerson sitting "solitary and silent" in melancholy thoughts.[29] But then he would offer the Mass and lift his eyes to the "works of the fingers of God, the moon and stars which Wisdom founded, so beautiful a sight."

Gerson combined such meditation with hard work: "You should not think of him as given to quiet and inactivity, as someone lying about for the whole day."[30] He spent his day, and often the night, in work as well as prayer, for which he would get up several times (560–61). Jean applauded his brother for this effort of refusing to give in to despair because it is so hard to correct evil and the number of fools is infinite.[31] Gerson had accepted his condition, and often told his brother that he now experienced a greater sense of peace and "eagerness of heart." At the same time, Gerson confided to Jean that he felt "a clearer and more lively understanding now within himself than ever before" (561).

Jean the Celestine's letter reveals intimacy with his brother. He reveals a social Gerson who, like the Desert Fathers he read, quoted and imitated, was willing to drop his other duties in order to be available for guests with their needs. Here is the solitary to whom people come for comfort and advice, a classic figure in Christian history. In fleeing the world such a person becomes more attractive for those who remain in it.[32]

Jean the Celestine's 1423 letter, however hagiographical, provides a sense of how Gerson lived his last years. Lyon with its political security and appreciative archbishop was the right place for Gerson to be. However dire the situation in France, Gerson could hope that one day he would return to Paris and resume his function as chancellor. The house in the corner of the cloister at Notre Dame of Paris was occupied by others, but it was still called Gerson's (554). In 1425 rumors circulated in Paris of Gerson's death, and various candidates jockeyed for the position he had held for so long (562). But the university records show that Gerson kept the title of chancellor.[33]

Beyond Jean the Celestine's letter, however, the sources reveal little about Gerson's daily life. Did he ever allow himself to take walks along the rivers? His only mention of them is a remark about how difficult it is to keep the Rhône within its banks.[34] Otherwise he remained as reticent as ever about his physical surroundings. He became what others needed him to be and yet, at the same time, he remained apart. In order to understand the man who settled at Lyon, I will retrace some of Gerson's steps, starting with the year of his migration east.

Praising Joseph and Mary

On the roads of Central Europe in 1418, Gerson had finished his great poem in twelve sections (*distinctiones*), the *Josephina*.[35] He opened it not with the angel's revelation that Mary's child was begotten by the Holy Spirit (Mt 1:18) but with the message of an angel to Joseph in a dream at Bethlehem that he was to take his wife and newborn son and flee into Egypt (Mt 2:13). The poem's first *distinctio* describes in detail the flight, while the second section concerns their arrival and settlement in Egypt, and the third their return from Egypt to Nazareth. It is only in the fourth distinction that Gerson reverts to the Annunciation, and from here his narrative is more conventional and closer to the biblical text, with the marriage of Joseph and Mary (distinction 5), the visitation of Mary to Elizabeth and the birth of John the Baptist (6), the birth of Christ (7) and his childhood (8–10), leading up to his temporarily being lost in the temple (11). In the twelfth distinction, in a description of the death of Joseph, Gerson returns to his practice from the first books of imagining events only implied in the biblical text. As he explains himself in the course of his poem: "Thus our meditation does not rashly assert anything about what is not known but only uses in a modest way the logic of conjectures. From what is written the mind can infer what is not written" (Gl 4.51).

In this way Gerson dramatized the life of Joseph and gave it a fullness lacking in the biblical narrative. The great historian Johan Huizinga once criticized Gerson for adding to the story of Joseph's life and emotions: "Gerson's seriousmindedness did not keep him from immodest curiosity about things that seem to be inevitably linked to Joseph's marriage."[36] Such interest, however, was very much in harmony with Gerson's concern to show a loving, caring man who was Mary's real husband and Jesus' real father, even if there was no sexual union with Mary.

In the scene of their leaving Bethlehem, Gerson seeks to capture the closeness between Mary and Joseph. "This is not the time for weeping, my dearest . . . we must flee and obey God's commands" (34). The child awoke and in recognizing its mother seemed to laugh. God himself had become for us "a fugitive and a foreigner" (*fugitivus et advena*; 35). We are to follow his example and to live as pilgrims (36).

While the rumor spread at Nazareth that Joseph, Mary, and the child had fled, the family rested in the desert. Joseph took the infant into his arms. Mary warmed the child before the fire. They ate and retired to bed: "Until he slept whose heart always keeps watch."[37]

Time and again in this first distinction, Gerson emphasized exile and its hardships: "How often the robber, how often thirst, cold, heat, and hunger could trouble the impoverished travellers" (37). Yet here in the desert they found, as Moses before them, a "refuge of freedom" (*libertatis asylum*). Gerson imagines the soothing hymns Mary would sing for her son. He describes Joseph's upsetting dreams and his telling Mary the next morning about them (38). She was certain that their trials, like Job's, were a condition of life and would lead to eternal life. Her considerations turned into a statement about determinism and liberty. Our liberty and free will do not perish in what seem to be events directed by fortune (38–39).

Joseph agreed with Mary, who added that people neither see heavenly matters nor perceive through the light of faith. Grace completes nature, which is not in itself evil (39–40). This learned travel dialogue (*doctus sermo viae*) between husband and wife ends with their seeking shelter for the night. Gerson turns the bitter trail of exile into pleasing theological instruction on the will of God as manifested in the world. He makes clear that it was Mary who taught her husband on their travels: *Qualia Virgo virum potuit docuisse viando.* The woman is wiser than the man, but the man is willing to learn. Mary and Joseph have become proto-professors of the university which would grow up near the great cathedral of Our Lady at Paris.

In the second distinction, Joseph and Mary have reached Memphis in Egypt, and Joseph is said to be afraid that Mary's beauty will attract Pharaoh. He asks her to pretend that she is his daughter, and in this way she will be safe. Here Mary is as courageous as she previously was wise: it is she who tells Joseph to dry his tears and not to give up hope (41).

Joseph addresses the people of Memphis and speaks of Mary as his only daughter. Her boy's father "lives in a remote place" (42). The story of the couple is spread throughout the land, and they are called before the king. Mary is silent, while Joseph tells the king that they are of royal stock but have come on hard times. They had been forced to flee the ferocious King Herod (42), and the child's father had asked Joseph to protect the infant. Joseph requests asylum and promises that the family will not be a burden on others but will work for its bread.[38]

The king is convinced of their sincerity. He grants them refuge and orders a house to be given to the family (43). Joseph answers all the questions of the Egyptian king truthfully but never tells the full story of his family's identity. The Egyptians treat the family well. The family is able to make an everyday life: Joseph makes food, while Mary feeds and bathes the child. They work hard to make a home and are careful not to waste time, in the true gersonian fashion of making good use of every available moment: *domus otia nulla recipit* (44).

Gerson combined the theme of pilgrimage in a strange land with tender details of everyday life. The poem depicts spiritual heroism, but with great gentleness, as in its description of the two-year-old Jesus:

> Now he could stand shakily and speak / He stammered with imperfect speech / Which seemed so sweet to both parents / He rushes into their embrace when called / Lifting his little arms he wants to hang on the necks of his parents / With tender embrace to give chaste kisses / He places his hand in yours, Mary and Joseph / And with his uneven step / He follows you all over the house. / Whatever he sees he marvels at, asking questions so he can know everything. / Maybe he sometimes interrupts your work. / Containers, strainer, baskets, thrashing instruments and small hatchets he handles and tries to carry about. (44)

In his late fifties, Jean Gerson had not forgotten how it was for him in his early teens to live in a family with infant siblings.

Gerson also remembered that childhood is not only a time for wonder: it also brings painful discoveries of the cruelty and harshness of life. In the poem, a playmate calls Jesus a "wretched foreigner" (*miser advena*), ignorant of an unknown father and fatherland (*Ignotus patriamque patrem qui dicere nescis*). The child runs crying to his mother, who dries his tears and adds her kisses. But he still asks: "Is not Joseph my father? Is not this our fatherland?" (45)

At this point Mary begins to tell Jesus about his life. His sorrow had been prophesied by Jeremiah. Jesus would come to take upon himself the crimes of humanity, she explains, with the story of creation and fall (45–46). Out of sorrow, such as Herod's killing of innocent children, redemption would come: "Alas, its price will be your death, most precious son" (46). Jesus, who was both God and man, reacts humanly with fear and joy. Then Joseph returns from work and "senses in entering the tears of both." He joins their weeping and tells the story of his namesake, Joseph the patriarch (47–48). The time will come, Joseph prophesies, when idols will no longer be worshipped in Egypt.

Mary and Joseph are both teachers, first of their son Jesus, and secondly of their neighbors, telling them of true religion and "what would come and what they should believe." The third book opens with Joseph's dream in which the angel tells him he and his family could return to their homeland. Once again Gerson adds details not even suggested in the biblical text, and yet quite believable in their everyday quality: the neighbors did not want their friends to leave; there was much weeping, kissing, and embracing at the family's departure.

Gerson wrote that he would have given anything to be able to see and hear the family on this journey, during which he imagined that they spoke of what was to come, but also enjoyed the birds and other creatures they met and saw "fields splendid with flowers of the season" and the rainbow with its pact, God's promise never to send another all-destroying flood (49; cf. Gen 9:15).

With the family secure at Nazareth, Gerson describes the full lineage of Mary. Her mother Anne married twice after losing Mary's father Joachim. From her marriage to Cleophas, the brother of Joseph, Anne gave birth to a second Mary, who had four sons: James the Less, Joseph, Simon, and Jude, called the brothers of Jesus because they were his close relatives (explaining the references in the biblical text to Jesus' brothers). Anne then had a third husband and they had a third Mary, who became the mother of the apostle James the Greater and John the Apostle. Thus we have the outline in Gerson's poem of what came to be called the Holy Kinship, the extended family of Christ, which fit perfectly into late medieval bourgeois notions of a fruitful and abundant family life.[39]

At Nazareth the child Jesus learned the trade of his father, and here Gerson once again extrapolates on the biblical text and reveals intimate knowledge of everyday life for working people: "Thus Christ was subject, as he was to you, Mary and Joseph. . . . Often he lights the fire and makes food. He does the dishes and fetches water. Now he sweeps the house, feeds and waters the donkey. He brings the neighbors his mother's weaving or gives himself to his father's carpentry in different types of wood; thus he was called a carpenter" (51–52). The lines that follow provide so technical a description of the carpenter's craft that one can imagine the young Jean Gerson hanging around his father's workshop observing and sometimes imitating his actions. Decades later, he recalled what it meant to make objects of wood. He made use of this portrayal of Christ the worker to cast shame on those who refuse to work and look down on physical labor (52).

At this point, Jesus asks his father about his family origin. Joseph takes the boy in his arms and tells him the story of his royal descent, but now Jesus wants to know how his father and mother found each other. This time it is Mary who explains. "I never wanted a man," she began. Her parents had sent her to the temple to be educated and where she learned to weave garments for the priests, to study, and to pray.[40] She acquiesced in her parents' wish that she marry Joseph but insisted on remaining a virgin.

At this point, says Gerson, a stranger perhaps entered and interrupted the conversation (55). Here the third distinction ends and Gerson returns to the biblical narrative starting with the Annunciation. The most original part of the poem is over, except for the final book with its tender description of Jesus parting with his dying father. Joseph is very much the father of Jesus. He cares for the child and teaches him love, a role he shares with Mary, his wife and companion. Parenthood and theological wisdom are combined in both mother and father in a way that precludes all gender preference!

Such a brief review cannot convey the rich texture of the *Josephina* in terms of thought and emotion. But here Gerson's search for an affective theology that combines creative imagination and logical clarity came to fruition. If it were not for the difficulty of the language and the many layers of meaning, the work might have received more attention. It seems that it has begun to be noticed only recently for its literary quality and spiritual insight.[41] Gerson did here what few medieval writers achieved: he described Jesus as a person who developed from childhood into adulthood, who had to discover the pain and sorrow of life and understand what it was to lose a parent. This story of growth and change undermines the popular conception, so common since the work of Philippe Ariès, that medieval people had little conception of childhood as a separate stage of life.

In the *Josephina* Gerson combined a lifetime of study in biblical theology with the freedom of a novelist. He invested in Joseph, Mary, and Jesus all he hoped and dreamed a good family life could be. Drawing on his own past, he recalled how a child learns from its parents. This process can flourish in an atmosphere of physical intimacy and tender concern.

Consoling the Self in Theology

Just as the *Josephina* summarized Gerson's affective spirituality, so did the *Consolation of Theology* provide the essence of what we might call his intellectual spirituality at this time. Gerson needed all the comfort and consolation he could get, whether from the Holy Family or from a personified theology.

Gerson's predecessor Boethius constructed a dialogue between the philosopher and philosophy, while Gerson's conversation takes place between *Volucer* and *Monicus,* cognitive intellect and affective inquisitiveness. In the course of the dialogue, however, it becomes clearer that Gerson saw in Monicus his youngest brother, who often refers to Gerson himself as "the wayfarer" (*advena*). *Volucer* and *Monicus* speak of the living Gerson as a third person in their discussion, in terms of his thoughts and experiences. Theology herself only enters and makes a speech at the end of the work, perhaps one of the weakest aspects in Gerson's refashioning of the Boethian model.

Mark S. Burrows has recently done a splendid job of showing the importance of this work as an indication of Gerson's theological reorientation later in his life.[42] But this interpretation goes too far in seeing the *Consolation of Theology* as a departure from Gerson's earlier teaching of the value of doing one's best (*facere quod in se est*), in a new awareness of the arbitrary grace of God as the only way to salvation.

Gerson's theology of grace is a subject in itself worthy of book-length treatment, but for our purposes it is sufficient to say that the *Consolation* does express Gerson's temporary abandonment of an earlier emphasis on individual effort in order to deserve salvation. After Constance, he was much more prone to place his trust in God and to give up thinking that his own exertions would make much difference. But this sense of impotence and flight into a mighty God did not remain with Gerson the rest of his days. As we shall see from a brief look at his writings from the mid-1420s, he returned, at least in part, to his earlier conviction that the individual person has an obligation to make the best use of his or her own abilities to contribute to God's plan for salvation.

The *Consolation of Theology* has to be seen together with its parallel piece, the *Dialogus Apologeticus.* Here Gerson looked back and found that his efforts had not been in vain. By that time he was in Melk and perhaps had gained some distance from the traumas of the spring of 1418. The *Consolation* alternates between prose sections and poems, just like Boethius's original work.[43] Gerson began with a scene of destruction in what used to be "happy France," introducing themes already found in his laments (Gl 9.185–86). Volucer tells Monicus that he has come from the Council of Constance, where he stayed with the brother of Monicus until after the pope's departure. It was then, says Volucer, that Gerson acted according to his name and became a pilgrim in foreign lands instead of returning to his own.

Monicus asks how his brother can survive "in unknown and distant places, where he does not know the tongue" (186). Is he not putting his light under a bushel or living in the shadows like those who are dead to the world?

Volucer's reply describes Gerson's way of life: "Do you not remember that our wayfarer always, even in the midst of crowds and cities, sought solitude for himself and loved it? I speak of solitude which is freedom (*vacatio*) from external cares and the calumnies of men." (186) Now he is in danger. Traps have been laid for him, and he has had to "swim away . . . from the shipwreck of the republic" (187). Heresy is found everywhere, "insulting catholic truth with their defenders," probably an allusion not only to Jean Petit but also to Martin Porrée.[44]

At this point Monicus asks what his brother had done in Constance. Gerson as author reveals his intention was not to go through the record of his earlier efforts (as he did in his *Dialogus apologeticus*), but to show how theology provides consolation. From childhood he had studied its holy writings, and "neither hostile fury nor terror could turn him aside from following its path." A poem in praise of wisdom and theology follows (Gl 4.28–29), summarizing the meaning of Gerson's life.

This very personal opening is followed by a discussion of free will, necessity, and eternal punishment (Gl 9.190–92). Volucer explains how "our wayfarer" distinguishes between grace and individual effort (*industria*;192). The third prose section continues the subject of human salvation and God's judgment. We simply have to trust in God and place a finger to the mouth of "human garrulity" (193). God does not want any wayfarer to be damned, and we must say as Job did: "Even if he shall kill me, still I will hope in him" (Job 13:13; 194).

It is a condition of human life to sin, and the only thing one can do is to hand oneself totally over to God (196). Faith and hope enable the wayfarer to stand firm on the top of life's mountain like the oak which, because of its deep roots, can resist the storm, as described in the fourth poem (Gl 4.146). The main theme of the *Consolation of Theology* appears as the centrality of hope, which will not confound or disappoint (Rom 5:5; Gl 9.201).

How does one respond, however, when all human hope seems to be gone? Monicus says he is fortunate because he is not forced to see with his own eyes the desolation of the city (202). He refers to the story that Augustine preferred to die rather than to live long enough to see his city taken by its enemies.[45]

Volucer sympathizes but claims that the wayfarer (Gerson), even though he too was spared witnessing the city's destruction, often sees in his mind his friends' sufferings. Some of them have been attacked because of their bond to him by blood and friendship (203). His enemies claim he is the root of the evil and that the time will come when he will be judged with them: "He hears that he has become an exile also, disgraced and despicable, unworthy in the sight of the public."[46]

Gerson asked himself why God had spared him from having to suffer in the way others did. Once again the dialogue resolves Gerson's personal doubts by means of a theological statement: nothing takes place outside of God's will (204). Somehow there will be meaning in everything that happens.

Monicus poses the question whether God made the world like a clockmaker, installing, as it were, in each created object its function and then leaving everything to itself.[47] But God participates in the world, and so "our prayers and hopes are not empty in being directed to God" (213).

Here, as so often in the poem, Gerson tried to reconcile an all-powerful God, who rules the universe in ways beyond our understanding, with a human need for comfort and hope. In the third book, Volucer describes the human zeal or effort that sometimes can be negative but also can be a positive force (215). Zeal can lead to heresy, as when people claim that no one in mortal sin has the right to rule others (216). The zealous man wants to take away the abuses he sees in the Church; but if he cannot do so, then he "tolerates and weeps" over them (218). Gerson was reflecting on his own situation. In spite of disappointment, he felt it his duty to remain faithful to the Church rather than condemn her.

The question of zeal also involves the administration of the state. Volucer describes its corruption due primarily to the giving of gifts and taking of bribes (218). This negative portrait of life at court leads to praise for those who are content with their solitude, as Pope Gregory desired.[48] The section ends with a poem praising monastic life for its solitude and isolation from the world (Gl 4.132–33).

Gerson had apparently abandoned his earlier reservations toward monastic life.[49] He now accepted its isolation as a way to cope with the cares of the world. But there follows a prose section in which Monicus warns Volucer not to ignore "the republic which perishes without rulers." At the same time, monastic life also has its dangers (219). Volucer and Monicus discuss the use of power in society. The desire to rule in itself is not wrong (221). The problem is, in one of Gerson's favorite quotations from the Old Testament, that "bad men are difficult to correct and the number of fools is infinite" (Eccles 1:15).[50]

Monicus asks here about those who seek benefices to which the care of souls is connected. In order to get or keep such offices, they get involved in lawsuits. It is acceptable for someone who wants to serve God to seek a benefice so that he has enough to support himself (221–22). This had been Gerson's guiding principle from the time he had been made chancellor, but our review of his life has shown how difficult it was for someone like him to combine office with a steady income.

Volucer's general principle in dealing with questions of power is the same Gerson proposed in Constance for ruling the Church: the exhortation in Matthew (18:15) to seek out your brother if he sins against you. If he will not hear you, then you must go to the Church. But here Volucer, probably in the light of Gerson's disappointment with the outcome of Constance, adds that even though we should act in such a way, we need not do so in every case. We can choose not to appeal to the judgment of the Church if we know it will be in vain. Passivity is acceptable when the odds make action useless: "No one should lightly fabricate scruples for himself about this matter, for instance, regarding the binding force of the precept."[51]

For Volucer all correction, whether of republic, church, or individual, should take place "in moderation." Only when sins become public and endanger religion is one obliged to speak out openly against them. This is the case when matters of faith are challenged "because of a depraved mind, from excessive fear of an errant power" (Gl 9.223). Here Monicus remarks: "I fear that this consideration touches our wayfarer, with his prosecution in the cause of faith, now before the episcopal judge, now in the presence of the holy general council."[52]

The poem that follows this section sums up Gerson's reaction to the ills of the world. We are to be content with what God calls us to be and not greedily seek new positions: "Be self-sufficient/ Let no one else's lot upset you."[53] Gerson was close to Boethius and to Stoic *apatheia,* but this did not mean lack of care or concern for what was going on around him.[54] In the next prose section, Volucer clarifies the matter by saying that someone who lives in solitude can profit others, "simply by living well." The person who is separated from others can be useful to them through prayer, and the solitary "prays more freely than the person who is busy" (224).

At the same time, we are not to rage against those who do evil (Ps 32:1). We are to live our own lives as well as possible: What matters is friendship with God, who is loved no matter what. Theology thus reaches beyond philosophy and reveals a God whose punishments we must accept: "We are used to smiling when boys are beaten and cry out . . . but we ourselves groan like grown-up little boys, we burn, we complain at the slightest blow from God."[55] God teaches us by beating us. In this way he cleanses and restores us. He forces those invited to enter the wedding feast, tearing off the garments of one guest, breaking another person's bones, taking out this person's eye, and crippling another: "You will be in tribulation and temptation: this is the common lot of all who live" (227).

This is the God of Job, who gives and takes away all good things, without any explanation. Here is the reverse side of Gerson's search for a loving, tender God: his experience of a God whose ways are harsh and inexplicable. The whole history of Christianity has been an attempt to reconcile the unbounded glory of God with the tenderness of Christ's love. Gerson at this time felt closer to a God who beats us and breaks our bones than to one who embraces us with his warmth. And so he could speak to the Lord: "Rip my clothing, drag me off/ At last as you wish, until I belong to you" (Gl 4.108). Long before John Donne's "Batter my heart," Gerson expressed a similar desire to be taken by God.

In such passages I read the *Consolation of Theology* as a highly autobiographical work.[56] Behind its intellectual and rhetorical framework, Gerson showed who he was in terms of what he had lived through. In the opening of the fourth book, Monicus asks Volucer whether "our wayfarer" did not regret his actions in France and at the council, "in writing of the power of the council, now concerning matters of faith, especially where he denounced a homicide committed without legitimate authority and its consequences" (Gl 9.228).

Volucer makes it clear that Gerson acted rightly in the past. He need have no scruples: "For he is not doubtful, but most certain, that the very thing which he pursued was catholic truth . . . and so he judges himself firmly obliged to believe and by no means doubt about the knowledge and understanding of divine precepts."[57] General belief is not enough. What is required is particular adhesion to God's commands, one more reference to declarations by the duke of Burgundy that he adhered to the faith of his fathers.[58]

The poem that follows deals, appropriately, with the ten commandments (Gl 4.112). The next prose section continues this theme. Volucer's moral exhortation describes in precise terms Gerson's reaction in 1413, after his earlier attempt to reconcile the warring factions at the French court: "We should not abandon the truth of life or of doctrine or justice while we are sure that it would be endangered by our silence and that the opposite error would be reinforced, for the rule is that error not opposed is approved."[59] Monicus, however, is not completely satisfied with this maxim. He asks whether "defense of catholic truth" in some cases does more harm than good. We have Christ's command that we are not to give what is holy to dogs (Mt 7:6). Monicus asks Volucer what the wayfarer does in such matters, when action seems pointless. The answer is that he accuses himself and so hands himself over to the grace of God, which "saves those who condemn themselves" (233). The passage concludes with a poem of hope.

The dialogue does not end here, but we can see by now Gerson's manner of representing different parts of his mind as teacher and student or as confident reason and impatient enquirer. Gerson returned time and again to questions concerning his actions or lack of action. At the same time he warned against expecting God to reward us for our efforts. We have to entrust ourselves to the Lord and expect nothing in return.

The *Consolation* condemns those whom Gerson saw as identifying faith in God with sentiment and emotion. One does not have to feel the presence and activity of God. The sense of sweetness (*suavitas*) of which some speak is not necessary (235). What matters is moral certitude, gained through the teaching of others and from experience (236). Moral principles are already visible in nature but were written with God's own finger "on stone tablets for imperishable memory," and then repeated a third time in the Gospels (237). Unfortunately a large number of those who claim to be professors of theology are so ignorant that they cannot learn from experience. They are caught up in other cares (237–38).

Toward the end of the *Consolation* Theology herself speaks, summarizing the themes of the work and returning to martyrdom for the sake of truth, a leitmotif of the work (240–44). Gerson regarded his own theology as one of grace and divine will, where human efforts are secondary. Yet, while he appealed to a merciful God who will provide consolation, he did not abandon his belief in doing whatever is humanly possible. In reconciling ourselves with his will, we show patience and find peace: *serenatio conscientiae* (244).

The work can be read solely as theology, but it also makes an existential statement. In reviewing his own belief, Gerson reconciled himself with the events of his life. He accepted his defeats at the Council of Constance without dismissing his efforts there to make changes in the Church. The *Consolatio,* just as the *Dialogus apologeticus,* is an apology for Gerson's attack on the justification of tyrannicide. It does so by placing his thoughts and actions in the larger context of God's will.

What might have ended in quietism instead asserts the necessity of affective involvement in order to complete intellectual understanding. As Volucer concludes: "We will now try to turn into affectivity (*in affectu*) what we for four days have discussed in terms of intellectuality (*per intellectum;* 244). Prayer, the solitary life, and a distance from events have replaced preaching, community living, and a *vita activa.* Gerson did not throw in the towel and walk away in disgust. However severely wounded, he was still involved.

Returning to Pastoral Concerns

The first indication of Gerson's continued attachment to the world around him comes a little more than a year after his arrival in Lyon. He wrote about contracts and obligations, at the request of a Carthusian community which had asked to what extent it could engage in purchases and sales.[60] He replied that they could do so, but by drawing up contracts that can be carried out in a proper way. Here as in so much else, the individual or the community must do its best, in this case to avoid abuses: *dum facit quod in se est ad preclusionem abusuum* (Gl 9.391).

The problem is that a financial agreement can hide the giving or taking of interest and thus be seen as usury. The Church provides guidance, "and where the pope fails, the general council has the supreme judgment." In church life, usury is forbidden, but in secular society some forms of usurious contracts may be permitted. As with the practice of prostitution, it is not approved but it is not to be punished either (393).

Gerson's discussion here assumes a wise civil *legislator.* The term may owe something to Marsilius of Padua's concept of a *legislator humanus* as supreme guide in human affairs.[61] Both dreamt of a better society, but Gerson gave the Church much more freedom than Marsilius would have done. At the same time,

Gerson believed that life would be better if prices were fixed so that people knew exactly how much to pay for the wine or cheese they bought: "Then the price would be given which was desired; he who refused [to do so] would go away without any quarrelling" (395).

From here Gerson turned to financial arrangements to support churchmen. Each person has the right to use the property he holds as if it were his own, and thus acquire an income from it. Gerson did not condone usury, which still meant taking any interest at all.[62] He did, however, approve that church properties be used to provide a regular income for clerics.

In the second part of the treatise, Gerson dealt with the concrete question submitted to him: a community has a grant of a piece of land from its lord in return for a fixed payment on whatever was sold as the produce of this land. For every pound earned, the lord was to be given two pennies. Beyond that payment, the community had the right to sell the fixed annual income at a discount to others and later to buy it back. A certain monastery bought the right from the community to receive a hundred florins annually from the land. This monastery paid two thousand florins in cash. The question was if this contract was usurious or in any other manner illegal.

Gerson responded that such a contract was not the same as a loan, and so interest was not being paid on what had been borrowed (397–98). But usury also is not present when money is handed over to someone else as a loan and there is a clause that if it is not repaid in time, there will be a penalty fee. Such a contract can be made with good intention and within the limits of charity. A product can also be sold on credit for a higher price than one would sell it for ready cash, so long as the intention is to help one's neighbor, not to harm him (398–99).

Gerson indicated here that it is acceptable to make a profit on exchanges of goods or property. In matters of doubt, where church authorities might have divergent opinions, the person or institution involved can choose either side! The view of one doctor of theology should not be decisive, if several theologians would allow a different course of action (402–3). More importantly, the Church respects what is customary. When laws or constitutions, even ecclesiastical ones, are forgotten or not generally observed, they do not have "the force of obligation" but are, as it were, "abolished through non-use or an opposing custom" (*vim obligationis, tamquam abolitae per non usum vel consuetudinem oppositam*, 404–5).

Gerson warned against the pope's or the Church's attempt to invalidate "useful laws for the distribution of such goods" (406). Admitting that he may be going against canon law, he gave the pope the benefit of the doubt but also asked that he be flexible. Church authorities were assumed to be reasonable and temperate and would not stand in the way of practices that benefited both sides in a contract.

What mattered was to avoid greed, as in the case of a person who on a Palm Sunday felt "the bite of avarice" (408). He put himself before the crucifix and cried out his need to the Lord. His appeal was not in vain, for "he soon felt the burden of avarice lifting from his heart." This anecdote could be from personal experience or from the confessional. Whatever the case, Gerson gave some leeway to human needs and desire for economic security but also set limitations.

The discussion on contracts and usury turned into a much broader consideration of ecclesiastical wealth, donations, and simony. Gerson referred to relevant sayings of his late teacher Pierre d'Ailly. One of them was that in human affairs contracts are natural and necessary, and so they should not be restricted or reduced to "the crime of usury" (*ad usurariam pravitatem*; 409). Gerson recalled how the Council of Constance had tried to remove simony, at the same time as usury, as being the worst diseases in the Church. Everyone wanted to get rid of them, but extreme measures could end up eliminating all endowments and offerings to the Church.

Gerson reviewed papal decisions contained in the Decretals and statements of theologians like Thomas Aquinas, "in so far as I have their books and can see them," an indication that his new situation in Lyon was not ideal for checking references (418). He also mentioned deliberations at the Council of Constance and added, perhaps humorously, that the opinions of "living doctors do not have less authority in doctrinally examining Sacred Scripture or interpreting laws than do dead ones" (420). He concluded with an appeal for independence of mind:

> It is thus clear that some people have too much humility or vanity. When they are asked to say what they think about a moral case, they immediately flee to one claim upon another, and to glosses on glosses. Sometimes they even dismiss the texts or universal principles which should provide a resolution. They say: "This [authority] says this, another that, yet another approves the one, and another agrees with this one. To all these it can rightly be said: Do not say what the others have written but what you yourself say or think!
>
> *Dic non quod alii scripserunt, sed quid tu ipse dicis vel sentis.* (420)

Gerson here challenged the technique of scholastic discourse, with its dependence on the accumulated weight of authorities. He had experienced a period in church history and a general council where normal rules of canon law were broken and experts had to be disregarded (421). He chose not to develop this approach further but insisted that he was not speaking rashly (*temerarie*).

The treatise ends with a condemnation of usury, and yet Gerson had approved of situations in which forms of interest or at least of profit-taking could be acceptable, even within church institutions. The treatise shows Gerson's continuing independence of mind in seeking viable solutions to questions of practical morality. He could have limited himself to canon law; instead he opened the question to larger issues of behavior and economic need. At the same time, he recommended himself and his fellow theologians as experts who could consider individual situations in light of universal ethical practices based on charity, not greed.

Also in 1421, Gerson preached the one sermon we have from this period of his life, probably at a synod before the archbishop of Lyon: *Redde quod debes* (Render what you owe; Gl 5.487–93). He spoke of the bishop's obligation to provide schools for boys and parish priests, thus anticipating the much more specific requirement at the Council of Trent for seminaries to train priests. He did not go into detail but referred to earlier treatises he had written. During these years, he often repeated himself. His writings are replete with references to earlier works.

Parish priests should have enough to live on, so it is wrong that the income from tithes often goes to other churchmen, while pastors themselves "are left naked" (491). At the same time, priests should be present in their parishes to administer the sacraments and preach to the people. On the subject of preaching, Gerson issued several warnings about discretion. Sermons, for example, should not openly attack the status of the lord, whether ecclesiastical or temporal; also the status of churchmen as such should not be undermined. The people are not to be incited to revolt.[63] Preaching to the laity against priests with concubines would lead people to miss mass and to the sacraments not being distributed.

Gerson had shown in earlier treatises that he could be tough on priests who live openly with their mistresses, but he did not want to be a firebrand.[64] The same was the case with condemnations of women who dress lavishly. Gerson praised what he heard the city of Nuremberg did to regulate the amount of money paid for garments (493). But he did not think sermons could change the ways of the fashion-conscious. The same was the case with verbal attacks on merchants. They should be encouraged to set a fixed price on their wares, but public sermons were not the right context for correcting the misbehavior of such people.

Gerson made a clear distinction between the learned, who could be excoriated in harsh language for their behavior, and the *gens simples,* who might misunderstand such language. Years before, he had complained how even a relatively learned audience had distorted one of his crucial sermons on papal power.[65] There was all the more reason to be cautious with uneducated people.

Another perennial concern was the laity's superstitions. A letter-treatise from March 1421 questions beliefs connected with certain days, especially the Feast of the Holy Innocents (28 December). The stars cannot take away human free will, Gerson wrote (Gl 2.228). Also we cannot blame demons for our misfortunes. Human unhappiness is our own fault. Those who belong to "the stupid crowd" often see causality on the basis of false premises, as when someone falls off a horse or drowns. Or they believe that if someone meets a cat on leaving home or one morning puts on his shirt on backwards or his right shoe on his left foot, then something bad is about to happen.

Such conceptions came from old wives' tales told by "foolish mothers and nurses" (230). Another cause is the pride of men who want to be known for their knowledge of wonders, or who try to deceive and ridicule others. Such people show off as schoolboys do. Another cause is the reading of "certain romances," books composed in French "of which the greatest part is fiction."[66] Gerson referred to a prince of his time who was urged to seek the counsel of the learned to give up his superstitions. The man refused to let himself be dissuaded, until he came to a sudden death and "will continue in eternal torments" (231).

Gerson denigrated the panoply of folk beliefs that was to provide fertile soil for clerical reaction and, from the end of the fifteenth century, set off the great witchcraft craze. Glorieux's dossier, listing writings on the subject of superstition, shows how much he was preoccupied with it during his last years (Gl10.73–76).

Even if his view was largely negative, Gerson here showed interest in the everyday lives and religious beliefs of ordinary people. It is likely that he was answering questions referred to him by the archbishop or by other members of the Lyon clergy. Another work showing his continuing involvement in church affairs is the brief treatise *De potestate absolvendi et peccatorum reservatione*, a plea for giving curates the authority to grant absolution for most sins (Gl 9.421–23). As Thomas Tentler has shown in his central book on confession during this period, Gerson in his Latin writings opposed the widespread practice of reserving many types of sin, especially those involving sexual behavior, so that only bishops or their officials could grant absolution for them.[67]

Gerson noted that he completed this work on 23 March 1422 and added that it remained *sub correctione* (Gl 10.423). He assumed that he might return to it later and adjust his statements according to further advice he might get. Even though most of the time he seems to have remained in the cloister of Saint Paul, he was responsive to the ecclesiastical world around him. In August 1423, at the request of his patron and benefactor the archbishop of Lyon, he completed a treatise *De nobilitate* (Gl 9.476–99). After treating the meaning of nobility, he initiated a dialogue between disciple and master. The question under discussion was whether it was legitimate to reserve canonries at the cathedral of Lyon for the successors of the noble families that had endowed the prebends.

Such an arrangement, replied the dialogue's *Magister*, was not only legitimate but also praiseworthy. When nobles became canons, they practiced humility in a way they otherwise would not have done (485–86). As canons they had to reach out to the poor and destitute and carry out functions in accord with the Church's practice. If nobles thereby learned to imitate Christ, venerate the Church, and show humility, then church foundations would do well to provide for representation of a certain number of noble families.

Gerson here not only supported his benefactor the archbishop but also backed the customs of a local church against what he may have seen as an oppressive universalism in canon law. In Gerson's dialogue the disciple points to a canon issued by Pope Gregory IX (1227–1241), according to which birth was not to be a criterion for being admitted to a prebend. The master answers that in spite of his respect for Gregory, it was necessary to understand the precise historical background for his pronouncement, which dealt with the situation of the church of Strasbourg (491–92).

The disciple replies by pointing to the scriptural foundation of Gregory's statement: There is no preference of persons with God (Rom 2:11). He quotes Paul (Gal 3:28): in Christ there is no longer male and female, gentile or Jew. We are all one. The master answers that canon law has to distinguish among different types of persons, as with women, slaves, the illegitimate, children, and others who cannot be admitted to church office (492). The text used by Gregory applies only to their salvation. It does not preclude exclusive access by nobles to some canonries.

Such deliberations gave Gerson an opportunity to repeat general principles that guided him after Constance. If a canon has no application to actual practice, then it can lose its validity. "Who does not see that in some cases decretals and decrees . . . are abolished because of non-usage?" (*per non usum*; 495) Secondly the pope does not have absolute authority over the Church. The church of Lyon has its own customs, and the pope cannot say, "Thus I wish, thus I order, let my will be the reason" (496).

The treatise ends with the text of a decree from the dauphin, the future Charles VII, as regent for his father. It confirms that the church of Lyon had fifty-seven prebends, of which thirty-two were to be given to nobles alone. The dauphin pointed out that the king's uncle, the duke of Berry, had been personally received as a canon of the church of Lyon.[68]

There could be no better indication that Gerson was in harmony with widespread efforts to defend the existence of a gallican church, just as the period also contributed to the growth of an *ecclesia anglicana*.[69] His intention, however, was not to increase the power of the king to decide matters in the churches of France. Gerson's goal was to ensure respect for local traditions and customs, so long as they conformed to the principles found in the Gospels. Scripture was the guide, not canon law. As the disciple said to his master in *De nobilitate:* "You have known the Scriptures from infancy."[70]

A final indication of Gerson's continuing interest during these years in church affairs is his *De sollicitudine ecclesiasticorum* (On the cares of churchmen; 434–58). He posed a number of questions about the obligations of clerics and monks to reciprocate for the temporal goods given them for masses and other services, "as is the common practice" (*usus communis*; 434). He emphasized individual circumstances. It is impossible to give rules that have no exceptions. We are not to go overboard in our search for moral probity: *ne quid nimis* in the classical tag, nothing too much (440). The cleric or church institution which has received a gift should be eager to pay its debt to its benefactor.

Church institutions are to fulfill their obligations, unless a dispensation is received. But such obligations are to take into consideration the circumstances: a promise to say a daily requiem mass, for example, cannot be enforced on Christmas, Easter, or Pentecost. When parishioners arrive to hear mass, "I think that none will say that a requiem is then to be sung" (443). The suggestion of mourning for a dead benefactor in the midst of a joyful solemnity indicates once again that Gerson now allowed himself ironic distance and perhaps even a smile.

He reviewed with great care the possible intentions and requirements of a donor, and the responses and limitations of the church benefiting from the gift. "What do you wish then for yourself, brother, in the individual Mass for you? Do you answer, 'I want it to be all mine'?" Such a position would be absurd, limiting the merit gained by the mass to the benefactor and excluding the priest and everyone else participating or being mentioned in the prayers offered there (445). Sometimes it is actually better for the recipient not even to think about the donor: Gerson, with his knowledge of the *Lives of the Fathers,* recalled the dour Arsenius who, when asked by a noble matron to remember her, said she should ask God to erase from his mind any memory of the woman.[71]

The priest or church receiving temporalities for spiritual services should carefully consider the obligations assumed (450). The burden can at first be tolerable but because of continual repetition become unbearable. We are reminded here of how R. W. Southern described this age in terms of inflation.[72] Everything increased, including the requirements for ensuring salvation. Wealthy people looked out for themselves by endowing local churches. The result was, as Gerson saw it, the growth of a vast tangle of obligations for chapters and monasteries to provide daily memorials for the living and the dead.

Gerson criticized what he saw as people's eagerness to found or expand religious houses. These efforts required financial investments and could involve greed on the part of the religious to gain new incomes (450). Religious needed to attract a growing number of benefactors, and this concern threatened the interior life of monastic and other church foundations. But as we might expect, his solution was not a radical one: gifts should be received in moderation, and communities should limit themselves in terms of their numbers, their material holdings, and their religious obligations.

Withdrawing into a Hermit's Life

By the spring of 1423, when Jean the Celestine wrote his loving portrait of his brother's life at Lyon, Gerson had found the pattern of living that would fill his remaining days. His intellectual contacts became more and more limited to monks, especially Celestines and Carthusians. Already in October of the previous year, he had written a long letter on monastic life to a monk of the Grande Chartreuse, William Minaud, a medical doctor whom Gerson praised for leaving his profession and joining the order. The letter-treatise is known as *De religionis perfectione et moderamine* (On the Perfection and Moderation of the Religious Life; Gl 2.232–45).

Gerson replied to three questions: whether a prayer or other spiritual exercise is to be criticized if it weakens bodily strength; if because of physical weakness one can live less ascetically than one's monastic order prescribes; if the solitary ought to say the canonical hours aloud or if it is sufficient to pray them silently in his heart.

These specific queries Gerson answered first with a general statement. The Christian religion, he began, is the way to salvation, so it is enough for us to follow Christ, our abbot (233). Every Christian thus belongs to this religious order, but the term is normally restricted to the religious orders whose members take the triple vow of poverty, chastity, and obedience. Gerson accepted a hierarchy among various orders or ways of life within the Church. One is more perfect than another to the degree that it helps getting close to the love of God and increases charity. Religious orders which dispose their practitioners to the contemplative life are to be called more perfect (234).

Gerson expresses here, as in other writings after Constance, a new receptiveness toward monastic life. His earlier reservations are gone, even though he warns his correspondent that just being a member of the Carthusians does not in itself mean a state of perfection (235). People are different and their differences need to be taken into consideration: "For what are members of religious orders except men?" (239). They should exercise zeal with discretion, in the saying of Bernard, and keep pride in check, by obeying their superiors, as Anthony the Great once exhorted.[73] When brothers have problems, as when they are ill, they can seek dispensation from the requirements of their religious order. They are not to complain about who gets permission and who is denied it. The superior is to avoid too much severity, especially if it endangers physical health, a consideration Gerson earlier showed in warning his Celestine brothers against ascetic excesses (240).

The first query has thus been answered: religious observances that drain physical strength are to be kept in check. In the second question, he found it acceptable to provide dispensations, as in giving more food to a brother who felt he needed it. This practice, he wrote, was especially viable in the Carthusian life, with brothers eating alone in their cells. An individual dispensation should not lead to complaints by other brothers (242).

As for the question concerning vocal or silent prayer, it was best to say prayers aloud or at least in opening the mouth slightly. Turning to the tears that can come in prayer, he warns that they can be a distraction. The person who weeps all the time can become incapacitated: "There is, I confess, in tears, something sweet and agreeable," but such sweetness could be a danger: flee as much as you can from such tears, for "the snake hides in the grass."[74]

"I do not want you to commit yourself to yourself alone." A life in a religious community is not exclusively intended for cultivating one's religious devotion. Self-love (*amor proprius*) can take over, and so we have to trust our superior's judgment (Gl 2.244). In a postscript Gerson observed that he had answered William's queries "more fully than was necessary," especially in dealing with tears. He also added that vocal prayer was desirable in part because it eliminates lack of occupation (*otium*), an indication of how Gerson was able to return to his writings and improve them.

Gerson certainly allowed himself very little *otium*, but he also would withdraw on occasion into what might be called "mystical affectivity." It has been argued that Gerson actually had a mystical experience on a given date in 1425, but his reference is obscure and ambiguous.[75] It is more likely that he experienced a gradual opening of his mind and heart to the presence of God, enabling him to write in a more immediate and less academic way about his perceptions. We can see this development, for example, in treatises on "The song of the heart," composed in the mid-1420s.[76] These are among the least known of Gerson's works, for their contents are a mixture of musical and theological learning hardly conceivable today. But for Gerson it was a natural step to reflect on how the language of the Psalms and the worship of the Lord through song expressed an interior music that he came to hear ever more clearly.

In writing *De canticorum originali ratione* (On the original basis of song), Gerson even compares song with friendship, combining Aristotle's definition in his *Politics* with the words of Paul, "Who clings to God is one spirit" (1 Cor 6:17; Gl 9.526). In friendship between human beings, the one person does not become the other, but through mutual conversation, friends can share "the hidden thoughts and passions of their hearts, their counsels and loves" (527). Gerson the solitary cleric with his skepticism about close human bonds now allowed himself to celebrate them!

He sought to show in these treatises that the meaning of human life resides in the praise of God and that song, especially religious chant, is central to expressing this praise. From a reflection on the sounds made by the musical instruments mentioned in the Psalms (532–35), he turned to the music that comes from the heart and reaches the mind on the threshold of mystical experience like "a certain spark flying above and flashing into eternal things" (537).

Mystical theology and song are thus connected. For a moment Gerson even gives a glimpse of his own interior life: "Yet it seemed to me sometimes meditating in the secret cubicle of my heart at night, with a sense of the present calamity all around me, that there could arise what seemed like a divine nuptial song. Here was shown a marriage of spirit and soul, especially in Christ. Again there was another spiritual marriage, of divine wisdom joined with the created spirit in the divine image, as seemed most evident in the spirit of Mary rejoicing" (546). This statement opens a reflection on the language of the Song of Songs, a work whose powerful language he had long kept at a distance. But in a way he was now returning to his student days, when he wrote on the theme of the marriage of the theologian and wisdom.[77] He seemed especially drawn to the opening passage, "He will kiss me with the kiss of his mouth," which he linked with the even more sensual verse: "Who will give you to me as my brother sucking the breasts of my mother, and I shall find you alone outside and now no one will despise me?" (Song 8:1; 552).

Gerson was thinking of composing his own commentary on the Song. He mentioned other commentators, but so far he had not found an interpretation in terms of the priest's marriage with the Church as his beloved (553). What he had in mind was a meeting of contemplative with intellectual life, and for this purpose he turned again to Possidius's *Life of Augustine,* this time for a description of how to combine tears with learning.[78]

Gerson's use of a vast array of sources, personal reminiscences, reflections on music, philosophy and theology deserves further analysis. However difficult it may be to fathom his true meaning, the treatise sheds light on how he interpreted his life. In one anecdote he tells of two "celebrated doctors in theology" he had known (568) who considered entering a religious order but conceded that because of age they could not accept the physical discipline of such a life. When they sought to compensate by "studying, teaching and meditation," they were told that these activities were not the same as "the institutes of religion."

Gerson had long been both attracted and repelled by the requirements of monastic asceticism. He had felt his vocation was not here, yet his praise of song, especially the routine of the monks' daily praise to the Lord, shows his abiding fascination. As he wrote to the dauphin's teacher in a letter accompanying a copy of this work, what is better than to offer a song to God for our salvation? (Gl 2.250).

Nevertheless, Gerson refused even to pay a visit to the monks whose life he praised so highly. In April 1424, he wrote to Oswald of Corda, vicar of the Grande Chartreuse, that he could not oblige his correspondent with a face-to-face visit.[79] It was more important, Gerson said, to share the spirit. He spoke of his own weakness (*fragilitatis*) but did not mention any specific illness (251). Instead he sent some of his writings and asked that the Carthusians edit and copy them.

In looking at the many letters of Gerson's last years, it is apparent how he tried to accomplish as much as possible in the briefest time. At the end of a letter-treatise on Christ's reception of humanity, he added that he had written it on 18

September 1426, "from morning until almost midday."[80] Was he telling his correspondent how much he had been able to write in under six hours? Similarly to his brother Jean the Celestine, he claimed he had composed his letter "this Wednesday morning in Lyon in a shorter period of time than it would have taken to go to you [at the Celestine house in Lyon] and to return" (247). Then, to avoid seeming to boast, he added, "Would that it be more fruitful [than a visit would have been]."

In the same letter Gerson laments that he scarcely ever engaged in conversation without afterwards regretting something he had said. He would reproach himself: "I do not know how I helped the other [person], but I see in myself what I obstructed." It was best to remain inside oneself. "And if advice is to be given, I prefer to reply with a written statement rather than with the tongue." Such a procedure was "more secure" (246). In this case the danger was not of wasting time but of avoiding foolish statements and being correctly understood. Silence and physical separation were best.

Though he rejected physical presence, Gerson remained a faithful correspondent, dealing with almost every imaginable question of conscience. He considered heretical writings (259–63), the books a monk should read (275–76), and especially the substance of monastic life. In several letters he returned to the case of a professed brother at the Grande Chartreuse who engaged in excessive penances and abstinence.[81]

Oswald of Corda, a resident at this monastery, was apparently Gerson's main correspondent during his last years. In a single letter, Gerson replied to his questions about the value of prayer, rightness of intention, and the occupation of the mind during the divine office (285–89). Gerson's answers may not always have pleased Oswald. The Carthusian had asked about pastoral care by monks for their lay workmen who lived near isolated monasteries at a great distance to parish churches. Gerson, who never forgot he was a secular priest, replied that contemplative monks had no business taking on the care of souls (292). But he did allow the monks to make use of Sundays and feast days, when laymen who owed them money would have been present, to collect debts (299–300). The monks could also hire laborers on such days by taking advantage of an occasion when people gathered. The brothers could also buy eggs, cheese, fish, and other items brought to them, but Gerson added it was best for the monks to choose "certain and licit hours" for such transactions. In general Gerson emphasized respect for local customs and practices (*usus patriae seu dyocesis*; 301).

There are other cases of conscience. A Carthusian brother who had not made his final profession and who for fifteen years had not been able to overcome the habit of masturbation was still to be given a chance to alter his ways (298–99). The delinquent should be absolved "in a spirit of gentleness" and be admitted to communion. Gerson remembered that he had written before on the subject, *sed apud me non habeo*: he no longer had the treatise with him. In these last years he probably only had access to a fraction of what he had written throughout his life. It must have been frustrating to remember that he had already dealt with a subject and not have the text available to him. Certainly here, with an individual case, Gerson showed himself to be much more the consoling doctor than when he had encouraged confessors to extract details about sexual behavior from their penitents (Gl 8.71). In another letter he told Oswald that his prior should not hesitate to grant dispensations to priest monks subject to nocturnal emissions. Also here he could refer to an earlier work, concerning the priest's worthiness to celebrate the mass (Gl 2.312–13).

In at least one case Gerson joked with his correspondent when he repeated a maxim about the contemplative life he had heard from a colleague. Its two "wings" or supports according to this doctor were "to sleep well and to eat well" (307). Gerson recalled how on hearing the phrase, "I laughed and agreed" (*Mox arrisi et consensi*). The colleague may have been poking fun at all the "wings of contemplation" Gerson had described in his *Practical Mystical Theology*, but he could take a joke and appreciate the moral: excessive sleeping and eating are an impediment to the contemplative life. But so is excessive lack of food and sleep.

Gerson's appreciation of the Carthusians comes across most directly in his *De laude scriptorum* (In praise of copyists), probably from April 1423 (Gl 9.423–34). A monk of La Grande Chartreuse had asked him if it was permitted to copy books of devotion on feast days. As before, Gerson responded to a specific question with a general statement before targeting the matter itself.

In giving praise to the lives of copyists, Gerson also mentions an order of brothers in Holland who follow the Rule of Saint Augustine, canons regular, thus showing his knowledge of one branch of what we call the *Devotio moderna* (426). Such copyists preached and prayed through their work. Each of us should do what we can (*faciendo quod in se est*). Monks cannot excuse themselves from copying books on the basis of ignorance of the technique: "Let them learn, let them learn, and they will not be embarrassed or despair" (427). Gerson quoted from Vergil (*Labor omnia vincit*)[82] and added the French saying "necessity makes old women run" (*besoin faict vielles trotter*). He believed that each human being has a duty to make use of his or her abilities. Always pushing himself to the limits of physical, intellectual, and spiritual performance, Gerson asked others to do the same. The message of the *Consolation of Theology*, to look for the gift of God's grace, has been complemented by the demand to sweat out one's salvation.

For Gerson the copyist was central in the life of the Church. He recalls, again looking to Possidius, the dying Augustine who asked his brothers to look after their church library "with great devotion, since he knew it was a great treasure."[83] Tyrants, by contrast, have no respect for books. Gerson cites incidents from the Old Testament as well as recent events in France, when the king's library had suffered losses (430). He quotes in French and translated to Latin what he called a common proverb: "Good books make good clerics." Not only clerics but also "lay persons and women" were meant to have books. And so Gerson favored translations of devotional books into the vernacular (432).

With such praise of books and their copyists, it is not surprising that Gerson answered the treatise's initial question with a declaration that there was no reason to refrain from writing books on feast days and Sundays. Not only monasteries but universities and collegial churches, especially cathedrals, should employ scribes "who will be excused from other tasks and be properly paid" (433–34). Even if inadequately compensated, such writers should still work in order to avoid lack of occupation, "the teacher of all vices" (434).

In spite of Gerson's professed awareness that Hussites and necromancers also copied books to spread their views, he believed it was worthwhile to take the risk and disseminate writings on almost all subjects. The only exception remained the complete text of Scripture itself, where he held to the standard medieval ecclesiastical view that lay people could not fathom the complexities and contradictions within the Bible (432).

Here as in other treatises from after 1421, Gerson was summarizing his own experience. In 1426, when he distributed his work on the books a monk should read, Gerson used the occasion to provide an intellectual and spiritual review of his life.[84] He emphasized the centrality of mystical theology and recommended the writings of various fathers, especially those of Bonaventure. He had read, reread, and meditated on such works for more than thirty years. He knew some of them almost by heart: "And behold in this time, in this leisure . . . I have scarcely begun to taste them." The more often he had returned to these works, the more they pleased him with their freshness. He quoted from Horace's *Ars poetica* that what is repeated ten times will please, but then, in his typical manner, he added a reference to Ecclesiasticus (24:29): "They who eat of me will hunger for more, and those who drink of me will still be thirsty."[85] One can never be completely satiated with spiritual writings.

Such passages, so balanced and clear, can make Gerson's last years sound idyllic. At the same time, however, he distanced himself more and more from the pious women who earlier had inspired him. In his *On the Examination of Teachings,* he deals for a third time with *discretio spirituum,* the discernment of spirits (458–75). As before he investigates claims by both men and women that they had received special revelations from God. But this time Gerson showed more reserve than ever toward women: "Every teaching of women, especially in an authoritative manner in word or writing (*maxime solemnis verbo seu scripto*), is to be considered suspect," unless it has been first investigated according to six criteria that Gerson set forward (468). Women were less dependable than men because they were "easier to seduce, and more stubborn as seducers." Gerson claimed that he could write a "huge book" if he brought together all the revelations, especially of women, he had heard (474). He thanks God for saving him from being seduced by such things even though he once, "through the narrative of some persons of outstanding reputation," had been close to accepting the revelations of Ermine of Reims. But he had moderated his response to her.[86]

There is nothing specific here about Gerson's dealings with the case of Birgitta of Vadstena. There is no indication he regretted his decision not to oppose the council's acceptance of her sanctity. But he was having second thoughts about holy women in general and retreated from his earlier interest in peering into the minds and hearts of visionary women to understand what they were saying.[87] At the end of the treatise, however, is a statement much more in character with his earlier work. After pages of warnings about listening only to "approved and learned doctors in both theology, scholastic and mystical," he said it was necessary that there be "the greatest effort to abandon any kind of effort" (*maxima sit industria deserere quamlibet industriam*; 475). The individual must surrender totally "to the magisterium of the Holy Spirit with all his faith, all his hope, all his love, all his devotion." Gerson thus deconstructed his own exhortation to listen only to recognized authorities and to be suspicious of individual religious experience. In the end, control is to be abandoned to the Holy Spirit, a requirement that covers both men and women, the learned and the unschooled.

Preparing for the Last Journey

The Gerson who was skeptical of women's revelations was the same man who wrote hundreds of pages praising Mary in his commentary on the *Magnificat,* his longest work (Gl 8.163–534). This product of his last years is part of an almost feverish period of literary production. "Devotion is sufficient for salvation in having nothing of philosophy or speculative scholastic theology," he wrote, undermining his own authority as professor of theology (303). Later, in the midst of a long discussion on the number and attributes of angels, he paused:

> This kind of studious pursuit can be fitting for theologians, but let curiosity cease in those who ought more fully to study devotion rather than subtle speculation. . . . Let us therefore seek more to live well than to dispute well.
>
> *Studeamus igitur plus bene vivere quam disputare.* (373–74)

Gerson did not discard decades of learning, but he put scholastic discourse in its proper place in Christian life. At the same time he returned to his childhood faith to show what really mattered. Explaining how we are all in the custody of a guardian angel, he added:

> I speak from experience. To a certain child a father placed himself up against the wall in the manner of the crucified and said, "See, my son: in this way your God was crucified and died. He who made you and saved you." This first image has remained, fixed in the memory of that age, its reflection still clear in that soul. It remains into old age and senility, growing with the increase of years. Blessed is that good father, for the day of the Exaltation of the Holy Cross [14 September] was the day of his death, when Christ went to meet him, the Christ who was lifted up through the humiliation of the cross. (369–70)

Now in his mid-sixties, Gerson recalled what he had seen and heard so many decades earlier. The image of his father as a guardian angel became ever clearer as the years passed by. By showing him the image of Christ, his father had furthered the faith that became a point of departure for everything else in his son's life.

The affective spirituality Gerson emphasized more than ever during these last years bore fruit in his commentary on the Song of Songs, written as an expression of his love of the Carthusian Order and allowing him at last to review the contents of a book that had long been on his mind (565–639). Rather than following his earlier suggestion to interpret the Song in terms of the love between the individual priest and the Church, he looked more broadly at the text as an expression of divine and human love.

In his usual systematic way, Gerson worked through the entire text, not lingering as his predecessor Bernard had done, with the result that Bernard's famed eighty-six sermons deal only with the first few chapters. Gerson almost completed the task he set out for himself, but his brother Jean the Celestine who ended the work, told posterity of Gerson setting down his pen on the ninth of July. Three days later, on 12 July 1429, he died. In Jean's words, his brother's soul came to enjoy the embraces and kisses of the groom for which he had longed (639).

We have no information about Gerson's final illness, but there are a few indications in this last work that he looked forward to dying.[88] With the strength left to him, he wrote about Joan of Arc and praised her efforts to restore the French monarchy and nation. There are two versions, but only one of them is from Gerson's hand. It belongs to the spring of 1429.[89] He ended up saying something quite different from what he had written a few years earlier about distancing oneself from the visions of women. Now he conceded that a contemporary woman could speak with the voice of God, for he saw in her initial success a hope for the restoration of France.

As ever, our Gerson was split. He wanted to control all forms of human affectivity and spirituality, especially when they came from women. Yet, at times, he threw away control and cast himself into the waves of his needs and instincts. The image of Joan of Arc in the mind of the dying Gerson takes on special meaning if we look back on the child who was overwhelmed by the image of the cross his father made. Behind his caution was a longing for the embrace of love.

In the last years he settled his affairs with help from the Carthusians and the Celestines. He willed his library to the Celestine house at Avignon and made provisions that the books be kept in a locked room at the priory. The collection, however, was also to be made available to those who could profit from it (Gl 2.334). To the Carthusians he expressed thanks for remembering his dead friend André in their masses and for instituting a trental or series of thirty masses to be said after Gerson's death (313). Later he asked the brothers to give him an advance on this gift's spiritual benefits by offering some of the masses before his death (330–31).

Gerson thirsted for such assurances and assistance. All his life he had been genuinely afraid of eternal damnation, a fear that was perhaps a motor for his ceaseless productivity. In asking the Carthusians to space out their prayers for him, he called them his spiritual friends (*spiritales amici*; 330), the only time in his writings I find him using this term.

A final hint of friendship in his life is a payment of a hundred florins made by a canon Jean Pernant, for a "perpetual anniversary" mass to be held in the church of Saint Paul on 12 July in memory not only of Jean Gerson but also of Gerson's companion Jacques de Cérisy, here called master of arts and canon of that church.[90] The endowment is a memorial to a friendship among three clerics.

Gerson can be interpreted and understood in many different ways, depending on how one reads him and what one reads of him. In trying to consider his life and work as a whole, I think of him neither as a defeated man, nor as a quietist nor as a misogynist. He was fair and sober in calling himself a foreigner and a pilgrim, for throughout his life he always felt (and often was) an outsider in terms of the people around him. In the last years at Lyon, however, he seems to have lived to a large degree in harmony with his surroundings, even if keeping a distance from them.

Gerson could have joined the Celestines or Carthusians and have done them honor, yet he remained the secular priest he was, giving advice and asking that rules should not be interpreted too strictly. He came to terms with his limited success in getting the defense of tyrannicide condemned and in restricting papal power. By the 1420s he knew the direction the Church was taking, but instead of withdrawing into silence or depression, he became active in other ways.

Gerson's vision of a church run by its bishops probably suited the archbishop of Lyon, and the two of them reached an understanding. The chancellor favored the prelate with some of his writings, while the archbishop must have provided financial and moral support. Having gained the political and material security he needed, Gerson could think, write, and pray until his dying day.

Jean Gerson's last years are a triumph of the human spirit over visible defeats and impotence to alter structures within medieval Christian society. He held to his convictions and did not allow himself to become cynical or bitter. Being loyal to his loves, Gerson withdrew into an almost Carthusian solitude. He never abandoned his scholastic learning, but united it with his religious affectivity. Like his beloved Carthusians, Jean Gerson worked hard and enriched the religious devotion and spirituality of his age.

Disappearing and Reappearing: The Legacy of Jean Gerson

The name Jean Gerson and the places associated with him have virtually disappeared from the European cultural map. One has to be a genuine Gerson aficionado to locate the site of the disappeared village of Gerson, to visit the nineteenth-century parish church next door at Barby, or to locate the cemetery at the other end of the village where the medieval church once stood.[1]

Similarly the Gerson tourist will be disappointed in coming to the great medieval center of ducal power at Bruges, with its Burg Square, where the collegial church of Saint Donatian once occupied a prominent place. Saint Donatian was demolished after the French Revolution, and the precinct today with its neo-gothic town hall reveals no trace of the great church going back to the Carolingians. Here Count Charles the Good was murdered, as we know from one of our most vivid twelfth-century chronicles.[2] Some decades ago there were important excavations of the church.[3] But the tourist who tries to find their location will have no success. No one has ever heard of the sign that once marked the site. The attendant at the nearby church of the Precious Blood guesses that it had to give way for what he calls "the car wash," an art installation in the midst of an artificial pond with a damp pontoon bridge.

In Paris the story of the disappearance of Jean Gerson continues. In the nineteenth century a statue of him was placed on the façade of the Sorbonne church, but today's tourist has to know exactly what to look for in order to locate it on the right of the entrance door to the church. The College of Navarre, the great educational institution that sheltered not only Gerson but also generations of scholars, is gone. Napoleon replaced it with the Ecole Polytéchnique, the military's engineering school, which, in turn, was replaced since 1990 by the Ministry of Research.

If we travel south to Lyon, we do find the church of Saint Paul, looking slightly out of place in a district known for its night clubs, and halfway hiding below the nineteenth-century suburban train station that took the church's name. The adjacent church of Saint Lawrence, which completed the cloister of Saint Paul and where Gerson was buried in 1429, also fell victim to the French Revolution and is completely gone.[4]

Gerson's grave was found in the seventeenth century and again in the nineteenth.[5] There is nothing to mark its location beneath the automobiles parked on the Place Gerson on the north side of the church of Saint Paul. Few townspeople have any idea about the identity of the curé represented in a statue next to a garage across from the west façade of the church. Gerson with his hand on the shoulder of a male pupil was thus commemorated in 1879 as teacher of children at Lyon, a tale that first appeared in the seventeenth century and has remained a fixed attribute of Gerson ever since.[6] Thus one of the greatest theologians and church reformers of the Middle Ages is either forgotten or remembered inaccurately, just as so much historical reminiscence is based on tales for tourists that sound good but have little to do with historical fact.

Perhaps one should not be so condescending about such memorials. What survives from the past is almost always accidental, the result of serendipity or tragedy, or a combination of both. The vanished village of Gerson bears witness to the movement of population in Europe and the world to city centers, while the demolished church of Saint Donatian reminds us of the bourgeois power that emerged from the French Revolution's challenge to royal and ecclesiastical prerogatives. As for the College of Navarre, its replacement by a military school for engineers points to nineteenth-century nation building, replacing the international university that preceded it.

In visiting places that once were part of Jean Gerson's everyday life, I have looked for the material foundation for his vision of reform in the Church and his search for union with God. Gerson's spirituality emerges from the institutions to which he dedicated himself. In his daily routines as canon of Notre Dame of Paris, Gerson expressed the kind of love of learning and desire for God the monk and scholar Jean Leclercq once described as characteristic of monastic life. Gerson's life was that of the scholastic, but his self-discipline and pursuit of affectivity were almost monastic.

Gerson's *Nachleben* includes not only physical memorials of his presence but also the transmission and reception of his writings. In this chapter I will briefly consider his intellectual and spiritual heritage. Afterwards I will turn to the aftermath of his reform program in the fifteenth and sixteenth centuries. This story does not end with the Protestant and Catholic Reformations of the sixteenth century. Gerson matters today not only for historians of Christian theology but also for historians and humanists in general. Anyone interested in the shaping of human identities can make use of Jean Gerson's heritage.

Inheriting the Works and Remembering the Man: Celestines and Carthusians

In November 1428 Gerson wrote to the Celestine brothers at Avignon: "I have decided in my old age to bestow a treasure [on you], in accord with my poverty, from salutary books."[7] The Celestine houses offered "some heavens and heavenly dwellings . . . especially because in your religious order I have had two professed brothers" (Gl 2.234). Gerson asked that the Celestines of Avignon look after his writings but also that they share them with others. He required that the collection be kept under lock and key "in a safe place specially made for this purpose." The letter is the closest we come to a testament for Gerson. It concludes with his exact age: "My sixty-sixth year will begin on 14 December, the Feast of Saint Nicaise of Reims, on which day I was born and reborn in the Lord Jesus Christ."

Gerson promised that the titles of his "books and treatises, both composed by myself and by others," would be affixed to a "special list."[8] In return he asked for the prayers of the Avignon brothers "for my final salvation." We do not have this list, and there is no trace of Gerson in the manuscript collection of the Avignon Celestines.[9] There is, however, a very incomplete list of Gerson's writings drawn up by his companion, Jacques de Cérisy, from April of 1429, a few months before his master's death.

The list is addressed to Oswald, monk of La Grande Chartreuse, "where already part has been placed" (*ubi jam pars posita est*; Gl 1.27). Part of what? Apparently part of the works of Gerson, which had been deposited at the Grande Chartreuse. The last paragraph of the description explains the elliptical opening:

> Finally the same Jean the chancellor wishes, asks and requests that without impediment or hesitation the venerable and most loved fathers and brothers of the Order of Celestines in Avignon hand over purely, simply and freely all and similar of his works which are with them, to the honored fathers and lords of the Grande Chartreuse, and that they be restored to them in good faith at their command at a given time and place. . . . And let the list, signed with [Gerson's] own hand, be a sufficient testimony for the same Celestines. (28)

Between November 1428 and April 1429 Gerson must have changed his mind about handing all his books over to the Celestines of Avignon. He was now asking them to turn most of them over to the Grande Chartreuse. Even in November, he had asked the Celestines that they should lend out his work. Now he was himself effectuating such a loan. His signed list was meant as a guarantee to the Celestines that they could get their Gerson manuscripts back.

The absence of Gerson manuscripts at Avignon indicates that the Grande Chartreuse may have kept the loan permanently. But Gerson was not alone in trying to keep track of his work. He had invaluable assistance from his youngest brother, Jean the Celestine, who also lived in Lyon. In 1423, in connection with his letter to the Grande Chartreuse concerning Gerson's life in exile, Jean the Celestine drew up what is known as the *annotatio prima* of his brother's works (23–26). Sometime before his death in 1434, Jean the Celestine compiled a second and more complete account, with eighty-two entries, the *annotatio secunda* (29–33).

This list ends with a general reference to "many other brief writings of his on various subjects which have been omitted for the sake of brevity." Jean the Celestine had put them together in a single volume, as "fragments so that they do not perish" (cf John 6:12). They would provide consolation (*solatium*) for those who read them (33). The word is worth noticing: it is perhaps a point of departure for the title later given Gerson as "consoling doctor" (*doctor consolatorius*).

The invention of printing is still used to explain the spread of the Protestant Reformation, but the new technique was just as important for the spread of the thoughts of theologians like Gerson who tried to reform the Christian Church from within. From 1483 until 1521, Gerson's collected works were printed and reprinted ten times in Cologne, Strasbourg, Nuremberg, Basel, and Paris (71–72). Already in the 1483 Cologne edition, we find what was to become a classic division of treatises dealing with the contemplative life, those concerned with church reform, and those concentrating on moral standards and behavior.[10] Gerson was thus made available not only as a church reformer but also as an expert on ethics and an authority on mystical theology.

Before the first printed edition of his works, individual writings had already appeared from the printing press. In 1475 the Brothers of the Common Life published in Brussels some of his works (72), while his *Alphabet of Divine Love* appeared under the name of the printer Ulrich Zell at Cologne in 1466. By 1511 it had been printed ten times: in Strasbourg, Louvain, Paris, and Delft (73). Even more popular was the *Donatus moralizatus,* Gerson's experiment in turning a grammatical treatise into one on morals (76). His various treatises on confession were also available in print before the first editions of the *Opera Omnia.*

During the thirty-seven years between Gerson's death and the first printed versions of his work, the primary purveyors of his writings were his brother Jean the Celestine and the Carthusians.[11] The Grande Chartreuse is only one of several charterhouses that recognized Gerson as a spiritual writer of great worth. There was also a Carthusian house at Basel that collected and distributed his works.[12]

Here was a monastic-humanistic milieu made up of university scholars who either went into the monastery or entered episcopal service and for whom Basel was a center for church reform. Expressing this commitment, the bishop of Basel, Christopher of Uthenim, wrote in 1504 to the chapter of the church of Saint Paul at Lyon and told the canons how important Gerson's teaching had been for him.[13] The bishop said he had heard that many pilgrims came to Gerson's burial place and that miracles took place there. According to these reports, the confessor of Charles VIII, a Carmelite, had composed a hymn in praise of Gerson and appended it to his tomb. This Carmelite had formerly shown contempt for Gerson but had been punished for his lack of faith with an ailment and so had changed his mind.

The chapter of Lyon responded that the reports reaching Basel were correct, except for the rumor that Lawrence Burel, the royal confessor, had initially held Gerson in contempt. But the bishop was right that there now was a painting of Gerson in the church. The chapter added that King Charles VIII (1483–1498) had, as a result of his chaplain's sermons on Gerson, established a chapel in his honor in the church of Saint Lawrence. The Carmelite, who apparently served as chaplain to both Charles VIII and his successor Louis XII, encouraged the king to gather information on Gerson's life and work for his canonization.[14]

The bishop of Basel wrote of Gerson as being a comforter (*consolatorius*). Two years earlier, Jacob Wimpheling, in the prologue of his collected works of Gerson, described him as "a consoling and most Christian doctor."[15] The remark of Jean the Celestine had been turned into a title for his brother. Wimpheling reflects the enthusiasm of a group of humanist scholars, printers, and churchmen clustered around the bishop of Basel. The editor promised his readers that they would find in Gerson's writings what they needed "for the love of God and neighbor, for the reformation of the Church, and for the salvation of souls."

Wimpheling's prologue also contains a defense of Gerson against potential detractors. "It seems to be impious, if the sweetest Gerson" were shown hatred instead of charity. Wimpheling did not make clear who it was that spread such ill will and tried to undermine his reputation. The assertion that there was nothing unorthodox in his writings perhaps answered criticism of Gerson for trying to limit papal power. Wimpheling's prologue ends with an *Exhortation to the Christian reader:* bishops and cardinals, lawyers, religious, youths, preachers, university and school teachers, inquisitors, parish priests, contemplatives, Friars Preachers (Dominicans), confessors, and those who are dying should all read Gerson! These representatives of Christian society were chosen according to the subjects with which he had dealt.

Gerson had something to say for just about everyone: "Every person, of each sex and each status." Thus women were included as readers, but not in the vernacular. Wimpheling explained in the prologue that he included many of Gerson's works translated from French into Latin. This had been done "by a certain German who was a student of philosophy and theology in Paris and had also learned the French language," perhaps Wimpheling himself.[16]

Jacob Wimpheling belonged to a group that made Gerson available to the learned Latin world of the early sixteenth century. Together with Geiler of Keysersberg, whose Strasbourg edition had already appeared in 1488, Wimpheling counted on the popularity of Gerson's theology in German-speaking regions, where the conciliar movement had been strongest. As for Paris, it was not until 1521 that a complete edition of Gerson appeared there, and its prologue takes up more space in praising the archbishop of Reims than in describing Gerson's achievement.[17]

With the coming of the Protestant Reformation, Gerson and his works lost some of their attraction.[18] The next *Opera omnia* appeared in Paris in 1606, by which time Gerson's memory at Lyon seems to have become obscured. Here for the first time is the incorrect assertion that Gerson taught the catechism to the young in Lyon. He was supposed to have taught them to say: *Mon Dieu mon createur, ayez pitié de vostre pauvre serviteur Jean Gerson* (My God and Creator, have pity on your poor servant Jean Gerson).[19]

The Huguenots ravaged Lyon in the 1560s and even destroyed the tomb of Saint Bonaventure there. The Gerson cult, which flowered at the beginning of the century, disappeared. The very place of his burial was forgotten until it was accidentally rediscovered in 1643. According to an account then written by a Stephen Verney for the chapter of Saint Paul, the Protestants had wrecked the chapel dedicated to Gerson.[20]

Gerson's wooden coffin was found in the church of Saint Lawrence in May of 1643 when a grave was being prepared for "a fine woman of the Grassi family." The news brought crowds from the town, for "everyone wanted to have a look."[21] The deceased woman was finally given a proper burial, but immediately miracles began to happen at the site of Gerson's tomb. A Marguerite Roux, who had lost the use of both legs after she had jumped out of a window in a fire, prayed for half an hour at the tomb and then could walk again. A crippled boy of five also regained his mobility. Amid such reports, the cardinal archbishop Richelieu, brother of the better-known minister, arrived but could not get to the tomb because of the press of people. He waited until the next day to investigate the site and the corpse: he found Gerson with his hands folded. They had once clasped a small tin chalice to his breast. It had slipped away from his grasp, but he still held a paten, which seemed to be worn out by use. Gerson's three fingers on his right hand were extended "as if in blessing."[22]

The corpse was lifted up so the cardinal could kiss it, and then the tomb was closed. But first some of his remaining hair and clothes were removed so they could be cut into pieces and distributed as relics. The people who had been eagerly waiting outside now rushed in, and so the miracles continued, for both children and adults. A woman with a tumor who had been abandoned by the doctors was healed. Prayers were offered at the tomb for King Louis XIII, who was ill. The writer says that it can only be believed that Louis was helped by the Gerson who had always been devoted to the royal family.[23] His description ends with an exhortation to praise Gerson, a model to all, and a saint. Happy is the Gaul that has given birth to him, the cities of Reims, Paris, Constance, Lyon, and every other place where he lived. The author wrongly describes Gerson here as canon of Saint Paul and as teacher of religion and minister of the sacraments to this church's parishioners.

From this description it would seem that the cult of Gerson, dormant for decades, had revived and that he even had a chance for canonization. But there is no more evidence of popular devotion or ecclesiastical intervention on his behalf. With the next edition of his works, that of Louis Du Pin in 1706, Gerson was brought into the fold of French prelates and theologians who opposed papal power, and so Du Pin's work is arranged to highlight this side of Gerson's teaching. Until the early eighteenth century, his reputation as theologian had remained international, as in the spread of his works in German-speaking regions. But after 1706, Gerson became a more parochial figure, celebrated by French academics and more or less forgotten elsewhere. His reputation rested on the mistaken attribution of the *Imitation of Christ* to his pen, the source of a debate that dragged on into the nineteenth century and engendered countless tracts of charges and countercharges.[24]

Gerson's cult thus never really became permanent, and when his burial place was located on the north side of the "Place Gerson" in the nineteenth century,[25] there was no attempt to transfer his bones to the still-standing church of Saint Paul. At the same time, however, Gerson was finally beginning to receive the appreciation he deserves. In 1837 the Académie Française announced a competition for a work celebrating Gerson, the first indication of a new enthusiasm for him, very much in harmony with the Catholic revival after the French Revolution.[26] Three years later, the great French historian Jules Michelet gave an insightful evaluation. He saw conflicts and paradoxes in Gerson, *cet homme de combat et de contradiction:* "Mystic, enemy of mystics, but even more the enemy of men of power and brutality; poor and powerless curé of Saint-Jean, . . . he censored princes, attacked butchers."[27]

Jean the Celestine and the Carthusians made it possible for Michelet and his successors to follow the life and thought of Gerson. In our time Gerson has once again become an international figure, transcending nineteenth-century nationalism and religious disputes.

Gerson was devoted to the French monarchy, but he was more than a protonationalist. He was a Christian humanist who contributed to the culture of scholastic humanism so well described by Sir Richard Southern.[28] In his catholic tastes and pursuits, Gerson learned to convey his thought and experience in literary forms that his thirteenth-century Parisian predecessors never attempted. At the same time, he opened scholastic culture to the vernacular. Thanks to Gilbert Ouy's labors in libraries and archives, Gerson can be seen as a great French as well as Latin writer. The important Paris edition of 1606 confirmed the practice of using only the Latin translations of the original French works made by German scholars.[29] It was not until the later twentieth century with the Glorieux edition that Ouy's *Gerson bilingue* became accessible.

Defending and Denying Conciliarism

Leaving aside Gerson's physical memorials, I want to look now at the aftermath of his life in terms of the Church's situation in the decades after his death. His form of conciliarism was not then doomed to self-destruction, an assertion sometimes found in later historical literature.[30] The Council of Basel, which lasted from 1431 to 1451, is a fascinating series of meetings and discussions that carried on the program of the Council of Constance. At moments Basel came close to success in developing a new model for governing the Western Christian Church.

The council is intertwined with the person and writings of Aeneas Sylvius Piccolomini, better known as Pope Pius II (1458–1464). Aeneas may seem to be the last person in the world whose career can be seen as a parallel to that of Gerson, for the one reached the top, while the other never came near the heights of power. Yet their origins are similar and their involvement in the conciliar movement also invites comparison. Like Gerson, Piccolomini came from a large, poor family and had to make his way on the basis of his connections and his pen. Unlike Gerson, however, he did not dedicate himself to a great institution like the University of Paris; rather he placed himself at the beck and call of various masters whom he served as secretary. In this capacity Piccolomini came to Basel to serve at the council in the 1430s.

In his *Commentaries* he described Basel in great detail during a crucial period in 1439 when the fathers were discussing the deposition of the Roman pope and the election of a more worthy successor.[31] It is still often stated in histories of the council that it was dominated by the lower clergy after the departure of some of its most influential members to join the Roman camp in the late 1430s.[32] But recent work has established that it was Piccolomini's own myth that the council fathers came from the lower ranks of the Church and even from menial professions.[33] Even after Pope Eugenius had dissolved the council and reopened it at Ferrara, the fathers who stayed at Basel were a distinguished company of bishops and theologians, who saw themselves as continuing the work begun at Constance.

In this company Aeneas Sylvius Piccolomini felt at home, at least so long as he remained in Basel. His modern editors are probably right that he was the kind of person who reflected whatever milieu he adopted: in Basel he was a conciliarist; later in Rome he was a papalist.[34] But Piccolomini was more than a creature who took on the colors of his immediate surroundings. He was an enthusiast, who when involved in a cause, could not imagine any other commitment. In reproducing arguments for the deposition of Pope Eugenius, he showed how the council fathers depended on the same passages in Matthew 18 that were so important for Gerson at Constance.[35]

Christ had told his apostles that if one brother had a grievance against another, they should talk over the matter. But if this approach did not work, they should take their dispute to the Church and there seek counsel. What was decided there would also apply in heaven. Thus the expression better known from Matthew 16, "What you bind on earth will be bound in heaven," is used in chapter 18 not for Peter's authority, but in relation to the power of the Church as a corporate body legislating for its members. Piccolomini did not quote directly from Gerson, but his dependence on this passage in Matthew shows that he was drawing on the same body of thought that had inspired his predecessor. The speeches delivered before the Council of Basel reveal the same spirit as at Constance: a belief that the Church is a corporate body which solves its problems through dialogue.

The proceedings of the council are well documented both in Piccolomini's account and elsewhere.[36] His discussions about how to deal with the pope and how to run the Church, however, have drawn little attention. The decrees of Basel are often seen mainly in terms of how they threatened the material and political basis of papal power, as in the abolition of annates as papal incomes. But one can also look at Basel as deciding on reform policies that never got off the ground at Constance after a universal pope had been elected.

The decisions made at Basel were very much in the gersonian spirit: the clergy was to set itself apart from the people by emphasizing its celibate vocation; it was to carry out its duties of prayer and devotion in a way that would engender respect; it was to show the difference between lay and clerical ways of life. The Council of Basel drew up a detailed program for church reform, not only in government but also in terms of everyday life. The electors lived together in one building and showed an asceticism that for Piccolomini reflected early Christian or monastic communities. His enthusiasm may seem almost boyish, but as clerk of ceremonies, he knew exactly how much food was brought in for the electors, who lived in what rooms, and how they spent their days and nights: "I will pass over that most holy blessed life, purer than all strict religion. Wherever is there such a band of Fathers, where such a splendour of knowledge, where the wisdom and the goodness that can be compared with the virtues of these Fathers. What a perfect brotherhood (*O integerrimam fraternitatem*)!"[37]

The Council of Basel, in the period when Piccolomini described it, from the election of Felix V as pope in November 1439 until his coronation in July 1440 continued the practice initiated at Constance: open discussion of church government. He did not hide the fact that there were times when disorder and disagreements dominated the sessions, but he describes the papal conclave as a gathering where "there were no quarrels and no disputes, everything took place in friendship and affection."[38] In the papal electors he saw the Desert Fathers, "either the great Anthony or Paul the Simple, and you would have compared one to Hilarion, one to Paphnutius, and one to Ammon." In the next sentence he mentions Jerome and Augustine, "whose writings were in the conclave but not in the wilderness."[39]

One can hardly imagine a greater contrast between such a conclave and the one in which Piccolomini himself some decades later was elected pope. Here we once again have his own description, but his idealism has turned into worldly wisdom, revealing jockeying for power, conspiracies, and ambitions: "Not a few were won over by Rouen's splendid promises and were caught like flies by their gluttony. And the tunic of Christ without Christ was being sold. Many cardinals met in the privies as being a secluded and retired place. . . . A fit place for such a pope to be elected! For where could one more appropriately enter into a foul covenant than in privies?"[40] These lines, together with other unedifying passages, were removed in a later censored edition of Pius II's memoirs. Their restoration to the text enables us to see his admission of the sordidness in the political negotiations connected with standard papal elections. He did his best to disassociate himself from such deliberations and to emerge as the pure candidate to the high office, but he had long since disowned the belief in conciliarism and constitutionalism maintained in Basel. As he wrote in his *Memoirs*, looking back at the council: "While the Schism lasted and the council was in session, since the authority which had belonged to bishops was now shared not only by abbots but by provosts, priors, canons, simple priests, and lowly monks, many of its decrees were promulgated contrary to virtue and justice in order to weaken the eminence of the Roman and Supreme See."[41] Thus Aeneas Silvius Piccolomini initiated the historical myth of the popularism of Basel. He also claimed that the churchmen who stayed there did so because they could not get high positions in the Roman Curia and so nursed a grudge against the papacy.

Pius II had a selective memory, as most of us do. He wanted to justify his own choice to join the papal court and to distance himself from his former colleagues. In the early 1440s, he had seen the election of Count Amadeus of Savoy as Felix V as "right and holy."[42] Now he claimed men did so in order to take their revenge on the papacy. Once again, there were two popes at the same time.

It would be easy to contrast Piccolomini as "opportunist-realist" with Gerson as "martyr-idealist." In many ways, however, the two are close. Like Gerson, he believed in the Christian Church as the instrument of the salvation of humankind. He loved to write, to describe life experiences, and to relate them to events around him. Similarly, he treasured classical learning and enjoyed displaying his mastery of it. And like Gerson, he never forgot his family and did what he could to protect and cherish its members.

Unlike Gerson, however, Piccolomini gave way to a natural human inclination to follow power and seek its exercise. At some point in the early 1440s, the future Pius II realized that the Council of Basel was a losing proposition, and he used his post as secretary to the German king to seek reconciliation with Rome. Here he was welcomed with open arms, as had been the case a few years earlier with the great theologian Nicholas of Cusa.

At this point the pope in Rome, Eugenius IV (1431–1447), looked like a winner because of his seeming success in reorganizing the council at Ferrara-Florence and obtaining reunion with the Eastern Church. If Basel had won the sympathies of the German king, however, it might have forced a compromise. As it was, the pope who succeeded Eugenius, Nicholas V (1447–1455), was successful in bringing most of Felix's supporters at Basel into his fold. There were no recriminations, and even Felix was able to end his life as a respected and loyal cardinal.[43]

The mildness and lack of vindictiveness of the triumphant papacy, however, had its reverse side. In Calixtus III (1455–1458), the first Borgia pope, we see a restoration of local family interests.[44] Whether it was the Colonnas or the Borgias or any other Roman family, the papacy once again, as so often earlier in its history, was used to serve brothers and nephews, to say nothing of illegitimate children. Pius II sacrificed his earlier vision of church community and desert asceticism to family aggrandizement, with grandiose building projects in his old hometown, renamed Pienza, complete with its palaces that today seem out of place in the Tuscan countryside.

In chapter 9 we met Pius II's bull *Execrabilis* of 1460. In it he condemned any future appeal from the pope to a new council, and in so doing reaffirmed what Martin V had already asserted in 1418, before he had even left the site of the council.[45] Gerson had done what he could to warn against the consequences and even claimed that the pope really did not mean what he said. But Martin meant every word, and so did his successors. They undermined the very conciliar movement that had reestablished papal rule.[46]

The language of *Execrabilis* shows how Piccolomini had abandoned Matthew 18 and its exhortation that those who disagree must seek dialogue within the Church. Instead Pius II stuck exclusively to Matthew 16, where it is Peter and his successors who alone bind on earth and thus in heaven:

> A horrible abuse, unheard-of in earlier times, has sprung up in our period. Some men, imbued with a spirit of rebellion and moved not by a desire for sound decisions but rather by a desire to escape the punishment for sin, suppose that they can appeal from the pope, vicar of Jesus Christ; from the pope, to whom in the person of the blessed Peter it was said,

> "Feed my sheep" (John 21:16) and "Whatever you bind on earth will be bound in heaven" (Mt 16:19)—from this pope to a future council. How harmful this is to the Christian republic, as well as how contrary to canon law, anyone who is not ignorant of the law can understand.[47]

The *respublica christiana* to which the text refers was a different construction from the gathering in Basel, which Piccolomini in his youth had envisaged as a new meeting of desert fathers. The council he now considered a mistake not to be repeated. The voices of reform were heard as threats to an institution governed by one absolute head, from whom there could be no appeal.

Abandoning North-South Dialogue

The church councils held in Constance and Basel had continued an old alliance between the Roman south and the Germanic north. This bond went back to the intervention of King Pepin of the Franks on the pope's behalf in the mid-eighth century. The pope crowned Charlemagne as a new Roman emperor on Christmas day 800 to strengthen this alliance and make it permanent. It was continued under Ottonian and Saxon emperors, as when Henry III removed all papal contenders in Rome and in 1049 chose one of his own men and relatives as the legitimate pope.[48]

Henry's restored papacy initiated the first medieval reformation of the Christian Church, and it remains an irony of history that the emperor thus created the papacy that so quickly turned against his family and its assumed prerogatives. But whatever Henry's son and his successors thought of the popes with whom they had to deal, they knew that they could not exist without them. So long as the Saxons and later Hohenstaufens sought to combine the title of king of the Germans with emperor of the Romans, they had to get to Rome and convince the pope to crown them. The conditions were always steep, and the road to Rome was littered with political obstructions and physical dangers. But the key to the rule of the North was the consent of the South.

After the papal war against the Hohenstaufen family and the legendary liquidation of its last member in 1268, the old alliance between empire and papacy seemed forever gone. But in the later Middle Ages new families vied for the old title, and new forms of government insisted on recognition. The residence of French popes in Avignon further upset the balance of power between North and South, and the schism between Roman and Avignon popes threatened to become a permanent fact in Christendom. As Gerson warned, it could become as much of a fact as the original schism between East and West.[49] Thus an unbridgeable rift would divide North and South, instead of their holding together in unity against the Turks who were encroaching on the Christian Republic.

In the aftermath of the Schism and the restoration of the papacy, it looked as if the old alliance between Roman pope and German king could be reestablished. It was, after all, the emperor-elect Sigismund who was instrumental in keeping the Council of Constance together. His death in 1437 was also the signal for the end of the role played by the Council of Basel in reconciling papal, imperial, and conciliar interests. In the years that followed, his successors tried to remain neutral in the dispute between pope and council. But when the Hapsburg Frederick III finally sided with the Roman pope, Nicholas V rewarded him in 1452 with the imperial crown.[50]

Frederick was the last emperor crowned in Rome. He was well served by secretaries such as Piccolomini, and for a time it looked as if North and South could maintain the precarious but necessary union they had maintained since the eighth century. But in the second half of the fifteenth century, the reestablished papacy began to look to the North not as an ideological challenge but as a source of income. Popes had, of course, long dispatched their emissaries to secure much-needed revenues, but now papal missions became more mercenary than ever.[51]

The papacy needed money in order to rebuild Rome in its image and especially, after 1503, for a new Saint Peter's.[52] The last reforming pope was Paul II (1464–1471), who tried to abolish money grants for offices that were "expectancies," reserved for the papal candidates. Paul's successors reverted to the practice.[53] Like them, he had been concerned with the governance of the papal states in Central Italy. His successor, Sixtus IV (1471–1484), became even more bogged down in Italian politics. The pope functioned now primarily as secular ruler of a choice piece of real estate that potentially provided him with income but in fact drained his resources.

The next three popes herald the end of medieval Christianity, with its internationalism, internal reformations, and search for a meeting between papal and episcopal power. Innocent VIII (1484–1492) was caught up in internecine wars and feuds between the Orsini and Colonna families. As Rome was marked by their violence, the pope exercised little control. In addition, there was the matter of his bastard son, for whom he tried to arrange a wealthy marriage. To increase his income, he sold offices, which became a source of enrichment for their holders.

Alexander VI (1492–1503) and Julius II (1503–1513) are better known (or more notorious) than their predecessor. The Borgia pope produced children and poisonings, while the warring pope created disputes in the papal states.[54] Leo X (1513–1521) continued in the same vein, in getting hold of all the land he could for the Medici family. At the same time, the Protestant Reformation had begun. The glories of the Italian Renaissance are intimately connected with the death of the medieval reforming spirit, for the Italian popes who paid for the great art seen today in the Vatican Museums are the same people who made it possible for an angry and bitter monk like Martin Luther to become the spokesperson of an enraged North. The pervasive arrogance, concupiscence, and greed of the South now came home to roost. The North refused to be milked any longer, and the reform ideas that the papacy had denied or condemned required separation from the papal Church. It is a familiar story in European history, but one that also can be told in terms of what might have been if Gerson's ideas had been followed. What if his appeal to corporatism and to discourse, inviting all those who had something worthwhile to say to participate, had been heeded?.

Like Jean Gerson, Aeneas Sylvius Piccolomini at first welcomed such discussion, a combination of scholastic reasoning and humanistic language in a Christian context. But it was the discourse of power that won out in the later fifteenth century. What mattered for Pius II and his successors was not reformation of the Church. It was perpetuation of the papal monarchy, now from the stronghold of the papal states.

The granting of indulgences as blank checks is still considered in some history books to be the main cause of the Protestant Reformation.[55] Even though such a cause-effect explanation is too simplistic, there is no doubt that the papacy at the opening of the sixteenth century was doing its best to collect money on this basis, in opposition to the efforts of the councils to limit such practices. Far more important than the misuse of indulgences, however, was the abandonment of the principle of constitutionalism that succeeded at Constance and failed at Basel. In the words of the great political historian John Nevill Figgis, who grasped the significance of the conciliar movement, "The principles of Constance are the last effort of medieval constitutionalism. Their failure marks the beginning of the modern world."[56] From here on, it was all downhill on the path to the absolutist monarchies of the seventeenth century.

It is a sad story that did not have to happen in the way it did. People made choices. They were not driven by some ineluctable determinism, even though historians sometimes act as if the past is governed by mechanisms still waiting to be discovered. As I see it, Aeneas Silvius chose to become the man who would be Pius: he selected papal monarchy instead of conciliar corporatism. Similarly other scholars and humanists chose the papacy as the best possible employer, a source of guaranteed income and patronage. When the papacy finally tried to revive the reformation of the Church and called a general council, it was too late.

We can look through the decisions of the Fifth Lateran Council (1512–1517) and see an awareness that abuses of ecclesiastical power and sacramental privilege had to stop.[57] But now the North was ready to strike out on its own. It had lived with one internal reformation of the Church after another; it had supported earlier councils in the hope of reform. Now reform would come from outside the church hierarchy, from people who no longer believed in the pope as the successor to Peter with the power to bind and loose on earth as in heaven.

We can leave the papal world with two portraits, one a painting by Jan van Eyck,

Fig. 15 Cardinal Niccolò Albergati, fifteenth-century papal emissary, in a painting by Jan van Eyck. Kunsthistorisches Museum, Vienna. An illustration of a man of power who has seen everything and is ready to retire.

the other a literary sketch by the Florentine historian Guicciardini. In 1438 van Eyck painted the cardinal and papal legate Niccolò Albergati. He based the painting on drawings made three years before at the meetings that led to the Treaty of Arras and a final reconciliation between the French monarchy and the duke of Burgundy, Philip the Good, who thus came to terms with the murder in 1419 of his father, John the Fearless. The pope sent Albergati to Arras, while the duke of Burgundy sent his in-house artist van Eyck from Bruges.

The portrait is now in Vienna, but I saw it in Bruges, where I was looking for memorials of Gerson. Here Albergati had taken up temporary residence in the midst of a great exhibition, "The Age of Van Eyck," marking the centennial of the 1902 exhibition in Bruges that had placed late medieval Flemish art on the European map.[58] Albergati is dressed in a red cope with what looks like an ermine lining around his neck and in the sleeves. He wears no symbols of power, but his face shows great authority. At the same time, his expression is almost naked with fatigue and disillusionment. His dark brown eyes have seen everything that is to be seen in the world. His ears have heard all too much, and his mouth reveals nothing.

What is in a picture? Whatever the viewer wants to behold? When I came upon Albergati, I knew I was in the presence of a man of power, but also one who had no illusions about pleasure to be had in its enjoyment. He has had his fill of delegations and intrigues and is ready to leave the world behind and withdraw into a study or a monastery. But he was doing his duty, trying to make peace in Northern Europe for the papacy, performing a papal role that stretched back centuries.

Albergati was one of the last successful representatives of a papal peacemaking initiative meant to hold North and South together. Eugenius IV needed such a diplomatic victory in order to ensure the papacy as a focal point of power and prestige in the *res publica christiana* of the 1430s, where the council fathers in Basel were trying to take over the leadership of the Church. Thus Albergati manifested the papacy's continuing presence in an international medieval culture.

A half-century later there were no more significant papal diplomats in the North. Roderigo Borgia had taken the name Alexander VI and was trying to cope with the French invasion of Italy. Sixty years after the Treaty of Arras in 1435, Alexander more or less surrendered to Charles VIII and accepted the French king's presence in Rome. The historian Guicciardini was scathing in his later portrait of Alexander, not because of his capitulation to French military power, but because the Borgia pope did so little to control the situation in his own realm: "The pope did nothing to prevent . . . disorders in the papal states, as he hated spending money on such things. And being by nature little troubled by the calamities of others, he was not disturbed by those things which offended his honor as long as his profit or pleasure was not interfered with. However he could not escape family misfortunes which disturbed his house with tragic events, and with lechery and cruelty which would be horrible even in any barbarian country."[59] By March of 1495, the pope had succeeded in forming a "Holy League" with Venice, Spain, Austria, and Milan. Charles VIII had to retreat, but in the words of one twentieth-century papal historian, "The removal of the French danger enabled the pope to revert to his schemes of family aggrandizement."[60]

His predecessor Eugenius IV, however suspicious he was of conciliar power, acted as a European leader, while Alexander was one more greedy, lecherous Italian prince who happened also to be titular leader of the Church. In this brave new world medieval reformations were dead, and new reformations were on the way.

Reforming by Attacking Instead of Talking

If we turn to the sixteenth-century reformations, we find a near-total breakdown of dialogue. The anger and hatred evident in some of Martin Luther's writings are remarkable, as if he managed to store up the frustrations not of one life but of centuries of resentment against the "whore of Babylon" whom he identified with the papacy.[61]

Instead of concentrating on Luther, however, it might be more fruitful to consider Philip Melanchton and his fellow theologians who in 1530 drew up the *Augsburg Confession*.[62] The first part of this fascinating document, steeped in the history of the Christian Church, states the beliefs considered to bind all Christians together, while the second part contains a relatively mild polemic against the abuses of the Roman Church. At the end of the first section, Melanchton and his colleagues claimed that their teaching was not in opposition to the Roman Church: "The whole controversy rests on a few abuses which without a proper basis have wormed their way into the churches."[63]

The document asked bishops to show mildness and give the reformers permission to preach. It pointed out that church law did not require universal uniformity. There could be different practices in different churches, while the reformers continued "for a great part to maintain the old ways." It was not true "that all ceremonies, all ancient ordinances are abolished in our churches."[64]

Melanchton was looking for a middle ground as a meeting place for the Roman Church and the new Reformed Church. He insisted it was still one church. Together with the other theologians behind the *Confessio augustana*, he called for a general council in order to resolve differences and heal this schism.[65] Just as their fifteenth-century predecessors had done.

It might be argued that the sixteenth-century reformers were not being sincere. Their statement can be seen as a masterly piece of political propaganda to calm the emperor and to hide the fact that a new Christian religion was growing up within his realms. The *Confessio*, however, is more than a political document.

It was an appeal to the bishops to allow a plurality not of belief but of practice. In the final sentences, it was argued that what were now considered to be abuses "perhaps originally had a reasonable basis; but they do not fit later times."[66]

If the passage was hinting at clerical celibacy, its authors were on solid historical ground. The clerical reformation of the eleventh century had brought in celibacy, but there was no doctrinal requirement that priests be celibate. The reformers believed that the time for clerical celibacy was over, an argument that continues to be heard today in the Roman Catholic Church.

In listing abuses, the Augsburg Confession not surprisingly turned to Jean Gerson and the reforming rhetoric of the fifteenth century. Considering monastic vows, Melanchton and his colleagues criticized the idea that the monastic way of life alone was the perfect Christian vocation. He was familiar with Gerson's claim that it was not necessary to take vows in order to follow the Gospels: "Before these times Gerson reproached monks their error concerning perfection and bears witness that in his time it was a new concept that monastic life is a state of perfection."[67]

Melanchton may have been referring to Gerson's letter-treatise *On the Perfection and Moderation of the Religious Life* (Gl 2.232–45). As we saw earlier (ch. 10), Gerson here had made it clear that the Christian life in itself and not any monastic order is the highest form of religion (233). Gerson did, however, see virtue in taking monastic vows, and so his criticism of monasticism is not as extreme as the Augsburg Confession makes it out to have been. He was here not a "precursor" of the Protestant Reformation but a representative of a medieval tradition on which Melanchton drew.

Gerson is also mentioned for lamenting that "many despaired, and some even killed themselves, because they realized that they could not satisfy the demands of tradition and at the same time they had not gained any comfort from the justification of the faith and of grace."[68] Once again we can turn to Gerson's letter on Christian perfection, for here he inveighed against excessive severity in maintaining what were mere customs. He saw men who were "sometimes inhuman, tyrannical, and cruel" in the exercise of their rules with no mildness or exceptions (238). I find no reference to suicide, and Melanchton was refashioning Gerson's text according to his own needs.[69] But fifteenth- and sixteenth-century reformers were in basic agreement that traditions, as in the monastic life, were not meant to be unchanging and inflexible. Human needs had to be taken into consideration.

In a polemical chapter of his Gerson biography, John Connolly states that these sixteenth-century reformers misconstrued Gerson's meaning.[70] I would not be quite so categorical; they took what they needed, but they did not abuse Gerson's critique of excessive demands on the human body and spirit. At the Council of Constance, he countered the view of the Dominican Matthew Graben that the way of perfection required formal vows and entrance into a monastic or religious order (Gl 10.70–72). Gerson came to admire the Celestines and the Carthusians, but he argued for moderation in their way of life.

This Gerson was still relevant in the mid-sixteenth century, but soon his basic acceptance of monasticism in Christian life would be forgotten in the course of the all-out attack on the Roman Church. Gerson had accepted papal authority, even when he disagreed with the prohibition of 1418 against appeal to future councils. His reforming successors, in appealing to such a council, must have known by 1530 that the papacy would not allow another general council to take place north of the Alps.

When the Council of Trent opened in 1545, the opportunity for compromise and negotiation had passed. The council's second decree enshrined the Vulgate Latin Bible as the basis for all future theological discussion, a slap in the face of the reformers who went back to the Hebrew and Greek texts.[71] There was to be no compromise with humanist reformers: the middle ground shared by men like Gerson, Erasmus, and Melanchton was no longer to be. The modern Roman Catholic Church was being born with an absolutist and triumphalist papacy and little room for dissent or new reformations. The old scholastic method of question and answer, challenge and response, thesis and antithesis was to be taken over by decrees and orders. Medieval discourse and plurality gave way to early modern regimentation, as expressed in the Counter Reformation papal army of the new Jesuit Order.[72]

Preferring Strong Monarchs to Council Challenges

The papacy emerging from the traumas of the fifteenth century and reestablishing itself in the reformations of the sixteenth century preferred strong kings to bothersome councils. From Martin V on, the restored papacy did its utmost to undermine the decisions of the Council of Constance while, at the same time, conceding power and privileges over the Church to kings. In the words of one of the most articulate interpreters of this development: "What is surprising . . . is the extent to which Eugenius IV was willing to promote this whole process of establishing rulers as masters of their respective churches so long as those rulers were willing to withdraw support from the conciliar idea and from the threat of reform in head and members that went with it. Possession of the actual substance of power mattered less, it seems, than the enjoyment of a theoretically supreme authority in the universal church."[73]

In 1438 the French king issued what is known as the Pragmatic Sanction of Bourges, denying appeals from the French clergy to the papacy and limiting papal incomes.[74] In the next decades kings used the decree as a point of departure for their relations with the pope, while they time and again promised to withdraw or mollify its provisions. Popes put up with such treatment in return for assurances that the monarchy would not support appeals to a future general council.

Royal policies had long undermined international bonds within the Church. By 1300 the henchmen of Philip the Fair had shown that they meant business in terms of making the king emperor in his own realm, with no appeal elsewhere, least of all to the pope. In Gerson's own Paris, more than one master had to pay dearly for opposing such a view. In February 1418, Raoul de la Porte, the head of the College of Navarre, preached before the king and the Parlement of Paris that "the collation or disposal of benefices of the Church was the province of clerics."[75] He claimed that the failure to observe this provision would be a disaster for the university and its clerics and students. The king, in future, should accept that papal ordinance disposed of such benefices.

As a leading Paris theologian associated with the College of Navarre, Raoul de la Porte would have been well known to Gerson. He merely asked for a return to the situation under the Avignon popes when university officials had been able to send petitions full of names of eligible scholars to the pope and were certain that his clerks would assign benefices to them. No better system for taking care of university graduates has ever been invented—practically everyone included on the roll was guaranteed a job!

Raoul required royal acceptance of papal power. The royal representative replied that the king has sovereign power in his kingdom, "which he holds from God alone without recognizing any sovereign lord on earth." The king rules alone and he cannot allow "any of his subjects or others to appeal."[76] And so Raoul's proposals were "iniquitous" and made him guilty of the crime of lèse-majesté. Together with the procurators of the university nations, he was arrested and thrown into the prison of the Conciergerie on the Ile-de-la-Cité. A final resolution of the matter was hindered by the entrance of the Burgundians into Paris at the end of May. But already on 1 March, in spite of attempts to reconcile university and monarchy, a statement was drawn up listing "the freedoms of the Gallican Church" and denying any papal right to exact payments from French clerics.[77]

Just as in the matter of appeal to a future council, it was already clear in 1418 what the future would bring in terms of royal claims to precedence over papal power. While the pope fought the council, he negotiated with the monarchy. To guarantee his theoretical supremacy, he chose what he must have considered the lesser of two evils.

The system of royal headship of the Church, which in the sixteenth century apparently arose as a new form in England, German lands, and Scandinavian countries, had been prepared much earlier in France. The long fight to distinguish between spiritual and temporal power, begun in the eleventh century, ended in the fifteenth with papal acceptance of royal power as definitive. The result was a strange blend of ideologies, with Luther's teaching about two *Regimente* (governments), one spiritual and one temporal, giving rulers virtually unlimited powers to crush unruly subjects.

The medieval concept of a right of disobedience to a tyrant disappeared in this ideological fortification of royal power. At the same time, popes were willing to accept their own loss of spiritual power, so long as they were guaranteed a place among temporal powers. They preferred to be in alliance with kings and other princes rather than challenge them. In this way the medieval foundation of a representative Church was ignored.

Where does Gerson belong in this discussion? In his sermons in praise of the king and a strong monarchy, he may seem to have sided with the new national churches. But however great his love of Christian monarchs, Gerson was not a French proto-nationalist. He represented a theological faculty which claimed a right to arbitrate in doctrinal disputes everywhere in the Church. In backing the conciliar movement, Gerson left behind his "national" origins and asserted the priority of his international involvement. In his writings condemning tyrannicide, he showed that churchmen have to speak out against princes, whatever the consequences for their careers and even lives. Like Raoul de la Porte, Gerson risked everything for the sake of belief in a church that had functions princes could not touch.

Gerson's successors in Paris compromised with the monarchy and abandoned the independence of their university from royal intervention.[78] With strong kings like Louis XI (1461–1483), the beginnings of consultative government in the Church and in secular society were crushed. Such rulers could join forces with the popes to make sure that bishops, theologians, and other church reformers would not disturb the power they exercised.

Turning Against Women and Their Inner Lives

Power is a word historians frequently use in describing and analyzing past societies, but human power is as elusive as divine grace. For centuries women had exercised power in the Church, even though they had no formal power and were kept out of the clergy, the universities, and all other spiritual assemblies. Yet, women had emerged, especially in the social, political and ecclesiastical crises of the period 1350–1450. Their voices were heard and made a difference in the Church, whether they were local spiritual figures such as Margery Kempe or prophetesses heard internationally such as Birgitta of Sweden.

The stories of such women are being told and retold today as never before, and I make no attempt here to go into detail concerning their significance.[79] However much some of the council fathers had been in doubt about the veracity of

Birgitta's revelations, they had confirmed her sainthood. However little liking Gerson had for the idea that a woman could speak with God's voice, he accepted the possibility. His profound ambivalence about women is representative of the situation of the medieval cleric, aware that God does not necessarily speak through his male theologians and may prefer the humble woman to the proud man. Even in his most pessimistic moments, Gerson left open a door that a woman could be the vessel of God's revelation. When Joan of Arc arrived on the scene, he gladly accepted her witness because he hoped for the restoration of the French monarchy.

At least until 1408, Gerson remained in contact with his sisters, responded to what he thought were their needs and provided advice. He was certain that women who wanted to live a devout life needed guidance from clerical men like himself, and he thereby accepted a continuing family bond. Although he may be looked upon as patronizing and paternalistic, Gerson expressed a tenderness and affection for which he had few other outlets in his carefully disciplined emotional life.

Women for Gerson were thus more than a necessary evil to continue the human race. They were recipients of divine grace and wisdom, as he saw Mary on the road to Egypt with her husband Joseph while she guided him through theological discussions. Gerson himself may have had similar conversations with his sisters, a point of departure for the treatises he later wrote for them.

As I have shown elsewhere, however, Gerson's various works on the discernment of spirits, which he had meant as guides for male clerics to spiritual women, by 1500 were used in the new literature to find out which women were witches.[80] The *Witches' Hammer,* the Dominican inquisitors' handbook on how to hunt them out, provided the main component in a packet of treatises that sometimes included Gerson's writings. The *Malleus Maleficiarum* of 1486 is hardly an original piece of work. It constitutes a scholastic compilation by the Dominicans Heinrich Kramer and Jakob Sprenger of all authorities on the subject of witches and brings together this misogynistic tradition reaching back beyond Christian Antiquity to pagan culture and the Old Testament. There are said to be more superstitious women than men; they have "slippery tongues and are unable to conceal from their fellow-women those things which by evil arts they know."[81] Here the biblical authority is Ecclesiasticus 19, while the statement that women are intellectually like children is attributed to Terence. Finally the central charge appears: women are "more carnal" than men. This carnal nature makes it easier for them to deceive, and so "a wicked woman is by her nature quicker to waver in her faith and consequently quicker to abjure the faith, which is the root of witchcraft."[82]

Women are creatures of their desires, and their main desire is for sex: "All witchcraft comes from carnal lust, which is in women insatiable."[83] Women are willing to seek out devils in order to get what they want. This statement may well appear to us as a male projection, but the Dominican brothers and their inquisitorial successors thought they had found the truth about women.

Gerson did not reduce women to such insatiable creatures. He was poised between rejecting them and admiring them, and so he expresses the medieval paradox of a society where women were both influential and powerless. The sixteenth century tried to dissolve such tensions. In Protestant Europe women were told to leave their convents and return to their families or get married. Now it was a time for fathers to rule. Even though their family regimes could be tender and caring, as Steven Ozment has shown, women were to listen submissively to the male voice and to restrain their own.[84]

Many women, of course, did not submit, and there were still those like Teresa of Avila (1515–1582) who knew how to play off confessors and even to outwit the Inquisition in order to live the lives they felt God had outlined for them.[85] Right into the seventeenth century, Ursuline women would try to combine preaching with their teaching function.[86] Even if women thus continued to exercise influence in the new churches, there no longer were men like Gerson to suggest the possibility that God does not distinguish between male and female when it comes to revealing his will to us. Gerson's fear of intellectual pride compelled him to listen to women and to make his theological inheritance available to them. Almost in spite of himself and his own inhibitions, he believed in female spiritual power.

Remembering a Piety of Active Resignation

In the centuries since his death, Jean Gerson's moral treatises have been read much more than his ecclesiological ones. In the years after 1500, Gerson's *Tripartitum* maintained its status as one of his most popular works, now translated into Latin and made available all over Europe. Here the final section, *The science of dying well,* also known as *The medicine of the soul,* summarizes his usefulness to both lay and clerical Christians.[87]

He opened the treatise with the message that "the true friends of a sick person" are those who show more interest in spiritual than in physical health. The body is secondary and the soul needs care. Gerson provides various considerations to encourage the dying person. Death is our common fate, and we have to resign ourselves to its coming: "My friend, whether you are man or woman, think of the grace that God has given you. We are all in his hands. There is no one, whether king or prince or anyone else, who does not have to come to this place. Here we have no tomorrow, for we have been placed in this world not in order to remain here always but to obtain a lodging and glory forever in paradise. We do so by living well and thus avoid the terrible sufferings of hell" (Gl 7.1.404). Gerson did not try to be poetic. He was here the teacher, reminding his reader or listener of what everyone knew was true but tended to forget. God will give us his grace, he insisted, to know our sins and repent them. Our purgatory can be here, in this life, rather than in the next. If we repent, then we can be certain of God's pardon. We should not be concerned with the affairs of the world, but hand ourselves over to God.

These exhortations are followed by six questions, as an examination of conscience. The dying person is asked, as a friend, if he or she wants "to live and die in the Christian faith of our savior Jesus Christ, as a loyal and true son or daughter of the holy Church? Answer yes." Here are simple formulae, to which one merely needs to answer affirmatively in order to do what needs to be done. Forgotten sins are accounted for; forgiveness is given to all and pardon is asked for; all worldly bonds are abandoned.

Next come brief prayers to be offered up. Here Gerson perhaps cites prayers he had spoken for himself: "My friend, say now with a good heart to God: God, my father, have pity on me. God, my good father, I place my soul in your hands. Father of mercy, have mercy on this your poor creature. Help me, Lord, in this last need. Help, Lord, my poor soul in its discomfort. Let it not be ravished and devoured by the dogs of hell" (406). The language is simple, prosaic, repetitive, brief sentences that can be gasped out by a dying person. He appealed to a "sweet father Jesus," to Our Lady, to the angels, and then to the patron saint: "I have through my life had confidence in you. Do not fail me in this final need."

Finally come practical suggestions, more for the helpers than for the dying person, about the reception of the sacraments, cases of excommunication, the reading aloud of prayers or stories which the dying person used during her life, the application of a cross or a saint's image. If necessary, the recommended prayers should be shortened. The person should not be plagued with thoughts or reminders about people or things being left behind, whether children, wife, or property. "He should concentrate only on what concerns his salvation, after taking care of their needs."

Those assisting the dying person should not delude him with the hope that he might be able to get well again: "For if one gives him a false and empty consolation, there is a risk of casting such a person into certain damnation" (407). The best way to provide comfort is to concentrate at this point on the needs of his soul, not his body. Therefore Gerson recommended that hospitals and hospices provide an opportunity for confession on the first day of admission. After being in charge of the Hôtel-Dieu in Paris, Gerson saw the care of the sick as both a medical and a pastoral concern.

This brief, unpretentious treatise deserves attention because it is quintessential Gerson. He combined calm resignation with inspired faith. If we see only the sense of powerlessness, we forget that he encouraged the helpers of the dying to make the journey easier and more peaceful. He did not hand over sick people arbitrarily to the will of God but called for the care of souls and bodies, with all that the Church could offer in prayers, sacraments, and tenderness.

Jesus maria.

S. Bernar. Floretus M. Jo. Jer.

Liber nomine floretus a san
cto Bernardo clareuallis abbate metrice ac-
cumulatus cum commento magistri iohan
nis Jersonis tractãs de virtutibus & vicijs
scdm precepta dei & ecclesie ad fugam peccato
rum. & electionem illorum operum. que hominem perdu-
cunt ad deum finaliter. cum maxima diligẽtia de nouo emẽ
datus & correctus.

Venundatur Lugduni a Johãne bu
guetan. eiusdem ciuitatis bibliopola & ciue. in vico mercu-
riali: prope imaginem sancte Marie magdalene.

Fig. 16 Gerson at his writing desk, across from Saint Bernard, with the mythical character "Floretus" in the middle. The book is pseudo-Bernard and shows how Gerson was considered to have been the great abbot's commentator. Lyon, 1513.

Gerson wrote of himself as a lonely pilgrim, but in this description of how he wanted fellow Christians to die, he showed that he did not want to be alone when he left this earth. He would have helpers to prepare him for the last journey. He would forget the concerns of this life and be able to draw on the care of the same Christian community for which he had lived.

Gerson's message can be interpreted as one of an isolated individual who abandons all hope and bonds with other people and turns to God alone. But I cannot see him as dying alone. In his pilgrimage, he could count on community, the communion of saints, a fellowship of men and women who remained with him, even as he distanced himself and feared getting too close to some of its members.

Gerson leaves us with the paradoxical Christian requirement to love both God and neighbor. In him as in so many other central figures from Late Antiquity on, the love of God at times seems to overwhelm everything else and to minimize human bonds. It is true that Gerson was deeply ambiguous about friendship and at times fled from it. But we need merely to return to the *Medicine of the Soul* to see that he counted on human company. For all his loneliness, he cried out, as in the apocryphal story in Lyon, "Have pity on me." He was speaking not only to God but also to the people in his life.

Gerson once sent a copy of this treatise to a dying man, someone whom he apparently had known well: "I am sending you a small treatise I once made to teach how one dies. You can have it read out to you and copied. And do not be displeased that I write to you in such a familiar manner and as if I am teaching you, for you have encouraged me. Love, moreover, makes me do so, as the God of good love knows (*ce scet le Dieu de bon amour*)."[88] However harsh and distant he could be in warning of the fires of damnation, he could be tender and caring in anticipating the God of good love. In becoming a most Christian doctor, Gerson learned to be a consoling one.

Seeking Meaning in a Battered World

A Unitary Vision

Beyond his ambiguities and dualism, Jean Gerson reveals a unitary vision of life in which polarities are dissolved in the vision of God. As he showed in rejecting what he thought was Jan van Ruusbroec's teaching, the human person in the vision of God, instead of being absorbed into the godhead, confirms its own individual identity.[89] In the vision of God, we become what we are meant to be: liberated from all restraint, we can at last love as we are meant to love.

Gerson looked forward to human unity as well as to ecclesiastical and social wholeness. His vision of mystical theology is matched by his hope for unity within the Church, in the healing not only of the Rome-Avignon Schism, but also that between Rome and Constantinople. When in 1409 the Council of Pisa elected a pope with Eastern roots, Alexander V, Gerson rejoiced because he saw this possibility.[90] East and West would meet in a common acknowledgment of their shared Gospel. Through the dialogue encouraged in Matthew 18, the claims of a single bishop would no longer dominate.

Gerson was not naive. He warned that schism might become a lasting fact. If the Church were not reformed, then future divisions awaited it. His teaching shows that Christianity as institutionalized religion requires a never-ending succession of reformations. The Samuel P. Huntington view of the world that places static religious systems at each other's throats may reflect the crusading mentality of some medieval Christians. But Gerson was not taken by the idea of crusade. For him what was necessary was not the recapture of Jerusalem or the triumph of Christians over Moslems. What mattered was the faithfulness of the Christian Church to its own message of repentance and reform. For him the Church, like the individual Christian, would always remain a pilgrim, a wanderer and a foreigner looking toward the everlasting country. The pilgrim Christian had no reason to delude himself into believing that it was his duty to conquer the world or uproot the heathen.

The Question of Power

Who decides in a world that is not worth conquering but which sets the conditions for our journey? Gerson was no anarchist. He looked to the king to be just and to provide order, even though he knew well that the king who was supposed to rule France was periodically ill and could not even rule himself. There can be something almost absurd in some of Gerson's sermons, an element of the play *Ubu Roi* in its praise of the king who was chronically insane.

Gerson believed in the power of the French monarchy, divided as it was, in the same way that he believed in the power of the Christian Church, divided as it was. He looked forward and worked for a resolution, but he refused to be guided by the royal servants who would have made the king absolute, emperor in his own kingdom, or by the canonists who would have made the pope absolute, a monarch in his own church.

Gerson was not afraid of the exercise of power: he saw it as necessary, but he insisted that the powerful must listen to the wise. This is probably why he accepted preaching at the royal court, even though he knew well that this function subjected him to intrigues. In accepting the post of university chancellor, Gerson tried to avoid the center of power, but here too he found that he had to humor those who mattered not because of their knowledge but because of family, riches, and social position. As he wrote to his colleagues: "I am forced because of the consideration of others or because of the custom of the age to promote those who lack knowledge and are morally corrupt, and sometimes to prefer them to those who are more capable."[91]

Disgusted with this milieu of favoritism and privileges, he tried to withdraw to his deanship at Bruges, only to find here too that privileges could be more important to his colleagues than commitment to discipline and reform. So he returned to Paris in 1400 and exercised the spiritual power that intellectual insight and communicative ability sometimes can bestow on a very few intellectuals in society.

Once again, however, power was the problem: the power of a member of the royal family who used his position to arrange the murder of his rival. John the Fearless thought he could make use of the same academic elite from which Gerson came to get away with his murder by calling it justifiable tyrannicide. But here he underestimated the chancellor's integrity. After first trying to reconcile the warring parties, Gerson began in 1413 his campaign against the defense of tyrannicide.

Gerson sealed his political fate by refusing to be silent. He would not give passive consent to the naked exercise of power. He turned into the pilgrim, wanderer, and foreigner he had long imagined himself to be. He joined the ranks of history's political refugees, a tragic group of outcasts who in our time continue to wander the roads of the world in an awareness that they have no abiding home.

In the end, Gerson's own power is the intellectual and spiritual force that reaches beyond a lifetime and finds its resurrection in new generations. On the whole Gerson was powerless to change the institutions of his own day, but his analyses continue to exercise power because of their spiritual and intellectual vitality.

The Role of the University

Gerson was a university man. The University of Paris and especially the College of Navarre were his home from the age of fourteen in 1377 until he left for Constance in 1415, with relatively brief interruptions. Gerson remained loyal to the institutions that had formed him, even as he, in letters from his self-imposed exile in Bruges, condemned university abuses and explained why he had left them behind. When he returned, he did not forget his reform program—his students were to be taught not just how to think but also how to live. Theology had to be a living process, not pure intellectual analysis. If it did not make them better Christians, it was a waste of time.

Gerson lived in a period when the university idea was catching on all over Europe, especially in the German lands to which his works spread so quickly. However hesitant he may have been about a loss of prestige for Paris as the great university, he probably would have welcomed the greater opportunities that the late medieval foundations gave young men to find alternative university instruction, especially in theology.

By the end of the fifteenth century, Europeans began to discover a hitherto unknown world far larger than anything previously imagined and they debated what to do with these new realms. Soldiers were accompanied by missionaries, who tried to convince the conquerors that the pagans were human beings who had to be taught the words of the Gospel and be baptized in accord with its precepts. Once there was a new Christian population in the Americas, universities also could be founded there, offshoots of their European mother institutions, primarily schools of theology, but also for the sake of disseminating other branches of knowledge.

The university idea had become a common inheritance of medieval culture. Gerson's contribution was largely forgotten, but scholastic discourse has until recently been a decisive factor within European and later American life. Harvard's Divinity School is not all that far from Gerson's University of Paris, for both sought to define God's ways toward humankind. Both medieval Paris and early modern Harvard took it for granted that their professors would play a leading role in the Christian society of their time.

Today such university visions are for the most part secularized, and yet the successors to the medieval university system continue to contribute to the growth of ideas and ideals in world society. Long before Gerson, Peter Abelard expressed the procedure that characterized what R. W. Southern has called scholastic humanism: "By doubting we come to inquiring and by inquiring we perceive the truth."[92] Only through open discussion and careful examination can one reach truth, however difficult and elusive it may be. Gerson lived for this approach, and we have inherited it.

Affective Conflicts Resolved in Common Affectivity

Gerson did not distinguish, as many people do today, between our public and our private lives. Everything held together in his culture, and so questions of personal morality were of central importance in religious and social life. Gerson condemned greed and was skeptical about the development of what we call capitalistic society. He thought that human needs and limitations should determine consumption, not the mechanisms of the market.

Exhortations to asceticism and self-restraint can look quite antiquated in the hedonistic culture of our time. But Gerson's warnings may not appear quite so old-fashioned if we put them in the context of the present debate about gender and sexuality. Where are the limits when people can have access to behavior and fantasies that our ancestors could hardly have imagined? Where are individual human bonds when the market and its exploiters encourage us to consume each other's bodies until virtually nothing is left untouched or untried?

Gerson probably had the same sexual impulses that most people have. So far as I can tell, he was drawn to women, but possibly with some fascination or attraction to his own sex. He did not have an easy time remaining celibate, as he himself indicates, and masturbatory fantasies may have plagued him, especially from what he heard in confession.

But Gerson made his way in celibate culture, and there is no reason to think of him as some deprived male who could not realize his "true" nature. He made choices and sacrifices and apparently kept a physical distance from other human beings. It was not easy at times, but eventually it became a matter of habit and perhaps even of inclination.

The result was not that Gerson came to hate women, as medieval clerics are still sometimes imagined to have done. However split he felt toward women in terms of sexual attraction, he saw the possibility that both men and women inside and outside religious orders could pool their affectivities to form communities based on sharing and spirituality. Gerson imagined such an arrangement for his sisters, and he defended such unofficial communities and thus was on the side of the *Devotio Moderna.* He maintained contact with his brothers in their more formalized Celestine houses, with Cistercians in Paris, as well as with members of the Grande Chartreuse.

Gerson remained on the fringes of these communities and never joined any of them. He was a secular priest, sometimes serving in parishes. He identified with the faculty of theology at the University of Paris, and he apparently did not feel the need for monastic commitment. He found his own niche in the great womb of the medieval Church, and here it is impossible to label him with any facile definitions about sexuality, celibacy, affectivity, and male-female relations.

Beyond gender roles, Gerson turned to God, the Virgin Mary, the angels, and the saints for help on the deathbeds of those he loved. He anticipated the day when the flesh stops its demands and believed that the spirit completely takes over. He was not afraid of this transition, so long as he felt he was in the care of a loving God. In Gerson affectivity, after being a threat, becomes a comfort.

The Desire for God as Metahistory

Did this affectivity lead Gerson to ponder the vision of God in this life? Can he be called a mystic? Scholars have long pondered over this question, and André Combes spent the better part of a lifetime trying to answer it, even taking a single obscure sentence in Gerson's later writings to pinpoint one day in 1425 when the vision may have come.[93]

I do not think it is possible to answer this question with any certitude, for Gerson himself chose not to make the answer available. There is no doubt, however, that both his treatises on *Mystical Theology* and his *Commentary on the Song of Songs* more than a quarter of a century later manifest a deep prayer life and an awareness of the centrality of spiritual experience beyond intellectual categories.

In Gerson we find the modesty and sense of God's ineffability that can characterize the mystic writer, without any guarantee that we are dealing with the actual experience of mystical union with God.[94]

Here, as with tired contemporary questions about sexual identities of people in the past, it is superfluous to provide some formula or phrase that satisfies our curiosity. Gerson's writings show that he was engaged in the tradition of Pseudo-Dionysius, the enigmatic writer whose negative theology is perhaps the most honest way of describing the search for the experience of God. When one gets there, there is no there there. And yet one is there.

Gerson saw that beyond scholastic discourse, there was prayer, the lifting up of mind and heart to God. He loved the phrase uttered by the priest in the transition from the Offertory to the Canon of the Latin Mass: *Sursum corda:* Lift up your hearts (Gl 2.199). In so doing, after having given our offerings, we let God come into our hearts, reenacting the offering of his Son Christ for our salvation.

Such a belief can turn into pious affectivity, with the individual isolated within personal experience. But Gerson looked beyond subjectivity and linked the coming of God's Spirit to the whole of the Church. In what is most individual, something happens to the entire community. The promise of salvation means that the grace of God takes us all.

In such an event we stand outside ourselves and complete the course of history. The individual person realizes his or her identity by being united to God, and the Church fulfills its mission on earth in bringing people to God through liturgy and sacraments. We are beyond time and yet in its fullness. Gerson strained to describe such a moment, but in the end he held back.

A Perennial Reformation

Jean Gerson believed in a *reformatio sempervirens,* an ever-renewed and self-renewing reform of individual, church, and society. In spite of all evidence to the contrary that human beings follow their own greed and lust, he thought Christian society could be refashioned in a better way through open discourse about the meaning of the Gospel and the organization of the Church.

Although he did not use the phrase, Gerson believed in universal human rights, in human prerogatives that were God-given and available to all.[95] There were reason and affectivity in each person, waiting to be reformed and transformed through baptism, membership in the Church, and education in school and university.

Gerson was an idealist, and idealists do not usually do well in the history books. It is easy to show how they fail to carry through their reform programs. But his beliefs remain with us. In the pain and energy of his pilgrimage is the story of generations of people who seek communities that work and believe in loves that last.

Chronology of Gerson's Life and Times

Note that only some of Gerson's works are listed. For more detail, see Glorieux 10.583–98, "Table chronologique" and his "La vie et les oeuvres de Gerson. Essai chronologique," summarized in 1.105–39. Gl6 also contains a helpful overview of the Schism and the conciliar movement, with references to the writings of Gerson and others. All references, unless otherwise given, are to the volumes in the Glorieux edition.

1337–1453	The Hundred Years War between France and England.
1348–1351	The plague makes its first visitation in Western Europe.
1356	Battle of Poitiers ends in French defeat.
1358	Revolt in Paris led by the provost of merchants Étienne Marcel; supported by a *Jacquerie* (peasant revolt) in the provinces.
1360	Treaties of Brétigny and Calais.
1363	The plague returns.
	14 December. **Jean Gerson born at Gerson-lès-Barby, the first child of Arnaut le Charlier and Elisabeth la Chardenière.**
1364	Death of King John. Reign of King Charles V the Wise 1364–1380.
1369–70	French victories in Aquitaine and Brittany.
1370–77	Reign of Pope Gregory XI at Avignon.
1375	French-English treaty of Bruges. Renewed plague epidemic.
1377	Death of King Edward III. Pope Gregory XI returns to Rome. **Fourteen-year-old Jean heads for Paris as a scholarship student of the faculty of arts at the College of Navarre.**
1378	Urban VI elected pope at Rome; Clement VII at Avignon.
	King of France, Charles V, supports Avignon pope.
1378–1417	Great Schism of the Western Church.
1379	Plague epidemic reaches Paris. Popular agitation in Flanders.
1380	King Charles V dies. His successor Charles VI reigns1380–1422.
1381	Popular uprising in England, the Peasants' Revolt. **Jean Gerson gains the licentiate in arts. He begins studies at the faculty of theology, attending lectures for four years on the Bible and two years on *The Sentences* of Peter Lombard.**
1382	Flanders in revolt. Uprisings in Paris and Rouen. **Gerson writes to his patron, probably Pierre d'Ailly** (2.1–4).
1381–83	***Pastorium Carmen,* political poem by Gerson on the Church** (10.290–95). **Also perhaps in 1380s, *Doctrinal aux simples gens,* his first catechism** (10.295–321).

1383	University of Paris declares allegiance to Pope Clement VII at Avignon.
1384	Gerson's teacher Pierre d'Ailly appointed head of the College of Navarre.
1386	Jean Blanchard removed from chancellorship of the university.
1388	**Gerson participates in delegation from the University of Paris, headed by Pierre d'Ailly, to the papal court at Avignon to counter the appeal of Dominican theologian Juan de Monzon.**
1389	**Begins theology lectures on *The Sentences*. Attacks Juan de Monzon** (10.7–24). Pierre d'Ailly elected chancellor of the faculty of theology. **Gerson begins to preach at the royal court: *Quaerite dominum dum inveniri potest*** (7.2.969–78).
1390	**Attains bachelor of theology degree (*baccalaureus formatus*).**
1392	First episodes of King Charles's mental illness. 29 June. **Sermon at royal chapel of Saint Paul for Feasts of Saints Peter and Paul** (7.2.720–39). December. **Gains licentiate in theology. His *resumptio, De jurisdictione spirituali* speaks of the Schism** (3.1–9). (Note that Connolly wrongly claims that Gerson did not receive his licentiate until 1394.)
1393 (?)	17 January. **Sermon in presence of duke of Burgundy, Philip the Bold, on the Feast of Saint Anthony** (7.2.561–72). April. **Named chaplain to the duke of Burgundy, with a stipend; later recommended for deanship of chapter at Saint Donatian, Bruges.** June. King Charles again ill after a period of recovery. 29 September. **Preaches again at royal chapel for Feast of Saint Michael the Archangel, *Factum est proelium*** (7.2.622–39).
1394	January. University delegation asks king to remove ban on public discussion of the Schism. 18 April. **Assumes deanship at Bruges *in absentia*.** 19 April. ***Pax vobis* deals with the Schism** (7.2.779–93). 30 June. King imposes silence on the university concerning the Schism. 16 September. Pope Clement VII dies at Avignon. 28 September. Cardinal Pedro de Luna elected Benedict XIII. October. University delegation to new pope is led by Pierre d'Ailly. 1 November (?). **University sermon, *Exsultabunt sancti in gloria*. Warns against *studiositas* and loss of purity** (5.265–78).
1395	2–18 February. Assembly of clergy (First Synod of Paris) recommends both popes resign (double cession) and considers withdrawal of obedience from Avignon pope. 4 April (?). **Sermon in French *Ecce rex tuus venit tibi mansuetus*. Asks both popes to resign** (7.2.615–22). 13 April. **Appointed chancellor of the University of Paris by Pope Benedict XIII, with the help of Pierre d'Ailly, who has been made bishop.** April–May. Requests by delegations from university and French court to Avignon for papal resignation declined. August–September. **Cautious statement: *De substractione obedientiae* or *De substractione schismatis*** (6.22–24).
1395–1400	**Religious instruction and guidance to his sisters, as in *Discours de l'excellence de la virginité*** (incomplete in Glorieux).

1396 17 January. **Sermon before duke of Burgundy: *Poenitimini* on Saint Anthony in the desert and temptation** (7.2.935–48).
March. Extension of truce between England and France. Richard II of England engaged to Isabelle, daughter of Charles VI of France. University appeals to a future pope against the present one.
Spring. **Gerson writes annotations to declaration of loyalty by Oxford masters for the pope in Rome** (10.324–45).
28 May. **Sermon *In nomine Patris et Filii et Spiritus Sancti:* uneducated persons can have deep spiritual insight** (7.2.671–79).
May–June. ***De papatu contendentibus* rebuts charges of Parisian masters against Benedict XIII** (6.24–28).
30 May. Jean de Varennes, preacher in Reims area, imprisoned.
16 August–14 September. Second Synod of Paris accepts in principle the withdrawal of obedience from the pope.
25 September. Disastrous defeat of crusading army at Nicopolis.

1396–97 **Gerson's youngest brothers, Nicolas (born 1382) and Jean (born 1384), come to Paris and live with him as university students. Letter to them from their mother** (2.6–8).
12 October. **Gerson exercises office of dean for first time at Bruges.**
16 October. **Gerson, as dean, publishes a new ordinance for the chapter of Saint Donatian** (10.432–33).

1397 **Rents rooms in house adjacent to the master's garden of College of Navarre in Paris.**
January or February. ***Requête pour les condamnés à mort,* asks that those condemned to death be allowed to confess** (7.1.341–43).
2 February. **French sermon *Suscepimus Deus*** (7.2.1048–57).

1397(?) 25 March. **Sermon *Ave Maria* on court ethics** (7.2.538–49).
19 April. **University sermon *Tradidit Jesum Judas*** (5.546–62).
21 October. **University sermon, *Vade in domum tuam,* concerning the meaning of "home"** (5.563–697).

1398 Late January–early March. **Negotiations for repair of the dean's house at Bruges. Letter of encouragement from Nicolas de Clamanges** (2.10–12).
March–April. ***De modo se habendi tempore schismatis* as guide to laity** (6.29–34).
14 May–28 July. Third Synod of Paris withdraws obedience from Benedict XIII. **Gerson does not participate.**
19 September. **Faculty of theology censures superstitious beliefs and practices** (10.86–90).
March 1398–March 1399. **Fails to obtain canonry and prebend at chapter of Notre Dame Cathedral** (10.444–46).

1399 27 March. **Sermon *Si non lavero te* on penance, contrition, and attack on reserving sins for special confessors** (5.498–511).

June 1399–Sept. 1400. **Self-imposed exile at Bruges.**

1399 King Richard II of England deposed and imprisoned.

1399–1400 Plague rages in Paris.

1399–1400 Winter. **Guide to his sisters' daily life** (2.14–17).

1400 1 March. **Requests chapter of Notre Dame to accept his resignation of the chancellorship. Leaves for Paris but takes ill and is forced to return to Bruges. Explains in a letter to his colleagues reasons for tendering his resignation** (2.17–35). Later he withdraws his resignation.

April–May. ***Montaigne de contemplation,* a guide in French to the mystical life** (7.16–66).

Spring and summer. Plague continues. Bruges canons allowed to disperse.

23 July. **Makes testament benefiting Saint Donatian** (10.455–56).

August–September. **Recovers from illness. Writes to his colleagues at College of Navarre** (2.42–43). **Perhaps now writes *Contra curiositatem scribendi plures libros*** (4.160).

Late September. **Renews attempt to obtain a prebend on return to Paris.**

1 November. **Sermon *Videns autem Jesus turbas ascendit in montem* on the contemplative life** (5.604–10).

1401 31 March. **Sermon *Omnia dedit ei Pater in manus* on joy in sharing with Christ our brother** (5.405–19).

29 May. **Sermon *Si terrena dixi vobis,* probably at Paris church of Saint-Jean-en-Grève** (7.2.1040–47).

8 June. **Gerson's mother dies. His brother Nicolas has left Paris and joined the Celestine Order.**

25 August. **Feast of Saint Louis. Sermon at College of Navarre: *Considerate lilia agri*** (5.151–68).

11 November. **Nicolas professed at Villeneuve-les-Soissons.**

5 December. **Writes to Nicolas about his sense of loss** (2.45–48).

November–December. **University lecture on Mark 1:4, later revised as *De distinctione verarum revelationum a falsis*** (3.36–56).

November. **Converts lecture on Mark 1:5 into *De comparatione vitae contemplativae ad activam*** (3.63–77).

December. **Lecture on Mark 1:6, *De non esu carnium,* defends abstinence from meat among the Carthusians** (3.77–95).

1400–1403. **Composes what becomes his most popular devotional work, *Tripertitum: Le miroir de l'âme*** (7.1.193–206)**; *Examen de conscience*** (7.1.393–400)**; *La science de bien mourir*** (7.1.404–7).

1402 January–July. **University lectures on Mark 1:8, dedicated to Pierre d'Ailly, become *De vita spirituali animae,* exposition of moral life for the individual and the Church as a whole** (3.113–202).

13 April. **Letter to his brother Nicolas (or to his superior) praising spiritual teaching in Saint Bernard's sermons** (2.54–55).

April–May. ***Protestatio super statum ecclesiae,* resists attempts to declare Pope Benedict a heretic** (3.34–35); ***De Schismate*** (6.42–51)**; *De concilio unius obedientiae*** (6.51–58), **opposes a general council to end the Schism; *Considerationes de restitutione obedientiae Benedicto XIII*** (6.58–69).

18 May. ***Contre le Roman de la Rose*** (7.1.301–16).

20 August. **Sermon on the Feast of Saint Bernard to Cistercians at the Collège de Saint Bernard: *Fulcite me floribus*** (5.325–39).

October. **Writes on topic of *Roman de la Rose* to Pierre Col** (2.65–70). **Soon after, issues appeal to civil and ecclesiastical power against** corruption of youth: *Expostulatio adversus correptionem juventutis* (10.27–28).

November. Lectures on Mark 1:15, *Contra curiositatem studentium* (3.224–49).

Advent 1402–Lent 1403. *Poenitimini,* twelve sermons preached in parish churches on seven capital sins (7.2.793–934).

Winter 1402–1403. Six university lectures, *De mystica theologia,* based on Mark 1:15, later reworked into his speculative treatise on mystical theology (3.250–92).

1403 13 April. *Ad Deum vadit,* Good Friday sermon, completing *Poenitimini* series (7.2.449–519).

May. French monarchy resumes obedience to Benedict XIII.

4 June. Gerson expresses his joy in new union with sermon at Notre Dame: *Emitte spiritum tuum* (5.255–65).

October. Participates in university delegation to Benedict XIII (10.464–66).

9 November. Holds sermon at Marseille in presence of Benedict: *Benedic haereditati tuae* (5.107–22).

18 November. Pope Benedict joins benefice of the church of Saint-Jean-en-Grève to the chancellorship of Paris.

24 December. Finally gains a canonry and prebend in the chapter of Notre Dame (10.467–68).

1404 1 January. Preaches again before Benedict XIII at Tarascon near Avignon: *Apparuit gratia Dei* (5.64–90).

25 and 28 January. Back in Paris, officially installed in his canonry and prebend at chapter of Notre Dame (10.468); purchases a residence in the corner of cathedral cloister later in June.

26 February. *Poenitimini et credite,* sermon on the life of clerics, delivered at Lenten synod in Paris (5.447–58).

27 April. Death of Philip the Bold, duke of Burgundy.

25 June. Becomes a supervisor of the *Hôtel Dieu,* hospital and poorhouse; also put in charge of Notre Dame choir school (10.470).

19 July. Condemns Charles of Savoisy, whose men attacked a religious procession of scholars on 14 July (7.326–40).

14 September. Gerson's father dies at monastery Saint Rémi of Reims, where Jean the Benedictine is a monk.

1405 July. Returns briefly to Bruges to meet challenge to his deanship due in part to his long absence.

August–October. Paris threatened with civil war; rivalry of dukes of Burgundy and Orléans.

7 November. *Vive le roy,* sermon at court advocating reform of the kingdom (7.2.1137–85).

21 November–end of January. University on strike against papal collections ordered by Benedict XIII. Growing resistance to the Avignon pope and agitation for renewed withdrawal of obedience.

1406 Intervenes in controversy over the relics of Saint Denis, the martyr and patron of Paris.

8 October. Sermon *Miserere nostri* expresses concern about the Hôtel Dieu in Paris (7.2.714–17).

(date uncertain) ***De arte audiendi confessiones*** (8.10–17); **probably same period: *De confessione mollitiei*** (8.71–75).

(date uncertain) October. ***De parvulis ad Christum trahendis*** (9.669–86).

November–December. ***Acta de schismate tollendo* warns that the Schism could last for generations** (6.97–98).

November. Fourth Synod of Paris; lasts to January 1407.

30 November. Gregory XII elected pope in Rome.

1407 January. French clergy partially withdraws obedience to Avignon pope, Benedict XIII. Decides to send an embassy to both popes on behalf of king and university.

18 March. ***Vade in pace*, sermon at Notre Dame cathedral on the unity of the Church** (7.2.1093–1100).

Mid-April. **Gerson is away from Paris until February 1408, perhaps until early May. Visits Benedict XIII with d'Ailly at Marseille; then on to Genoa in early June, Lucca, Florence, Viterbo, and Rome in July, where they have two audiences with Gregory XII. *Dialogue spirituel* for sisters possibly written during this trip** (7.1.158–93).

17 May. **Preaches before the cardinals at Avignon; sermon is lost.**

September–November. ***De theologia mystica practica*, second half of his *Mystical Theology*, probably written at Genoa; resides there from end of August to end of January** (Glorieux, "La vie et les oeuvres," 171)**; returns to France but not Paris.**

15 September. **With d'Ailly at Genoa writes to Roman pope, Gregory XII, insisting on latter's resignation** (2.84–86).

23 November. King's brother Louis, the duke of Orléans, is assassinated by henchmen of the duke of Burgundy, John the Fearless, who flees Paris but returns on 28 February 1408.

1408 19 February. **Granted benefice of church of Saint Jean-en-Grève but it is not attached to the office of chancellor. Protest by the abbot of Bec, who lays claim to the church.**

8 March. Theologian Jean Petit defends the killing of Charles of Orléans as justifiable tyrannicide.

Spring (?). **Writes to his brother Nicolas concerning youngest brother, Jean, who has become a Celestine monk** (2.86–90).

29 April. **Sermon *Bonus Pastor* at a diocesan synod in Reims: an outline for reform of the episcopal church** (5.123–44).

Early May. ***Diligite justiciam*, discourse against provost of Paris, William of Tignonville, for hanging two clerics** (7.2.598–615).

1 June. **Temporary reconciliation with canons of Saint Donatian at Bruges, after they had seized his incomes** (10.500–501).

Summer (?). ***Rememoratio agendorum per praelatum durante substractione*** (6.108–14).

4 November. ***Veniat pax*, asks dauphin to end attempts to avenge Duke Louis of Orléans** (7.2.1100–123).

Autumn (?). **Sends letter of spiritual consolation to d'Ailly** (2.105–7).

15 November 1408 to 25 March 1409. **Writes *De auctoritate concilii universalem ecclesiam repraesentantis*** (6.114–23).

1409 January. ***Propositio facta coram Anglicis*, discourse for the English delegation to Pisa** (6.125–35).

January. Beginning controversy, lasting to April 1411, between secular masters and Dominican theologians over position of the friars within the Church.

2 January. **Chancellor and faculty of theology reprove errors of the Dominican Jean Gorrel** (20.32–34).

23 March. Opening of the Council of Pisa. **Gerson not present.**

15 June–8 July. ***De auferabilitate sponsi*, perhaps first given as university lecture on Mark 2:19** (3.294–313).

19 June. ***Domine si in tempore hoc*, sermon later revised and probably sent to the pope elected at Pisa** (6.204–17).

26 June. Council elects a new pope, Alexander V, in vain hopes of the Roman and Avignon popes' resignation.

Late July–mid-August. **Gains canons' consent for arrangements with the chapter at Bruges** (10.501–2).

18 December. ***Pax hominibus bonae voluntatis*, sermon at court advocates peace in the Church and union with the Eastern Orthodox Church** (7.2.763–78).

1410 23 February. ***Quomodo stabit regnum eius?* Sermon attacks the privileges of the mendicants** (7.2.978–92).

5 March. **Protests, with other masters of theology, a bull of Alexander V favoring the mendicants** (10.34–39).

26 March. ***De gravato debitis*, based on Mark 2:23** (3.313–19).

April. ***Dominus his opus habet*, address to graduates in canon law** (5.218–29).

1410. **Letter-treatise to his brother Nicolas on absolution** (2.133–42).

23 May. John XXIII elected successor to Pisa pope, Alexander V.

19 September. **Falls ill and remains absent from chapter of Notre Dame until 21 March 1411** (10.499).

December. **In proceedings lasting until June 1411, the chapter at Bruges takes over the dean's house and removes Gerson from office *in absentia*.**

1411 April (?) **Sets down rules for choir boys at Notre Dame** (9.686–89).

December. Civil war breaks out in Paris between Burgundian and Armagnac factions, lasting until August 1412.

1412 (?) **Treatises on chastity for priests: *De pollutione nocturna et praeparatione ad missam*, also called *De dignitate celebrationis*** (9.35–50); ***De cognitione castitatis* or *De pollutione diurna*** (9.50–64).

1413 11 March (?) **Letter to Basel Carthusians concerning popular practice of honoring saints by saying "Our Father"** (2.151–54).

27 April. Supporters of duke of Burgundy initiate Cabochien revolt in Paris. **Gerson's house pillaged. Flees to the "high vaults" of Notre Dame, where he remains until early September** (10.513–14).

17 August. **Letter to "all churches" asking for a new feast day in honor of the marriage of Virgin Mary and Joseph** (8.61–67).

August–September. **Writes *Considérations sur St. Joseph*** (7.1.63–94).

4 September. **Preaches before the king, after departure of duke of Burgundy from Paris and return of the Armagnac faction: *Rex in sempiternum vive,* his first public attack on Jean Petit's teaching concerning tyrannicide** (7.2.1005–30).
September. **Receives backing from faculty of theology in campaign against defense of tyrannicide** (10.171–79).
30 November. Council of the Faith meets at Paris until 23 February; deals with tyrannicide.

1414 23 February. The Paris council, with the bishop's authority, issues nine propositions condemning justification of tyrannicide.
16 November. First solemn session of the Council of Constance.
4 December. **Gerson preaches on tyrannicide at the royal residence of Saint Paul: *Ecce rex*** (5.243–55).
24 December. King Sigismund, the emperor-elect, arrives at Constance.

1415 5 January. **Solemn Requiem Mass at Notre Dame for the duke of Orléans. Gerson's sermon is lost, but known to have been an attack on the duke of Burgundy.**
Early February. **Sets out for the Council of Constance.**
2 March. Pope John XXIII promises to resign his office.
20 March. John XXIII flees Constance.
23 March. **Gerson rallies the council with *Ambulate dum lucem habetis*** (5.39–50).
6 April. *Haec sancta* decree affirms council is highest governing body in the Church with power to depose popes.
11 April. **Reads a statement (in anger according to Martin Porrée) condemning defense of tyrannicide at the residence of now Cardinal Pierre d'Ailly** (10.529).
21 April. **Sermon *Obsecro vos,* we are all foreigners and pilgrims.**
29 May. The council formally deposes John XXIII.
4 July. The Roman pope, Gregory XII, through his representative, formally "convokes" the council and then resigns. Benedict XIII refuses to resign but is marginalized.
6 July. The council passes sentence against John Hus. It condemns the justification of tyrannicide (*Quilibet tyrannus*).
21 July. **After King Sigismund's departure, sermon *Prosperum iter faciet nobis Deus*** (5.471–80).
3 August. **Hesitant about Birgitta of Vadstena's revelations: *De probatione spirituum,* on the discernment of spirits** (9.177–85).
22 August. **Repeats denunciation of nine assertions condemned by the Council of the Faith at Paris** (10.538).
September. ***Nova positio* asserts council's right to condemn moral propositions such as defense of tyrannicide** (6.146–54).
October. Martin Porrée, representative of the duke of Burgundy, ascribes twenty-two doubtful propositions to Gerson (10.220–25).
October. ***Tractatus de simonia.* Launches relatively mild attack on the buying and selling of Church offices** (6.167–74).
21 October. ***Oportet haereses esse,* sermon before the council, attacks heresies ascribed to Jean Petit** (5.420–35).

25 October. French defeated at Agincourt.

30 October and 13 November. **Replies to Porrée** (10.226–32).

November. Council appoints a commission to deal with the nine assertions concerning tyrannicide.

4 December. **Response to the commission** (10.232–53).

1416 15 January. Three cardinals revoke the decision of the Council of Faith at Paris concerning Jean Petit (Du Pin 5.500–507).

2 February. **Sermon *Suscepimus Deus misericordiam tuam,* urges the council to condemn any teaching that threatens God's commandments** (5.538–46); **memorandum on the right of bishops to define questions of faith** (6.175–78).

19 March. **Beseeches the council, on behalf of the French king, to hold a public hearing on tyrannicide** (10.254–55).

5 May. **Sermon *Deus judicium tuum,* concerned once again with teaching of Jean Petit and necessity for condemning it** (5.190–204).

7 June. **Pentecost sermon *Spiritus Domini;* nothing on tyrannicide, life of contemplation** (5.520–38).

8 September. **Sermon *Jacob autem genuit,* deals with the marriage of Joseph and Mary (5.344–62).**

After 8 September. ***Declaratio compendiosa quae veritates sint de necessitate salutis credendae*** (6.181–89).

28 September. **Letter-treatise *De modo orandi*** (2.169–74).

Autumn. **Brief memorandum on simony** (6.179–81).

1417 1 January. **Letter to Jean the Celestine; spiritual testament as pilgrim and exile** (2.199).

17 January. **Sermon for Feast of Saint Anthony: *Nuptiae factae sunt*** (5.376–98).

After 17 January. **Returns to subject of tyrannicide in sermon *De nuptiis Christi et ecclesiae,*** (6.190–210).

27 January. King Sigismund returns to Constance.

6 February. ***Tractatus de potestate ecclesiastica,* fullest statement on power in the Church** (6.210–50).

26 April. ***Libellus articulorum contra Petrum de Luna*** (6.265–77).

5 June. Council declares Pedro de Luna (Benedict XIII) a heretic.

9 and 21 June. **Letter (with d'Ailly postscript) to Dominican Vincent Ferrier; issues warning against the Flagellants** (2.200–202).

18 July. ***Contra sectam flagellantium*** (10.45–51).

Summer. **Spiritual treatises, ending with *De directione seu rectitudine cordis*** (8.97–115).

26 July. Benedict XIII formally deposed.

15 August. **Discussion on tyrannicide** (10.280–84; Glorieux wrongly claims that it is directed against Dominican John of Falkenberg).

Before 19 August. ***Ad obviandum multis erroribus,* memorandum accepting a papal election prior to Church reform** (6.278–90).

5 October. **Appeals again to the council, in the king's name, to return to question of tyrannicide** (10.260–61).

9 October. *Frequens* decree at Constance; frequent and regular councils of the entire Church to be held in the future.

20 October. Commissioners dealing with question of tyrannicide reject the French appeal as frivolous (Du Pin 5.691).
11 November. Election of a new pope, Odo Colonna of Rome, on Feast of Saint Martin. He takes the name Martin V.

1418 February. ***Considerent zelatores,*** **exhorting council to reconsider condemnation of tyrannicide due to an appeal to a future council by Polish lords** (6.301–2).
3 April. ***Contra conclusiones Matthaei Graben,*** **response to Dominican assertion that members of religious orders are more perfect in their vocations than parish priests** (10.70–72).
15 April. Papacy concludes concordats with Germans and French.
22 April. Council of Constance adjourns.
10 May. Martin V prohibits appeals to future councils.
Soon after 10 May. ***An liceat in causis fidei a papa appellare,*** **attempts to avoid consequences of Martin V's decision** (6.283–90).
May. ***De sententia pastoris semper tenenda,*** **asks for return to ancient liberties of the Gallican Church** (6.291–94).
17 May. **Leaves Constance the day after Martin V's departure**
July–August. ***Deploratio super civitatem*** **mourns the destruction of Paris and the killings by supporters of the duke of Burgundy** (10.407–14). ***Deploratio studii parisiensis,*** **written probably soon thereafter** (4.5–7).
Summer–Autumn. **Stays at Rattenberg and Neuburg am Inn in Bavaria, and later at Melk,** ***Consolatio Theologiae*** (9.185–245).
27 July. **At Rattenberg in Tyrol, completes** ***Josephina,*** **the great poem of the Holy Family with Joseph as central figure** (3.31–100).
September. ***Dialogus apologeticus.*** **From the abbey of Melk on the Danube, looks back on the council and defends his record, especially his stance on tyrannicide** (6.296–304). **Apparently continues on to Vienna.**

1419 10 September. Duke John of Burgundy killed by supporters of the dauphin at meeting on the bridge of Montereau.
September–October. ***Carmen in laudem ducis Austriae*** (4.169–70), **for Frederick of Austria. Leaves Vienna soon thereafter.**
November. ***Trilogium astrologiae theologizatae*** (10.90–109).
November–December. **Pierre d'Ailly writes from Avignon about arrangements for his visit to Lyon** (2.222).
December (?). **Arrives back in French-speaking regions and settles at Lyon, under Archbishop Amédée de Talaru's protection.**

1420 January. **The dauphin, future Charles VII, at Lyon grants Gerson compensation for what he lost in Paris** (10.553).
21 March. Treaty of Troyes, according to which the son of English King Henry V and Catherine of France stand to inherit both kingdoms
9 August. Pierre d'Ailly dies.
Sometime that year. **Letter-poems consoling brother Jean (probably the Celestine, not the Benedictine as Glorieux states) on death of their brother Nicolas and sister Raulina** (2.224–26).

1421 **Youngest brother, Jean the Celestine, until then prior at Marcoussis, moves to Lyon to become prior of Celestine house there.**

January. *De contractibus,* at request of Carthusians (9.385–422).
18 March. *Contra superstitiosam dierum observantiam* (10.116–21); same day: letter-treatise on the same question (2.227–32).
8 October. Sermon before the archbishop, *Redde quod debes,* calls for a synod at Lyon, (5.487–93).

1422 23 March. *De potestate absolvendi et peccatorum reservatione* asks that parish priests be granted authority to absolve most sins (9.421–23).
August. *De nobilitate* for the archbishop of Lyon. Accepts that some canonries in collegial churches be reserved for sons of noble families (9.476–99).
31 August. Henry V of England dies.
21 October. Charles VI of France dies.
30 October. Letter-treatise, *De religionis perfectione et moderamine,* to William Minaud of the Grande Chartreuse (2.232–45).
November. Completes revision of *Mystical Theology,* which he sends to the Grande Chartreuse.

1423 April. *De laude scriptorium,* in praise of copyists (9.423–34).
Before May. *De sollicitudine ecclesiasticorum* (9.434–58).
May. Letter from Jean the Celestine to the Grande Chartreuse describes Gerson's life and work at Lyon and contains a first list of his writings (10.554–61; 1.23–26).
About May. Letter to Jean the Celestine at Lyon concerning Gerson's hesitation to leave his life of silence (2.245–47).
May. *De examinatione doctrinarum,* third treatise about discernment of spirits (9.458–75).
Begins *Tractatus de canticis,* concerning music, song, and their spiritual manifestations; finishes August 1426 (9.524–602).

1424 April. Letter to Oswald of Corda, vicar of the Grande Chartreuse, declines invitation to visit him (2.251).

1426 9 June. Letter to monk of the Grande Chartreuse with *De libris legendis a monacho,* summarizes his life in terms of his readings (2.275–76; 9.609–13).
18 September. Letter-treatise *De susceptione humanitatis christi,* written "from early morning until almost noon" (2.263–74).

1427 January. Begins his longest work, *Collectorium super Magnificat;* finishes 4 April 1428 (8.163–534).

1427–28. Several letter-treatises on spiritual and ethical questions to Oswald of Corda and other Carthusians (2.285–331).

1428 6 October. *De indulgentiis* (9.654–58).
November. Letter to Celestines asks to keep his writings at their house in Avignon (2.334). Later changes his mind, sends part of his writings to the Grande Chartreuse (1.27).

1429 29 April. Joan of Arc at Orléans under siege by the English.
8 May. The English abandon siege of Orléans.
14 May. *De puella Aurelianensi,* defends Jeanne d'Arc (9.661–65).
15 May–9 July. *Amo te sacer ordo,* commentary on the Song of Songs (8.565–639).

	12 July. **Gerson dies.** Jeanne d'Arc and the dauphin are on their way to Reims, where he is crowned Charles VII.
	17 July. **Archbishop of Lyon writes to Jean the Celestine in praise of his brother** (1.144). Charles VII is anointed king of France at Reims .
1430	23 May. Jeanne d'Arc captured at Compiègne.
1431	9 January. Trial of Joan of Arc opens at Rouen.
30 March.	Joan burned at the stake as a relapsed heretic.
1431–1451	Council of Basel.
1434	**Jean the Celestine dies; he has been Gerson's literary executor with *annotatio secunda* of his writings** (1.29–33).
1437	Pope Eugenius IV (1431–47) transfers the council to Ferrara (later to Florence). Most clerics remain at Basel.
1438	The Pragmatic Sanction of Bourges guarantees virtual independence of Gallican Church. Van Eyck paints Cardinal Niccolò Albergati.
1439	Council of Basel elects Count Amadeus of Savoy as Felix V, a second pope.
1439	Council of Florence declares union of the Roman and Greek Churches; never implemented.
1449	Felix V abdicates and accepts Nicolas V (1447–1455).
1450	French reconquer Normandy.
1452	Hapsburg Frederick III elected Holy Roman Emperor, the last medieval king to go to Rome to be crowned.
1453	Turks conquer Constantinople; end of Eastern Roman Empire.
1456	Joan of Arc rehabilitated.
1458	Aeneas Sylvius Piccolomini, former fervid conciliarist, elected as Pope Pius II at Basel.
1460	*Execrabilis;* Pius II forbids appeals of papal decisions by future councils.
1464	Paul II becomes the last medieval pope who sought reform.
1471	Sixtus IV, a Franciscan, attempts to designate 19 March as feast day for Saint Joseph. Gets bogged down in family and Italian politics.
1483–1521	**Gerson's collected works printed and reprinted in Cologne, Strasbourg, Nuremberg, Basel, and Paris**
1483–1498	**King Charles VIII shows special devotion to Gerson and makes chapel in his honor at Lyon.**
1486	*Malleus maleficarum* signals beginning of the witch craze in Western Europe, lasting into the seventeenth century.
1492–1503	Pope Alexander VI's reign riddled with scandals.
1503–1513	Reign of the warrior Pope Julius II. Construction of a new Saint Peter's cathedral funded with indulgence collections.
1504	**Bishop of Basel writes to chapter of Saint Paul at Lyon on importance of Gerson's writings for him** (Du Pin vol. 1, clxxi).
1512–17	Fifth Lateran Council makes last ditch reform attempt.
1517	Martin Luther launches the Protestant Reformation.
1530	*Confessio Augustana* (The Augsburg Confession) seeks compromise by calling for a general council.
1545	Opening of the Council of Trent begins the Catholic Reformation and lays the foundation of the modern Roman Catholic Church.
	Gerson's medieval Christian Church comes to an end.
1606	**Gerson's collected works published in Paris.**

1643	Gerson's grave accidentally discovered; reports of miracles (Du Pin 1.cxc–cxcv).
1706	Gerson's works and other contemporary conciliar writings published by Louis Ellies Du Pin, in defense of his concept of church government under a council and a Gallican church.
1836	First indications of new interest in Gerson in Paris.
1858	After twelve years of reading and research, Johann Baptist Schwab of Würzburg publishes a two-volume Gerson biography.
1928	James L. Connolly's Gerson biography portrays him as "reformer and mystic" to plead for him in Catholic circles as orthodox.
1960–1973	Palemon Glorieux's publishes new edition of Gerson's works.

Notes

Chapter 1

1. See the introduction in *Jean Gerson. Early Works,* 4–21; abbreviated as EW. For a review of previous work on Gerson and his times, see the final chapter.

2. *Collectorium super Magnificat,* in Glorieux, *Jean Gerson. Oeuvres complètes,* vol. 8, 369. References to Gerson's writings in this edition will be to "Gl" with the volume and page number.

3. EW, 154–56. Original text in Gl 2.6–8.

4. Francis Ledwidge, "Relations de famille," esp. 7–8.

5. Gl 2.47, Letter 9, trans. EW, 198.

6. See William Chester Jordan, *The Great Famine.* Also Denys Hay, *Europe in the Fourteenth and Fifteenth Centuries,* 36–39.

7. Samuel K. Cohn, *The Black Death Transformed,* argues that the plague could be transmitted directly by human contact and not necessarily by rats. For the role of the Church in one diocese, see William J. Dohar, *The Black Death and Pastoral Leadership.*

8. Skibby and Bregninge churches northwest of Copenhagen. Danish church wall paintings are now on www.kalkmalerier.dk, thanks to professor Axel Bolvig of Copenhagen University and his students.

9. A new standard history is being written by Jonathan Sumption, *The Hundred Years War,* vol. 1, *Trial by Battle,* reaches from 1337 to the Battle of Crécy; vol. 2, *Trial by Fire,* from the truce of Calais in 1347 to the resumption of the war in 1369.

10. Emile Rebouis, *Etude historique . . . sur la peste.* See Gerson's remark in Gl 2.28, Letter 3; EW, 174.

11. For a classic account see, Etienne Gilson, *History of Christian Philosophy.* For medieval intellectuals in their social context see, Alexander Murray, *Reason and Society.*

12. A good introduction is still David Knowles, *The Evolution of Medieval Thought,* 318–326. Also Julius Rudolf Weinberg, *A Short History of Medieval Philosophy,* 235–265.

13. See Arthur Stephen McGrade, *The Political Thought of William of Ockham.*

14. See Gilbert Ouy, "Humanism and Nationalism in France," in McGuire, *The Birth of Identities,* 107–125, esp. 112.

15. *Letters on Familiar Matters,* trans. Aldo S. Bernardo: *Fam.* 24:4, 319.

16. In *Fam.*17:1, Petrarch wrote to his monastic brother about "true philosophy" and quoted from Augustine, whom he called "the philosopher of Christ" (trans. Aldo S. Bernardo, 2).

17. The phrase is from *Fam.*11:6. See Morris Bishop, *Petrarch and his World,* 41–50.

18. See Abelard, *Ethics,* ed. D. E. Luscombe, 31–33. Also Michael T. Clanchy, *Abelard. A Medieval Life,* esp. 128–29.

19. See Jean Froissart's *Chronicles,* as in the Penguin Classics translation and abridgement. For the original text, *Chroniques de Froissart,* a critical edition is still in progress at the Société de l'Histoire de France (1869–1975), 15 volumes. The last volume covers the years 1387–1389.

20. Emmanuel Le Roy Ladurie, *Montaillou,* 33. Statement of the parish priest Pierre Clergue: "It would be better for a brother to marry his sister rather than to receive a wife who was a stranger."

21. C. H. Lawrence, *Medieval Monasticism,* 227. An illuminating study is Dennis D. Martin's *Fifteenth-Century Carthusian Reform.*

22. *Inferno* 3.59–60.

23. See, for example, Richard Kieckhefer, *Unquiet Souls.*

24. In general, Oliver Davies, *God Within. The Mystical Tradition of Northern Europe.* For texts: *John Ruusbroec. The Spiritual Espousal and other Works.*

25. *Ruusbroec,* 115.

26. Gl 2.55–62, Letter 13; EW, 202–10; Gl 2.97–103, Letter 26; EW, 249–56.

27. For central texts and a superb introduction, see John Van Engen, *Devotio Moderna. Basic Writings.*

28. *Angela of Foligno. Complete Works,* 221. Bernard McGinn, *The Flowering of Mysticism,* 141–152.

29. *On Distinguishing True from False Revelations,* 356, n. 53 in EW.

30. Trans. F. Hopman. The first complete English translation, with Huizinga's original footnotes was only issued in 1996, *The Autumn of the Middle Ages.* This translation is harshly criticized by Edward Peters and Walter P. Simons in "The New Huizinga and the Old Middle Ages," with valuable analyses of new work on the period.

31. My colleague and friend Henrik Jensen has greatly increased my understanding of the twentieth century, especially with his landmark study *Ofrets århundrede* ("The Century of the Victim").

32. Tuchman, *A Distant Mirror,* conceded little understanding for medieval spirituality, but she was a master of military history.

33. *Ruusbroec,* 46.

34. *The Cloud of Unknowing,* trans. Clifton Wolters.

35. For the dance of death, the church of Nørre Alslev on the island of Falster (*Jeg ser på kalkmalerier,* ed. Niels Saxtorph, 202–3). For a courtly "dance of life," the *dansefrise* at Ørslev church on southwestern Zealand (reproduced on the cover of the guidebook), dates to about 1325.

36. The phrase *Oremus et pro perfidis Judaeis* was used in the Good Friday prayers of the Roman Catholic Church as late as the early 1960s. For background, see Gavin I. Langmuir, "The Faith of Christians and Hostility to Jews." Also Langmuir, *Toward a Definition of Antisemitism.*

37. Helen Waddell, *Mediaeval Latin Lyrics,* 225. I have adapted her translation.

38. Daniel Hobbins, "The Schoolman as Public Intellectual."

CHAPTER 2

1. *Jean de Gerson. Recherches sur son origine,* esp. 53–60. Abbreviated as "Jadart."

2. Gl 4.147, *Memoriale nativitatis.*

3. The village seems to have been attractive property for the Abbey of Saint Rémi. As late as 1370, the monks added five new parcels of property to their land in and around the village. See Jadart, 71.

4. Another distinguished theologian and churchman who came from a modest background was Robert Grosseteste. See R. W. Southern, *Robert Grosseteste.*

5. Gilbert Ouy, "L'humanisme et les mutations politiques et sociales."

6. *De simplificatione cordis,* 15.3; Gl 8.93.

7. Gilbert Ouy, "Trois prières françaises inédites," 34.

8. Maurice H. Keen, *England in the Later Middle Ages,* 69–70. Also Alfred Coville, *Les premiers Valois et la guerre de cent ans,* 160–61.

9. See Bibliographical Guide.

10. Jadart, 110.

11. Gl 4.52. I am grateful to Gilbert Ouy for this observation.

12. Jadart, 109–118. See page 113 for his claim that Gerson's sisters later became nuns or nurses at Reims. There is no evidence that any, except for Marion, ever left the family home.

13. For literacy, see Michael T. Clanchy, *From Memory to Written Record,* 224–252. In forthcoming work, Clanchy shows, especially on the basis of late medieval art, how mothers taught their children to read. Also R. W. Southern, *Scholastic Humanism,* esp. ch. 5.

14. See chapter 1, note 5.

15. Favier, *La guerre,* esp. ch. 11; "La reconquête de Charles V," 327–366. Christine de Pizan, today far better known than her contemporary Jean Gerson, in 1404 chronicled the attractive reign of Charles V in her *Le livre des fais.*

16. Keen, *England in the Later Middle Ages,* 260.

17. There are many studies. See especially Rodney Hilton, *Bond Men Made Free* and Michel Mollat and Philippe Wolff, *The Popular Revolutions of the Late Middle Ages.*

18. As in writing to his brother Jean the Celestine (from Constance, 1 January 1417, Gl 2.199): "Ego peregrinus et advena, sic enim Gerson interpretatum significat." Also Gl 2.226.

19. Georges Duby, *Les trois ordres,* trans. as *The Three Orders.*

20. For the baptism of Clovis, see Gregory of Tours, *The History of the Franks* II.31, 143–44 in the Penguin translation. Also Nathalie Nabert, "La référence à Clovis chez Jean Gerson," 231–248.

21. *Sermo de officio pastoris,* 29 April 1408, Gl 5.123–144.

22. Hastings Rashdall, "Previous Education of the Medieval Student," *The Universities of Europe,* vol. 3, 341–352. Abbreviated as "Rashdall."

23. Pierre Desportes, *Reims et les rémois.*

24. *Abbot Suger. On the Abbey Church of St. Denis and Its Art Treasures,* ed. Erwin Panofsky. Also *Peter of Celle. Selected Works,* with an excellent introduction. Pierre was an advocate of monastic friendship: McGuire, *Friendship and Community,* 270–279. For the church of Saint Rémi, see Patrick Demouy, *Saint-Rémi de Reims.*

25. Gl 4.31–100. See chapter 10.

26. Gilbert Ouy, *Gerson bilingue.*

27. Louis Mourin, *Jean Gerson. Prédicateur français,* 381–426.

28. Gl 2.67, Letter 15; EW, 216. Cf. *Disticha Catonis* 1.4.2.

29. Mourin, *Prédicateur français,* 368–377. See also the "Table des auteurs cités" in Gl 10.631–644.

30. As Letter 13, Gl 2.62; EW, 209: "Something to which the Apostle and Aristotle in their experience bear witness."

31. McGuire, "In Search of Bernard's Legacy."

32. *De parvulis ad Christum trahendis,* Gl 9.669–686. See McGuire, "Education, Confession and Pious Fraud," esp. 320–324.

33. Gl 5.331; EW, 137. Gl 5.331.

34. See the family tree in Jadart, 131.

35. Letter B, Gl 2.7 EW, 156.

36. Rashdall, vol. 1, 507.

37. Gerson appears in a list sent in July 1387 to Clement VII in Avignon, in order to obtain prebends: *Johanni Arnaudo de Gersonio, cler. Remens. dioc., mag. in art. stud in theol.* (Gl 10.421).

38. Rashdall, vol. 1, 510.

39. *Paradiso* 10: *Che leggendo nel Vico de li strami/sillogizzò invidiosi veri.* Glorieux has provided a rare glimpse into the life and thoughts of a Paris student in "L'année universitaire 1392–1393."

40. A. Combes, "Gerson et la naissance de l'humanisme." Gilbert Ouy, "Pétrarque et les premiers humanistes français."

41. Perhaps not so surprising, however, in view of greater skepticism toward friendship in late medieval Christian life. See McGuire, *Friendship and Community,* 413–23.

42. Gl 2.35, Letter 5; EW, 183. McGuire, "Jean Gerson and the End of Spiritual Friendship."

43. Jacques Le Goff has shown how concepts of time changed in the later Middle Ages and how "a humanism based on a nice computation of time was born." See "Labor Time in the 'Crisis' of the Fourteenth Century," *Time, Work, and Culture,* 43–57, esp. 51.

44. Gl 2.3; EW, 152.

45. *The Register of Eudes of Rouen* as for 16 October 1248: "William, priest of Notre-Dame, is publicly known for incontinence with a certain woman whom, it is said, he has been keeping for the last twenty years," 16.

46. A good example of such a sensationalistic treatment is James Cleugh, *Love Locked Out.*

47. As seen by the arrangement of hell in the *Divine Comedy.* Here I disagree with Lester Little's claim that after the eleventh century avarice was seen as the greater sin. See *Religious Poverty and the Profit Economy,* 36.

48. See *On Distinguishing True from False Revelations,* Gl 3.52; EW, 357.

49. "Une lettre de jeunesse de Jean Gerson."

50. Bernard Guenée, *Between Church and State,* 126.

51. Gl 2.1; EW, 149.

52. Gl 2.2; EW, 151.

53. Gl 2.3; EW, 151.

54. Gl 2.3; EW, 152.

55. Lynn Thorndike, *University Records.*

56. Gl 2.4; EW, 153–54.

57. R. W. Southern, *Robert Grosseteste,* 52.

58. Rashdall, vol. 1, 457. Glorieux, "La vie et les oeuvres de Gerson," 151.

59. Alan E. Bernstein, *Pierre d'Ailly and the Blanchard Affair,* esp. 82–105.

Chapter 3

1. Gordon Leff, *Paris and Oxford Universities;* Stephen Ferruolo, *The Origins of the University.*

2. Rashdall, vol. 1, 461–62. Jacques Verger, "Teachers," ch. 5 in Hilde de Ridder-Symoens, *A History of the University in Europe,* vol. 1, 144–168, esp. 144–47.

3. Rashdall, vol. 1, 472.

4. Glorieux, "La vie et les oeuvres de Gerson," esp. 152. For background, Marcia L. Colish, *Peter Lombard,* 1–2.

5. For the traditional view: Glorieux, "L'enseignement universitaire de Gerson," esp. 108–113. As Daniel Hobbins now has shown in his important article "The Schoolman as Public Intellectual," 1317: "We have no evidence that Gerson ever prepared such a work for publication."

6. Gilbert Ouy, "Le 'Pastorium Carmen'." Note that Glorieux in vol. 4 only gave a fragment of the text, but in vol 10, 290–95 included Ouy's edition.

7. Francis Oakley, *The Western Church,* 55–70. For more detail, E. Delaruelle, *L'église au temps du grand schisme,* 3–200.

8. Bernstein, *Pierre d'Ailly,* 37–39.

9. Ouy, "Le *Pastorium Carmen,*" 199.

10. As did other commentators on the Song of Songs, from Origen to Bernard and other Cistercian writers. Among many rich new studies, see Denys Turner, *Eros and Allegory.*

11. Gl 10.295–321. Glorieux (10.287) promised an article to explain his reasons for dating the work to about 1387, "Une oeuvre de jeunesse de Gerson," but it never appeared.

12. Desportes, *Reims et les remois,* 206, thought the work was edited by the archbishop himself.

13. D. Catherine Brown, *Pastor and Laity,* esp. 1–3.

14. *Jacobi a Voragine Legenda Aurea,* 253–54. Trans. *The Golden Legend* for 7 December, 28.

15. *Prédicateur français,* 425.

16. Thomas Tentler, *Sin and Confession,* 307–314.

17. R. W. Southern, "The English Origin of the 'Miracles of the Virgin'."

18. Jacobus a Voragine, *Legenda Aurea,* 221–22; trans., 207–8.

19. Cf. *Waning of the Middle Ages,* ch. 12, "Religious Thought Crystallizing into Images."

20. Jacobus a Voragine, *Legenda Aurea,* 17; trans, 12. For Gregory the Great, see Homily 37 of his *XL homiliarum in Evangelia libri duo,* trans. *Forty Gospel Homilies,* 334, concerning Cassius, Bishop of Narni. Gerson's summary of this *exemplum* is very precise. He must have read the sermon. His knowledge of the Church Fathers has not been studied in detail.

21. For background, Michael T. Clanchy, *From Memory to Written Record,* 187.

22. Perhaps a variant of "Qu'aprent poulains en denteüre/ Tenire le veut tant come il dure," in Joseph Morawski, *Proverbes français,* nr. 1765.

23. It is a commonplace of medieval studies that descriptions and depictions of hell are more vivid and "convincing" than those of heaven. One medieval writer who invested his creativity in a detailed description of heaven was Dante. See Jeffrey Burton Russell, *A History of Heaven.*

24. As Gl 8.10–17; EW, 365–377.

25. I have been unable to find a written source for this story. A similar story concerns a woman in the diocese of Reims who hid her sins. See the thirteenth-century collection by the Dominican preacher, Stephen of Bourbon, *Anecdotes historiques d'Etienne de Bourbon,* nr. 186.

26. For chronology and sources, a helpful "dossier" is in Gl 10.3–5. Also Ouy's pioneering article, "La plus ancienne oeuvre retrouvée de Jean Gerson."

27. Rashdall, vol. 1, 486.

28. The Roman Catholic Church proclaimed the doctrine of the Immaculate Conception in 1854 (*Catechism of the Catholic Church,* nr. 490–92). There was an ongoing theological discussion in the Middle Ages concerning this teaching. Bernard of Clairvaux opposed it. See his letter to the canons of Lyon (*The Letters of Saint Bernard,* nr. 215, 289–293; *Sancti Bernardi Opera,* vol. 7, nr. 174). For background, Marielle Lamy, *L'Immaculée conception,* 562–575.

29. Gl 2.39, Letter 6; EW, 188.

30. Ibid.

31. See Gl 1.23, a list of Gerson's works from 1423 by his brother, Jean the Celestine. Also Glorieux, "Autour de la liste des oeuvres de Gerson," esp. 96–97.

32. I have dealt briefly with this work in "Anti-clerical Invective and the Growth of Clerical Satire," esp. 88–91.

33. *Adversus Vigilantium* 4.2.

34. Gilbert Ouy, "Humanism and Nationalism in France," 112–15.

35. John of Salisbury reflects the twelfth-century combination of school learning and humanism, especially in his *Policraticus* and his *Historia Pontificalis.*

36. In the opening of *Cligès,* as translated in *Arthurian Romances,* 123: "Our books have taught us that chivalry and learning first flourished in Greece; then to Rome came chivalry and the sum of knowledge, which now has come to France." Original in Chrétien de Troyes, *Oeuvres complètes,* 174.

37. Bernstein, *Pierre d'Ailly,* chs. 3 and 4, also provides an excellent edition of the two treatises.

38. Guillaume Mollat, *The Popes at Avignon,* 21–23; Christian Trottmann, *La vision béatifique,* esp. 446–455. See also the detailed review by Kent Emery, Jr., in *Vivarium* 37 (1999), 258–281. Russell Friedman kindly gave me this reference.

39. Rashdall, vol. 1, 461.

40. Cf. *Contra curiositatem studentium,* Gl 3.224–249, partly trans. in *Jean Gerson: Selections,* 26–45. Also Gerson's Letters 2–7 (Gl 2. 17–43; EW, 160–194).

41. Gl 10.14. Cf. Horace, *Ars poetica,* line 139: "Parturient montes, nascetur ridiculus mus."

42. Morawski, *Proverbes français,* nr. 186: *Au plus fol la machue.* Cf. Gl 10.21: "Juxta vulgare proverbium, stolidiori clava ab eis data esset."

43. Gilbert Ouy, "La plus ancienne oeuvre," esp. 456.

44. See Michael Clanchy's superb *Abelard. A Medieval Life,* especially ch. 7, "Knight."

45. For the political background, there are several good studies, but I am especially indebted to R. C. Famiglietti, *Royal Intrigue.*

46. *Quaerite dominum dum inveniri potest,* for Ash Wednesday, Gl 7.2.969–278. The dating is not certain. See Mourin, *Prédicateur français,* 55–60.

47. The story is redolent of the *Golden Legend* or the *Lives of the Fathers,* but I have been unable to find Gerson's source.

48. As Gilbert Ouy has pointed out ("Pétrarque et les premiers humanistes français," 424), Gerson was borrowing here directly from Petrarch's *De remediis.*

49. Important recent work includes: *Medieval Monastic Preaching,* ed. Carolyn Muessig; Hervé Martin, *Le métier de prédicateur à la fin du Moyen Age (1350–1520);* David L. d'Avray, *The Preaching of the Friars;* Jussi Hanska, *"And the Rich Man also died".*

50. See Catherine Brown, *Pastor and Laity,* ch. 2, "The Art of the Preacher," esp. 11–17. As in all sermon literature, there is the question to what extent the text reflects what actually was said. Gerson's sermons are sometimes so long and detailed that one can hardly imagine their being preached *in toto.* At other times his texts seem to be merely his notes for the sermon.

51. Ernst H. Kantorowicz, *The King's Two Bodies,* 44–45, 118–125. Also Sarah Hanley, *The Lit de Justice of the Kings of France.*

52. Cf. Gl 10.10. See Jerome's polemic *Contra Vigilantium.*

53. Actually it is in the sixth book of the *Aeneid* (l. 854), an indication that Gerson was quoting from memory.

54. Gl 7.2.528: *Titi Livi. Ab Urbe Condita* 2.32.

55. See Gl 10.421. This may be the curate of Champeaux-en-Brie in the diocese of Paris, which Gerson had before 1395; Glorieux, "La vie et les oeuvres," 152, n. 5.

56. Cf. *Legenda Aurea* on Ambrose, 250; *The Golden Legend,* 25.

57. It is a medieval commonplace that kings do bad things because of bad advisors. The king's person is rarely blamed. See Froissart on Edward II of England, "who governed his realm very harshly on the advice of others." (*Chronicles,* trans. Brereton, 39).

58. *In Dominica Septuagesimae,* Gl 6.362–376.

59. The phrase "a mari usque ad mare" is found in Ps 71 (72):8 and was already used by the Cistercian Order. Today it is a motto for Canada and is found in the patriotic US hymn *America the Beautiful*: "From sea to shining sea."

60. "He compared the time of youth to a piece of wax of the right consistency for the impress of a seal." Eadmer, *The Life of Saint Anselm,* ch. xi, 20.

61. Jacques Le Goff, "Merchant's Time and Church's Time in the Middle Ages," *Time, Work and Culture,* 29–42.

62. Gl 2.3; EW, 152.

63. Alan Bernstein, *Pierre d'Ailly.*

64. As in a letter (nr. 44) from exile, 10 August 1418, to his brothers Nicolas and Jean the Celestine, Gl 2.216–217.

65. See "Otium et quies," *Dictionnaire de spiritualité* vol. 12, col. 2746–56. Also Edith Scholl, "The Cistercian Vocabulary," esp. 78–82.

66. See Glorieux's dossier of Gerson's works on superstition (Gl 10.73–76).

67. Glorieux, "La vie," 154. Also Glorieux, "L'année universitaire 1392–1393," 470.

68. *Gerson and the Great Schism,* 36. For more recent bibliography, John J. Ryan, *The Apostolic Conciliarism of Jean Gerson.*

69. Cf. L. Salembier's "Gerson," *Dictionnaire de Théologie Catholique,* referring (col. 1321) to Gerson's "erreurs" and "fausses doctrines."

70. Morrall, *Gerson and the Great Schism,* 34–38.

71. Famiglietti, *Royal Intrigue,* 1–2.

72. *Pour la Pentecôte,* Gl 7.2.431–449.

73. *Enarrationes in psalmos* 83. See PL 36:765.

74. This theme is not mentioned in the otherwise very detailed study by P. S. Lewis, *Later Medieval France.*

75. For the "Ghent War" of 1379–1385, see David Nicholas, *Medieval Flanders,* 227–231.

76. Gl 7.2.446. Cf. Morawski, *Proverbes français,* nr. 273: "Bonne est la maille qui garde le denier."

77. For what happened in the forest of Le Mans, Froissart (trans. Brereton), 392–96. Also *Chronique du religieux de Saint-Denys,* livre 13, ch. 5; tome 2, vol. 1, 16–19. Abbreviated as CRSD.

78. Famiglietti, *Royal Intrigue,* tried on the basis of contemporary chronicles to diagnose the mental illness of the king in late twentieth-century terminology. See "The Mental Disorder of Charles VI," ch. 1, esp. 7–14.

79. Ouy, "Trois prières françaises," and *The Prayers and Meditations of Saint Anselm,* 152.

80. Gl 5.240. The same point as in Gl 7.2.435, the Sermon for Pentecost mentioned above.

81. Famiglietti, *Royal Intrigue,* 3.

82. CRSD for 1392, livre 13, ch.9; tome 2, vol. 1, 35.

83. As Famiglietti, *Royal Intrigue* or Richard Vaughan, *John the Fearless,* ch. 2, 29–48.

84. Famiglietti, *Royal Intrigue,* 233, n 88.

85. Gl 10.429. See E. Vansteenberghe, "Gerson à Bruges."

86. Peter Moraw, "Careers of Graduates," in Hilde de Ridder-Symoens, *Universities in the Middle Ages,* 244–279.

87. Gl 2.19; EW, 162.

88. Gl 2.19; EW, 163. See Glorieux, "Gerson au chapitre de Notre-Dame," esp. 428–438.

89. Richard Vaughan, *Philip the Bold,* 198–99, 202–4. Also Henri David, *Claus Sluter,* who (127) rejected the claim made in 1935 that one of the *pleurants* at the tomb of Philip the Bold was modeled on Gerson.

90. Louis Mourin, *Prédicateur français,* 84–85.

91. Cf. *De cognitione castitatis,* Gl 9.69.

92. *Athanasius. The Life of Antony,* ch. 10–12, 39–40. Gerson's source, however, may have been the *Legenda Aurea,* ch. 21, 104 (trans., 100).

CHAPTER 4

1. Hefele-Leclercq, *Histoire des Conciles* tome 6.2, 1145–46.

2. CRSD Livre 14, ch. 10; tome 2, vol. 1, 98.

3. CRSD Livre 14, ch. 11; tome 3, vol. 2, 100.

4. Heinrich Denifle, *Chartularium Universitatis Parisiensis* vol. 3, nr. 1679. Abbreviated as CUP.

5. E. Vansteenberghe, "Gerson à Bruges", esp., 8–9.

6. Gl 7.2.779–83. King Philip VI is referred to (780) as *vostre aieul,* but Gerson could have been speaking to members of the royal family and not necessarily the king.

7. CRSD Livre 15, ch. 3; tome 2, vol. 1, 136–183.

8. Ibid., 138.

9. Ibid., 168.

10. Hefele-Leclercq 6.2.1147.

11. CRSD Livre 15, ch. 4; tome 2, vol. 1, 184.

12. Ibid., 186.

13. CRSD Livre 15, ch. 7; tome 2, vol. 1, 192.

14. The sermon appears in MS BN nouv. acq. lat. 3043. See Ouy, *Gerson bilingue,* lxiii–iv. Ouy has pointed out to me that the text here does not completely agree with Glorieux's edition.

15. As indicated in the opening salutation, *o doctissimi viri patres et fratres* (Gl 5.265).

16. Gl 5.275. From Ecclesiasticus (Sirach) 33:29: *multam enim malitiam docuit otiositas.*

17. Gerson refers to *De disciplina scholarium.* See PL 64:1227, where the work is attributed to Boethius.

18. "De clerico immundo desperate moriente," bk. 22, ch. 30, 323–24. I am grateful to Markus Schürer of Dresden University for his help in procuring the edition of Douai, 1627.

19. Cf. *De confessione mollitiei,* Gl 8.73–74. Perhaps Gerson's concern about protecting youths from pedophiles seems more relevant and less "medieval" today than it would have been some years ago.

20. I cannot agree with Christopher Bellitto who in his otherwise illuminating *Nicolas de Clamanges* (3) claims that Gerson, in contrast to Clamanges, "saw personal reform as the result of hierarchical reform."

21. Cf. his advice to a newly elected bishop, Gl 2.108–16, Letter 29, esp. 113–14

22. CRSD Livre 15, ch. 11; tome 2, vol. 1, 224.

23. Ibid., ch. 12, 226–244. For background, Howard Kaminsky, *Simon Cramaud and the Great Schism*, esp. ch. 4.

24. Francis Oakley, *The Political Thought of Pierre d'Ailly* says (12) that Benedict was "regrettably successful" in buying d'Ailly's support. D'Ailly was attacked in his own time for accepting the bishopric: cf. Bernard Guenée, *Between Church and State*, 180–81.

25. There is the remark "se tu prens excusation pour la presence du roy," indicating the king's presence (Gl 7.2.617).

26. See, for example, CRSD Livre 15, ch. 4; tome 2, vol. 1, 184, where the royal chancellor blamed the duke for prohibiting discussion of the Schism (30 June 1394).

27. There were, of course, other monastic colleges at Paris. See the list in Rashdall, vol. 3, 536.

28. *Regula Benedicti. Praefatio* 45: "Constituenda est ergo nobis dominici scola servitii."

29. Gl 2.6. Benedict XIII on 12 July 1395 permitted Gerson to hold the benefice of a church in the diocese of Paris whose income did not exceed a hundred pounds, since there was no canonry or prebend for him at the church of Notre Dame in Paris (CUP, vol. 4, 8).

30. Alan Bernstein, *Pierre d'Ailly*, 70–81.

31. As pointed out by Vansteenberghe ("Gerson à Bruges," 40): "La notoire insuffisance des revenus de la chancellerie permettait à Gerson de conserver avec elle le décanat de Saint-Donatien."

32. For the chancellor's prerogatives, and the limitations of his office, see Rashdall, vol. 1, 338–340.

33. Ouy, "Le brouillon," 460.

34. CRSD Livre 16, ch. 1; tome 2, vol. 1, 248–252. Cf. Hefele-Leclercq 6.2.1168–83 and Noël Valois, *La France et le grand schisme d'Occident*, vol. 3, 44–67.

35. See the summary in chapter 3.

36. Morrall, *Gerson and the Great Schism*, 40–41. See also Hefele-Leclercq 6.2.1185.

37. For dating, Louis Mourin, *Jean Gerson: Prédicateur français*, 103–8. Mourin's judgments about dating are usually better argued than Glorieux's.

38. *Athanasius. The Life of Antony*, ch. 10, 39. See above, ch. 3, n. 92.

39. CRSD Livre 16, ch. 20; tome 2, vol. 1, 402–6.

40. Hefele-Leclercq 6.2.1189–92. Also Valois, *La France et le grand schisme*, vol.3, 86–88.

41. For dating, Mourin, *Prédicateur français*, 109–11.

42. "Gerson et l'Angleterre." Howard Kaminsky (*Simon de Cramaud*, 175, n 90) rejected Ouy's attribution of the glosses to Gerson, mainly because he thought several of the statements were not consistent with Gerson's views. However much I admire Kaminsky's superb work, I have to disagree here. Gerson's views were in flux at the time; the glosses underline his general commitment to the "way of cession"; since the glosses were not meant for any eyes except Gerson's, he could have revealed here opinions that he did not yet want to make public. Finally, Ouy's identification of the handwriting as Gerson's remains unchallenged. See also note 48 below.

43. For the full texts of marriage contract and truce, see CRSD livre 16, ch. 15; tome 2, vol. 1, 328–386.

44. There was the possibility of a meeting at Compiègne in July 1396, but it never came to anything. As Ouy has shown ("Gerson et l'Angleterre," 50), the Oxford academics refused to discuss the Schism with their Parisian confrères.

45. Gl 10.325: "Non debet dici spoliatus, quia nulla fuit ejus electio."

46. Morrall, *Gerson and the Great Schism*, 36–38.

47. Only Gregory VII's much discussed *Dictatus papae* comes to mind, his list of papal pregrogatives. Volumes have been written about this source to Gregory's thinking, but its precise intent will probably never be clear.

48. Gl 10.342: "Licet in hiis quae fidei sunt, non sit dicendum concilium posse errare, cum in illis a Spirito Sancto rogatur, in aliis tamen quae facti sunt, falli et errare potest ex falsis testibus aut instrumentis et falsa suggestione."

This statement is very close to what Gerson wrote in 1402, *De schismate,* before he came to accept the council as the solution to the Schism, Gl 6.47: "Nec valet hoc dicere quod Dominus non permittet errare concilium; quoniam in eis quae sunt facti aut juris positivi, et breviter in omnibus aliis praeterquam in materiis quae sunt pure de fide, Ecclesia fallit et fallitur, servata caritate." We thus have further evidence for Gerson as the author of the remarks appended to the Oxford text.

49. Gl 6.24–28. For dating, see Gl 6.ix.

50. Morrall, *Gerson and the Great Schism,* 43.

51. *De modo se habendi tempore schismatis,* Gl 6.29–34. See below in this chapter.

52. Hefele-Leclercq 6.l.1193–95; Valois, *La France et le grand schisme,* vol. 3, 104–7; Kaminsky, *Simon de Cramaud,* 161–69.

53. Hefele-Leclercq 6.2.1161–62, note 2. See CRSD livre 14, ch. 19; tome 2, vol. 1, 124–26 for a positive description of his preaching.

54. See Claude Arnaud-Gillet, *Entre Dieu et Satan. Les visions d'Ermine de Reims,* 20, 232. Also Gl 2.93–96, Letter 25; EW, 244–49.

55. *Responsiones ad capita accusationum,* in Johannes Gerson, *Opera Omnia,* ed. Louis Ellies Du Pin, vol. 1.905–44. Abbreviated as Du Pin.

56. The autograph is contained in a Saint Victor manuscript of Gerson's works. See Gilbert Ouy, *L'oeuvre de Gerson à Saint-Victor,* 125.

57. Du Pin 1.932: The fortieth accusation against Jean de Varennes concludes: "Populum incitando, si voluisset, per ejus praedicationes."

58. Du Pin 1.932C: "Per hoc autem populum non incitabam ad rebellionem. . . . Sed contra illos praedicabam, ut a populi cessarent comestione et ut populus inde cessaret a rebellione."

59. Du Pin I.933D: "Item. Publice praedicavit quod omnia mala quae in hoc mundo eveniebant, evenerant per gentes ecclesiasticas.
"Respondeo. Non recordor me sic dixisse; sed si dixi, a veritate non multum deviavi."

60. Du Pin 1.920–21.

61. This claim apparently occasioned Huizinga's memorable but exaggerated assertion that "according to popular belief, current towards the end of the fourteenth century, no one, since the beginning of the great Western Schism, had entered Paradise" (*The Waning of the Middle Ages,* 29).

62. *De duplici logica,* Gl 3.62. The supposed quotation from Bernard ("zelus sine discretione praecipitat") seems to be a simplified version of *De consideratione* 2.20.

63. "Gerson au chapitre de Notre-Dame," esp., 426.

64. Glorieux, "La vie," 156.

65. Gl 2.7; Letter B, EW, 155.

66. Schwab, *Johannes Gerson* (vol. 1, 54): "Eine durch wahre Frömmigkeit getragene gegenseitige Liebe"; Connolly, *John Gerson,* 22. For the opposite view, Francis Ledwidge, "Relations de famille," esp., 6–8.

67. Gl 2.8; EW, 156.

68. Gl 7.1.55–57, trans. as "Eleven Rules" in EW, 125–27.

69. Gl 2.9; EW, 156.

70. CRSD livre 17, ch. 29; tome 2, vol. 1, 522: "Ubique luctus occupat universa; anxietas corda sibi vendicat singulos."

71. Richard Vaughan, *Philip the Bold,* 59–78. Also Barbara Tuchman, *A Distant Mirror* contains a well-written chapter 26, "Nicopolis."

72. CRSD livre 17, ch. 30–31; tome 2, vol. 1, 522–26.

73. CRSD livre 17, ch. 34; tome 2, vol. 1, 532–34.

74. For the chronicle's composition, see Bernard Guenée's excellent introduction in the reprint of the Bellaguet edition, esp., xvi–xviii.

75. Gl 7.2.1048–57. For dating, see Mourin, *Prédicateur français,* 111–112.

76. CRSD livre 17, ch. 33; tome 2, vol. 1, 528.

77. CRSD livre 18, ch. 2; tome 2, vol. 1, 542–44.

78. Ibid., 544.

79. Gl 7.2.538–49. For dating, Mourin, *Prédicateur français,* 112–13.

80. Gl 7.2.545: "Ce fut la doctrine saint Loys a son filz." Probably the teachings included by Joinville at the end of his biography of the king. See *Chronicles of the Crusades,* 347. Also David O'Connell, *Les propos de Saint Louis,* 183–85.

81. Gl 7.2.546: "Toute seulette en sa chambre, non mie parlant a Birthe ou a Gaultier." The remark about "Bertha or Walter" is Gerson's addition to Bernard's statement in *Sermones in laudibus Virginis Matris,* Homilia 3, *Sancti Bernardi Opera,* vol. 4, 36. See McGuire, "In Search of Bernard's Legacy," 298–99.

82. Gl 7.2.547–48: "Veultz tu qu'elles soient vestues comme femmes de village ou comme beguinez? Response: je ne reprouve que l'excez et l'abuz et l'orgueil et le mal acquest." For Gerson on the Beguines, Ernest W. McDonnell, *The Beguines and Beghards,* 430, 501, 557.

83. Gl 5.546–62. Gerson gave Latin sermons on Holy Thursday in 1395, 1397, 1399, 1401, 1402, and 1403. See Gl 5.ix, xiii, xv. In the 1397 sermon he referred to a now lost Holy Thursday sermon for 1396: "Tractavimus litteraliter thema praesens incipientes ab hoc verbo: cum jam diabolus misisset in cor Judae etc. (Gl 5.547; cf. Jn 13:2).

84. See *Fables of Aesop,* nr. 118, 122.

85. Gerson was referring here to the climax of the Franciscan discussion on apostolic poverty in the time of John XXII (1316–1334). He is ambiguous about his sympathies here.

86. Hefele-Leclercq, vol. 6.2.1196–201.

87. Valois, *La France et le grand schisme* vol. 3, 123.

88. Ibid., 144–47.

89. Hefele-Leclercq, 6.2.1209.

90. Glorieux, "La vie," 158.

91. Gl 5.577–78: "Veniunt indociles pueri, vagi, moribus incompositissimi; affirmant se alto claroque sanguine progenitos familiares regum, ducum amicos: miscent cum precibus minas."

92. Gl 5.581: "Et quo fugietis cum vindicta advenerit, infelicissimi? Qualiter horrendas Dei viventis manus evadere confiditis, perditissimi hominum?"

93. Cf. R. W. Southern, *Saint Anselm and His Biographer,* as 141.

94. Gl 5.583: "Et ecclesiastici debent, ut non fiat domus orationis domus negotationis" (cf. John 2:16).

95. Gl 5.584: "Eisdem vero verbis quibus praeceptor meus, dominus Cameracensis, tractatum suum de anima exorsus est incipio." Pierre d'Ailly had transferred from the bishopric of Puy to that of Cambrai.

96. Philippians 3:20, as in Letter 25 to his brother Jean the Celestine, from Constance in 1417: "Assidua meditatione recordarer verbi coelestis peregrini Pauli: nostra conversatio in coelis est" (Gl 2.199).

97. Vansteenberghe, "Gerson à Bruges," 14.

98. Gl 2.10, dated to January-February 1398: "Tuas pridie litteras accepi quibus incredibilia mihi fore significas quae apud vos geruntur."

99. Gl 2.11: "Quoniam non est qui pro domo Israel miserabiliter corruente se murum opponat" (Ezechiel 13:15).

100. Gl 6.29–34. One version adds the words *specialiter in patria Flandrensi* (Du Pin 2.3).

101. Gl 6.33: "Possunt homines secundum credulitatem suae partis et suam seipsos quietare, tenendo pro facto id quod eorum superior creditus fecerit."

102. *Peter Abelard's Ethics* (53): "That a work is good by reason of a good intention."

103. Morrall, *Gerson and the Great Schism,* 45

104. Glorieux, "Gerson au chapitre de Notre-Dame," 428–431.

105. CRSD livre 18, ch. 10; tome 2, vol. 1, 564–570.

106. Hefele-Leclercq 6.2.1210–21; Kaminsky, *Simon de Cramaud,* 212–243.

107. CRSD livre 19, ch. 2; tome 2, vol. 1, 582: "Auctoritate regia dominorum et nobilium Francie necnon et ecclesie gallicane statutum est, ut amodo domino Benedicto non modo beneficiorum regni collacio, sed et omnis obediencia substrahatur, donec viam cessionis acceptaverit, ut juravit." The full text of the royal decree is in CRSD livre 19, ch. 5, 598–642.

108. crsd livre 19, ch 8; tome 2, vol. 1, 654–56. Valois, *La France et le grand schisme,* vol. 3, ch. 3, 189–323.

109. Gl 10.86–90, included by Gerson at the end of a later treatise on the errors of magic.

110. Glorieux, "Gerson au chapitre de Notre-Dame," 430.

111. "Gerson au chapitre," 431. For some of these negotiations, see Gl 10.446–47.

112. Gl 5.504. For his later censure of the group: *Contra sectam flagellantium,* from the Council of Constance in 1417: Gl 10.46–51.

113. Gl 5.504: "In consideratione passionis Domini nostri Jesus Christi, de qua dicit Bernardus quod nullum cor tam durum est quod non molliatur si passio domini ad memoriam revocetur." This is an apt summary of the opening from Bernard's first sermon for Holy Thursday, "De Passione Domini," *Sancti Bernardi Opera,* vol. 5, 56. See McGuire, "In Search of Bernard's Legacy," 321–22.

114. Gl 8.10–17; ew, 365–377.

115. Cf. Tentler, *Sin and Confession,* 304–318.

116. D. Catherine Brown, *Pastor and Laity,* 68.

117. See the sermon *Exsultabunt sancti in gloria,* mentioned in the early part of this chapter.

118. "Gerson à Bruges," 15–20.

119. crsd livre 20, ch. 1; tome 2, vol. 1, 684.

120. crsd livre 20, ch. 10; tome 2, vol. 1, 716–18.

121. See Denifle, cup 4, nr. 1759: the faculty of medicine decided on 8 November 1399 to suspend lessons and disputations until after Epiphany, *propter mortalitatem, que tunc vigebat Parisius.*

Chapter 5

1. E. Vansteenberghe, "Gerson à Bruges," with documents, 41–52, reprinted in Gl 10, "Actes et documents."

2. For background, David Nichols, *Medieval Flanders,* esp. chs. 11 and 12. As of page 384: "The major generator of foreign capital for Flanders in the fifteenth century was not exports but the commercial facilities and tolls at Bruges."

3. "Gerson à Bruges," 13: "Il semble pourtant n'avoir agi qu'avec quelque hésitation ou quelque scrupule."

4. Glorieux, "Gerson au chapitre de Notre-Dame," 427: "Gerson résidait encore alors au Collège de Navarre. C'est en 1397 seulement en effet qu'il louera à vie la maison qui était contigüe au jardin du Grand-Maître. Sa nomination de chancelier ne modifia pas cette résidence."

5. As Vansteenberghe pointed out ("Gerson à Bruges," 15), at a provincial synod at Reims in 1408, Gerson sought to limit payment for spiritual services by priests (Gl 5.137).

6. Colin Morris, *The Papal Monarchy,* as 1ol–103.

7. "Gerson à Bruges," 18.

8. Ibid., 32.

9. Ibid., 14.

10. Ibid., 25, n 4.

11. As indicated in a letter to his colleagues at the College of Navarre, 27 April 1400 (Gl 2.29).

12. In the same letter of 27 April: "Mandatus sum quippe ab illo cui, post Deum, me et omnes operas meas debeo, dominum meum, dominum Burgundiae loquor" (Gl 2.29).

13. The relative values of these sums are difficult, if not impossible, to determine. See N. J. G. Pounds, *An Economic History of Medieval Europe,* 114–16, 426–430. From the early thirteenth century on, France had two currencies, from royal mints at Paris and at Tours: "The Parisian penny was . . . larger than the 'Tournois' and served as the basis of a separate system of money and accounting" (115).

14. I know of no complete study for France, but see Ann K. Warren, *Anchorites and Their Patrons in Medieval England.* Her conclusion that "anchoritism was a significant religious

phenomenon in medieval England and a wide range of persons were touched by it" (280) probably applies also to other parts of Western Europe.

15. Karma Lochrie, *Margery Kempe and Translations of the Flesh,* sees Gerson as showing "horror and disgust at the insufficiently mortified female flesh" (1). She fails to see that Gerson's problem was not women but human sensuality in general.

16. See McGuire, "Late Medieval Care and Control of Women."

17. See E. Vansteenberghe, "Trois règlements de vie de Gerson pour ses soeurs," esp. 195–96. Glorieux without explanation dated the treatise to after 11 November 1399 (Gl 10.585). Also the text he provides is incomplete: a major part is excluded (see my "Late Medieval Care," 11, note 23). I follow the text in Du Pin, vol. 3:829–841, corrected by Gilbert Ouy in an unpublished edition he has kindly lent me.

18. Du Pin 3.831C: "A propos, tresamées Sueurs, n'est ja necessité quant à vous que soiez mariees charnelement pour avoir ligné, car assez en y a d'autres pour acroistre Crestienté."

19. Vansteenberghe, "Trois règlements," 192, n 3.

20. Beatrice Beech, former librarian at the Rare Book Room of the Waldo Library, Western Michigan University, made me aware of this economic argument. I am also grateful for her unpublished translation of this treatise, the basis of the translations I provide below.

21. Du Pin 3.840C: "Et vivrez de vostre labeur ensemble, et de l'eritage qui vous puet ou pourra appartenir, qui doit estre soufisant pour vostre vie: car, quant a nous vos freres, je cuide que jamais riens n'en prendrons."

22. See McDonnell, *The Beguines and Beghards,* esp. part 5.

23. Du Pin 3.832A. As Renate Blumenfeld-Kosinski has kindly pointed out to me, Gerson may have been influenced by *Les XV joies de mariage,* edited by Jean Rychner, dated to the 1390s.

24. Du Pin 3.832B: "Et toute la perte et douleur cherra sur la povre femme qui coupe n'y avra; et bien souvent en avra du pis car, avec la perte, le mari, qui sera couroucié ou ivre, la tensera et riotera jusques a coups ferir."

25. Du Pin 3.832D.

26. Du Pin 3.832D-833A.

27. Du Pin 3.833C.

28. Du Pin 3.834B.

29. Du Pin 3.834B: "Et par ainsi ont enfer en ce monde et en l'autre."

30. Du Pin 3.834D.

31. Du Pin 3.835B.

32. Du Pin 3.834D.

33. Du Pin 3.834C.

34. Du Pin 3.835D and 836B-838B.

35. Du Pin 3.836D: "Ainsi, quant tu cuideras que le feu de la charnalité soit apetissié par ce que tu l'avras acompli, dedens brief fauldra plus grandement ou aussi comme par avant."

36. Du Pin 3.837A.

37. Du Pin 3.838A.

38. Du Pin 3.838B.

39. Du Pin 3.836A: "Toutesfoix, tresamées sueurs, je vous supply que vous me pardonnez se je parle de ceste matiere plus avant, par aventure, que vous ne vauriez ou devriez oïr, car verité me contraint a ce cy faire et la grant amour que j'ai a vous, affin que vous preniez et creiez bon conseil."

40. Du Pin 3.829D-830A.

41. Du Pin 3.839A: "Si croy et tien en bonne foy que Dieu a envoyé ce meschief de la morte son mari pour son grant bien, jasoit ce que ce soit fort qu'elle n'en ait pris tristece."

42. Du Pin 3.839B: "Et, se je ne suy deceü, elle a maintenant plus de repos, de plaisance et de bonne leesse que par avant en mariage, et je m'en raporte a ce qu'elle en treuve."

43. Gl 2.9; EW, 156.

44. Du Pin 3.839D-840A.

45. Du Pin 3.840C.

46. Du Pin 3.840D-841A.

47. Du Pin 3.841A: "Telles viandes qui engendrent mauvaises chaleurs et perilleux esmovemens."

48. Du Pin 3.841B: "Et ne vous chaille d'aler a dances et autres fols esbatemens ou plus de folie y a que de bien."

49. Du Pin 3.841B.

50. McGuire, "The Cistercians and the Transformation of Monastic Friendships," in *Friendship and Faith.*

51. As Aelred of Rievaulx in his *Rule of Life for a Recluse.* See McGuire, *Brother and Lover,* 30–31.

52. Du Pin 3.836C–D: "Gette du bois un pou vert dedens le feu: il se apetissera au commencement, mais incontinent s'alumera plus habondanment."

53. Gl 9.684: "Olim quoque circa sorores germanas dum eas ad coelibatum perpetuum inducerem, tale aliquid carnale patiebar. Turbabat nonnunquam me et rationes meas omnes tumultus vulgaris consuetudinis; insolitum mihi proponebatur id quod agere moliebatur mea devotio. Fluctuabam et nutabam, et pene quaerebam dissolvere sanctitatem propositi ac retro pedem flectere."

54. According to Gl 7.1.xiv, the *Pitieuse complainte* is "about 1399," while Gl 10.584–85 puts the prayer both at the end of 1399 and in January-March 1400. It was completed before the *Montaigne de contemplation,* which belongs to 1400. See E. Vansteenberghe, "La 'Pitieuse complainte de l'âme dévote'," esp. 395.

55. *Sancti Anselmi Cantuariensis Archiepiscopi Opera Omnia,* vol. 3; trans. *The Prayers and Meditations of Saint Anselm,* 221–24.

56. EW, 157.

57. Vansteenberghe, "Lettre à ses soeurs sur la méditation." For parallels with earlier writings, see esp. 380.

58. *The Waning,* esp. ch. 12.

59. Gl 2.16; EW, 159.

60. Gl 2.16; EW, 159.

61. Gl 2.17; EW, 160.

62. See *Introduction à la vie dévote,* as well as *Francis de Sales, Jane de Chantal: Letters of Spiritual Direction.*

63. Gl 7.1.x places the work to about 1396, while in Gl 10.585, the date is November-December 1399. This is more realistic, in relation to the Bruges period when Gerson was most involved with his sisters.

64. Gl 7.1.1–2. Such a recommendation is also in the *De cognitione castitatis,* or *De pollutione diurna* (Gl 9.60), meant for priests to maintain purity. Gerson thus gave the same advice to religious women as to clerical men.

65. The opening indicates a memorandum rather than a letter: "The following contains some of the difficulties and calamities I have experienced in the office of chancellor of the University of Paris. This list I have drawn up in a direct and free way in order to consider the counsels of most holy persons who fear God" (EW, 161). The second sentence hints that Gerson intended to make the list public, in order to seek advice.

66. Here and in the following I use my translation from EW, 161–68.

67. Gl 2.21: "Est autem natura mea et consuetudo ad agibilia prorsus inepta, scrupulosa, iners, formidolosa, levissime perturbata ut plus millies experior jugiter." EW, 165.

68. Gl 2.23; EW, 167.

69. Gl 2.23; EW, 168.

70. Louis Salembier, *Le cardinal Pierre d'Ailly,* 169.

71. Valois, *La France et le grand schisme,* vol. 3, 189–257.

72. See Letter 28, from 1408 or 1411, where Gerson acted almost as d'Ailly's spiritual advisor (Gl 2.105–7; EW, 258–261).

73. "Sed omitto me; perdidi enim scripta jam verbaque innumera," Gl 2.24; EW, 169.

74. Gl 2.24; EW, 169.

75. *Contre la fête des fous,* possibly from August 1402, Gl 7.1.409–11.

76. Gl 2.26; EW, 171.

77. Gl 2.28; EW, 174.

78. As his *A.B.C. des simples gens,* also known as *Alphabetum puerorum,* from 1401–2, Gl 7.1.154–57.

79. Gl 2.27–28; EW, 174.

80. Gl 7.1.16–55; EW, 75–127.

81. Gl 7.1.17; EW, 76.

82. Gl 7.1.20; EW, 80.

83. See the seminal articles of Giles Constable, "Twelfth-Century Spirituality and the Late Middle Ages" and "The Popularity of Twelfth-Century Spiritual Writers in the Late Middle Ages."

84. Chapter 14: "How reading and listening to the lives of the saints is profitable," Gl 7.1.24–25; EW, 85–86.

85. Gl 7.1.26; EW, 88–89. In a later letter, from 13 April 1402, Gerson says that he had just recently discovered that his distinction already was to be found in Bernard of Clairvaux (Gl 2.54). Actually Gerson was borrowing from Gilbert of Hoyland's continuation of Bernard's *Sermons on the Song of Songs* (EW, 200 and 402, n 34).

86. Gl 7.1.28; EW, 90: "Car hermitaige et reclusaige ne sont mie seulement es boys et es desers, mais en tous lieus on lez puet avoir et exercer par eschever le bruit du monde et toutes ses sollicitudes et occupations."

87. McGuire, "Loving the Holy Order."

88. In the famed Letter to Eustochium (esp. 22.7).

89. Gl 7.1.32; EW, 96.

90. For example, Christina, who had to fight for years to get her family and the Church to accept her desire to live as a recluse: C.H. Talbot, *The Life of Christina of Markyate.*

91. Gl 7.1.34; EW, 98. See William's *Rhetorica divina,* ch. 26, in *Guilelmi Alverni Opera Omnia* vol. 1, 365.

92. See John Baldwin, *Masters, Princes, and Merchants. The Social Views of Peter the Chanter and his Circle,* 1–2, esp. 1, 47–59.

93. "Ceulx qui sont experts scevent que ie voel dire." Gl 7.1.37; EW, 102.

94. The *Orloge de sapience* refers to the French translation of Henry Suso's *Horologium sapientiae,* the Latin version of Suso's German *Little Book of Eternal Wisdom.* See *Henry Suso: The Exemplar,* 32–36, 207–304.

95. Gl 7.1.50; EW, 118: "Car on ne puet mie escripre les affections ne les engendrer par lettres ou par parolles."

96. Gl 7.1.55–57; EW, 125–27. Vansteenberghe, "Trois règlements de vie," esp. 200–204.

97. Gl 2.32; EW, 178–79.

98. Gl 2.33; EW, 181: "Pro illa quae legentis mores aedificet, regulet et componat."

99. Gl 2.34; EW, 182.

100. See above, chapter 2, note 42.

101. Gl 2.37, EW, 186: "Alter alterum pessimis modis maculantes." See *Sermon on the Feast of Saint Bernard* in Gl 5.331; EW, 137.

102. Gl 2.38; EW, 187.

103. Gl 2.40; EW, 190.

104. Gl 2.41; EW, 190.

105. Gl 2.42; EW, 192.

106. *Metrum contra curiositatem scribendi plures libros,* Gl 4.160.

Chapter 6

1. Glorieux, "La vie et les oeuvres," (158), says Gerson in 1397 rented this house for life and referred to Jean de Launoy, *Regii Navarrae gymnasii parisiensis historia* (Paris, 1677). Olivier Legendre was kind enough to check this reference for me: Launoy, Pars I, liber 1, chap. 11, 84.

Launoy added that when Gerson became resident at the cloister of Notre Dame three years later, his house at the College was rented to Pierre d'Ailly. The dating is not correct, but the fact that d'Ailly took over the lease indicates continuing contact between the two men.

For a sense of Paris at this time, see the superb catalogue for the 2004 Louvre exhibition, *Paris 1400. Les arts sous Charles VI,* an indication of a new interest for this neglected period in French history.

2. Glorieux, "La vie," 167.

3. Valois, *La France et le grand schisme* vol. 3, 269–70.

4. Gerson's inspiration was the *Soul's Journey into God,* trans. Ewert Cousins in *Bonaventure.*

5. See the epitaph for Elisabeth la Chardenière, Gl 10.463, which Jadart (108) concluded was composed by Gerson.

6. Gl 2.45; EW, 196

7. EW, 423, n152.

8. Gl 2.46; EW, 197.

9. Gl 8.71–75, *De confessione mollitiei,* which cannot be more precisely dated than to 1400–1415.

10. Gl 9.47; EW, 198.

11. Gl 2.86–90; EW, 236–240.

12. Gl 2.48; EW, 199.

13. Gerson addressed five sisters in his *Eleven Rules* (EW, 125), when six sisters were still alive. On this basis, and because of mention in *Dialogue spirituel* from 1408, Vansteenberghe concluded that Marion had probably remarried and was no longer at home ("Trois règlements," 201–2).

14. McGuire, *Friendship and Community,* esp. chps. 2 and 6.

15. Glorieux, "Gerson au chapitre de Notre-Dame," esp. 432–36. Also Gl 10.446–47, 458–461.

16. Gl 5.407–8. See Jerome's Letter 53 (PL 22:549).

17. André Combes, *La théologie mystique de Gerson,* esp. vol. 2, 465–568.

18. *On Distinguishing True from False Revelations,* Gl 3.54; EW, 360.

19. Glorieux thought Gerson lectured on the entire Gospel but that only some of these lessons survived. I think Gerson did not plan an exhaustive commentary but chose a certain number of texts. See "L'enseignement universitaire de Gerson," esp. 92–93.

20. A comparison of Pierre d'Ailly's Latin sermons with Gerson's indicates d'Ailly was more traditional in categories and definitions. Gerson's text has greater vitality. See, for example, *Super omnia vincit veritas,* ed. Bernstein in *Pierre d'Ailly,* 237–298.

21. Gl 3.38; EW, 336.

22. Gl 3.43; EW, 344.

23. Gl 3.44; EW, 345.

24. Gl 3.51; EW, 356: "Non esse tutam mulierum quantumcumque sanctarum cum viris etiam religiosissimis cohabitationem et familiaritatem."

25. Robert Lerner, *The Heresy of the Free Spirit,* 165–66, esp. n 6.

26. Gl 3.52, EW, 357. Note the use of the Pauline "I know a man" (2 Cor 12:2–3) to allow one to speak of personal experience.

27. Gl 3.52; EW, 52.

28. *De non esu carnium,* Gl 3.77–95. See EW, 194–95. For Gerson and the Carthusians, McGuire, "Loving the Holy Order."

29. Pascoe, *Jean Gerson,* 50–53. For the text of this remarkable document, see Henry Bettenson, *Documents of the Christian Church,* 135–140. The volume of literature is enormous. See Walter Ullmann, *Medieval Political Thought,* 59–63. Gerson had already denounced the Donation in his *Pastorium Carmen.* See chapter 3 above.

30. A translation of Lorenzo Valla's proof from 1440 that the Donation was a forgery is in Werner L. Gundersheimer, ed., *The Italian Renaissance,* 55–68.

31. John Moorman, *A History of the Franciscan Order,* 180.

32. Gl 3.224–49. The lectures are dated to 8–9 November 1402. Partial translation by Stephen Ozment, *Jean Gerson: Selections,* 30–45.

33. As Gerson already had written to Pierre d'Ailly, Gl 2.27–28; EW, 174. See chapter 5 above.

34. For an appreciation of the *Sentences,* R. W. Southern, *Scholastic Humanism,* vol. 2, 142–46.

35. See Francis Oakley, *The Political Thought of Pierre d'Ailly* (22): "The basic tenet of his thought, as of Ockham's, is the unity, freedom, and omnipotence of God."

36. Gl 3.242. It has been discussed whether Gerson was a nominalist, a problematic term representing the direction in medieval thought that denied the real existence of intellectual categories outside the mind. Gerson's nominalism consisted in his rejection of such categories within God. The most thorough recent study of Gerson's philosophical allegiance is Zenon Kaluza's *Les querelles doctrinales,* esp. ch. 2. Kaluza shows how Gerson, in much of his commentary on the teaching of philosophy, describes the situation as it was when he was a student. This is an important point, but it should be added that Gerson's main purpose was not to defend a given philosophical system but to convey a theological attitude about intellectual life in an ethical dimension.

37. See Simon Tugwell, *Albert and Thomas,* 74–76.

38. The definitive text is in André Combes, *Mystica Theologia.* References, however, are to the Glorieux edition. Part of the *Speculative Mystical Theology* (SMT) is translated in EW, while all of the *Practical Mystical Theology* (PMT) is there.

39. Gl 3.255; EW, 271: "Quidam amor et ardor experiendi ea quae sola interim fide tenent et quae docta ratiocinatione conferunt ad invicem."

40. Gl 3.257; EW, 274.

41. Gl 3.276: "Nullus unquam intelliget verba Apostoli et prophetarum quantumcumque illa resonent exterius, si non imbiberit affectum scribentium." See William of Saint Thierry, *The Golden Epistle* 31.120 (trans., 51): "The Scriptures need to be read and understood in the same spirit in which they were written." For background, McGuire, "La présence de la *Lettre aux frères du Mont-Dieu,*" in Nicole Boucher, *Signy l'abbaye.*

42. Gl 3.290. From Gregory the Great, *Homiliae Quadraginta in Evangelia,* 27, in PL 76:1207. Trans. *Forty Gospel Homilies,* 215.

43. See "Table des auteurs cités," Gl 10.637. Of patristic authors, Gregory is outdone only by Gerson's use of Augustine.

44. Gerson's source was Cassian's *Collationes* 9.31, trans. *John Cassian. The Conferences,* 349.

45. Gl 3.291: "Contemplatio namque si nude consideretur sine dilectione vel affectu subsequente jam arida est, inquieta est, curiosa est, ingrata est, inflata est."

46. See the Preface by Louis Dupré in *John Ruusbroec: The Spiritual Espousals,* esp. 20–21.

47. Gl 2.54–55; EW, 200–202; also 425, n 171. The sermon was actually by the Cistercian Gilbert of Hoyland.

48. Gl 5.325–39; EW, 128–148. McGuire, "Gerson and Bernard: Languishing with Love."

49. Gl 5.331; EW, 137.

50. Louis Mourin, *Prédicateur français,* 509.

51. Gl 5.151–68, dated to 1393, but the subjects of concern indicate the period after the return from Bruges. See Max Lieberman, "Chronologie gersonienne," *Romania* 83 (1962), 52–89, esp. 71, n 1.

52. Gl 5.156. Gerson later used a similar image for Paris in the prologue to his epic poem *Josephina,* Gl 4.31.

53. Gl 5.163. Gobard may have been an arts master. His name is not on the list of masters of theology at Paris in 1403 (Gl 10.466).

54. See Gl 7.2.793–934, from 3 December 1402 to 18 March 1403. For background, Mourin, *Prédicateur français,* 138–148.

55. It would be worthwhile to compare Gerson's views with those James A. Brundage considers representative of the medieval Church and especially of its canon lawyers. See his *Law, Sex, and Christian Society.* I disagree that Gerson "considered solitary sex so serious an offense that only a bishop was empowered to pardon the offender and prescribe suitable punishment" ("Sex and Canon Law," *Handbook of Medieval Sexuality,* ed. Vern L. Bullough and James A. Brundage, 41). See Gl 9.422: "Casus carnalium lapsuum, praesertim in sexu muliebri ac puerili, qui secreti sunt, videntur curatis dimittendi."

56. See chapter 11 below. I find the earliest use of *doctor consolatorius* in the 1502 edition of Gerson by Jacob Wimpheling (Du Pin, vol. 1, clxxix).

57. See chapter 5 above, n 64.

58. Gl 7.2.829. See chapter 7 on humility, in Benedict's *Rule,* especially its twelfth degree on how the eyes always should be lowered.

59. Gl 7.2.829: "Je respon que regulierement c'est chose a s'en garder puis que les enfans ont plus de deux ans, car jasoit ce que ceulx de quatre ou six ans n'y pansent lors mal, touteffois apres quant ilz viennent en aage, la remambrance leur vient et les temptent griefment."

60. Gl 7.2.865. See McGuire, "Education, Confession and Pious Fraud," 314–16.

61. *On the Art of Hearing Confessions,* Gl 8.15; EW, 373.

62. See the *Vita Prima* 1.1, in PL 185:227C.

63. Richard Kieckhefer, "Major Currents in Late Medieval Devotion."

64. See "Le chemin de la croix" in Delaruelle, *L'église au temps du grand schisme,* 760–61. The chapter, "L'homme devant le Christ et Marie" is a superb summary of the period's devotion to the Passion of Christ.

65. Gl 7.2.477. Note the difference here from Mel Gibson's approach in his 2004 film *The Passion of the Christ.* Gerson pictures Jesus' sufferings through Mary's inner life, while Gibson chose to make everything physical and graphic. A commentary on the difference between late medieval and postmodern cultures?

66. Gl 10.463. For background, André Combes, *Jean de Montreuil,* 591–609.

67. For background, Michel Zink, *La prédication en langue romane avant 1300* and David L. D'Avray, *The Preaching of the Friars.*

68. Catherine Brown, *Pastor and Laity,* 49.

69. Ibid., 23.

70. Valois, *La France et le grand schisme,* vol. 3, 261.

71. Ibid., 257.

72. *Protestatio super statum ecclesiae,* Gl 6.34–35: "Insequendo consilium regis et regni pro mea facultate et vocatione."

73. Morrall, *Gerson and the Great Schism,* 59.

74. Gl 5.55: "Vel redeundum esset ad statum ecclesiae tempore Silvestri et Gregorii, quando quilibet praelatus dimittebatur in sua jurisdictione et sollicitudinis parte et papa tenebat quae sua erant absque tot reservationibus, tot et continuis magnisque exactionibus pro sustinendo statum curiae et capitis nimis forte crescentem supra ceteros membrorum status."

75. See for example, "The Church as Apostolic Council," the final chapter in Ryan, *The Apostolic Conciliarism.*

76. Gl 5.67, dated to after 15 April 1402. The opening uses the term "ad pacificationem et informationem domini," presumably meaning the Lord Benedict, whom Gerson thereby avoided calling pope.

77. Valois, *La France et le grand schisme,* vol. 3, 325–332

78. CRSD, Livre 24, ch. 5; tome 3, vol. 2, 92.

79. For an introduction and central writings from this period, Eric Hicks, *Le débat sur le Roman de la Rose.*

80. For an excellent introduction, see Renate Blumenfeld-Kosinski, ed., *The Selected Writings of Christine de Pizan.*

81. Earl Jeffrey Richards, "Christine de Pizan and Jean Gerson: An Intellectual Friendship." Also his "Rejecting Essentialism and Gendered Writing: The Case of Christine de Pizan," in *Gender and Text in the Later Middle Ages.*

82. Gl 7.1.301–16; EW, 378–398. Also in Hicks, *Le débat,* 59–87.

83. Gl 7.1.303; EW, 380.

84. Gl 7.1.306; EW, 385.

85. Gl 7.1.309; EW, 389.

86. Gl 7.1.312; EW, 393. See Alan of Lille, *The Plaint of Nature,* Meter 1, trans. James J. Sheridan, 68: "A man turned woman blackens the fair name of his sex."

87. Gl 2.65–70; EW, 213–220.

88. Gl 2.66; EW, 215.

89. Gl 2.67; EW, 216: "Istud positum mihi visum est magis ad diffamationem theologorum quam pertinenter ad rem."

90. Gl 2.69; EW, 218.

91. Gl 2.70; EW, 220.

92. Gl 2.70; EW, 220: "Pudebit te forsan audaciae allegandi ea quae non plene prospexeris."

93. Gl 7.1.409–11. See E. K. Chambers, *The Medieval Stage,* vol. 1, esp. 292–97 and 325–27.

94. Gl 10.28: "Jam ei neque praedicationes publicae, neque admonitiones secretae seu fraternales, quidquam possunt; irridentur potius, et in canticum ac fabulam convertuntur." Gerson was apparently thinking of 2 Tim 4:3–4: *ad fabulas autem convertentur.*

95. Gl 3.150. For Wycliffe's teaching, Gordon Leff, *Heresy in the Later Middle Ages,* vol. 2, 546–49.

96. Gl 3.153: "Quo in loco nimis delirant quidam juristarum qui textibus suis adeo fixi."

97. See his amazing statement (Gl 3.199): "Sic absque consensu Occidentalium non fuissent apud suos sacerdotes interdicta matrimonia, nam Orientales quia dissenserunt ipsi, ut nubant licet. Ita de plurimis in qualibet politia."

98. Gl 3.202: "Consolatur me praeterea dictum cujusdam Hismenii ab Jeronymo repetitum: mihi cecini et Musis, etsi nemo alius audierit." See PL 23:452A. Gerson seems to have been quoting from memory. I am grateful to Mark Williams of Calvin College for this reference.

Chapter 7

1. See Howard Kaminsky, *Simon de Cramaud and the Great Schism,* a superb biography.

2. McGuire, "Jean Gerson and the End of Spiritual Friendship: Dilemmas of Conscience", in Julian Haseldine, ed., *Friendship in Medieval Europe,* 229–250.

3. G.H.M. Posthumus Meyjes, *Jean Gerson. Apostle of Unity,* 100.

4. John B. Morrall, *Jean Gerson and the Great Schism,* 66.

5. Heinrich Denifle, ed., *Chartularium Universitatis Parisiensis* (abbreviated CUP), vol. 4, nr. 1781, 21 August 1403.

6. CUP vol. 4, nr. 1796, p. 85: "Johanni de Gersonno, cler. Remens. dioc. mag. in art., stud. in theol. in secundo anno sue auditionis."

7. See Thomas Tentler, *Sin and Confession on the Eve of the Reformation,* 307–314.

8. For the concept of equity or *epikie,* see Posthumus Meyjes, esp. 242–46.

9. Gl 6.47. See chapter 6 above.

10. *Jean Gerson. Apostle of Unity,* 115.

11. As asserted by Morrall (65–66), who provides a "hypothesis" based on "rapid disillusionment."

12. It would be interesting to write a psychological portrait of Benedict XIII. Most of the relevant materials can be found in Valois, *La France et le grand schisme,* esp. t. 3.

13. Gl 2.71; EW, 221.

14. Gl 2.71; EW, 221.

15. Gl 2.79; EW, 227.

16. CUP, vol. 4, nr. 1801.

17. The chapter's decision is in Gl 10.467–68. For background, see Glorieux, "Gerson au chapitre de Notre-Dame", esp. 438–39.

18. Glorieux, "La vie et les oeuvres de Gerson," 167.

19. Glorieux, "Gerson au chapitre de Notre-Dame," esp. 841–42. Also Noël Valois, "Gerson. Curé de Saint-Jean-en-Grève."

20. Glorieux, "Gerson au chapitre" (444), referred to the seventeenth-century cloister plan in F.L. Chartier, *L'ancien chapitre de Notre Dame et sa maîtrise* (Paris, 1897), 9.

21. Glorieux, "Gerson au chapitre," 439–441.

22. "Gerson au chapitre," 839–40, for 16 August 1407, where Gerson with the two other commissioners supervised the veiling of the "girls or women of the said house." See E. Coyecque, *L'Hôtel-Dieu de Paris au Moyen Age,* vols. 1–2.

23. E. Vansteenberghe, "Gerson à Bruges," 28–30.

24. Alan Bernstein, *Pierre d'Ailly and the Blanchard Affair* (174): "To exchange money . . . for the theological license is simony, and it violates natural and divine law."

25. As indicated in the sermon *Vive le roy,* Gl 7.2.1183.

26. Gl 2.104; *Early Works,* 258.

27. Gl 2.104: "Cum error in materia religionis atque mendacium culpae notam denominet."

28. Gl 8.29; EW, 305.

29. Gl 8.34; EW, 313

30. See the *Vitae patrum,* esp. book 5, on fornication, in PL 73, and partly trans. Helen Waddell, *The Desert Fathers,* esp. 74–76.

31. Gilbert Ouy, "Gerson and the Celestines," in *Reform and Renewal in the Middle Ages and the Renaissance,* eds. Thomas Izbicki and Christopher Bellitto. See nr. 101: "Scio quemdam qui ad occursum talium solitus est in animo subridere quasi subsannans."

32. See Gilbert Ouy, "Gerson, émule de Pétrarque: le 'Pastorium Carmen,' poème de jeunesse de Gerson."

33. Gl 2.87; EW, 236.

34. Gl 2.88; EW, 238–39.

35. Gl 2.89; EW, 239–40.

36. Gl 7.1.158. My translation is based on that of Valerie Beech, Kalamazoo College, 1987, in typescript.

37. Gl 7.1.172. This story is probably taken from *Legenda aurea,* ch. 21, 105; trans. Ryan and Ripperger, 100.

38. Francis Ledwidge, "La correspondance de Gerson."

39. Yelena Matusevich, "From Monastic to Individual Spirituality."

40. Louis Mourin, *Jean Gerson. Prédicateur Français,* 163–65.

41. The dating to 1406 is provisional (Glorieux, "La vie et les oeuvres de Gerson," 169). I agree that the treatises may result from Gerson's new duties as canon of Notre Dame cathedral. In 1406 he was resident in Paris, while he was absent for much of 1407 and 1408.

42. See Tentler, *Sin and Confession.* Also McGuire, "Education, Confession, and Pious Fraud."

43. Gl 8.11; EW, 367.

44. Gl 8.14; EW, 371.

45. Gl 8.14; EW, 371.

46. See the famous twenty-first constitution of the Fourth Lateran Council of 1215, "Omnis utriusque sexus fidelis" about yearly confession and communion. The confessor's function is described as that of "a skilled doctor" (*periti medici,* Alberigo, 221).

47. As in the classic manual, *Raymundina:* "I advise that in his questions he not descend to special circumstances and special sins; for many fall severely after such an interrogation who otherwise never would have dreamt of it," quoted in Tentler, *Sin and Confession,* 88.

48. Gl 8.16; EW, 374.

49. "Sed experientiam totalem non habeo." Gl 8.15; EW, 373.

50. Gl 9.673–74. See chapter 6 above.

51. Gl 9.678: "Quod mihi, quia in talibus esse putor momenti alicujus, in fabulam et improprium cesserit."

52. *Phormio,* l. 454: "Suus cuique mos est." Gerson still used classical tags, though not as frequently as a decade earlier.

53. Gl 9.682: "Si non liceret cuiquam aliquid praeclarae novitatis arripere, male iret respublica." So far as I know, this is one of the first times a medieval ecclesiastical writer emphasized the positive value of novelty.

54. See Gl 3.xii and Gl 8.47. Also chapter 6, n 38 above.

55. Gl 8.22; EW, 294.

56. Gl 8.26; EW, 301.

57. See Hugh's *Expositio in hierarchiam coelestem S. Dionysii areopagitae* 6 (PL 175:1038D): "Et intrat dilectio, et appropinquat, ubi scientia foris est."

58. Gl 8.31; EW, 308. Horace, *Sermonum libri* (*Satires* 1.9.59–60). Gerson used *Deus* instead of Horace's term *vita.*

59. Gl 8.46; EW, 331. See Bernard's *Sermones super Cantica,* 3.

60. Gl 3.293; EW, 332–33. Glorieux (3.xiii) dated this *Annotatio* to winter 1402–3, when Gerson was writing his lecture notes for the *Speculative Mystical Theology.* Max Lieberman, "Chronologie gersonienne," *Romania* 79 (1958), claimed this addition was written by Jean the Celestine in 1419–1422. It would resemble Gerson, however, to add a booklist to his exposition, either in 1403–43 or in 1407–8.

61. For the classic medieval theology of grace, see Aage Rydstrøm-Poulsen, *The Gracious God.*

62. *Gerson bilingue,* esp. xviii–xxi.

63. Ibid., 34–35. For details, McGuire, "Jean Gerson and Bilingualism in the Late Medieval University," esp. 125.

64. Gl 2.72–3; EW, 222–23.

65. Gl 2.74. In EW, 224. I followed Glorieux's assertion that the work was sent to an unknown person, but as Ouy has shown (*Gerson bilingue,* xvii, n 1), Gerson was posing as an anonymous writer to all Christendom: *Christianitati suus qualiscumque zelator.*

66. "Pour tant je m'en suis estudié vous escrire aucunes consideracions briefves." (Gl 7.1.370).

67. For this development, see Miri Rubin, *Corpus Christi,* esp. 63–64, 69–70.

68. Gl 7.1.140. See Joseph Morawski, *Proverbes français antérieurs au XVe siècle,* 52, n 1424.

69. *Traité des diverses tentations de l'ennemi,* Gl 7.2.343–60.

70. Once again Gerson applies to all Christians what used to be a monastic concern. For *singularitas* in a twelfth-century Cistercian context, McGuire, "A Lost Clairvaux Exemplum Collection Found," in *Friendship and Faith,* IV, 34–35.

71. Gl 5.454: "Quae blasphemia si fiat sub ludi specie, debet per superiores seriose reparari." See Gl 7.1.409–11 and chapter 6 above, n 93.

72. See note 37 above.

73. See chapter 4 above.

74. Gl 5.126: "Est, inquiunt, hoc officum vel mendicantium vel pauperum theologorum."

75. Gl 5.138. See McGuire, "Anti-clerical Invective."

76. Similar recommendations are found in a memorandum for bishops, *De visitatione praelatorum,* dated 30 April 1408, the day after Gerson's sermon, Gl 8.47–55.

77. Gl 5.140, "Nonne tangitur altare per laicos incompositos comitatos canibus mingentibus ad pallas altaris?"

78. Gl 2.82; EW, 231.

79. CRSD livre 25, ch. 14; tome 3, vol. 2, 185–89.

80. The reference could have come from the opening of the first book in Augustine's *City of God.* It was also available, however, in Jerome (Ep. 27:13).

81. CRSD livre 25, ch. 14; tome 3, vol. 2, 190–92.

82. CRSD livre 26, ch.21; tome 3, vol. 2, 346.

83. CRSD livre 26, ch. 13; tome 3, vol. 2, 294.

84. CRSD livre 26, ch. 15; tome 3, vol. 2, 306: "Et quia tunc inter eos vigere odium inexpiabile videbatur, a circumspectis viris timebatur ne divisionem principum, in detrimentum regni, guerrarum discrimina sequerentur."

85. CRSD livre 26, ch. 16; tome 3, vol. 2, 314: "Recedentes igitur, studendo ministerium vestrum debite compleatis, quoniam, et si filia regis Universitas vocetur, tamen de regimine regni ipsam intromittere non decet."

86. For this development, see the still useful analysis by Hastings Rashdall, *The Universities of Europe,* vol. 1, 579–581.

87. CRSD livre 26, ch. 19; tome 3, vol. 2, 333.

88. Ibid., 334–36. The situation is described more briefly in *Journal d'un bourgeois de Paris 1405–1449*, ed. Alexandre Tuetey, 1–3.

89. CRSD livre 26, ch. 20; tome 3, vol. 2, 344.

90. Gerson's assumption of a common heritage for monarchy and people hints at national feeling long before the French Revolution. See Gilbert Ouy, "Humanism and Nationalism in France at the Turn of the Fifteenth Century."

91. CRSD livre 26, ch.1; tome 3, vol. 2, 236–38.

92. CRSD livre 26, ch. 24; tome 3, vol. 2, 352–54.

93. For Benedict XIII's earlier efforts to invade Italy with French help, see Noël Valois, *La France et le grand schisme*, vol. 3, 398–416.

94. Ibid., 455–476.

95. Glorieux, "La vie et les oeuvres," 170, n 7. Glorieux, however, may have been confusing this sermon with the *Vade in pace* of 18 March.

96. CRSD livre 27, ch. 22; tome 3, vol. 2, 542–44.

97. CRSD livre 28, ch. 9; tome 3, vol. 2, 604.

98. CRSD livre 28, ch. 11; tome 3, vol. 2, 614–18.

99. Gl 2.84; EW, 234.

100. A good background study is Bernard Guenée, *Un meurtre, une société.*

101. The text of the Parlement de Paris decision is in Gl 10.493–98. For background, Valois, "Gerson, curé de Saint Jean-en-Grève."

102. Gl 6.108–14: *Rememoratio agendorum per praelatum durante subtractione.*

103. Gl 5.113. See *On the Spiritual Life of the Soul,* Gl 3.176 and chapter 6 above.

104. Gl 6.113. See also Gerson's more detailed letter-treatise to a bishop concerning moderation in reserved cases, Gl 2.90–93; EW, 240–44.

105. For background, CRSD livre 28, ch. 29; tome 3, vol. 2, 722–28. Gerson's oration is not mentioned here.

106. Mourin, *Prédicateur français,* 187–196, rejected an earlier assumption that Gerson was addressing the duke of Burgundy.

107. This is a Celestine (d. 1408) close to Gerson. Also known as Pierre Pocquet, he became vicar general of the Order. See Max Lieberman, "Pierre Pocquet: *Dictamen de Laudibus Beati Josephi.*" Also note 31 above.

108. Gl 2.106–7; EW, 260.

Chapter 8

1. See Posthumus Meyjes, *Jean Gerson. Apostle of Unity,* 146, n 1, for a review of the evidence that troubles in Bruges explain Gerson's staying home from Pisa.

2. Glorieux, "Gerson au chapitre de Notre-Dame," 841–42.

3. Vansteenberghe, "Gerson à Bruges," esp. 28–38.

4. Ibid., 34–35.

5. Ibid., 38–39.

6. Gerson's colleague Nicolas de Clamanges, for example, was painfully aware of his weakness in this matter: Christopher M. Bellitto, *Nicolas de Clamanges,* 104–5.

7. Remarkably enough, we have no sermons by Gerson in French from Parisian parish churches dating from these years. While he had earlier invested a great deal of himself in composing "guest sermons" for such churches, his regular duties at Saint-Jean may have meant more spontaneous preaching without writing down a sermon before or after he gave it.

8. Glorieux, "La vie et les oeuvres de Gerson," 174–75; also Gl 9.29–31.

9. Gl 2.140: The dating of 1410 is given in a manuscript from Trier (Gl 2.xviii).

10. Glorieux, "L'enseignement universitaire de Gerson," esp. 103 and 112–13.

11. Gl 2.143: "Qui apostolicam illam sententiam a puerilibus pene annis imbuisti: virtus in infirmitate perficitur" (Rom 7:24).

12. cup, vol. 4, nr. 1916, 203.

13. crsd livre 32, ch. 3; tome 4, vol. 2, 400.

14. Louis Mourin, *Jean Gerson. Prédicateur français,* 206.

15. See Alfred Coville, *Jean Petit. La question du tyrannicide,* 421–26, who claimed Gerson could not have written this work and thought it must have been authored by a theologian trying to make him seem to contradict himself. Coville made Gerson too consistent. The confused contents of this treatise represent to my mind Gerson's thinking during this period.

16. Gl 10.288, where Glorieux stated (with a question mark) that Gerson edited or transmitted this report.

17. crsd livre 32, ch. 9; tome 4, vol. 2, 416.

18. crsd (418): "Sed cum die dicta propter hoc comparuisset, a peritis in jure canonico et divino, visa ejus proposicione scriptis data, dictum fuit et in regis presencia quod id exemplariter referebat." The written declaration referred to here may well be the *cédule* printed in Glorieux.

19. Gl 7.1.363: "Et Augustinus Quarto de Civitate Dei: remota justicia quid sunt regna nisi magna latrocinia." This is an exact quote from *City of God,* bk. 4, ch. 4.

20. Gl 7.1.219, in a reply to criticisms made against the university, 4 October 1413: "Qui es cas dessus dits empesche par violence et par menaces et par puissance ou par corruption de dons et de promesses."

21. The classic work remains Alfred Coville, *Les cabochiens et l'ordonnance de 1413.*

22. Gl 7.2.1030, from *Rex in sempiternum vive,* 4 September 1413.

23. Coville, *Les cabochiens,* esp. ch. 3, "Commentaire de l'ordonnance."

24. crsd livre 34, ch. 30; tome 5, vol. 3, 128.

25. Coville, *Les Cabochiens,* 362–64, as well as Mourin, *Prédicateur français,* 210.

26. crsd livre 34, ch. 32; tome 5, vol. 3, 136. The chronicler claimed he did not want to tire his readers by repeating the sermon but reported that Gerson praised God for a miracle (*velud pro miraculo manifesto*) of bringing the civil war so quickly to an end. Glorieux (10.590) claims the sermon was about Saint Joseph but provides no evidence.

27. In one sermon, Gerson refers to exams for the licentiate in theology (*Pax hominibus bonae voluntatis,* from December 1409, Gl 7.2.764.

28. The work of Posthumus Meyjes is authoritative and provides a detailed review of Gerson's writings on the schism. See my review in *Speculum* 76 (2001), 1092–93.

29. For Henry of Langenstein, R. N. Swanson, *Universities, Academics and the Great Schism,* 54–55 and 59–62. The development of Pierre d'Ailly's conciliar thought deserves fresh treatment. See Francis Oakley, *The Political Thought of Pierre d'Ailly,* 11.

30. See *Propositiones utiles ad exterminationem praesentis schismatis,* in Du Pin as Gerson's work (vol 2, 112–13). Glorieux (6.lii) attributes it to d'Ailly.

31. Gerson's ecclesiastical thinking needs to be examined in greater detail in terms of its contribution to late medieval and early modern philosophies of political power in church and state. Antony Black, *Council and Commune,* provides a beginning.

32. For background in Gerson's use of this term, see Posthumus-Meyjes, *Apostle of Unity,* 242–46.

33. Gerson was apparently referring to the Second Philippic 13, but admitted that he did not have the passage on hand and so only provided its essence: *cujus est sententia quia verba non habeo* (Gl 6.139). He often recalled what he thought he remembered without checking quotations (McGuire, "In Search of Bernard's Legacy").

34. For background, Valois, *La France et le grand schisme,* vol. 4, 102–7.

35. Gl 5.204. See Anselm of Canterbury, *Cur deus homo,* ch. 17.

36. Morrall, *Gerson and the Great Schism* (88), calls the treatise *De auferibilitate papae ab ecclesia,* on the removal of the pope from the Church. It may have been revised and completed at the Council of Constance (cf. Glorieux, "L'enseignement universitaire," 101).

37. Posthumus Meyjes, *Apostle of Unity,* 176, n 118.

38. Gl 3.305: "Quanto magis erronea et damnanda est assertio quod licet unicuique subditorum mox ut aliquis est tyrannus, ipsum viis omnius fraudulentis et dolosis sine quavis auctoritate vel

declaratione judiciaria morti tradere." The statement could, of course, have been added by Gerson later when he revised the treatise at Constance.

39. Gerson traced the view linking power with holiness back to the "poor of Lyon and others like them" in a reference he found in Bonaventure's *Commentary on the Sentences,* 4:25.

40. Posthumus Meyjes, *Apostle of Unity,* 178–182.

41. Gerson did not take it for granted that Boniface had asserted such temporal jurisdiction. He merely said "some people impose on Boniface VIII" such a claim (*comme aucuns emposent a Boniface le VIIIe,* Gl 7.2.770)—a judicious distinction.

42. Gl 7.2.772: "La reformacion de l'Esglise de France et de ses libertés nonobstant la contradiction que vauroient faire par aventure aucunus de la cour de Romme." For the concept of a semi-autonomous Gallican Church, see Victor Martin, *Les origines du gallicanisme,* vols. 1–2.

43. Gl 7.2.775: "C'est fort; mais n'est riens que bonne voulenté ne mette affin par grant labeur et diligence; labor improbus omnia vincit" (Vergil *Georgics* 1:144).

44. See Glorieux's helpful "dossier," Gl 10.30–31. The role of the mendicants in university history needs to be researched for this period. See the "Additional Note" in Hastings Rashdall, *The Universities of Europe,* vol. 1, 396–97. Also remarks by Monika Asztalos in "The Faculty of Theology," in Hilde de Ridder-Symoens, ed., *A History of the University in Europe,* vol. 1, 414–17.

45. Gl 10.32–34, which begins with reference to the fifth year "from the election of Pedro de Luna as pope, who *dudum* (formerly) was called Benedict XIII." The expression captures Gerson's attitude toward the Avignon pope at this point.

46. See Rashdall, vol. 1, 370–395.

47. See chapter 3 above.

48. CUP vol. 4, nr. 1868, 165–67.

49. Note that Glorieux (10.31) says the sermon was given in the cathedral, while Mourin, *Jean Gerson* (203), claims it was given in the course of a solemn procession.

50. The eleventh-century Gregorian Reform of the secular clergy was inspired by men of monastic background. See H.E.J. Cowdrey, *The Cluniacs and the Gregorian Reform.*

51. CUP, vol. 4, nr. 1879, 173. The decision refers to the faculty of theology as a whole and indicates nothing about the possible dissent or absence of mendicant masters.

52. Gl 10.35: "Et parata semper esse reddere rationem de ea quae in nobis est fide et spe." Cf. *Regula Benedicti,* ch.2.

53. The literature on the Spiritual Franciscans is a growth industry. Classic and central remains Marjorie Reeves, *The Influence of Prophecy in the Later Middle Ages.*

54. Gl 10.39: "Quod maneat imperturbatus hierarchicus ordo et essentialis ecclesiae, praelatorum et curatorum, quorum potissime papa defensor, non destitutor esse debet."

55. CUP vol. 4, nr. 1917, 204–6.

56. Ibid., 204.

57. A privilege first granted for ecclesiastical jurisdiction in 1245. See Rashdall, vol. 1, 342.

58. *Tractatus de duplici statu in ecclesia dei, curatorum et privilegiatorum,* Gl 9.25.35. See Posthumus Meyjes, *Apostle of Unity,* 294–98. Glorieux 9.viii dated the treatise to before June of 1409, prior to Alexander V's election. In view of Gerson's concern, in 1410–12, with the mendicants, I think it belongs to these years.

59. As in Britain, see www.nolanreview.org.uk. The "Programme for Action" 2.9.5 recommends that confession, especially for children, take place "in a setting where both priest and lay person can be seen but not heard."

60. Gl 9.35: "Ne si ad invicem, more cornicum, se mordeant, consumantur."

61. Gl 3.320: "Hoc praemisi quia vidi quaedam scripta nomini meo ascripta quae truncate recitata erant, ponendo partem unam, dimittendo alteram." See Gerson's earlier letter in which he claims that his writings had been tampered with (Gl 2.43; EW, 193).

62. See chapter 6 above, note 28.

63. Gerson followed Augustine's *City of God* (bk. 10.23): "We must speak according to a fixed rule" or standard. This reference turns up regularly in Gerson's work from these years. See chapter 9, n 34.

64. Gl 5.227: "Addito quod agibilium istorum vehemens consideratio a pueritia vel ab adolescentia non tantum erudit neque clarificat ingenium quantum exercitatio in speculabilibus principiis." The "neque" is problematic here and may be a misreading.

65. Gl 9.24: "Nihil quidem sublimius sed nihil periculosius et tentationibus magis expositum, quam ambulare per viam affectionis amorosae."

66. *Pro pueris ecclesiae parisiensis,* Gl 9.686–89. Glorieux gives this date (9.xix) because on 2 April 1411, the chapter of Notre Dame provided six general rules for the masters of the choir school (Gl 10.509). These show similar concerns to Gerson's.

67. This recommendation may come originally from the *Rule of Saint Benedict* (ch 22), but Benedict wrote nothing about deeds that shun the light.

68. For Gerson's contribution in terms of the history of education, see McGuire, "Education, Confession and Pious Fraud," esp. 318–20. See also Philippe Ariès and Georges Duby, *A History of Private Life,* vol. 2.

69. An excellent introduction to Gerson's moral theology is Sven Grosse, *Heilsungewissheit und Scrupulositas.*

70. Gl 9.106, nr. 44: "Nulli facienti quod in se est, hoc est bene utenti donis Dei jam habitis, deest deus in necessariis ad salutem, sive sint illa credenda, sive operanda." For Gerson on "doing what one has in oneself," see Brown, *Pastor and Laity,* 61, 65.

71. Gl 2.151. Gerson merely said some pages (*cedulae*) had been brought to him at Paris. The messenger asked for an answer in order to calm a scandal that had arisen.

72. Gilbert Ouy has established that one of the manuscripts in the Basel University Library is the original letter with Gerson's own signature. See "Enquête sur les manuscrits autographes du chancelier Gerson," 299–301.

73. See chapter 4 above.

74. See E. Vansteenberghe, "Consultation sur une forme de dévotion populaire," esp. 176–183.

75. Ibid., 178.

76. CRSD livre 33, ch. 30–31; tome 4, vol. 2, 736–768.

77. Gl 10.512, taken from Juvenal des Ursins (*Histoire de Charles VI,* ed. D Godefroy, Paris, 1653, 320). He says Gerson was accustomed to act faithfully ("de s'en acquitter loyaulement"). The same information is given in the CRSD livre 34, ch. 18; tome 5, vol. 3, 62.

78. According to the CRSD the crowd removed Gerson's *substanciam,* probably referring to his books and furnishings, presumably to be sold in lieu of what he "owed" in taxes.

79. Vansteenberghe, "Gerson à Bruges," 32 and 37, n 5.

80. Gl 10.511 and Glorieux, "Gerson au chapitre de Notre-Dame," 845.

81. See chapter 2 above.

82. See Christopher M. Bellitto, *Nicolas de Clamanges.*

83. Max Lieberman, "Pierre d'Ailly, Jean Gerson et le culte de Saint Joseph," 271–314.

84. Gl 2.139: "Nihilominus condescendendum est quandoque fragilitati et debili devotioni hominum."

85. *De pollutione nocturna et praeparatione ad missam* (*De dignitate celebrationis*), Gl 9.35–50, and *De cognitione castitatis* (*De pollutione diurna*), Gl 9.50–64. There are many more surviving manuscripts of the first treatise than of the second. See Gl 9.viii-ix.

86. See chapter 7 above.

87. The 22nd Conference of Cassian is dedicated to nocturnal illusions, as in *John Cassian: The Conferences,* 763–778. See Terrence Kardong, "John Cassian's Teaching on Perfect Chastity." For Gerson's teaching on sex as a whole, see McGuire, "Sexual Control and Spiritual Growth."

88. Gerson was not a pioneer here. Already in the early thirteenth century, Thomas of Chobham "devoted no less than four chapters of his *Summa* to nocturnal emissions, a problem of great concern in clerical circles." See James A. Brundage, *Law, Sex, and Christian Society,* 400–401.

89. Gl 9.39: "Dixit ei devotus et circumspectus Bernardus postquam hoc accepit: vade frater et in fide mea celebres."

90. Conrad of Eberbach, *Exordium magnum cisterciense,* Distinctio secunda, cap. 6, 102: "De

monacho quem sacramentis altaris fidem non adhibentem iussit pater sanctus communicare fide sua."

91. Gl 9.40: "Evenit insuper plerumque illud dictum Nasonis: Qui non est hodie cras minus aptus erit." See *Remedia amoris,* 94.

92. I have been unable to find Evagrius connected with this anecdote in the *Vitae patrum,* but Cassian's *Conference* 23, on sinlessness, section 21.1–2 makes the same observation.

93. Gl 9.46. Gerson also used "I know a man" in describing a failure, probably on his part, to maintain spiritual friendship with a nun. See chapter 6 above.

94. Gl 9.47: "Fornicata es, o anima mea, cum amatoribus tuis." Cf. Anselm's Meditation 2, "Lament for virginity unhappily lost," *The Prayers and Meditations of Saint Anselm,* 225.

95. According to this *Vita,* Peter was bothered by the question of nocturnal emissions and then had this dream about the donkey. This is almost certainly the source of Gerson's story: *Acta Sanctorum Maii IV* for 9 May, 487. Peter's dream is followed by an excursus on the causes of nocturnal pollution. For the various *vitae,* see [Anonymous], "Saint Pierre Célestin et ses premiers biographes."

96. Gl 7.1.412–16: *Contre les tentations de blasphème.*

97. Gl 9.60: "Phy, phy de vobis, cogitationes vilissimae; procul hinc abite, in malam horam veneritis; sum occupatus in aliis."

98. Gl 9.62: "Ipsa placeat non quia delectatio est sed quia alleviationem corporis operatur."

99. In making this point three times, Gerson indicates a sense of unease about the matter. Gl 9.57,60 and 63.

100. Mourin, *Prédicateur français,* 211, n 4.

101. *Prédicateur français,* 214.

102. Gl 7.2.1018. Coville, *Les Cabochiens,* ch. 3, "Commentaire de l'ordonnance."

103. For disagreement, see Ole Feldbæk, "Is there Such a Thing as a Medieval Danish Identity?" in McGuire, ed., *The Birth of Identities,* 127–134.

104. Alfred Coville, *Jean Petit. La question du tyrannicide,* 442.

105. *Oportet haereses esse,* dated 4–6 September 1413, Gl 10.174–79.

106. Gl 10.175. Gerson had earlier dealt with this question and had insisted that those condemned to death receive confession. See chapter 4.

107. Coville, *Jean Petit,* p. 445.

108. Gl 7.1.216: "Selon la doctrine de Saint Grégoire: Rectius oriri scandalum permittitur quam veritas deseratur." Cf. *Homiliae in Ezechielem.* PL 76:842C: "Si autem de veritate scandalum sumitur, utilius permittitur nasci scandalum quam veritas relinquatur." Gerson, as so often, apparently was quoting from memory and did not give the precise wording. For his earlier use on 4 September, Gl 7.2.1029.

109. The only treatment of Gerson's use of such language comes in brief remarks by Louis Mourin, *Prédicateur français,* 381–85.

110. CUP vol.4, nr 1999, 270. Also in Gl 10.514.

111. Cf. his protest from the spring of 1402 about his previous role in the Schism: "Nunquam fui praesens ubi haec materia pro facultate tractaretur" (Gl 6.35).

112. CUP vol. 4, nr. 1995, 266.

113. Ibid. (266–67): "Alii fugam velud exules capere, alii semet obcludere et templis se tueri, alii digitum ori suo apponere."

114. Coville, *Jean Petit,* 472–73.

115. CUP vol.4, nr. 2014, 280–82.

116. Gl 5.244. See note 108 above.

117. Gl 5.245. For the peace of Chartres (4 March 1409), Bernard Guenée, *Un meurtre, une société,* 218–222.

118. Gl 5.250, cf. Gratian, *Concordia discordantium canonum,* dist. 83, c. 3.

119. For John XXII, see G. Mollat, *The Popes at Avignon,* 21–23.

120. Gl 5.253: "Proinde lecto tenore protestationis, sensi tristis aliter esse quam credidi, nec purgationem sed sordidationem esse."

121. "Lettre de Gerson au duc de Berry," esp. 228–232. As from 17 August 1413 (Gl 8.62): "Movit rursus operatio miraculorum quae ad invocationem ipsius justi Joseph deputant in seipsis et in aliis contigisse." Cf. *Considerations sur Saint Joseph,* Gl 7.1.72.

122. For background, McGuire, "When Jesus did the Dishes: The Transformation of Late Medieval Spirituality," in *The Making of Christian Communities.* Also Palemon Glorieux, "Saint Joseph dans l'oeuvre de Gerson," 414–428.

123. Gl 7.1.76: "Nous disons cecy en especial pour un livre que on intitule: De l'enfance du Sauveur." (*Considérations sur Saint Joseph*). Gerson was reacting against the so-called *Liber de infantia,* also known as the *Gospel of Pseudo-Matthew.* See Montague Rhodes James, *The Apocryphal New Testament.* Gerson said that Saint Jerome was supposed to have translated what Saint Matthew had written in Hebrew. See James, 70–71, for the "letter" written to Jerome with these claims.

124. As in the letter of 17 August 1413 (Gl 8.65).

125. Gl 8.64: "Sit denique liberum cuilibet, super hac re vel simili non decisa per ecclesiam, quae neque auctoritate neque ratione certis fulcita est, sentire salva pietate fidei, quod voluerit."

126. Gerson used a term that shows how keen he was to prove this was a genuine marriage. He described the consent as being given *per verba de praesenti,* the canon law term required for a marriage (Gl 8.58).

127. Gl 7.1.66: "Et a brief dire il accompli toute la cure que bon et loyal et saige pere peut et doit faire a son vray fils."

128. Gl 2.155–57. See Lieberman, "Lettre de Gerson au duc de Berry."

129. See chapter 7. Lieberman may have exaggerated the importance of Henri Chiquot's death as an incentive for Gerson's devotion ("Lettre de Gerson au duc de Berry," 233–34).

130. Gl 7.1.88: "Pour parler par aventure plus a plain de la disposition de leurs noces. . . . et quelles personnes y estoient ou seroient appelees."

CHAPTER 9

1. For the Council of Constance, I have used Charles-Joseph Hefele and H. Leclercq, *Historie des conciles,* vol. 7.2; Valois, *La France et le grand schisme,* vol. 4, ch. 3, 227–408; E. Delaruelle, E.-R. Labande and Paul Ourliac, *L'église au temps du grand schisme et de la crise conciliare,* 167–200. Also Walter Brandmüller, *Papst und Konzil im Grossen Schisma (1378–1431). Studien und Quellen,* esp. 225–242.

The council sources are collected in Hermann von der Hardt, *Rerum concilii Oecumenici Constantiensis,* vols. 1–4. Also Heinrich Finke, *Acta Concilii Constanciensis,* vols. 1–4. Central sources are translated, with a good introduction, in C. M. D. Crowder, *Unity, Heresy and Reform 1378–1460: The Conciliar Response to the Great Schism,* esp. 65–138. Also L. R. Loomis, trans., and John H. Mundy and K. M. Woody, eds., *The Council of Constance. The Unification of the Church.*

2. For tyrannicide and Gerson, see the sources in Du Pin, vol. 5. Finke, vol. 4, 237–432, has materials not in Du Pin, especially writings by the Burgundian party.

3. CUP vol. 4, nr. 2011, 277–79, where the assertions are given in French. Gerson in a memorandum from October 1416 translated the statements into Latin (Gl 10.267–68).

4. Crowder, *Unity, Heresy and Reform,* 18. See also Valois, *La France et le grand schisme,* vol. 4, 331, who called this quarrel a "heartbreaking conflict." To my knowledge the fullest modern account of tyrannicide disputes at Constance is Alfred Coville, *Jean Petit. La question de tyrannicide.* Even here, however, there is little about Gerson's role after 1416.

5. For the proceedings, Joseph Alberigo et al., *Conciliorum Oecumenicorum Decreta,* esp. 381–82, the bull of John XXIII read out and approved at the first session.

6. Crowder, *Unity, Heresy and Reform* (9) says that Cardinal Zabarella and King Sigismund had "probably" agreed at a meeting at Como in 1413 that Pope John must be removed. Crowder sees in the French cardinal Fillastre's early 1415 recommendation that the pope be ready to lay

down his life for his flock a "plain recommendation of a voluntary withdrawal" (10). Text in Hardt, vol. 2, 208–213. For translations: Crowder, 69–74; Loomis, 209–212.

7. *Cedula Joanni XXIII exhibita, de molli via,* Hardt 2.198–201.

8. Wilhelm Baum, *Kaiser Sigismund,* 106–7.

9. See Hardt, vol. 4.

10. For background, see Valois, *La France and le grand schisme,* vol. 4, 228–237.

11. Otto Feger, *Kleine Geschichte der Stadt Konstanz,* 124–25.

12. As in the 1416 excursion of Poggio Bracciolini to Saint-Gall with three humanist friends. See L. D. Reynolds and N. G. Wilson, *Scribes and Scholars,* 120–22.

13. See the *Konzilstagebücher* in Finke, vol. 2. In the *Liber gestorum* of Cerretanus, for example, Gerson's sermon after the flight of John XXIII in March 1415 is mentioned, but he is only called "a certain doctor of the University of Paris" (Finke 2.224).

14. See John McGowan, *Pierre d'Ailly and the Council of Constance.* Simon de Cramaud was only at Constance from March 1417 until January 1418 and contributed with a brief treatise on combining the college of cardinals with the nations for the papal election of November 1417. See Kaminsky, *Simon de Cramaud,* 301–3.

15. *Chronique d'Enguerran de Monstrelet,* bk. 1, ch. 133, 55–56, in vol. 3, ed. L. Douët-d'Arcq. Trans. Thomas Johnes, *The Chronicles of Enguerrand de Monstrelet,* vol. 2, 320.

16. Gl 10.521. See chapter 8, n 118.

17. On 4 February, Gerson formally asked permission at the chapter of Notre Dame to go to Constance. On 8 February, a reference to the "seals of the church sent" to the dean of the chapter indicates that he was no longer in Paris (Gl 10.517–18).

18. On 4 December 1415, in response to a commission investigating tyrannicide, he referred to himself as "ambassador of the most Christian king of the Franks and the University of Paris and the Gallican Church for the province of Sens" (Gl 10.253).

19. Valois, *La France et le grand schisme,* vol. 4, 273–74.

20. Ibid., 275ff, remains the best account of day-to-day events at the council, even though the author maintains a French point of view and is often harsh on Sigismund.

21. Gl 5.39–50, partly translated in Crowder, 76–82. See the analysis in Posthumus Meyjes, *Jean Gerson,* 192–94.

22. Gl 5.44: "Concilium generale est congregatio legitima auctoritate facta ad aliquem locum ex omni statu hierarchico totius ecclesiae catholicae, nulla fideli persona quae audiri requirat exclusa, ad salubriter tractandum et ordinandum ea quae debitum regimen ejus ecclesiae in fide et moribus respiciunt."

23. The term *personarum acceptio* from the Vulgate (James 2:1 and 1 Pet. 1:17) is translated from the Greek in the New Revised Standard Version as "acts of favoritism," close to Gerson's understanding of the term.

24. Gl 5.46: "Sed impeditus tunc, partim amicorum suasione partim temporis arctatione . . . silentio praeteriit."

25. Gilbert Ouy, "Le Célestin Jean Gerson. Copiste et éditeur de son frère."

26. For the text: Alberigo, 385–86. Partial translation in Crowder, 83. For the still lively discussion about *Haec sancta,* Francis Oakley, *The Western Church,* 65–66, and his *Council over Pope?,* 105–141.

27. Gl 10.214–15: "Ita quod nullus non praemonitus nec diffidatus potest voluntarie interfici." There is a reference here to the declaration "Quilibet tyrannus," condemned by the council in July, but this may have been added later. Note, however, that Glorieux at one point (10.xv) dated this work to July, while in his dossier on Gerson and tyrannicide, he dated it to 9 June, in accord with Coville, *Jean Petit,* 519.

28. Alberigo (408): "Quilibet tyrannus potest et debet licite et meritorie occidi per quemcumque vassallum suum vel subditum, etiam per insidias, et blanditias vel adulationes, non obstante quocumque praestito iuramento, seu confoederatione facta cum eo, non expectata sententia vel mandato iudicis cuiuscumque."

29. For Sigismund's involvement, see Valois, *La France et le grand schisme,* vol. 4, 323–24.

30. For council events and dates, I draw on the overview in Glorieux, vol. 6, xxxix–lx. His main source is Valois, but he refers also to central works of Gerson and other theologians. For an attack on John XXIII as pirate, seducer of wives, and notorious simoniac, see Thierry de Niehm, *De vita, facinoribus et fatis Balthasaris,* in Hardt, vol. 2, esp. col. 336–341. The name John was not used again by popes for centuries, until Pope John XXIII (1958–1963).

31. See, for example, Eric John, ed., *The Popes,* where the names of Gregory XII's rivals are given in quotation marks, to show that they were not genuine popes.

32. A comparison of the two texts shows how Gerson switched the original emphasis on humility to the difficulty of avoiding traps: *Verba seniorum* 17.3, *De humilitate:* "Vidi omnes laqueos inimici tensos in terra et ingemiscens dixi: Quis putas transiet istos? Et audivi vocem dicentem: Humilitas" (PL 73:953).
Gerson, Gl 5.473: "Quis non cum Antonio pavescens exclamaverit: hoc Domine laqueos omnes, haec scandalorum retia quis evadet?" As so often in his writings, especially at Constance, he apparently quoted from memory.

33. *Viae Sion lugent* is taken from Lamentations 1:4 and is the title of a treatise on the mystical life by the Carthusian Hugh of Balma, a work known to Gerson. See *Carthusian Spirituality,* trans. Dennis D. Martin.

34. *Civitas dei* Bk. 10.23: "Nobis autem ad certam regulam loqui fast est, ne verborum licentia etiam et rebus quae his significantur impiam gignat opinionem."

35. See Crowder (96), in introducing translations of letters written by Hus shortly before he was executed. Matthew Spinka, *John Hus at the Council of Constance* (171, n 25) claims Gerson wrongly associated Hus with Wycliffe's view that someone in mortal sin has no dominion or ownership in Christian community.

36. For a translation, see Paschal Boland, *The Concept of Discretio Spirituum,* 25–38. Also Cornelius Roth, *Discretio spirituum.* and Nancy Caciola, *Discerning Spirits,* esp. ch. 6.

37. Boland, *The Concept,* 28. Text in Gl 9.179.

38. As Gerson pointed out in a letter from 1402 (Gl 2.54), he had reread Bernard's *Sermons on the Song of Songs* while he was ill. From this time on, Bernard's emphasis on the spiritual experience of the individual soul can clearly be seen in Gerson's writings.

39. Gl 9.182. See *Vitae patrum* 15.68 and 70, in PL 73:965.

40. Gl 9.184: "Habet insatiabilem videndi loquendique, ut interim de tactu silentium sit, puriginem; evenitque illud de Didone, apud poetam, '. . . haerent infixi pectore vultus, / Verbaque nec placidam membris dat cura quietem'." Cf. *Aeneid* 4.4–5, where Dido falls in love with Aeneas while he recounts his adventures.

41. Compare this treatise with his earlier one on the subject. See chapter 6 above.

42. Gl 9.184. Cf. *Sermones in Cantica* 74.5–6, in *Sancti Bernardi Opera,* vol. 2, 242–43.

43. Gl 6.154: "Oportet enim tales auditores esse theologos eruditissimos et incorruptissimos, et talium quanta fuerit et sit raritas in curia romana, nimis proh dolor, docuit experientia."

44. Gl 6.154. For this important phrase in Gerson's ecclesiastical thinking, Posthumus Meyjes, *Jean Gerson et l'assemblée de Vincennes (1329),* 24–25.

45. Jürgen Miethke and Lorenz Weinrich, *Quellen zur Kirchenreform,* 36–37, esp. n 84.

46. Porrée was correct in ascribing this view to Gerson, who opposed Ockham's teaching that the Church can exist in a single person. See Gordon Leff, *Heresy in the Later Middle Ages,* vol. 2, 436–37.

47. Such a claim was a typical defense in medieval academic heresy trials. See J.M.M.H. Thijssen, *Censure and Heresy at the University of Paris, 1200–1400.* Also Luca Bianchi, *Censure et liberté intellectuelle à l'université de Paris aux XIIIè et XIVè siècles.*

48. *Political Thought from Gerson to Grotius,* originally published in 1907.

49. According to Edouard Perroy, "A soixante-dix-neuf ans de distance, l'erreur de Crécy se renouvela," *La guerre de cent ans,* 298.

50. Jean Favier, *La guerre de cent ans,* esp. 438–445.

51. For their deliberations and depositions, see Du Pin 5.721–1012, with a list of seventy-seven masters and bachelors of theology.

52. Du Pin 5.919–20. Gl 10.233.

53. Gl 10.238. See the Council of Lyon (1245), article 18, *De homicidio* (cf. Alberigo, 266).

54. See Finke 4.244–45.

55. The full text of this long-winded declaration (Du Pin 5.500–507) reveals that the cardinals were eager to please the duke of Burgundy.

56. Coville, *Jean Petit,* 534–37.

57. Gl 5.538–46. Note that Glorieux in his dossier on tyrannicide dates this sermon to 2 February 1416 (Gl 10.168), while in Gl 5.xv, it is supposed to have been preached in 1418. The tone of regret and frustration with the council's failure to condemn tyrannicide points to 1416 rather than 1418. Glorieux is unfortunately full of such inconsistencies.

58. Gl 5.543: "Horresco referens, lamentabilis derepente vox insonuit ex ore prophetico clamans et conquerens; corruit in platea veritas (Isa 59:14). 'Obstupui visu subito gelidusque pererrat/Ossa tremor'" (*Aeneid* 2.120).

59. Gl 5.544: "Quid dicerem? Quid responderem sic pulsatus, sic obtestatus in ipso meditationis meae secreto per misericordiam condolentem veritati quae tam infeliciter et foede corruerat in plateis."

60. Gl 5.546. Cf. Gregory's *Homiliae in Ezechielem,* 1.7, PL 76.842. For an earlier use, see chapter 8, n 108 above.

61. For the relationship between temporal and spiritual power, see *De jurisdictione spirituali et temporali* (Gl 6.259–64) and the helpful study by Posthumus Meyjes, *Jean Gerson et l'assemblée de Vincennes.* He dates Gerson's brief treatise on the subject to August or September 1405 (53), long before he left for Constance, instead of Glorieux's dating (Gl 6.xv) to sometime after February of 1417. The content nevertheless reflects Gerson's views also at Constance.

62. The steady stream of royal missives to Constance during these years shows that someone was representing the king. Most likely "the king" means the Armagnac party, which was able to get Charles VI to do what it wanted, just as the Burgundians after 1418 did with him.

63. Gl 5.193. See *Liber Usualis* (1123) for the Antiphon sung at the Magnificat: "Iste sanctus pro lege Dei sui certavit usque ad mortem et a verbis impiorum non timuit: fundatus enim erat supra firmam petram." The words of the liturgy are ever present in Gerson's writings. More work deserves to be done on his link to this rich world.

64. Gl 5.196: "Notum est illud Ciceronis: inter arma silent leges; qui audit intelligat," cf. *Oratio pro Milone* 4.10 and *Epistolae ad Atticum* 7.3.5. Glorieux has a misprint here with a reference to one of the Psalms.

65. Gl 5.200: "Dico secundo quod antequam rex veniret hic in causam, assumpsi mihi causam ipsam modo qui decebat theologum, a quo modo neque discessi neque discedo neque discedam."

66. Gl 5.203: "Denique cognitum est quod mortem hanc mox ut patefacta est et annotata, sic ipse dominus dux praesens exhorruit detestatusque est ut diceret dominis de regio sanguine: diabolus, inquit, mihi persuasit." See CRSD liber 28, ch. 31; tome 3, vol. 2, 740: "Instiguante dyabolo."

67. Du Pin 5.585–86.

68. Wilhelm Baum, *Kaiser Sigismund,* 133–34.

69. Du Pin 5.640. Gl 10.169 gives the date as 23 July. I do not see the basis for this conclusion. Here as in so much else, Glorieux needs to be used with care.

70. See note 16 above.

71. Gl 10.263: "Alioquin frustraretur intentio concilii quae satagebat hunc errorem funditus tollere."

72. Du Pin 5.691: "Respondent quod cum appellationibus frivolis jura non deferant."

73. Hefele-Leclercq, *Historie des conciles,* vol. 7.l, 419–424.

74. Gl 5.345–46: "Sic eorum quae dicentur plurima volo posterius intelligi ita ut non tam quae facta sunt quam quae fieri potuisse pia quadam religiositate credi possunt." Compare with Gl 8.64, chapter 8, n 125.

75. Gl 5.347. Gerson described what is known as the Holy Kinship. See Kathleen Ashley and Pamela Sheingorn's excellent "Introduction" in *Interpreting Cultural Symbols. Saint Anne in Late Medieval Society.*

76. Gl 5.355–56. Cf. the text of the *Josephina*, dist. 12, Gl 4.95.

77. Gl 5.362, a fascinating passage: "Esset utinam apud tales hujusmodi numerus festivitatum minor, sicut in reformatione hic in concilio notatum est; sed apud ecclesiasticos et de ecclesiasticis talia loquimur." For d'Ailly on the danger in the multiplication of feast days, "quia dies operabiles vix sufficiunt pauperibus ad vitae necessaria procuranda," see *Tractatus de reformatione ecclesie,* 1 November 1416, Du Pin 2.911, less than two months after Gerson's sermon.

78. Gl 2.169–74. Glorieux said that Jean the Celestine was prior at Lyon, but Max Lieberman has shown that he did not take this post until 1421. See "Pierre d'Ailly, Jean Gerson et le culte de Saint Joseph," *Cahiers de Joséphologie* 15 (1967), esp. 77.

79. Du Pin 2.903–16, dated to 1 November 1416, with a wonderful opening quoting from Bernard of Clairvaux (*Sermo 33 in Cantica*). The Latin text (here called *De reformacione ecclesie*) and a German translation are in Miethke and Weinrich, *Quellen zur Kirchenreform,* 338–377.

80. Du Pin 2.904: "Et post ista tonitrua tam horrenda, alia horribiliora, in proximo audiemus. Eapropter summopere vigilandum est circa reformationem ecclesie."

81. Du Pin 5.908. Also Peter the Chanter and other late twelfth- to early thirteenth-century Parisian writers are mentioned, col. 907.

82. Du Pin 2.916.

83. Matthew Spinka (*Advocates of Reform*) claimed that d'Ailly incorporated almost all of chapters 16–19 of Conrad of Gelnhausen's *Letter on Behalf of a Council of Peace* (Du Pin 2.835–40) into his treatise. I find agreement in terms of what needed to be reformed, but Conrad provided a shopping list while d'Ailly gave a fuller description of the evils of the day.

84. Max Lieberman, "Autour de l'iconographie gersonienne," 307–353, esp. 327–331, for the *Icon peregrini.*

85. McGuire, "*Ego peregrinus et advena:* Jean Gerson, Mystical Theology and Late Medieval Interior Pilgrimage," in Morten Nøjgaard, *The Epic Journey in Classical and Medieval Romance.*

86. See James A. Weisheipl, *Friar Thomas d'Aquino. His Life, Thought and Works,* 320–23.

87. Gl 7.2.563. See chapter 3 above.

88. *Conferences* 9.31, "On Prayer."

89. At the opening of the treatise, Gerson refers to his sermon, addressed to the council, about Saint Anthony (Gl 6.190).

90. For Sigismund's trip, see Hefele-Leclercq, *Historie des conciles,* vol. 7.1, 425–27. Also Baum, *Kaiser Sigismund,* ch. 11, 130–38.

91. For background see Valois, vol. 4, 535–36.

92. See Hardt vol. 4, 345–47 for a statement concerning Nicolas by the Burgundian delegation at Constance and King Sigismund, made in the Franciscan priory. The instructions recovered on his person when he was taken provide a fascinating document of a medieval *aide-memoire* by a diplomatic messenger (Hardt, vol. 4, 343–45). On 13 April 1417, the Burgundian delegates protested against Capella's complaint (733–36) and said they were innocent of his capture.

93. The most complete and probably best summary is in Posthumus Meyjes, *Apostle of Unity,* 247–286.

94. Gl 6.239. Posthumus Meyjes, *Apostle of Unity* (280), translates the term as "considered opinion."

95. Gl 6.240, cf. Gl 5.44.

96. Gl 6.lix. For background, Hefele-Leclercq, *Historie des conciles,*vol. 7.1, 429–436.

97. According to Posthumus Meyjes, *Apostle of Unity* (201), Gerson's *Libellus* contains nothing new from the point of view of his ecclesiology.

98. Gl 6.268: "Intelligebat ergo de ecclesia quae est congregatio fidelium." Cf. Acts 15, providing a model for a collegial church.

99. For text of the condemnation see Alberigo, 413–14. Partial translation in Crowder, 126–28

100. Also the French and the English could not agree. The French claimed that there were too few English representatives to make up a nation. See Crowder, 108–126. This dispute led to "the exchange of blows" (109).

101. For background, Gordon Leff, *Heresy in the Late Middle Ages,* vol. 2, 485–493.

102. Gl 10.48: "Sectam hujusmodi cruentam et sanguinolentem, gallice sanglante." Here, as in his attacks on the nine assertions, Gerson at times uses French words to explain his Latin.

103. Gl 8.77–84, *De meditatione cordis,* dated prior to July 1417, because the last treatise in the series, *De directione cordis,* is dated to 28 July 1417.

104. Gl 8.84. See note 41 above.

105. Gl 8.84: "Ubi sicut vulgo dicitur. neque est caput neque cauda." See Mourin, *Prédicateur français,* 381–84, for the chancellor's delight in proverbs and sayings.

106. *Expositio in hierarchiam coelestem S. Dionysii areopagitae* 6, PL 174:1038. See Gl 8.26; EW, 301.

107. Gl 8.92: "Sed et ipse amor, sicut dicit Gregorius, quaedam cognitio est." From *XL Homiliarum in Evangelio* 27.4, PL 76:1204. Gregory's influence on Gerson's mystical theology was immense and deserves further study, as so much else in the sources of his learning.

108. See chapter 1 for my previous use of this important recollection and *exemplum* from Gerson's life.

109. Gl 8.93. Gerson's reference was correct (Eusebius, *Ecclesiastica historia,* bk 5.1). He was drawing on the readings of a lifetime.

110. Gl 8.94. A fascinating story, so different from what Sir Richard Southern once told me, that it was through reading these same meditations in the early 1930s that he became a Christian.

111. Gerson did, however, in his own prayers come to accept Anselm's affective mode of expression. See chapter 1.

112. Gl 8.94: "Nihil est, inquit, magis mihi suspectum quam amor, etiam circa Deum. Posui hoc in lectione quadam edita per modum tractatuli De probatione verarum revelationum." See Gl 3.51 and EW, 356 and 459, n 53.

113. Gl 8.97–115, according to Gl 8.xvi from 28 July 1417, but no evidence is given. *De directione cordis,* follows almost word for word the letter-treatise *De valore orationis* (Gl 2.175–91) but from page 107 at the bottom on, the text is new.

114. Du Pin 1.clxxix, the prologue of Jacob Wimpheling, probably Strasbourg 1502 (see Gl 1.72 and chapter 11 below).

115. See the condemnation by the council, Session 13, 15 June 1415, in Alberigo, 394–95.

116. For other universities and the council, see R. N. Swanson, *Universities, Academics and the Great Schism,* esp. 187–201. Some of the letters of Peter de Pulka, official representative of the University of Vienna, are translated in Crowder, 129–138.

117. Gl 10.168–69. Falkenberg's *Satira contra haereses et cetera infanda Polonorum* is not among the three treatises of his concerning tyrannicide printed in Du Pin 5.1013–32.

118. Finke vol. 4, 356–363. Among other sources contained in this valuable collection are drafts of a statement of condemnation of Falkenberg's attack on the Poles made by Pierre d'Ailly and Cardinal Zabarella (410–13), from August or September 1417.

119. Finke, vol. 4, 378–387.

120. "Mémoire pour l'éléction avant la réforme," *Ad obviandum multis erroribus qui nunc oriri videntur.* Gl 6.278–82.

121. See the eighteen items listed by the council's fortieth plenary session, on 30 October 1417, a few days before the papal election: *Reformationes fiendae per papam una cum concilio antequam dissolvatur* (Alberigo, 420).

122. Crowder (179): "It can be accepted as a symbol marking the end of the conciliar epoch in the history of the fifteenth-century Church, even if it was not finally definitive."

123. Alberigo, 426–27. Hefele-Leclercq, vol. 4, 567–68; Hardt vol. 4, 1557. Note that Morrall, *Gerson and the Great Schism* (108), dates this constitution to 10 March, but Gerson in his *An liceat in causis fidei a papa appellare* gives the date as 10 May (Gl 6.283).

124. See the texts of the concordats given in German and Latin in Miethke and Weinrich, *Quellen zur Kirchenreform,* 516–545. To the German Church the pope promised to limit in future the "excessive spread of indulgences" (530). To the Gallican Church, he promised no changes

("nichil intendimus circa eas immutare seu ordinare," 536), while to the English Church he made detailed provisions for limiting abuses.

125. Alberigo, 423–27; Miethke and Weinrich, 506–515.

126. Hefele-Leclercq, vol. 4, 567–68. See also "Das Konstanzer Dekret 'Haec sancta'" in Brandmüller, *Papst und Konzil*, esp. 242–44. The interpretation of this adverb seems to have enabled the papalist party to distance itself from conciliar authority.

127. Morrall, *Gerson and the Great Schism*, 109–110.

128. James Connolly, *John Gerson. Reformer and Mystic*, 220.

Chapter 10

1. Gl 2.3; EW, 152. See chapter 2 above.

2. It was probably his brother Jean the Celestine who gives us the place and date, Gl 4.x.

3. *Deploratio studii parisiensis*, Gl 4.5–7 and *Deploratio super civitatem*, Gl 10.407–14. See the new edition with full annotation and an introduction by Gilbert Ouy, "Gerson et la guerre civile à Paris."

4. CRSD livre 39, ch. 8; tome 6, vol. 3, 243–253.

5. Andre Combes, *La théologie mystique de Gerson*, vol. 2, 306–311.

6. Glorieux writes (2.216) "Neuenburg sur le Danube." I was unable to find such a place, but there is a Neuburg on the Inn. Gerson wrote at the end of the letter "Novum Burgum in Bavaria," corresponding to the location of Neuburg.

7. See chapter 8 above.

8. See Burrows, *Jean Gerson and De Consolatione Theologiae (1418)*, 36–38.

9. Pierre d'Ailly, however, did write to Gerson (Gl 2.221): "Et contra vero tyrannus ille suo demerito turpissima morte temporali, utinam non aeterna, vitam finivit." See Bernard Guenée, *Between Church and State*, 254.

10. Glorieux (1.134) gives this date. The only evidence I find for it is Jean the Celestine's letter, dated to May 1423, saying that Gerson had been in Lyon "jam fere per quadriennium" (Gl 10.559).

11. Pierre Wuilleumier, *Lyon. Métropole des Gaules.*

12. Marcel Pacaut, *Guide de Lyon médiéval*, 40–50.

13. Eadmer, *The Life of Saint Anselm*, bk. 2, ch. xxxix, 116.

14. Ibid., 116.

15. Gl 10.553. Glorieux's edition states 1419, but there is no doubt the correct date is 1420.

16. There is a poem dedicated to d'Ailly, *Quod vita somnium sit* (That Life is a Dream, Gl 4.148–49). Glorieux gives no date, but the contents do not point to the aftermath of d'Ailly's death.

17. Du Pin 1.xxxvi. Gl 1.134.

18. Lieberman, "Pierre d'Ailly, Jean Gerson et le culte de Saint Joseph," esp. 76–77. Unfortunately Lieberman's article has not been widely noticed. See, for example, Brown, *Pastor and Laity*, 10.

19. See the excellent contribution of Hervé Chopin in *Quartier Saint-Paul Lyon*, esp. 86–88.

20. Lieberman, "Pierre d'Ailly," 78: "On voit encore dans le cloître de Saint-Paul les pièces qu'occupaient Gerson." Lieberman, normally very cautious, accepted a story that has no firm basis in the sources. More work remains to be done on Gerson at Lyon. The *Acta* of the chapter of Saint Paul are contained in the Archives du Département du Rhône at Lyon (13G6) and contain several unpublished references to Gerson, as f. 156v from 26 June 1423.

21. Gl 1.136, followed in Brown, *Pastor and Laity*, 10.

22. Schwab, *Johannes Gerson*, vol. 2, 773.

23. Connolly, *John Gerson*, 198, wrote, "In Lyons, Gerson resumed the work of catechizing children which had characterized his activity in Paris," and referred to Schwab (773) as his source!

24. Anne-Louise Masson, *Jean Gerson*, 406.

25. For background on the formation of this bond, McGuire, "Loving the Holy Order: Jean Gerson and the Carthusians."

26. Gl 10.559: "Vitam quietissimam ducens et tam solitariam ut unum ex eremiciolis crederes nisi quod deserti recessus nondum petiit sed habitat in medio populi sui" (cf. 2 Chron 4:13).

27. Gl 10.559. Gerson used the rare but appropriate verb *debacchantur,* to rave oneself to exhaustion.

28. For the ideal in another setting, see *De Cella in Seculum,* Michael G. Sargent, ed..

29. Gl 9.560: "Sedet solitarius et tacet," from Lamentations 3:28.

30. Gl 10.561: "Non igitur putes illum datam quietem male exequi et inerti otio tota die torpescere." Gerson himself used the phrase *inerti otio* in his sermon *Jacob autem* concerning Joseph, Gl 5.348, an indication of Jean the Celestine's use of his brother's vocabulary. See chapter 9.

31. Gl 10.561: "Quando perversi difficile corriguntur et stultorum infinitus est numerus." The last phrase is from Eccles 1:15, one of Gerson's favorite quotations, as in *Consolatio Theologiae,* Gl 9.191.

32. See Irénée Hausherr, *Spiritual Direction in the Early Christian East,* esp. ch. 4, "The Duties of the Spiritual Father."

33. On 6 July 1418, after the June massacres, the rector and university delegates handed over the chancellor's function to the theologian Jean Cortecuisse "propter absentiam domni cancelarii Parisiensis ecclesie," CUP vol. 4, nr. 2106, 344.

34. Gl 2.285, Letter 60, about the difficulty of answering questions posed by Oswald of Corda: "Aut praeterea simile est quasi si niteretur aliquis fluctus Rhodani vel maris fluxus aut refluxus vel describere vel certis concludere metis."

35. Gl 4.31–100. A critical edition is available on CD-Rom, with a full introduction, ed.G. Matteo Roccati. Also McGuire, "When Jesus did the Dishes: Jean Gerson and the Transformation of Late Medieval Spirituality."

36. *The Autumn of the Middle Ages,* trans. Rodney J. Payton and Ulrich Mammitzsch, 195.

37. Gl 4.36: "Donec dormiat is cujus semper vigilat cor." Cf. "Ego dormio et cor meum vigilat," Song of Songs 5:2. Gerson wove the biblical text into his narrative. This method is almost banal in medieval spiritual literature, but Gerson was a master of it.

38. Gl 4.43: "Nulli nos erimus oneri, panem neque gratis/ Sed partum propriis manibus quaesisse voluntas."

39. See Ton Brandenburg, "Saint Anne. A Holy Grandmother and Her Children." Also chapter 9 above, n 75.

40. These details, as well as others in the poem, could be taken from the *Legenda aurea* in its account for the feastday of the Nativity of the Virgin Mary (8 September). The compiler, Jacobus a Voragine, gave his source as a letter of Jerome (Edition of Graesse, 589). See the translation, 523.

41. As so often in gersonian studies, we are indebted to Gilbert Ouy. But Max Lieberman also made a major contribution in the 1960s in the *Cahiers de Joséphologie.*

42. *Jean Gerson and De Consolatione Theologiae.* See especially his introduction. For a translation, with excellent references to biblical and classical literature: Clyde Lee Miller, *Jean Gerson. The Consolation of Theology.*

43. Unfortunately Glorieux printed the poems separately from the prose. The first are spread around volume 4 according to first lines, while the second is found in Gl 9.185–245.

44. Lee's translation (49) is "It insults the Catholic truth and its defenders," but the Latin is: "Insultans catholicae veritati cum defensoribus suis," thus "with their defenders," the supporters of these heretics (the Latin would have had to have been "defensoribus eius" for Lee's translation to work). The term "defensores" points to the defense of tyrannicide. In general both Burrows and Lee interpret Gerson's attack on heretics as limited to the followers of Wycliffe and Hus, without taking into account that Gerson was much more concerned at Constance with the heresy of defending tyrannicide.

45. Gl 9.202–3. See Possidius, *Vita Augustini,* ch. 29; trans. Hoare, *The Western Fathers,* 231. Gerson at this time seems to have felt especially close to Augustine's life and writings and frequently referred to Possidius.

46. Gl 9.203. Lee's translation, 113.

47. Gl 9.213: "Artifex aliquod horologium; ipse vero deinceps manet quietus, neque sollicitus per singula." This point of view later characterized the Enlightenment. See Carl L. Becker, *The Heavenly City of the Eighteenth-Century Philosophers,* ch. 2.

48. Gl 9.219. Cf. the introduction to the *Dialogues,* where Gregory expressed sadness at leaving monastic life for the papal court.

49. As in Letter 23, on how extreme ascetic practices can be dangerous for his brother Jean, Gl 2.86–90.

50. See note 31 above.

51. Gl 9.222: "Nemo debet sibi fabricare leviter scrupulos tamquam de necessitate praecepti." Lee's translation, 195.

52. Gl 9.223: "Quam vereor, Volucer, ne tangat haec consideratio peregrinum nostrum, cum sua prosecutione in causa fidei, nunc coram ordinario judice, nunc in praesentia sacri generalis concilii." Lee translates as "before the regularly appointed judge" and thus misses Gerson's reference to the Council of Faith held by the bishop of Paris at the behest of Gerson.

53. Gl 4.155; trans., 201.

54. For *apatheia,* see McGuire, *Friendship and Community,* xlii and 13–15.

55. Gl 9.227: "Hinc pueros, dum flagellantur et clamant, ridere solemus. . . . Nos vero grandiusculi pueri gemimus, excandescimus, murmuramus ad modicum Dei flagellum."

56. Cf. Burrows (30): "In this sense the text is never far from autobiography, standing as a peculiar dialogical narrative through which Gerson offers glimpses of his own plight and comments, often in an oblique way." I would add, however, that the debate on tyrannicide provides a key to understanding.

57. Gl 9.229, Lee has a note here (n 9, 308) linking Gerson's statements with the errors of Wycliffe and Hus. Once again I think the chancellor meant primarily the defense of tyrannicide.

58. Gl 9.229. See chapter 9 above and Gl 5.252–53.

59. Gl 9.230. Trans. Lee (229), who (309, n 25) gives the reference to Gratian's *Decretum* 83.1.3, one of Gerson's favored quotations during these years.

60. Gl 9.385–421. According to Du Pin 3.166, it was written "ad instantiam prioris et conventus domus Carthusiae in Sabaudia."

61. See *Defensor pacis,* Discourse 2.4, trans. Gewirth, 113–126.

62. According to Colin Morris, however, "Already in the generation after Gratian . . . usury was being redefined so as to permit interest in normal commercial transactions." *The Papal Monarchy,* 334.

63. Gerson had not forgotten the case of Jean de Varennes. See chapter 4 above.

64. See especially *De vita spirituali animae,* Gl 3.172–73, analyzed at the end of chapter 6.

65. Letter 16, to the Duke of Orléans, Gl 2.71: "Nec ignoro posse ea a tot capitibus in varias facile traduci sententias."

66. Gl 2.231: "Ex lectione quorumdam romanciorum, id est librorum compositorum in gallico, quasi poeticorum de gestis militaribus in quibus maxima pars fabulosa est."

67. *Sin and Confession,* 308–313. See chapter 7 above, esp. n 104.

68. Gl 9.499. Duke Jean of Berry, was actually the great uncle of King Charles VII.

69. Victor Martin, *Les origines du Gallicanisme,* vol. 2, esp. 325–338. Note how E. F. Jacob, *The Fifteenth Century* (266), made the careful point that legally the English Church "was an integral part of the western system, acknowledging the primacy of Rome," but he still used the term *Ecclesia Anglicana.*

70. Gl 9.491: "Laudo quod ad pauca te revocas quae possint tractari per sacras Scripturas quas ab infantia, non adulans loquor, nosti."

71. Gl 9.447: "Ora, inquit, Deum ut Deus deleat ex animo meo memoriam tui." Cf. *Verba Seniorum,* 2.7, in PL 73:859: "Ora Deum ut deleat memoriam tui de corde meo."

72. *Western Society and the Church,* 133–169.

73. Gl 2.239. Gerson was probably thinking of the description of Anthony in Cassian's Second Conference, On Discretion. See *Conferences* 2.1–4.4, trans., 84–87.

74. Gl 2.243: "Est fateor in lacrimis aliquid dulce et mulcebre. . . . Propterea fuge quantum poteris interim tales lacrimas, quoniam latet anguis in herba." The last phrase is taken from Vergil's *Eclogues* 3.93.

75. Gl 2.262: "Nunc autem hodie primo mysticum nescio quid aliud aperitur." See André Combes, *La théologie mystique de Gerson,* vol. 2, 535–39.

76. Glorieux gathered these writings under the general title "Tractatus de canticis," (9.524–602) and dated them between May 1423 and August 1426 (9.xv).

77. See chapter 3 above and the annotation of Gerson's works by his brother Jean the Celestine, Gl 1.23.

78. Gl 9.554: "Hinc Augustino fuerunt profundissimae pro pia matre lacrimae. Hinc sibi jam seni fuerunt lacrimae panes die et nocte" (cf. Ps 41:4). *Vita Augustini,* ch. 28, trans. Hoare, 229.

79. Gl 2.251. For Oswald, see James Hogg, "Oswald de Corda, a forgotten Carthusian of Nordlingen."

80. Gl 2.274: "Sub anno Domini 1426, decima octava septembris de mane usque ad prope meridiem."

81. As to Oswald of Corda, dated to 1427, Gl 2.292. Also 2.306–8 and 311.

82. From *Georgica* 1.145.

83. Gl 9.429, cf. *Vita Augustini* ch. 31, trans. Hoare, 243.

84. Gl.9.609–13, *De libris legendis a monacho,* also called, significantly enough, *De serenatione conscientiae et perseverantia.*

85. Gl 9.613. The passage is indicative of Gerson's practice of combining classical and Christian sources: "Et ecce hac aetate, hoc otio, velut ad votum vix perveni usque ad initium gustus eorumdem, qui repetiti mihi semper novi fiunt et placet, juxta illud Flacci de poemate vel imagine compositi eleganter: decies repetita placebit [*Ars poetica* 365] . . . sicut illa eadem Sapientia se collaudans dicit: qui edunt me adhuc esurient et qui bibunt me adhuc sitient, quia scilicet in edendo saturitas est ne quid desit, et in desiderio aviditas continua manet, ne fastidium sit."

86. See Letter 25, Gl 2.93–96. For the full discussion, but without asking why late in life Gerson changed his view, see Claude Arnaud-Gillet, *Entre Dieu et Satan. Les visions d'Ermine de Reims.*

87. It is this sense of the development of Gerson's attitude that I miss in an otherwise brilliant treatment of Gerson's views of female spirituality by Dyan Elliott, "Seeing Double: John Gerson, the Discernment of Spirits, and Joan of Arc."

88. As "Faciat utinam languor iste mihi mortem qualis est illa justorum," Gl 8.623.

89. For an unsatisfactory discussion, followed by both texts, see Dorothy G. Wayman, "The Chancellor and Jeanne d'Arc." Note that the version called "De mirabili victoria" in Wayman was printed in Glorieux (9.661–65) as "De puella aurelianensi." The other text, not in Glorieux, Wayman calls "De quadam puella." Dyan Elliott's article provides full bibliography of recent work on Gerson and Joan of Arc. See also Deborah Fraioli, *Joan of Arc: The Early Debate.* Daniel Hobbins has worked on the manuscript tradition and has confirmed that the Glorieux text is genuine Gerson.

90. Georges Guigue and J. Laurent, *Obituaires de la province de Lyon,* vol. 2, 132–33: "Eadem die ob. vir inclite memorie et magne devocionis dom. Johannes Gerson, quondam sacre theologie doctor famosissimus ac cancellarius Parisiensis, pro cujus necnon et viri venerabilis magistri Jacobi de Ciresio, quondam in artibus magistri et hujus ecclesie S. Paul canonici, generali anniversario perpetuo in ipsa ecclesia fundanda et dicta die celebrando, venerabilis vir. dom. Johannes Pernant, canonicus et prepositus de Varena ecclesie Beatissimi Martini Turonensis, dedit et realiter solvit centum florenos." I am grateful to Hervé Chopin for this reference.

Chapter 11

1. For the gersonian memorials near his birthplace, see Jadart, *Jean Gerson.*

2. Galbert of Bruges, *The Murder of Charles the Good,* ed. James Bruce Ross.

3. See the description by Joseph Mertens of the 1955 excavations, in *Murder of Charles the Good,* 318–320.

4. See Anne-Louise Masson, *Jean Gerson*, 402. This study has excellent illustrations of places concerned with Gerson's life, but unfortunately with no data about the origins of the prints used. The pictorial map showing the district of Saint Paul and Saint Laurent is from 1550.

5. Masson, 402.

6. For the earliest assertion that Gerson taught catechism to the boys of Lyon, see the brief *vita* included in the 1606 edition of his works and reprinted by Ellies Du Pin in his edition of Gerson at Antwerp in 1706, vol. 1, clxviii.

7. Gl 2.334: "Disposui in senectute thesaurizare juxta paupertaculam meam de libris salutaribus."

8. Gl 2.334: "Denique nomina librorum et tractatuum, tam ab aliis quam a me compositorum, disposui colligere in speciali schedula."

9. Information kindly supplied by Gilbert Ouy.

10. For a detailed review of contents, see Schwab, *Johannes Gerson*, vol. 2, 788–790. A fourth volume of Gerson's works appeared in 1484, but the next edition, from Strasbourg in 1488, sufficed with three volumes.

11. See Gilbert Ouy, "Le célestin Jean Gerson, copiste et éditeur de son frère."

12. Veronika Gerz-Von Büren, *La tradition de l'oeuvre de Jean Gerson chez les Chartreux: La Chartreuse de Bâle.*

13. Du Pin 1.clxxi: "Quoniam a multis annis, doctrinae et scriptis magistri Joannis Gerson, singulariter affecti fuimus; in eisdem legendis, usque hodie plurimum delectamur (quod nobis solidus, ecclesiae utilis, et omni statui consolatorius visus est).

14. Du Pin 1.clxxi. See also P. M. Gonon, *Séjours de Charles VIII et Loys XII à Lyon sur le Rosne*, 34.

15. Du Pin 1.clxxix: "Joannis Gerson consolatorii christianissimique doctoris."

16. Du Pin 1.clxxix: "A Germano quodam qui apud Parisios philosphiam et sacras literas audiens, Gallicum quoque sermonem didicerat."

17. Du Pin 1.clxii-clxiii, with the incorrect date of 1421. Elisabeth Mornet has made an excellent study of Gerson's reception in Scandinavia, especially Sweden: "Gerson en Scandinavie."

18. Erasmus was generally positive about Gerson's theology, even though he mainly used the consoling doctor for his own polemics. See István Bejczy, "Érasme explore le moyen âge: Bernard de Clairvaux et Jean Gerson." For an appreciation of Gerson and his contemporaries in terms of the sixteenth-century reformations, see the important work of Berndt Hamm, now available in *The Reformation of Faith in the Context of Late Medieval Theology and Piety.*

19. Du Pin 1.clxix.

20. Du Pin 1.cxc.

21. Du Pin 1.cxc: "Subito rumor exoritur de tumulo gersoniano; fama volat per urbem. . . . Omnes introspicere cupiunt, interrogant, sermonem habent."

22. Du Pin 1.cxcii: "Cujusmodi erat etiam attrita uso patena, quae contractam extremis digitis manum habebat in medio sculptam, tribus primis extentis, velut benedicentem."

23. Du Pin 1.cxciii.

24. As late as the 1890s it was still being argued that Gerson had written thc *Imitation*. See Masson, *Jean Gerson*, 352–364.

25. According to Masson, *Jean Gerson*, 392, Gerson was buried "in the precinct of [the church of] Saint Lawrence, north side of the square, to the right of the preacher's pulpit." I have not been able to locate the source of this information.

26. Masson introduced a mention of the 1837 *concours* with the words: "Notre siècle . . . révilla dans les esprits la mémoire de ce saint homme" (402). For details, see Schwab's "Vorwort," an excellent overview of Gerson studies in the first half of the nineteenth century.

27. From *Histoire de France*, vol. 7.2, quoted in Gl 1.150. Gl 1.141–52 has a selection of appreciations of Gerson from his lifetime and until 1944, ending with Etienne Gilson's *La philosophie au moyen-âge.* The list notably has no mentions of Gerson between 1702 and 1840.

28. *Scholastic Humanism and the Unification of Europe*, vols. 1–2.

29. As explained by the 1606 editor at the end of his *vita* of Gerson, included by Du Pin a century later (1.clxxi).

30. As in R. N. Swanson, *Religion and Devotion in Europe, c. 1215–c. 1515*, 46.

31. I use the excellent edition and translation of Denys Hay and W. K. Smith, *De Gestis Concilii Basiliensis Commentariorum libri II*, abbreviated as *Commentaries.*

32. As in the Introduction by Hay and Smith to the *Commentaries*, xviii.

33. Gerald Christianson, "Aeneas Sylvius Piccolomini and the Historiography of the Council of Basel," esp. 177–181. I am grateful to the author for sending me this important article.

34. *Commentaries* (xxvii): "One of those personalities who readily assume the colour and the convictions of a given time and place."

35. See chapter 9 above. The central gersonian text is *Libellus articulorum contra Petrum de Luna*, Gl 6.267–68. For Aeneas and Matthew 18, see the *Commentaries*, 50–53.

36. An overview is Erich Methuen, *Das Basler Konzil als Forschungsproblem der europaïschen Geschichte.* An excellent historical review, with outstanding appendices, is in Joachim W. Stieber, *Pope Eugenius IV, the Council of Basel and the Secular and Ecclesiastical Authorities in the Empire.* There is a section on Amédée de Talaru, the archbishop of Lyon, whom Gerson knew from Constance and who played an important role at Basel, in Heribert Müller, *Die Franzosen, Frankreich und das Basler Konzil (1431–1449).*

37. *Commentaries*, 238–39.

38. *Commentaries* (240–41): "Nullae illic rixae, nullae contentiones, omnia in amicitia, omnia in dilectione fiebant."

39. *Commentaries* (241): "Quorum literae in conclavi fuerunt, in eremo non fuerunt."

40. *Memoirs of a Renaissance Pope*, 81.

41. Ibid., 209.

42. *Commentaries*, 252–53.

43. See the Introduction to the *Commentaries*, xx–xxi, with references to earlier literature on Felix V.

44. For the later fifteenth- and early sixteenth-century popes, I have used Eric John, *The Popes. A Concise Biographical History.* Calixtus III is on pages 296–98. In spite of confessional bias, many of the portraits for the later medieval period give a sense of the human and moral dimension of these people which is lacking, for example, in the more academic study by John A. F. Thomson, *Popes and Princes 1417–1517. Politics and Polity in the Late Medieval Church.*

45. See above, chapter 9, the final section "Apologizing: January-May 1418."

46. For an excellent appreciation of the conciliar movement, see Antony Black, *Council and Commune: The Conciliar Movement and the Council of Basle.*

47. Trans. C.M.D. Crowder, *Unity, Heresy and Reform, 1378–1460*, 179–180. Crowder argued that even though it was not "epoch-making," the bull "can be accepted as a symbol marking the end of the conciliar epoch in the history of the fifteenth-century Church."

48. Colin Morris, *The Papal Monarchy*, 82–89.

49. As in Gerson's sermon to Benedict XIII, "Apparuit," which apparently upset the pope greatly (Gl 5.84).

50. For a summary of developments in the North, Daniel Waley, *Later Medieval Europe from St. Louis to Luther*, esp. chs. 4 and 14.

51. Papal collections were possible because secular rulers often cooperated, for their own gain: See Thomson, *Popes and Princes*, 175–180.

52. Thomson, 208–9.

53. Eric John, *The Popes*, 299.

54. Ibid., 326. For details on his military policy, see Thomson, *Popes and Princes*, 137–141.

55. As a teacher of history at a Danish university, I still have to explain to students that what they may have learned in high school about indulgences and the Protestant Reformation is misleading. Even though Denmark is a secular society, versions of the old Lutheran polemic against the Middle Ages still dominate. An excellent summary of the growth of indulgences in the later Middle Ages is to be found in R. N. Swanson, *Religion and Devotion in Europe*, 217–225. It was Pope Sixtus IV who in 1476 extended the benefit of indulgences to the souls of the dead (224).

56. Figgis, "The Conciliar Movement and the Papalist Reaction," in *Political Thought from Gerson to Grotius 1414–1625*, 44.

57. See Alberigo, 571–631, esp. 584–85, for the decree on the reformation of the curia.

58. Till-Holger Borchert, *The Age of Van Eyck,* 235, nr. 24.

59. Guicciardini, *History of Italy,* trans. Cecil Grayson, ch. 13, 357.

60. John, *The Popes,* 323. See also Thomson, *Popes and Princes,* 132–34.

61. See, for example, Luther, "The Pagan Servitude of the Church," also known as "The Babylonian Captivity of the Church," trans. John Dillenberger, *Martin Luther: Selections from His Writings,* 249–359.

62. Melanchton, et al., *Die Bekenntnisschriften der evangelisch-lutherischen Kirche,* 44–137, abbreviated as *Confessio.*

63. *Confessio* (83c): "Tota dissensio est de paucis quibusdam abusibus qui sine certa autoritate in ecclesias irrepserunt."

64. *Confessio* (83d): "Quamquam apud nos magna ex parte veteres ritus diligenter servantur. Falsa enim calumnia est, quod omnes caerimoniae, omnia vetera in ecclesiis nostris aboleantur."

65. See the *Praefatio* or *Vorrede,* 48. The text existed in both Latin and German, a sign of new times but also in continuity with the efforts of theologians like Gerson to make theology available in the vernacular.

66. *Confessio* (132): "Fortassis initio habuerunt illae constitutiones causas probabiles, quae tamen posterioribus temporibus non congruunt."

67. *Confessio* (118–19): "Et ante haec tempora reprehendit Gerson errorem monachorum de perfectione et testatur, suo tempore novam hanc vocem fuisse, quod vita monastica sit status perfectionis."

68. *Confessio* (102–3): "Gerson scribit multos incidisse in desperationem, quosdam etiam sibi mortem conscivisse, quia senserant se non posse satisfacere traditionibus, et interim consolatione nulla de iustitia fidei et de gratia audierant."

69. The notes to the critical edition of the *Confessio Augustana* say that this assertion is "nicht nachweisbar" (cannot be documented) but do point to Gerson's treatise, *De vita spirituali animae,* lectiones 2 and 4.

70. Connolly, *John Gerson. Reformer and Mystic,* 366: "They did not consider his intention, nor did they stop to make a comparative study between what they wanted him to say and the whole tenor of his writings."

71. Alberigo, Sessio IV, 8 April 1546, 640–41.

72. See Michael A. Mullett, *The Catholic Reformation,* as 90: "As far as the individual Jesuit was concerned, it is true that his hallmark was unquestioning obedience."

73. Francis Oakley, *The Western Church in the Later Middle Ages,* 73. Also Francis Rapp, *L'église et la vie religieuse en occident à la fin du moyen âge,* 88–95.

74. Victor Martin, *Les origines du Gallicanisme,* esp. the review in vol. 2 of the Pragmatic Sanction, 303–315 and the conclusion, 325–338.

75. CUP, vol. 4, n. 296, 337: "Et aussi ou regard de la collacion ou disposicion des benefices de l'Eglise qui estoient deubz aux clers, laquelle collacion ou disposicion les prelas de ce royaume vouloient à eulx atraire, à leur plaine et franche disposicion."

76. CUP 4 (337): "Et disoit en effect, entre autres choses, que le roy est empereur en son royaume, qu'il tient de Dieu seul sans recognoistre souverain seigneur terrien, et a acoustumé, comme lui est loisible, pour regir et gouverner sondit royaume. . . . desquellez il n'est loisible á aucuns de ses subgiez ou autres appeller."

77. CUP 4, nr. 2097, 338. On 2 March the university threatened to strike in protest of the imprisonment (n. 2098). A compromise seems to have been reached at the end of March (nr. 2101). But it was made clear that the king and the dauphin intended to maintain what they entitled *ecclesiam gallicanam* (nr. 2100, 340).

78. See Rashdall, who already in 1895 (vol. 1, 580) wrote: "This nationalization of the Catholic Church throughout Europe—this breaking down, so to speak, of the solidarity of the ecclesiastical order—almost involved the destruction of the ecumenical character of the University of Paris." For the development "From internationalism to regionalism" in terms of student numbers, see ch. 9, Hilde de Ridder-Symoens, *A History of the University in Europe,* vol. 1, esp. 285–290.

79. See, for example, the studies from a June 2002 workshop at Groningen University, The Netherlands, under Anneke Mulder-Bakker and edited by Martin Gosman, "The Prime of Their Lives: Wise Old Women," including McGuire, "Visionary women who did what they wanted and men who helped them," with bibliography. Publication in preparation.

80. McGuire, "Late Medieval Care and Control of Women," esp. 34–36.

81. In the translation by Montague Summers, *Malleus Maleficarum,* part 1, qn.6, 116.

82. Ibid., 117.

83. Ibid., 122.

84. *When Fathers Ruled. Family Life in Reformation Europe.* Later studies have greatly nuanced Ozment, but his view of a new control over women has been confirmed in Lyndal Roper, *The Holy Household. Women and Morals in Reformation Augsburg.*

85. Religious houses for women still continued to be founded right up to the Protestant Reformation. For example, the Sankt Annen-Kloster was founded in Lübeck in 1502. It belonged to the Augustinian nuns of the Windesheimer Congregation at Zwolle and was thus associated to the *Devotio Moderna.* The former convent is today a museum of religious art, much of which comes from late medieval Lübeck and Sankt Annen-Kloster itself. Here we sense the presence of female spirituality and religious power in the first decades of the sixteenth century. See Brigitte Heise, *Das St. Annen-Kloster zu Lübeck.* Also Brigitte Heise and Hildegard Vogeler, *Die Altäre des St. Annen-Museums.*

86. Linda Lierheimer, "Preaching or Teaching?" and "Introduction" to *The Life of Antoinette Micolon.* I am grateful to Professor Lierheimer for sending me her important work.

87. I have translated from Glorieux's edition, 7.1.404–7.

88. Gl 2.77; EW, 226.

89. Gl 2.57–59; EW, 204–7.

90. See chapter 7, "Healing the Schism."

91. Gl 2.18; EW, 161.

92. Trans. from the Prologue to *Sic et Non* in Brian Pullan, *Sources for the History of Medieval Europe,* 103.

93. *La théologie mystique de Gerson,* esp. vol. 2, 535–39. See chapter 9 above, n 75.

94. The Carthusian prior of Aggsbach complained in a bitter attack from 1453 that Gerson's conception of mystical theology was too intellectual (Gl 10.567–76). See the summary of the debate in Connolly, *Jean Gerson,* 309–315.

95. Richard Tuck, *Natural Rights Theories: Their Origin and Development,* 25–29.

Bibliographical Guide

After a long period of neglect in the twentieth century when study of Gerson was limited to specialists, evaluations of his life and writings have now become part of mainstream medieval studies. Here I shall limit this introduction to the literature to publications that have been central for my biography of Gerson. For a fuller list of background literature see the bibliography.

Editions

A central point of departure is Palemon Glorieux's ten-volume edition of Gerson's work: *Jean Gerson. Oeuvres Complètes* (Paris: Desclée, 1960–73). Volume 1 contains a general introduction; 2, the letters; 3, the scholastic writings (*L'oeuvre magistrale*); 4, poems; 5, Latin sermons; 6, ecclesiological treatises; 7, part 1, treatises in French; 7, part 2, sermons in French; 8, spiritual and pastoral works; 9, doctrinal and pedagogical works (continuing in large part volume 3); 10, polemical writings.

Glorieux unfortunately seems to have been working in such haste that he often did little more than gather Gerson's writings from earlier editions. For identification of biblical and classical references, he depended on prior work, without any further checking for accuracy. Glorieux does, however, in volume 10, provide a useful chronological listing of Gerson's writings and references to authors Gerson is known to have used. This volume also includes "Actes et Documents," with rich documentation of events in Gerson's life.

An example of Glorieux's limitations is the text *Sur l'excellence de la virginité* (Gl 7.1.416–21). Here a central section is omitted. In such and other cases one must consult the 1706 Antwerp edition by Louis Ellies Du Pin, *Johannes Gerson. Opera Omnia,* reprinted in 1987 (Hildesheim: Georg Olms Verlag) in 5 volumes. The treatise on virginity is printed in Du Pin 3.829–41.

Hitherto unknown works by Gerson have been uncovered in recent years. Some of them are included in a supplement to Glorieux's tenth volume. Important for me has been Gilbert Ouy's publication of "Trois prières françaises inédites de Jean Gerson" in Charles Brucker, *Mélanges de langue et de littérature françaises du Moyen Age offerts à Pierre Demarolle* (Paris: Honoré Champion, 1998), 27–38.

Gerson's important narrative poem, the *Josephina,* is now available on CD-ROM, with a significant introduction and useful indices by Matteo Roccati (Paris: Lamop, 2001).

English Translations

Even though many translations of Gerson's writings into English have been made, they are by no means always easily available. Such is the case, for example, with some of his poems, which can be found in a flowery Victorian rendition by Sebastian Evans, *In the Studio. A Decade of Poems* (London: Macmillan, 1875), 194–221.

Steven E. Ozment has given invaluable access to some of Gerson's writings in his work *Jean Gerson. Selections from "A Deo exivit," "Contra curiositatem studentium," and "De Mystica theologia speculativa"* (Leiden: Brill, 1969).

For the Classics of Western Spirituality series, *Jean Gerson. Early Works* (New York: Paulist Press, 1998), I translated the *Mountain of Contemplation,* the *Sermon on Saint Bernard,* Gerson's known letters from the 1380s to 1408, part of the *Mystical Theology. The First and Speculative Treatise,* all of the *Mystical Theology. The Second and Practical Treatise, Distinguishing True from False Revelations, On Hearing Confessions,* and the *Treatise against the Romance of the Rose.*

Paschal Boland earlier translated *On Distinguishing True from False Revelations* together with another of Gerson's three treatises on the subject, published in *The Concept of Discretio Spirituum in John Gerson's De Probatione Spirituum and the De Distinctione Verarum Visionum a Falsis* (Washington, D.C.: Catholic University of America Press, 1959). The notes here are unfortunately not very helpful.

Clyde Lee Miller has produced an excellent and most welcome annotated translation, with full references, in *Jean Gerson. The Consolation of Theology* (Abaris Books, 1998). The incunabulum edition of Gerson's Latin text on facing pages is, however, difficult to read due to inferior reproduction.

Biographies and Their Background

The study of Jean Gerson still owes much to the first modern biography, published in two volumes by Johann Baptist Schwab, *Johannes Gerson. Professor der Theologie und Kanzler der Universität Paris* ((Würzburg, 1858; reissued by Burt Franklin, New York, no date, but probably in the 1970s). In eighteen solid chapters, with full references, Schwab presents Gerson in the context of the politics and theology of his age. His "Vorwort" provides a judicious evaluation of earlier studies, such as that of R. Thomassy from 1843. Only in the last chapter, however, does Schwab allow himself specific considerations on Gerson's person and character.

A review of the main events of Gerson's life to which I have returned time and again is P. Glorieux, "La vie et les oeuvres de Gerson. Essai chronologique," *Archives d'histoire doctrinale et littéraire du Moyen Age* 25–26 (1951), 149–52, abbreviated in Glorieux's edition of Gerson, vol. 1.105–39. Some dating of Gerson's works needs to be revised, but on the whole the content is reliable. Two other important biographical articles are Glorieux, "Gerson au chapitre de Notre-Dame de Paris," *Revue d'histoire ecclésiastique* (RHE) 56 (1961), 424–448 and 827–854 and E. Vansteenberghe, "Gerson à Bruges," RHE 31 (1935), 5–51. Vansteenberghe did pioneering work during the 1930s in bringing Gerson's writings to light. His twelve studies, on which Glorieux drew copiously, are published in the *Revue des sciences religieuses* between 1933 (13) and 1936 (16) as "Quelques écrits de Jean Gerson. Textes inédits et études."

Still useful for information about Gerson's background in the Champagne-Ardennes area of what today is northeastern France is Henri Jadart's detailed study, *Jean de Gerson. Recherches sur son origine, son village natal et sa famille* (Reims: Deligne et Renart, 1881).

Nineteenth-century French biographies of Gerson are mostly hagiographic and seek to defend him against charges of unorthodoxy in his views on papal power. I nevertheless turned frequently to Anne-Louise Masson, *Jean Gerson. Sa vie, son temps, ses oeuvres*

(Lyon: Emmanuel Vitte, 1894). The book lacks footnotes, but the last chapters, on Gerson at Lyon, are a guide to little-known facts about the last years of his life.

A much more accessible and trustworthy study is that of James L. Connolly, *John Gerson. Reformer and Mystic* (Louvain: Librairie Universitaire and Herder, 1928). Connolly, a Catholic historian trained at Louvain, disproves the charge that Gerson anticipated the teachings of Luther and other Protestant reformers. Although Connolly idealizes certain aspects of Gerson's life, the book can still be read with profit and deserves to be reprinted. A more superficial treatment, but entertaining to read and with a special sensitivity for Gerson's life in Paris, is M.-J. Pinet, *La vie ardente de Gerson* (Paris: Bloud & Gay, 1929).

An excellent biography of Gerson could have been one by Max Lieberman had it ever been written. His numerous studies of aspects of Gerson's life and writings appeared regularly in the journal *Romania* between 1948 (70) and 1970 (91). One series of articles has the common title "Chronologie Gersonienne" but deals with many aspects of Gerson's writings: 70 (1948), 51–67; 73 (1952), 480–496; 74 (1953), 289–337; "Gerson poète," 76 (1955), 289–333; "Gerson et d'Ailly," 78 (1957), 433–462; "Gerson ou d'Ailly," 79 (1958), 339–375; "Gerson et d'Ailly (II)," 80 (1959), 289–336; "Gerson et d'Ailly (III), 81 (1960), 44–98; "Jean Gerson et Philippe de Mézières," 81 (1960), 338–379; "Le sermon *Memento Finis*," 83 (1962): 52–89.

Lieberman displays immense knowledge of the subject, but the thread of his thought is at times hard to follow. The amount of detail is overwhelming and at times excessive. See also his studies "Autour de l'iconographie gersonienne" in *Romania* 84 (1963): 307–353; 85 (1964): 49–100 and 230–268; and 91 (1970): 341–377.

An excellent collection of biographical portraits of the period, though without one of Gerson, is Bernard Guenée, *Between Church and State. The Lives of Four French Prelates in the Late Middle Ages* (Chicago: University of Chicago Press, 1997), trans. Arthur Goldhammer from *Entre l'église et l'état* (Paris: Gallimard, 1987). The biography of Pierre d'Ailly is superb and a good background toward any understanding of Gerson.

Gerson as Theologian and Preacher

I am presently editing for Brill a companion to Jean Gerson with contributions by gersonian scholars on many aspects of his thinking. For the background of Gerson's theology at Paris, Zenon Kaluza, *Les querelles doctrinales à Paris. Nominalistes et réalistes aux confins du quatorzième et du quinzième siècles* (Bergamo: Pierluigi Lubrina, 1988) is vital.

The most comprehensive English presentation of Gerson's theology is D. Catherine Brown, *Pastor and Laity in the Theology of Jean Gerson* (Cambridge, U.K.: Cambridge University Press, 1987). I have learned an immense amount from this superb presentation about Gerson as preacher and the late medieval preaching tradition. My one criticism is the lack of any chronological distinctions in his thought as it developed from one period to the next.

Louis Mourin was a pioneer in the appreciation of Gerson's French sermons. See his *Six sermons français inédits de Jean Gerson* (Paris: Librairie J. Vrin, 1946) and his *Jean Gerson. Prédicateur français* (Bruges: De Tempel, 1952), an essential guide to the chronology and content of the sermons. We need a corresponding study of the Latin sermons.

The question of Gerson as a mystical theologian was inspiration for the life work of André Combes. His work is difficult to read, due to an excess of detail. I also find his historical arguments not always convincing. See *Jean Gerson. Commentateur dionysien* (Paris: J. Vrin, 1940) and *La théologie mystique de Gerson: Profil de son évolution* 1–2 (Rome:

Desclée, 1963–64). Combes's best work is his edition of the *Mystical Theology: Joannis Carlerii de Gerson de Mystica Theologia* (Lugano: Thesaurus Mundi, 1958). In the course of preparing my English translation, however, I discovered many notes and references that are not only superfluous but may even be misleading in terms of the actual sources on which Gerson drew. See the remarks below on Gerson the humanist.

The best English summary of Gerson's mystical theology is probably still David Schmiel's brief *Via Propria and Via Mystica in the Theology of Jean le Charlier de Gerson* (Saint Louis: Concordia Seminary, 1969). A challenging and important study of the development of Gerson's theology in the last decade of his life is Mark S. Burrows, *Jean Gerson and De Consolatione Theologiae* (Tübingen: J.C.B. Mohr, 1991).

German-language studies on Gerson are numerous and often reward close reading. See Johann Stelzenberger, *Die Mystik des Johannes Gerson* (Breslau: Müller & Seiffert, 1928). Christoph Burger, *Aedificatio, Fructus, Utilitas. Johannes Gerson als Professor der Theologie und Kanzler der Universität Paris* (Tübingen: J.C.B. Mohr, 1986) is excellent. Sven Grosse's study is central: *Heilsungewissheit und Scrupulositas im späten Mittelalter. Studien zu Johannes Gerson und Gattungen der Frömmigkeitstheologie seiner Zeit* (Tübingen: J.C.B. Mohr, 1994). Less specialized than the title sounds is Karlheinz Diez, "Das Kirchenväterverständnis bei Johannes Gerson," in *Väter der Kirche. Ekklesiales Denken von den Anfängen bis in die Neuzeit*, eds. Johannes Arnold, Rainer Berndt, Ralf M. W. Stammberger (Paderborn: Ferdinand Schöningh, 2004), 823–840.

Gerson looms large in Thomas Tentler's important study *Sin and Confession on the Eve of the Reformation* (Princeton, N.J.: Princeton University Press, 1977)

The question of the discernment of spirits as a central part of Gerson's theology has attracted much attention of late. Independently of each other, a German Roman Catholic priest and a University of Chicago graduate student dealt with the subject: Cornelius Roth, *Discretio spirituum. Kriterien geistlicher Unterscheidung bei Johannes Gerson* (Würzburg: Echter, 2001) and Wendy Love Anderson, *Free Spirits, Presumptuous Women, and False Prophets: The Discernment of Spirits in the Late Middle Ages* (Ph.D. dissertation, University of Chicago, 2002). A further contribution, with many brilliant insights, but some narrowness, can be found in Dyan Elliott, "Seeing Double: Jean Gerson, the Discernment of Spirits, and Joan of Arc," *American Historical Review* 107 (2002), 26–54. Much of this article is contained in Elliott, *Proving Woman: Female Spirituality and Inquisitional Culture in the Late Middle Ages* (Princeton, N.J.: Princeton University Press, 2004). Also Nancy Caciola, *Discerning Spirits: Divine and Demonic Possession in the Middle Ages* (Ithaca, N.Y.: Cornell University Press, 2003).

Gerson appears frequently in the works of Heiko Augustinus Oberman. Even though this author never dedicated a special study to the consoling doctor, Gerson is one of the central late medieval figures in Oberman's lifelong quest for sources of sixteenth-century, especially Lutheran, theology. See *The Harvest of Medieval Theology: Gabriel Biel and Late Medieval Nominalism* (originally published by Harvard University Press, 1963). Also *Die Reformation. Von Wittenberg nach Genf* (Göttingen: Vandenhoeck & Ruprecht, 1986) and *The Dawn of the Reformation: Essays in Late Medieval and Early Reformation Thought* (Grand Rapids, Mich.: William B. Eerdmans, 1986, 1992).

Gerson and Church Reform

Here the point of departure remains John B. Morrall's brief and indispensable *Gerson and the Great Schism* (Manchester, U.K.: Manchester University Press, 1960). The principles behind Gerson's writings and actions are presented in an approachable, clear manner in the work of Louis B. Pascoe, S.J., *Jean Gerson. Principles of Church Reform* (Leiden, Netherlands: Brill, 1973). John J. Ryan, *The Apostolic Conciliarism of Jean Gerson* (Atlanta: Scholars Press, 1998) is an interesting but not completely successful attempt to understand the background for Gerson's conciliar thinking. See my review in *The Journal of Religion* 79 (1999): 661–62.

The Dutch historian G.H.M. Posthumus Meyjes wrote a thesis in 1963 on the topic, which he has now made available in English in revised and expanded form. This is an outstanding and central study: *Jean Gerson. Apostle of Unity. His Church Politics and Ecclesiology* (Leiden: Brill, 1999). See my review in *Speculum* 76 (2001): 1092–93. See the accompanying *Jean Gerson et l'Assemblée de Vincennes. Ses conceptions de la juridiction temporelle de l'église* (Leiden: Brill, 1978).

Gerson figures largely in R. N. Swanson, *Universities, Academics, and the Great Schism* (Cambridge, U.K.: Cambridge University Press, 1979). Still useful for placing Gerson in a fuller context is Noël Valois, *La France et le grand schisme d'Occident*, especially volumes 3 and 4, for developments from 1394 to 1418 (Paris: Alphonse Picard, 1901–02). Gerson is present in Howard Kaminsky's important study, *Simon de Cramaud and the Great Schism* (New Brunswick, N.J.: Rutgers University Press, 1983). There are also numerous references to Gerson in Phillip H. Stump, *The Reforms of the Council of Constance (1414–1418)* (Leiden: Brill, 1994).

The work of the French historian Alfred Coville is almost forgotten but has been invaluable to me in seeing the background for Gerson's involvement at Constance with the question of tyrannicide. See his *Jean Petit. La question du tyrannicide au commencement du quinzième siècle* (Paris: August Picard, 1932).

Gilbert Ouy and Gerson the Humanist

The French philologist, manuscript scholar, and humanist Gilbert Ouy has perhaps done more than any other person in the last decades to define Gerson's contribution to late medieval humanism in Northern Europe. Many of his articles are published in journals and *Festschrifts* that are difficult to acquire outside of France. See, however, together with Danièle Calvot, *L'oeuvre de Gerson à Saint-Victor de Paris: Catalogue des manuscrits* (Paris: Centre National de la Recherche Scientifique, 1990). Also *Gerson bilingue: Les deux rédactions, latines et françaises, de quelques oeuvres du chancelier parisien* (Paris: Honoré Champion, 1998).

A mere selection of Gilbert Ouy's articles includes: "Gerson et l'Angleterre: A propos d'un texte polémique retrouvé du chancelier de Paris contre l'Université d'Oxford (1396)" in *Humanism in France at the End of the Middle Ages and in the Early Renaissance*, ed. A.H.T. Levi (Manchester, U.K.: Manchester University Press, 1970); "L'humanisme et les mutations politiques et sociales en France aux quatorzième et quinzième siècles," *L'Humanisme français au début de la Renaissance* (Paris: J.Vrin, 1973); "Le Collège de Navarre, berceau de l'humanisme français," in *Bulletin philologique et historique du Comité des travaux historiques* 1 (1975): 276–299; "In Search of the Earliest Traces of French Humanism: The Evidence from Codicology," *The Library Chronicle* 43 (Philadelphia, 1978): 3–38; "L'humanisme du jeune Gerson," *Genèse et débuts du grand schisme d'Occident* (Colloques internationaux du Centre National de Recherche Scientifique, Paris, 1980), 256–268; "Humanism and Nationalism in France at the Turn of the Fifteenth Century" in *The Birth of Identities. Denmark and Europe in the Middle Ages*, ed. Brian

P. McGuire (Copenhagen: C.A. Reitzel, 1996), 107–125; "Gerson et l'infanticide: Défense des femmes et critique de la pénitence publique," in *Etudes sur l'art d'écrire au Moyen Age offertes à Eric Hicks* (Geneva: Éditions Slatkine, 2001), 45–66.

Ouy is in the midst of revising several of his earlier articles, and we can look forward to their appearance under the title, *A la recherche de Gerson.*

Others who have worked on Gerson and French humanism are Alfred Coville, *Gontier et Pierre Col et l'humanisme en France au temps de Charles VI* (Paris: Droz, 1934); André Combes, "Gerson et la naissance de l'humanisme," *Revue du Moyen Age latin* 1 (1945): 259–284 and *Jean de Montreuil et le chancelier Gerson. Contribution à l'histoire des rapports de l'humanisme et de la théologie en France au début du quinzième siècle* (Paris: Vrin, 1942); Ezio Ornato, *Jean Muret et ses amis Nicolas de Clamanges et Jean de Montreuil. Contribution à l'étude des rapports entre les humanistes de Paris et ceux d'Avignon (1394–1420)* (Geneva and Paris: Librairie Droz, 1969).

Nicolas de Clamanges, Gerson's contemporary from the College of Navarre, who is usually seen mainly as what the French used to call "homme de lettres," is now being appreciated also in his religious dimension: Christopher M. Bellitto, *Nicolas de Clamanges: Spirituality, Personal Reform, and Pastoral Renewal on the Eve of the Reformations* (Washington, D.C.: Catholic University of America Press, 2001). See, however, the review by Dennis Martin on the Internet Medieval Review for 24.07.02 (tmr-l@wmich.edu).

Gerson's name is often associated with that of Christine de Pizan. The best collection of sources for their common interests is Eric Hicks, *Le débat sur le Roman de la Rose* (Paris: Honoré Champion, 1977).

The Political Background

I make no attempt here to provide even a semi-complete list of studies of the complicated politics of this period in French and European history but merely include some of the central works that have guided me. Alfred Coville, *Les Cabochiens et l'ordonnance de 1413* (Geneva: Slatkine, 1974) is a reprint of the 1888 edition, a careful and enlightening study of the political ideas behind the Paris uprising that changed Gerson's life.

Among Richard Vaughan's studies of the dukes of Burgundy from which I have benefited are *Philip the Bold. The Formation of the Burgundian State* (London: Longmans, 1962) and *John the Fearless. The Growth of Burgundian Power* (London: Longmans, 1966). Extremely detailed but essential for understanding the period's background is Michael Nordberg, *Les ducs et la royauté. Études sur la rivalité des ducs d'Orléans et de Bourgogne, 1392–1407* (Uppsala: Svenska Bokförlaget, 1964). Some of Nordberg's conclusions are challenged in the equally competent work of R. C. Famiglietti, *Royal Intrigue. Crisis at the Court of Charles VI 1392–1420* (New York: AMS Press, 1986).

The best English study of the way late medieval France was governed (and misgoverned) is perhaps P. S. Lewis, *Later Medieval France. The Polity* (London and New York: Macmillan and St. Martin's Press, 1968). Bernard Guenée has written a dramatic account of the murder of the duke of Orleans in 1407, *Un meurtre, une société* (Paris: Gallimard, 1992). This book richly deserves translation into English.

A classic account of the Hundred Years War is Édouard Perroy, *La guerre de cent ans* (Paris: Gallimard, 1945). Much more detailed is Jean Favier, *La guerre de cent ans* (Paris: Fayard, 1980). A recent English summary is Christopher Allmand, *The Hundred Years War. England and France at War c. 1300–c. 1450*(Cambridge, U.K.: Cambridge University Press, 1989). Also Jonathan Sumption, *The Hundred Years War,* vol. 1: *Trial by Battle;* vol.2: *Trial by Fire* (Philadelphia: University of Pennsylvania Press, 1992 and 1999).

Church History

An excellent treatment of the period is found in the great French series, *Histoire de l'église,* founded by Augustin Fliche and Victor Martin. See especially tome 14 (two volumes of more than 1200 pages) by E. Delaruelle, E.-R. Labande, and Paul Ourliac, *L'église au temps du grand schisme et de la crise conciliaire (1378–1449),* 1–2 (Paris: Bloud & Gay, 1962–64). See especially "Le siècle de Gerson," 837–860, with "Note additionelle. État actuel des études gersoniennes," 861–69.

More modest but very insightful is Francis Rapp, *L'église et la vie religieuse en Occident à la fin du Moyen Age,* (Paris: Presses Universitaires de France, 1971).

Francis Oakley has written several important and helpful studies on the thought and life in this period. His most general treatment is *The Western Church in the Later Middle Ages* (Ithaca, N.Y.: Cornell University Press, 1979). See also Steven Ozment, *The Age of Reform 1250–1550* (New Haven, Conn.: Yale University Press, 1980).

A good introduction to church life and spirituality of this period is R. N. Swanson, *Religion and Devotion in Europe, c. 1215–c.1515* (Cambridge, U.K.: Cambridge University Press, 1995).

Broad Cultural and Intellectual History

The Dutch historian Johan Huizinga's masterpiece from 1919 *Herfsttij der Middeleeuwen (The Waning of the Middle Ages)* depends heavily on Gerson's writings for its interpretation of the late medieval Church and religious belief. Two translations are available: the original one, supervised by Huizinga and made by F. Hopman in 1924, frequently republished by Penguin; the other by Rodney J. Payton and Ulrich Mammitzsch, *The Autumn of the Middle Ages* (Chicago: University of Chicago Press, 1996). The newer translation contains the original footnotes but lacks the poetic quality of Hopman's version. See Edward Peters and Walter P. Simons, "The New Huizinga and the Old Middle Ages," *Speculum* 74 (1999): 587–620.

Gerson's bonds with other members of his circle at the College of Navarre remains a subject for future exploration. But there are already two studies of Pierre d'Ailly that are essential for understanding Gerson's background: Alan E. Bernstein, *Pierre d'Ailly and the Blanchard Affair. University and Chancellor of Paris at the Beginning of the Great Schism* (Leiden: Brill, 1978) and Francis Oakley, *The Political Thought of Pierre d'Ailly. The Voluntarist Tradition* (New Haven, Conn.: Yale University Press, 1964).

Gerson's involvement in the matter of the visions of a woman of Reims appears within a larger context in the excellent edition and translation into modern French: Claude Arnaud-Gillet, *Entre Dieu et Satan. Les visions d'Ermine de Reims* (Florence, Italy: Sismel. Edizioni del Galluzzo, 1997).

Gerson is a frequent guest in Jean Delumeau's work *Sin and Fear. The Emergence of a Western Guilt Culture, 13th–18th Centuries* (New York: St. Martin's Press, 1990). Originally published as *Le péché et la peur* (Paris: Fayard, 1983), this book promises to tie together several centuries in the transition between the medieval and the modern world. In reality it oversimplifies complex questions, as Heiko Oberman points out in a review in *The Sixteenth Century Journal* 33 (1992): 149–150.

Gerson's discovery of Saint Joseph has inspired important new work by Pamela Sheingorn, as for example "'*Illustris patriarca Joseph*': Jean Gerson, Representations of Saint Joseph and Imagining Community among Churchmen in the Fifteenth Century," in

Visions of Community in the Pre-Modern World, ed. Nicholas Howe (Notre Dame, Ind.: University of Notre Dame Press, 2002), 75–108.

It is almost inevitable that I have left out writings of significance. From those scholars whose work I have neglected, I beg pardon and absolution. I would appreciate further guidance and information via email brianmcqu@gmail.com.

Bibliography

Primary Sources

Abelard, Peter. *Peter Abelard's Ethics,* ed. David E. Luscombe. Oxford, U.K.: Clarendon Press, 1971.

———. *The Letters of Abelard and Heloise,* trans. Betty Radice. Harmondsworth, U.K.: Penguin, 1974.

Aeneas Sylvius Piccolominus (Pius II). *De Gestis Concilii Basiliensis Commentariorum libri II,* ed. and trans. Denys Hay and W. K. Smith. Oxford, U.K.: Clarendon Press, 1992.

———. *Memoirs of a Renaissance Pope. The Commentaries of Pius II,* trans. Florence A. Grabb. New York: Capricorn Books, 1962.

Aesop, *The Fables of Aesop,* trans. S. A. Handford. Harmondsworth, U.K.: Penguin, 1979.

Alan of Lille, *The Plaint of Nature,* trans. James J. Sheridan. Toronto: Pontifical Institute of Mediaeval Studies, 1980.

Alberigo, Joseph, *Conciliorum Oecumenicorum Decreta,* eds. Perikle-P. Joannou, Claudio Leonardi, Paulo Prodi, et al. Basel: Herder. Centro di Documentazione, Istituto per le Scienze Religiose, Bologna, 1962.

Albert the Great and Thomas Aquinas. *Albert and Thomas. Selected Writings,* ed. Simon Tugwell. New York: Paulist Press, 1988.

Angela of Foligno. Complete Works, trans. Paul Lachance. New York: Paulist, 1993.

Anselm of Canterbury. *Sancti Anselmi Cantuariensis Archiepiscopi Opera Omnia,* vol. 3, ed. F. S. Schmitt. Edinburgh: Nelson, 1946.

———. *The Letters of Saint Anselm of Canterbury,* vol. 1, trans. Walter Fröhlich. Kalamazoo, Mich.: Cistercian Publications, 1990.

———. *The Prayers and Meditations of Saint Anselm,* trans. Benedicta Ward. Harmondsworth, U.K.: Penguin, 1973.

Athanasius. *The Life of Antony,* trans. Robert C. Gregg. New York: Paulist Press, 1980.

Bellaguet, M. L., ed. *Chronique du Religieux de Saint-Denys,* tome 1–6. Paris: 1842–52. Reprinted in three volumes, with introduction by Bernard Guenée. Éditions du Comité des travaux historiques et scientifiques, 1994.

Bernard of Clairvaux. *The Letters of Bernard of Clairvaux,* trans. Bruno Scott James. Kalamazoo, Mich.: Cistercian Publications, 1998.

———. *Sancti Bernardi Opera,* vol. 1–8, eds. Jean Leclercq and Henri Rochais, esp. vol. 1–2, *Sermones super Cantica Canticorum.* Rome: Editiones Cistercienses, 1957–1977.

Bettenson, Henry. *Documents of the Christian Church.* London: Oxford University Press, 1950.

Boland, Paschal, ed. and trans. *The Concept of Discretio Spirituum in John Gerson's 'De Probatione Spirituum' and the 'De Distinctione Verarum Visionum a Falsis'.* Washington, D.C.: Catholic University of America Press, 1959.

Bonaventure, *The Soul's Journey into God,* trans. Ewert Cousins. New York: Paulist Press, 1978.

Calvot, Danièle and Ouy, Gilbert. *L'oeuvre de Gerson à Saint-Victor de Paris. Catalogue des manuscrits.* Paris: Éditions du Centre National de la Recherche Scientifique, 1990.

Cassian, John. *The Conferences,* trans. Boniface Ramsey. New York: Newman Press, 1997.

Celestine V (Peter Celestine or Peter of Morrone). "Saint Pierre Célestin et ses premiers biographes." *Analecta Bollandiana* 16 (1897): 365–487.

Chrétien de Troyes. *Oeuvres complètes,* ed. Daniel Poiron et al. Paris: Gallimard, 1994.

———. *Arthurian Romances,* trans. William W. Kibler. London: Penguin, 1991.

Christine de Pizan. *Le livre des fais et bonnes meurs du sage roy Charles V,* vol. 1–2, ed. S. Solente. Paris: Honoré Champion, 1936–1940.

———. *The Selected Writings of Christine de Pizan,* ed. Renate Blumenfeld-Kosinski. New York: W. W. Norton, 1997.

Conrad of Eberbach. *Exordium Magnum Cisterciense,* ed. Bruno Griesser. Rome: Editiones Cistercienses, 1961.

Crowder, C.M.D., ed. and trans. *Unity, Heresy and Reform 1378–1460. The Conciliar Response to the Great Schism.* London: Edward Arnold, 1977.

Denifle, Heinrich, ed. *Chartularium Universitatis Parisiensis,* vols. 3–4. Paris: Delalain, 1894, 1897.

Devotio Moderna. Basic Writings, trans. John Van Engen. New York: Paulist Press, 1988.

Eadmer. *The Life of Saint Anselm,* ed. R. W. Southern. Oxford, U.K.: Clarendon Press, 1972.

Ermine de Reims. *Entre Dieu et Satan. Les visions d'Ermine de Reims,* ed. Claude Arnaud-Gillet. Florence, Italy: Sismel, 1997.

Eudes de Rouen. *The Register of Eudes of Rouen,* trans. Sydney M. Brown; ed. Jeremiah F. O'Sullivan. New York and London: Columbia University Press, 1964.

Evans, Sebastian, trans. *In the Studio. A Decade of Poems.* London: Macmillan, 1875. (Gerson's poems, 194–221)

Finke, Heinrich, ed. *Acta Concilii Constanciensis,* vols. 1–4. Münster in Westfalen: Regensbergsche Buchhandlung, 1896–1928.

Francis de Sales. *Francis de Sales. Jane de Chantal. Letters of Spiritual Direction,* trans. Péronne Marie Thibert. New York: Paulist Press, 1988.

———. *Introduction à la vie dévote.* Montreal: Fides, 1947.

Froissart, Jean. *Chronicles,* trans. Geoffrey Brereton. London: Penguin, 1978.

———. *The Chronicles of England, France and Spain,* ed. H. P. Dunster, trans. Thomas Johnes (1805). New York: E. P. Dutton, 1961.

———. *Chroniques,* vol. 15, ed. Albert Miron. Société de l'Histoire de France. Paris: Librairie C. Klincksieck, 1975.

Galbert of Bruges. *The Murder of Charles the Good, Count of Flanders,* ed. and trans. James Bruce Ross. New York: Columbia University Press, 1959.

Gerson, Jean. *Jean Gerson. The Consolation of Theology,* trans. Clyde Lee Miller. npp: Abaris Books , 1998.

———. *Jean Gerson. Early Works,* trans. Brian Patrick McGuire. New York: Paulist Press, 1998.

———. *Jean Gerson. Josephina* (CD-Rom), ed. G. Matteo Roccati. Paris: Lamop, 2001.

———. *Jean Gerson. Oeuvres Complètes,* vols. 1–10, ed. Palemon Glorieux. Paris, Tournai, Rome, New York: Desclée, 1960–73.

———. *Jean Gerson. Selections from "A Deo exivit," "Contra curiositatem studentium," and "De mystica theologia speculativa,"* trans. Stephen Ozment. Leiden: Brill, 1969.

———. *Ioannis Carlerii de Gerson de Mystica Theologia,* ed. André Combes. Lugano: Thesaurus Mundi, 1958.

———. *Johannes Gerson. Opera Omnia,* vols. 1–5, ed. Louis Ellies Du Pin. Antwerp: 1706. Reprinted Hildesheim: Georg Olms Verlag, 1987.

Glorieux, Palemon. "L'année universitaire 1392–1393 à la Sorbonne à travers les notes d'un étudiant." *Revue des sciences religieuses* 19 (1939): 419–482.

Gregory the Great. *Forty Gospel Homilies.* Trans. David Hurst. Kalamazoo, Mich.: Cistercian Publications, 1990.

Gregory of Tours. *The History of the Franks.* Trans. Lewis Thorpe. Harmondsworth, U.K.: Penguin, 1974.

Guicciardini. *History of Italy.* Trans. Cecil Grayson. New York: Washington Square Press, 1964.

Guigue, Georges and Laurent, J. "Obituaires de la province de Lyon," tome 2 in *Recueil des historiens de la France, Obituaires.* Paris, 1965.

Gundersheimer, Werner L., ed. *The Italian Renaissance.* Englewood Cliffs, N.J.: Prentice-Hall, 1965.

Hardt, Hermann von der, ed. *Rerum Concilii Oecumenici Constantiensis,* vols. 1–4. Frankfurt and Leipzig: Christian Genschius, 1697–1700.

Hicks, Eric, ed. *Le débat sur le Roman de la Rose.* Paris: Honoré Champion, 1977.

Jacobus a Voragine. *Legenda Aurea,* ed. Th. Graesse. Osnabrück: Otto Zeller, 1965 (reproduction of the third edition from 1890).

———. *The Golden Legend of Jacobus de Voragine,* trans. Granger Ryan and Helmut Ripperger. New York: Arno Press, 1969.

James, Montague Rhodes. *The Apocryphal New Testament.* Oxford, U.K.: Clarendon Press, 1953.

John of Salisbury. *Historia Pontificalis,* ed. Marjorie Chibnall. London: Thomas Nelson, 1956.

———. *Policraticus,* ed. Cary J. Nederman. Cambridge, U.K.: Cambridge University Press, 1990.

Joinville, Jean de. *Chronicles of the Crusades,* trans. M. R. B. Shaw. Harmondsworth, U.K.: Penguin, 1970.

Julian of Norwich. *Revelations of Divine Love,* trans. A. C. Spearing. Harmondsworth, U.K.: Penguin, 1998.

Kramer, Heinrich and Sprenger, James. *Malleus Maleficarum,* trans. Montague Summers. London: Arrow Books, 1971.

Langland, William. *Piers the Ploughman,* trans. F. F. Goodridge. Baltimore: Penguin, 1966.

———. *Piers Plowman.* Ed. Derek Pearsall. London: Edward Arnold, 1978.

Liber Usualis. Tournai and New York: Desclée, 1959.

Lieberman, Max. "Pierre Pocquet: *Dictamen de Laudibus Beati Josephi.*" *Cahiers de Joséphologie* 12 (1964): 5–23.

Lierheimer, Linda, ed. *The Life of Antoinette Micolon.* Milwaukee, Wis.: Marquette University Press, 2004.

Loomis, L. R., trans. *The Council of Constance. The Unification of the Church,* ed. John H. Mundy and K. M. Woody. New York: Columbia University Press, 1961.

Luther, Martin. *Martin Luther: Selections from his Writings,* trans. John Dillenberger. Garden City, N. Y.: Doubleday, 1961.

Margery Kempe. *The Book of Margery Kempe,* trans. B. A. Windeatt. London and New York: Penguin, 1994.

Marsilius of Padua. *Defensor Pacis,* trans. Alan Gewirth. Medieval Academy Reprints for Teaching. Toronto: University of Toronto Press, 1980.

Martin, Dennis, trans. *Carthusian Spirituality.* New York: Paulist Press, 1997.

Melanchton, Philip (and others). *Die Bekenntnisschriften der evangelisch-lutherischen Kirche.* Göttingen: Vandenhoeck & Ruprecht, 1992.

Miethke, Jürgen and Weinrich, Lorenz. *Quellen zur Kirchenreform im Zeitalter der grossen Konzilien des 15. Jahrhunderts. Erster Teil.* Darmstadt: Wissenschaftliche Buchgesellschaft, 1995.

Monstrelet. *The Chronicles of Enguerrand de Monstrelet,* trans. Thomas Johnes. London: George Routledge, 1867; Kraus Reprint: Millwood N.Y., 1975.

———. *Chronique d'Enguerran de Monstrelet,* vol. 3, ed. L. Douët-d'Arcq. Paris: Jule Renouard, 1859.

Morawski, Joseph, ed. *Proverbes français antérieurs au quinzième siècle.* Paris: Edouard Champion, 1925.

O'Connell, David. *Les propos de Saint Louis.* Paris: Gallimard. 1974.

Ouy, Gilbert. *Gerson bilingue. Les deux rédactions, latine et française, de quelques oeuvres du chancelier parisien.* Paris: Honoré Champion, 1998.

———. "Gerson, émule de Pétrarque. Le 'Pastorium Carmen', poème de jeunesse de Gerson." *Romania* 88 (1967): 175–231.

———. "Gerson et la guerre civile à Paris," *Archives d'Histoire doctrinale et littéraire du Moyen Age* 72 (2005).

———. "La plus ancienne oeuvre retrouvée de Jean Gerson: Le brouillon inachevé d'un traité contre Juan de Monzon (1389–1390)." *Romania* 83 (1962): 433–492.

———. "Trois prières françaises inédites de Jean Gerson." In *Mélanges de langue et de littérature françaises du moyen âge offerts à Pierre Demarolle.* Paris: Honoré Champion, 1998: 27–38.

———. "Une lettre de jeunesse de Jean Gerson." *Romania* 80 (1959): 461–472.

Peter of Celle. *Selected Works,* trans. Hugh Feiss. Kalamazoo, Mich.: Cistercian Publications, 1987.

Petrarch: *Letters on Familiar Matters,* trans. Aldo S. Bernardo. Baltimore and London: The Johns Hopkins University Press, 1985.

Pierre d'Ailly, "Vita S. Petri Coelestini." In *Acta Sanctorum Maii,* vol. 4 (Antwerp 1685): 485–498.

Possidius. "The Life of Augustine." In *The Western Fathers,* trans. F. R. Hoare. London: Sheed and Ward, 1980.

Pullan, Brian. *Sources for the History of Medieval Europe.* Oxford, U.K.: Basil Blackwell, 1966.

Ruusbroec. *John Ruusbroec. The Spiritual Espousal and other Works,* trans. James A. Wiseman. New York: Paulist Press, 1985.

Rychner, Jean, ed. *Les XV joies de mariage.* Geneva: Droz, 1967.

Stephen of Bourbon. *Anecdotes historiques d'Etienne de Bourbon,* ed. A. Lecoy de la Marche. Paris: Renouard, 1877.

Suger of Saint Denis. *Abbot Suger. On the Abbey Church of St. Denis and its Art Treasures,* ed. Erwin Panofsky. Princeton, N.J.: Princeton University Press, 1979.

Suso, Henry. *Henry Suso. The Exemplar.* New York: Paulist, 1989.

Talbot, C. H. *The Life of Christina of Markyate.* Oxford, U.K.: Clarendon Press, 1987.

Thomas of Cantimpré. *Bonum universale de apibus.* Douai: Baltazaris Bellerus, 1627.

Thorndike, Lynn. *University Records and Life in the Middle Ages.* New York: Norton, 1974.

Tuetey, Alexandre, ed. *Journal d'un bourgeois de Paris 1405–1449.* Paris: Honoré Champion, 1881.

Vansteenberghe, E. "La 'Pitieuse complainte de l'âme dévote' faussement attribuée à Pierre d'Ailly." *Revue des sciences religieuses* 13 (1933): 393–410.

———. "Lettre à ses soeurs sur la méditation et les dévotions quotidiennes." *Revue des sciences religieuses* 14 (1934): 370–395.

———. "Trois règlements de vie de Gerson pour ses soeurs." RSR 14 (1934), 191–218.

Vitae patrum (The Lives of the Desert Fathers). *Patrologia Latina,* vol. 73, ed. J. P. Migne, 1844–1855. The complete work is available on an electronic database. See http://pld.chadwyck.com.

Waddell, Helen, trans. *The Desert Fathers.* Ann Arbor: University of Michigan Press, 1966.

———. *Mediaeval Latin Lyrics.* Harmondsworth, U.K.: Penguin, 1968.

William of Auvergne. *Guilelmi Alverni Opera Omnia,* vol. 1. Paris, 1674; reprinted Frankfurt am Main: Minerva, 1963.

William of Saint Thierry. *The Golden Epistle. A Letter to the Brethren at Mont Dieu,* trans. Theodore Berkeley. Kalamazoo, Mich.: Cistercian, 1976.

Secondary Sources

Allmand, Christopher. *The Hundred Years War.* Cambridge, U.K.: Cambridge University Press, 1989.

Andrieu, E. "La personnalité des pleurants du tombeau de Philippe le Hardi." *Revue belge d'archéologie et de l'histoire de l'art* 5 (1935): 221–230.

Ariès, Philippe. *L'enfant et la vie familiale sous l'Ancien Régime.* Paris: Editions du Seuil, 1973.

Ariès, Philippe, and Duby, Georges. *A History of Private Life,* vol. 2: *Revelations of the Medieval World.* Cambridge, Mass.: Belknap Press, 1988.

Ashley, Kathleen and Sheingorn, Pamela. *Interpreting Cultural Symbols. Saint Anne in Late Medieval Society.* Athens: The University of Georgia Press, 1990.

Baldwin, John. *Masters, Princes and Merchants. The Social Views of Peter the Chanter and his Circle,* vols. 1–2. Princeton, N.J.: Princeton University Press, 1970.

Baum, Wilhelm. *Kaiser Sigismund: Hus, Konstanz, und Türkenkrieg.* Graz, Austria: Verlag Styria, 1993.

Becker, Carl L. *The Heavenly City of the Eighteenth-Century Philosophers.* New Haven, Conn.: Yale University Press, 1964.

Bejczy, István. "Erasme explore le moyen âge: Sa lecture de Bernard de Clairvaux et de Jean Gerson." *Revue d'histoire ecclésiastique* 93 (1998): 460–476.

Bellitto, Christopher M. *Nicolas de Clamanges. Spirituality, Personal Reform and Pastoral Renewal on the Eve of the Reformations.* Washington, D.C.: The Catholic University of America Press, 2001.

Bernstein, Alan E. *Pierre d'Ailly and the Blanchard Affair. University and Chancellor of Paris at the Beginning of the Great Schism.* Leiden: Brill, 1978.

Bianchi, Luca. *Censure et liberté intellectuelle à l'université de Paris.* Paris: Les Belles Lettres, 1999.

Bishop, Morris. *Petrarch and His World.* Bloomington: Indiana University Press, 1963.

Black, Antony. *Council and Commune: The Conciliar Movement and the Council of Basle.* London: Burns and Oates, 1979.

Borchert, Till-Holger, *The Age of Van Eyck. The Mediterranean World and Early Netherlandish Painting 1430–1530.* Ghent-Amsterdam: Ludion, 2002.

Brandenburg, Ton. "Saint Anne. A Holy Grandmother and her Children." In *Sanctity and Motherhood: Essays on Holy Mothers in the Middle Ages,* ed. Anneke B. Mulder-Bakker, 31–65. New York: Garland, 1995.

Brandmüller, Walter. *Papst und Konzil im Grossen Schisma (1378–1431). Studien und Quellen.* Paderborn: Ferdinand Schöningh, 1990.

Brown, D. Catherine. *Pastor and Laity in the Theology of Jean Gerson.* Cambridge, U.K.: Cambridge University Press, 1987.

Brundage, James A. *Law, Sex, and Christian Society in Medieval Europe.* Chicago: University of Chicago Press, 1987.

Bullough, Vern L. and Brundage, James A. *Handbook of Medieval Sexuality.* New York: Garland, 1996.

Burrows, Mark Stephen. *Jean Gerson and De Consolatione Theologiae. The Consolation of a Biblical and Reforming Theology for a Disordered Age.* Tübingen: J.C.B. Mohr (Paul Siebeck), 1991.

Caciola, Nancy. *Discerning Spirits. Divine and Demonic Possession in the Middle Ages.* Ithaca, N.Y.: Cornell University Press, 2003.

Cantor, Norman F. *In the Wake of the Plague. The Black Death and the World It Made.* New York: The Free Press, 2001.

———. *Inventing the Middle Ages. The Lives, Works, and Ideas of the Great Medievalists of the Twentieth Century.* New York: Quill. William Morrow. 1991.

Catechism of the Catholic Church. New York: Doubleday, 1995.

Chambers, E. K. *The Medieval Stage,* vol. 1. Oxford, U.K.: Oxford University Press, 1903.

Chopin, Hervé. "Une église à travers les âges: L'ancienne collégiale Saint-Paul." In *Quartier Saint-Paul, Lyon,* ed. Max Bobichon et al., 83–105. Lyon: Chirat, 2000.

Christianson, Gerald. "Aeneas Sylvius Piccolomini and the Historiography of the Council of Basel." In *Ecclesia Militans: Studien zur Konzilien- und Reformationsgeschichte Remigius Bäumer zum 70. Geburtstag gewidmet* 1, ed. Walter Brandmüller, Herbert Immenkötter and Erwin Iserloh, 157–184. Paderborn: Ferdinand Schöningh, 1988.

Clanchy, Michael T. *Abelard. A Medieval Life.* Oxford, U.K.: Blackwell, 1997.

———. *From Memory to Written Record.* Oxford, U.K.: Blackwell, 1993.

Cleugh, James. *Love Locked Out.* London and New York: Spring Books, 1970.

Cohn, Samuel K. *The Black Death Transformed. Disease and Culture in Early Renaissance Europe.* London: Arnold. 2002.

Colish, Marcia L. *Peter Lombard,* vols. 1–2. Leiden: Brill, 1994.

Combes, André. "Gerson et la naissance de l'humanisme." *Revue du Moyen Age latin* 1 (1945): 259–284.

———. *Jean de Montreuil et le chancelier Gerson.* Paris: J. Vrin, 1942.

———. *La théologie mystique de Gerson. Profil de son évolution,* vols. 1–2. Rome: Libraria Editrix and Desclée, 1963–64.

Connolly, James L. *John Gerson. Reformer and Mystic.* Louvain: Librairie Universitaire and Herder, 1928.

Constable, Giles. "The Popularity of Twelfth-Century Spiritual Writers in the Late Middle Ages." *Renaissance Studies in Honor of Hans Baron,* ed. Anthony Molho and John A. Tedeschi, 5–28. DeKalb: Northern Illinois University Press, 1971.

———. "Twelfth-Century Spirituality and the Late Middle Ages." *Medieval and Renaissance Studies* 5, ed. O. B. Hardison Jr., 27–60. Chapel Hill: University of North Carolina Press, 1971.

Coville, Alfred. *Les Cabochiens et l'ordonnance de 1413.* Geneva: Slatkine-Megariotis, 1888 [1974].

———. *Jean Petit. La question du tyrannicide au commencement du quinzième siècle.* Paris: Auguste Picard, 1932.

———. *Les premiers Valois et la guerre de cent ans (1328–1422).* Paris: Hachette, 1902.

Cowdrey, H. E. J. *The Cluniacs and the Gregorian Reform.* Oxford, U.K.: Clarendon Press, 1970.

Coyecque, E. *L'Hôtel-Dieu de Paris au Moyen Age,* vols. 1–2. Paris: Honoré Champion, 1889–1891.

David, Henri. *Claus Sluter.* Paris: Editions Pierre Tisné, 1951.

Davies, Oliver. *God Within. The Mystical Tradition of Northern Europe.* New York: Paulist Press, 1988.

D'Avray, David L. *The Preaching of the Friars. Sermons diffused from Paris before 1300.* Oxford, O.K.: Clarendon Press, 1985.

Delaruelle, E., Labande, E.-R., Ourliac, Paul. *L'église au temps du grand schisme et de la crise conciliaire,* vol. 14 in *Histoire de l'église.* Paris: Bloud & Gay, 1962.

Demouy, Patrick. *Saint-Rémi de Reims.* Saint Ouen: Editions La Goélette, 1997.

Desportes, Pierre. *Reims et les Rémois aux treizième et quatorzième siècles.* Paris: Picard, 1979.

Dohar, William J. *The Black Death and Pastoral Leadership. The Diocese of Hereford in the Fourteenth Century.* Philadelphia: University of Pennsylvania Press, 1995.

Duby, Georges. *The Three Orders: Feudal Society Imagined.* Chicago and London: University of Chicago Press, 1980.

Duplain, L. and Giraud J. *Saint-Paul de Lyon. Etudes d'histoire lyonnaise.* Lyon: Rey Imprimeurs, 1899.

Elliott, Dyan. "Seeing Double: John Gerson, the Discernment of Spirits, and Joan of Arc." *American Historical Review* 107 (2002): 26–54.

Emery, Kent. "A Forced March Towards Beatitude: Christian Trottman's *History of the Beatific Vision.*" *Vivarium* 37 (1999): 258–281.

Famiglietti, R. C. *Royal Intrigue. Crisis at the Court of Charles VI, 1392–1420.* New York: AMS Press, 1986.

Favier, Jean. *La guerre de cent ans.* Paris: Fayard, 1980.

Feger, Otto. *Kleine Geschichte der Stadt Konstanz.* Constance: Rosgarten Verlag, 1972.

Ferruolo, Stephen. *The Origins of the University.* Stanford, Calif.: Stanford University Press, 1985.

Figgis, J. N. *Political Thought from Gerson to Grotius: 1414–1625.* New York: Harper, 1960.

Fraioli, Deborah. *Joan of Arc: The Early Debate.* Woodbridge, Suffolk: Boydell Press, 2000.

Gerz-Von Büren, Veronika. *La tradition de l'oeuvre de Jean Gerson chez les Chartreux: La Chartreuse de Bâle.* Paris: Institut de Recherche et d'Histoire des Textes. Editions du Centre National de la Recherche Scientifique, 1973.

Gilson, Etienne. *History of Christian Philosophy in the Middle Ages.* London: Sheed and Ward, 1955.

Glorieux, Palemon. "Autour de la liste des oeuvres de Gerson." *Recherches de théologie ancienne et médiévale* 22 (1995): 95–109.

———. "Gerson au chapitre de Notre-Dame de Paris." *Revue d'histoire ecclésiastique* 56 (1961): 424–448 and 827–854.

———. "L'année universitaire 1392–1393 à la Sorbonne à travers les notes d'un étudiant." *Revue de sciences religieuses* 19 (1939): 429–482.

———. "La vie et les oeuvres de Gerson: Essai chronologique." *Archives d'histoire doctrinale et littéraire du Moyen-Age* 25–26 (1950–51): 149–192.

———. "L'enseignement universitaire de Gerson." *Recherches de théologie ancienne et médiévale* 23 (1956): 88–113.

———. "Saint Joseph dans l'oeuvre de Gerson." In *Saint Joseph durant les quinze premiers siècles de l'église.* Centre de Recherche et de Documentation Oratoire Saint-Joseph Montréal. Published as *Cahiers de Joséphologie* 19 (1971): 414–428.

Grosse, Sven. *Heilsungewissheit und Scrupulositas im späten Mittelalter.* Tübingen: J. C. B. Mohr, 1994.

Guenée, Bernard. *Between Church and State. The Lives of Four French Prelates in the Late Middle Ages.* Chicago: University of Chicago Press, 1991.

———. *Un meurtre, une société. L'assassinat du duc d'Orléans 23 novembre 1407.* Paris: Gallimard, 1992.

Hamm, Berndt. *The Reformation of Faith in the Context of Late Medieval Theology and Piety,* ed. Robert J. Bast. Leiden: Brill, 2004.

Hanley, Sarah. *The "Lit de Justice" of the Kings of France: Constitutional Ideology in Legend, Ritual, and Discourse.* Princeton, N.J.: Princeton University Press, 1983.

Hanska, Jussi. *And the Rich Man also died; and he was buried in Hell: The Social Ethos in Mendicant Sermons.* Helsinki: Suomen Historiallinen Seura, 1997.

Hausherr, Irénée. *Spiritual Direction in the Early Christian East.* Kalamazoo, Mich.: Cistercian, 1990.

Hay, Denys. *Europe in the Fourteenth and Fifteenth Centuries.* London: Longman, 1989.

Hefele, Charles-Joseph and Leclercq, Henri. *Histoire des conciles,* vols. 6.2, 7.1 and 7.2. Paris: Letouzey et Ané, 1915–16.

Heise, Brigitte. *Das St. Annen-Kloster zu Lübeck.* Lübeck: Museum für Kunst und Kulturgeschichte der Hansestadt Lübeck, 1989.

Heise, Brigitte, and Vogeler, Hildegard. *Die Altäre des St. Annen-Museums.* Lübeck: Museum für Kunst und Kulturgeschichte der Hansestadt Lübeck, 1993.

Herlihy, David. *The Black Death and the Transformation of the West.* Cambridge, Mass.: Harvard University Press, 1997.

Hilton, Rodney. *Bond Men Made Free.* London: Methuen, 1980.

Hobbins, Daniel. "Jean Gerson's Authentic Tract on Joan of Arc: *Super facto puellae et credulitate sibi praestanda* (14 May 1429)." *Mediaeval Studies* 67 (2005).

———. "The Schoolman as Public Intellectual. Jean Gerson and the Late Medieval Tract." *American Historical Review* 108 (2003): 1308–1335.

Hogg, James. "Oswald de Corda, a Forgotten Carthusian of Nordlingen." *Kartäusermystik und -Mystiker. Analecta Cartusiana* (55):181–85. Salzburg: Institut für Anglistik und Amerikanistik, Universität Salzburg, 1982.

Huizinga, Johan. *The Autumn of the Middle Ages,* trans. Rodney J. Payton and Ulrich Mammitzsch. Chicago: University of Chicago Press, 1996.

———. *The Waning of the Middle Ages,* trans. 1924 by F. Hopman. Harmondsworth, U.K.: Penguin, 1965.

Hyma, Albert. *The Christian Renaissance. A History of the "Devotio Moderna."* Hamden, Conn.: Archon Books, 1965.

Jacob, E. F. *The Fifteenth Century.* Oxford, U.K.: Clarendon Press, 1961.

Jadart, Henri. *Jean de Gerson. Recherches sur son origine, son village natal et sa famille.* Reims: Deligne et Renart, 1881.

Jensen, Henrik. *Den sorte død og livet i senmiddelalderen* [The Black Death and Life in the Late Middle Ages]. Copenhagen: Gyldendal, 1987.

———. *Ofrets århundrede* [The Century of the Victim]. Copenhagen: Samleren, 1998.

John, Eric, ed. *The Popes. A Concise Biographical History.* New York: Hawthorn Books, 1964.

Jordan, William Chester. *The Great Famine: Northern Europe in the Early Fourteenth Century.* Princeton, N.J.: Princeton University Press, 1996.

Kaluza, Zenon. *Les querelles doctrinales à Paris. Nominalistes et réalistes aux confins du quatorizième et quinzième siècles.* Bergamo, Italy: Pierluigi Lubrina Editore, 1988.

Kaminsky, Howard. *Simon Cramaud and the Great Schism.* New Brunswick, N.J.: Rutgers University Press: 1983.

Kantorowicz, Ernst H. *The King's Two Bodies.* Princeton, N.J.: Princeton University Press, 1997.

Kardong, Terrence. "John Cassian's Teaching on Perfect Chastity." *American Benedictine Review* 30 (1979): 249–263.

Keen, Maurice H. *England in the Later Middle Ages.* London: Methuen, 1973.

Kieckhefer, Richard. "Major Currents in Late Medieval Devotion." In *Christian Spirituality. High Middle Ages and Reformation,* ed. Jill Raitt, 75–108. New York: Crossroad, 1988.

———. *Unquiet Souls. Fourteenth-Century Saints and Their Religious Milieu.* Chicago: University of Chicago Press, 1984.

Knowles, David. *The Evolution of Medieval Thought.* New York: Addison-Wesley, 1989.

Lamy, Marielle. *L'Immaculée Conception. Etapes et enjeux d'une controverse au Moyen Age.* Paris: Institut Augustiniennes/Brepols, 2000.

Langmuir, Gavin. "The Faith of Christians and Hostility to Jews." In *Christianity and Judaism,* ed. Diana Wood, 77–92. Oxford: Blackwell, 1992.

———. *Towards a Definition of Antisemitism.* Berkeley, Los Angeles, London, 1996.

Lawrence, C. H. *Medieval Monasticism.* London: Longman, 1984.

Leclercq, Jean. "Were the *Sermons on the Song of Songs* Delivered in Chapter?" In *Bernard of Clairvaux on the Song of Songs II,* vii–xxx. Kalamazoo, Mich.: Cistercian, 1976.

Ledwidge, Francis. "Relations de famille dans la correspondance de Gerson."*Revue historique* 271 (1984): 3–23.

Leff, Gordon. *Heresy in the Later Middle Ages,* vols. 1–2. Manchester and New York: Manchester University Press and Barnes and Noble, 1967.

———. *Paris and Oxford Universities in the Thirteenth and Fourteenth Centuries.* Huntington, N.Y.: R. E. Krieger, 1975.

Le Goff, Jacques. *Time, Work, and Culture in the Middle Ages.* Chicago: University of Chicago Press, 1980.

Lerner, Robert. *The Heresy of the Free Spirit in the Later Middle Ages.* Notre Dame, Ind.: University of Notre Dame Press, 1972.

Le Roy Ladurie, Emmanuel. *Montaillou: Cathars and Catholics in a French Village 1294–1324.* London: Scolar Press, 1978. American version *Montaillou: The Promised Land of Error,* ed. Barbara Bray. New York: George Braziller, 1978.

Lewis, P. S. *Later Medieval France. The Polity.* London and New York: Macmillan and Saint Martin's Press, 1968.

Lieberman, Max. "Autour de l'iconographie gersonienne." *Romania* 84 (1963): 307–353.

———. "Chronologie gersonienne." *Romania* 79 (1958): 339–375.

———. "Lettre de Gerson au Duc de Berry." *Cahiers de Joséphologie* 9 (1961): 199–265.

———. "Pierre d'Ailly, Jean Gerson et le culte de Saint Joseph." *Cahiers de Joséphologie* 13 (1965): 227–272; 14 (1966): 271–314; 15 (1967): 5–106.

Lierheimer, Linda. "Preaching or Teaching? Defining the Ursuline Mission in Seventeenth-Century France." In *Women Preachers and Prophets through Two Millenia of Christianity,* ed. Beverly Mayne Kienzle and Pamela J. Walker, 212–226. Los Angeles and Berkeley: University of California Press, 1998.

Little, Lester. *Religious Poverty and the Profit Economy.* London: Paul Elek, 1978.

Lochrie, Karma. *Margery Kempe and Translations of the Flesh.* Philadelphia: University of Pennsylvania Press, 1991.

Martin, Dennis D. *Fifteenth-Century Carthusian Reform. The World of Nicholas Kempf.* Leiden: Brill, 1992.

Martin, Victor. *Les origines du Gallicanisme,* vols. 1–2. Paris: Bloud & Gay, 1939.

Masson, Anne-Louise. *Jean Gerson. Sa vie, son temps, ses oeuvres.* Lyon: Emmanuel Vitte, 1894.

Matusevich, Yelena. *L'âge d'or de la mystique française: Étude de la littérature spirituelle de Jean Gerson à Jacques Lefevre d'Étaples.* Paris: Editions Sarl-Arche, 2004.

———. "From Monastic to Individual Spirituality: Another Perspective on Jean Gerson's Attitude toward Women." *Magistra* 6 (2000): 61–88.

McDonnell, Ernest W. *The Beguines and Beghards in Medieval Culture.* New York: Octagon Books, 1969.

McGinn, Bernard. *The Flowering of Mysticism. Men and Women in the New Mysticism 1200–1350.* New York: Crossroad, 1998.

McGowan, John P. *Pierre d'Ailly and the Council of Constance.* Washington, D.C.: Catholic University of America Press, 1936.

McGrade, Arthur Stephen. *The Political Thought of William of Ockham.* Cambridge, U.K.: Cambridge University Press, 1974.

McGuire, Brian Patrick. "Anti-clerical Invective and the Growth of Clerical Satire, 1075–1400." In *Master Golyas and Sweden: The Transformation of a Clerical Satire,* eds. Olle Ferm and Bridget Morris, 45–93. Stockholm: Sällskapet Runica et Mediaevalia, 1997.

———. *Brother and Lover. Aelred of Rievaulx.* New York: Crossroad, 1994.

———, ed. *A Companion to Jean Gerson.* Leiden: Brill, 2006.

———. "Education, Confession, and Pious Fraud: Jean Gerson and a Late Medieval Change." *American Benedictine Review* 47 (1996): 310–338.

———. *Friendship and Community. The Monastic Experience 350–1250.* Kalamazoo, Mich.: Cistercian Publications, 1988.

———. *Friendship and Faith: Cistercian Men, Women and their Stories, 1100–1250.* Aldershot, Hampshire, U.K. and Burlington, Vt.: Ashgate, 2002.

———. "Gerson and Bernard: Languishing with Love." *Cîteaux. Commentarii Cistercienses* 46 (1995): 127–156.

———. "In Search of Bernard's Legacy: Jean Gerson and a Lifetime of Devotion." In *Praise No Less Than Charity. Studies in Honor of M. Chrysogonus Waddell,* ed. E. Rozanne Elder, 285–328. Kalamazoo, Mich.: Cistercian Publications, 2002.

———. "Jean Gerson and the End of Spiritual Friendship: Dilemmas of Conscience." In *Friendship in Medieval Europe,* ed. Julian Haseldine, 229–250. Stroud, Gloucestershire: Sutton, 1999.

———. "Jean Gerson and Bilingualism in the Late Medieval University." In *Pratiques de traduction au Moyen Age,* ed. Peter Andersen, 121–29. Copenhagen: Museum Tusculanum, 2004.

———. "Jean Gerson, the Shulammite, and the Maid." In *Joan of Arc and Spirituality,* ed. Ann W. Astell and Bonnie Wheeler, 183–192. New York: Palgrave Macmillan, 2003.

———. "Late Medieval Care and Control of Women: Jean Gerson and His Sisters." *Revue d'histoire ecclésiastique* 92 (1997): 1–37.

———. "Loving the Holy Order: Jean Gerson and the Carthusians." In *Die Kartäuser und ihre Welt: Kontakte und gegenseitige Einflüsse. Analecta Cartusiana* 62, ed. James Hogg, 100–139. New York: Edwin Mellen Press, 1993.

———. "La présence de la *Lettre aux frères de Mont-Dieu* dans les oeuvres de Jean Gerson." In *Signy l'abbaye et Guillaume de Saint-Thierry,* ed. Nicole Boucher, 565–574. Signy l'Abbaye: Associations des Amis de l'Abbaye de Signy, 2000.

———. "Sexual Control and Spiritual Growth in the Late Middle Ages: The Case of Jean Gerson." In *Tradition and Ecstasy: The Agony of the Fourteenth Century,* ed. Nancy van Deusen, 123–152. Ottawa: Institute of Mediaeval Music, 1997.

———. "'Shining Forth like the Dawn.' Jean Gerson's Sermon to the Carthusians." In *Medieval Monastic Preaching,* ed. Carolyn Muessig, 37–52. Leiden: Brill, 1998.

———. "When Jesus did the Dishes. The Transformation of Late Medieval Spirituality." In *The Making of Christian Communities,* ed. Mark F. Williams, 131–152. London: Anthem Press, 2005.

———, ed. *The Birth of Identities. Denmark and Europe in the Middle Ages.* Copenhagen: C. A. Reitzel, 1996.

Martin, Hervé. *Le métier de prédicateur à la fin du Moyen Age (1350–1520).* Paris: Editions du Cerf, 1988.

Methuen, Erich. *Das Basler Konzil als Forschungsproblem der europaïschen Geschichte.* Kleve: Westdeutscher Verlag, 1985.

Mollat, Guillaume. *The Popes at Avignon.* London: Thomas Nelson, 1963.

Mollat, Michel and Wolff, Philippe. *The Popular Revolutions of the Late Middle Ages.* London: Allen and Unwin, 1973.

Moorman, John. *A History of the Franciscan Order.* Oxford, U.K.: Clarendon Press, 1968.

Mornet, Elisabeth. "Gerson en Scandinavie." In *Pratiques de la culture écrite en France au quinzième siècle,* eds. M. Ornato and N. Pons, 93–108. Louvain-la-Neuve: Fidem Publications, 1995.

Morrall, John B. *Gerson and the Great Schism.* Manchester, U.K.: Manchester University Press, 1960.

Morris, Colin. *The Papal Monarchy. The Western Church from 1050 to 1250.* Oxford, U.K.: Clarendon Press, 1991.

Mourin, Louis. *Jean Gerson. Prédicateur français.* Brugge: De Tempel, 1952.

Muessig, Carolyn, ed. *Medieval Monastic Preaching.* Leiden: Brill, 1999.

Müller, Heribert. *Die Franzosen, Frankreich, und das Basler Konzil (1431–1449).* Paderborn: Ferdinand Schöningh, 1990.

Mullett, Michael A. *The Catholic Reformation.* London: Routledge, 1999.

Murray, Alexander. *Reason and Society in the Middle Ages.* Oxford, U.K.: Clarendon Press, 1978.

Nabert, Nathalie. "La référence à Clovis chez Jean Gerson et chez Christine de Pisan." In *Clovis histoire et mémoire,* ed. Michel Rouche, 231–248. Paris: Presses de l'Université de Paris-Sorbonne, 1997.

Nichols, David. *Medieval Flanders.* London: Longman, 1992.

Nuth, Joan M. *Wisdom's Daughter. The Theology of Julian of Norwich.* New York: Crossroad, 1991.

Oakley, Francis. *Council over Pope? Towards a Provisional Ecclesiology.* New York: Herder and Herder, 1969.

———. *The Medieval Experience.* Toronto: University of Toronto Press, 1988.

———. *The Political Thought of Pierre d'Ailly.* New Haven, Conn.: Yale University Press, 1964.

———. *The Western Church in the Later Middle Ages.* Ithaca, N.Y.: Cornell University Press, 1979.

Ouy, Gilbert. "Le Célestin Jean Gerson. Copiste et éditeur de son frère." In *La collaboration dans la production de l'écrit médiéval,* ed. Harald Spilling, 281–308. Paris: Ecole des Chartes, 2003.

———. "Enquête sur les manuscrits autographes du chancelier Gerson et sur les copies faites par son frère le Célestin Jean Gerson." *Scriptorium* 16 (1962): 275–301.

———. "Gerson et l'Angleterre: A propos d'un texte polémique retrouvé du chancelier de Paris contre l'université d'Oxford." In *Humanism in France at the End of the Middle Ages and in the Early Renaissance,* ed. A.H.T. Levi, 43–81. Manchester, U.K.: Manchester University Press, 1970.

———. "Gerson and the Celestines: How Jean Gerson and His Friend Pierre Poquet Replied to Various Questions of Discipline and Points of Conscience (ca. 1400)." In *Reform and Renewal in the Middle Ages and the Renaissance,* eds. Thomas Izbicki and Christopher Bellitto, 113–140. Leiden: Brill, 2000.

———."Humanism and Nationalism in France at the Turn of the Fifteenth Century." In *The Birth of Identities: Denmark and Europe in the Middle Ages,* ed. Brian Patrick McGuire, 107–125. Copenhagen: C. A. Reitzel, 1996.

———. "L'humanisme et les mutations politiques et sociales en France aux quatorzième et quinzième siècles." In *L'humanisme français au début de la Renaissance,* 27–44. Paris: Collège International de Tours J. Vrin, 1973.

———. "Pétrarque et les premiers humanistes français." In *Petrarca, Verona e l'Europa. Studi sul Petrarca* 26, 415–434. Padua: Antenore, 1997.

———. "Quelques conseils de Gerson aux confesseurs." In *Codex in Conflict. Studies over codicologie . . . aangeboden aan Prof. Dr. A. Gruijs,* eds. Chr. de Bacher, A. J. Geurts, and A. G. Weiler, 289–312. Nijmegen/Grave: Alfa, 1985.

Ozment, Steven. *The Age of Reform 1250–1550.* New Haven, Conn.: Yale University Press, 1980.

———. *When Fathers Ruled. Family Life in Reformation Europe.* Cambridge, Mass.: Harvard University Press, 1983.

Pacaut, Marcel. *Guide de Lyon médiéval.* Lyon: Editions lyonnaises d'art et d'histoire, 2000.

Pascoe, Louis B. *Jean Gerson: Principles of Church Reform.* Leiden: Brill, 1973.

Perroy, Edouard. *La guerre de cent ans.* Paris: Gallimard, 1945.

Peters, Edward and Simons, Walter P. "The New Huizinga and the Old Middle Ages." *Speculum* 74 (1999): 587–620.

Posthumus Meyjes, G.H.M. *Jean Gerson. Apostle of Unity. His Church Politics and Ecclesiology.* Leiden: Brill, 1999.

Pounds, N.J.G. *An Economic History of Medieval Europe.* London: Longman, 1974.

Rapp, Francis. *L'église et la vie religieuse en Occident à la fin du Moyen Age.* Paris: Presses Universitaires de France, 1971.

Rashdall, Hastings. *The Universities of Europe in the Middle Ages,* 1895. Revised by F. M. Powicke and A. B. Emden. Oxford, U.K.: Oxford University Press, 1936.

Rebouis, Emile. *Etude historique et critique sur la peste.* Paris: Picard, 1888.

Reeves, Marjorie. *The Influence of Prophecy in the Later Middle Ages. A Study in Joachimism.* Oxford, U.K.: Clarendon Press, 1969.

Reynolds, L. D. and Wilson, N. G. *Scribes and Scholars.* Oxford, U.K.: Clarendon Press: 1974.

Richards, Earl Jeffrey. "Christine de Pizan and Jean Gerson: An Intellectual Friendship." In *Christine de Pizan 2000,* ed. John Campbell and Nadia Margolis, 197–208. Amsterdam: Rodopi, 2000.

———. "Rejecting Essentialism and Gendered Writing: The Case of Christine de Pizan." In *Gender and Text in the Later Middle Ages,* ed. Jane Chance, 96–131. Gainesville: University Press of Florida, 1996.

Ridder-Symoens, Hilde de, ed. *A History of the University in Europe,* vol. 1: *Universities in the Middle Ages.* Cambridge, U.K.: Cambridge University Press, 1994.

Roper, Lyndal. *The Holy Household. Women and Morals in Reformation Augsburg.* Oxford, U.K.: Clarendon Press, 1991.

Rouche, Michel, ed. *Clovis. Histoire et mémoire.* Paris: Presses de l'Université de Paris-Sorbonne, 1997.

Roth, Cornelius. *Discretio spirituum. Kriterien geistlicher Unterscheidung bei Johannes Gerson.* Würzburg: Echter Verlag, 2001.

Rubin, Miri. *Corpus Christi. The Eucharist in Late Medieval Culture.* Cambridge, U.K.: Cambridge University Press, 1991.

Russell, Jeffrey Burton. *A History of Heaven. The Singing Silence.* Princeton, N.J.: Princeton University Press, 1997.

Ryan, John J. *The Apostolic Conciliarism of Jean Gerson.* Atlanta, Ga.: Scholars Press, 1998.

Rydstrøm-Poulsen, Aage. *The Gracious God: Gratia in Augustine and the Twelfth Century.* Copenhagen: Akademisk, 2002.

Salembier, Louis. "Gerson." *Dictionnaire de théologie catholique* 6 (1915): 1314–1330.

———. *Le cardinal Pierre d'Ailly.* Tourcoing: Georges Frère, 1932.

Saxtorph, Niels, ed. *Jeg ser på kalkmalerier* [Looking at Wall Paintings]. Copenhagen: Politiken, 1979.

Schwab, Johann Baptist. *Johannes Gerson. Professor der Theologie und Kanzler der Universität Paris,* vols. 1–2. Würzburg: np., 1858; republished New York: Burt Franklin, nd.

Scholl, Edith. "The Cistercian Vocabulary: A Proposal." *Cistercian Studies Quarterly* 27 (1992): 77–89.

Sargent, Michael G., ed. *De Cella in Seculum. Religious and Secular Life and Devotion in Late Medieval England.* Woodbridge, Suffolk: D. S. Brewer, 1989.

Seitz, Joseph. *Die Verehrung des hl. Joseph in ihrer geschichtlichen Entwicklung bis zum Konzil von Trient dargestellt.* Freiburg im Breisgau: Herdersche Verlagshandlung, 1908.

Southern, Richard W. "The English Origin of the 'Miracles of the Virgin.'" *Medieval and Renaissance Studies* 4 (1958): 176–216.

———. *Robert Grosseteste. The Growth of an English Mind in Medieval Europe,* 2nd ed. Oxford, U.K.: Clarendon Press, 1992.

———. *Saint Anselm and His Biographer.* Cambridge, U.K.: Cambridge University Press, 1963.

———. *Saint Anselm. A Portrait in a Landscape.* Cambridge, U.K.: Cambridge University Press, 1990.

———. *Scholastic Humanism and the Unification of Europe,* vol. 1: *Foundations.* Oxford, U.K.: Blackwell, 1995.

______. *Scholastic Humanism and the Unification of Europe,* vol. 2: *The Heroic Age,* with notes and additions by Lesley Smith and Benedicta Ward. Oxford, U.K.: Blackwell, 2001.

———. *Western Society and the Church in the Middle Ages.* Harmondsworth, U.K.: Penguin, 1970.

Spinka, Matthew. *Advocates of Reform. From Wyclif to Erasmus.* Philadelphia: Westminster Press, 1963.

Stieber, Joachim W. *Pope Eugenius IV, the Council of Basel and the Secular and Ecclesiastical Authorities in the Empire.* Leiden: Brill, 1978.

Sumption, Jonathan. *The Hundred Years War,* vol. 1: *Trial by Battle.* Philadelphia: University of Pennsylvania Press, 1999.

———. *The Hundred Years War,* vol. 2: *Trial by Fire.* Philadelphia: University of Pennsylvania Press, 2001.

Swanson, R. N. *Religion and Devotion in Europe c.1215–c.1515.* Cambridge, U.K.: Cambridge University Press, 1995.

———. *Universities, Academics, and the Great Schism.* Cambridge, U.K.: Cambridge University Press, 1979.

Taburet-Delahaye, Elisabeth and Avril, François. *Paris 1400. Les arts sous Charles VI.* Paris: Musée du Louvre/Fayard, 2004.

Tentler, Thomas N. *Sin and Confession on the Eve of the Reformation.* Princeton, N.J.: Princeton University Press, 1977.

Thijssen, J.M.M.H. *Censure and Heresy at the University of Paris, 1200–1400.* Philadelphia: University of Pennsylvania Press, 1998.

Thomson, John A. F. *Popes and Princes 1417–1517. Politics and Polity in the Late Medieval Church.* London: George Allen and Unwin, 1980.

Trottmann, Christian. *La vision béatifique des disputes scolastiques à sa définition par Benoît XII.* Rome: École française de Rome, 1995.

Tuck, Richard. *Natural Rights Theories: Their Origin and Development.* Cambridge, U.K.: Cambridge University Press, 1979.

Tuchman, Barbara. *A Distant Mirror. The Calamitous Fourteenth Century.* New York: Alfred A. Knopf, 1978.

Turner, Denys. *Eros and Allegory. Medieval Exegesis of the Song of Songs.* Kalamazoo, Mich.: Cistercian Publications, 1995.

Ullmann, Walter. *Medieval Political Thought.* Harmondsworth, U.K.: Penguin, 1970.

Valois, Noël. *La France et le grand schisme d'Occident,* vols. 1–4. Paris: Alphonse Picard, 1896–1902.

———. "Gerson. Curé de Saint-Jean-en-Grève." *Bulletin de la Société de l'Histoire de Paris et de l'Ile de France* 28 (1901): 49–53.

Van Ortroy, A. "Saint Pierre Célestin et ses premiers biographes." *Analecta Bollandiana* 16 (1897): 365–487.

Vansteenberghe, E. "Gerson à Bruges." *Revue d'histoire écclésiastique* 31 (1935): 5–52.

———. "Consultation sur une forme de dévotion populaire, 11 mars 1413." *Revue des sciences religieuses* 13 (1933): 165–185.

Vaughan, Richard. *John the Fearless.* London: Longman, 1966.

———. *Philip the Bold.* London: Longman, 1962.

Waley, Daniel. *Later Medieval Europe from Saint Louis to Luther.* London: Longman, 1989.

Warren, Ann K. *Anchorites and Their Patrons in Medieval England.* Los Angeles and Berkeley: University of California Press, 1985.

Wayman, Dorothy G. "The Chancellor and Jeanne d'Arc: February–July 1429." *Franciscan Studies* 17 (1957): 273–305.

Weinberg, Julius Rudolf. A short History of Medieval Philosophy. Princeton, N.J.: Princeton University Press, 1964.

Weisheipl, James A. *Friar Thomas d'Aquino. His Life, Thought, and Works.* Washington, D.C.: Catholic University of America Press, 1983.

Wuilleumier, Pierre. *Lyon. Métropole des Gaules.* Paris: Les Belles Lettres, 1953.

Zink, Michel. *La prédication en langue romane avant 1300.* Paris: Honoré Champion, 1976.

Index

Please note that the index follows surnames (such as "Gerson, Jean") when they are well known and thus does not follow the practice of listing first names first for persons born before 1500. This index is not a lexicon, but it does include a number of key words and concepts found in Gerson, whether in Latin, French, or English. The names included by no means exhaust the possibilities. Future research will provide a richness of detail for which there is insufficient space in what must primarily be an index of persons and titles of writings.

Brian Patrick McGuire